Lecture Notes in Computer Science 7796

Commenced Publication in 1973
Founding and Former Series Editors:
Gerhard Goos, Juris Hartmanis, and Jan van Leeuwen

Editorial Board

David Hutchison, UK
Josef Kittler, UK
Alfred Kobsa, USA
John C. Mitchell, USA
Oscar Nierstrasz, Switzerland
Bernhard Steffen, Germany
Demetri Terzopoulos, USA
Gerhard Weikum, Germany

Takeo Kanade, USA
Jon M. Kleinberg, USA
Friedemann Mattern, Switzerland
Moni Naor, Israel
C. Pandu Rangan, India
Madhu Sudan, USA
Doug Tygar, USA

Advanced Research in Computing and Software Science
Subline of Lectures Notes in Computer Science

Subline Series Editors

Giorgio Ausiello, *University of Rome 'La Sapienza', Italy*
Vladimiro Sassone, *University of Southampton, UK*

Subline Advisory Board

Susanne Albers, *University of Freiburg, Germany*
Benjamin C. Pierce, *University of Pennsylvania, USA*
Bernhard Steffen, *University of Dortmund, Germany*
Madhu Sudan, *Microsoft Research, Cambridge, MA, USA*
Deng Xiaotie, *City University of Hong Kong*
Jeannette M. Wing, *Carnegie Mellon University, Pittsburgh, PA, USA*

David Basin   John C. Mitchell (Eds.)

Principles of Security and Trust

Second International Conference, POST 2013
Held as Part of the European Joint Conferences
on Theory and Practice of Software, ETAPS 2013
Rome, Italy, March 16-24, 2013. Proceedings

 Springer

Volume Editors

David Basin
ETH Zurich, Department of Computer Science
Universitätsstr. 6, CNB F, 8092 Zürich, Switzerland
E-mail: basin@inf.ethz.ch

John C. Mitchell
Stanford University
Department of Computer Science
Gates 476, Stanford, CA 94305-9045, USA
E-mail: mitchell@cs.stanford.edu

ISSN 0302-9743   e-ISSN 1611-3349
ISBN 978-3-642-36829-5   e-ISBN 978-3-642-36830-1
DOI 10.1007/978-3-642-36830-1
Springer Heidelberg Dordrecht London New York

Library of Congress Control Number: 2013931844

CR Subject Classification (1998): C.2.0, C.2.2, E.3, K.4.4, K.6.5

LNCS Sublibrary: SL 4 – Security and Cryptology

© Springer-Verlag Berlin Heidelberg 2013
This work is subject to copyright. All rights are reserved, whether the whole or part of the material is
concerned, specifically the rights of translation, reprinting, re-use of illustrations, recitation, broadcasting,
reproduction on microfilms or in any other way, and storage in data banks. Duplication of this publication
or parts thereof is permitted only under the provisions of the German Copyright Law of September 9, 1965,
in ist current version, and permission for use must always be obtained from Springer. Violations are liable
to prosecution under the German Copyright Law.
The use of general descriptive names, registered names, trademarks, etc. in this publication does not imply,
even in the absence of a specific statement, that such names are exempt from the relevant protective laws
and regulations and therefore free for general use.

Typesetting: Camera-ready by author, data conversion by Scientific Publishing Services, Chennai, India

Printed on acid-free paper

Springer is part of Springer Science+Business Media (www.springer.com)

Foreword

ETAPS 2013 is the sixteenth instance of the European Joint Conferences on Theory and Practice of Software. ETAPS is an annual federated conference that was established in 1998 by combining a number of existing and new conferences. This year it comprised six sister conferences (CC, ESOP, FASE, FOSSACS, POST, TACAS), 20 satellite workshops (ACCAT, AiSOS, BX, BYTECODE, CerCo, DICE, FESCA, GRAPHITE, GT-VMT, HAS, Hot-Spot, FSS, MBT, MEALS, MLQA, PLACES, QAPL, SR, TERMGRAPH and VSSE), three invited tutorials (*e-education*, by John Mitchell; *cyber-physical systems*, by Martin Fränzle; and *e-voting* by Rolf Küsters) and eight invited lectures (excluding those specific to the satellite events).

The six main conferences received this year 627 submissions (including 18 tool demonstration papers), 153 of which were accepted (6 tool demos), giving an overall acceptance rate just above 24%. (ETAPS 2013 also received 11 submissions to the software competition, and 10 of them resulted in short papers in the TACAS proceedings). Congratulations therefore to all the authors who made it to the final programme! I hope that most of the other authors will still have found a way to participate in this exciting event, and that you will all continue to submit to ETAPS and contribute to making it the best conference on software science and engineering.

The events that comprise ETAPS address various aspects of the system development process, including specification, design, implementation, analysis, security and improvement. The languages, methodologies and tools that support these activities are all well within its scope. Different blends of theory and practice are represented, with an inclination towards theory with a practical motivation on the one hand and soundly based practice on the other. Many of the issues involved in software design apply to systems in general, including hardware systems, and the emphasis on software is not intended to be exclusive.

ETAPS is a confederation in which each event retains its own identity, with a separate Programme Committee and proceedings. Its format is open-ended, allowing it to grow and evolve as time goes by. Contributed talks and system demonstrations are in synchronised parallel sessions, with invited lectures in plenary sessions. Two of the invited lectures are reserved for 'unifying' talks on topics of interest to the whole range of ETAPS attendees. The aim of cramming all this activity into a single one-week meeting is to create a strong magnet for academic and industrial researchers working on topics within its scope, giving them the opportunity to learn about research in related areas, and thereby to foster new and existing links between work in areas that were formerly addressed in separate meetings.

ETAPS 2013 was organised by the *Department of Computer Science of 'Sapienza' University of Rome*, in cooperation with

▷ European Association for Theoretical Computer Science (EATCS)
▷ European Association for Programming Languages and Systems (EAPLS)
▷ European Association of Software Science and Technology (EASST).

The organising team comprised:

General Chair: *Daniele Gorla;*

Conferences: *Francesco Parisi Presicce;*

Satellite Events: *Paolo Bottoni* and *Pietro Cenciarelli;*

Web Master: *Igor Melatti;*

Publicity: *Ivano Salvo;*

Treasurers: *Federico Mari* and *Enrico Tronci.*

Overall planning for ETAPS conferences is the responsibility of its Steering Committee, whose current membership is:

Vladimiro Sassone (Southampton, chair), Martín Abadi (Santa Cruz), Erika Ábrahám (Aachen), Roberto Amadio (Paris 7), Gilles Barthe (IMDEA-Software), David Basin (Zürich), Saddek Bensalem (Grenoble), Michael O'Boyle (Edinburgh), Giuseppe Castagna (CNRS Paris), Albert Cohen (Paris), Vittorio Cortellessa (L'Aquila), Koen De Bosschere (Gent), Ranjit Jhala (San Diego), Matthias Felleisen (Boston), Philippa Gardner (Imperial College London), Stefania Gnesi (Pisa), Andrew D. Gordon (MSR Cambridge and Edinburgh), Daniele Gorla (Rome), Klaus Havelund (JLP NASA Pasadena), Reiko Heckel (Leicester), Holger Hermanns (Saarbrücken), Joost-Pieter Katoen (Aachen), Paul Klint (Amsterdam), Jens Knoop (Vienna), Steve Kremer (Nancy), Gerald Lüttgen (Bamberg), Tiziana Margaria (Potsdam), Fabio Martinelli (Pisa), John Mitchell (Stanford), Anca Muscholl (Bordeaux), Catuscia Palamidessi (INRIA Paris), Frank Pfenning (Pittsburgh), Nir Piterman (Leicester), Arend Rensink (Twente), Don Sannella (Edinburgh), Zhong Shao (Yale), Scott A. Smolka (Stony Brook), Gabriele Taentzer (Marburg), Tarmo Uustalu (Tallinn), Dániel Varró (Budapest) and Lenore Zuck (Chicago).

The ordinary running of ETAPS is handled by its management group comprising: Vladimiro Sassone (chair), Joost-Pieter Katoen (deputy chair and publicity chair), Gerald Lüttgen (treasurer), Giuseppe Castagna (satellite events chair), Holger Hermanns (liaison with local organiser) and Gilles Barthe (industry liaison).

I would like to express here my sincere gratitude to all the people and organisations that contributed to ETAPS 2013, the Programme Committee chairs and members of the ETAPS conferences, the organisers of the satellite events, the speakers themselves, the many reviewers, all the participants, and Springer-Verlag for agreeing to publish the ETAPS proceedings in the ARCoSS subline.

Last but not least, I would like to thank the organising chair of ETAPS 2013, Daniele Gorla, and his Organising Committee, for arranging for us to have ETAPS in the most beautiful and historic city of Rome.

———————   ■   ———————

My thoughts today are with two special people, profoundly different for style and personality, yet profoundly similar for the love and dedication to our discipline, for the way they shaped their respective research fields, and for the admiration and respect that their work commands. Both are role-model computer scientists for us all.

ETAPS in Rome celebrates *Corrado Böhm*. Corrado turns 90 this year, and we are just so lucky to have the chance to celebrate the event in Rome, where he has worked since 1974 and established a world-renowned school of computer scientists. Corrado has been a pioneer in research on programming languages and their semantics. Back in 1951, years before FORTRAN and LISP, he defined and implemented a *metacircular compiler* for a programming language of his invention. The compiler consisted of just 114 instructions, and anticipated some modern list-processing techniques.

Yet, Corrado's claim to fame is asserted through the breakthroughs expressed by the *Böhm-Jacopini Theorem* (CACM 1966) and by the invention of *Böhm-trees*. The former states that any algorithm can be implemented using only sequencing, conditionals, and while-loops over elementary instructions. Böhm trees arose as a convenient data structure in Corrado's milestone proof of the decidability inside the λ-calculus of the equivalence of terms in β-η-normal form.

Throughout his career, Corrado showed exceptional commitment to his roles of researcher and educator, fascinating his students with his creativity, passion and curiosity in research. Everybody who has worked with him or studied under his supervision agrees that he combines an outstanding technical ability and originality of thought with great personal charm, sweetness and kindness. This is an unusual combination in problem-solvers of such a high calibre, yet another reason why we are ecstatic to celebrate him. *Happy birthday from ETAPS, Corrado!*

ETAPS in Rome also celebrates the life and work of *Kohei Honda*. Kohei passed away suddenly and prematurely on December 4th, 2012, leaving the saddest gap in our community. He was a dedicated, passionate, enthusiastic scientist and –more than that!– his enthusiasm was contagious. Kohei was one of the few theoreticians I met who really succeeded in building bridges between theoreticians and practitioners. He worked with W3C on the standardisation of web services choreography description languages (WS-CDL) and with several companies on *Savara* and *Scribble*, his own language for the description of application-level protocols among communicating systems.

Among Kohei's milestone research, I would like to mention his 1991 epoch-making paper at ECOOP (with M. Tokoro) on the treatment of asynchrony in message passing calculi, which has influenced all process calculi research since. At ETAPS 1998 he introduced (with V. Vasconcelos and M. Kubo) a new concept in type theories for communicating processes: it came to be known as '*session types*,' and has since spawned an entire research area, with practical and multi-disciplinary applications that Kohei was just starting to explore.

Kohei leaves behind him enormous impact, and a lasting legacy. He is irreplaceable, and I for one am proud to have been his colleague and glad for the opportunity to arrange for his commemoration at ETAPS 2013.

My final ETAPS '*Foreword*' seems like a good place for a short reflection on ETAPS, what it has achieved in the past few years, and what the future might have in store for it.

On April 1st, 2011 in Saarbrücken, we took a significant step towards the consolidation of ETAPS: the establishment of *ETAPS e.V.* This is a *non-profit association* founded under German law with the immediate purpose of supporting the conference and the related activities. ETAPS e.V. was required for practical reasons, e.g., the conference needed (to be represented by) a legal body to better support authors, organisers and attendees by, e.g., signing contracts with service providers such as publishers and professional meeting organisers. Our ambition is however to make of '*ETAPS the association*' more than just the organisers of '*ETAPS the conference*'. We are working towards finding a voice and developing a range of activities to support our scientific community, in cooperation with the relevant existing associations, learned societies and interest groups. The process of defining the structure, scope and strategy of ETAPS e.V. is underway, as is its first ever membership campaign. For the time being, ETAPS e.V. has started to support community-driven initiatives such as open access publications (LMCS and EPTCS) and conference management systems (Easychair), and to cooperate with cognate associations (European Forum for ICT).

After two successful runs, we continue to support POST, *Principles of Security and Trust*, as a candidate to become a permanent ETAPS conference. POST was the first addition to our main programme since 1998, when the original five conferences met together in Lisbon for the first ETAPS. POST resulted from several smaller workshops and informal gatherings, supported by IFIP WG 1.7, and combines the practically important subject of security and trust with strong technical connections to traditional ETAPS areas. POST is now attracting interest and support from prominent scientists who have accepted to serve as PC chairs, invited speakers and tutorialists. I am very happy about the decision we made to create and promote POST, and to invite it to be a part of ETAPS.

Considerable attention was recently devoted to our *internal processes* in order to streamline our procedures for appointing Programme Committees, choosing invited speakers, awarding prizes and selecting papers; to strengthen each member conference's own Steering Group, and, at the same time, to strike a balance between these and the ETAPS Steering Committee. A lot was done and a lot remains to be done.

We produced a *handbook* for local organisers and one for PC chairs. The latter sets out a code of conduct that all the people involved in the selection of papers, from PC chairs to referees, are expected to adhere to. From the point of view of the authors, we adopted a *two-phase submission* protocol, with fixed deadlines in the first week of October. We published a *confidentiality policy* to set high standards for the handling of submissions, and a *republication policy* to clarify what kind of material remains eligible for submission to ETAPS after presentation at a workshop. We started an *author rebuttal phase*, adopted by most of the conferences, to improve the author experience. It is important to acknowledge that – regardless of our best intentions and efforts – the quality of reviews is not always what we would like it to be. To remain true to our commitment to the authors who elect to submit to ETAPS, we must endeavour to improve our standards of refereeing. The rebuttal phase is a step in that direction and, according to our experience, it seems to work remarkably well at little cost, provided both authors and PC members use it for what it is. ETAPS has now reached a healthy paper acceptance rate around the 25% mark, essentially uniformly across the six conferences. This seems to me to strike an excellent balance between being selective and being inclusive, and I hope it will be possible to maintain it even if the number of submissions increases.

ETAPS signed a favourable three-year publication contract with Springer for publication in the ARCoSS subline of LNCS. This was the result of lengthy negotiations, and I consider it a good achievement for ETAPS. Yet, publication of its proceedings is possibly the hardest challenge that ETAPS – and indeed most computing conferences – currently face. I was invited to represent ETAPS at a most interesting Dagstuhl Perspective Workshop on the *'Publication Culture in Computing Research'* (seminar 12452). The paper I gave there is available online from the workshop proceedings, and illustrates three of the views I formed also thanks to my experience as chair of ETAPS, respectively on open access, bibliometrics, and the roles and relative merits of conferences versus journal publications. Open access is a key issue for a conference like ETAPS. Yet, in my view it does not follow that we can altogether dispense with publishers – be they commercial, academic, or learned societies – and with their costs. A promising way forward may be based on the *'author-pays'* model, where publications fees are kept low by resorting to learned-societies as publishers. Also, I believe it is ultimately in the interest of our community to de-emphasise the perceived value of conference publications as viable – if not altogether superior – alternatives to journals. A large and ambitious conference like ETAPS ought to be able to rely on quality open-access journals to cover its entire spectrum of interests, even if that means promoting the creation of a new journal.

Due to its size and the complexity of its programme, hosting ETAPS is an increasingly challenging task. Even though excellent candidate *locations* keep being volunteered, in the longer run it seems advisable for ETAPS to provide more support to local organisers, starting e.g., by taking direct control of the organisation of satellite events. Also, after sixteen splendid years, this may be a good time to start thinking about exporting ETAPS to other continents. The US East Coast would appear to be the obvious destination for a first ETAPS outside Europe.

The strength and success of ETAPS comes also from presenting – regardless of the natural internal differences – a homogeneous interface to authors and

Preface

The second conference on Principles of Security and Trust (POST) was held March 18–19, 2013, in Rome, Italy, as part of ETAPS 2013. POST attracted 59 submissions, from which the committee selected 14. Aside from these contributions, POST also featured an invited talk given by Jean-Pierre Hubaux, of the Swiss Federal Institute of Technology, Lausanne. The proceedings include the selected papers as well as abstracts from ETAP's two unifying speakers, Gilles Barthe and Cédric Fournet.

We would like to thank our dedicated and collegial Program Committee, the ETAPS Steering Committee, the ETAPS Local Organizing Committee, and our invited speakers for their help in making this conference a success.

January 2013

David Basin
John Mitchell

Organization

Program Committee

Martin Abadi — Microsoft Research and UCSC, USA
Alessandro Acquisti — Carnegie Mellon University, USA
Gilles Barthe — IMDEA Software Institute, Spain
Lujo Bauer — Carnegie Mellon University, USA
Bruno Blanchet — INRIA, Ecole Normale Supérieure, CNRS, France
Jan Camenisch — IBM Research, Zurich Research Laboratory, Switzerland
Mihai Christodorescu — IBM T.J. Watson Research Center, USA
Veronique Cortier — CNRS, Loria, France
Pierpaolo Degano — Università di Pisa, Italy
Deepak Garg — Max Planck Institute for Software Systems, Germany
Andy Gordon — Microsoft Research, UK
Joshua Guttman — Worcester Polytechnic Institute, USA
Steve Kremer — INRIA Nancy, Loria, France
Ralf Kuesters — University of Trier, Germany
Boris Köpf — IMDEA Software, Spain
Benjamin Livshits — Microsoft Research, USA
Gavin Lowe — University of Oxford, UK
Sjouke Mauw — University of Luxembourg, UK
Sebastian A. Mödersheim — DTU, Denmark
Alexander Pretschner — Karlsruhe Institute of Technology (KIT), Germany
Andrei Sabelfeld — Chalmers University of Technology, Sweden
Dominique Unruh — Saarland University, Germany
Luca Viganò — University of Verona, Italy

Additional Reviewers

Armando, Alessandro
Bana, Gergei
Birgisson, Arnar
Bodei, Chiara
Ciancia, Vincenzo
Clarkson, Michael
Crespo, Juan Manuel

Dong, Naipeng
Dupressoir, Francois
Ferrari, Gianluigi
Fredrikson, Matt
Gibson-Robinson, Thomas
Haralambiev, Kris
Hedin, Daniel

Jia, Limin
Jonker, Hugo
Kelbert, Florian
Kifer, Daniel
Kordy, Barbara
Kumari, Prachi
Lopez, Javier
Mezzetti, Gianluca
Nori, Aditya

Rafnsson, Willard
Sanchez, Cesar
Truderung, Tomasz
Tuengerthal, Max
Vogt, Andreas
Warinschi, Bogdan
Wüchner, Tobias
Zhang, Chenyi

Computer-Aided Cryptographic Proofs
(Invited Talk)

Gilles Barthe

IMDEA Software Institute

Cryptography plays a central role in the security of computer and communication systems. Yet, designing, implementing, and deploying cryptographic constructions is notoriously difficult, mainly for two factors. First, security proofs typically rest on elaborate arguments from information theory, complexity theory, and possibly algebra or number theory. Second, attacks frequently exploit characteristics such as execution time or power consumption, as well as implementation issues, such as error messages, rounding errors, or message formatting, that are elided in proofs. Over the last thirty years, cryptographers have strived to develop models and proof methods that simultaneously address these factors. Thanks to these efforts, it is becoming possible to provide rigorous security proofs for detailed, "real world", descriptions of cryptographic standards. On the downside, security proofs are becoming extremely complex, making formal verification an appealing alternative for building and verifying them.

Over the last six years, we have built two tools for computer-aided cryptographic proofs: CertiCrypt [2] and EasyCrypt [1]. Both tools adopt the code-based approach, in which cryptographic schemes and assumptions are modeled as probabilistic programs, or games. Moreover, they use deductive verification, and in particular relational program logics, to support the game-based approach, in which security is proved using a sequence of games and probability claims about pairs of games. We have used both tools to verify a representative set of emblematic cryptographic constructions, including public-key encryption schemes, modes of operation, signature schemes, hash function designs, zero-knowledge proofs.

Our most recent work intends to accomodate real world descriptions of cryptographic constructions, and to provide support for modular proofs. We have also started to use CertiCrypt and EasyCrypt as certifying back-ends for cryptographic compilers and synthesizers.

References

1. Barthe, G., Grégoire, B., Heraud, S., Béguelin, S.Z.: Computer-Aided Security Proofs for the Working Cryptographer. In: Rogaway, P. (ed.) CRYPTO 2011. LNCS, vol. 6841, pp. 71–90. Springer, Heidelberg (2011)
2. Barthe, G., Grégoire, B., Béguelin, S.Z.: Formal certification of code-based cryptographic proofs. In: 36th ACM SIGPLAN-SIGACT Symposium on Principles of Programming Languages, POPL 2009, pp. 90–101. ACM, New York (2009)

An Implementation of TLS 1.2
with Verified Cryptographic Security

(Invited Talk)

Cédric Fournet[1], Karthikeyan Bhargavan[3], Markulf Kohlweiss[1],
Alfredo Pironti[2,3], and Pierre-Yves Strub[2,4]

[1] Microsoft Research
[2] MSR-INRIA Joint Centre
[3] INRIA
[4] IMDEA

Abstract. SSL/TLS is possibly the most used and most studied protocol for secure communications, with a 19-year history of flaws and fixes, ranging from its protocol logic to its cryptographic design, and from the Internet standard to its diverse implementations.

We develop a new, verified, reference implementation of TLS 1.2. Our code fully supports its wire formats, ciphersuites, sessions and connections, re-handshakes and resumptions, alerts and errors, and data fragmentation, as prescribed in the RFCs; it interoperates with mainstream web browsers and servers. At the same time, our code is carefully structured to enable its modular, automated verification, from its main API down to computational assumptions on its cryptographic algorithms such as AES and RSA.

Our implementation is written in F# and specified in F7. We present security specifications for its main components, such as authenticated stream encryption for the record layer and key establishment for the handshake. We describe their automated verification using the F7 refinement typechecker. To this end, we equip each cryptographic primitive and construction of TLS with a new typed interface that captures its security properties, and we gradually replace concrete implementations with ideal functionalities. We finally typecheck the protocol state machine, and thus obtain precise security theorems for TLS, as it is implemented and deployed. We also revisit classic attacks and report a few new ones.

References

1. Implementing TLS with verified cryptographic security: source code, technical report, and details at http://msr-inria.inria.fr/projects/sec/tls (2012)
2. Dierks, T., Rescorla, E.: The transport layer security (TLS) protocol version 1.2. RFC 5246 (2008)

Table of Contents

Formal Analysis of Privacy for Routing Protocols in Mobile Ad Hoc Networks*

Rémy Chrétien and Stéphanie Delaune

LSV, ENS Cachan & CNRS & INRIA Saclay Île-de-France

Abstract. Routing protocols aim at establishing a route between distant nodes in ad hoc networks. Secured versions of routing protocols have been proposed to provide more guarantees on the resulting routes, and some of them have been designed to protect the privacy of the users.

In this paper, we propose a framework for analysing privacy-type properties for routing protocols. We use a variant of the applied-pi calculus as our basic modelling formalism. More precisely, using the notion of equivalence between traces, we formalise three security properties related to privacy, namely *indistinguishability*, *unlinkability*, and *anonymity*. We study the relationship between these definitions and we illustrate them using two versions of the ANODR routing protocol.

1 Introduction

Mobile ad hoc networks consist of mobile wireless devices which autonomously organise their communication infrastructure. They are being used in a large array of settings, from military applications to emergency rescue; and are also believed to have future uses in *e.g.* vehicular networking. In such a network, each node provides the function of a router and relays packets on paths to other nodes. Finding these paths is a crucial functionality of any ad hoc network. Specific protocols, called *routing protocols*, are designed to ensure this functionality known as *route discovery*.

Since an adversary can easily paralyse the operation of a whole network by attacking the routing protocol, substantial efforts have been made to provide efficient and secure routing protocols [21,14,18]. For instance, in order to prevent a malicious node to insert and delete nodes inside a path, cryptographic mechanisms such as encryption, signature, and MAC are used. However, there is a privacy problem related to the way routes are discovered by those routing protocols. Indeed, most routing protocols (*e.g.* [14,18]) flood the entire network with a route request message containing the names of the source and the destination of the intended communication. Thus, an eavesdropper can easily observe who wants to communicate with whom even if he is not on the route between the communicating nodes. Since then, in order to limit privacy issues, several anonymous routing protocols have been developed, *e.g.* ANODR [15], AnonDSR [20] to resist against passive adversaries showing no suspicious behaviours.

---

* This work has been partially supported by the project JCJC VIP ANR-11-JS02-006.

D. Basin and J.C. Mitchell (Eds.): POST 2013, LNCS 7796, pp. 1–20, 2013.
© Springer-Verlag Berlin Heidelberg 2013

Because security protocols are in general notoriously difficult to design and analyse, formal verification techniques are particularly important. For example, a flaw has been discovered in the Single-Sign-On protocol used *e.g.* by Google Apps [4]. It has been shown that a malicious application could very easily gain access to any other application (*e.g.* Gmail or Google Calendar) of their users. This flaw has been found when analyzing the protocol using formal methods, abstracting messages by a term algebra and using the AVISPA platform [5].

Whereas secrecy and authentication are well-understood notions, anonymity itself is ill-defined: behind the general concept lie distinct considerations which share the general idea of not disclosing any crucial information to an attacker on the network. Thus, formalizing privacy-type properties is not an easy task and has been the subject of several papers in the context of electronic voting (*e.g.* [12,7]), RFID systems (*e.g.* [3,9]), or anonymizing protocols (*e.g.* [16,13]). Whereas some of them rely on a probabilitistic notion of anonymity (*e.g.* [19]), we focus on deterministic ones, for which formal analysis appears more natural. All these definitions share a common feature: they are based on a notion of equivalence that allows one to express the fact that two situations are similar, *i.e.* indistinguishable from the point of view of the attacker.

Our contributions. In this paper, we propose a formal framework for analyzing privacy-type properties in the context of routing protocols. We use a variant of the applied-pi calculus as our basic modeling formalism [1], which has the advantage of being based on well-understood concepts and to allow us to model various cryptographic primitives by the means of an equational theory (see Sections 2 and 3). However, in order to model route discovery protocols, we have to adapt it to take into account several features of those protocols, *e.g.* the topology of the network, broadcast communication, internal states of the nodes, *etc*

Then, we investigate the different properties a routing protocol could achieve to be considered indeed anonymous in presence of a passive attacker. We propose three different families of such properties: *indistinguishability*, which deals with the possibility to distinguish some external action undertaken by an agent from another (see Section 4); *unlinkability*, which is related to the ability for the attacker to link certain actions together (see Section 5); and finally *anonymity* which concerns the disclosure of information such as the identity of the sender, or the identity of the receiver (see Section 6). We formalise those properties using a notion of equivalence between traces. Some difficulties arise due to the application under study. In particular, to achieve those security properties, we have to ensure that the network is *active enough*, and thus we have to provide a formal definition of this notion. We study the relationship between these privacy-type properties and we illustrate our definitions on two versions of the ANODR routing protocol [15].

Related work. Notions of privacy have been studied for RFID protocols [3] such as the key establishment protocol used in the electronic passport application. Similarly, formal definitions and proofs of anonymity for anonymizing protocols, like the onion routing, were proposed in [16,13]. Nevertheless these formalisms do not allow one to freely specify network topologies, a crucial feature for mobile ad-hoc routing. Moreover, as an extension of the applied pi-calculus, our formalism is not bound to a fixed set of primitives but make our definition usable for a large class of routing protocols. A more detailed version of this paper is available in [10].

2 Messages and Attacker Capabilities

As often in protocol analysis, cryptographic primitives are assumed to work per-fectly. However, we do *not* consider an active attacker who controls the entire network as generally done when analyzing more classical protocols. We will con-sider an eavesdropper who listens to some nodes of the network or even all of them. Basically, he can see messages that are sent from locations he is spying on, and can only encrypt, decrypt, sign messages or perform other cryptographic operations if he has the relevant keys.

2.1 Messages

For modeling messages, we consider an arbitrary term algebra, which provides a lot of flexibility in terms of which cryptographic primitives can be modelled. In such a setting, messages are represented by terms where cryptographic primitives such as encryption, signature, and hash function, are represented by *function symbols*. More precisely, we consider a *signature* $(\mathcal{S}, \Sigma)$ made of a set of sorts $\mathcal{S}$ and a set of *function symbols* Σ together with arities of the form $ar(\mathsf{f}) = s_1 \times \ldots \times s_k \to s$ where $\mathsf{f} \in \Sigma$, and $s, s_1, \ldots, s_k \in \mathcal{S}$. We consider an infinite set of *variables* $\mathcal{X}$ and an infinite set of *names* $\mathcal{N}$ which are used for representing keys, nonces, *etc* We assume that names and variables are given with sorts. *Terms* are defined as names, variables, and function symbols applied to other terms. Of course function symbol application must respect sorts and arities. For $\mathcal{A} \subseteq \mathcal{X} \cup \mathcal{N}$, the set of terms built from $\mathcal{A}$ by applying function symbols in Σ is denoted by $\mathcal{T}(\Sigma, \mathcal{A})$.

We write $vars(u)$ (resp. $names(u)$) for the set of variables (resp. names) that occur in a term u. A term u is said to be a *ground* term if $vars(u) = \emptyset$. Regarding the sort system, we consider a special sort agent that only contains names and variables. These names represent the names of the agents, also called the nodes of the network. We assume a special sort msg that subsumes all the other sorts, *i.e.* any term is of sort msg.

For our cryptographic purposes, it is useful to distinguish a subset Σ_{pub} of Σ, made of *public symbols*, *i.e.* the symbols made available to the attacker. A *recipe* is a term in $\mathcal{T}(\Sigma_{\mathsf{pub}}, \mathcal{X} \cup \mathcal{N})$, that is, a term containing no private (non-public) symbols. Moreover, to model algebraic properties of cryptographic primitives, we define an *equational theory* by a finite set E of equations $u = v$ with $u, v \in \mathcal{T}(\Sigma, \mathcal{X})$ (note that u, v do not contain names). We define $=_{\mathsf{E}}$ to be the smallest equivalence relation on terms, that contains E and that is closed under application of function symbols and substitutions of terms for variables.

Example 1. A typical signature for representing secured routing protocols is the signature $(\mathcal{S}, \Sigma)$ defined by

- $\mathcal{S} = \{\text{agent}, \text{msg}\}$, and
- $\Sigma = \{\langle\rangle, \text{proj}_1, \text{proj}_2, \text{senc}, \text{sdec}, \text{aenc}, \text{adec}, \text{pub}, \text{prv}, \text{req}, \text{rep}, \text{src}, \text{dest}, \text{key}\}$

with the following arities:

$$\text{senc}, \text{sdec}, \text{aenc}, \text{adec}, \langle\,\rangle : \text{msg} \times \text{msg} \to \text{msg} \qquad \text{pub}, \text{prv} : \text{agent} \to \text{msg}$$
$$\text{req}, \text{rep}, \text{src}, \text{dest}, \text{key} : \ \to \text{msg} \qquad \text{proj}_1, \text{proj}_2 : \ \text{msg} \to \text{msg}$$

The constants req and rep are used to identify the request phase and the reply phase, src, dest, and key are some other public constants. The function symbols sdec, senc (resp. adec and aenc) of arity 2 represent symmetric (resp. asymmetric) decryption and encryption. Pairing is modelled using a symbol of arity 2, denoted $\langle\,\rangle$, and projection functions are denoted proj_1 and proj_2. We denote by $\text{pub}(A)$ (resp. $\text{prv}(A)$) the public key (resp. the private key) associated to the agent A. Moreover, we assume that $\text{prv} \notin \Sigma_{\text{pub}}$. Then, we consider the equational theory E, defined by the following equations ($i \in 1, 2$):

$$\text{sdec}(\text{senc}(x, y), y) = x \quad \text{adec}(\text{aenc}(x, \text{pub}(y)), \text{prv}(y)) = x \quad \text{proj}_i(\langle x_1, x_2\rangle) = x_i$$

For sake of clarity, we write $\langle t_1, t_2, t_3\rangle$ for the term $\langle t_1, \langle t_2, t_3\rangle\rangle$.

Substitutions are written $\sigma = \{x_1 \triangleright u_1, \ldots, x_n \triangleright u_n\}$ where its *domain* is written $dom(\sigma) = \{x_1, \ldots, x_n\}$, and its *image* is written $img(\sigma) = \{u_1, \ldots, u_n\}$. We only consider *well-sorted* substitutions, that is substitutions for which x_i and u_i have the same sort. The application of a substitution σ to a term u is written $u\sigma$. A *most general unifier* of two terms u and v is a substitution denoted by $mgu(u, v)$. We write $mgu(u, v) = \perp$ when u and v are not unifiable.

2.2   Attacker Capabilities

To represent the knowledge of an attacker (who may have observed a sequence of messages $t_1, \ldots, t_\ell$), we use the concept of *frame*. A frame $\phi = \text{new } \tilde{n}.\sigma$ consists of a finite set $\tilde{n} \subseteq \mathcal{N}$ of *restricted* names (those unknown to the attacker), and a substitution σ of the form $\{y_1 \triangleright t_1, \ldots, y_\ell \triangleright t_\ell\}$ where each t_i is a ground term. The variables y_i enable an attacker to refer to each t_i. The *domain* of the frame ϕ, written $dom(\phi)$, is $dom(\sigma) = \{y_1, \ldots, y_\ell\}$.

In the frame $\phi = \text{new } \tilde{n}.\sigma$, the names $\tilde{n}$ are bound in σ and can be renamed. Moreover names that do not appear in ϕ can be added or removed from $\tilde{n}$. In particular, we can always assume that two frames share the same set of restricted names. Thus, in the definition below, we will assume w.l.o.g. that the two frames ϕ_1 and ϕ_2 have the same set of restricted names.

Definition 1 (static equivalence). *We say that two frames* $\phi_1 = \text{new } \tilde{n}.\sigma_1$ *and* $\phi_2 = \text{new } \tilde{n}.\sigma_2$ *are statically equivalent,* $\phi_1 \sim_E \phi_2$, *when* $dom(\phi_1) = dom(\phi_2)$, *and for all recipes* M, N *such that* $names(M, N) \cap \tilde{n} = \emptyset$, *we have that:* $M\sigma_1 =_E N\sigma_1$ *if, and only if,* $M\sigma_2 =_E N\sigma_2$.

Intuitively, two frames are equivalent when the attacker cannot see the difference between the two situations they represent, *i.e.*, his ability to distinguish whether two recipes M, N produce the same term does not depend on the frame.

Example 2. Let $\phi_{\mathsf{req}} = \mathsf{new}\, n.\{y_1 \triangleright \mathsf{senc}(\langle \mathsf{req}, n \rangle, k)\}$ and $\phi_{\mathsf{rep}} = \mathsf{new}\, n.\{y_1 \triangleright \mathsf{senc}(\langle \mathsf{rep}, n \rangle, k)\}$ be two frames. Considering the equational theory E introduced in Example 1, we have that $\phi_{\mathsf{req}} \not\sim_{\mathsf{E}} \phi_{\mathsf{rep}}$ since the recipes $M = \mathsf{proj}_1(\mathsf{sdec}(y_1, k))$ and $N = \mathsf{req}$ allow one to distinguish the two frames. However, we have that $\mathsf{new}\, k.\phi_{\mathsf{req}} \sim_{\mathsf{E}} \mathsf{new}\, k.\phi_{\mathsf{rep}}$. Indeed, without knowing the key k, the attacker is unable to observe the differences between the two messages. This is a non-trivial equivalence that can be established using an automatic tool (*e.g.* ProVerif [8]).

3 Models for Protocols

In this section, we introduce the cryptographic process calculus that we will use for describing protocols. Several well-studied calculi already exist to analyse security protocols and privacy-type properties (*e.g.* [2,1]). However, modelling ad-hoc routing protocols requires several additional features. Our calculus is actually inspired from some other calculi (*e.g.* [17,6,11]) which allow mobile wireless networks and their security properties to be formally described and analysed. We adapt those formalisms in order to be able to express privacy-type properties such as those studied in this paper.

3.1 Syntax

The intended behavior of each node of the network can be modelled by a *process* defined by the grammar given below (u is a term that may contain variables, n is a name, and Φ is a formula). Our calculus is parametrized by a set $\mathcal{L}$ of formulas whose purpose is to represent various tests performed by the agents (*e.g.* equality tests, neighbourhood tests). We left this set unspecified since it is not relevant for this work. For illustration purposes, we only assume that the set $\mathcal{L}$ contains at least equality and disequality tests.

$P, Q := 0$	null process
$\quad$ in$(u).P$	reception
$\quad$ out$(u).P$	emission
$\quad$ if Φ then P else Q	conditional $\Phi \in \mathcal{L}$
$\quad$ store$(u).P$	storage
$\quad$ read $u[\Phi]$ then P else Q	reading
$\quad$ $P \mid Q$	parallel composition
$\quad$ $!P$	replication
$\quad$ new $n.P$	fresh name generation

The process "in$(u).P$" expects a message m of the form u and then behaves like $P\sigma$ where σ is such that $m = u\sigma$. The process "out$(u).P$" emits u, and then behaves like P. The variables that occur in u will be instantiated when the evaluation will take place. The process $\mathsf{store}(u).P$ stores u in its storage list and then behaves like P. The process $\mathsf{read}\ u[\varPhi]$ then P else Q looks for a message of the form u that satisfies $\varPhi$ in its storage list and then, if such an element m is found, it behaves like $P\sigma$ where σ is such that $m = u\sigma$. Otherwise, it behaves like Q. The other operators are standard.

Sometimes, for the sake of clarity, we will omit the null process. We also omit the else part when $Q = 0$. We write $fvars(P)$ for the set of *free variables* that occur in P, *i.e.* the set of variables that are not in the scope of an input or a read. We consider *ground processes*, *i.e.* processes P such that $fvars(P) = \emptyset$, and *parametrized* processes, denoted $P(z_1, \ldots, z_n)$ where $z_1, \ldots, z_n$ are variables of sort agent, and such that $fvars(P) \subseteq \{z_1, \ldots, z_n\}$. A *routing protocol* is a set of parametrized processes.

3.2   Example: ANODR

ANODR is an anonymous on-demand routing protocol that has been designed to prevent traffic analysis in ad hoc networks [15]. We consider a simplified version of this protocol, denoted $\mathcal{P}_{\mathsf{ANODR}}^{\mathsf{simp}}$. For sake of readability, we give below an Alice and Bob version of this two-phase protocol where we omit some $\langle \cdots, \cdot \rangle$ and we use $\{\cdot\}$. instead of senc and aenc.

$$S \ \rightarrow V_1 : \langle \mathsf{req}, id, \{D, chall\}_{\mathsf{pub}(D)}, \{S, \mathsf{src}\}_{k_S} \rangle$$
$$V_1 \rightarrow V_2 : \langle \mathsf{req}, id, \{D, chall\}_{\mathsf{pub}(D)}, \{V_1, \{S, \mathsf{src}\}_{k_S}\}_{k_1} \rangle$$
$$V_2 \rightarrow D : \langle \mathsf{req}, id, \{D, chall\}_{\mathsf{pub}(D)}, \{V_2, \{V_1, \{S, \mathsf{src}\}_{k_S}\}_{k_1}\}_{k_2} \rangle$$

$$D \ \rightarrow V_2 : \langle \mathsf{rep}, N_D, chall, \{V_2, \{V_1, \{S, \mathsf{src}\}_{k_S}\}_{k_1}\}_{k_2} \rangle$$
$$V_2 \rightarrow V_1 : \langle \mathsf{rep}, N_2, chall, \{V_1, \{S, \mathsf{src}\}_{k_S}\}_{k_1} \rangle$$
$$V_1 \rightarrow S \ : \ \langle \mathsf{rep}, N_1, chall, \{S, \mathsf{src}\}_{k_S} \rangle$$

Request phase. The source initiates route discovery by locally broadcasting a request. The constant req is used to identify the request phase whereas id is an identifier of the request. The third component of the request is a cryptographic trapdoor that can only be opened by the destination; and the last one is a cryptographic onion that is used for route establishment. At this stage, the onion built by the source contains only one layer.

Then, intermediate nodes relay the request over the network, except if they have already seen it. However, contrary to what happen in many routing protocols, the names of the intermediate nodes are not accumulated in the route request packet. This is important to prevent traffic analysis.

Reply phase. When the destination D receives the request, it opens the trapdoor and builds a route reply.

During the reply phase, the message travels along the route back to S. The intermediary node decrypt the onion using its own key which has been generated during the request phase. If its own identity does not match the first field of the decrypted result, it then discards the packet. Otherwise, the node is on the anonymous route. It generates a random number (namely N_D, N_1, or N_2), stores the correspondence between the nonce it receives and the one it has generated. It peels off one layer of the onion, replaces the nonce with its own nonce, and then locally broadcasts the reply packet.

Formally, this protocol is composed of four parametrized processes that can be modelled using the signature given in Example 1. Let id be a name, z_S, z_V, z_D be variables of sort agent, and x_N, x_{id}, x_{tr} and x_{onion} be variables of sort msg.

The process executed by the agent z_S initiating the search of a route towards a node z_D is:

$$P_{\mathsf{src}}(z_S, z_D) = \mathsf{new}\ id.\mathsf{new}\ chall.\mathsf{new}\ k_S.\mathsf{out}(u_1).\mathsf{in}(u_2).\mathsf{store}(\langle z_D, x_N \rangle)$$

where $\begin{cases} u_1 = \langle \mathsf{req}, id, \mathsf{aenc}(\langle z_D, chall \rangle, \mathsf{pub}(z_D)), \mathsf{senc}(\langle z_S, \mathsf{src} \rangle, k_S) \rangle \\ u_2 = \langle \mathsf{rep}, x_N, chall, \mathsf{senc}(\langle z_S, \mathsf{src} \rangle, k_S) \rangle \end{cases}$

The source z_S builds a request message and sends it. Then, the source is waiting for a reply containing the same cryptographic onion as the one used in the request, a proof of global trapdoor opening (here modelled as a nonce $chall$), and a locally unique random route pseudonym N. Lastly, the source will store that destination D can be reached using the route pseudonym N as the next hop.

The process executed by an intermediary node z_V during the request phase is described below. For sake of simplicity, we did not model the fact that a duplicated request message is directly discarded.

$$P_{\mathsf{int}}^{\mathsf{req}}(z_V) = \mathsf{in}(w_1).\mathsf{if}\ \neg \Phi_{\mathsf{req}}\ \mathsf{then}\ (\mathsf{new}\ k_V.\mathsf{store}(\langle \mathsf{key}, k_V \rangle).\mathsf{out}(w_2))$$

where $\begin{cases} w_1 = \langle \mathsf{req}, x_{id}, x_{tr}, x_{onion} \rangle \qquad \Phi_{\mathsf{req}} = \mathsf{proj}_1(\mathsf{adec}(x_{tr}, \mathsf{prv}(z_V))) = z_V \\ w_2 = \langle \mathsf{req}, x_{id}, x_{tr}, \mathsf{senc}(\langle z_V, x_{onion} \rangle, k_V) \rangle \end{cases}$

The process executed by the destination node z_D is the following:

$$P_{\mathsf{dest}}(z_D) = \mathsf{in}(v_1).\ \mathsf{if}\ \Phi_{\mathsf{dest}}\ \mathsf{then}\ (\mathsf{new}\ N.\mathsf{out}(v_2))$$

where $\begin{cases} v_1 = \langle \mathsf{req}, x_{id}, x_{tr}, x_{onion} \rangle \qquad \Phi_{\mathsf{dest}} = \mathsf{proj}_1(\mathsf{adec}(x_{tr}, \mathsf{prv}(z_D))) = z_D \\ v_2 = \langle \mathsf{rep}, N, \mathsf{proj}_2(\mathsf{adec}(x_{tr}, \mathsf{prv}(z_D))), x_{onion} \rangle \end{cases}$

The process executed by an intermediary node z_V during the reply phase is as follows:

$$P_{\mathsf{int}}^{\mathsf{rep}}(z_V) = \mathsf{in}(w_1').\mathsf{read}\ \langle \mathsf{key}, y \rangle\ [\Phi_{\mathsf{rep}}]\ \mathsf{then}\ (\mathsf{new}\ N'.\mathsf{store}(\langle x_N, N' \rangle).\mathsf{out}(w_2'))$$

where $\begin{cases} w_1' = \langle \mathsf{rep}, x_N, x_{pr}, x_{onion} \rangle \qquad \Phi_{\mathsf{rep}} = \mathsf{proj}_1(\mathsf{sdec}(x_{onion}, y)) = z_V \\ w_2' = \langle \mathsf{rep}, N', x_{pr}, \mathsf{proj}_2(\mathsf{sdec}(x_{onion}, y)) \rangle \end{cases}$

Once, a route between S and D has been established using this protocol, a data packet can then be sent from S to D using the route pseudonyms that nodes have stored in their storage list.

3.3   Configuration and Topology

Each process is located at a node of the network, and we consider an eavesdropper who observes messages sent from particular nodes. More precisely, we assume that the *topology* of the network is represented by a pair $\mathcal{T} = (G, \mathcal{M})$ where:

- $G = (V, E)$ is an undirected finite graph with $V \subseteq \{A \in \mathcal{N} \mid A$ of sort agent$\}$, where an edge in the graph models the fact that two agents are neighbors.
- $\mathcal{M}$ is a set of nodes, the *malicious nodes*, from which the attacker is able to listen to their outputs.

We consider several malicious nodes, and our setting allows us to deal with the case of a global eavesdropper (*i.e.* $\mathcal{M} = V$). A *trivial topology* is a topology $\mathcal{T} = (G, \mathcal{M})$ with $\mathcal{M} = \emptyset$.

A *configuration* of the network is a quadruplet $(\mathcal{E}; \mathcal{P}; \mathcal{S}; \sigma)$ where:

- $\mathcal{E}$ is a finite set of names that represents the names restricted in $\mathcal{P}$, $\mathcal{S}$ and σ;
- $\mathcal{P}$ is a multiset of expressions of the form $\lfloor P \rfloor_A$ that represents the process P executed by the agent $A \in V$. We write $\lfloor P \rfloor_A \cup \mathcal{P}$ instead of $\{\lfloor P \rfloor_A\} \cup \mathcal{P}$.
- $\mathcal{S}$ is a set of expressions of the form $\lfloor u \rfloor_A$ with $A \in V$ and u a ground term. $\lfloor u \rfloor_A$ represents the term u stored by the agent $A \in V$.
- $\sigma = \{y_1 \triangleright u_1, \ldots, y_n \triangleright u_n\}$ where $u_1, \ldots, u_n$ are ground terms (the messages observed by the attacker), and $y_1, \ldots, y_n$ are variables.

3.4   Execution Model

Each node broadcasts its messages to all its neighbors. The communication system is formally defined by the rules of Figure 1. They are parametrized by the underlying topology $\mathcal{T}$. The COMM rule allows nodes to communicate provided they are (directly) connected in the underlying graph, without the attacker actively interfering. We do not assume that messages are necessarily delivered to the intended recipients. They may be lost. The exchange message is learnt by the attacker as soon as the node that emits it is under its scrutiny.

The other rules are quite standard.

We write $\rightarrow$ instead of $\rightarrow_\mathcal{T}$ when the underlying network topology $\mathcal{T}$ is clear from the context. Let $\mathcal{A}$ be the alphabet of actions where the special symbol $\tau \in \mathcal{A}$ represents an unobservable action. For every $\ell \in \mathcal{A}$, the relation $\xrightarrow{\ell}$ has been defined in Figure 1. For every $w \in \mathcal{A}^*$ the relation $\xrightarrow{w}$ on configurations is defined in the usual way. By convention $K \xrightarrow{\epsilon} K$ where ϵ denotes the empty word. For every $s \in (\mathcal{A} \setminus \{\tau\})^*$, the relation $\xRightarrow{s}$ on configurations is defined by: $K \xRightarrow{s} K'$ if, and only if, there exists $w \in \mathcal{A}^*$ such that $K \xrightarrow{w} K'$ and s is obtained from w by erasing all occurrences of τ. Intuitively, $K \xRightarrow{s} K'$ means that K transforms into K' by experiment s.

An *initial configuration associated to a topology* $\mathcal{T} = (G, \mathcal{M})$ *and a routing protocol* $\mathcal{P}_{\text{routing}}$ is a configuration $K_0 = (\mathcal{E}_0; \mathcal{P}_0; \mathcal{S}_0; \sigma_0)$ such that:

$$\mathcal{P}_0 = \bigcup_{\substack{P \in \mathcal{P}_{\text{routing}} \\ A, B_1, \ldots, B_k \in V}} \lfloor !P(A, B_1, \ldots, B_k) \rfloor_A.$$

COMM $(\mathcal{E}; \lfloor \mathsf{out}(t).P \rfloor_A \cup \{\lfloor \mathsf{in}(u_j).P_j \rfloor_{A_j} \mid mgu(t, u_j) \neq \perp \wedge (A, A_j) \in E\} \cup \mathcal{P}; \mathcal{S}; \sigma)$
$$\xrightarrow{\ell}_{\mathcal{T}} (\mathcal{E}; \{\lfloor P_j \sigma_j \rfloor_{A_j}\} \cup \lfloor P \rfloor_A \cup \mathcal{P}; \mathcal{S}; \sigma')$$

where $\begin{cases} \sigma_j = mgu(t, u_j) \\ \sigma' = \sigma \cup \{y \triangleright t\} \text{ where } y \text{ is a fresh variable and } \ell = (\mathsf{out}(y), A) \text{ if } A \in \mathcal{M}; \\ \sigma' = \sigma \text{ and } \ell = \tau \text{ otherwise} \end{cases}$

STORE $(\mathcal{E}; \lfloor \mathsf{store}(t).P \rfloor_A \cup \mathcal{P}; \mathcal{S}; \sigma) \xrightarrow{\tau}_{\mathcal{T}} (\mathcal{E}; \lfloor P \rfloor_A \cup \mathcal{P}; \lfloor t \rfloor_A \cup \mathcal{S}; \sigma)$

READ-THEN $(\mathcal{E}; \lfloor \mathsf{read}\ u[\Phi]\ \mathsf{then}\ P\ \mathsf{else}\ Q \rfloor_A \cup \mathcal{P}; \lfloor t \rfloor_A \cup \mathcal{S}; \sigma)$
$$\xrightarrow{\tau}_{\mathcal{T}} (\mathcal{E}; \lfloor P\lambda \rfloor_A \cup \mathcal{P}; \lfloor t \rfloor_A \cup \mathcal{S}; \sigma)$$
$$\text{when } \lambda = mgu(t, u) \text{ exists and } \Phi\lambda \text{ is evaluated to true}$$

READ-ELSE $(\mathcal{E}; \lfloor \mathsf{read}\ u[\Phi]\ \mathsf{then}\ P\ \mathsf{else}\ Q \rfloor_A \cup \mathcal{P}; \mathcal{S}; \sigma)$
$$\xrightarrow{\tau}_{\mathcal{T}} (\mathcal{E}; \lfloor Q \rfloor_A \cup \mathcal{P}; \mathcal{S}; \sigma)$$
$$\text{if for all } t \text{ such that } \lfloor t \rfloor_A \in \mathcal{S}, mgu(t, u) = \perp \text{ or } \Phi mgu(t, u) \text{ is evaluated to false}$$

IF-THEN $(\mathcal{E}; \lfloor \mathsf{if}\ \Phi\ \mathsf{then}\ P\ \mathsf{else}\ Q \rfloor_A \cup \mathcal{P}; \mathcal{S}; \sigma) \xrightarrow{\tau}_{\mathcal{T}} (\mathcal{E}; \lfloor P \rfloor_A \cup \mathcal{P}; \mathcal{S}; \sigma)$
$$\text{if } \Phi \text{ is evaluated to true}$$

IF-ELSE $(\mathcal{E}; \lfloor \mathsf{if}\ \Phi\ \mathsf{then}\ P\ \mathsf{else}\ Q \rfloor_A \cup \mathcal{P}; \mathcal{S}; \sigma) \xrightarrow{\tau}_{\mathcal{T}} (\mathcal{E}; \lfloor Q \rfloor_A \cup \mathcal{P}; \mathcal{S}; \sigma)$
$$\text{if } \Phi \text{ is evaluated to false}$$

PAR $(\mathcal{E}; \lfloor P_1 \mid P_2 \rfloor_A \cup \mathcal{P}; \mathcal{S}; \sigma) \xrightarrow{\tau}_{\mathcal{T}} (\mathcal{E}; \lfloor P_1 \rfloor_A \cup \lfloor P_2 \rfloor_A \cup \mathcal{P}; \mathcal{S}; \sigma)$

REPL $(\mathcal{E}; \lfloor !P \rfloor_A \cup \mathcal{P}; \mathcal{S}; \sigma) \xrightarrow{\tau}_{\mathcal{T}} (\mathcal{E}; \lfloor P \rfloor_A \cup \lfloor !P \rfloor_A \cup \mathcal{P}; \mathcal{S}; \sigma)$

NEW $(\mathcal{E}; \lfloor \mathsf{new}\ n.P \rfloor_A \cup \mathcal{P}; \mathcal{S}; \sigma) \xrightarrow{\tau}_{\mathcal{T}} (\mathcal{E} \cup \{n'\}; \lfloor P\{^{n'}/_n\} \rfloor_A \cup \mathcal{P}; \mathcal{S}; \sigma)$
$$\text{where } n' \text{ is a fresh name}$$

Fig. 1. Transition system

Such a configuration represents the fact that each node can play any role of the protocol an unbounded number of times. Moreover, the agent who executes the process is located at the right place. A typical initial configuration will consist of $\mathcal{E}_0 = \mathcal{S}_0 = \sigma_0 = \emptyset$, but depending on the protocol under study, we may want to populate the storage lists of some nodes.

Example 3. Let $\mathcal{T}_0 = (G_0, \mathcal{M}_0)$ be a topology where G_0 is described below, and consider a global eavesdropper, *i.e.* $\mathcal{M}_0 = \{A, B, C, D\}$.

We consider the execution of the protocol $\mathcal{P}_{\mathsf{ANODR}}^{\mathsf{simp}}$ where B acts as a source to obtain a route to D. Receiving this request, and not being the destination, its neighbour C acts as a request forwarding node. We have that:

$$\mathrm{tr} = K_0 \xrightarrow{\tau} \xrightarrow{\tau} \xrightarrow{\tau} \xrightarrow{\mathsf{out}(y_1), B} (\mathcal{E}_1; \mathcal{P}_1; \mathcal{S}_1; \sigma_1) \xrightarrow{\tau} \xrightarrow{\tau} \xrightarrow{\tau} \xrightarrow{\mathsf{out}(y_2), C} (\mathcal{E}_2; \mathcal{P}_2; \mathcal{S}_2; \sigma_2)$$

where:
$$
\begin{cases}
K_0 = (\emptyset; \mathcal{P}_0; \emptyset; \emptyset) \text{ initial configuration associated to } \mathcal{T}_0 \text{ and } \mathcal{P}_{\mathsf{ANODR}}^{\mathsf{simp}}. \\
\mathcal{E}_1 = \{id, chall, k_B\} \quad \mathcal{E}_2 = \{id, chall, k_B, k_C\} \\
\mathcal{S}_1 = \emptyset \qquad\qquad\quad \mathcal{S}_2 = \{\lfloor\langle\mathsf{key}, k_C\rangle\rfloor_C\} \\
\sigma_1 = \{y_1 \rhd u\} \qquad\quad \sigma_2 = \{y_1 \rhd u, y_2 \rhd v\} \\
u = \langle\mathsf{req}, id, \mathsf{aenc}(\langle D, chall\rangle, \mathsf{pub}(D)), \mathsf{senc}(\langle B, \mathsf{src}\rangle, k_B)\rangle \\
v = \langle\mathsf{req}, id, \mathsf{aenc}(\langle D, chall\rangle, \mathsf{pub}(D)), \mathsf{senc}(\langle C, \mathsf{senc}(\langle B, \mathsf{src}\rangle, k_B)\rangle, k_C)\rangle
\end{cases}
$$

The process $\lfloor P_{\mathsf{src}}(B, D)\rfloor_B$ that occurs in K_0 will first follow the rule NEW three times to generate the nonces id, $chall$ and k_B leading to a new set of restricted names $\mathcal{E}_1$. The rule COMM is then applied between nodes B and C. As $B \in \mathcal{M}_0$, the message is included in σ_1 to represent the knowledge gained by the attacker. As the node C is not the destination, $\lfloor P_{\mathsf{int}}^{\mathsf{req}}(C)\rfloor_C$ can evolve (rule IF-THEN). It generates a key (rule NEW) added in $\mathcal{E}_2$, and stores it in $\mathcal{S}_2$ (rule STORE) and finally it uses COMM to broadcast the resulting message, which is also added to current substitution σ_2. Actually, in case we are only interested by the visible actions, this trace tr could also be written as follows:

$$
\mathsf{tr} = K_0 \xRightarrow{\mathsf{out}(y_1), B} (\mathcal{E}_1; \mathcal{P}_1; \mathcal{S}_1; \sigma_1) \xRightarrow{\mathsf{out}(y_2), C} (\mathcal{E}_2; \mathcal{P}_2; \mathcal{S}_2; \sigma_2).
$$

3.5   Extension and Equivalence of Traces

We cannot expect that privacy-type properties hold in any situation. We have to ensure that the traffic is sufficient. For this we need to introduce the notion of *extension of a trace*. Roughly, we say that a trace tr^+ is an extension of a trace tr if tr^+ contains at least all the actions that are exhibited in tr. In order to track of the actions, we consider annotated traces. This need comes from the fact that our calculus (and many others cryptographic calculi) does not provide us with information that allow us to retrieve who performed a given action.

We will denote $K \xrightarrow[A,R]{\tau} K'$ (resp. $K \xrightarrow[A,R]{\mathsf{out}(y), A} K'$) instead of $K \xrightarrow{\tau} K'$ (resp. $K \xrightarrow{\mathsf{out}(y), A} K'$) to explicit the annotations. We have that $A \in V$ and R is a constant. Intuitively A is the node that performs the action (resp. the output) whereas R is a constant that represents the role who is responsible of this action (resp. output). Thus, to formalise this notion of annotated trace, we associate a constant to each parametrized process part of the routing protocol under study. Theses annotations are nonetheless invisible to the attacker: she has only access to the labels of the transitions defined in our semantics. Annotations are meant to be used to specify privacy properties.

Example 4. Going back to our running example, $\mathcal{P}_{\mathsf{ANODR}}^{\mathsf{simp}}$ is made up of 4 roles and we associate a constant to each of them, namely Src, Req, Dest, and Rep. The annotated version of the trace tr described in Example 3 is:

$$
K_0 \xrightarrow[B,\mathsf{Src}]{\tau} \xrightarrow[B,\mathsf{Src}]{\tau} \xrightarrow[B,\mathsf{Src}]{\tau} \xrightarrow[B,\mathsf{Src}]{\mathsf{out}(y_1), B} K_1 \xrightarrow[C,\mathsf{Req}]{\tau} \xrightarrow[C,\mathsf{Req}]{\tau} \xrightarrow[C,\mathsf{Req}]{\tau} \xrightarrow[C,\mathsf{Req}]{\mathsf{out}(y_2), C} K_2
$$

with $K_1 = (\mathcal{E}_1; \mathcal{P}_1; \mathcal{S}_1; \sigma_1)$ and $K_2 = (\mathcal{E}_2; \mathcal{P}_2; \mathcal{S}_2; \sigma_2)$.

Given two configurations $K = (\mathcal{E}; \mathcal{P}; \mathcal{S}; \sigma)$ and $K^+ = (\mathcal{E}^+; \mathcal{P}^+; \mathcal{S}^+; \sigma^+)$, we write $K \subseteq K^+$ if $\mathcal{E} \subseteq \mathcal{E}^+$, $\mathcal{P} \subseteq \mathcal{P}^+$, $\mathcal{S} \subseteq \mathcal{S}^+$, and $\sigma^+_{|dom(\sigma)} = \sigma$.

Definition 2 (extension of a trace). *Let* tr^+ *be an annotated trace:*

$$\mathsf{tr}^+ = K_0 \xrightarrow[A_1,R_1]{\ell_1} K_1^+ \xrightarrow[A_2,R_2]{\ell_2} \cdots \xrightarrow[A_n,R_n]{\ell_n} K_n^+.$$

We say that tr^+ *is an* extension *of* tr, *denoted* $\mathsf{tr} \preccurlyeq \mathsf{tr}^+$, *if*

$$\mathsf{tr} = K_0 \xrightarrow[A_{k_1},R_{k_1}]{\ell_{k_1}} K_{k_1} \xrightarrow[A_{k_2},R_{k_2}]{\ell_{k_2}} \cdots \xrightarrow[A_{k_\ell},R_{k_\ell}]{\ell_{k_\ell}} K_{k_\ell}$$

where $0 < k_1 < k_2 < \ldots < k_\ell \leq n$, *and* $K_{k_i} \subseteq K_{k_i}^+$ *for each* $i \in \{1,\ldots,\ell\}$.

Given an indice i *corresponding to an action in* tr *(*$1 \leq i \leq \ell$*), we denote by* $\mathsf{ind}_i(\mathsf{tr},\mathsf{tr}^+)$ *the indice of the corresponding action in* tr^+, *i.e.* $\mathsf{ind}_i(\mathsf{tr},\mathsf{tr}^+) = k_i$.

Example 5. An extension of the trace tr described in Example 3 could be to let A initiate a new session before B tries to discover a route to D. Such an execution is formalised by the trace tr^+ written below:

$$K_0 \xrightarrow[A,\mathsf{Src}]{\tau} \xrightarrow[A,\mathsf{Src}]{\tau} \xrightarrow[A,\mathsf{Src}]{\tau} \xrightarrow[A,\mathsf{Src}]{\mathsf{out}(y_0),A} K_0^+ \xrightarrow[B,\mathsf{Src}]{\tau} \xrightarrow[B,\mathsf{Src}]{\tau} \xrightarrow[B,\mathsf{Src}]{\tau} \xrightarrow[B,\mathsf{Src}]{\mathsf{out}(y_1),B} K_1^+$$

$$\xrightarrow[C,\mathsf{Req}]{\tau} \xrightarrow[C,\mathsf{Req}]{\tau} \xrightarrow[C,\mathsf{Req}]{\tau} \xrightarrow[C,\mathsf{Req}]{\mathsf{out}(y_2),C} K_2^+.$$

where the configurations are not detailed, but $(\mathcal{E}_i; \mathcal{P}_i; \mathcal{S}_i; \sigma_i) \subseteq K_i^+$ $(i \in \{1,2\})$.

Privacy-type security properties are often formalised using a notion equivalence (see *e.g.* [12,3,9]). Here, we consider the notion of *equivalence between two traces*.

Definition 3 (equivalence of two traces). *Let* $\mathsf{tr}_1 = K_1 \xRightarrow{s_1} (\mathcal{E}_1; \mathcal{P}_1; \mathcal{S}_1; \sigma_1)$ *and* $\mathsf{tr}_2 = K_2 \xRightarrow{s_2} (\mathcal{E}_2; \mathcal{P}_2; \mathcal{S}_2; \sigma_2)$ *be two traces. They are* equivalent, *denoted* $\mathsf{tr}_1 \approx_\mathsf{E} \mathsf{tr}_2$, *if* $s_1 = s_2$ *and* new $\mathcal{E}_1.\sigma_1 \sim_\mathsf{E}$ new $\mathcal{E}_2.\sigma_2$.

Note that only observable actions are taken into account in the definition of equivalence between two traces. Roughly, two traces are equivalent if they process the same sequence of visible outputs. The two sequences may differ (we do *not* require the equality between σ_1 and σ_2) but they should be indistinguishable from the point of view of the attacker.

Example 6. In the execution tr^+ provided in Example 5 one could hope to hide the fact that the node B is initiating a route discovery and let the attacker think A is the actual source. Let tr' be the execution below where A initiates a route discovery towards D, while nodes B and C act as forwarders.

$$K_0 \xrightarrow[A,\mathsf{Src}]{\tau} \xrightarrow[A,\mathsf{Src}]{\tau} \xrightarrow[A,\mathsf{Src}]{\tau} \xrightarrow[A,\mathsf{Src}]{\mathsf{out}(y_0),A} K_0' \xrightarrow[B,\mathsf{Req}]{\tau} \xrightarrow[B,\mathsf{Req}]{\tau} \xrightarrow[B,\mathsf{Req}]{\tau} \xrightarrow[B,\mathsf{Req}]{\mathsf{out}(y_1),B} K_1'$$

$$\xrightarrow[C,\mathsf{Req}]{\tau} \xrightarrow[C,\mathsf{Req}]{\tau} \xrightarrow[C,\mathsf{Req}]{\tau} \xrightarrow[C,\mathsf{Req}]{\mathsf{out}(y_2),C} K_2'.$$

where the configurations are not detailed.

Unfortunately the attacker is able to tell the difference between tr^+ and tr'. Indeed, we have $\mathsf{tr}^+ \not\approx_\mathsf{E} \mathsf{tr}'$ since the test $\mathsf{proj}_2(\mathsf{proj}_1(y_0)) \overset{?}{=} \mathsf{proj}_2(\mathsf{proj}_1(y_1))$ can be used to distinguish the two traces. The equality test will hold in tr' and not in tr^+. Note that, as the annotations are invisible to the attacker, she cannot know *a priori* that B is playing a forwarder in tr'.

4   Indistinguishability

Intuitively, indistinguishability deals with the ability for the attacker to distinguish a specific action from another. For a routing protocol such actions take the form of the various roles of the protocol. In particular we could hope, in an execution of the protocol, to make actions of the initiator or recipient indistinguishable from actions of forwarding nodes. Our definition of indistinguishability, and later of other privacy properties, depends on the network topology we are considering. Incidentally, when designing anonymous protocols, these properties should hold for large enough classes of topologies.

4.1   Formalizing Indistinguishability

Let Roles be a set of roles for which indistinguishability has to be preserved. A very naive definition would be to ensure that for any annotated trace tr issued from K_0 (the initial configuration associated to the protocol under study) where at some position i the role $\mathsf{R} \in$ Roles is played and observed by the attacker, there exists an equivalent annotated trace tr' where the role played at position i is not in the set Roles. However, without appropriate traffic on the network, this definition is far too strong. Indeed, as soon as the source role is the only role able to spontaneously start a session, we will have no hope to achieve indistinguishability.

Definition 4 (indistinguishability). *Let K_0 be an initial configuration associated to a routing protocol and a topology, and* Roles *be a set of roles. We say that K_0 preserves* indistinguishability *w.r.t.* Roles *if for any annotated trace* tr

$$\mathsf{tr} = K_0 \xrightarrow[A_1,R_1]{\ell_1} K_1 \xrightarrow[A_2,R_2]{\ell_2} \dots \xrightarrow[A_n,R_n]{\ell_n} K_n = (\mathcal{E}; \mathcal{P}; \mathcal{S}; \sigma)$$

and for any $i \in \{1, \dots, n\}$ such that $\mathsf{R}_i \in$ Roles and $\ell_i \neq \tau$ (i.e. ℓ_i is an action observed by the attacker), there exist two annotated traces tr^+ *and* tr' *such that:* $\mathsf{tr} \preccurlyeq \mathsf{tr}^+$, $\mathsf{tr}^+ \approx \mathsf{tr}'$, *and* $\mathsf{R}'_{\mathsf{ind}_i(\mathsf{tr},\mathsf{tr}^+)} \notin$ Roles *where*

$$\mathsf{tr}' = K_0' \xrightarrow[A_1',R_1']{\ell_1'} K_1' \xrightarrow[A_2',R_2']{\ell_2'} K_2' \dots \xrightarrow[A_{n'}',R_{n'}']{\ell_{n'}'} K_{n'}'.$$

The trace tr^+ enables us to deal with the aforementioned traffic needed to aim at preserving indistinguishability. Indeed rather than imposing the equivalence of tr with another trace, indistinguishability will be achieved if there exist two other traces tr^+ and tr' which look the same to the attacker, and in which the action of interest is played by a different role.

4.2   Analysis of ANODR

Now, we apply our formalisation of indistinguishability to the ANODR protocol.

Proposition 1. *Let $\mathcal{T}$ be a topology with a malicious node that has only malicious neighbours, and K_0 be an initial configuration associated to P_{ANODR}^{simp} and $\mathcal{T}$. We have that K_0 does not preserve indistinguishability w.r.t.* Src *(resp.* Dest*).*

Indeed, given a node A which is, together with its neighbors, under the scrutiny of the attacker, consider a situation, *i.e.* a trace tr, where the node A starts a new session by acting as a source. Of course, if this action is the only activity of the network, there is no hope to confuse the attacker. The idea is to see whether the attacker can be confused when the traffic is sufficient. In particular, we may want to consider a situation, *i.e.* a trace tr^+, where a request also arrives at node A at the same time, so that the node A has also the possibility to act as a forwarder. However, since a request conveys a unique identifier *id*, it will be easy for the attacker to observe whether A is acting as a source (the request will contain a fresh identifier) or as a forwarder (the request will contain an identifier that has been previously observed by the attacker). Actually, the same reasoning allows us to conclude that indistinguishability is not preserved w.r.t. the role Dest: a reply conveys a globally unique nonce (namely *chall*).

The updated version of ANODR proposed in [15] and informally described below (see the appendice for a formal description) fixes the issue regarding indistinguishability w.r.t. Roles = {Dest}. In this version, K_T is a symmetric encryption key shared between the source A and the destination D; K_A, K_B and K_C are symmetric keys known only to their owners A, B, C, whereas K_{seedB}, K_{seedC}, K_{seedD} are fresh keys shared between consecutive nodes on the reply route. The key K_D is generated by A and will be known by every node on the route by the end of a session. The routes are stored as a correspondence between route pseudonyms (the N_i) by each intermediate node. The proof of opening takes the form of the key K_D which is embedded in an onion which is different from the onions used during the request phase. For sake of clarity, we use $\{\cdot\}$ instead of senc and aenc, and we omit some $\langle \cdot, \cdot \rangle$.

$A \to B : \langle \text{req}, id, \text{pub}(A), \{\text{dest}, K_D\}_{K_T}, \{\text{dest}\}_{K_D}, \{\text{src}\}_{K_A} \rangle$
$B \to C : \langle \text{req}, id, \text{pub}(B), \{\text{dest}, K_D\}_{K_T}, \{\text{dest}\}_{K_D}, \{N_B, \{\text{src}\}_{K_A}\}_{K_B} \rangle$
$C \to D : \langle \text{req}, id, \text{pub}(C), \{\text{dest}, K_D\}_{K_T}, \{\text{dest}\}_{K_D}, \{N_C, \{N_B, \{\text{src}\}_{K_A}\}_{K_B}\}_{K_C} \rangle$

$D \to C : \langle \text{rep}, \{K_{seedD}\}_{\text{pub}(C)}, \{K_D, \{N_C, \{N_B, \{\text{src}\}_{K_A}\}_{K_B}\}_{K_C}\}_{K_{seedD}} \rangle$
$C \to B : \langle \text{rep}, \{K_{seedC}\}_{\text{pub}(B)}, \{K_D, \{N_B, \{\text{src}\}_{K_A}\}_{K_B}\}_{K_{seedC}} \rangle$
$B \to A : \langle \text{rep}, \{K_{seedB}\}_{\text{pub}(A)}, \{K_D, \{\text{src}\}_{K_A}\}_{K_{seedB}} \rangle$

Considering a topology $\mathcal{T}$ such that any malicious node has at least two distinct neighbours other than itself, and an initial configuration K_0 associated to the updated version of ANODR and $\mathcal{T}$, we have that K_0 preserves indistinguishability w.r.t. Roles = {Dest}, according to Definition 4.

Intuitively, for each trace tr in which the node A (under the scrutiny of the attacker) acts as a destination, we will consider a trace tr^+ which extends tr and such that the node A has at least two reply to treat (one as a destination and one as a forwarder). Since the proof of opening and the onion are modified at each hop of the route, the attacker will not be able to observe whether two reply packets come from the same session or not. Thus, he can not be sure that the action of interest has been done by the role Dest.

5   Unlinkability

We focus here on a different kind of anonymity: the (un)ability for the attacker to determine whether two messages belong to the same session. Note that an attacker able to determine whether two reply messages belong to the same session will gain valuable information about the route being established.

5.1   Augmented Process

To define unlinkability, we need a notion of session. Note that, in our setting, a session may involve an arbitrary number of actions since we do not know in advance the length of the path from the source to the destination. In order to define this notion formally, we need to be able to track an execution of the process through the entire network, goal which is achieved through a notion of *augmented processes*. Thus, given a routing protocol $\mathcal{P}_{\text{routing}}$, we define its augmentation $\tilde{\mathcal{P}}_{\text{routing}}$ and modify the operational semantics accordingly to trace an execution of one session of the protocol. We also add some information about the source and the destination. This information will be useful later on to define our notion of anonymity (see Section 6).

For sake of simplicity, we consider a routing protocol that is made up of parametrized processes of two different kinds. Even if these syntactic restrictions seem to be very specific, our definition actually captures most of the routing protocols and are quite natural.

Initiator: a parametrized process with two parameters $P(z_S, z_D)$ such that its first communication action is an output possibly followed by several inputs. In such a case, its *augmentation* $\tilde{P}(z_S, z_D)$ is obtained from $P(z_S, z_D)$ by adding the prefix new sid. to it, by replacing the action out(u) with out$(\langle u, \langle sid, z_S, z_D \rangle \rangle)$, and replacing each action in(u) with in$(\langle u, \langle x_1, x_2, x_3 \rangle \rangle)$ where x_1, x_2, x_3 are fresh variables.

Responder: a parametrized process with one parameter $P(z_V)$ such that its first communication action is an input possibly followed by several outputs. In such a case, its *augmentation* $\tilde{P}(z_V)$ is obtained from $P(z_V)$ by replacing the action in(u) with in$(\langle u, \langle x_1, x_2, x_3 \rangle \rangle)$ where x_1, x_2, x_3 are fresh variables, and each action out(u) with out$(\langle u, \langle x_1, x_2, x_3 \rangle \rangle)$.

Now, to prevent the additional information that is conveyed by the messages to occur in the frame, we need to adapt our operational semantics. Basically, when we perform a communication, we only add the first projection of the outputted term in the frame. The second projection of the outputted term is added under the arrow as an annotation.

Example 7. Back to Example 3, the counterpart of the trace tr, where only visible actions have been exhibited, is succinctly depicted below:

$$\tilde{K}_0 \xrightarrow[B,\mathsf{Src},sid,B,D]{\mathsf{out}(y_1),B} \tilde{K}_1 \xrightarrow[C,\mathsf{Req},sid,B,D]{\mathsf{out}(y_2),C} \tilde{K}_2$$

where the configurations $\tilde{K}_0$, $\tilde{K}_1$ and $\tilde{K}_2$ are the counterpart of K_1, K_2, and K_3. The annotations under the arrows witness the fact that the two messages come from the same session *sid* which was initiated by B to obtain a route towards D.

Note that only observable action will benefit from this annotation. For sake of simplicity, we write $K \xrightarrow[A,R,[sid,S,D]]{\ell} K'$ even in presence of an unobservable action ℓ (*i.e.* when $\ell = \tau$) and we add the brackets to emphasize the fact that $[sid, S, D]$ is optional. Actually, the annotation is undefined in this case.

5.2   Formalising Unlinkability

Intuitively, unlinkability means that an attacker cannot tell whether two visible actions of a trace tr belong to the same session. As it was the case for indistinguishability, one cannot expect to achieve this goal without any sufficient traffic on the network. Moreover, due to the globally unique identifier that occur for efficiency purposes in many routing protocols (*e.g.* the nonce *id* in ANODR), there is no hope to achieve unlinkability for request messages. However, this is not a big issue since these messages are flooded in the network and thus tracking them is useless. We may want to study unlinkability for particular sets of roles, and our definition allows one to do that.

Definition 5 (unlinkability). *Let K_0 be an initial configuration associated to a routing protocol and a topology, and* Roles$_1$, Roles$_2$ *be two sets of roles. We say that K_0 preserves* unlinkability *w.r.t.* Roles$_1$/Roles$_2$ *if for any annotated trace* tr

$$\mathsf{tr} = K_0 \xrightarrow[A_1,R_1,[sid_1,S_1,D_1]]{\ell_1} K_1 \xrightarrow[A_2,R_2,[sid_2,S_2,D_2]]{\ell_2} \cdots \xrightarrow[A_n,R_n,[sid_n,S_n,D_n]]{\ell_n} K_n$$

and for any $i, j \in \{1, \ldots, n\}$ such that $R_i \in$ Roles$_1$, $R_j \in$ Roles$_2$, $sid_i = sid_j$, and $\ell_i, \ell_j \neq \tau$ (i.e. ℓ_i, ℓ_j are actions observed by the attacker), there exist two annotated traces tr$^+$ *and* tr$'$ *such that:* tr $\preccurlyeq$ tr$^+$, tr$^+ \approx$ tr$'$, *and* $sid'_{\mathsf{ind}_i(\mathsf{tr,tr}+)} \neq sid'_{\mathsf{ind}_j(\mathsf{tr,tr}+)}$ *where*

$$\mathsf{tr}' = K'_0 \xrightarrow[A'_1,R'_1,[sid'_1,S'_1,D'_1]]{\ell'_1} K'_1 \xrightarrow[A'_2,R'_2,[sid'_2,S'_2,D'_2]]{\ell'_2} \cdots \xrightarrow[A'_{n'},R'_{n'},sid'_{n'},S'_{n'},D'_{n'}]{\ell'_{n'}} K'_{n'}.$$

Unlinkability versus indistinguishability. Note that unlinkability is a distinct notion from the indistinguishability notion exposed in Section 4. Protocols unlinkable w.r.t. any reasonable topology can be designed so as not to be indistinguishable for any role. An example of such a protocol would be $\mathcal{P} = \{P_1(z_S, z_D), P_2(z_V)\}$ defined as follows:

$$P_1(z_S, z_D) = \text{out(src).in}(x) \qquad P_2(z_V) = \text{in}(x).\text{out(dest)}$$

where src and dest are two constants. The unlinkability is a consequence of emitting the same messages for every session, whereas the indistinguishability fails as the constant src (resp. dest) identifies the role P_1 (resp. P_2).

Reciprocally one can design protocols preserving indistinguishability for certain roles but not unlinkability for any two subsets of roles. The protocol $\mathcal{P}'$ made up of the three roles described below fails clearly at preserving the unlinkability w.r.t. any non-trivial topology for any sets of roles Roles_1 and Roles_2 as it mimicks the session identifiers introduced formerly.

$$P_1'(z_S, z_D) = \text{new } n.\text{out}(n).\text{in}(x) \qquad P_2'(z_V) = \text{in}(x).\text{out}(x)$$
$$P_3'(z_V) = \text{in}(x).\text{store}(x).\text{out}(x)$$

On the other hand, the indistinguishability w.r.t. any topology for either P_2' or P_3' is trivially preserved as the roles are essentially the same.

5.3   Analysis of **ANODR**

As discussed at the beginning of Section 5.2, ANODR, as many other routing protocols, does not preserve unlinkability (as soon as the underlying topology is non-trivial topology) for sets $\text{Roles}_1 = \text{Roles}_2 = \{\text{Src}, \text{Req}\}$ due to the forwarding of the same *id* by every intermediate node during the request phase. Actually, the simplified version of ANODR presented in Section 3.2 does not preserve unlinkability for sets $\text{Roles}_1 = \text{Roles}_2 = \{\text{Dest}, \text{Rep}\}$ due to the forwarding of the nonce *chall* by every intermediate node during the reply phase. This version does not preserve unlinkability for sets $\{\text{Src}, \text{Req}\}/\{\text{Dest}, \text{Rep}\}$ either. Indeed, during the request phase, the nodes will emit a message containing an onion, and during the reply phase, they are waiting for a message that contains exactly the same onion. This allows the attacker to link a request message with a reply message and to identify them as coming from the same session.

The updated version of ANODR (see Section 4.2) actually fixes the two last issues. Again, we need for this to consider topologies $\mathcal{T}$ for which any malicious node has at least two distinct neighbours other than itself. In such a situation, following the same ideas as the one used to establish indistinguishability, we can show that an initial configuration K_0 preserves unlinkability w.r.t. $\{\text{Dest}, \text{Rep}\}/$ $\{\text{Dest}, \text{Rep}\}$, and $\{\text{Src}, \text{Req}\}/\{\text{Dest}, \text{Rep}\}$ (according to Definition 5).

6   Anonymity

Anonymity is concerned with hiding who performed a given action. Here, we are not concerned by hiding the identity of the sender (or the receiver) of a given message, but we would like to hide the identity of the source (or the destination) of the request/reply message. When the identity of the source is hidden, we speak about *source anonymity*. Similarly, when the identity of the destination is hidden, we speak about *destination anonymity*. Again, we consider both types of anonymity with respect to an external eavesdropper that is localised to some nodes (possibly every one of them) of the network.

As in Section 5, to define the anonymity, we need to link messages occurring at various places in the network to their respective source and destination, thus we consider the augmented version of the protocol as in Section 5.1

6.1   Formalising Anonymity

Intuitively, source (resp. destination) anonymity can be achieved if the attacker is unable to tell the source (resp. the destination) of an observed message. This idea can actually be interpreted as the existence of anonymity sets of cardinal greater or equal than two. As for the previous privacy-type notions, one cannot expect to hide the source (resp. destination) of an action in a trace tr without any sufficient traffic as it would be easy for an attacker to observe the first node to output a request (resp. a reply) and deduce the source (resp. destination) of this execution. For this reason, anonymity will be achieved if there exist two other traces tr^+ and tr' of the system which look the same to the attacker, and in which the corresponding transitions have different sources (resp. destinations).

Definition 6 (anonymity). *Let K_0 be an initial configuration associated to a routing protocol and a topology. We say that K_0 preserves source anonymity (resp. destination anonymity) if for any annotated trace* tr

$$\text{tr} = K_0 \xrightarrow[A_1,R_1,[sid_1,S_1,D_1]]{\ell_1} K_1 \xrightarrow[A_2,R_2,[sid_2,S_2,D_2]]{\ell_2} \cdots \xrightarrow[A_n,R_n,[sid_n,S_n,D_n]]{\ell_n} K_n$$

and for any $i \in \{1,\ldots,n\}$ such that $\ell_i \neq \tau$ (i.e. ℓ_i is an action observed by the attacker), there exist two annotated traces tr^+ and tr' such that $\text{tr} \preccurlyeq \text{tr}^+$, $\text{tr}^+ \approx \text{tr}'$, and $S'_{\text{ind}_i(\text{tr},\text{tr}^+)} \neq S_i$ (resp. $D'_{\text{ind}_i(\text{tr},\text{tr}^+)} \neq D_i$) where

$$\text{tr}' = K_0' \xrightarrow[A_1',R_1',[sid_1',S_1',D_1']]{\ell_1'} K_1' \xrightarrow[A_2',R_2',[sid_2',S_2',D_2']]{\ell_2'} \cdots \xrightarrow[A_{n'}',R_{n'}',[sid_{n'}',S_{n'}',D_{n'}']]{\ell_{n'}'} K_{n'}'$$

6.2   Anonymity versus Indistinguishability/Unlinkability

The notions of source and destination anonymity are distinct from indistinguishability for a set of roles and unlinkability of two sets of roles. The protocol $\mathcal{P} = \{P_1(z_S, z_D), P_2(z_V)\}$ where $P_1(z_S, z_D) = \text{out}(z_S).\text{in}(x)$, and $P_2(z_V) = \text{in}(x).\text{out}(x)$ preserves both the indistinguishability of P_1 (a node can play P_2 as a response to a session it initiated previously as P_1) and the unlinkability of any two subsets of $\{P_1, P_2\}$ (as every session with the same node as a source will generate the exact same messages) but not source anonymity as the identity of the source is obvious for any attacker along the route. A symmetrical protocol can be built by replacing z_S with z_D in P_1 to disclose the destination of a session without breaking the indistinguishability.

Conversely, the protocol $\mathcal{P} = \{P_1(z_S, z_D), P_2(z_V)\}$ defined as

$$P_1(z_S, z_D) = \text{new } n.\text{out}(\langle \text{src}, n \rangle).\text{in}(x) \qquad P_2(z_V) = \text{in}(\langle x, y \rangle).\text{out}(\langle \text{dest}, y \rangle)$$

preserves destination anonymity as any node can play P_2 in response to a request, whatever the original destination was. Indeed, given such a topology $\mathcal{T}$, a trace tr of the protocol, and a visible action $\ell_i = (\mathsf{out}(y), A)$ associated to a a source $S_i = S$ and a destination $D_i = A$, we can let tr^+ be equal to tr and define tr' to be the trace mimicking tr but with S as the source and destination of the request associated to ℓ_i. The equivalence of tr and tr' comes from the content of their frames which is limited to the names of the request sources, identical in both cases. On the other hand, $\mathcal{P}$ does not preserve indistinguishability of P_1 or P_2, nor unlinkability of any two subsets of $\{P_1, P_2\}$ as session identifiers and constants to distinguish roles are embedded in the protocol.

However, intuitively, there is a relation between source anonymity (resp. destination anonymity) and indistinguishability of the role source (resp. destination). Indeed, source anonymity seems to imply that the action of interest can be mimicked by someone different from source, and thus who should not play the role source. Thus, restricting ourselves to "reasonable" routing protocols, we are indeed able to establish this relation. For this, we define *source* and *destination roles* as roles which are only used by nodes acting as sources or destinations.

Definition 7 (acting as a source (resp. destination)). *Let K_0 be an initial configuration associated to a routing protocol and a topology. We say that* Roles *is the set of roles* acting as a source *(resp.* acting as a destination*) if for any annotated trace* tr *with* $\ell_1, \ldots, \ell_n \neq \tau$

$$\mathsf{tr} = K_0 \xrightarrow[A_1,\mathsf{R}_1,sid_1,S_1,D_1]{\ell_1} K_1 \xrightarrow[A_2,\mathsf{R}_2,sid_2,S_2,D_2]{\ell_2} \cdots \xrightarrow[A_n,\mathsf{R}_n,sid_n,S_n,D_n]{\ell_n} K_n$$

and for any $i \in \{1, \ldots, n\}$, $\mathsf{R}_i \in$ Roles *if and only if* $A_i = S_i$ *(resp. if and only if* $A_i = D_i$*).*

In case of ANODR (both versions), the set of roles acting as a source is {Src}. This is the only role able to spontaneously start a session and it is unable to reply to a request. The set of roles acting as a destination is limited to {Dest}. The proof of opening prevents any node other than the destination to play it and, conversely, a destination node can only play the role Dest as a response to such a request. Note that, for some badly designed routing protocols, it may happen that the set of roles acting as a source (resp. destination) is empty. In such a case, the proposition below is trivially true.

Proposition 2. *Let K_0 be an initial configuration associated to a routing protocol and a topology. If K_0 preserves source (resp. destination) anonymity, then it preserves indistinguishability w.r.t. the set of roles acting as a source (resp. destination).*

6.3   Analysis of ANODR

In this section, we apply our formalisation of anonymity to the ANODR routing protocol. As a consequence of Propositions 1 and 2, we have the following result.

Corollary 1. *Let $\mathcal{T}$ be a topology with a malicious node that has only malicious neighbours, and K_0 be an initial configuration associated to $\mathcal{P}_{\mathsf{ANODR}}^{\mathsf{simp}}$ and $\mathcal{T}$. We have that K_0 preserves neither source nor destination anonymity.*

For the updated version of ANODR, similarly, we can show that it does not preserve source anonymity. However, this protocol seems to have been designed to achieve destination anonymity. Indeed, considering topologies for which any malicious node has at least one neighbour other than itself, we can show that any trace tr can be extended to tr$^+$ so that the node of interest has at least two reply to treat (one as the destination of the request, and the other one as the forwarder). This is actually sufficient to confuse the attacker who observes the network, and to establish anonymity of the destination according to Definition 6.

7 Conclusion

We have defined a framework for modeling routing protocols in ad hoc networks in a variant of the applied pi-calculus. Within this framework we can stipulate which agents are subject to the attention of a global eavesdropper. We were able to propose several definitions for privacy-type properties that encompass the specificity of a given network topology. We illustrate these definitions on the anonymous routing protocol ANODR, considered in two versions, and thus provide a partial formal security analysis of its anonymity.

As future work, it would be interesting to have a more general model of protocols to represent high-level operations in routing protocols (*e.g.* reversing a list). However, since our definitions are expressed in terms of traces, this should not impact so much the privacy definitions proposed in this paper. Another direction is the enrichment of our attacker model, so as to model fully compromised nodes which disclose their long-term keys or fresh nonces generated during the execution of the protocols, and active attackers able to forge messages and interact with honest agents. Finally, from the point of view of the verification, a reduction result on network topologies as presented in [11] would make the perspective of automated proofs of anonymity easier.

References

1. Abadi, M., Fournet, C.: Mobile values, new names, and secure communication. In: Proc. 28th Symposium on Principles of Programming Languages, POPL 2001, pp. 104–115. ACM Press (2001)
2. Abadi, M., Gordon, A.: A calculus for cryptographic protocols: The spi calculus. In: Proc. 4th Conference on Computer and Communications Security, CCS 1997, pp. 36–47. ACM Press (1997)
3. Arapinis, M., Chothia, T., Ritter, E., Ryan, M.: Analysing unlinkability and anonymity using the applied pi calculus. In: Proc. 23rd Computer Security Foundations Symposium, CSF 2010, pp. 107–121. IEEE Computer Society Press (2010)
4. Armando, A., Carbone, R., Compagna, L., Cuéllar, J., Tobarra, M.L.: Formal analysis of SAML 2.0 web browser single sign-on: breaking the SAML-based single sign-on for google apps. In: Proc. of the 6th ACM Workshop on Formal Methods in Security Engineering, FMSE 2008, pp. 1–10. ACM (2008)

5. Armando, A., Basin, D., Boichut, Y., Chevalier, Y., Compagna, L., Cuellar, J., Hankes Drielsma, P., Heám, P.C., Kouchnarenko, O., Mantovani, J., Mödersheim, S., von Oheimb, D., Rusinowitch, M., Santiago, J., Turuani, M., Viganò, L., Vigneron, L.: The AVISPA Tool for the Automated Validation of Internet Security Protocols and Applications. In: Etessami, K., Rajamani, S.K. (eds.) CAV 2005. LNCS, vol. 3576, pp. 281–285. Springer, Heidelberg (2005)

6. Arnaud, M., Cortier, V., Delaune, S.: Modeling and verifying ad hoc routing protocols. In: Proc. 23rd IEEE Computer Security Foundations Symposium, CSF 2010, pp. 59–74. IEEE Computer Society Press (July 2010)

7. Backes, M., Hritcu, C., Maffei, M.: Automated verification of remote electronic voting protocols in the applied pi-calculus. IEEE Comp. Soc. Press (2008)

8. Blanchet, B.: An efficient cryptographic protocol verifier based on prolog rules. In: Proc. 14th Computer Security Foundations Workshop, CSFW 2001. IEEE Comp. Soc. Press (2001)

9. Bruso, M., Chatzikokolakis, K., den Hartog, J.: Formal verification of privacy for RFID systems. In: Proc. 23rd Computer Security Foundations Symposium, CSF 2010, IEEE Computer Society Press (2010)

10. Chrétien, R., Delaune, S.: Formal analysis of privacy for routing protocols in mobile ad hoc networks. Research Report LSV-12-21, Laboratoire Spécification et Vérification, ENS Cachan, France, 24 pages (December 2012)

11. Cortier, V., Degrieck, J., Delaune, S.: Analysing Routing Protocols: Four Nodes Topologies Are Sufficient. In: Degano, P., Guttman, J.D. (eds.) Principles of Security and Trust. LNCS, vol. 7215, pp. 30–50. Springer, Heidelberg (2012)

12. Delaune, S., Kremer, S., Ryan, M.D.: Verifying privacy-type properties of electronic voting protocols. Journal of Computer Security (4), 435–487 (2008)

13. Garcia, F.D., Hasuo, I., Pieters, W., van Rossum, P.: Provable anonymity. In: Proc. ACM Workshop on Formal Methods in Security Engineering, FMSE 2005, pp. 63–72. ACM (2005)

14. Hu, Y.-C., Perrig, A., Johnson, D.: Ariadne: A Secure On-Demand Routing Protocol for Ad Hoc Networks. Wireless Networks 11, 21–38 (2005)

15. Kong, J., Hong, X.: ANODR: anonymous on demand routing with untraceable routes for mobile ad-hoc networks. In: Proc. 4th ACM Interational Symposium on Mobile Ad Hoc Networking and Computing, MobiHoc 2003. ACM (2003)

16. Mauw, S., Verschuren, J.H.S., de Vink, E.P.: A Formalization of Anonymity and Onion Routing. In: Samarati, P., Ryan, P.Y.A., Gollmann, D., Molva, R. (eds.) ESORICS 2004. LNCS, vol. 3193, pp. 109–124. Springer, Heidelberg (2004)

17. Nanz, S., Hankin, C.: A Framework for Security Analysis of Mobile Wireless Networks. Theoretical Computer Science 367(1), 203–227 (2006)

18. Papadimitratos, P., Haas, Z.: Secure routing for mobile ad hoc networks. In: Proc. SCS Communication Networks and Distributed Systems Modelling Simulation Conference, CNDS (2002)

19. Serjantov, A., Danezis, G.: Towards an Information Theoretic Metric for Anonymity. In: Dingledine, R., Syverson, P.F. (eds.) PET 2002. LNCS, vol. 2482, pp. 41–53. Springer, Heidelberg (2003)

20. Song, R., Korba, L., Lee, G.: AnonDSR: Efficient anonymous dynamic source routing for mobile ad-hoc networks. In: Proc. ACM Workshop on Security of Ad Hoc and Sensor Networks, SASN 2005. ACM (2005)

21. Zapata, M.G., Asokan, N.: Securing ad hoc routing protocols. In: Proc. 1st ACM Workshop on Wireless SEcurity, WiSE 2002, pp. 1–10. ACM (2002)

Practical Everlasting Privacy

Myrto Arapinis[1], Véronique Cortier[2], Steve Kremer[2], and Mark Ryan[1]

[1] School of Computer Science, University of Birmingham
[2] LORIA, CNRS, France

Abstract. Will my vote remain secret in 20 years? This is a natural question in the context of electronic voting, where encrypted votes may be published on a bulletin board for verifiability purposes, but the strength of the encryption is eroded with the passage of time. The question has been addressed through a property referred to as *everlasting privacy*. Perfect everlasting privacy may be difficult or even impossible to achieve, in particular in remote electronic elections. In this paper, we propose a definition of *practical everlasting privacy*. The key idea is that in the future, an attacker will be more powerful in terms of computation (he may be able to break the cryptography) but less powerful in terms of the data he can operate on (transactions between a vote client and the vote server may not have been stored).

We formalize our definition of everlasting privacy in the applied-pi calculus. We provide the means to characterize what an attacker can break in the future in several cases. In particular, we model this for perfectly hiding and computationally binding primitives (or the converse), such as Pedersen commitments, and for symmetric and asymmetric encryption primitives. We adapt existing tools, in order to allow us to automatically prove everlasting privacy. As an illustration, we show that several variants of Helios (including Helios with Pedersen commitments) and a protocol by Moran and Naor achieve practical everlasting privacy, using the ProVerif and the AKiSs tools.

1 Introduction

Electronic voting schemes such as Helios [2], JCJ/Civitas [14,8], and Prêt-à-Voter [7] aim simultaneously to guarantee *vote privacy* (that is, the link between the voter and her vote will not be revealed), and *outcome verifiability* (that is, voters and observers can check that the declared outcome is correct). A common way to achieve verifiability is to publish a "bulletin board" that contains all encrypted votes (indeed, this is the way it is done in the systems cited above). The strength and key-length of the encryption should be chosen so that decryption by an attacker is impossible for as long as the votes are expected to remain private. To prevent coercer reprisal not just to the voter but also to her descendants, one may want vote privacy for up to 100 years.

Unfortunately, however, it is not possible to predict in any reliable way how long present-day encryptions will last. Weaknesses may be found in encryption algorithms, and computers will certainly continue to get faster. A coercer can plausibly assert that a voter should follow the coercer's wishes because the bulletin board will reveal in (say) 10 years whether the voter followed the coercer's instructions. For this reason, systems with "everlasting privacy" have been introduced by [18]. These systems do not rely

D. Basin and J.C. Mitchell (Eds.): POST 2013, LNCS 7796, pp. 21–40, 2013.
© Springer-Verlag Berlin Heidelberg 2013

on encryptions whose strength may be eroded, but on commitments that are *perfectly* or *information-theoretically hiding*. These systems have computational verifiability instead of perfect verifiability, and are considered less usable and computationally more expensive than systems relying on encryptions. More recently, schemes have been proposed with a weaker form of everlasting privacy (e.g., [10,12]); they rely on encryptions for counting votes, but use commitments rather than encryptions for verifiability purposes. Thus, the bulletin board which only publishes the commitments does not weaken the privacy provided by the underlying scheme. Although the encrypted votes must be sent to the election administrators, it is assumed that these communications cannot be intercepted and stored *en masse*. We call this weaker form of everlasting privacy *practical everlasting privacy*.

Symbolic models for security protocol analysis have been used to model both privacy properties (e.g., [11,3,13]) and verifiability properties (e.g.,[16,17]) of voting systems, but they are currently not capable of distinguishing *perfect* versus *computational* notions of privacy, or indeed, of verifiability. Our aim in this paper is to extend the model to allow these distinctions. We focus on practical everlasting privacy, and use our definitions to verify whether particular schemes satisfy that property.

Our contributions. Our first and main contribution is a general and practical definition of everlasting privacy. The key idea is that, in the future, an attacker will be more powerful in terms of computation (he may be able to break cryptography) but less powerful in terms of the data he can operate on (transactions between a vote client and the vote server may not have been stored). We therefore distinguish between standard communication channels (on which eavesdropping may be possible, but requires considerable effort) and *everlasting channels*, on which the information is intentionally published and recorded permanently (e.g. web pages that serve as a public bulletin board). Formally, we model everlasting privacy in the applied-pi calculus [1], a framework well-adapted to security protocols and already used to define privacy [11] and verifiability [16]. Our definitions apply not only to voting protocols but also to situations where forward secrecy is desirable, such as for instance untraceability in RFID protocols.

Modeling everlasting privacy also requires to precisely model what an attacker can break in the future. Our second contribution is a characterization, for several primitives, of what can be broken. The first natural primitive is encryption, for which we provide an equational theory that models the fact that private keys can be retrieved from public keys, or even from ciphertexts. Some other primitives have been primarily designed to achieve everlasting privacy. This is the case of *perfectly hiding* and *computationally binding* primitives, such as Pedersen commitments [19]. Intuitively, perfectly hiding means that the hidden secret cannot be retrieved even by a computationally unbounded adversary, while computationally binding means that, binding is ensured only for a (polynomially) limited attacker. We provide an equational theory that models such perfectly hiding and computationally binding primitives in general.

As an application, we study everlasting privacy for several variants of Helios [2], an e-voting protocol used for electing the president of the University of Louvain and board members of the IACR[1]. We study in particular its latest variants with Pedersen

---

[1] International Association for Cryptologic Research.

commitments [12], designed to achieve everlasting privacy, still providing full verifiability. We also model and prove everlasting privacy of a (simplified) version of Moran
and Naor's protocol [18]. Interestingly, we were able to adapt algorithms in existing
tools to automate the verification of everlasting privacy and we use adapted versions of
the AKiSS [6] and ProVerif [4] tools to analyze everlasting privacy for half a dozen of
protocols.

Outline. In the following section we recall the applied pi calculus and introduce notations and basic definitions. In Section 3 we define new equivalence relations, namely
forward and everlasting indistinguishability. Then, in Section 4 we instantiate these
equivalences to the case of voting protocols, define everlasting privacy and illustrate
this property on several examples. In Section 5 we present a modeling of perfectly hiding and computationally binding (and vice-versa) primitives in the applied pi calculus.
In particular we model Pedersen commitments, which are for studying two protocols
that provide everlasting privacy. In Section 6 we discuss tool support for automatically
proving everlasting indistinguishability before concluding.

2   The Applied Pi Calculus

The applied pi calculus [1] is a language for modeling distributed systems and their
interactions. It extends the pi calculus with an equational theory, which is particularly
useful for modeling cryptographic protocols. The following subsections describe the
syntax and semantics of the calculus.

2.1   Syntax

Terms. The calculus assumes an infinite set of names $\mathcal{N} = \{a, b, c, \ldots\}$, an infinite set of variables $\mathcal{V} = \{x, y, z, \ldots\}$ and a finite signature Σ, that is, a finite set
of function symbols each with an associated arity. We use meta-variables u, v, w to
range over both names and variables. Terms $M, N, T, \ldots$ are built by applying function symbols to names, variables and other terms. Tuples $M_1, \ldots, M_l$ are occasionally
abbreviated $\tilde{M}$. We write $\{M_1/u_1, \ldots, M_l/u_l\}$ for substitutions that replace $u_1, \ldots, u_l$
with $M_1, \ldots, M_l$. The applied pi calculus relies on a simple type system. Terms can
be of sort Channel for channel names or Base for the payload sent out on these channels. Function symbols can only be applied to, and return, terms of sort Base. A term is
ground when it does not contain variables.

The signature Σ is equipped with an equational theory E, that is a finite set of equations of the form $M = N$. We define $=_E$ as the smallest equivalence relation on terms,
that contains E and is closed under application of function symbols, substitution of
terms for variables and bijective renaming of names.

Example 1. A standard signature for pairing and encryption is:

$$\Sigma_{enc} = \{0, 1, \langle \_, \_ \rangle, \mathsf{fst}(\_), \mathsf{snd}(\_), \mathsf{pk}(\_), \mathsf{aenc}(\_, \_, \_), \mathsf{adec}(\_, \_), \mathsf{senc}(\_, \_, \_), \mathsf{sdec}(\_, \_)\}$$

The term $\langle m_1, m_2 \rangle$ represents the concatenation of m_1 and m_2, with associated projec-
tors $\mathsf{fst}(\_)$ and $\mathsf{snd}(\_)$. The term $\mathsf{aenc}(k, r, m)$ represents the asymmetric encryption of

$$
\begin{array}{lll}
P, Q, R ::= & & \text{processes} \\
\quad 0 & & \text{null process} \\
\quad P \mid Q & & \text{parallel composition} \\
\quad !P & & \text{replication} \\
\quad \nu n.P & & \text{name restriction} \\
\quad u(x).P & & \text{message input} \\
\quad \overline{u}\langle M \rangle.P & & \text{message output} \\
\quad \text{if } M = N \text{ then } P \text{ else } Q & & \text{conditional} \\
& & \\
A, B, C ::= & & \text{extended processes} \\
\quad P & & \text{plain process} \\
\quad A \mid B & & \text{parallel composition} \\
\quad \nu n.A & & \text{name restriction} \\
\quad \nu x.A & & \text{variable restriction} \\
\quad \{M/x\} & & \text{active substitution}
\end{array}
$$

where u is either a name or variable of channel sort.

Fig. 1. Applied pi calculus grammar

message m with public key k and randomness r while the associated decryption operator is adec. Similarly, $\mathsf{senc}(k, r, m)$ represents the symmetric encryption of message m with key k and randomness r. The associated decryption operator is sdec. The properties of these primitives are modeled by the following standard equational theory $\mathsf{E_{enc}}$:

$$
\mathsf{E_{enc}} = \left\{
\begin{array}{r}
\mathsf{fst}(\langle x, y \rangle) = x \\
\mathsf{snd}(\langle x, y \rangle) = y \\
\mathsf{adec}(x, \mathsf{aenc}(\mathsf{pk}(x), y, z)) = z \\
\mathsf{sdec}(x, \mathsf{senc}(x, y, z)) = z
\end{array}
\right\}
$$

Processes. The grammar for processes is shown in Figure 1. Plain processes are standard. Extended processes introduce *active substitutions* which generalize the classical let construct: the process $\nu x.(\{M/x\} \mid P)$ corresponds exactly to the process let $x = M$ in P. As usual names and variables have scopes which are delimited by restrictions and by inputs. All substitutions are assumed to be cycle-free.

The sets of free and bound names, respectively variables, in process A are denoted by $\mathsf{fn}(A)$, $\mathsf{bn}(A)$, $\mathsf{fv}(A)$, $\mathsf{bv}(A)$. We also write $\mathsf{fn}(M)$, $\mathsf{fv}(M)$ for the names, respectively variables, in term M. An extended process A is *closed* if it has no free variables. A *context* $C[\_]$ is an extended process with a hole. We obtain $C[A]$ as the result of filling $C[\_]$'s hole with A. An *evaluation context* is a context whose hole is not under a replication, a conditional, an input, or an output.

Example 2. Throughout the paper we illustrate our definitions with a simplified version of the Helios voting system [2]. Two techniques can be used for tallying in Helios: either a homomorphic tally based on El Gamal encryption, or a tally based on mixnets. We present here the version with mixnets.

1. The voter V computes her ballot by encrypting her vote with the public key $\mathsf{pk}(skE)$ of the election. The corresponding secret key is shared among several election authorities. Then she casts her ballot together with her identity on an authenticated channel. Upon receiving the ballot, the administrator simply publishes it on a public web page (after having checked that V is entitled to vote).
2. Once the voting phase is over, the votes are shuffled and reencrypted through mixnets. The permuted and rerandomized votes are again published on the public web page (together with a zero knowledge proof of correct reencryption and mixing).
3. Finally, the authorities decrypt the rerandomized votes and the administrator publishes the decrypted votes (with a zero knowledge proof of correct decryption).

The process representing the voter is parametrized by her vote v, and her identity id.

$$V(auth, id, v) \stackrel{\mathsf{def}}{=} \nu r.\overline{auth}\langle\langle id, \mathsf{aenc}(\mathsf{pk}(skE), r, v)\rangle\rangle$$

The administrator BB receives votes on private authenticated channels and publishes the votes. It is parametrized by the authenticated channels of the voters. Then the ballots are forwarded to the tally T over the private channel c. The tally consists in decrypting the vote. The shuffle through mixnets is modeled simply, by non deterministic parallel composition after all ballots have been received. For simplicity, we consider here an election system for three voters.

$$BB(a_1, a_2, a_3) \stackrel{\mathsf{def}}{=} \nu c.\, a_1(x).\, \overline{bb}\langle x\rangle.\, \overline{c}\langle x\rangle \mid a_2(y).\, \overline{bb}\langle y\rangle.\, \overline{c}\langle y\rangle \mid a_3(z).\, \overline{bb}\langle z\rangle.\, \overline{c}\langle z\rangle \mid T$$

$$T \stackrel{\mathsf{def}}{=} c(x').c(y').c(z').$$
$$(\overline{bb}\langle \mathsf{adec}(skE, \mathsf{snd}(x'))\rangle \mid \overline{bb}\langle \mathsf{adec}(skE, \mathsf{snd}(y'))\rangle \mid \overline{bb}\langle \mathsf{adec}(skE, \mathsf{snd}(z'))\rangle)$$

The process H then represents the whole Helios system with two honest voters and one dishonest voter (which does therefore not need to be explicitly specified and whose authenticated channel is public).

$$H \stackrel{\mathsf{def}}{=} \nu skE.\, \nu auth_1.\, \nu auth_2.$$
$$\overline{bb}\langle\mathsf{pk}(skE)\rangle.\, (V(auth_1, id_1, a) \mid V(auth_2, id_2, b) \mid BB(auth_1, auth_2, auth_3))$$

The first honest voter casts the vote a while the second honest voter casts the vote b.

2.2 Semantics

The operational semantics of the applied pi calculus is defined by the means of two relations: structural equivalence and internal reductions. *Structural equivalence* ($\equiv$) is the smallest equivalence relation closed under α-conversion of both bound names and variables and application of evaluation contexts such that:

$$A \mid 0 \equiv A \qquad\qquad \nu n.0 \equiv 0$$
$$A \mid (B \mid C) \equiv (A \mid B) \mid C \qquad\qquad \nu u.\nu w.A \equiv \nu w.\nu u.A$$
$$A \mid B \equiv B \mid A \qquad\qquad A \mid \nu u.B \equiv \nu u.(A \mid B)$$
$$!P \equiv P \mid !P \qquad\qquad \text{if } u \notin \mathsf{fn}(A) \cup \mathsf{fv}(A)$$
$$\nu x.\{M/x\} \equiv 0 \qquad\qquad \{M/x\} \equiv \{N/x\}$$
$$\{M/x\} \mid A \equiv \{M/x\} \mid A\{M/x\} \qquad\qquad \text{if } M =_\mathsf{E} N$$

$$a(x).P \xrightarrow{a(M)} P\{M/x\} \qquad \frac{A \xrightarrow{\alpha} A' \quad u \text{ does not occur in } \alpha}{\nu u.A \xrightarrow{\alpha} \nu u.A'}$$

$$\overline{a}\langle u\rangle.P \xrightarrow{\overline{a}\langle u\rangle} P \qquad \frac{A \xrightarrow{\alpha} A' \quad \mathrm{bv}(\alpha) \cap \mathrm{fv}(B) = \mathrm{bn}(\alpha) \cap \mathrm{fn}(B) = \emptyset}{A \mid B \xrightarrow{\alpha} A' \mid B}$$

$$\frac{A \xrightarrow{\overline{a}\langle u\rangle} A' \quad u \neq a}{\nu u.A \xrightarrow{\nu u.\overline{a}\langle u\rangle} A'} \qquad \frac{A \equiv B \quad B \xrightarrow{\alpha} B' \quad A' \equiv B'}{A \xrightarrow{\alpha} A'}$$

Fig. 2. Labelled reductions

Internal reduction ($\rightarrow$) is the smallest relation closed under structural equivalence, application of evaluation contexts satisfying the following rules:

COMM	$\overline{c}\langle x\rangle.P \mid c(x).Q \rightarrow P \mid Q$
THEN	if $N = N$ then P else $Q \rightarrow P$
ELSE	if $L = M$ then P else $Q \rightarrow Q$
	for ground terms L, M where $L \neq_E M$

Labelled reduction ($\xrightarrow{\alpha}$) extends the internal reduction and enables the environment to interact with the processes as defined in Figure 2. The label α is either an input, or the output of a channel name or a variable of base type.

We write $\Rightarrow$ for an arbitrary (possibly zero) number of internal reductions and $\xrightarrow{\alpha}$ for $\Rightarrow \xrightarrow{\alpha} \Rightarrow$. Whenever the equational theory is not clear from the context we annotate the above relations by the equational theory and write e.g. $\rightarrow_E$.

A *trace* of a process is the sequence of actions (i.e. labels) together with the corresponding sent messages. Formally, the set of traces of a process A is defined as follows. Note that it depends on the underlying equational theory E.

$$\mathsf{trace}_E(A) = \{(\alpha_1 \cdot \alpha_2 \cdot \ldots \cdot \alpha_n, \varphi(B)) \mid A \xRightarrow{\alpha_1}_E A_1 \xRightarrow{\alpha_2}_E \cdots A_{n-1} \xRightarrow{\alpha_n}_E B\}$$

Example 3. Consider the process H representing the Helios protocol as defined in Example 2. A possible execution for H is:

$$H \xRightarrow{\nu xk.\ \overline{bb}\langle xk\rangle} H_1$$

$$\xRightarrow{\nu x.\ \overline{bb}\langle x\rangle \quad \nu y.\ \overline{bb}\langle y\rangle \quad auth_3(\langle id_3,x\rangle) \quad \nu z.\ \overline{bb}\langle z\rangle \quad \nu x'.\ \overline{bb}\langle x'\rangle \quad \nu y'.\ \overline{bb}\langle y'\rangle \quad \nu z'.\ \overline{bb}\langle z'\rangle} H_2$$

where H_1 and H_2 are defined below (we omit the other intermediate processes). Note that H_2 is simply an active substitution.

$$H_1 = \nu skE.\ \nu auth_1.\ \nu auth_2.\ \nu r_1.$$

$$(\{\mathsf{pk}(skE)/xk\} \mid V(auth_1, id_1, a) \mid V(auth_2, id_2, b) \mid BB(auth_1, auth_2, auth_3))$$

$$H_2 = \nu skE.\ \nu auth_1.\ \nu auth_2.\ \nu r_1.\ \nu r_2.\{\mathsf{pk}(skE)/xk\} \mid \{a/x', b/y', a/z'\} \mid$$

$$\{\langle id_1, \mathsf{aenc}(\mathsf{pk}(skE), r_1, a)\rangle/x, \langle id_2, \mathsf{aenc}(\mathsf{pk}(skE), r_2, b)\rangle/y, \langle id_3, \mathsf{aenc}(\mathsf{pk}(skE), r_1, a)\rangle/z\}$$

This execution trace corresponds to the case where the two honest voters cast their vote as expected, while the dishonest voter replays the first voter's ballot. As we shall see in Example 5, this corresponds to the attack on privacy discovered in [9].

2.3 Equivalence Relations for Processes

Privacy is often stated in terms of equivalence [11]. We recall here the definitions of static and trace equivalence.

Sequences of messages are often stored as *frames*. Formally, a frame is an extended process built from 0 and active substitutions $\{M/x\}$, and closed by parallel composition and restriction. The *domain* of a frame $\phi = \nu\tilde{n}. \{M_1/x_1, \ldots, M_n/x_n\}$ such that $x_i \notin \tilde{n}$ is $\mathrm{dom}(\phi) = \{x_1, \ldots, x_n\}$. Every extended process A can be mapped to a frame $\varphi(A)$ by replacing every plain process in A with 0. The frame $\varphi(A)$ represents the static knowledge output by a process to its environment.

Two frames are indistinguishable to an attacker if it is impossible to build a test that allows to differentiate between the two.

Definition 1 (Static equivalence). *Given an equational theory* E *two frames* ϕ *and* ψ *are are statically equivalent, denoted* $\phi \sim_E \psi$, *if* $\mathrm{dom}(\phi) = \mathrm{dom}(\psi)$ *and there exist* $\tilde{n}, \sigma, \tau$ *such that* $\phi \equiv \nu\tilde{n}.\sigma$, $\psi \equiv \nu\tilde{n}.\tau$ *and for all terms* M, N *such that* $\tilde{n} \cap (\mathrm{fn}(M) \cup \mathrm{fn}(N)) = \emptyset$, *we have* $M\sigma =_E N\sigma$ *if and only if* $M\tau =_E N\tau$. *By abuse of notation, we may write* $M\phi$ *instead of* $M\sigma$ *when* σ *is clear from the context.*

Example 4. Let E_{enc} be the equational theory defined at Example 1. Let H_2 be the process/frame defined in Example 3. Let $\phi = \varphi(H_2)$ (= H_2 actually). Consider the following frame ψ.

$$\psi = \nu skE.\, \nu r_1.\, \nu r_2. \{\mathrm{pk}(skE)/_{xk}\} \mid \{^a/_{x'}, {}^b/_{y'}, {}^b/_{z'}\} \mid$$
$$\{\langle id_1, \mathrm{aenc}(\mathrm{pk}(skE), r_1, b)\rangle/_x, \langle id_2, \mathrm{aenc}(\mathrm{pk}(skE), r_2, a)\rangle/_y, \langle id_3, \mathrm{aenc}(\mathrm{pk}(skE), r_1, b)\rangle/_z,\}$$

The two frames ϕ and ψ are not statically equivalent for the equational theory E_{enc}. Indeed, consider for example $M = z'$ and $N = a$, we have $M\phi = a = N\phi$ but $M\psi = b \neq N\psi$. Therefore, $\phi \not\sim_{E_{enc}} \psi$.

The active counterpart of static equivalence is trace equivalence. Intuitively, two processes A and B are indistinguishable to an attacker if any execution of A can be matched to an execution of B that is equal for their observable actions and such that the corresponding sequences of sent messages are statically equivalent.

Definition 2 (Trace equivalence). *Given an equational theory* E *two processes* A *and* B *are trace equivalent, denoted* $A \overset{tr}{\approx}_E B$, *if for any trace* $(tr_A, \phi_A) \in \mathrm{trace}_E(A)$ *there is a corresponding trace* $(tr_B, \phi_B) \in \mathrm{trace}_E(B)$ *such that* $tr_A = tr_B$ *and* $\phi_A \sim_E \phi_B$ *(and reciprocally).*

Example 5. We consider the Helios system H' with two honest voters and one dishonest voter where one honest voter casts the vote b while the other one casts the vote a.

$$H' \stackrel{\text{def}}{=} \nu skE. \, \nu auth_1. \, \nu auth_2.$$

$$\overline{bb}\langle \text{pk}(skE) \rangle. \, (V(auth_1, id_1, b) \mid V(auth_2, id_2, a) \mid BB(auth_1, auth_2, auth_3))$$

Let (tr, ϕ) be the trace corresponding to the execution of H described in Example 3 where $\phi = \varphi(H_2) = H_2$ (as defined in Example 3) and $tr = \nu xk. \, \overline{bb}\langle xk \rangle \cdot \nu x. \, \overline{bb}\langle x \rangle \cdot \nu y. \, \overline{bb}\langle y \rangle \cdot auth_3(\langle id_3, x \rangle) \cdot \nu z. \, \overline{bb}\langle z \rangle \cdot \nu x'. \, \overline{bb}\langle x' \rangle \cdot \nu y'. \, \overline{bb}\langle y' \rangle \cdot \nu z'. \, \overline{bb}\langle z' \rangle$. Then $(tr, \phi) \in \text{trace}_{\mathsf{E}_{\text{enc}}}(H)$ and for any $(tr, \phi') \in \text{trace}_{\mathsf{E}_{\text{enc}}}(H')$, it is easy to check that we have $\phi \not\approx_{\mathsf{E}_{\text{enc}}} \phi'$. (In fact, $\phi' = \psi$ from Example 4.) Therefore, $H \overset{tr}{\not\approx}_{\mathsf{E}_{\text{enc}}} H'$

Intuitively, if the dishonest voter's strategy is to replay the first voter's vote, then he would cast a vote of the form $\langle id_3, \text{aenc}(\text{pk}(skE), r_1, a) \rangle$ in the system H while he would cast a vote of the form $\langle id_3, \text{aenc}(\text{pk}(skE), r_1, b) \rangle$ in the system H'. Once the result is published, an attacker would be then able to distinguish H from H' since the tally in H is $\{a, b, a\}$ while it is $\{b, a, b\}$ in H'. This corresponds exactly to the replay attack against Helios, explained in [9].

3 Forward and Everlasting Indistinguishability

In this section we introduce and illustrate our definitions of forward and everlasting indistinguishability. In the next section we will show how the here presented definitions can be used to define practical everlasting privacy in electronic voting.

3.1 Definitions of Forward and Everlasting Indistinguishability

From now on we suppose that Σ is a signature and that E_0 and E_1 are equational theories over Σ. We want to model that an attacker may interact with a protocol today and store some data which may be exploited in the future when his computational power has increased. We model the fact that the attacker's computational power may change by using two different equational theories: E_0 models the attacker's capabilities while interacting with the protocol at the time of the election, while E_1 models his capabilities when exploiting the published data in the future when the strength of cryptography has been eroded.

We also argue that in many situations it is reasonable to suppose that the attacker does not store all of the data that was sent over the network. We will therefore consider some channels to be *everlasting*: data sent over such channels will remain in the attacker's knowledge for future analysis while other data will be "forgotten" and can only be used during the interaction with the protocol. Typically, everlasting channels are media such as web-pages published on the Internet (that can easily be accessed by anyone, for a rather long period of time) while public but non-everlasting channels can be communications over the Internet, which can be recorded only by the active and costly involvement of an attacker.

In order to reason about data that has been sent on certain channels we introduce the following notation. Let P be a process, $\mathcal{C}$ a set of channels (corresponding to the everlasting channels), and $tr = (\alpha_1 \cdot \alpha_2 \cdot \ldots \cdot \alpha_n, \varphi) \in \mathsf{trace}_E(P)$ a trace of P. We define the set of variables in the domain of φ corresponding to terms sent on channels in $\mathcal{C}$ as $\mathcal{V}_\mathcal{C}(\alpha_1 \cdot \alpha_2 \cdot \ldots \cdot \alpha_n) = \{x \mid c \in \mathcal{C}, \ 1 \leq i \leq n, \ \alpha_i = \nu x.\ \bar{c}\langle x \rangle\}$ and denote by $\phi_\mathcal{V}(P_n)$ the substitution $\phi(P_n)$ whose domain is restricted to the set of variables $\mathcal{V}$.

Two processes A and B are said to be forward indistinguishable if, informally, an attacker cannot observe the difference between A and B being given the computational power modeled by E_1 (where it can break keys for example), but for executions that happened in the past, that is over E_0 (the standard theory) and observing only the information that was passed through everlasting channels.

Definition 3 (Forward indistinguishability). *Let A and B be two closed extended processes and $\mathcal{C}$ a set of channels. We define $A \stackrel{\mathsf{fwd}}{\sqsubseteq} {}^\mathcal{C}_{\mathsf{E}_0,\mathsf{E}_1} B$, if for every trace $(\alpha_1 \cdot \alpha_2 \cdots \alpha_n, \varphi_A) \in \mathsf{trace}_{\mathsf{E}_0}(A)$ there exists φ_B s.t. $(\alpha_1 \cdot \alpha_2 \cdots \alpha_n, \varphi_B) \in \mathsf{trace}_{\mathsf{E}_0}(B)$*

$$and \quad \phi_{A\mathcal{V}} \sim_{\mathsf{E}_1} \phi_{B\mathcal{V}}.$$

where $\mathcal{V} = \mathcal{V}_\mathcal{C}(\alpha_1 \cdot \alpha_2 \cdots \alpha_n)$. A and B are forward indistinguishable w.r.t. $\mathcal{C}$, E_0 and E_1, denoted $A \stackrel{\mathsf{fwd}}{\approx} {}^\mathcal{C}_{\mathsf{E}_0,\mathsf{E}_1} B$, if $A \stackrel{\mathsf{fwd}}{\sqsubseteq} {}^\mathcal{C}_{\mathsf{E}_0,\mathsf{E}_1} B$ and $B \stackrel{\mathsf{fwd}}{\sqsubseteq} {}^\mathcal{C}_{\mathsf{E}_0,\mathsf{E}_1} A$.

Note that in the above definition we only check equivalence of messages that were sent on channels in the set $\mathcal{C}$. We may also require that A and B are indistinguishable in the standard way (over E_0). Standard indistinguishability and forward indistinguishability yield *everlasting indistinguishability*.

Definition 4 (Everlasting indistinguishability). *Let A and B be two closed extended processes, $\mathcal{C}$ a set of channels. A and B are everlasting indistinguishable w.r.t. $\mathcal{C}$, E_0 and E_1, denoted $A \stackrel{\mathsf{ev}}{\approx} {}^\mathcal{C}_{\mathsf{E}_0,\mathsf{E}_1}$ if*

1. *$A \stackrel{\mathsf{tr}}{\approx}_{\mathsf{E}_0} B$, i.e. A and B are trace equivalent w.r.t. E_0; and*
2. *$A \stackrel{\mathsf{fwd}}{\approx} {}^\mathcal{C}_{\mathsf{E}_0,\mathsf{E}_1} B$, i.e. A and B are forward indistinguishable w.r.t. $\mathcal{C}$, E_0 and E_1.*

3.2 Examples

We illustrate the above definitions on a simple RFID protocol. In the context of RFID systems, forward secrecy is often a desired property: even if an RFID tag has been tampered with, and its secrets have been retrieved by a malicious entity, its past transactions should remain private. This can be seen as a form of everlasting security requirement. Indeed, RFID tags being devices vulnerable to tampering, one would like to make sure that when an intruder gains access to an honest device, he is not able to trace back the movements of the tag. Such tampering can be modelled by the following equational theory $\mathsf{E}_{\mathsf{break}}$, that gives direct access to keys.

$$\mathsf{E}_{\mathsf{break}} = \left\{ \begin{array}{l} \mathsf{break}_{\mathsf{aenc}}(\mathsf{aenc}(\mathsf{pk}(x), y, z)) = x \\ \mathsf{break}_{\mathsf{senc}}(\mathsf{senc}(x, y, z)) = x \end{array} \right\}$$

We also use this equational theory later to model that in 20 or 30 years an adversary will be able to break nowadays encryption keys.

Consider the following toy RFID protocol

$$session = \nu r.\ \overline{c}\langle \mathsf{enc}(k, r, id)\rangle$$
$$tag \quad\ = \nu k.\ \nu id.\ !session$$
$$system = !tag$$

where a tag identifies itself to a reader by sending its tag identifier id encrypted with a long-term symmetric key shared between the tag and the reader.

We can model unlinkability as being the property that an attacker cannot distinguish the situation where the same tag is used in several sessions from the situation where different tags are used. Formally unlinkability is modelled as the trace equivalence:

$$system \overset{\mathsf{tr}}{\approx}_{\mathsf{E_{enc}}} system'$$

where

$$system' = !\nu k.\nu id.\ session.$$

Intuitively, this protocols satisfies unlinkability only as long as the keys are not leaked. Indeed, since each identification uses a different random in the encrypted message sent to the reader, each of the sent messages is different and looks like a random message to the intruder. However, $system$ and $system'$ are not forward indistinguishable when considering a theory $\mathsf{E_1}$ which allows to break keys, i.e.,

$$system \overset{\mathsf{fwd}\,\{c\}}{\not\approx}_{\mathsf{E_{enc}},\mathsf{E_{enc}}\cup\mathsf{E_{break}}} system'$$

where $\mathsf{E_{enc}}$ is the equational theory introduced in Example 1. Indeed, once the key k of a tag is obtained by the intruder, he can retrieve the identity behind each blob he has seen on channel c, and thus distinguish the set of messages obtained by an execution of $system$ where the same tag executes at least two sessions, from the set of messages obtained by the corresponding execution of $system'$ where each tag has executed at most one session. Thus this protocol does not satisfy the stronger requirement of everlasting indistinguishability either:

$$system \overset{\mathsf{ev}\,\{c\}}{\not\approx}_{\mathsf{E_{enc}},\mathsf{E_{enc}}\cup\mathsf{E_{break}}} system'$$

4   Application to Practical Everlasting Privacy

We model a practical version of everlasting privacy in voting protocols based on everlasting indistinguishability.

4.1   Definition of Practical Everlasting Privacy

We first recall the definition of vote privacy introduced in [15].

Definition 5   (Vote privacy). *Let* $\mathsf{VP}(v_1, v_2)$ *be an extended process with two free variables* v_1, v_2. $\mathsf{VP}(v_1, v_2)$ *respects vote privacy for an equational theory* E *if*

$$\mathsf{VP}(a, b) \overset{\mathsf{tr}}{\approx}_{\mathsf{E}} \mathsf{VP}(b, a)$$

Intuitively, the free variables refer to the votes of two honest voters id_1 and id_2. Then this equivalence ensures that an attacker cannot distinguish the situations where voter id_1 voted for candidate a and voter id_2 voted for candidate b, from the situation where the voters swapped their votes, i.e., voter id_1 voted for candidate b and voter id_2 voted for candidate a.

Example 6. Let $\mathsf{Helios}(v_1, v_2)$ be the process

$$\nu\, skE.\ \nu\, auth_1.\ \nu\, auth_2.$$

$$\overline{bb}\langle \mathsf{pk}(skE)\rangle.\ (V(auth_1, id_1, v_1)\mid V(auth_2, id_2, v_2)\mid BB(auth_1, auth_2, auth_3))$$

where processes V and BB are defined in Example 2.

In Example 5, when we illustrated trace equivalence we showed that Helios does not satisfy vote privacy due to a vote replay attack discovered in [9].

A simple fix of the attack consists in weeding duplicates. The corresponding tally is

$$T' \overset{\text{def}}{=} c(x').c(y').c(z').$$
$$\text{if } \mathsf{snd}(x') \neq \mathsf{snd}(y') \ \wedge\ \mathsf{snd}(x') \neq \mathsf{snd}(z') \wedge \mathsf{snd}(y') \neq \mathsf{snd}(z') \text{ then}$$
$$\overline{bb}\langle\mathsf{adec}(skE, \mathsf{snd}(x'))\rangle \mid \overline{bb}\langle\mathsf{adec}(skE, \mathsf{snd}(y'))\rangle \mid \overline{bb}\langle\mathsf{adec}(skE, \mathsf{snd}(z'))\rangle$$

In other words, the tally is performed only if there are no duplicates amongst the cast votes. We define the voting protocol $\mathsf{Helios}^{\mathsf{noreplay}}$ as Helios but with the revised version T' of the tally. Using the tools ProVerif and AKISS we have shown that this protocol satisfies vote privacy.

$$\mathsf{Helios}^{\mathsf{noreplay}}(a, b) \overset{\mathsf{tr}}{\approx}_{\mathsf{E_{enc}}} \mathsf{Helios}^{\mathsf{noreplay}}(b, a)$$

The above definition of vote privacy does however not take into account that most cryptographic schemes rely on computational assumptions and may be broken in the future. In order to protect the secrecy of votes against such attacks in the future we propose a stronger definition based on forward indistinguishability.

Definition 6 (Everlasting vote privacy). *Let* $\mathsf{VP}(v_1, v_2)$ *be an extended process with two free variables* v_1, v_2. $\mathsf{VP}(v_1, v_2)$ *satisfies everlasting privacy w.r.t. a set of channels* $\mathcal{C}$ *and equational theories* $\mathsf{E_0}$ *and* $\mathsf{E_1}$, *if*

$$\mathsf{VP}(a, b) \overset{\mathsf{ev}}{\approx}_{\mathsf{E_0},\mathsf{E_1}}^{\mathcal{C}} \mathsf{VP}(b, a)$$

We note that everlasting vote privacy is strictly stronger than vote privacy as it requires trace equivalence of $\mathsf{VP}(a, b)$ and $\mathsf{VP}(b, a)$ (which is exactly vote privacy) and additionally forward indistinguishability of these processes. Our definition is parametric with respect to the equational theories and the channels we suppose to be everlasting. The equational theory $\mathsf{E_1}$ allows us to exactly specify what a future attacker may be able to break. The set of everlasting channels $\mathcal{C}$ allows us to specify what data a future attacker has access to. When $\mathcal{C}$ corresponds to all channels we typically get a requirement which is too strong for practical purposes. We argue that it is reasonable to suppose that in, say 50 years, an attacker does not have access to the transmissions between individual voters and the system while a bulletin board published on the Internet could easily have been stored.

4.2 Examples

Helios with Identities. As discussed In Example 6, $\text{Helios}^{\text{noreplay}}$ does satisfy vote privacy. However, this protocol does not satisfy everlasting vote privacy with $E_0 = E_{\text{enc}}$, $E_1 = E_{\text{enc}} \cup E_{\text{break}}$ and $C = \{bb\}$. Intuitively, this is due to the fact that a future attacker can break encryption and link the recovered vote to the identity submitted together with the cast ballot. Formally, we can show that

$$\text{Helios}^{\text{noreplay}}(a, b) \overset{\text{fwd}}{\not\approx} \text{Helios}^{\text{noreplay}}(b, a)$$

Consider the trace $(\nu x k. \overline{bb}\langle x k\rangle \cdot \nu x. \overline{bb}\langle x\rangle \cdot \nu y. \overline{bb}\langle y\rangle, \varphi_A) \in \text{trace}_{E_{\text{enc}}}(\text{Helios}^{\text{noreplay}}(a, b))$ where

$$\varphi_A = \nu skE, r_1, r_2.\{ \ \text{pk}(skE)/x k,$$
$$\langle id_1, \text{aenc}(\text{pk}(skE), r_1, a)\rangle/x,$$
$$\langle id_2, \text{aenc}(\text{pk}(skE), r_2, b)\rangle/y \}$$

Traces $(\nu x k. \overline{bb}\langle x k\rangle \cdot \nu x. \overline{bb}\langle x\rangle \cdot \nu y. \overline{bb}\langle y\rangle, \varphi_B) \in \text{trace}_{E_{\text{enc}}}(\text{Helios}^{\text{noreplay}}(b, a))$ are either such that

$$\varphi_B \equiv \nu skE, r_1, r_2.\{ \ \text{pk}(skE)/x k,$$
$$\langle id_1, \text{aenc}(\text{pk}(skE), r_1, b)\rangle/x,$$
$$\langle id_2, \text{aenc}(\text{pk}(skE), r_2, a)\rangle/y \}$$

or

$$\varphi_B \equiv \nu skE, r_1, r_2.\{ \ \text{pk}(skE)/x k,$$
$$\langle id_2, \text{aenc}(\text{pk}(skE), r_1, a)\rangle/x,$$
$$\langle id_1, \text{aenc}(\text{pk}(skE), r_2, b)\rangle/y \}$$

In both cases we have that $\varphi_A \not\approx_{E_{\text{enc}} \cup E_{\text{break}}} \varphi_B$. In the first case this is witnessed by the test $M = a$ and $N = \text{break}_{\text{aenc}}(\text{snd}(x))$ as

$$M\varphi_A = a =_{E_{\text{enc}} \cup E_{\text{break}}} N\varphi_A \quad \text{but} \quad M\varphi_B = a \neq_{E_{\text{enc}} \cup E_{\text{break}}} b =_{E_{\text{enc}} \cup E_{\text{break}}} N\varphi_B$$

In the second case non equivalence is witnessed by the test $M = id_1$ and $N = \text{fst}(x)$.

Helios without Identities. As we just saw $\text{Helios}^{\text{noreplay}}$ does not satisfy everlasting privacy. This is due to the fact that encrypted votes are published together with the identity of the voter on the bulletin board. A simple variant (used e.g. in Louvain for student elections) consists in publishing the encrypted vote without the identity of the voter. We define $\text{Helios}^{\text{noid}}$ as $\text{Helios}^{\text{noreplay}}$ but redefining the process BB as

$$BB'(a_1, a_2, a_3) \overset{\text{def}}{=} \nu c. \, a_1(x). \, \overline{bb}\langle\text{snd}(x)\rangle. \, \overline{c}\langle x\rangle \mid a_2(y). \, \overline{bb}\langle\text{snd}(y)\rangle. \, \overline{c}\langle y\rangle \mid$$
$$a_3(z). \, \overline{bb}\langle\text{snd}(z)\rangle. \, \overline{c}\langle z\rangle \mid T'$$

where T' is as defined at Example 6. As we shall see in Section 6, we prove everlasting privacy of $\text{Helios}^{\text{noid}}$ w.r.t E_{enc}, E_{break} and everlasting channel bb, using (adaptations of) ProVerif and AKISS.

5   Modeling Commitments

Commitment schemes allow a sender to commit to a value v while keeping this value hidden until an 'opening' phase, where the sender reveals v to the receiver of the commitment $\mathsf{commit}(v)$. The receiver should then be able to verify that the revealed value is indeed the one used to compute $\mathsf{commit}(v)$, and in that sense that the sender had indeed committed to the revealed value. The two main security properties of such schemes are *binding* (the sender can't claim that $\mathsf{commit}(v)$ is a commitment to some $v' \neq v$), and *hiding* (the receiver can't deduce v from $\mathsf{commit}(v)$). These two properties can hold 'perfectly' or merely 'computationally'. It is known that there are no commitment schemes which are both perfectly hiding and perfectly binding, so one has to choose between perfectly hiding and computationally binding (PHCB) and perfectly binding and computationally hiding (PBCH). In this section, we characterize in our formal model what it means for a primitive to be PHCB and PBCH. We also give equational theories to model such primitives, which we then use for the verification of two voting protocols that rely on such primitives to ensure everlasting vote privacy.

5.1   Modeling Hiding and Binding Cryptographic Primitives

PBCH Primitives. Informally, an n-ary function f is *perfectly binding* if the inputs are totally determined by the output. In other words, f is perfectly binding if it admits no collisions. It is *computationally hiding* if it is hard to retrieve the inputs from the output.

To model a PBCH primitive f using the applied pi calculus, we introduce two equational theories $\mathsf{E}_0^{\mathsf{f}}$ and $\mathsf{E}_1^{\mathsf{f}}$ over the signature $\Sigma = \{\mathsf{f}, \mathsf{break}_{\mathsf{f}}^1, \ldots, \mathsf{break}_{\mathsf{f}}^n\}$, such that no equation of the form

$$\mathsf{f}(M_1, \ldots, M_n) =_{\mathsf{E}} \mathsf{f}(N_1, \ldots, N_n)$$

is derivable, where $(M_1, \ldots, M_n) \neq_{\mathsf{E}} (N_1, \ldots, N_n)$ and $\mathsf{E} \in \{\mathsf{E}_0^{\mathsf{f}}, \mathsf{E}_1^{\mathsf{f}}\}$; and that the equation

$$\mathsf{break}_{\mathsf{f}}^i(\mathsf{f}(v_1, \ldots, v_n)) =_{\mathsf{E}_1^{\mathsf{f}}} v_i.$$

is derivable. As before, $\mathsf{E}_0^{\mathsf{f}}$ models the capabilities of a computationally bounded attacker interacting with the protocol, while $\mathsf{E}_1^{\mathsf{f}}$ models the capabilities of a computationally unbounded attacker in the future.

Example 7. A trivial example of a perfectly binding function is the identity function id. However, id is not hiding.

Example 8. An example of a PBCH primitive is the ElGamal public key derivation function. Given multiplicative cyclic group G of order q with generator g, to generate a private and public key pair Alice does the following:

1. she chooses at random her private key $sk \in \{1, \ldots, q - 1\}$,
2. she computes and publishes her public key $\mathsf{pk}_{G,g,q}(sk) = g^{sk}$.

The secret key sk is totally determined by the public key $\mathsf{pk}_{G,g,q}(sk) = g^{sk}$. It is however as hard to find sk from $\mathsf{pk}_{G,g,q}(sk)$ as it is to compute discrete logarithms.

Thus, to reason about protocols relying on ElGamal encryption we consider the following equational theories over the signature $\{\text{aenc}_{G,g,q}, \text{adec}_{G,g,q}, \text{pk}_{G,g,q}, \text{break}_{\text{pk}_{G,g,q}}\}$ (we omit the subscripts G, g, q for readability):

$$E_0^{\text{ElGamal}} = \{\text{adec}(xk, \text{aenc}(\text{pk}(xk), xr, xm)) = xm\}$$

$$E_1^{\text{ElGamal}} = \left\{ \begin{array}{l} \text{adec}(xk, \text{aenc}(\text{pk}(xk), xr, xm)) = xm \\ \text{break}_{\text{pk}}(\text{pk}(xk)) = xk \end{array} \right\}$$

The function $\text{pk}_{G,g,q}$ is PBCH. Note however that the encryption algorithm $\text{aenc}_{G,g,q}$ is not PBCH, since it is not perfectly binding. Indeed, given the parameters G, q, and g, to encrypt the message m with the public key g^{sk}, Alice would

1. pick a random $r \in \{0, \ldots, q-1\}$ and comput $c_1 = g^r$;
2. compute the secret shared key $s = (g^{sk})^r$; and
3. computer $c_2 = m.s$

The computed ciphertext is then $\text{aenc}(\text{pk}(sk), r, m) = (c_1, c_2) = (g^r, m.(g^{sk})^r)$. Hence, for any public key $\text{pk}(sk') = g^{sk'}$, there exists a message $m' = m.(g^{sk})^r/(g^{sk'})^r$ such that $\text{aenc}(\text{pk}(sk), r, m) = \text{aenc}(\text{pk}(sk'), r, m')$. Thus, ElGamal encryption is not perfectly binding.

PHCB Primitives. Informally, an n-ary function f is perfectly hiding if given the output, it is impossible to retrieve any of the inputs. So even enumerating all the possible inputs shouldn't allow one to retrieve the inputs from the output of the function. But this implies that f should admit collisions for each possible input. On the other hand, f is computationally binding if it is computationally not feasible to find such collisions.

Example 9. Any constant function $f(x_1, \ldots, x_n) = c$ is obviously perfectly hiding but not computationally binding. The $\oplus$ function is also perfectly hiding since for all $z = x \oplus y$

- for all x', we have that $y' = z \oplus x'$ is such that $x \oplus y = x' \oplus y'$; and
- for all y'', we have that $x'' = z \oplus y''$ is such that $x \oplus y = x'' \oplus y''$.

However, it is not computationally binding since it is easy to compute x'' and y'.

Example 10. Pedersen commitments are PHCB. The Pedersen commitment over a cyclic group G of order q and two generators $h, g \in G$ such that $\log_g h$ is not known is the function $P_{h,g}^G(x, y) = h^x \cdot g^y (\bmod q)$. Pedersen commitments are perfectly hiding since for all $z = P_{h,g}^G(x, y)$,

- for all x', we have that $y' = y + (x - x') \cdot \log_g h \bmod q$ is such that $P_{h,g}^G(x, y) = P_{h,g}^G(x', y')$;
- for all y'', we have that $x'' = x + (y - y'') \cdot \log_h g \bmod q$ is such that $P_{h,g}^G(x, y) = P_{h,g}^G(x'', y'')$.

but they are computationally binding because finding these x'' and y' is as hard as computing discrete logarithms.

To reason about protocols relying on Pedersen commitments using the applied pi calculus, we introduce the function symbols $\mathsf{forge}^1_{\mathsf{Ped}}$, and $\mathsf{forge}^2_{\mathsf{Ped}}$ and the two following equational theories

$$\mathsf{E}^{\mathsf{Ped}}_0 = \emptyset$$

$$\mathsf{E}^{\mathsf{Ped}}_1 = \left\{ \begin{array}{l} \mathsf{Ped}(\mathsf{forge}^1_{\mathsf{Ped}}(v, y'), y') = v \\ \mathsf{Ped}(x', \mathsf{forge}^2_{\mathsf{Ped}}(v, x')) = v \\ \mathsf{forge}^1_{\mathsf{Ped}}(\mathsf{Ped}(x, y), y) = x \\ \mathsf{forge}^2_{\mathsf{Ped}}(\mathsf{Ped}(x, y), x) = y \\ \mathsf{forge}^1_{\mathsf{Ped}}(v, \mathsf{forge}^2_{\mathsf{Ped}}(v, x)) = x \\ \mathsf{forge}^2_{\mathsf{Ped}}(v, \mathsf{forge}^1_{\mathsf{Ped}}(v, y)) = y \end{array} \right\}$$

For the first equation, suppose $v = \mathsf{Ped}(x, y)$, and we have some y'; then $\mathsf{forge}^1_{\mathsf{Ped}}$ allows us to compute a value $x' = \mathsf{forge}^1_{\mathsf{Ped}}(v, y')$ such that $v = \mathsf{Ped}(x', y')$. The second equation is similar. The third and fourth equation allow us to recover one of the arguments, given that the other argument is known. In other words the third equation expresses that when forging $x' = \mathsf{forge}^1_{\mathsf{Ped}}(v, y)$ and $v = \mathsf{Ped}(x, y)$ then we must have that $x' = x$, and similarly for the fourth equation. The fifth and sixth equations are also seen to be mathematically valid, given that $\mathsf{forge}^1_{\mathsf{Ped}}(v, y)$ and $\mathsf{forge}^2_{\mathsf{Ped}}(v, x)$ respectively model the terms $\log_g(v/h^y)$ and $\log_h(v/g^x)$.

5.2 Applications: Electronic Voting Protocols and Everlasting Privacy

Pedersen commitments have been used in several voting protocols for achieving everlasting privacy. In particular we study the protocol by Moran and Naor [18] and a recent version of Helios [12] based on Pedersen commitments.

Moran-Naor Protocol. Moran and Naor [18] designed a protocol to be used with voting machines in a polling station. The protocol aims to achieve both verifiability and everlasting privacy. From a high level point of view the protocol works as follows.

1. The voter enters his vote into the voting machine inside the voting booth. The machine then computes a Pedersen commitment to this vote and provides a zero knowledge proof to the voter that the computed value commits to the voter's choice. The commitment is then published on a bulletin board so that the voter can verify the presence of his ballot.
2. After all ballots have been cast, the votes are published (in random order) on the bulletin board together with a zero knowledge proof asserting that the published votes correspond to the votes of the published commitments.

As we are only interested in privacy and not verifiability we ignore the zero knowledge proofs in our modeling and simply represent the protocol by the process

$$\mathsf{MoranNaor}(v_1, v_2) \stackrel{\mathsf{def}}{=} \nu priv_1. \, \nu priv_2.$$
$$V(priv_1, v_1) \mid V(priv_2, v_2) \mid \nu c.(DRE(priv_1, priv_2, priv_3) \mid T)$$

where

$$V(priv, v) \stackrel{\text{def}}{=} \overline{priv}\langle v\rangle$$

$$DRE(p_1, p_2, p_3) \stackrel{\text{def}}{=} \overline{p_1(x_1).\nu r_1.\overline{bb}\langle\text{Ped}(x_1, r_1)\rangle.\overline{c}\langle x_1\rangle \mid}$$
$$\overline{p_2(x_2).\nu r_2.\overline{bb}\langle\text{Ped}(x_2, r_2)\rangle.\overline{c}\langle x_2\rangle \mid}$$
$$\overline{p_3(x_3).\nu r_3.\overline{bb}\langle\text{Ped}(x_3, r_3)\rangle.\overline{c}\langle x_3\rangle}$$
$$T = c(y_1).\overline{bb}\langle y_1\rangle \mid c(y_2).\overline{bb}\langle y_2\rangle \mid c(y_3).\overline{bb}\langle y_3\rangle$$

As the voter enters his vote in a private ballot booth, we have modelled this communication on a private channel. We have been able to show that MoranNaor verifies everlasting privacy with respect to the channel bb and the equational theories introduced for Pedersen commitments.

Helios with Pedersen Commitments. In [12], the authors propose a version of the Helios voting system that provides everlasting vote privacy *w.r.t.* the bulletin board. They rely for this on Pedersen commitments. In this section, we present this new version of the Helios system.

1. The voter V chooses her candidate v and commits to it by generating a random number r and computing the Pedersen commitment $\text{Ped}(r, v)$. She then separately encrypts the decommitment values r and v using the public key $\text{pk}(skE)$ of the election; and casts her commitment together with the encrypted decommitment values and her identity on a private authenticated channel. Upon reception of the ballot, the Bulletin Board (BB) publishes on a public web page the commitment $\text{Ped}(r, v)$ (after having checked that V is entitled to vote).
2. Once the voting phase is over, the ballots (*i.e.* the commitments together with the encrypted decommitment values) are shuffled and rerandomized through mixnets. The random permutation of the rerandomized ballots is published on the public webpage (together with a zero knowledge proof of correct reencryption and mixing).
3. Finally, the authorities decrypt the rerandomized and shuffled decommitment values and the BB publishes them.

The voter can be modelled by the following process:

$$V(id, auth, v) \stackrel{\text{def}}{=} \nu s.\nu rv.\nu rs.$$
$$\overline{auth}\langle\langle id, \langle\text{Ped}(s, v), \langle\text{aenc}(\text{pk}(skE), rv, v), \text{aenc}(\text{pk}(skE), rs, s)\rangle\rangle\rangle\rangle$$

She sends to the BB on the private authenticated channel $authCh$, her commitment $\text{Ped}(s, v)$ to vote v, together with her identity and the encrypted decommitment values $\text{aenc}(\text{pk}(skE), rv, v)$, $\text{aenc}(\text{pk}(skE), rs, s)$.

The ballot box publishes her commitment for verifiability purposes. After having received all votes, the BB publishes the votes in a random order through the process T.

$$BB(a_1, a_2, a_3) \stackrel{\text{def}}{=} a_1(x).\ \overline{bb}\langle\langle\text{fst}(x), \text{fst}(\text{snd}(x))\rangle\rangle.\ \overline{c}\langle x\rangle \mid$$
$$a_2(y).\ \overline{bb}\langle\langle\text{fst}(x), \text{fst}(\text{snd}(x))\rangle\rangle.\ \overline{c}\langle x\rangle \mid$$
$$a_3(z).\ \overline{c}\langle z\rangle \mid T$$

$$T \overset{\text{def}}{=} c(x).\ c(y).\ c(z).\text{if } \mathsf{fst}(\mathsf{snd}(\mathsf{snd}(x))) \neq \mathsf{fst}(\mathsf{snd}(\mathsf{snd}(z)))$$
$$\wedge\ \mathsf{fst}(\mathsf{snd}(\mathsf{snd}(y))) \neq \mathsf{fst}(\mathsf{snd}(\mathsf{snd}(z)))$$
$$\wedge\ \mathsf{fst}(\mathsf{snd}(\mathsf{snd}(x))) \neq \mathsf{fst}(\mathsf{snd}(\mathsf{snd}(y)))\ \text{then}$$
$$\overline{bb}\langle\mathsf{adec}(skE, \mathsf{fst}(\mathsf{snd}(\mathsf{snd}(x))))\rangle\ |$$
$$\overline{bb}\langle\mathsf{adec}(skE, \mathsf{fst}(\mathsf{snd}(\mathsf{snd}(y))))\rangle\ |$$
$$\overline{bb}\langle\mathsf{adec}(skE, \mathsf{fst}(\mathsf{snd}(\mathsf{snd}(z))))\rangle$$

Finally we can define the voting protocol $\mathsf{Helios}^{\mathsf{Ped}}$ as

$$\mathsf{Helios}^{\mathsf{Ped}}(v1, v2) \overset{\text{def}}{=} \nu skE.\ \nu auth_1.\ \nu auth_2.$$
$$\overline{bb}\langle\mathsf{pk}(skE)\rangle.\ (V(auth_1, id_1, v_1)\ |\ V(auth_2, id_2, v_2)\ |\ BB(auth_1, auth_2, auth_3))$$

which verifies everlasting privacy with respect to the channel bb and the previously introduced equational theories.

6 Tool Support for Everlasting Indistinguishability

In order to verify everlasting indistinguishability on the examples presented in the previous section we have adapted two tools for automated verification of equivalence properties, AKiSs [6] and ProVerif [5]. The two tools have shown themselves to be complementary and the results obtained using the tools are summarized in Figure 3.

AKiSs. AKiSs is a recent tool that has been designed to automatically prove trace equivalence by translating processes into Horn clauses and using a dedicated resolution algorithm. More precisely it can both under- and over-approximate trace equivalence in the case of a bounded number of sessions, i.e. for processes without replication. The tool has currently two limitations: it does not support private channels, or else branches in conditionals. However, it is able to deal with a wide range of equational theories, including the theory for Pedersen commitments introduced in the previous section.

We have adapted the tool in order to check forward indistinguishability and adapted the syntax to declare everlasting channels and an everlasting equational theory. More precisely we implemented an algorithm to check an under-approximation of forward indistinguishability, yielding a proof of forward indistinguishability whenever the tool responds positively. While false attacks are possible, we did not encounter any in our case studies.

Absence of support for private channels and else branches required us to adapt some of the examples. In particular we rewrote the processes by directly *inlining* private communications, which in the examples maintained the same set of traces, hence preserving everlasting indistinguishability. The weeding operation in $\mathsf{Helios}^{\mathsf{noreplay}}$, $\mathsf{Helios}^{\mathsf{noid}}$ and $\mathsf{Helios}^{\mathsf{ped}}$ requires the use of an else branch. We encoded a different weeding procedure using cryptographic proofs of knowledge. While the vote replay attack on the simple Helios protocol is found in less than 10 seconds, the verification of other examples ranged from a few minutes to several hours. While attempting to verify $\mathsf{Helios}^{\mathsf{ped}}$ the tool ran out of memory and we were only able to verify a version of $\mathsf{Helios}^{\mathsf{ped}}$ with two honest voters and no dishonest voter. As the tool is still in a prototype status we are confident that future optimizations will allow the tool to scale up to this kind of protocols. The tool and example files are available at https://github.com/ciobaca/akiss.

ProVerif. The ProVerif tool [4] is an automatic cryptographic protocol verifier. It is based on the representation of protocols by Horn clauses and relies on several approximations. ProVerif can handle several types of properties and in particular equivalence based properties [5] like the privacy-type ones which we are interested in this work. Moreover, ProVerif can handle many different cryptographic primitives, including Pedersen commitments as our case studies show.

The ProVerif tool works by translating biprocesses into Horn clauses built over the two predicates attacker2 and message2. For equivalence checking, biprocess is used to represent the pair of processes for which ProVerif is called to check equivalence. The fact attacker2(M, M') means that the attacker can learn the value M (*resp. M'*) from the first (*resp.* second) process encoded by the biprocess. The fact message2(M, N, M', N') means that the message N (*resp. N'*) has appeared on the channel M (*resp. M'*) while executing the first (*resp.* second) process encoded by the biprocess.

As for the AKISS tool, our extension of ProVerif consists in the addition of constructs for declaring *everlasting channels* and a *future equational theory* (different from the *present* one). We introduce the extra binary predicate attacker2_ev for the generation of Horn clauses from biprocesses of our extended ProVerif language. The fact attacker2_ev(M, M') means that in the future, the attacker will either remember or be able to compute from messages he remembers, the value M (*resp. M'*). The declaration of an everlasting channel c generates the following *inheritance* Horn clause:

$$\text{message2} : c[], xm, c[], ym \;\rightarrow\; \text{attacker2\_ev} : xm, ym$$

This clause transports messages sent on the everlasting channel to the "future". The declaration of future equations generates the same equations as present ones but using our new attacker2_ev predicate. For example, the everlasting equation

$$\text{break}(\text{aenc}(\text{pk}(xk), xr, xm)) = xk$$

will generate the two following clauses

$$\text{attacker2\_ev} : x, \text{aenc}(\text{pk}(xk), xr, xm) \;\rightarrow\; \text{attacker2\_ev} : \text{break}(x), xk$$
$$\text{attacker2\_ev} : \text{aenc}(\text{pk}(xk), xr, xm), x \;\rightarrow\; \text{attacker2\_ev} : xk, \text{break}(x)$$

These clauses model the "future" ability of the attacker to recover the decryption key of ciphertexts he remembers.

Using our extension of the ProVerif tool, we managed to find the attack on Helios[noreplay] presented in section 4.2, but also to prove that Helios[noid], Helios[pedersen] and that Moran − Naor satisfy everlasting vote privacy. However, because of the abstractions made by ProVerif, we had to adapt our models of Helios[noid] and Helios[pedersen] in order for ProVerif to succeed in proving that satisfy everlasting privacy. Indeed, these

	AKISS	ProVerif
Helios	attack on privacy	attack on privacy
Helios^{noreplay}	proof of privacy attack on everlasting privacy	proof of privacy attack on everlasting privacy
Helios^{noid}	proof of everlasting privacy	proof of everlasting privacy (voters casting their votes in fixed order)
Helios^{ped}	proof of everlasting privacy (2 honest voters only)	proof of everlasting privacy (voters casting their votes in fixed order)
Moran-Naor	proof of everlasting privacy	proof of everlasting privacy

Fig. 3. Automated verification using AKISS and ProVerif

two protocols do not satisfy uniformity under reductions, and ProVerif reported false attacks on these two protocols. To overcome this limitation of ProVerif, we fixed the order in which the three voters cast their votes.

The tool and example files are available at http://markryan.eu/research/EverlastingPrivacy/.

7 Conclusion

The key idea of "practical" everlasting privacy is that in the future, an attacker will be more powerful in terms of computation (he may be able to break the cryptography) but less powerful in terms of the data he can operate on (transactions between a vote client and the vote server may not have been stored). We realized this idea in the "symbolic" model by allowing different equational theories in different phases, and restricting the information flow from the earlier phase to the later one. We modified ProVerif and AKISS to verify our examples automatically.

We foresee to apply our results to more evolved case studies, e.g. taking into account the zero knowledge proofs that we omitted here for simplicity. Our case studies also show the limitations of the tools for checking equivalence properties which motivates further work to increase their efficiency and scope. Finally, the ability to model different equational theories with restricted information passing between them opens up possibilities for modeling breakable cryptography and other kinds of forward security. In particular it would be interesting to apply the notion of everlasting security to other flavors of anonymity and untraceability.

Acknowledgements. The research leading to these results has received funding from the European Research Council under the European Unions Seventh Framework Programme (FP7/2007-2013) / ERC grant agreement no 258865, project ProSecure, the ANR projects ProSe (decision ANR 2010-VERS-004) and JCJC VIP (decision ANR-11-JS02-006). We also acknowledge funding from EPSRC projects EP/G02684X/1 "Trustworthy Voting Systems" and EP/H005501/1 "Analysing Security and Privacy Properties".

References

1. Abadi, M., Fournet, C.: Mobile values, new names, and secure communication. In: 28th Symposium on Principles of Programming Languages, POPL 2001. ACM Press (2001)
2. Adida, B.: Helios: web-based open-audit voting. In: 17th Conference on Security Symposium, SS 2008. USENIX Association (2008)
3. Backes, M., Hritcu, C., Maffei, M.: Automated verification of remote electronic voting protocols in the applied pi-calculus. In: 21st IEEE Computer Security Foundations Symposium, CSF 2008. IEEE (2008)
4. Blanchet, B.: An efficient cryptographic protocol verifier based on Prolog rules. In: 14th Computer Security Foundations Workshop, CSFW 2001. IEEE (2001)
5. Blanchet, B., Abadi, M., Fournet, C.: Automated verification of selected equivalences for security protocols. Journal of Logic and Algebraic Programming 75(1) (2008)
6. Chadha, R., Ciobâcă, Ş., Kremer, S.: Automated Verification of Equivalence Properties of Cryptographic Protocols. In: Seidl, H. (ed.) ESOP 2012. LNCS, vol. 7211, pp. 108–127. Springer, Heidelberg (2012)
7. Chaum, D., Ryan, P.Y.A., Schneider, S.: A Practical Voter-Verifiable Election Scheme. In: De Capitani di Vimercati, S., Syverson, P.F., Gollmann, D. (eds.) ESORICS 2005. LNCS, vol. 3679, pp. 118–139. Springer, Heidelberg (2005)
8. Clarkson, M., Chong, S., Myers, A.: Civitas: Toward a secure voting system. In: 29th IEEE Symposium on Security and Privacy, S&P 2008 (2008)
9. Cortier, V., Smyth, B.: Attacking and fixing helios: An analysis of ballot secrecy. In: 24th IEEE Computer Security Foundations Symposium, CSF 2011. IEEE (June 2011)
10. Cuvelier, E., Peters, T., Pereira, O.: Election verifiabilty or ballot privacy: Do we need to choose? SecVote, Dagstuhl (2012),
    secvote.uni.lu/slides/opereira-verif-or-priv.pdf
11. Delaune, S., Kremer, S., Ryan, M.D.: Verifying privacy-type properties of electronic voting protocols. Journal of Computer Security 17(4), 435–487 (2009)
12. Demirel, D., Van De Graaf, J., Araújo, R.: Improving helios with everlasting privacy towards the public. In: International conference on Electronic Voting Technology/Workshop on Trustworthy Elections, EVT/WOTE 2012. USENIX Association (2012)
13. Dreier, J., Lafourcade, P., Lakhnech, Y.: Defining Privacy for Weighted Votes, Single and Multi-voter Coercion. In: Foresti, S., Yung, M., Martinelli, F. (eds.) ESORICS 2012. LNCS, vol. 7459, pp. 451–468. Springer, Heidelberg (2012)
14. Juels, A., Catalano, D., Jakobsson, M.: Coercion-resistant electronic elections. In: ACM Workshop on Privacy in the Electronic Society, WPES 2005. ACM (2005)
15. Kremer, S., Ryan, M.: Analysis of an Electronic Voting Protocol in the Applied Pi Calculus. In: Sagiv, M. (ed.) ESOP 2005. LNCS, vol. 3444, pp. 186–200. Springer, Heidelberg (2005)
16. Kremer, S., Ryan, M., Smyth, B.: Election Verifiability in Electronic Voting Protocols. In: Gritzalis, D., Preneel, B., Theoharidou, M. (eds.) ESORICS 2010. LNCS, vol. 6345, pp. 389–404. Springer, Heidelberg (2010)
17. Küsters, R., Truderung, T., Vogt, A.: Accountability: definition and relationship to verifiability. In: ACM Conference on Computer and Communications Security, CCS 2010 (2010)
18. Moran, T., Naor, M.: Receipt-Free Universally-Verifiable Voting with Everlasting Privacy. In: Dwork, C. (ed.) CRYPTO 2006. LNCS, vol. 4117, pp. 373–392. Springer, Heidelberg (2006)
19. Pedersen, T.P.: Non-interactive and Information-Theoretic Secure Verifiable Secret Sharing. In: Feigenbaum, J. (ed.) CRYPTO 1991. LNCS, vol. 576, pp. 129–140. Springer, Heidelberg (1992)

A Differentially Private Mechanism of Optimal Utility for a Region of Priors*

Ehab ElSalamouny[1,2], Konstantinos Chatzikokolakis[1], and Catuscia Palamidessi[1]

[1] INRIA and LIX, Ecole Polytechnique, France
[2] Faculty of Computer and Information Science, Suez Canal University, Egypt

Abstract. The notion of differential privacy has emerged in the area of statistical databases as a measure of protection of the participants' sensitive information, which can be compromised by selected queries. Differential privacy is usually achieved by using mechanisms that add random noise to the query answer. Thus, privacy is obtained at the cost of reducing the accuracy, and therefore the *utility*, of the answer. Since the utility depends on the user's side information, commonly modelled as a prior distribution, a natural goal is to design mechanisms that are optimal *for every prior*. However, it has been shown that such mechanisms *do not exist* for any query other than (essentially) counting queries ([1]).

Given the above negative result, in this paper we consider the problem of identifying *a restricted class of priors* for which an optimal mechanism *does exist*. Given an arbitrary query and a privacy parameter, we geometrically characterise a special region of priors as a convex polytope in the priors space. We then derive upper bounds for utility as well as for min-entropy leakage for the priors in this region. Finally we define what we call the *tight-constraints mechanism* and we discuss the conditions for its existence. This mechanism reaches the bounds for all the priors of the region, and thus it is optimal on the whole region.

1 Introduction

Statistical databases are commonly used to provide aggregate information about the individuals of a certain population, to attain a social benefit. In general, certain data of the participants in the database may be confidential, and we should not allow queries that can reveal them. On the other hand we would like to allow global queries, like, for instance, the average salary of the inhabitants of a certain region, the percentage of individuals having a certain disease, or the cities with the highest rates of crime. This kind of information can be extremely useful for e.g. financial planning, medical research, and anti-crime measures.

Unfortunately, even though these kinds of queries do not refer directly to the individual data, they still represent a major threat to the privacy of the participants in the databases. To illustrate the problem, consider a database whose records contain personal data, among which the salary, regarded as confidential. Suppose we are allowed to query the number of participants and their average salary. Then, by querying the

---

* This work is partially funded by the Inria large scale initiative CAPPRIS, the EU FP7 grant no. 295261 (MEALS), and the project ANR-09-BLAN-0169-01 (PANDA).

D. Basin and J.C. Mitchell (Eds.): POST 2013, LNCS 7796, pp. 41–62, 2013.
© Springer-Verlag Berlin Heidelberg 2013

database before and after the insertion of a new record "Bob", we can easily infer, by an easy calculation, the exact salary of Bob.

A successful approach to solve the above problem is to report to the user an approximate answer instead of the exact one. The approximate answer is produced by adding controlled *random noise* to the exact answer. The overall procedure, representing the sanitized query, is a (probabilistic) *mechanism* $\mathcal{K}$ which takes as input the database v and reports to the user an output o in some domain O, according to some probabilistic distribution. Intuitively, the uncertainty introduced at the level of the global answer induces uncertainty about the value of the individual data in the database, thus making it difficult for an attacker to guess such value. However it is crucial to know *exactly* what kind of protection is achieved this way. *Differential privacy*, introduced by Dwork ([2–5]), is a formalization of the privacy property that can be guaranteed by such mechanism. It is a quantitative notion, in the sense that it depends on a parameter ϵ representing the provided level of privacy.

Following common lines (e.g. [6–8]), in this paper we assume that the mechanism $\mathcal{K}$ is *oblivious* with respect to the given query f. Namely, its output depends only on the exact query result and not on the underlying database. Furthermore, we consider only the case in which the domains of the answers (exact and reported) are finite. Under these assumptions, the mechanism $\mathcal{K}$ is determined by an underlying stochastic *noise matrix* X whose generic element x_{io} is the conditional probability of reporting the answer o when the exact query answer is i.

Besides guaranteeing differential privacy, a mechanism should of course provide an answer which is still "useful" enough to the user asking the query. This second goal is measured in terms of *utility*, which represents the average gain that a rational user obtains from the reported answer. More precisely, on the basis of the reported answer o the user can make a guess k (remapping) about the exact hidden query result i. His gain $g(i, k)$ is established by a given function g. The utility is then defined as *the expected gain under the best possible remapping*. While the gain function can take various forms, in this paper we restrict our analysis to the *binary* gain function, which evaluates to 1 when the user's guess is the same as the query result ($k = i$) and evaluates to 0 otherwise.

The utility of a mechanism depends on the side-information which the user may have about the database. This knowledge induces a probability distribution, called 'prior', over the possible query results. Suppose for example that a user "Alice" knows that all people in the database have a salary of at least 20K €. Thus Alice expects the average of the salaries to be at least 20K €. This is reflected on Alice's prior over the average-salary query results: the total probability mass is distributed on the range of values $\geq$ 20K, while it is 0 on lower values. Given this prior, a mechanism X producing only outputs $\geq$ 20K is intuitively more useful to Alice than another one generating also values < 20K, which are less informative for Alice.

The *optimal* mechanism for a given prior and level of privacy ϵ is defined as the mechanism which maximises the utility function, while satisfying ϵ-differential privacy. Naturally, we do not want to change the mechanism depending on the user, so we would like to devise mechanisms which are *universally optimal*, i.e. optimal for *any* prior. A famous result by Gosh et al. [6] states that this is possible for the so-called *counting queries*, which are queries concerned with questions of the kind "how many records in the database have the property $\mathcal{P}$?" (for some $\mathcal{P}$). In [6] it was proved that the *truncated geometric mechanism* is optimal, for this type of queries, for all priors. Of course the question immediately arises whether we can obtain a similar result for other queries as well. Unfortunately Brenner and Nissim answered this question negatively, by showing that for any query other than (essentially) counting queries a universally optimal mechanism does not exist [1]. However, one can still hope that, also for other queries, by restricting the class of users (i.e. the domain of priors), one could find mechanisms that are optimal for all the users of the class. This is exactly the objective of the present paper: given a query, we aim at identifying a mechanism, and a class of users, for whom that same mechanism provides ϵ-differential privacy and maximal utility at the same time.

Given an arbitrary query and a privacy level $\epsilon > 0$, we call ϵ-*regular* the priors, for which, the probabilities of two adjacent answers (i.e. answers obtained from databases that differ for only one record) are not very different (their ratio is bounded by e^{ϵ}). At the same time, they may assign significantly different probabilities to "distant" answers. As an example of such prior, consider a researcher "Alice" in a medical school who is interested in the incidence of a certain disease in a statistical medical database containing 1000 records. (Each record represents a person and contains a field saying whether or not the person is infected.) Assume that Alice's side knowledge lets her to expect that the percentage of infected people is likely to be, say, between 1% and 2%, while it is highly unlikely to be higher than 5%. Also, assume that Alice does not have "sharp" enough information to assign significantly different probabilities to adjacent answers, e.g. 1.5% (15 people affected) and 1.6% (16 people affected). It is precisely this kind of users that we target in this paper: we will see that, under certain conditions, we can design a mechanism which maximises the utility for all of them.

A related issue that we consider in this paper is the amount of information leaked by a mechanism, from the point of view of the so-called *quantitative information flow* framework. There have been various proposal for quantifying the information flow; we consider here the *information-theoretic approach*, in which the system (in this case the mechanism) is regarded as a *noisy channel*, and the leakage is defined as the difference between the a priori *entropy* of the input (the secret – in this case the database entries), and the a posteriori one, after revealing the output (in this case the reported answer). Depending on the notion of entropy adopted one can model different kinds of adversaries [9]. In particular, Shannon entropy (used, for instance, in [10–13]) is suitable for adversaries who can probe the secret repeatedly, while Rényi min-entropy (used, for instance, in [14, 15]) is suitable for one-try attacks. In both cases, the main difference with differential privacy is that the information-theoretic approaches measure the *expected* threat to confidentiality (i.e. the average amount of leakage, where each leak is weighted by its probability to occur), while differential privacy considers catastrophic any disclosure of confidential information, no matter how unlikely it is.

Computing and bounding the information leakage has been pursued in several papers, we mention for instance [16, 17]. Recently, researchers have investigated the relation between differential privacy and information leakage [18–20, 8], and in particular it has been proved in [20] that differential privacy induces a bound on the min-entropy leakage, which is met by a certain mechanism for the uniform prior (for which min-entropy leakage is always maximum). In this paper, we extend the above result so to provide a more accurate bound for any fixed ϵ-regular prior distribution. More precisely, we provide a bound to the leakage specific to the prior and that can be met, under a certain condition, by a suitable mechanism. It is worth noting that this mechanism is defined similarly to the one that is optimal for the ϵ-regular priors. In fact, min-entropy leakage and utility are strongly related: the main difference is what we regard as the input of the channel. For the former is the database, for the latter the exact answer to the query. Correspondingly, min-entropy leakage measures the correlation between the reported answer and the database entries, while utility measures the correlation between the reported answer and the exact answer.

Contribution

- We identify, for an arbitrary query and a privacy parameter ϵ, the class of the ϵ-regular prior distributions on the exact answers. The interest of this class is that for each prior in it we are able to provide a specific upper bound to the utility of any ϵ-differentially-private mechanism. We characterise this class as a geometric region, and we study its properties.
- We describe an ϵ-differentially-private mechanism, called "tight-constraints mechanism", which meets those upper bounds for every ϵ-regular prior, and is therefore universally optimal in this region. We provide necessary and sufficient conditions for the existence of such mechanism, and an effective method to test the conditions and to construct the mechanism.
- Switching view, and considering the correlation between the databases and the reported answers (instead than between the exact and reported answers) we recast the above definitions and results in terms of quantitative information flow. The outcome is that we are able to improve the upper bounds for the min-entropy leakage of an ϵ-differentially-private mechanism, for all the ϵ-regular prior distributions on the databases. A construction similar to the one in previous point yields the tight-constraints mechanism which reaches those upper bounds.

Plan of the paper. In the next section we recall the basic definitions of differential privacy and utility. Section 3 introduces the notion of ϵ-regular prior, investigates the properties of these priors, and gives a geometric characterisation of their region. Section 4 shows that for all ϵ-regular priors on the exact answers (resp. databases), ϵ-differential privacy induces an upper bound on the utility (resp. on the min-entropy leakage). Section 5 identifies a mechanism which reaches the above bounds for every ϵ-regular prior, and that is therefore the universally optimal mechanism (resp. the maximally leaking mechanism) in the region. Section 6 illustrates our methodology and results using the example of the sum queries. Section 7 concludes and proposes some directions for future research.

For reasons of space we have omitted several proofs. The interested reader can find them in the report version of this paper [21].

2   Preliminaries

2.1   Differential Privacy

The notion of ϵ-differential privacy, introduced by Dwork in [2], imposes constraints on data reporting mechanisms so that the user is unable to distinguish, from an output, between two databases differing only for one record. This indistinguishability property represents a protection for the individual corresponding to that record. In the following, the mechanism is represented as a probabilistic function $\mathcal{K}$ from the set of possible databases $\mathcal{V}$ to the set of possible reported outputs O. The relation of 'differing only for one record' for two databases v and v' is represented by the *adjacency* relation and written as $v \sim v'$.

Definition 1 (Differential privacy [2]). *A probabilistic mechanism $\mathcal{K}$ from $\mathcal{V}$ to O satisfies ϵ-differential privacy if for all pairs $v, v' \in \mathcal{V}$, with $v \sim v'$, and all $S \subseteq O$, it holds that*

$$P(\mathcal{K}(v) \in S) \leq e^{\epsilon} P(\mathcal{K}(v') \in S).$$

Note that the indistinguishability property is independent from the a priori knowledge the user may have about the database.

Consider a query $f : \mathcal{V} \to \mathcal{R}_f$, where $\mathcal{R}_f$ is the set of the query results. Then a mechanism $\mathcal{K}$ is said to be *oblivious* if for every database $v \in \mathcal{V}$, the output of the mechanism, $\mathcal{K}(v)$, depends only on $f(v)$, the result of applying the query to the database v, regardless of v itself. More formally,

Definition 2 ([1]). *Let $f : \mathcal{V} \to \mathcal{R}_f$ be a query. A mechanism $\mathcal{K} : \mathcal{V} \to O$ is oblivious if there exists a randomised function $\mathcal{M} : \mathcal{R}_f \to O$ such that, for all $v \in \mathcal{V}$, and all $S \subseteq O$, it holds that*

$$P(\mathcal{K}(v) \in S) = P(\mathcal{M}(f(v)) \in S).$$

According to the above definition, any oblivious mechanism $\mathcal{K}$ can be seen as a cascade of two functions: the deterministic query f and a randomised function $\mathcal{M}$. The role of $\mathcal{M}$ is to add random noise to the exact query result $f(v)$ and produce a 'noisy' output $o \in O$ to the user. The privacy guarantees are therefore provided by the function $\mathcal{M}$ which we implement by a stochastic matrix $X = (x_{io})$, called the *noise matrix*. The rows of X are indexed by the elements of $\mathcal{R}_f$ and the columns are indexed by the elements of O. With this representation x_{io} is the probability of giving the output o when the exact query result is i. In this paper, we consider only oblivious mechanisms and therefore our results concern the design of the noise matrix X. Similarly, the query function f and the mechanism can be represented as matrices and hence it holds by Def. 2 that $\mathcal{K} = f X$.

Given a query f, The adjacency relation on databases $\mathcal{V}$ induces another adjacency relation on the set of query results $\mathcal{R}_f$ as follows.

Definition 3 (Adjacent query results). *Given a query function f with a range $\mathcal{R}_f$, two different results $i, h \in \mathcal{R}_f$ are said to be 'adjacent', and written as $i \sim_f h$, if and only if there exists two databases v, v' such that $f(v) = i$ and $f(v') = h$, and $v \sim v'$.*

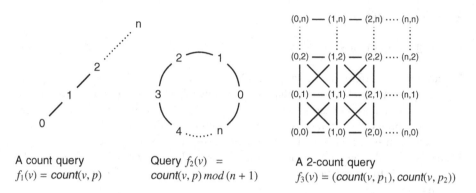

A count query	Query $f_2(v) =$	A 2-count query
$f_1(v) = count(v, p)$	$count(v, p) \bmod (n + 1)$	$f_3(v) = (count(v, p_1), count(v, p_2))$

Fig. 1. Examples for the graph structures of different queries

Informally, $i, h \in \mathcal{R}_f$ are adjacent if they discriminate between two adjacent databases. Using the introduced notion of adjacency between query results, a graph structure can be used to model these results along with their adjacency relationship. More precisely, the set of nodes in this graph represents the set of query results $\mathcal{R}_f$, while edges represent the adjacency relationship among them. It is worth noting that this graph structure of queries have been used also in [8, 1] to analyse the differentially private mechanisms. Figure 1 shows examples of the graph structures of different queries. In these examples $count(v, p)$ refers to a counting query which returns the number of records in the database v which satisfy a certain property p. Other queries in the figure are expressed using the $count$ function.

Let $\mathcal{K}$ be an oblivious mechanism for which X is the underlying noise matrix. It is intuitive to see that satisfying the indistinguishability between adjacent databases (i.e. satisfying differential privacy) corresponds to the satisfying indistinguishability (by means of X) between adjacent query results. Formally,

Lemma 1. *Given a noise matrix X, An oblivious mechanism $\mathcal{K}$ satisfies ϵ-differential privacy if and only if for all query results i, h where $i \sim_f h$ and all outputs $o \in O$, it holds that $x_{io} \le e^\epsilon x_{ho}$.*

Note that Lemma 1 provides an equivalent characterisation for differential privacy in terms of adjacent query results rather than adjacent databases.

With the graph structure of a query, the 'distance' between two query results i, h, denoted by $d(i, h)$ is defined as the shortest graph distance between i and h. Using this distance measure, differential privacy constraints can be further lifted from conditions on pairs of adjacent query results (Lemma 1) to a general condition on any pair of query results according to the following proposition.

Proposition 1. *Given a noise matrix X, the oblivious mechanism $\mathcal{K}$ satisfies ϵ-differential privacy if and only if for all query results i, h and all outputs $o \in O$, it holds that $x_{io} \le e^{\epsilon d(i,h)} x_{ho}$.*

That is, the ratio between the probability of reporting an answer o given that the query result is r and the probability of reporting the same output o given that the query result is h does not exceed $e^{\epsilon d(i,h)}$. We call the noise matrix that satisfies this condition ϵ-differentially private. Note that, while Lemma 1 describes differential privacy in terms of only adjacent query results, the equivalent characterisation given by Proposition 1 specifies the privacy constraints imposed on any pair of results (whether or not they are adjacent to each other). This feature abstracts our analysis to arbitrary pairs of graph nodes rather than reasoning about only adjacent ones.

2.2 Utility Model

For an oblivious mechanism $\mathcal{K}$, the objective of the underlying noise matrix X is to guarantee the differential privacy of the database, while providing the user with 'useful' information about the true query result. That is to satisfy a trade-off between the privacy and utility. For quantifying the utility of $\mathcal{K}$ we follow the model adopted in [6]. Given a query f, let $i \in \mathcal{R}_f$ be the result of executing f on some database. After processing i by the noise matrix X, let o be the reported output to the user. In practice, the user may use the output o, to 'guess' the value of the real query result. Therefore she may apply a *remap* (or guess) function which maps the mechanism output o to a guess $k \in \mathcal{R}_f$ for the exact query answer. The remap function (or simply 'remap') can be described as a stochastic matrix R, where its entry r_{ok} is the probability of guessing k when the observed mechanism output is o. With this representation, it can be easily seen that the probabilities of the user's guesses given individual query results are described by the matrix product $X R$. We say here that X is remapped to $X R$ by the remap R. Note that this remapping procedure models the post-processing done by the user for the mechanism output o. Now, with the user's guessed value k, a real-valued *gain function* $g : (\mathcal{R}_f \times \mathcal{R}_f) \to \mathbb{R}$ quantifies how informative k is compared to the real result i.

The *utility* of a given mechanism to the user is described as the expected value of the gain function g. The evaluation of this expected value depends on the a priori probability distribution π over the real query results, which models the side knowledge of the user about the database. The utility of the mechanism depends therefore on the definition of the gain function g, the mechanism's underlying noise matrix X, the user's remap R, and also the probability distribution π over the real query results.

One choice for the gain function is the binary gain defined as $g_b(i, j) = 1$ iff $i = j$ and 0 otherwise. The binary gain function formalises the requirement of a user to guess the exact query result using the mechanism output. In the current work we restrict our analysis to this gain function. An important feature of this function, is that it is applicable to the ranges of various queries including numerical and non-numerical one. Moreover, it will be shown that this gain function is strongly connected to the information theoretic notions of conditional entropy and information leakage. Hence, our results about the utility of private mechanism imply corresponding results regarding quantifying information leaked by these mechanisms. These results go inline with a recent trend of research aiming at quantifying information leaked by security protocols, and privacy mechanisms specifically (see e.g. [16, 17, 8, 18]). We leave considering other gain functions to future work.

Now, for formulating the utility we represent the a priori probability distribution (called the 'prior') over the real query results by a row vector π, indexed by $\mathcal{R}_f$, where

π_i is the probability that the query in hand yields the result i. The prior is therefore relative to the user and depends on her knowledge. With a generic gain function g, the utility of a mechanism for a prior π using the remap R is denoted by $\mathcal{U}(X, \pi, R)$, and defined as follows.

$$\mathcal{U}(X, \pi, R) = \mathbf{E}\left[g(i, k)\right] = \sum_{i,k} \pi_i (X R)_{ik}\, g(i, k), \qquad (1)$$

where X is the noise matrix of the given mechanism. In our case, where the binary gain function g_b is used, the utility reduces to a convex combination of the diagonal elements of $X R$ as follows.

$$\mathcal{U}(X, \pi, R) = \sum_i \pi_i (X R)_{ii}. \qquad (2)$$

Accordingly, for a given prior π, an oblivious ϵ-differentially private mechanism, with a noise matrix X, is said to be *optimal* if and only if there is a remap R such that the above function is maximised over all ϵ-differentially private mechanisms and all remaps [1]. As exemplified in the introduction, the optimality of a mechanism depends, in general, on the prior (user); that is a mechanism can be optimal for a prior while it is not for another one. It has been proved by [1] that for arbitrary queries (except the counting ones), there is no such a mechanism that is optimal for all priors simultaneously. Nevertheless, we identify in the following section a region of priors, where it is possible to find a single mechanism which is optimal to all of them.

3 ϵ-Regular Priors

In this section we describe a region of priors, called 'ϵ-regular'. These priors are determined by the given query f and privacy parameter ϵ. In our way to specify these priors, we first represent the ϵ-differential privacy constraints in a matrix form. By Proposition 1, observe that each ϵ-differential privacy constraint imposed on a noise matrix X can be written as $x_{io}/x_{ho} \geq e^{-\epsilon d(i,h)}$. Since the lower bound $e^{-\epsilon d(i,h)}$ depends only on i, h, all constraints can be described altogether by a square matrix Φ formed by such lower bounds. We refer to this matrix as the *privacy-constraints* matrix. Note that the rows, and also columns of Φ are indexed by the elements of $\mathcal{R}_f$, the set of query results.

Definition 4 (privacy-constraints matrix). *The* privacy-constraints matrix Φ *of a query f with a range $\mathcal{R}_f$, and a privacy parameter $\epsilon > 0$ is a square matrix, indexed by $\mathcal{R}_f \times \mathcal{R}_f$, where $\phi_{ih} = e^{-\epsilon d(i,h)}$ for all $i, h \in \mathcal{R}_f$.*

Note that Φ is symmetric ($\phi_{ih} = \phi_{hi}$) due to the symmetry of the distance function $d(i, h)$. Observe that when $\epsilon \to \infty$, i.e. exclude privacy at all, Φ converges to the identity matrix where each diagonal entry is 1 and other entries are zeros. In terms of the privacy-constraints matrix of a query and ϵ, we define now the ϵ-regular priors as follows (note that we use $\mathbf{y} \geq 0$ to denote $\forall i : y_i \geq 0$).

Definition 5 (ϵ-regular prior). *For a given query f and a privacy parameter $\epsilon > 0$, a prior π is called ϵ-regular iff there exists a row vector $\mathbf{y} \geq 0$ such that $\pi = \mathbf{y}\, \Phi$.*

---

[1] Note that there may exist many optimal mechanism for a given prior.

In the following we describe the common properties of these priors and also give a geometric characterisation for their region comparing it to the whole prior space. As the first observation, note that, as privacy is excluded ($\epsilon \to \infty$), this region converges to the entire prior space. This is because Φ approaches the identity matrix where the vector y exists for each prior.

An important property of any ϵ-regular prior is that the ratio between any two of its entries π_i, π_j is always bound as follows, depending on ϵ and the distance $d(i, j)$. Because of this property, such a prior is called ϵ-regular.

Proposition 2. *Consider a query f and $\epsilon > 0$. Then for any ϵ-regular prior π, it holds for all $i, j \in \mathcal{R}_f$: $\pi_i/\pi_j \leq e^{\epsilon d(i,j)}$.*

While the above property restricts the ratio between probabilities of adjacent query results, this restriction, in practice, holds for a large class of users who have no sharp information suggesting discrimination between adjacent results. This class is exemplified in the introduction. Note that the above property is not equivalent to Definition 5. Namely, it is not true that all priors having such a property are ϵ-regular.

A consequence of the above proposition is that for any ϵ-regular prior π, the probability π_i associated with any query result i is restricted by upper and lower bounds as follows.

Proposition 3. *Consider a query f and $\epsilon > 0$. Then for any ϵ-regular prior π, it holds for all $i \in \mathcal{R}_f$ that*

$$1 \Big/ \sum_{j \in \mathcal{R}_f} e^{\epsilon d(i,j)} \leq \pi_i \leq 1 \Big/ \sum_{j \in \mathcal{R}_f} e^{-\epsilon d(i,j)}.$$

One implication is that any ϵ-regular prior must have full support, that is $\pi_i > 0$ for all $i \in \mathcal{R}_f$.

In the following we go further and describe the region of ϵ-regular priors as a region of points in the prior space, where each point represents a member in this region. For doing so, we identify by the following definition a set of priors which describe the 'corner points' or vertices of the region.

Definition 6 (corner priors). *Given a query f and a privacy parameter $\epsilon > 0$, then for each query result $i \in \mathcal{R}_f$, a corresponding corner prior, denoted by c^i, is defined as*

$$c^i_j = \frac{\phi_{ij}}{\sum_{k \in \mathcal{R}_f} \phi_{ik}} \qquad \forall j \in \mathcal{R}_f.$$

Note that the above definition is sound, i.e. c^i is a probability distribution. By the above definition, for a given query with the domain $\mathcal{R}_f$ of results, the region of ϵ-regular priors has $|\mathcal{R}_f|$ corner priors. Each one corresponds to a query result $i \in \mathcal{R}_f$. Note that each corner prior c^i is maximally biased (relative to the region) to the query result i; that is the entry c^i_i meets its maximum value given in Proposition 3. It can be seen that each corner prior is ϵ-regular. Namely for any corner c^i, define the vector y as $y_i = 1/\sum_{k \in \mathcal{R}_f} \phi_{ik}$ and $y_j = 0$ for all $j \neq i$; thus it holds that $c^i = y \Phi$.

The region of the ϵ-regular priors can be characterised in terms of the corner priors. More precisely, this region consists of all priors that can be composed as a convex combination of the corner priors.

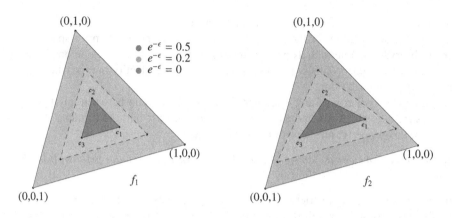

Fig. 2. Regions of ϵ-regular priors for queries described in Example 1

Proposition 4 (convexity). *For a given a query f and privacy parameter $\epsilon > 0$, a prior π is ϵ-regular iff there exist real numbers $\gamma_i \geq 0$, $i \in \mathcal{R}_f$ such that*

$$\pi = \textstyle\sum_{i \in \mathcal{R}_f} \gamma_i \, c^i.$$

It is easy to see that it must hold that $\sum_{i \in \mathcal{R}_f} \gamma_i = 1$ for any ϵ-regular prior. This is obtained by summing the components of the π as follows.

$$\textstyle\sum_{j \in \mathcal{R}_f} \pi_j = \sum_i \gamma_i \sum_j c^i_j \quad \text{and} \quad \sum_j \pi_j = 1, \forall \pi.$$

From Proposition 4 and the above observation, the region of ϵ-regular priors is a convex set, where each point (prior) in this region is a convex combination of the corner priors. This region is therefore geometrically regarded as a convex polytope in the prior space. Since the corner points always exists, this region is never empty.

For a prior π in this region, the coefficients γ_i model the 'proximity' of π to each corner prior c^i. Observe that $0 \leq \gamma_i \leq 1$, and $\gamma_i = 1$ iff $\pi = c^i$. We demonstrate this geometric interpretation using the following examples.

Example 1. Priors having 3 entries can be represented as points in the 3-dimensional euclidean space. These priors correspond to queries whose graph structures contain 3 nodes. These nodes can be arranged in either a sequence or a cycle, corresponding to queries f_1 and f_2 respectively shown in Figure 1, with $n = 2$ in both cases. Figure 2 shows - for each of these queries - the region of ϵ-regular priors. The corner priors of each region are represented by points c^1, c^2, c^3. For each query in Fig. 2, we depict the regions for $e^{-\epsilon} = 0.5$ and $e^{-\epsilon} = 0.2$. Note that the level of privacy set by ϵ imposes a restriction on the region of ϵ-regular priors. With $e^{-\epsilon} = 0.2$ (less privacy), this region is larger than the one with $e^{-\epsilon} = 0.5$. In fact, as $e^{-\epsilon} \to 0$ (i.e. no privacy), the region of ϵ-regular priors converges to the entire region of priors defined by the corner points $\{(0, 0, 1), (0, 1, 0), (0, 0, 1)\}$.

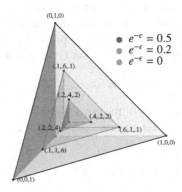

Fig. 3. Regions of ϵ-regular priors for the query described in Example 2

Example 2. Let v be database containing at most one record. Consider a bundle of two counting queries $f_3 = (count(v, p_1), count(v, p_2))$ which counts the records satisfying properties p_1 and p_2 respectively in the database v. The graph structure of this query is depicted in Figure 1 (with $n = 1$). Note that in this case the adjacency graph (and also the set $\mathcal{R}_f$ of query results) consists of 4 nodes: $\{(0, 0), (1, 0), (0, 1), (1, 1)\}$. Any prior π corresponds therefore to a point in a 4-dimensional space. However, since the 4th component of the prior is redundant ($\sum_i \pi_i = 1$), each prior is defined by its 'projection' onto the 3- dimensional subspace. Given this observation, Figure 3 shows the projection of the ϵ-regular prior region for different values of $e^{-\epsilon}$. It is again seen that the region is getting larger as the level of privacy $e^{-\epsilon}$ decreases, and coincides with the full space of priors when $e^{-\epsilon} \to 0$ (i.e. when no privacy is provided).

4 Upper Bounds for Utility and Min-mutual Information

In this section, we further describe the ϵ-regular priors in terms of the utility that can be achieved for these priors by ϵ-differentially private mechanisms. We also describe the amount of information that can be conveyed by these mechanisms to users with such priors. More precisely, we identify for any ϵ-regular prior π upper bounds for the utility and min-mutual information, considering all ϵ-differentially private mechanisms and all possible remaps. These bounds are indeed induced by the privacy constraints parameterised by ϵ and the query f as stated by Proposition 1. They also depend on the given prior π.

4.1 Utility

Given a query f and a privacy parameter $\epsilon > 0$, let π be a prior on the set R_f of the query results. For any noise matrix X satisfying ϵ-differential privacy (as in Proposition 1), and a remap R, we derive in the following a linear algebraic expression for $\mathcal{U}(X, \pi, R)$, the utility of X for π using the remap R. Such an expression will play the main role in the subsequent results. We start by observing that the matrix product of the noise matrix X and the remap R describes an ϵ-differentially private noise matrix $XR : \mathcal{R}_f \to \mathcal{R}_f$. Hence the entries of XR satisfy (by Proposition 1) the following subset of constraints.

$$e^{-\epsilon d(i,k)} (XR)_{kk} \leq (XR)_{ik}$$

for all $i, k \in \mathcal{R}_f$. Using Definition 4 of the privacy-constraints matrix Φ, and taking into account that $\sum_{k \in \mathcal{R}_f} (XR)_{ik} = 1$ for all i (as both X and R are stochastic), we imply the following inequalities.

$$\sum_{k \in \mathcal{R}_f} \phi_{ik} (XR)_{kk} \leq 1, \quad \forall i \in \mathcal{R}_f.$$

The inequality operators can be replaced by equalities while introducing *slack* variables $0 \leq s_i \leq 1$ for all $i \in \mathcal{R}_f$. The above inequalities can therefore be written as follows.

$$\sum_{k \in \mathcal{R}_f} \phi_{ik} (XR)_{kk} + s_i = 1, \quad \forall i \in \mathcal{R}_f.$$

Let the slack variables s_i form a column vector $\mathbf{s}$ indexed by $\mathcal{R}_f$. Let also $\mathbf{1}$ denote another column vector of the same size having all entries equal to 1. Using these vectors and the privacy-constraints matrix Φ (for the given query and ϵ), the above equations can be rewritten in the following matrix form.

$$\Phi \text{ diag}(XR) + \mathbf{s} = \mathbf{1}, \tag{3}$$

where $\text{diag}(XR)$ is the column vector consisting of the diagonal entries of XR. Now, for any noise matrix $X : \mathcal{R}_f \to O$ and a remap $R : O \to \mathcal{R}_f$ satisfying Eq. (3), and for a prior π, we want to refine the generic expression (2) of the utility by taking Eq. (3) into account. We start by rewriting Eq. (2) in the following matrix form.

$$\mathcal{U}(X, \pi, R) = \pi \text{ diag}(XR). \tag{4}$$

Now, let $\mathbf{y}$ be a row vector such that

$$\pi = \mathbf{y} \Phi. \tag{5}$$

Note that, the above matrix equation is in fact a system of $|\mathcal{R}_f|$ linear equations. The kth equation in this system is formed by the kth column of Φ, and the kth entry of π as follows.

$$\mathbf{y} \Phi_k = \pi_k \quad \forall k \in \mathcal{R}_f.$$

Solving this system of equations for the row vector $\mathbf{y}$ has the following possible outcomes: If the matrix Φ is invertible, then, for any prior π, Eq. (5) has exactly one solution. If Φ is not invertible (i.e. it contains linearly dependent columns), then there are either 0 or an infinite number of solutions, depending on the prior π: If the entries of π respect the linear dependence relation then are infinitely many solutions. Otherwise, the equations are '*inconsistent*', in which case there are no solutions.

Since the matrices Φ have a precise format, one may wonder whether it could be that they are all invertible or all non invertible. In fact, this is not the case: In the report version of this paper [21] we show an example of a matrix Φ that, for certain values of ϵ is invertible, while for others is non invertible.

Whether Φ is invertible or not, we consider here only the priors where the matrix equation (5) has at least one solution y. Note that, by definition, all the ϵ-regular priors have this property, but there can be others for which the solution y has some negative components. In some of the results below (in particular in Lemma 2) we consider this larger class of priors, for the sake of generality.

Multiplying Equation (3) by y yields

$$y \, \Phi \, \mathrm{diag}(X R) + y \, s = y \, \mathbf{1}. \tag{6}$$

Substituting Equations (5) and (4) in the above equation consecutively provides the required expression for the utility and therefore proves the following lemma.

Lemma 2. *For a given query f and a privacy parameter $\epsilon > 0$, let π be any prior. Then for every row vector y satisfying $\pi = y \, \Phi$, the utility of any ϵ-differentially private mechanism with a noise matrix X for the prior π using a remap R is given by*

$$\mathcal{U}(X, \pi, R) = y \, \mathbf{1} - y \, s, \tag{7}$$

for a vector s satisfying $0 \leq s_i \leq 1$ for all $i \in \mathcal{R}_f$.

Lemma 2 expresses the utility function for any ϵ-private noise matrix X for a prior π with a remap R as a function of the vector y and the slack vector s. Although the matrix X and the remap R do not explicitly appear on the right hand side of Equation (7), the utility still depends on them indirectly through the vector s. Namely, according to Equation (3), the choice of X and R determines the slack vector s. The utility function depends also on the prior π, because the choice of π determines the set of vectors satisfying Eq. (5). Substituting any of these vectors y in Eq. (7) yields the same value for $\mathcal{U}(X, \pi, R)$.

By Definition 5, of ϵ-regular priors, the above lemma specifies the utility for any of them. Therefore, we use Lemma 2, and obtain an upper bound for the utility of ϵ-differentially private mechanisms for ϵ-regular priors.

Theorem 1 (utility upper bound). *For a given query f and a privacy parameter $\epsilon > 0$, let π be an ϵ-regular prior and X be an ϵ-differentially private noise matrix. Then for all row vectors $y \geq 0$ satisfying $y \, \Phi = \pi$, it holds for any remap R that*

$$\mathcal{U}(X, \pi, R) \leq \sum_{i \in \mathcal{R}_f} y_i, \tag{8}$$

where the equality holds iff $\Phi \, \mathrm{diag}(X R) = \mathbf{1}$.

The above result can be also seen from the geometric perspective. As shown by Proposition 4, each member in the region of ϵ-regular priors is described as a convex combination of the corner priors. That is there are coefficients $\gamma_i \geq 0$ for $i \in \mathcal{R}$ which form this combination. It can be shown (as in the proof of Proposition 4) that $\gamma_i = y_i \left(\sum_{k \in \mathcal{R}_f} \phi_{ik} \right)$. Hence, the upper bound given by Theorem 1 can be written as follows using the coefficients γ_i.

$$\mathcal{U}(X, \pi, R) \leq \sum_{i \in \mathcal{R}_f} \frac{\gamma_i}{\sum_{k \in \mathcal{R}_f} \phi_{ik}}.$$

Inspecting the above result for corner priors, recall that for a corner c^i, γ_j is 1 for $j = i$ and is 0 otherwise; thus, the utility upper bound for c^i is therefore $1/\sum_k \phi_{ik}$. Moreover, the upper bound for each ϵ-regular prior π can be regarded (according to the above equation) as a convex combination of the upper bounds for the corner priors. That is, from the geometric perspective, the utility upper bound for π linearly depends on its proximity to the corner priors.

4.2 Min-mutual Information

In this section, we employ an information-theoretic notion, namely mutual information, to quantify the amount of information conveyed by a noise matrix X as an information theoretic channel. We use this notion in two distinct ways: first, mutual information is used to measure the information conveyed about the result of a specific query, similarly to the use of "utility" in the previous section. Mutual information and utility (under the binary gain function) are closely related, which allows us to transfer the bound obtained in the previous section to the information-theoretic setting.

Second, we use mutual information to quantify the information *about the database* that is revealed by a mechanism, a concept known in the area of quantitative information flow as "information leakage". This allows us to obtain bounds on the information leaked by any mechanism, even non-oblivious ones, independently from the actual query. For arbitrary priors, we obtain in a more natural way the bound conjectured in [18] and proven in [8]. Moreover, if we restrict to specific (ϵ-regular) priors, then we are able to provide more accurate bounds.

Following recent works in the are of quantitative information flow ([14–17, 8, 18]), we adopt *Rényi's min-entropy* ([22]) as our measure of uncertainly. The min-entropy $\mathcal{H}_\infty(\pi)$ of a prior π, defined as $\mathcal{H}_\infty(\pi) = -\log_2 \max_i \pi_i$, measures the user's uncertainty about the query result. Then, the corresponding notion of *conditional* min-entropy, defined as $\mathcal{H}_\infty(X, \pi) = -\log_2 \sum_o \max_i \pi_i x_{io}$, measures the uncertainty about the query result after observing the output of the noise matrix X. Finally, subtracting the latter from the former brings us to the notion of min-mutual information:

$$\mathcal{L}(X, \pi) = \mathcal{H}_\infty(\pi) - \mathcal{H}_\infty(X, \pi)$$

which measures the amount of information about the query result conveyed by the noise matrix. In the area of quantitative information flow this quantity is known as *min-entropy leakage*; the reader is referred to [14] for more details about this notion.

Min-mutual information is closely related to the notion of utility under the binary gain function and using an *optimal* remap. A remap $\hat{R}$ is optimal for X, π if it gives the best utility among all possible remaps for this noise matrix and prior. The following result from [8] connects min-mutual information and utility:

Proposition 5. *Given a noise matrix X and a prior π, let $\hat{R}$ be an optimal remap for π, X. Then, it holds*

$$\mathcal{L}(X, \pi) = \log_2 \frac{\mathcal{U}(X, \pi, \hat{R})}{\max_i \pi_i}$$

This connection allows us to transfer the upper-bound given by Theorem 1 to min-mutual information.

Proposition 6 (min-mutual information upper bound). *Let f be a query, let $\epsilon > 0$, let π be an ϵ-regular prior and let X be the noise matrix of any ϵ-differentially private mechanism. Then for all row vectors $y \geq 0$ satisfying $y\,\Phi = \pi$, it holds that:*

$$\mathcal{L}(X, \pi) \leq \log_2 \frac{\sum_{i \in \mathcal{R}_f} y_i}{\max_i \pi_i} \tag{9}$$

The above bound holds only for ϵ-regular priors. However, it is well-known ([15]) that min-mutual information is maximised by the uniform prior u, i.e. $\mathcal{L}(X, \pi) \leq \mathcal{L}(X, u)$ for all X, π. Thus, in cases when u is ϵ-regular, we can extend the above bound to *any* prior.

Corollary 1. *Let f be a query, let $\epsilon > 0$ such that the uniform prior u is ϵ-regular, and let X be the noise matrix of any ϵ-differentially private mechanism. Then for all row vectors $y \geq 0$ satisfying $y\,\Phi = u$, and for all priors π, it holds that:*

$$\mathcal{L}(X, \pi) \leq \log_2(|\mathcal{R}_f| \sum_{i \in \mathcal{R}_f} y_i)$$

4.3   Quantifying the Leakage about the Database

In the previous section we considered the information about the query result conveyed by an oblivious mechanism. This information was measured by the min-mutual information $\mathcal{L}(X, \pi)$, where X is noise matrix, mapping query results $\mathcal{R}_f$ to outputs.

We now turn our attention to quantifying the information about the *database* that is conveyed by the complete mechanism $\mathcal{K}$ (even in the case of non-oblivious mechanisms). Intuitively, we wish to minimise this information to protect the privacy of the users, contrary to the utility which we aim at maximising. Quantifying this information can be done in a way very similar to the previous section. The only difference is that we use a stochastic matrix Y that models the mechanism $\mathcal{K}$, mapping databases $\mathcal{V} = V^u$ to outputs (recall that u is the number of individuals in the database and V the set of possible values for each individual). Moreover, the underlying graph $\sim$ is the *Hamming graph*, induced by the adjacency relation on databases, and ϵ-regularity concerns priors π on databases.

In this case, $\mathcal{L}(Y, \pi)$ measures the information about the database conveyed by the mechanism, which we refer to as "min-entropy leakage", and the bounds from the previous section can be directly applied. However, since we now work on a specific graph $(\mathcal{V}, \sim)$, we can obtain a closed expression for the bound of Corollary 1. We start by observing that due to the symmetry of the graph, the uniform prior u is ϵ-regular for all $\epsilon > 0$. More precisely, we can show that the vector y, defined as

$$y_i = \left(\frac{e^\epsilon}{|V|(|V| - 1 + e^\epsilon)} \right)^u \qquad i \in \mathcal{V}$$

satisfies $y\,\Phi = u$ and $y \geq 0$. Thus, applying Corollary 1 we get the following result.

Theorem 2 (min-entropy leakage upper bound). *Let $\mathcal{V} = V^u$ be a set of databases, let $\epsilon > 0$, and let Y be an ϵ-differentially private mechanism. Then for all priors π, it holds that:*

$$\mathcal{L}(Y, \pi) \leq u \log_2 \frac{|V| e^\epsilon}{|V| - 1 + e^\epsilon}$$

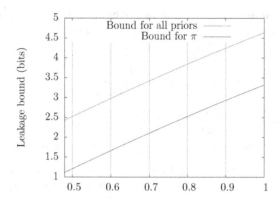

Fig. 4. Leakage bounds for various values of ϵ

This bound determines the maximum amount of information that *any* differentially privacy mechanism can leak about the database (independently from the underlying query). The bound was first conjectured in [18] and independently proven in [8]; our technique gives an alternative an arguably more intuitive proof of this result.

Note that the above bound holds for *all priors*. If we restrict to a *specific ϵ-regular prior* π, then we can get better results by using the bound of Proposition 6 which depends on the actual prior. This is demonstrated in the following example.

Example 3. Consider a database of 5 individuals, each having one of 4 possible values, i.e. $\mathcal{V} = V^u$ with $V = \{1, 2, 3, 4\}$ and $u = 5$. Assume that each individual selects a value independently from the others, but not all values are equally probable; in particular the probabilities of values $1, 2, 3, 4$ are $0.3, 0.27, 0.23, 0.2$ respectively. Let π be the corresponding prior on $\mathcal{V}$ that models this information. We have numerically verified that for all $0.48 \le \epsilon \le 1$ (with step 0.01) π is ϵ-regular. Thus we can apply Proposition 6 to get an upper bound of $\mathcal{L}(Y, \pi)$ for this prior.

The resulting bound, together with the general bound for all priors from Theorem 2, are shown in Figure 4. We see that restricting to a specific prior provides a significantly better bound for all values of ϵ. For instance, for $\epsilon = 0.5$ we get that $\mathcal{L}(Y, \pi) \le 1.2$ for this π, while $\mathcal{L}(Y, \pi) \le 2.5$ for all priors π.

Note that, in general, the above bounds for the utility and the min-mutual information are not tight. For a given query and a privacy parameter ϵ, there may be no noise matrix X that meets these bounds. Nevertheless, they provide ultimate limits, induced by the privacy constraints, for all ϵ-differential private mechanisms and ϵ-regular priors. Note also that these bounds are simultaneously tight if the *common* condition $\Phi \, \text{diag}(X R) = \mathbf{1}$ is satisfied (note that this condition is independent of the underlying prior). From this point we investigate the mechanisms that, whenever exist, they satisfy such a condition and are therefore optimal for the entire class of ϵ-regular priors.

5   Tight-Constraints Mechanisms

In this section we introduce the notion of *tight-constraints* mechanism and we investigate their properties in terms of privacy guarantees and optimality for ϵ-regular priors.

Definition 7 (A tight-constraints mechanism). *For a given query f with range $\mathcal{R}_f$, and a given privacy parameter $\epsilon > 0$, an oblivious mechanism with a noise matrix $X :$ $\mathcal{R}_f \to \mathcal{R}_f$ is called a* tight-constraints *mechanism iff it satisfies the following conditions for all $i, k \in \mathcal{R}_f$.*

$$e^{-\epsilon\, d(i,k)}\, x_{kk} = x_{ik}. \tag{10}$$

It is important to note that, in general, there may exist zero, one or more tight-constraints mechanisms for a given query f and a privacy parameter $\epsilon > 0$. The above definition enforces $|\mathcal{R}_f|(|\mathcal{R}_f| - 1)$ linearly independent equations, referred to as the '*tight constraints*'. Additionally it must also hold that $\sum_{k \in \mathcal{R}_f} x_{ik} = 1$ for all $i \in \mathcal{R}_f$. Thus we have, in total, $|\mathcal{R}_f| |\mathcal{R}_f|$ equations. If these equations are linearly independent, then they solve to unique values. If these values are non-negative, then they determine a *unique* tight-constraints mechanism. On the other hand, if these equations are not linearly independent, then there may be multiple solutions with non-negative entries, in which case we have multiple tight-constraints mechanisms for the given query and privacy parameter ϵ.

5.1   Properties

It has been seen from Definition 7, that the choice of a query f and a value $\epsilon > 0$ correspond to a set of tight-constraints mechanisms. The first important feature of these mechanisms is that they satisfy ϵ-differential privacy as confirmed by the following proposition.

Proposition 7 (differential privacy). *For a given query f and a privacy parameter $\epsilon > 0$, every tight-constraints mechanism is ϵ-differentially private.*

Thanks to the above fact, we can give a further useful characterisation of the tight-constraints mechanisms in comparison to other ϵ-differentially private mechanisms. More precisely, the following proposition identifies a linear algebraic condition that is satisfied *only by* the tight-constraints mechanisms for given f, ϵ:

Lemma 3 (diagonal characterisation). *Let f be a query and let $\epsilon > 0$. Then for any oblivious ϵ-differentially private mechanism $\mathcal{K}$ with a noise matrix $X : \mathcal{R}_f \to \mathcal{R}_f$, the following equation holds iff $\mathcal{K}$ is a tight-constraints mechanism.*

$$\Phi \operatorname{diag}(X) = \mathbf{1}. \tag{11}$$

The above proposition provides a way to check the existence of, and also compute, the tight-constraints mechanisms for given f, ϵ. Since Condition (11) is satisfied only by these mechanisms, then there is at least one tight-constraints mechanism if there is a vector z, with non-negative entries, that satisfies the equation $\Phi\ z = \mathbf{1}$. In this case the noise matrix $\hat{X}$ of a tight-constraints mechanism is obtained by setting its diagonal to z, and evaluating the non-diagonal entries from the diagonal using Eqs. (10).

Now we turn our attention to the region of ϵ-regular priors and we identify the oblivious mechanisms which are optimal wrt both utility and min-mutual information in this region. It turns out that the set of these optimal mechanisms consists exactly of all the mechanisms that can be *mapped to* a tight-constraints one using a remap R.

Theorem 3 (Optimality). *Let f be a query and let $\epsilon > 0$ such that at least one tight-constraints mechanism exists. Then any oblivious mechanism $\mathcal{K} : \mathcal{V} \to O$ is optimal (wrt both utility and min-mutual information) for every ϵ-regular prior π iff there is a remap $R : O \to \mathcal{R}_f$ such that $\mathcal{K} R$ is a tight-constraints mechanism for f, ϵ.*

Proof. If there exists a tight-constraints mechanism for given f, ϵ, then its noise matrix $\hat{X}$ must satisfy Eq (11). This implies that the upper-bound in Theorem 1 is reachable by $\hat{X}$ and the identity remap. Thus that upper-bound, in this case, is tight. By Theorem 1, a mechanism $\mathcal{K}$ with a noise matrix X meets such an upper bound for the utility (and therefore is optimal) iff it satisfies the condition $\Phi \operatorname{diag}(X R) = \mathbf{1}$, with some remap R. Since any mechanism with noise matrix $X R$ is ϵ-differentially private, then by Lemma 3, this condition is satisfied iff $X R$ is the noise matrix of a tight-constraints mechanism (for f, ϵ). That is iff $f X R = \mathcal{K} R$ is a tight-constraints mechanism. Using the relation, given by Proposition 5, between utility and min-mutual information, the same argument holds for the latter.   □

Note that tight-constrains mechanisms are themselves optimal as they are mapped to themselves by the identity remap.

As a consequence of the above general result, we consider the special case of the uniform prior, denoted by u, where all exact query results in $\mathcal{R}_f$ are equally likely. Note that this prior corresponds to users having unbiased knowledge about the query results, i.e. they assume that all the exact results $\mathcal{R}_f$ are yielded, by executing the query, with the same probability. Firstly, the following lemma proves an equivalence between the existence of at least one tight-constraints mechanism on one hand and the uniform prior u being ϵ-regular on the other hand.

Lemma 4. *For a given query f and privacy parameter $\epsilon > 0$, there exists at least one tight-constraints mechanism iff the uniform prior u is ϵ-regular.*

It is worth noticing that in general the region of ϵ-regular priors may or may not include the uniform prior. However, as shown earlier in Section 3, this region is enlarged and converges to the entire prior space as less privacy is imposed (that is as ϵ increases). This means that for the values of ϵ above certain threshold ϵ^*, depending on the query, the region of ϵ-regular priors accommodates the uniform prior u, and therefore (by Lemma 4), there is at least one tight-constraints mechanism. This provides a design criteria to *select* a setting for ϵ such that we have an optimal mechanism for the whole region.

Using Lemma 4, we can describe the optimal mechanisms for the uniform prior as a corollary of Theorem 3.

Corollary 2. *Let f be a query and let $\epsilon > 0$ such that there exists at least one tight-constrains mechanism. Then a mechanism $\mathcal{K} : \mathcal{V} \to O$ is optimal for the uniform prior iff $\mathcal{K} R$ is a tight-constraints mechanism for some remap $R : O \to \mathcal{R}_f$.*

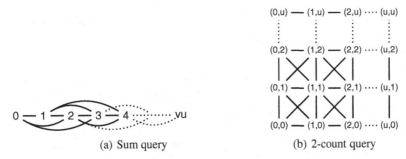

(a) Sum query   (b) 2-count query

Fig. 5. Adjacency graphs

In fact when we consider arbitrary queries, we find that our specification for the tight-constraints mechanisms covers other well known differentially-private mechanisms. In particular, when we consider a counting query, we find that a tight-constraints mechanism for this query is exactly the *truncated-geometric mechanism*, which is shown by [6] to be optimal for every prior. Furthermore, we are able to show that this mechanism, as a tight-constraints one, exists for the selected query with any $\epsilon > 0$.

Another class of queries, studied in [8] are the ones whose graph structures are either *vertex-transitive* or *distance-regular*. The authors in [8] were able to construct a mechanism which is optimal for the uniform prior for any $\epsilon > 0$. In the context of our results, when we consider a query f in this class, it is easy to show that such an optimal mechanism is in fact a tight-constraints mechanism for f. We can also show that this tight-constraints mechanism exists for all $\epsilon > 0$.

6   Case-Study: Sum and 2-Count Queries

In this section we show the usefulness of the tight-constraints mechanism by applying it to two particular families of queries, namely sum and 2-count queries. For each family, we evaluate the tight-constraint mechanism on databases consisting of u individuals each having an integer value between 0 and v, and we compare its utility to the geometric mechanism.

It is well-known that no universally optimal mechanism exists for these families; in particular, the geometric mechanism, known to be optimal for a single counting query, is not guaranteed to be optimal for sum queries or multiple counting queries. On the other hand, as discussed in the previous section, tight-constraints mechanisms, whenever they exist, are guaranteed to be optimal within the region of ϵ-regular priors.

The comparison is made as follows: for each query, we numerically compute the smallest ϵ (using a step of 0.01) for which a tight-constraints mechanism exists (i.e. for which the uniform prior u is ϵ-regular, see Lemma 4). Then we compute the utility (using an optimal remap) of both the tight constraints and the geometric mechanisms, for a range of ϵ starting from the minimum one. Note that the tight constraint mechanism exists for any ϵ greater than the minumum one.

Sum query. Let f be the query returning the sum of the value for all individuals, thus it has range $\mathcal{R}_f = \{0, \ldots, vu\}$. By modifying the value of a single individual, the outcome

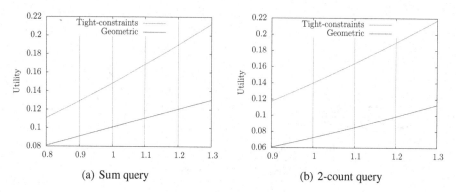

Fig. 6. Utility for various values of ϵ

of the query can be altered by at most v (when changing the value from 0 to v), thus two elements $i, j \in \mathcal{R}_f$ are adjacent iff $|i - j| \leq v$. The induced graph structure on $\mathcal{R}_f$ is shown in Figure 5(a) (for the case $v = 3$).

For our case-study we numerically evaluate this query for $u = 150, v = 5$ and for the uniform prior. We found that the minumum ϵ for which a tight-constraints mechanism exists (and is in fact unique since Φ is invertible) is 0.8. Figure 6(a) shows the utility of the tight-constraint mechanism, as well as that of the geometric mechanism, for values of ϵ between 0.8 and 1.3, the uniform prior and using and optimal remap. We see that the tight-constraint mechanism provides significantly higher utility than the geometric mechanism in this case.

2-count query. Consider now the query f consisting of 2 counting queries (i.e. reporting the number of users satisfying properties p_1 and p_2), thus it has range $\mathcal{R}_f = \{0, \ldots, u\} \times \{0, \ldots, u\}$. By modifying the value of a single individual, the outcome of each counting query can be altered by at most 1, thus two anwers $(i_1, i_2), (j_1, j_2) \in \mathcal{R}_f$ are adjacent iff $|i_1 - j_1| \leq 1$ and $|i_2 - j_2| \leq 1$. The induced graph structure on $\mathcal{R}_f$ is shown in Figure 5(b).

We evaluate this query for $u = 30$ and for the uniform prior. We found that the minumum ϵ for which a tight-constraints mechanism exists is 0.9. Figure 6(b) shows the utility of the tight-constraint mechanism, as well as that of the geometric mechanism (applied independently to each counting query), for values of ϵ between 0.9 and 1.3 and the uniform prior. Similarly to the sum query, we see that the tight-constraint mechanism provides significantly higher utility than the geometric mechanism in this case.

7   Conclusion and Future Work

In this paper we have continued the line of research initiated by [6, 1] about the existence of universally-optimal differentially-private mechanisms. While the positive result of [6] (for counting queries) and the negative one of [1] (for essentially all other queries) answer the question completely, the latter sets a rather dissatisfactory scenario for differential privacy and the typical mechanisms used in the community, since counting queries are just one of the (infinitely many) kinds of queries one can be interested in. In practice the result of [1] says that for essentially any query other than counting queries one cannot devise a mechanism that gives the best trade-off between privacy and utility for all users. Hence one has to choose: either design a different mechanism for every user, or be content with a mechanism that, depending on the user, can be far from providing the best utility. We have then considered the question whether, for a generic query, the optimality is punctual or can actually be achieved with the same mechanism for a class of users. Fortunately the answer is positive: we have identified a class of priors, called ϵ-regular, and a mechanism which is optimal for all the priors in this class. We have also provided a complete and effectively checkable characterisation of the conditions under which such mechanism exists, and an effective method to construct it. As a side result, we have improved on the existing bounds for the min-entropy leakage induced by differential privacy. More precisely, we have been able to give specific and tight bounds for each ϵ-regular prior, in general smaller than the bound existing in literature for the worst-case leakage (achieved by the uniform prior [20]).

So far we have been studying only the case of utility for binary gain functions. In the future we aim at lifting this limitation, i.e. we would like to consider also other kinds of gain. Furthermore, we intend to study how the utility decreases when we use a tight-constraints mechanism outside the class of ϵ-regular priors. In particular, we aim at identifying a class of priors, larger than the ϵ-regular ones, for which the tight-constraints mechanism is close to be optimal.

The definition of tight-constrains mechanism is related to the connectivity condition of the column graphs introduced by Kifer and Lin [23, 24]. They show that this property implies maximality w.r.t. the postprocessing preorder. Following the suggestion of an anonymous reviewer, we will try to exploit the above result to strengthen our results in Section 5, in particular Theorem 3.

The negative result of [1] is stated in terms of the graph induced by $\sim_f$: a universally optimal mechanism can exist only if such graph is a line. This is the case of counting queries, but not only: any composition of a counting query with a function that preserves the graph structure would induce the same kind of graph, and it is for this reason that the authors of [1] write "*essentially* counting queries". As pointed out by an anonymous reviewer, we can use the techniques of our paper to prove that a universally optimal mechanism exists if and only if the query is derivable from a counting query by a bijection, thus making the result of [1] more precise, and extending the result of [6].

Acknowledgement. We would like to thank the anonymous reviewers for their valuable recommendations for improving the paper, and their suggestion for future work.

References

1. Brenner, H., Nissim, K.: Impossibility of differentially private universally optimal mechanisms. In: Proc. of FOCS, pp. 71–80. IEEE (2010)
2. Dwork, C.: Differential Privacy. In: Bugliesi, M., Preneel, B., Sassone, V., Wegener, I. (eds.) ICALP 2006, Part II. LNCS, vol. 4052, pp. 1–12. Springer, Heidelberg (2006)
3. Dwork, C., Lei, J.: Differential privacy and robust statistics. In: Proc. of STOC, pp. 371–380. ACM (2009)
4. Dwork, C.: Differential privacy in new settings. In: Proc. of SODA, pp. 174–183. SIAM (2010)

5. Dwork, C.: A firm foundation for private data analysis. Communications of the ACM 54(1), 86–96 (2011)
6. Ghosh, A., Roughgarden, T., Sundararajan, M.: Universally utility-maximizing privacy mechanisms. In: Proc. of STOC, pp. 351–360. ACM (2009)
7. Gupte, M., Sundararajan, M.: Universally optimal privacy mechanisms for minimax agents. In: Proc. of PODS, pp. 135–146. ACM (2010)
8. Alvim, M.S., Andrés, M.E., Chatzikokolakis, K., Palamidessi, C.: On the Relation between Differential Privacy and Quantitative Information Flow. In: Aceto, L., Henzinger, M., Sgall, J. (eds.) ICALP 2011, Part II. LNCS, vol. 6756, pp. 60–76. Springer, Heidelberg (2011)
9. Köpf, B., Basin, D.A.: An information-theoretic model for adaptive side-channel attacks. In: Proc. of CCS, pp. 286–296. ACM (2007)
10. Clark, D., Hunt, S., Malacaria, P.: Quantitative information flow, relations and polymorphic types. J. of Logic and Computation 18(2), 181–199 (2005)
11. Boreale, M.: Quantifying Information Leakage in Process Calculi. In: Bugliesi, M., Preneel, B., Sassone, V., Wegener, I. (eds.) ICALP 2006, Part II. LNCS, vol. 4052, pp. 119–131. Springer, Heidelberg (2006)
12. Malacaria, P.: Assessing security threats of looping constructs. In: Proc. of POPL, pp. 225–235. ACM (2007)
13. Chatzikokolakis, K., Palamidessi, C., Panangaden, P.: Anonymity protocols as noisy channels. Inf. and Comp. 206(2-4), 378–401 (2008)
14. Smith, G.: On the Foundations of Quantitative Information Flow. In: de Alfaro, L. (ed.) FOSSACS 2009. LNCS, vol. 5504, pp. 288–302. Springer, Heidelberg (2009)
15. Braun, C., Chatzikokolakis, K., Palamidessi, C.: Quantitative notions of leakage for one-try attacks. In: Proc. of MFPS. ENTCS, vol. 249, pp. 75–91. Elsevier (2009)
16. Köpf, B., Smith, G.: Vulnerability bounds and leakage resilience of blinded cryptography under timing attacks. In: Proc. of CSF, pp. 44–56. IEEE (2010)
17. Andrés, M.E., Palamidessi, C., van Rossum, P., Smith, G.: Computing the Leakage of Information-Hiding Systems. In: Esparza, J., Majumdar, R. (eds.) TACAS 2010. LNCS, vol. 6015, pp. 373–389. Springer, Heidelberg (2010)
18. Barthe, G., Köpf, B.: Information-theoretic bounds for differentially private mechanisms. In: Proc. of CSF, pp. 191–204. IEEE (2011)
19. Clarkson, M.R., Schneider, F.B.: Quantification of integrity. Tech. Rep. (2011), http://hdl.handle.net/1813/22012
20. Alvim, M.S., Andrés, M.E., Chatzikokolakis, K., Degano, P., Palamidessi, C.: Differential Privacy: On the Trade-Off between Utility and Information Leakage. In: Barthe, G., Datta, A., Etalle, S. (eds.) FAST 2011. LNCS, vol. 7140, pp. 39–54. Springer, Heidelberg (2012)
21. ElSalamouny, E., Chatzikokolakis, K., Palamidessi, C.: A differentially private mechanism of optimal utility for a region of priors. Technical report, INRIA (2013), http://hal.inria.fr/hal-00760735/
22. Rényi, A.: On Measures of Entropy and Information. In: Proc. of the 4th Berkeley Symposium on Mathematics, Statistics, and Probability, pp. 547–561 (1961)
23. Kifer, D., Lin, B.R.: Towards an axiomatization of statistical privacy and utility. In: Proc. of PODS, pp. 147–158. ACM (2010)
24. Kifer, D., Lin, B.R.: An axiomatic view of statistical privacy and utility. Journal of Privacy and Confidentiality 4(1), 5–49 (2012)

Proved Generation of Implementations from Computationally Secure Protocol Specifications

David Cadé and Bruno Blanchet

INRIA Paris-Rocquencourt, France
{david.cade,bruno.blanchet}@inria.fr

Abstract. In order to obtain implementations of security protocols proved secure in the computational model, we have previously implemented a compiler that takes a specification of the protocol in the input language of the computational protocol verifier CryptoVerif and translates it into an OCaml implementation. However, until now, this compiler was not proved correct, so we did not have real guarantees on the generated implementation. In this paper, we fill this gap. We prove that this compiler preserves the security properties proved by CryptoVerif: if an adversary has probability p of breaking a security property in the generated code, then there exists an adversary that breaks the property with the same probability p in the CryptoVerif specification. Therefore, if the protocol specification is proved secure in the computational model by CryptoVerif, then the generated implementation is also secure.

1 Introduction

The verification of security protocols is an important research area since the 1990s: the design of security protocols is notoriously error-prone, and errors can have serious consequences. Formal verification first focused on verifying formal specifications of protocols. However, verifying a specification does not guarantee that the protocol is correctly implemented from this specification. It is therefore important to make sure that the implementation is secure, and not only the specification. Moreover, two models were considered for verifying protocols. In the symbolic model, the so-called Dolev-Yao model, messages are terms. This abstract model facilitates automatic proofs. On the other hand, in the computational model, typically used by cryptographers, messages are bitstrings and attackers are polynomial-time probabilistic Turing machines. Proofs in the latter model are more difficult than in the former, but yield a much more precise analysis of the protocol. Therefore, we would like to obtain implementations of protocols proved secure in the computational model.

To reach this goal, we have proposed the following approach in [7]. We start from a formal specification of the protocol. In order to prove the specified protocol secure in the computational model, we rely on the automatic protocol verifier CryptoVerif [4,5]. This verifier can prove secrecy and authentication properties. The generated proofs are proofs by sequences of games, like the manual proofs written by cryptographers. These games are formalized in a probabilistic process

D. Basin and J.C. Mitchell (Eds.): POST 2013, LNCS 7796, pp. 63–82, 2013.
© Springer-Verlag Berlin Heidelberg 2013

calculus. In order to obtain a proved implementation from the specification, we have written a compiler that takes a CryptoVerif specification and returns an implementation in the functional language OCaml (http://caml.inria.fr). This compiler starts from a CryptoVerif specification annotated with implementation details: the annotations specify how to divide the protocol in different roles, for example, key generation, server, and client, and how to implement the various cryptographic primitives and types. The compiler then generates an OCaml module for each role in the input file. In order to get a full implementation of the protocol, this module is combined with manually written network code, responsible in particular for sending and receiving messages from the network. From the point of view of security, the network code can be considered as part of the adversary, so we do not need to prove its security.

To make sure that the generated implementation is actually secure, we need to prove the correctness of our compiler. This proof was still missing in [7]. It is the topic of this paper. To make this proof, we needed a formal semantics of OCaml. We adapted the operational small-step semantics of a core part of OCaml by Owens et al. [13]. We added to this language support for simplified modules, multiple threads where only one thread can run at any given time, and communication between threads by a shared part of the store.

An adversary against the generated implementation is an OCaml program using the modules generated by our compiler. On the CryptoVerif side, an adversary is a process running in parallel with the verified protocol. In our proof, for each OCaml adversary, we construct a corresponding CryptoVerif adversary that simulates the behavior of the OCaml adversary. When the OCaml adversary calls one of the functions generated by our compiler, which comes from an oracle in the CryptoVerif process, the CryptoVerif adversary calls this oracle. Then we establish a precise correspondence between the traces of the CryptoVerif process with that CryptoVerif adversary and the traces of the OCaml program. This correspondence allows us to show that the probability of success of an attack is the same on the CryptoVerif side and on the OCaml side. Therefore, if CryptoVerif proves that the protocol is secure, then the generated OCaml implementation is also secure, and the bound on the probability of success of an attack computed by CryptoVerif is also valid for the implementation.

We have made several assumptions to get this proof; the important ones are:

A1. The cryptographic primitives are correct with respect to the assumptions made on them in the specification.

A2. The roles are executed in the order specified in CryptoVerif (e.g., in a key-exchange protocol, the key generation is called before the servers and clients).

A3. The adversary and the network code do not access files created by our implementation (e.g. private key files).

A4. The network code is a well-typed OCaml program, which does not use unsafe OCaml functions to bypass the type system.

A5. We represent bitstrings by the OCaml type `string`. We assume that the network code does not mutate `string`s passed to or received from generated code. This could be guaranteed by using an abstract type instead of string. In our semantics, strings are immutable values.

A6. Our semantics of threads is obeyed, which implies that two processes that read or write the same file are not run concurrently (which can be enforced using locks), and that one cannot fork in the middle of a role.

Related work. Several approaches have been considered in order to obtain proved implementations of security protocols. In the symbolic model, several approaches generate protocols from specifications, e.g. [12,14]. Other approaches analyze implementations by extracting a specification verified by a symbolic protocol verifier, e.g. [3,1], or analyze them by other tools such as the model-checker ASPIER [8], the general-purpose C verifier VCC [9] or typing [15].

In contrast, the following approaches provide computational security guarantees, by analyzing implementations. The tool FS2CV [11] translates a subset of F# to the input language of CryptoVerif, which can then prove the protocol secure. The tool F7, which uses a dependent type system to prove security properties on protocols implemented in F#, has been adapted to the computational model in [10]; it uses type annotations to help the proof. The symbolic execution approach of [1] provides computational security guarantees by applying a computational soundness result, which however restricts the class of protocols that can be considered. The tool of [2] generates a CryptoVerif model from a C implementation; however, it can analyze only a single execution path.

To the best of our knowledge, our approach is the first one for generating implementations with a computational proof. The work of [2] and ours are the only ones to provide an explicit bound on the probability of success of an attack against the verified protocol implementation.

Outline. Section 2 describes the common input language of CryptoVerif and of our compiler. Section 3 describes OCaml, the output language of our compiler. Section 4 describes the compiler itself. Sections 5 to 8 present our proof. The long version [6] provides additional details on the semantics of the CryptoVerif input language, on the compiler, and on the proof.

2   The CryptoVerif Input Language

This section presents the syntax and semantics of the CryptoVerif input language, as well as the annotations that specify implementation details.

Syntax and Informal Semantics. Let us first introduce the syntax of the CryptoVerif language in Fig. 1. The language is typed, and types T are subsets of $bitstring_\perp = bitstring \cup \{\perp\}$ where $bitstring$ is the set of all bitstrings and $\perp$ is a symbol that is not a bitstring, used, for example, to represent the failure of a decryption. The boolean type $bool = \{\text{true}, \text{false}\}$ with true being the bitstring 1 and false 0, $bitstring$, and $bitstring_\perp$ are predefined.

Variables $x[i_1, \ldots, i_m]$ represent arrays of bitstrings of a given type T indexed by the values of the indices i of the replications foreach $i \leq N$ do Q present above the definition of the variable. We call these indices *replication indices*, and we

$$M ::= x[i_1, \ldots, i_m] \quad | \quad f(M_1, \ldots, M_m) \hspace{4cm} \text{(Terms)}$$

$$Q ::= 0 \quad | \quad Q \mid Q' \quad | \quad \text{foreach } i \leq N \text{ do } Q \quad | \quad O[\widetilde{i}](x_1[\widetilde{i}], \ldots, x_k[\widetilde{i}]) := P$$
$$\text{(Oracle definitions)}$$

$$P ::= \text{return}(M_1, \ldots, M_k); Q \quad | \quad \text{end} \quad | \quad x[i_1, \ldots, i_m] \xleftarrow{R} T; P$$
$$| \quad x[i_1, \ldots, i_m] \leftarrow M; P \quad | \quad \text{if } M \text{ then } P \text{ else } P' \quad | \quad \text{event } e(M_1, \ldots, M_k); P$$
$$| \quad \text{insert } Tbl(M_1, \ldots, M_k); P$$
$$| \quad \text{get } Tbl(x_1[\widetilde{i}], \ldots, x_k[\widetilde{i}]) \text{ suchthat } M \text{ in } P \text{ else } P'$$
$$| \quad \text{let } (x_1[\widetilde{i}], \ldots, x_{k'}[\widetilde{i}]) = O[M_1, \ldots, M_l](M_1', \ldots, M_k') \text{ in } P \text{ else } P'$$
$$| \quad \text{let } x[\widetilde{i}] = \text{loop } O[M_1, \ldots, M_n](M') \text{ in } P \text{ else } P' \hspace{1.5cm} \text{(Oracle bodies)}$$

Fig. 1. Syntax of the CryptoVerif language

abbreviate $i_1, \ldots, i_m$ by $\widetilde{i}$. Each function f comes with its type $T_1 \times \cdots \times T_m \to T$; all CryptoVerif functions are deterministic and efficiently computable. Some functions are predefined, and some are infix, like the equality test $=$ and boolean operations. The cryptographic primitives used in the protocol are represented by CryptoVerif functions. Terms M represent computations over bitstrings: they can be variable accesses $x[i_1, \ldots, i_m]$ or function applications $f(M_1, \ldots, M_m)$.

The oracle definitions Q represent the oracles that will become available to the adversary at this point. The nil construct 0 provides no oracle. The parallel composition $Q \mid Q'$ provides oracles in Q and Q'. The replication foreach $i \leq N$ do Q provides N copies of Q, indexed by $i \in \{1, \ldots, N\}$. The parameter N is unspecified and is used by CryptoVerif to express the maximum probability of breaking the protocol, which typically depends on the number of calls to the various oracles. The oracle definition $O[\widetilde{i}](x_1[\widetilde{i}] : T_1, \ldots, x_k[\widetilde{i}] : T_k) := P$ makes available the oracle $O[\widetilde{i}]$, and when called by the adversary with arguments $a_1, \ldots, a_k$, it executes the oracle body P with $x_j[\widetilde{i}]$ set to a_j.

The oracle bodies P represent the behavior of the oracle. A return statement return$(M_1, \ldots, M_k); Q$ returns the result of $M_1, \ldots, M_k$ to the caller, and makes available oracles in Q. An end statement end returns to the caller on an error. A random number assignment $x[\widetilde{i}] \xleftarrow{R} T; P$ puts a uniformly chosen random value of type T in variable $x[\widetilde{i}]$, and continues with P. The type T must consist of all bitstrings of a given size. An assignment $x[\widetilde{i}] \leftarrow M; P$ puts the result of M in the variable $x[\widetilde{i}]$, and continues with P. A conditional statement if M then P else P' executes P if M evaluates to true and P' otherwise.

An insert statement insert $Tbl(M_1, \ldots, M_k); P$ inserts the result of $M_1, \ldots, M_k$ into the table Tbl. Tables are lists of tuples, used for example to store tables of keys. A get statement get $Tbl(x_1[\widetilde{i}], \ldots, x_k[\widetilde{i}])$ suchthat M in P else P' searches for an element $a_1, \ldots, a_k$ in the table Tbl such that the term M evaluates to true when $x_1[\widetilde{i}] = a_1, \ldots, x_k[\widetilde{i}] = a_k$. If there is no such element, we continue with P', and otherwise we choose randomly one of the elements that correspond, store it in the variables $x_1[\tilde{i}], \ldots, x_k[\tilde{i}]$, then continue with P. An event statement event $e(M_1, \ldots, M_k); P$ is used to log events. Events serve for specifying security properties of protocols, but do not change the execution of the process.

An oracle call let $(x_1[\tilde{i}], \ldots, x_{k'}[\tilde{i}]) = O[M_1, \ldots, M_l](M'_1, \ldots, M'_k)$ in P else P' calls oracle $O[M_1, \ldots, M_l]$, stores its returned values in the variables $x_1[\tilde{i}], \ldots, x_{k'}[\tilde{i}]$, and continues with P if the oracle terminates with a return statement, and continues with P' if the oracle terminates with end.

A loop let $x[\tilde{i}] = \mathsf{loop}\ O[M_1, \ldots, M_n](M')$ in P else P' calls oracle O in a loop. Oracle O takes a unique argument (the internal state of the loop) and returns a pair containing a result of the same type and a boolean indicating whether the loop should continue or not. $O[M_1, \ldots, M_n](M')$ is first called. If it returns (a_1, true), $O[M_1 + 1, M_2, \ldots, M_n](a_1)$ is called. If it returns (a_2, true), $O[M_1 + 2, M_2, \ldots, M_n](a_2)$ is called, and so on, until $O[M_1 + k, M_2, \ldots, M_n](a_k)$ returns $(a_{k+1}, \mathsf{false})$. Then we run P with $x[\tilde{i}]$ set to a_{k+1}. If O terminates with end, we run P'. Oracle call and loop statements cannot appear in the CryptoVerif process representing the protocol, but are used for representing the adversary.

Formal Semantics. The complete formal semantics of the language can be found in [6]. The semantics is defined as a reduction relation on semantic configurations, which are tuples of the form $\mathfrak{C} = E, P, \mathcal{T}, \mathcal{Q}, \mathcal{R}, \mathcal{E}$. The environment E is a mapping from variables with their replication indices to bitstring values. The oracle body P is the oracle body currently running. The mapping $\mathcal{T}$ maps table names to their contents, which is the multiset of elements inserted in the table. The set $\mathcal{Q}$ contains the set of the callable oracle definitions. The list $\mathcal{R}$ is the call stack, which consists of triplets containing the variables with which the result should be bound and two oracle bodies, the first will be executed if the oracle returns a result with a return statement, and the second will be executed if the oracle returns on an end statement. The sequence $\mathcal{E}$ is the list of events $e(a_1, \ldots, a_k)$ executed so far, by the construct event $e(M_1, \ldots, M_k)$.

The notation $E, M \Downarrow a$ means that the term M evaluates to the bitstring a under the environment E. We say that an oracle definition $O[\tilde{i}](x_1[\tilde{i}], \ldots, x_k[\tilde{i}]) := P$ is defined *at the beginning of* Q when this oracle definition is present in Q without entering into oracle bodies. The list $\mathrm{reduce}'(Q) = [(Q_1, b_1), \ldots, (Q_n, b_n)]$ contains all oracle definitions at the beginning of Q, ordered from left to right, with the boolean b_i to true if Q_i is under a replication in Q, and false otherwise. The set $\mathrm{reduce}(Q)$ contains all oracle definitions present in $\mathrm{reduce}'(Q)$. The semantics is probabilistic: $\mathfrak{C} \rightarrow_p \mathfrak{C}'$ means that $\mathfrak{C}$ reduces into $\mathfrak{C}'$ with probability p. The initial configuration for running the oracle definition Q is $\mathfrak{C}_i(Q) = \emptyset, \mathsf{let}\ x = O_{\mathrm{start}}()$ in $\mathsf{return}(x)$ else end, $\emptyset, \mathrm{reduce}(Q), \emptyset, \emptyset$, which starts by calling oracle O_{start}. The oracle definition Q typically contains a protocol in parallel with an adversary.

Annotations. In order to compile a CryptoVerif process into an implementation, we added annotations to the language, to specify implementation details.

First, we separate the parts of the process that correspond to different roles, such as client and server, which will be included in different OCaml programs in the generated implementation. We annotate processes to specify roles: the beginning of *role* is specified in oracle definitions *role*{Q; the end of *role* is specified by a closing brace } between a return(...) and its following oracle definition Q. We denote by $Q(role)$ the part of the process corresponding to the role *role*.

The process for a role $Q(role)$ may have free variables, but CryptoVerif requires that these free variables be defined under no replication, so that they can be passed from the process that defines them to the process $Q(role)$, which uses them, simply by storing each variable in a file. (There must be a single value to store, not one for each value of the replication indices.) The user must also declare, for each free variable $x[]$ in a role, the file f in which the variable will be stored. Let files be the set of these pairs $(x[], f)$. Let also tables be the set of pairs (Tbl, f) such that the table Tbl will be stored in file f.

Finally, the user annotations provide, for each CryptoVerif type T, the corresponding OCaml type $\mathbb{G}_T(T)$ as well as several OCaml functions: a function $\mathbb{G}_{\mathsf{random}}(T)$: unit $\rightarrow \mathbb{G}_T(T)$ that generates random numbers uniformly in T (when T is used in a random number generation), serialization and deserialization functions $\mathbb{G}_{\mathsf{ser}}(T)$: $\mathbb{G}_T(T) \rightarrow$ string and $\mathbb{G}_{\mathsf{deser}}(T)$: string $\rightarrow \mathbb{G}_T(T)$ (when T is written or read from tables and files), and a predicate function $\mathbb{G}_{\mathsf{pred}}(T)$: $\mathbb{G}_T(T) \rightarrow$ bool that returns true if its argument corresponds to an element of type T and false otherwise (when T is present in the interface of the oracle definitions). The user annotations also provide, for each CryptoVerif function f, a corresponding OCaml function $\mathbb{G}(f)$. We assume that these functions are all provided in an OCaml module μ_{prim}.

Requirements. CryptoVerif verifies the following requirements:

1. Variables are renamed so that each variable has a single definition. The indices $\tilde{i}$ of a variable $x[\tilde{i}]$ are always the indices of replications above the definition of x.
2. The processes are well-typed. (In particular, functions receive arguments of their expected types. See [4] for a similar type system.)
3. Oracles with the same name can be defined only in different branches of an if or get construct.
   We define types of oracles as follows. The type of a return($M_1, \ldots, M_n$); Q statement consists of the types of $M_1, \ldots, M_n$ and the type of the oracle definitions at the beginning of Q. The type of an oracle definition consists of the role that it starts (if it starts a role), the oracle name, the bounds of the replications above that oracle definition, the types of the arguments of the oracle, and the common type of its return statements.
   An oracle may have several return statements, but they must be of the same type. When there are several definitions of an oracle with the same name O, they must be of the same type.

Item 1 makes sure that a distinct array cell is used in each copy of a process, so that all values of the variables during execution are kept in memory. (This helps in cryptographic proofs.) To lighten notations, we often omit the indices since they are determined by Item 1. Item 3 guarantees that the various definitions of an oracle are consistent, and can in fact be compiled into a single function in OCaml. Furthermore, for simplicity, we also require the following points:

1. All oracle definitions are included in a role.
2. No replication occurs directly under a replication.

We can encode nested replications by adding a dummy oracle between the two replications. These assumptions are relaxed in our implementation.

3   The OCaml Language

We do not repeat the syntax of OCaml, which is standard (see the manual at http://caml.inria.fr). To define its formal semantics, we adapted the semantics by Scott Owens et al. [13]. This semantics is a small step, operational semantics of the core part of the OCaml language. We modified it in several ways.

First, this semantics substitutes directly variables with their values. Instead, we define an environment Env that maps variables to their values. This way, it is easier to relate the OCaml state to the CryptoVerif state which also contains an environment. Then, we need to define explicit closures function$[Env, pm]$ where pm is a pattern matching. A pattern matching is a list of tuples containing a pattern and an expression, which is denoted $pat_1 \to e_1 \mid \ldots \mid pat_m \to e_m$. When matching a value v, this executes the first expression e_j such that the pattern pat_j matches v. We also need to add an explicit call stack $Stack$. The stack is a list of pairs (Env, C), where C is an *evaluation context*, that is, an expression with a hole $[\cdot]$, such that the expression inside the hole can be immediately evaluated. For instance, $e\ [\cdot]$ and $[\cdot]\ v$ are evaluation contexts, so we evaluate the argument of applications first, and when it becomes a value v, we evaluate the function. In order to evaluate an expression $C[e]$, that is, C with e in the hole, we push the context C on the stack with the current environment, evaluate the expression e until it becomes a value v, and finally pop the context C from the stack, inserting the obtained value in it, yielding $C[v]$. As usual, the contents of references are stored in a *store*, which maps locations to their current values. Hence, the semantic configuration of an OCaml program is $\langle Env, pe, Stack, store \rangle$, where pe is the program or expression currently evaluated.

Moreover, a security protocol typically involves several programs running in parallel on different machines. We model this by considering several threads. Each thread has a configuration $Th_i = \langle Env_i, pe_i, Stack_i, store_i \rangle$ and the semantic configuration becomes

$$[Th_1, \ldots, Th_n], globalstore, j \,,$$

where j is the number of the thread currently being executed, and *globalstore* is a store for locations shared between threads. We use it to model the communication between threads by storing messages in shared locations, and to store the files containing private data from the CryptoVerif process (free variables of roles and tables). In practice, these files may for example be copied from one machine to another by the user. The values in the global store contain no closure and no reference. Let S_g be the set of locations of the global store and $S_{priv} \subset S_g$ be the ones reserved for private CryptoVerif data. (The latter cannot be used by the adversary, following Assumption A3.) We define the new primitives addthread(pe), which starts the program pe in a new thread, and schedule(j), which stops execution of the current thread and continues execution of the thread j. The primitive addthread does not allow using the same local store in several threads, which corresponds to forbidding fork in the middle of a role. Moreover, we reduce only the active thread, and we change threads only with schedule. So we can only change threads in code defined by the adversary, because neither the primitives nor the generated modules use schedule. So a call to an oracle cannot be interleaved with other threads. This corresponds to Assumption A6: if multiple oracles cannot interleave reads and writes in the same table file, one can reconstruct a well-defined call order for these oracles in the CryptoVerif process, which processes one oracle call after another, so that the calls can be simulated in our semantics.

In order to represent random choices, we add the primitive random (), which returns a random boolean true or false with equal probability.

OCaml programs typically contain several modules. A module named μ consists of an OCaml program pe_μ and its interface $interface_\mu$ that is the set of OCaml identifiers defined in μ and usable in other modules. A correct OCaml program is then of the form $pe_{\mu_1};; \ldots ;; pe_{\mu_n}$, where, for all $i \leq n$, the free variables of μ_i are defined in the interfaces of μ_j with $j < i$.

Finally, we instrument OCaml code in three ways. First, we add a new kind of functions and closures tagfunction that behave exactly in the same way as the regular closures. We use these to differentiate closures coming from our generated code and closures coming from the adversary.

Second, we need to be able to match CryptoVerif events, so we add to the semantic configuration an element $events$ that contains the list of the events executed until now. We add the primitive event $e(e_1, \ldots, e_k)$ that adds the event $e(v_1, \ldots, v_k)$ to $events$ where $e_1, \ldots, e_k$ evaluate to the values $v_1, \ldots, v_k$ respectively. Events serve in specifying security properties of protocols, so they appear in generated code, but cannot be used by the adversary.

Third, the roles of a CryptoVerif process cannot be executed in any order: if a role is defined after the return from an oracle, it can be executed only after the previous oracle has returned. For instance, we can run a server only after generating its keys. We need to enforce this constraint also in the OCaml program. Each CryptoVerif role $role$ is translated by our compiler into an OCaml module μ_{role}. We add to the OCaml configuration the multiset of callable modules $\mathcal{MI}$ that contains tuples (μ_{role}, b) of a module μ_{role} and a boolean b, indicating, if true, that the module can be called any number of times and if false that the module can be called only once. The construct addthread is then modified to reject new programs that contain a module that cannot be called. We add the primitive return($\mathcal{MI}'$, e) that adds to the module list $\mathcal{MI}$ the generated modules present in $\mathcal{MI}'$, and returns the result of e. This primitive is useful to add modules newly defined at the return from an oracle.

$$G(x \xleftarrow{R} T; P) = \text{let } G_{\text{var}}(x) = G_{\text{random}}(T_x) \text{ () in } (G_{\text{file}}(x); G(P)) \qquad \text{(Random)}$$

$$G(x \leftarrow M; P) = \text{let } G_{\text{var}}(x) = G_{\text{M}}(M) \text{ in } (G_{\text{file}}(x); G(P)) \qquad \text{(Let)}$$

$$G(\text{if } M \text{ then } P \text{ else } P') = \text{if } G_{\text{M}}(M) \text{ then } G(P) \text{ else } G(P') \qquad \text{(If)}$$

$$\frac{[(Q_1, b_1), \ldots, (Q_l, b_l)] = \text{reduce}'(Q)}{G(\text{return}(N_1, \ldots, N_k); Q) = (G_{\text{O}}(Q_1, b_1), \ldots, G_{\text{O}}(Q_l, b_l), G_{\text{M}}(N_1), \ldots, G_{\text{M}}(N_k))} \qquad \text{(Return1)}$$

$$G(\text{return}(N_1, \ldots, N_k)\}; Q) = (\text{return}(G_{\text{get}_{\mathcal{MI}}}(Q), (G_{\text{M}}(N_1), \ldots, G_{\text{M}}(N_k)))) \qquad \text{(Return2)}$$

$$G(\text{end}) = (\text{raise Match\_failure}) \qquad \text{(End)}$$

$$G(\text{event } e(M_1, \ldots, M_k)) = \text{event } e(G_{\text{M}}(M_1), \ldots, G_{\text{M}}(M_k)) \qquad \text{(Event)}$$

$$G_{\text{O}}(Q, \text{false}) = \text{let } token = \text{ref true in tagfunction } pm_{\text{false}}(Q)$$
$$pm_{\text{false}}(O(x_1 : T_1, \ldots, x_k : T_k) := P) = (G_{\text{var}}(x_1), \ldots, G_{\text{var}}(x_k)) \rightarrow$$
$$\quad \text{if } (!token) \,\&\&\, (G_{\text{pred}}(T_1) \; G_{\text{var}}(x_1)) \,\&\&\, \ldots \,\&\&\, (G_{\text{pred}}(T_k) \; G_{\text{var}}(x_k)) \qquad \text{(Oracle1)}$$
$$\quad \text{then } (token := \text{false}; G(P)) \text{ else raise Bad\_Call}$$

$$G_{\text{O}}(Q, \text{true}) = \text{tagfunction } pm_{\text{true}}(Q)$$
$$pm_{\text{true}}(O(x_1 : T_1, \ldots, x_k : T_k) := P) = (G_{\text{var}}(x_1), \ldots, G_{\text{var}}(x_k)) \rightarrow$$
$$\quad \text{if } (G_{\text{pred}}(T_1) \; G_{\text{var}}(x_1)) \,\&\&\, \ldots \,\&\&\, (G_{\text{pred}}(T_k) \; G_{\text{var}}(x_k)) \text{ then } G(P) \qquad \text{(Oracle2)}$$
$$\quad \text{else raise Bad\_Call}$$

Fig. 2. Translation function G, excerpt

Hence, the instrumented semantic configuration is

$$\mathcal{C} = [Th_1, \ldots, Th_n], globalstore, j, \mathcal{MI}, events$$

We have shown that this instrumentation does not alter the semantics of OCaml: an instrumented program behaves exactly in the same way as that program with the instrumentation deleted, provided only allowed roles are executed, as assumed by Assumption A2. Below, when the current thread of $\mathcal{C}$ is $Th_j = \langle Env_j, pe_j, Stack_j, store_j \rangle$, we denote by $\mathcal{C}_{pe}(\mathcal{C}) = pe_j$ and $\mathcal{C}_{store}(\mathcal{C}) = store_j$ the current program and store of $\mathcal{C}$.

4 Translation

Our compiler translates each CryptoVerif role *role* into an OCaml module μ_{role} and each CryptoVerif oracle into a function. Let G_{var} be an injective function taking a CryptoVerif variable name and returning an OCaml variable name. The function G_{M} transforms a term M into an OCaml expression as follows: $G_{\text{M}}(x[\widetilde{i}]) = G_{\text{var}}(x)$ and $G_{\text{M}}(f(M_1, \ldots, M_m)) = G_{\text{f}}(f) \, (G_{\text{M}}(M_1), \ldots, G_{\text{M}}(M_m))$. To translate an oracle, we translate the body of the oracle using the function G defined in Fig. 2, except the translation of get and insert, which is shown in [6]. Most cases are straightforward.

After defining a variable, we store it in a file if needed, using $G_{\text{file}}(x)$ which is () when $x[]$ is not present in files, and $f := G_{\text{ser}}(T_x) \, G_{\text{var}}(x)$ when $(x[], f)$ is present in files.

For the return case, if the return is not at the end of a role, we return the closures corresponding to the oracles defined after the return (Return 1). Otherwise, we update the set of available roles using the primitive return introduced in the previous section (Return 2). We let $\mathbb{G}_{\text{get}_{\mathcal{MI}}}(Q)$ be the set of pairs (μ_{role}, b) where $role$ is defined at the beginning of Q, and the boolean b is true if the role $role$ is under a replication and false otherwise.

An oracle $O(x_1, \ldots, x_n) := P$ is transformed in a closure by the function $\mathbb{G}_O$ as shown in Fig. 2. When the oracle O is not under replication (second argument of $\mathbb{G}_O$ false, in (Oracle 1)), we use a boolean token $token$ to make sure that it can be called only once: $token$ is initially true, it is set to false in the first call. In subsequent calls, an exception will be raised. The translation of an oracle always checks that the arguments are correct values for their CryptoVerif types.

Finally, we generate an OCaml module μ_{role} for each role $role$ in the CryptoVerif process. This module provides a single function init which returns the functions implementing the oracles defined at the beginning of $Q(role)$, so its interface is $interface_{\mu_{role}} = \{\mu_{role}.\text{init}\}$ and its program is

$$
\begin{aligned}
pe_{\mu_{role}} &= \text{let } \mu_{role}.\text{init} = \text{let } token = \text{ref true in tagfunction } pm_{role} \\
pm_{role} &= () \to \text{if } (!token) \text{ then} \\
&\qquad \mathbb{G}_{\text{read}}(x_1[]) \text{ in } \ldots \mathbb{G}_{\text{read}}(x_m[]) \text{ in} \\
&\qquad (token := \text{false}; (\mathbb{G}_O(Q_1, b_1), \ldots, \mathbb{G}_O(Q_k, b_k))) \\
&\qquad \text{else raise Bad\_Call}
\end{aligned}
$$

where $[(Q_1, b_1), \ldots, (Q_n, b_n)] = \text{reduce}'(Q(role))$ and $x_1[], \ldots, x_k[]$ are the free variables of $Q(role)$, which are the variables we need to retrieve from the files. These variables are read by $\mathbb{G}_{\text{read}}(x) = \text{let } \mathbb{G}_{\text{var}}(x) = \mathbb{G}_{\text{deser}}(T_x) \ !(f)$ where $(x[], f) \in \text{files}$.

The generated modules are included in manually-written programs that represent the full implementation of the protocol, for instance a client and a server. In particular, these programs are responsible for sending the result of oracles to the network and receiving messages to be passed as arguments to oracles. We consider that these programs are run by the adversary using the addthread primitive. We represent the adversary by an OCaml program pe_0. For simplicity, we require that the programs added by addthread in pe_0 contain modules in the following order $pe_{\mu_{\text{prim}}};; pe_{\mu_{role_1}};; \ldots;; pe_{\mu_{role_k}};; pe$ where pe contains no generated module. We assume that pe_0 uses the generated modules only inside addthread, and that pe_0 is a well-typed OCaml program. (The network code is well-typed by Assumption A4. The adversary itself is any probabilistic Turing machine, which can be implemented by a well-typed OCaml program.) The program pe_0 is run in the initial OCaml configuration $\mathcal{C}_0(Q_0, pe_0)$ defined as follows:

$$\mathcal{C}_0(Q_0, pe_0) = [\langle \emptyset, pe_0, [], \emptyset \rangle], globalstore_0, 1, \mathbb{G}_{\text{get}_{\mathcal{MI}}}(Q_0)$$

where $\mathbb{G}_{\text{get}_{\mathcal{MI}}}(Q_0)$ is the set of modules available at the beginning of the execution and $globalstore_0 = \{x \mapsto [] \mid x \in S_g\}$ is the initial value of global store. We use the empty list $[]$ as initial value, representing that the file has not been created yet, or that the table is empty.

5   Correctness of the Translation of Oracle Bodies

Let us first define precisely the notion of trace.

Definition 1 (Traces). *A trace $\mathcal{CT}$ is a sequence of reductions: $\mathcal{CT} = \mathcal{C}_0 \rightarrow_{p_1}$ $\cdots \rightarrow_{p_n} \mathcal{C}_n$. The trace $\mathcal{CT}$ is* complete *when there is no possible reduction from its last configuration $\mathcal{C}_n$. The probability of the trace $\mathcal{CT}$ is $\Pr[\mathcal{CT}] = p_1 \times \cdots \times p_n$. The probability of a set of traces is the sum of the probabilities of its elements.*

We write $\mathcal{C} \rightarrow_p^* \mathcal{C}'$ when there exists a trace from $\mathcal{C}$ to $\mathcal{C}'$ and p is the probability of the set of all traces from $\mathcal{C}$ to $\mathcal{C}'$ that contain a single occurrence of $\mathcal{C}'$. The notation $\mathcal{C} \rightarrow^* \mathcal{C}'$ means $\mathcal{C} \rightarrow_1^* \mathcal{C}'$.

We denote OCaml traces by $\mathcal{CT}$ and CryptoVerif traces by $\mathfrak{CT}$.

For expressions that do not use addthread, return, event, nor schedule operations and do not use the store nor the global store, we use the shortened OCaml configuration $Env, pe, Stack$. The rest of the OCaml configuration is unchanged. We make the following assumptions on the code of primitives.

Assumption 1. *1. There are no addthread, return, event, nor schedule operations and no mention of global store locations in $pe_{\mu_{\text{prim}}}$.*

2. There are no operations that touch the store (ref, !, :=) and no mention of store locations in $pe_{\mu_{\text{prim}}}$.

3. There exists Env_{prim} such that for all programs pe, we have $\emptyset, pe_{\mu_{\text{prim}}} ;; pe, [\,]$ $\rightarrow^* Env_{\text{prim}}, pe, [\,]$.

Item 2 may not be realistic (the primitives often use the store internally). This assumption is made here only for simplicity; it can be relaxed at the cost of a much more complex proof: when the primitives use the store, we need to make sure that the part of the store used by the primitives is disjoint from the one used by the rest of the program. We are finishing this proof. Item 3 requires that there are no random choices during the initialization of primitives, so that the obtained environment is always the same. This is not restrictive since random choices are allowed during calls to primitives.

To establish the correspondence between CryptoVerif values and OCaml values, we define a function $\mathbb{G}_{\text{val}_T}$, which maps each CryptoVerif bitstring a to its associated value v in OCaml. For a given type T, $\mathbb{G}_{\text{val}_T}$ must be a bijection between T and the set of OCaml values of type $\mathbb{G}_T(T)$ satisfying the predicate function $\mathbb{G}_{\text{pred}}(T)$. We extend this function to events by $\mathbb{G}_{\text{ev}}(e(a_1,\ldots,a_j)) = e(\mathbb{G}_{\text{val}_{T_1}}(a_1),\ldots,\mathbb{G}_{\text{val}_{T_j}}(a_j))$ if e is of type $T_1 \times \cdots \times T_j$. This function is naturally extended to lists of events. The next assumption states that the primitives have been correctly implemented, following Assumption A1.

Assumption 2 (Correct primitives). *For each CryptoVerif function f of type $T_1 \times \cdots \times T_n \rightarrow T$, for all CryptoVerif values $a_1,\ldots,a_n$ of types $T_1,\ldots,T_n$, $Env_{\text{prim}}, \mathbb{G}_f(f)\ (\mathbb{G}_{\text{val}_{T_1}}(a_1),\ldots,\mathbb{G}_{\text{val}_{T_n}}(a_n)), [\,] \rightarrow^* Env', \mathbb{G}_{\text{val}_T}(f(a_1,\ldots,a_n)), [\,].$*

For each CryptoVerif type T used for getting fresh values, for each value $a \in T$, $Env_{\text{prim}}, \mathbb{G}_{\text{random}}(T)\ (), [\,] \rightarrow_{1/|T|}^* Env', \mathbb{G}_{\text{val}_T}(a), [\,].$

For each CryptoVerif type T used to check predicates, for each value v of the OCaml type $\mathbb{G}_T(T)$, $Env_{\text{prim}}, \mathbb{G}_{\text{pred}}(T) \ v, [\,] \to^* Env', v', [\,]$ where $v' = \text{true}$ if $\mathbb{G}_{\text{val}_T}^{-1}(v)$ exists, and $v' = \text{false}$ otherwise.

For each CryptoVerif type T used for serialization/deserialization, for each value $a \in T$, there exists an OCaml string value $\text{ser}(T, a)$, such that

$$Env_{\text{prim}}, \mathbb{G}_{\text{ser}}(T) \ \mathbb{G}_{\text{val}_T}(a), [\,] \to^* Env', \text{ser}(T, a), [\,]$$
$$\text{and } Env_{\text{prim}}, \mathbb{G}_{\text{deser}}(T) \ \text{ser}(T, a), [\,] \to^* Env', \mathbb{G}_{\text{val}_T}(a), [\,]$$

We denote by $\text{fv}(P)$ the free variables of the oracle body P, with their indices, defined as usual. Let us define the minimal environments and global stores corresponding to CryptoVerif variables and tables.

Definition 2 (Minimal environments and stores).

$$Env(E, P) = \{\mathbb{G}_{\text{var}}(x) \mapsto \mathbb{G}_{\text{val}_{T_x}}(a) \mid x[\tilde{a}] \in \text{fv}(P), E, x[\tilde{a}] \Downarrow a\} \quad \text{(Environment)}$$

$$\begin{aligned}
globalstore(E, \mathcal{T}) = \{ \\
&\{f \mapsto \text{ser}(T_x, \mathbb{G}_{\text{val}_{T_x}}(a)) \mid (x[\,], f) \in \text{files}, E, x[\,] \Downarrow a\} \cup \\
&\{f \mapsto [\,] \mid (x[\,], f) \in \text{files}, x \text{ not defined in } E\} \cup \quad \text{(Global store)} \\
&\{f_1 \mapsto l_1, \ldots, f_k \mapsto l_k\} \\
&\mid \{(Tbl_1, f_1), \ldots, (Tbl_k, f_k)\} = \text{tables}, l_i \in \mathbb{G}_{\text{tbl}}(\mathcal{T}(Tbl_i))\}
\end{aligned}$$

where $\mathbb{G}_{\text{tbl}}(t)$ is the set of OCaml lists corresponding to the table contents t, defined as follows. Suppose the table has type $T = T_1, \ldots, T_l$. Let $\mathbb{G}_{\text{tblel}}(b_1, \ldots, b_l)$ be the OCaml value $(\text{ser}(T_1, \mathbb{G}_{\text{val}_{T_1}}(b_1)), \ldots, \text{ser}(T_l, \mathbb{G}_{\text{val}_{T_l}}(b_l)))$ corresponding to the table element $(b_1, \ldots, b_l)$. If $t = \{a_1, \ldots, a_k\}$, $\mathbb{G}_{\text{tbl}}(t)$ is the set of all lists containing elements $\mathbb{G}_{\text{tblel}}(a_1), \ldots, \mathbb{G}_{\text{tblel}}(a_k)$ in any order.

We also define $Env(E, Q)$ and $Env(E, M)$ in the same way as $Env(E, P)$.

The *globalstore* function above returns the set of all the possible minimal global stores in which the contents of the files and the tables is correct with respect to the CryptoVerif configuration.

The next lemma shows that CryptoVerif terms are correctly translated into OCaml. It is proved by induction on the syntax of the term M.

Lemma 1 (Term reduction). *For all CryptoVerif terms M of type T and all CryptoVerif environments E, if $Env \supseteq Env_{\text{prim}} \cup Env(E, M)$ and $E, M \Downarrow a$, then $Env, \mathbb{G}_M(M), Stack \to^* Env', \mathbb{G}_{\text{val}_T}(a), Stack$.*

The next lemma shows that CryptoVerif oracle bodies are correctly translated into OCaml.

Lemma 2 (Inner reduction). *Consider a CryptoVerif configuration $\mathfrak{C}$ whose program part P is not in a return, end, call or loop form. Suppose we have n reductions beginning at this configuration:*

$$\mathfrak{C} = E, P, \mathcal{T}, \mathcal{Q}, \mathcal{R}, \mathcal{E} \to_{p_i} \mathfrak{C}_i = E_i, P_i, \mathcal{Q}, \mathcal{T}_i, \mathcal{R}, \mathcal{E}_i$$

for $i \leq n$. Let $\mathcal{C}$ be an OCaml configuration such that $\mathcal{C} = [Th_1, \ldots, Th_j, \ldots, Th_m]$, $globalstore, j, \mathcal{MI}, \mathbb{G}_{\mathsf{ev}}(\mathcal{E})$ with $Th_j = \langle Env, \mathbb{G}(P), Stack, store \rangle$, $Env_{\mathsf{prim}} \cup Env(E, P) \subseteq Env$, and $G \subseteq globalstore$ for some $G \in globalstore(E, \mathcal{T})$.

Then there exist m disjoint sets of OCaml traces $\mathcal{CTS}_1, \ldots, \mathcal{CTS}_m$, all starting at $\mathcal{C}$, such that none of these traces is a prefix of another of these traces, $\Pr[\mathcal{CTS}_i] = p_i$, and the last configurations of traces in $\mathcal{CTS}_i$ are of the form $[Th_1, \ldots, Th'_j, \ldots, Th_m]$, $globalstore', j, \mathcal{MI}, \mathbb{G}_{\mathsf{ev}}(\mathcal{E}_i)$ with $Th'_j = \langle Env', \mathbb{G}(P_i), Stack, store \rangle$, $Env_{\mathsf{prim}} \cup Env(E_i, P_i) \subseteq Env'$, and $G' \subseteq globalstore'$ for some Env', $globalstore'$, and some $G' \in globalstore(E_i, \mathcal{T}_i)$.

This lemma is proved by cases on the process P. We use Lemma 1 when we need to evaluate a term. Similar lemmas can be proved for return and end, adapting the form of the final configuration. The oracle bodies that we translate into OCaml do not contain calls nor loops.

6   Simulation of OCaml Code

In this section, we show how to simulate in CryptoVerif any OCaml program pe_0 corresponding to an adversary interacting with the protocol implementation generated from the CryptoVerif process Q_0. Basically, we run the OCaml program pe_0 inside a CryptoVerif primitive f (which is possible since these primitives can represent any deterministic Turing machine). When pe_0 needs to call an oracle of Q_0, the primitive returns and the call is made by CryptoVerif. When pe_0 needs to generate a random number, this generation is performed by CryptoVerif.

We assume that the OCaml program pe_0 runs in bounded time, so makes a bounded number of oracle calls. When oracle O is under replication, we let N_O be the maximum number of calls to $\mathbb{G}_O(Q, \mathsf{true})$ for each call to the oracle defined above O. We use N_O as the bound of the replication above O. When a role $role$ is under replication, we let N_{role} be the maximum number of executions of $\mathsf{addthread}(pe)$ for some pe that contains μ_{role} for each call to the oracle defined above $role$. We use N_{role} as the bound of the replication above $role$. These replication bounds are chosen such that the OCaml program never exhausts the number of oracle calls allowed by the CryptoVerif process.

From the OCaml program pe_0, we build a CryptoVerif adversary $Q_{\mathsf{adv}}(Q_0, pe_0)$ given in Fig. 3. The initial CryptoVerif configuration is then $\mathfrak{C}_0(Q_0, pe_0) = \mathfrak{C}_{\mathsf{i}}(Q_0 \mid Q_{\mathsf{adv}}(Q_0, pe_0))$. In Fig. 3, we use a let construct with pattern matching, which can easily be encoded in the syntax shown in Fig. 1, by defining functions for creating tuples and their corresponding projections. Let $O_1, \ldots, O_n$ be the oracle names in Q_0. We define n constants $o_1, \ldots, o_n$ which are used to designate the oracles $O_1, \ldots, O_n$ respectively, o_R which corresponds to a random choice, and o_S which corresponds to the end of the OCaml program.

The adversary is mainly encoded by the function f. This function takes as argument the bitstring representation $s = \mathsf{repr}(\mathcal{CS})$ of a simulator configuration $\mathcal{CS} = \mathcal{C}, \mathcal{RI}, \mathcal{I}$, which consists of an OCaml configuration $\mathcal{C}$ (without $\mathcal{MI}$ and events) and sets $\mathcal{RI}$ and $\mathcal{I}$ that finitely represent the callable oracles Q of CryptoVerif. The set $\mathcal{RI}$ represents the callable roles with their replication indices.

$Q_{\mathrm{adv}}(Q_0, pe_0) = (O_{\mathrm{start}}() = \mathsf{let}\ r = \mathsf{loop}\ O_{loop}(s_0(Q_0, pe_0))\ \mathsf{in}\ \mathsf{end}\ \mathsf{else}\ \mathsf{end})$
$\qquad\qquad\quad |\ Q_c(Q_0, pe_0)$

$Q_c(Q_0, pe_0) = \mathsf{foreach}\ i' \leq N'\ \mathsf{do}\ O_{loop}[i'](s : bitstring) :=$
(1) $\mathsf{let}\ (s', o, i, args) = f(s)\ \mathsf{in}$
(2) $\mathsf{if}\ o = o_S\ \mathsf{then}$
(3) $\mathsf{return}(s', \mathsf{false})$
     $\mathsf{else\ if}\ o = o_1\ \mathsf{then}$
        $\mathsf{let}\ (a_{1_1}, \ldots, a_{1_{m_1}}) = args\ \mathsf{in}\ \mathsf{let}\ (i_{1_1}, \ldots, i_{1_{n_1}}) = i\ \mathsf{in}$
(4) $(r_{1_1}, \ldots, r_{1_{k_1}}) \leftarrow O_1[i_{1_1}, \ldots, i_{1_{n_1}}](a_{1_1}, \ldots, a_{1_{m_1}});$
(5) $\mathsf{return}(f'_{O_1}(s', (r_{1_1}, \ldots, r_{1_{k_1}})), \mathsf{true})$
(6) $\mathsf{else\ return}(f''_{O_1}(s'), \mathsf{true})$
     $\mathsf{else\ if}\ o = o_2\ \mathsf{then}\ \ldots$
     $\mathsf{else\ if}\ o = o_R\ \mathsf{then}$
(7) $b_R \overset{R}{\leftarrow} bool; \mathsf{return}(f_R(s', b_R), \mathsf{true})$

Fig. 3. The program $Q_c(Q_0, pe_0)$

Its elements are as follows: $role\,[[a, +\infty[, \widetilde{a}']$ means that role $role$ is under replication and the roles $role[1, \widetilde{a}']$ to $role[a-1, \widetilde{a}']$ have been used, and the roles $role[a, \widetilde{a}']$ to $role[N_\mu, \widetilde{a}']$ are callable; $role\,[\widetilde{a}]$ means that $role$ is not under replication and $role[\widetilde{a}]$ is callable. Similarly, the set $\mathcal{I}$ represents the callable oracles (inside an already started role), using $O\,[[a, +\infty[, \widetilde{a}']$ to mean that the oracles $O[a, \widetilde{a}']$ to $O[N_O, \widetilde{a}']$ are usable, and $O[\widetilde{a}]$ to mean that oracle $O[\widetilde{a}]$ can be called.

The OCaml configuration $\mathcal{C}$ is slightly modified with respect to a standard OCaml configuration. It uses the additional constructs $\mathsf{call}(O[\widetilde{a}])$ and $\mathsf{call}(O[\_, \widetilde{a}])$ which are functional values and correspond to our generated closures for oracle O (the latter for oracles under replication, for which the first index is the first available index value; the former for oracles not under replication). The semantics of $\mathsf{call}(O[\widetilde{a}])\ (v_1, \ldots, v_k)$ is defined as follows. If the required oracle $O[\widetilde{a}]$ is not in $\mathcal{I}$, or the number of arguments of O is not k, or $v_1, \ldots, v_k$ are not values of the types expected by O, then it reduces into $\mathsf{raise\ Bad\_Call}$, as the OCaml translation of the oracle does. Otherwise it blocks; the oracle call succeeds but will be handled outside f by the process $Q_c(Q_0, pe_0)$ as we detail below. The semantics of $\mathsf{call}(O[\_, \widetilde{a}])$ is defined similarly. The semantics of random is modified so that random () blocks; the random number generation is handled outside f by the process $Q_c(Q_0, pe_0)$. The semantics of $\mathsf{addthread}$ is also modified so that it updates the sets of available roles and oracles $\mathcal{RI}$ and $\mathcal{I}$, and it replaces the program of generated modules μ_{role} from CryptoVerif code with:

$program'(role[\widetilde{a}]) = \mathsf{let}\ \mu_{role}.\mathsf{init} = \mathsf{let}\ token = \mathsf{ref\ true\ in\ tagfunction}\ pm'_{role[\widetilde{a}]}$
$pm'_{role[\widetilde{a}]} = () \rightarrow \mathsf{if}\ (!token)\ \mathsf{then}\ (token := \mathsf{false}; (\mathsf{call}(O_1[\widetilde{a}]), \ldots, \mathsf{call}(O_k[\widetilde{a}])))$
$\qquad\qquad\qquad \mathsf{else\ raise\ Bad\_Call}$

where $\widetilde{a}$ are the smallest replication indices such that $role[\widetilde{a}]$ is present in $\mathcal{RI}$, $O_1, \ldots, O_k$ are the oracles defined at the beginning of $Q(role)$, which are supposed not to be under replication. (When O_j is under replication, we use the form call($O_j[\_, \tilde{a}]$) instead of call($O_j[\tilde{a}]$).) All oracle calls are then performed using call rather than directly in OCaml.

Then $f(\text{repr}(\mathcal{CS}))$ is defined as follows. Let $\mathcal{CS}'$ be the configuration such that $\mathcal{CS} \rightarrow^* \mathcal{CS}'$ and $\forall \mathcal{CS}'', \mathcal{CS}' \not\rightarrow \mathcal{CS}''$, using the semantics outlined above.

- If $\mathcal{C}_{pe}(\mathcal{CS}') = \text{call}(O[\tilde{a}])\ (v_1, \ldots, v_l)$, let $T_1, \ldots, T_l$ be the type of the arguments of the oracle O and let o be the constant associated to O. We define

$$f(\text{repr}(\mathcal{CS})) = (\text{repr}(\mathcal{CS}'), o, \tilde{a}, (\mathbb{G}^{-1}_{\text{val}|_{T_1}}(v_1), \ldots, \mathbb{G}^{-1}_{\text{val}|_{T_l}}(v_l))).$$

The case $\mathcal{C}_{pe}(\mathcal{CS}') = \text{call}(O[\_, \tilde{a}])\ (v_1, \ldots, v_l)$ can be defined similarly, calling $O[a', \tilde{a}]$ when $O[[a', +\infty[, \tilde{a}]$ is in the component $\mathcal{I}$ of $\mathcal{CS}'$.
- If $\mathcal{C}_{pe}(\mathcal{CS}') = \text{random}\ ()$, we define $f(\text{repr}(\mathcal{CS})) = (\text{repr}(\mathcal{CS}'), o_R, (), ())$.
- Otherwise, we define $f(\text{repr}(\mathcal{CS})) = (\text{repr}(\mathcal{CS}'), o_S, (), ())$.

The function f can be implemented by a deterministic Turing machine (since the random choices are handled outside f), so it can be used as a CryptoVerif primitive.

When f returns $(\text{repr}(\mathcal{CS}'), o, \tilde{a}, (a_1, \ldots, a_l))$, the CryptoVerif process $Q_c(Q_0, pe_0)$ performs the corresponding oracle call $O[\tilde{a}](a_1, \ldots, a_l)$ (lines (4)–(6) of Fig. 3). Similarly, when f returns $(\text{repr}(\mathcal{CS}'), o_R, (), ())$, the process $Q_c(Q_0, pe_0)$ performs a random choice (lines (7)–(8)), and when f returns $(\text{repr}(\mathcal{CS}'), o_S, (), ())$, the process $Q_c(Q_0, pe_0)$ terminates (lines (2)–(3); the corresponding OCaml program also terminates).

The functions f'_O and f''_O replace, in the simulator configuration, the call expression by the result returned by the oracle, or raise the Match_failure exception, respectively. More formally,

- $f'_O(\text{repr}(\mathcal{C}, \mathcal{RI}, \mathcal{I}), (r_1, \ldots, r_n)) = \text{repr}(\mathcal{C}', \mathcal{RI}, \mathcal{I}')$ where the current program is $\mathcal{C}_{pe}(\mathcal{C}) = \text{call}(O[\tilde{a}])\ (v_1, \ldots, v_l)$, $T_1, \ldots, T_n$ are the types of the return value of O, the oracles defined after the return from O in Q_0 are $O_1, \ldots, O_k$, $\mathcal{C}'$ is the configuration $\mathcal{C}$ where the current expression is replaced with the translated result $(\text{call}(O_1[\tilde{a}]), \ldots, \text{call}(O_k[\tilde{a}]), \mathbb{G}_{\text{val}|_{T_1}}(r_1), \ldots, \mathbb{G}_{\text{val}|_{T_n}}(r_n))$, $\mathcal{I}' = \mathcal{I} \setminus \{O[\tilde{a}]\} \cup \{O_1[\tilde{a}], \ldots, O_k[\tilde{a}]\}$ is obtained from $\mathcal{I}$ by removing the called oracle $O[\tilde{a}]$ and adding the newly available oracles $O_1[\tilde{a}], \ldots, O_k[\tilde{a}]$. (For simplicity, the previous notations assume that the oracles $O, O_1, \ldots, O_k$ are not under replication; they can be easily adapted to situations in which these oracles are under replication. We also assumed that the return of oracle O does not terminate a role. When it terminates a role, the oracles $O_1, \ldots, O_k$ are not returned nor added to $\mathcal{I}$, but the roles that start after the return from O are added to $\mathcal{RI}$.)
- $f''_O(\text{repr}(\mathcal{C}, \mathcal{RI}, \mathcal{I})) = \text{repr}(\mathcal{C}', \mathcal{RI}, \mathcal{I} \setminus \{(O[\tilde{a}]\}))$ where $\mathcal{C}_{pe}(\mathcal{C}) = \text{call}(O[\tilde{a}])\ (v_1, \ldots, v_l)$ and $\mathcal{C}'$ is the configuration $\mathcal{C}$ in which the current expression is replaced with raise Match_failure. (The case $\mathcal{C}_{pe}(\mathcal{C}) = \text{call}(O[\_, \tilde{a}])\ (v_1, \ldots, v_l)$ can be defined similarly.)
- $f_R(\text{repr}(\mathcal{C}, \mathcal{RI}, \mathcal{I}), b) = \text{repr}(\mathcal{C}'(b), \mathcal{RI}, \mathcal{I})$ where $\mathcal{C}'(b)$ is the configuration $\mathcal{C}$ in which the current expression is replaced with $\mathbb{G}_{\text{val}|_{bool}}(b)$.

Finally, the initial state of the simulator is

$$s_0(Q_0, pe_0) = \mathsf{repr}(([\langle \emptyset, pe_0, [\,], \emptyset \rangle], global store_0, 1), \mathcal{RI}_0(Q_0), \emptyset)$$

where $\mathcal{RI}_0(Q_0)$ is the set of the initially callable roles of Q_0.

7   Correctness of the Simulation

This section proves the correctness of the simulator, by showing a precise relation between the state of the simulator and the state of the OCaml program. Basically, the OCaml configuration is obtained by replacing the call present in the simulator configuration with the corresponding closures. We show that the tables and files in the OCaml global store correspond to the CryptoVerif tables $\mathcal{T}$ and environment E, and that the OCaml events match the CryptoVerif events.

Definition 3 (Preliminary definitions). *Let us first define the set of oracles* $\mathcal{O}(\mathcal{I})$ *and* $\mathcal{O}(\mathcal{RI})$ *represented by* $\mathcal{I}$ *and* $\mathcal{RI}$ *respectively:*

$\mathcal{O}(\mathcal{I}) = \{O[b, \widetilde{a'}] \mid O[[a, +\infty[, \widetilde{a'}] \in \mathcal{I}, a \le b \le N_O\} \cup \{O[\widetilde{a}] \mid O[\widetilde{a}] \in \mathcal{I}\}$

$\mathcal{O}(\mathcal{RI}) = \{O[b, \widetilde{a}] \mid role[\widetilde{a}] \in \mathcal{RI}, O$ *defined under replication at the beginning of role in* $Q_0, 1 \le b \le N_O\}$
  $\cup \{O[\widetilde{a}] \mid role[\widetilde{a}] \in \mathcal{RI}, O$ *defined not under replication at the beginning of role in* $Q_0\}$
  $\cup \{O[b, \widetilde{a'}] \mid role[[a, +\infty[, \widetilde{a'}] \in \mathcal{RI}, O$ *defined at the beginning of role in* $Q_0, a \le b \le N_O\}$

We say that $\mathcal{I}$ *and* $\mathcal{RI}$ *represent the set of callable processes* $\mathcal{Q}$, *and we write* $\mathcal{Q} \leftrightarrow \mathcal{RI}, \mathcal{I}$, *when* $\mathcal{Q}$ *contains exactly one element* $O[\widetilde{a}](\widetilde{x}) := P$ *for each* $O[\widetilde{a}]$ *in* $\mathcal{O}(\mathcal{I}) \cup \mathcal{O}(\mathcal{RI})$. *In this case, we denote by* $\mathcal{Q}(O[\widetilde{a}])$ *this element of* $\mathcal{Q}$.

 Given a simulator thread $Th = \langle Env, pe, Stack, store \rangle$, $\mathcal{O}_{\mathsf{call}}(Th)$ *is the set of oracles* $O[\widetilde{a}]$ *not under replication such that* $\mathsf{call}(O[\widetilde{a}])$ *occurs in* Th *outside* tagfunction *functions or closures. Let* rolelist(Th) *be the set of roles* role$[\widetilde{a}]$ *such that* tagfunction$[Env, pm'_{role[\widetilde{a}]}]$ *occurs in thread* Th, *and the store of* Th *binds* $Env(token)$ *to true. Let* rolefunlist(Th) *be the set of roles* role$[\widetilde{a}]$ *such that* program$'(role[\widetilde{a}])$ *occurs in* Th.

 We also define $\mathcal{O}_{\mathsf{call}}(\mathcal{CS})$ *(resp.* rolelist$(\mathcal{CS})$, rolefunlist$(\mathcal{CS})$) *as the union of* $\mathcal{O}_{\mathsf{call}}(Th)$ *(resp.* rolelist(Th), rolefunlist(Th)) *for all threads present in* $\mathcal{CS}$.

 The set $\mathcal{O}_{\mathsf{willbeavailable}}(\mathcal{CS})$ *contains the set of oracles that can eventually become available in* $\mathcal{O}(\mathcal{I})$ *or* $\mathcal{O}(\mathcal{RI})$ *in a future configuration, and that are not available now. More precisely,* $\mathcal{O}_{\mathsf{willbeavailable}}(\mathcal{CS})$ *is the set of* $O'[\widetilde{a'}, \widetilde{a}]$ *such that there is an oracle* O *defined above* O' *in* Q_0 *such that* $O[\widetilde{a}] \in \mathcal{O}(\mathcal{I}) \cup \mathcal{O}(\mathcal{RI}) \cup \mathcal{O}(\mathsf{rolelist}(\mathcal{CS})) \cup \mathcal{O}(\mathsf{rolefunlist}(\mathcal{CS}))$.

 The function replaceinitpm *replaces everywhere in a simulator thread the pattern matchings corresponding to role initialization of the simulator by the OCaml module initialization for the given role. Formally,* replaceinitpm(Th) *replaces each occurrence of* $pm'_{role[\widetilde{a}]}$ *in* Th *with* pm_{role}.

Suppose that $\mathcal{Q} \leftrightarrow \mathcal{RI}, \mathcal{I}$, and l_{tok} is a function that associates to each oracle $O[\widetilde{a}]$ the location of its token. We define the set of closures that correspond to an oracle:

- $\mathsf{correctclosures}(O[\widetilde{a}], \mathcal{I}, E, \mathcal{Q}, l_{\mathsf{tok}}) = \{\mathsf{tagfunction}[Env, pm_{\mathsf{false}}(\mathcal{Q}(O[\widetilde{a}]))] \mid Env_{\mathsf{prim}} \cup Env(E, \mathcal{Q}(O[\widetilde{a}])) \subseteq Env, Env(token) = l_{\mathsf{tok}}(O[\widetilde{a}])\}$ *if* $O[\widetilde{a}] \in \mathcal{I}$;
- $\mathsf{correctclosures}(O[\widetilde{a}], \mathcal{I}, E, \mathcal{Q}, l_{\mathsf{tok}}) = \{\mathsf{tagfunction}[Env, pm_{\mathsf{false}}(Q)] \mid$ *for any* $Q, Env(token) = l_{\mathsf{tok}}(O[\widetilde{a}])\}$ *if* $O[\widetilde{a}] \notin \mathcal{I}$;
- $\mathsf{correctclosures}(O[\_, \widetilde{a}], \mathcal{I}, E, \mathcal{Q}, l_{\mathsf{tok}}) = \{\mathsf{tagfunction}[Env, pm_{\mathsf{true}}(\mathcal{Q}(O[a', \widetilde{a}]))] \mid Env_{\mathsf{prim}} \cup Env(E, \mathcal{Q}(O[a', \widetilde{a}])) \subset Env\}$ *if* $O\big[[a', +\infty[, \widetilde{a}\big] \in \mathcal{I}$;
- $\mathsf{correctclosures}(O[\_, \widetilde{a''}], \mathcal{I}, E, \mathcal{Q}, l_{\mathsf{tok}}) = \emptyset$ *if* $O\big[[a', +\infty[, \widetilde{a''}\big] \notin \mathcal{I}$.

The function $\mathsf{replacecalls}$ *replaces in its argument the calls* $\mathsf{call}(O[\widetilde{a}])$ *with closures that correspond to the oracle.*

$\mathsf{replacecalls}(\langle Env, pe, Stack, store \rangle, \mathcal{I}, E, \mathcal{Q}, l_{\mathsf{tok}}) = \{\langle Env', \sigma(pe), \sigma(Stack), store' \rangle \mid Env'$ *is any environment if pe is a value v or an exception* raise v, $Env' = \sigma(Env)$ *otherwise; store'* $\supseteq \sigma(store)$ *with σ a function that replaces each occurrence of a* $\mathsf{call}(R)$ *with an element of* $\mathsf{correctclosures}(R, \mathcal{I}, E, \mathcal{Q}, l_{\mathsf{tok}})\}$

The function $\mathsf{gettokens}$ *returns the store part corresponding to the tokens of the closures of oracles not under replication:*

$$\mathsf{gettokens}(\mathcal{I}, \mathcal{O}, l_{\mathsf{tok}}) = \{l_{\mathsf{tok}}(O[\widetilde{a}]) \mapsto \mathsf{true} \mid O[\widetilde{a}] \in \mathcal{O} \cap \mathcal{I}\}$$
$$\cup \{l_{\mathsf{tok}}(O[\widetilde{a}]) \mapsto \mathsf{false} \mid O[\widetilde{a}] \in \mathcal{O} \setminus \mathcal{I}\}$$

Definition 4 (Relation between CryptoVerif and OCaml states). *Let CS be a configuration of the simulator, $E, \mathcal{T}, \mathcal{Q}, \mathcal{E}$ be parts of a CryptoVerif configuration, and C be an OCaml configuration. We say that $CS, E, \mathcal{T}, \mathcal{Q}, \mathcal{E} \equiv C$ when the following properties are all true:*

1. $CS = ([Th_1, \ldots, Th_n], globalstore, i), \mathcal{RI}, \mathcal{I}$.
2. $C = [Th'_1, \ldots, Th'_n], globalstore', i, \mathcal{MI}, events$.
3. $\mathcal{Q} \leftrightarrow \mathcal{RI}, \mathcal{I}$.
4. *The environment E contains values for every free variable in the oracle definitions present in $\mathcal{Q}$.*
5. *There exists an injective function l_{tok} that associates to each oracle $O[\widetilde{a}]$ a store location that does not occur in CS such that*
   - $\forall i \leq n, Th'_i \in \mathsf{replacecalls}(\mathsf{replaceinitpm}(Th_i), \mathcal{I}, E, \mathcal{Q}, l_{\mathsf{tok}})$,
   - $\forall i \leq n, \mathsf{gettokens}(\mathcal{I}, \mathcal{O}_{\mathsf{call}}(Th_i), l_{\mathsf{tok}}) \subseteq store'_i$ *where $store'_i$ is the store part of Th'_i.*
6. *There exists an injective function l'_{tok} that associates to each role role$[\widetilde{a}]$ a store location such that for all i, for all closures* $\mathsf{tagfunction}[Env, pm'_{role[\widetilde{a}]}]$, *present in thread Th_i, $l'_{\mathsf{tok}}(role[\widetilde{a}]) = Env(token)$.*
7. $\forall l \in S_{priv}, globalstore(l) = [\,]$.
8. $G' \subseteq globalstore'$ *for some $G' \in globalstore(E, \mathcal{T})$.*
9. $\forall l \notin S_{priv}, globalstore(l) = globalstore'(l)$.

10. $\mathcal{MI} = \{(\mu_{role}, \text{false}) \mid role\,[\tilde{a}] \in \mathcal{RI}\} \cup \{(\mu_{role}, \text{true}) \mid role\,[[a', +\infty[, \tilde{a}] \in \mathcal{RI}\}$.
11. $events = \mathbb{G}_{\text{ev}}(\mathcal{E})$.
12. The sets $\mathcal{O}(\mathcal{I}) \cup \mathcal{O}_{\text{call}}(\mathcal{CS})$, $\mathcal{O}(\mathcal{RI})$ and $\mathcal{O}_{\text{willbeavailable}}(\mathcal{CS})$ are pairwise disjoint.
13. The $3n$ sets $\mathcal{O}_{\text{call}}(Th_i)$, $\mathcal{O}(\text{rolefunlist}(Th_i))$, and $\mathcal{O}(\text{rolelist}(Th_i))$ for $i \leq n$ are pairwise disjoint, and are all included in $\mathcal{O}(\mathcal{I}) \cup \mathcal{O}_{\text{call}}(\mathcal{CS})$.

Item 3 is an invariant on the CryptoVerif side: it relates the CryptoVerif available oracles in $\mathcal{Q}$ to elements of the simulator configuration. Item 4 is also an invariant of the CryptoVerif semantics.

Item 5 relates the threads of the simulator and of the OCaml semantics. Basically, the simulator uses call while OCaml uses the corresponding tagfunction. The tokens that determine whether oracles can be called are absent from the simulator: the value of these tokens is determined from $\mathcal{I}$ by the function gettokens, and we require that they are present in the OCaml store with their correct value.

Item 6 assures that all instances of a closure of a given role initialization $role\,[\tilde{a}]$ share the same store location for their tokens.

Items 7 to 9 relate the values of the global store in the simulator and in the OCaml semantics. The public part of the global store is the same on both sides (Item 9). The private part (files and tables) is empty in the simulator, since this part is handled by CryptoVerif itself (Item 7). We require that the private part of the OCaml global store corresponds to the CryptoVerif configuration (Item 8).

Item 10 relates the OCaml set of callable modules $\mathcal{MI}$ and the simulator set of callable roles $\mathcal{RI}$, and Item 11 relates the OCaml and CryptoVerif events.

Finally, Items 12 and 13 are required to keep the injections of Items 5 and 6.

Given a CryptoVerif configuration $\mathfrak{C}$, it is easy to recover the corresponding simulator configuration $\mathcal{CS}$. The next definition formalizes this point.

Definition 5 (Simulator configuration). Let $\mathfrak{C} = E, P, \mathcal{T}, \mathcal{Q}, \mathcal{R}, \mathcal{E}$ be a CryptoVerif configuration. If $E(r[])$ is defined (we are at the end of the loop), then $\mathcal{CS}(\mathfrak{C}) = \text{repr}^{-1}(E(r[]))$. Otherwise, if $E(s[\alpha])$ is defined and $E(s'[\alpha])$ is not defined (we are just before line (1) of Fig. 3 in iteration number α), then $\mathcal{CS}(\mathfrak{C}) = \text{repr}^{-1}(E(s[\alpha]))$. Otherwise, if $E(s'[\alpha])$ is defined and $E(s[\alpha+1])$ is not defined (we are after line (1) in iteration number α), then $\mathcal{CS}(\mathfrak{C}) = \text{repr}^{-1}(E(s'[\alpha]))$.

Definition 6 (Invariant). Let $\mathfrak{C} = E, P, \mathcal{T}, \mathcal{Q}, \mathcal{R}, \mathcal{E}$ be a CryptoVerif configuration and C be an OCaml configuration. We say that $\mathfrak{C} \equiv C$ if and only if $\mathcal{CS}(\mathfrak{C}), E, \mathcal{T}, \mathcal{Q}, \mathcal{E} \equiv C$.

We say that a CryptoVerif configuration $\mathfrak{C} = E, P, \mathcal{T}, \mathcal{Q}, \mathcal{R}, \mathcal{E}$ is at a *checkpoint* when the process P corresponds to the process at lines marked (1), (2), (4), (7) of Fig. 3 and the stack $\mathcal{R}$ contains one element or P is end and $\mathcal{R}$ is empty. The following lemma shows that the invariant of Definition 6 is preserved at checkpoints during execution.

Lemma 3. Let $\mathfrak{C}\mathfrak{T}_1, \ldots, \mathfrak{C}\mathfrak{T}_n$ be CryptoVerif traces starting at $\mathfrak{C}$, such that $\mathfrak{C}$ and the last configuration of these traces are at checkpoints, and there is no other checkpoint in these traces. Let C be an OCaml configuration such that $\mathfrak{C} \equiv C$.

Then there exist disjoint sets of OCaml traces $CTS_1, \ldots, CTS_n$ *all starting at* C *such that none of these traces is a prefix of another of these traces, for all* $i \leq n$, $\Pr[\mathfrak{CT}_i] = \Pr[CTS_i]$, *and if* $\mathfrak{C}'$ *is the last configuration of* $\mathfrak{CT}_i$ *and* C' *is the last configuration of a trace in* CTS_i, *then* $\mathfrak{C}' \equiv C'$. *Furthermore, if* $\mathfrak{C}'$ *cannot be reduced, then neither can* C'.

From this lemma, we can prove:

Proposition 1. *Let* $\mathfrak{CT}_1, \ldots, \mathfrak{CT}_n$ *be complete CryptoVerif traces starting at* $\mathfrak{C}_0(Q_0, pe_0)$. *Then there exist disjoint sets of complete OCaml traces* $CTS_1, \ldots,$ CTS_n *all starting at* $C_0(Q_0, pe_0)$ *such that for all* $i \leq n$, $\Pr[\mathfrak{CT}_i] = \Pr[CTS_i]$, *and if* $\mathfrak{C}$ *is the last configuration of* $\mathfrak{CT}_i$ *and* C *is the last configuration of a trace in* CTS_i, *then* $\mathfrak{C} \equiv C$.

8   Security Result

CryptoVerif security properties are defined using distinguishers D which are functions that take a list of events $\mathcal{E}$ and return true or false. We denote by $\Pr[\mathfrak{C} : D]$ the probability of the set of complete CryptoVerif traces starting at $\mathfrak{C}$ and such that the list of events $\mathcal{E}$ in their last configuration satisfies $D(\mathcal{E}) = \text{true}$. For instance, to show that a protocol Q_0 satisfies a correspondence of the form "for all a, if $e_1(a)$ has been executed, then $e_2(a)$ has also been executed", we define D by $D(\mathcal{E}) = \text{true}$ if and only if the correspondence does not hold, that is, $\mathcal{E}$ contains $e_1(a)$ but not $e_2(a)$ for some a. Then we bound the probability $\Pr[\mathfrak{C}_i(Q_0 \mid Q_{\text{adv}}) : D]$, that is, the probability that the adversary Q_{adv} breaks the correspondence in Q_0. We can also define secrecy using events and distinguishers [5]. We use a similar definition in OCaml: $\Pr[C : D]$ is the probability of the set of complete OCaml traces starting at C and such that the list of events *events* in their last configuration satisfies $D(\mathbb{G}_{\text{ev}}^{-1}(events)) = \text{true}$. Our main theorem is then:

Theorem 1 (Security result). $\Pr[\mathfrak{C}_0(Q_0, pe_0) : D] = \Pr[C_0(Q_0, pe_0) : D]$.

This theorem is easy to prove from Proposition 1, noticing that, when $\mathfrak{C} \equiv C$ and the events of $\mathfrak{C}$ are $\mathcal{E}$, the events of C are $\mathbb{G}_{\text{ev}}(\mathcal{E})$ (Definition 4, Item 11).

In other words, the adversary pe_0 against the OCaml program has the same probability of breaking the security property as the adversary $Q_{\text{adv}}(Q_0, pe_0)$ against the CryptoVerif process. If CryptoVerif bounds the probability $\Pr[\mathfrak{C}_0(Q_0, pe_0) : D]$, then the same bound also holds for the generated implementation.

As detailed in [7], CryptoVerif shows that our model of the SSH Transport Layer Protocol guarantees the authentication of the server to the client and the secrecy of the session keys. By Theorem 1, our generated implementation of this protocol satisfies the same properties, provided assumptions A1 to A6 hold.

9   Conclusion

We have proved that our compiler preserves security. Therefore, by using CryptoVerif, we can prove the desired security properties on the protocol specification, and then by using our compiler, we get a runnable implementation of the protocol, which satisfies the same security properties as the specification. Making such a proof is also useful because it clarifies the assumptions needed to ensure that the implementation is secure (Assumptions A1 to A6 in our case). The proof technique presented in this paper, simulating any adversary by a CryptoVerif process, is also useful to show that any Turing machine can be encoded as a CryptoVerif adversary, which is important for the validity of the verification by CryptoVerif. We have done the proof by hand. Formalizing it using a proof assistant (e.g. Coq) would be interesting future work.

Acknowledgments. This work was partly done while the authors were at École Normale Supérieure, Paris. It was partly supported by the ANR project ProSe (decision ANR 2010-VERS-004).

References

1. Aizatulin, M., Gordon, A.D., Jürjens, J.: Extracting and verifying cryptographic models from C protocol code by symbolic execution. In: CCS 2011, pp. 331–340. ACM, New York (2011)
2. Aizatulin, M., Gordon, A.D., Jürjens, J.: Computational verification of C protocol implementations by symbolic execution. In: CCS 2012, pp. 712–723. ACM, New York (2012)
3. Bhargavan, K., Fournet, C., Gordon, A., Tse, S.: Verified interoperable implementations of security protocols. ACM TOPLAS 31(1) (2008)
4. Blanchet, B.: A computationally sound mechanized prover for security protocols. IEEE Transactions on Dependable and Secure Computing 5(4), 193–207 (2008)
5. Blanchet, B.: Automatically verified mechanized proof of one-encryption key exchange. In: CSF 2012, pp. 325–339. IEEE, Los Alamitos (2012)
6. Cadé, D., Blanchet, B.: Proved generation of implementations from computationally secure protocol specifications,
   http://prosecco.gforge.inria.fr/personal/dcade/post2013full.pdf
7. Cadé, D., Blanchet, B.: From computationally-proved protocol specifications to implementations. In: ARES 2012, pp. 65–74. IEEE, Los Alamitos (2012)
8. Chaki, S., Datta, A.: ASPIER: An automated framework for verifying security protocol implementations. In: CSF 2009, pp. 172–185. IEEE, Los Alamitos (2009)
9. Dupressoir, F., Gordon, A.D., Jürjens, J., Naumann, D.A.: Guiding a general-purpose C verifier to prove cryptographic protocols. In: CSF 2011, pp. 3–17. IEEE, Los Alamitos (2011)
10. Fournet, C., Kohlweiss, M., Strub, P.Y.: Modular code-based cryptographic verification. In: CCS 2011, pp. 341–350. ACM, New York (2011)
11. http://msr-inria.inria.fr/projects/sec/fs2cv/
12. Milicia, G.: χ-spaces: Programming security protocols. In: NWPT 2002 (2002)
13. Owens, S.: A Sound Semantics for OCaml$_{light}$. In: Drossopoulou, S. (ed.) ESOP 2008. LNCS, vol. 4960, pp. 1–15. Springer, Heidelberg (2008)
14. Pironti, A., Sisto, R.: Provably correct Java implementations of spi calculus security protocols specifications. Computers and Security 29(3), 302–314 (2010)
15. Swamy, N., Chen, J., Fournet, C., Strub, P.Y., Bharagavan, K., Yang, J.: Secure distributed programming with value-dependent types. In: ICFP 2011, pp. 266–278. ACM, New York (2011)

Sound Security Protocol Transformations*

Binh Thanh Nguyen and Christoph Sprenger

Institute of Information Security, ETH Zurich, Switzerland
{thannguy,sprenger}@inf.ethz.ch

Abstract. We propose a class of protocol transformations, which can be used to (1) develop (families of) security protocols by refinement and (2) abstract existing protocols to increase the efficiency of verification tools. We prove the soundness of these transformations with respect to an expressive security property specification language covering secrecy and authentication properties. Our work clarifies and significantly extends the scope of earlier work in this area. We illustrate the usefulness of our approach on a family of key establishment protocols.

1 Introduction

It is well-known that security protocols are notoriously hard to get right. This motivates the use of formal methods for their design and development. The last decade has witnessed substantial progress in the formal verification of security protocols' properties such as secrecy and authentication. However, methods for transforming protocols have received much less attention.

Protocol transformations are interesting for at least two applications: we can use them (1) to develop (families of) protocols by refinement [17,9,16,7,6,4] and (2) to abstract existing protocols for the more efficient tool-based verification of their properties [11]. Abstraction and refinement correspond bottom-up and top-down views on (the same) protocol transformations. To be useful, protocol transformations must be sound with respect to a relevant class of security properties, i.e., refinement must be property-preserving, or equivalently, abstraction must be attack-preserving.

In this work, we propose a class of syntactic protocol transformations covering a wide range of protocols and security properties. Following Hui and Lowe [11], we support both message-based transformations, which we lift to protocol roles, and structural transformations, which directly operate on protocol roles. Message-based transformations include the removal of hashes or encryptions, pulling cleartext fields out of an encryption, and rearranging pair components. To guarantee the uniform transformation (e.g., removal) of variables and the messages they are supposed to receive, we work with typed messages. We use the type system of Arapinis and Duflot [2], which enables a fine-grained control over the message transformations. We establish the soundness of our typed

---

* This work is partially supported by the EU FP7-ICT-2009.1.4 Project No. 256980, NESSoS: Network of Excellence on Engineering Secure Future Internet Software Services and Systems.

D. Basin and J.C. Mitchell (Eds.): POST 2013, LNCS 7796, pp. 83–104, 2013.
© Springer-Verlag Berlin Heidelberg 2013

transformations with respect to an expressive property specification language based on [14].

We make the following contributions. First, our work provides a sound formal underpinning for protocol transformations, which can serve as a foundation for rigorous security protocol development by refinement as well as for the abstraction of existing protocols. As an example of the latter, our approach helps to improve the performance of security protocol verifiers that are sensitive to message sizes such as SATMC [3]. Second, we extend existing work with respect to the expressiveness of the protocol specifications, the protocol transformations, and the preserved properties. In particular, we extend [11] in several ways: (1) we clarify and formally justify the application of transformations to protocol specifications, which contain variables not only ground terms as in [11]; (2) we support composed keys under a mild restriction; (3) we cover additional transformations (e.g., splitting encryptions) including many of those in [5,7,6]; and (4) we extend soundness to a more expressive property language based on predicates expressing event occurrence and ordering, intruder knowledge, and including quantification over thread identifiers.

The full version of this paper [15] includes the proofs of all our results and the treatment of structural transformations.

A Motivating Example. We discuss the abstraction and refinement of key establishment protocols. We first take the abstraction view and defer a brief discussion of the refinement view to the end of this section. We start from a core version of Kerberos IV, called K4, which we simplify in several steps with the aim of optimizing the performance of verification tools. In Alice&Bob notation, the protocol K4 reads as follows.

K4(1). $A \rightarrow S : A, B, n_A$
K4(2). $S \rightarrow A : \{\!|B, t_S, n_A, k_{AB}, \{\!|A, t_S, k_{AB}\}\!|_{\mathsf{sh}(B,S)}\}\!|_{\mathsf{sh}(A,S)}$
K4(3). $A \rightarrow B : \{\!|A, t_S, k_{AB}\}\!|_{\mathsf{sh}(B,S)}, \{\!|c, t_A\}\!|_{k_{AB}}$
K4(4). $B \rightarrow A : \{\!|t_A\}\!|_{k_{AB}}$

The security properties we are interested in include: (P1) the secrecy of the session key k_{AB}, (P2) A authenticates S on k_{AB}, n_A, and t_S, and (P3) A and B authenticate each other on k_{AB} and t_A. To improve the performance of verification tools, we remove protocol elements that we deem unnecessary for a given property to hold and verify that property on the simplified protocol. If there is no attack then the soundness of our abstractions allows us to conclude that the original protocol also satisfies the property.

In the first abstraction step, we pull B's ticket out of the encryption in message K4(2). The result is the core of Kerberos V, called K5, which differs from K4 as follows.

K5(2). $S \rightarrow A : \{\!|B, t_S, n_A, k_{AB}\}\!|_{\mathsf{sh}(A,S)}, \{\!|A, t_S, k_{AB}\}\!|_{\mathsf{sh}(B,S)}$

In the second step, we eliminate the forwarding of B's ticket by A by applying structural transformations. This yields protocol K3, on which we verify mutual authentication of A and B (P3). We omit the message K3(1) which equals K5(1).

K3(2). $S \to A : \{\!|B, t_S, n_A, k_{AB}|\!\}_{\mathsf{sh}(A,S)}$
K3(3). $S \to B : \{\!|A, t_S, k_{AB}|\!\}_{\mathsf{sh}(B,S)}$
K3(4). $A \to B : \{\!|c, t_A|\!\}_{k_{AB}}$
K3(5). $B \to A : \{\!|t_A|\!\}_{k_{AB}}$

In the third step, we remove the key confirmation phase, i.e., messages K3(4) and K3(5). For the resulting protocol, K2, which we omit here, we verify the authentication property (P2).

In a final transformation, we remove the server timestamp t_S and the initiator nonce n_A. The result is protocol K1 for which we verify secrecy (P1).

K1(1). $A \to S : A, B$
K1(2). $S \to A : \{\!|B, k_{AB}|\!\}_{\mathsf{sh}(A,S)}$
K1(3). $S \to B : \{\!|A, k_{AB}|\!\}_{\mathsf{sh}(B,S)}$

The protocols and transformations above will serve as running examples throughout the paper. We will report on experiments with SATMC in Section 4.

We can also view these transformations in the other direction, as a development of K4 by refinement. We start from the abstract protocol K1 satisfying session key secrecy (P1) and add new properties or modify the protocol structure with each refinement step. We verify properties (P2) and (P3) for K2 and K3, respectively, knowing that they are preserved by further refinements. By refining given protocols in different ways, we can develop entire protocol families, whose members share structure and properties. For example, most server-based key establishment protocols can be derived from K1.

2 Security Protocol Model

2.1 Term Algebra

We define a generic set of terms $\mathcal{T}(V, U, F, C)$ parametrized by four sets V, U, F, and C. We will instantiate these parameters to generate different sets of terms including those in protocol descriptions, network messages, and types, i.e., V to variables, U to roles or agents, F to fresh values, and C to constants, as well as to their associated types.

$\mathcal{T} ::= V$	variables
$\mid U \mid F \mid C$	atoms: agents/roles, fresh values, constants
$\mid \mathsf{pk}(U) \mid \mathsf{pri}(U) \mid \mathsf{sh}(U,U)$	atoms: long-term keys (public, private, shared)
$\mid \mathsf{h}(\mathcal{T}) \mid \langle \mathcal{T}, \mathcal{T} \rangle \mid \{\!|\mathcal{T}|\!\}_{\mathcal{T}}$	composed terms: hashing, pairing, encryption

We use $\mathcal{T}$ as a shorthand for $\mathcal{T}(V, U, F, C)$ in the generic case where the concrete parameters do not matter. We denote by $|t|$ the size of a term t. The set $St(t)$ denotes the set of subterms of t. For $T \subseteq \mathcal{T}$, $vars(T)$ and $atoms(T)$ denote the sets of variables and atoms in $St(T)$. A term without variables is called *ground*.

The terms $\mathsf{pk}(A)$, $\mathsf{pri}(A)$, and $\mathsf{sh}(A,B)$ for $A, B \in U$ denote the public key of A, the private key of A, and a symmetric key shared by A and B. We define the function $(\cdot)^{-1}$ on ground terms t as follows: $\mathsf{pk}(A)^{-1} = \mathsf{pri}(A)$, $\mathsf{pri}(A)^{-1} = \mathsf{pk}(A)$, and $t^{-1} = t$ otherwise. Next, we define a number of functions on terms in $\mathcal{T}$.

A multiset m over a set S is a function $m: S \to \mathbb{N}$, where $m(x)$ denotes the multiplicity of x in m. The relations $\sqcap, \sqcup, \sqsubseteq$ denote multiset intersection, union, and inclusion, respectively, and $set(m) = \{x \in S \mid m(x) > 0\}$.

Definition 1. *We define the* pair splitting function *on terms as follows.*

$$split(u) = \{u\} \qquad\qquad \text{if } u \text{ is not a pair}$$
$$split(\langle u_1, u_2 \rangle) = split(u_1) \sqcup split(u_2)$$

We also define $split(U) = \bigsqcup_{u \in U} split(u)$ for a set U of terms.

Definition 2. *We define the set $acc(t)$ of* accessible subterms *of a term t by*

$$acc(u) = \{u\} \qquad\qquad \text{if } u \text{ is a variable, atom, or hash}$$
$$acc(\langle u_1, u_2 \rangle) = acc(u_1) \cup acc(u_2)$$
$$acc(\{\!|u|\!\}_k) = acc(u)$$

2.2   Protocols

Let $\mathcal{V}$, $\mathcal{R}$, $\mathcal{F}$, and $\mathcal{C}$ be infinite and pairwise disjoint sets of variables, role names, fresh names, and constants. We define the set of *messages* by $\mathcal{M} = \mathcal{T}(\mathcal{V}, \mathcal{R}, \mathcal{F}, \mathcal{C})$.

We specify protocols in terms of roles. A *role* is a sequence of send and receive events of the form $\mathsf{snd}(t)$ or $\mathsf{rcv}(t)$ for a term $t \in \mathcal{M}$. We denote the set of all events by *Event*. We write $term(e)$ for the term contained in the event e. Let $mgu(t, u)$ denote the most general unifier of the terms t and u.

Definition 3 (Protocol). *A protocol* role *is a sequence of events. We define* $Role = Event^*$. *A protocol $P : \mathcal{R} \rightharpoonup Role$ is a partial function from role names to roles such that*

1. *the sets of variables and fresh values in different roles are pairwise disjoint,*
2. *variables first occur in accessible positions of receive events, i.e., for all events e in a role $P(R)$ and all variables $X \in vars(term(e))$ there is an event $\mathsf{rcv}(t)$ in $P(R)$ such that $\mathsf{rcv}(t)$ equals or precedes e in $P(R)$ and $X \in acc(t)$.*
3. *the events in P's roles can be exhaustively enumerated in a list of pairs of send and receive events $[(s_1, r_1), \ldots, (s_m, r_m)]$. We require that, for each $i \in \{1, \ldots, m\}$, there exist a substitution δ_i such that*
   - $\delta_1 = mgu(term(s_1), term(r_1))$, *and, for $1 < k \leq m$,*
   - $\delta_k = mgu(term(s_k)(\delta_{k-1} \circ \cdots \circ \delta_1), term(r_k)(\delta_{k-1} \circ \cdots \circ \delta_1))$.
   We define $\delta_P = \delta_m \circ \ldots \circ \delta_1$ and call it the honest substitution *of P.*

The second condition of this definition ensures that δ_P is a ground substitution.

Given a protocol P, let $\mathcal{V}_P$, $\mathcal{R}_P$, $\mathcal{F}_P$, and $\mathcal{C}_P$ be the sets of variables, role names, fresh values, and constants appearing in the roles of P (i.e., $\mathcal{R}_P = dom(P)$). We assume a constant $\mathsf{nil} \in \mathcal{C} \setminus \mathcal{C}_P$ and define $\mathcal{C}_P^{\mathsf{nil}} = \mathcal{C}_P \cup \{\mathsf{nil}\}$. We denote by $Event_P$ the set of all events in the protocol P and $Rt_P = term(Event_P)$. Moreover, we define the set of protocol messages (over the atomic messages of the protocol P) by $\mathcal{M}_P = \mathcal{T}(\mathcal{V}_P, \mathcal{R}_P, \mathcal{F}_P, \mathcal{C}_P^{\mathsf{nil}})$.

$$\frac{u \in T}{T \vdash u} \ \text{Axiom} \qquad \frac{T \vdash t \quad T \vdash u}{T \vdash \langle t, u \rangle} \ \text{Pair} \qquad \frac{T \vdash \langle t_1, t_2 \rangle}{T \vdash t_i} \ \text{Proj}_i$$

$$\frac{T \vdash u}{T \vdash \mathsf{h}(u)} \ \text{Hash} \qquad \frac{T \vdash t \quad T \vdash u}{T \vdash \{\!|t|\!\}_u} \ \text{Enc} \qquad \frac{T \vdash \{\!|t|\!\}_u \quad T \vdash u^{-1}}{T \vdash t} \ \text{Dec}$$

Fig. 1. Intruder deduction rules

2.3 Attacker Model and Operational Semantics

Let $\mathcal{A}$ and *TID* be infinite sets of agents and thread identifiers. We partition $\mathcal{A}$ into non-empty sets of honest and compromised agents: $\mathcal{A} = \mathcal{A}_H \cup \mathcal{A}_C$.

When we instantiate a role into a thread for execution, we mark variables, role names, and fresh values of the respective role script with the thread identifier to distinguish them from those of other threads. Given a thread identifier $tid \in$ *TID*, we define the instantiation function $inst_{tid}$ as the homomorphic extension of the following definition to all messages:

$$
\begin{aligned}
inst_{tid}(w) &= w^{tid} && \text{if } w \in \mathcal{V} \cup \mathcal{F} \cup \mathcal{R} \\
inst_{tid}(c) &= c && \text{if } c \in \mathcal{C} \\
inst_{tid}(k(R)) &= k(R^{tid}) && \text{if } R \in \mathcal{R}, k \in \{\mathsf{pk}, \mathsf{pri}\} \\
inst_{tid}(\mathsf{sh}(R, S)) &= \mathsf{sh}(R^{tid}, S^{tid}) && \text{if } R, S \in \mathcal{R}
\end{aligned}
$$

We define by $T^{\sharp} = \{inst_i(t) \mid t \in T \wedge i \in \textit{TID}\}$ the set of instantiations of terms in a set T. Hence, the set of *instantiated messages* of protocol P is $\mathcal{M}_P^{\sharp}$. We lift this to sets of events by instantiating the terms they contain, e.g., to define $Event_P^{\sharp}$. We also define the set of *network messages*, i.e., the ground messages transmitted over the network, by $\mathcal{N}_P = \mathcal{T}(\emptyset, \mathcal{A}, \mathcal{F}_P^{\sharp} \cup \mathcal{F}_P^{\bullet}, \mathcal{C}_P^{\mathsf{nil}})$, where $F^{\bullet} = \{f^{\bullet} \mid f \in F\}$ for $F \subseteq \mathcal{F}$ are attacker-generated fresh values. Furthermore, we abbreviate $\mathcal{M}_P^{\square} = \mathcal{M}_P \cup \mathcal{M}_P^{\sharp} \cup \mathcal{N}_P$.

Attacker model. We use a standard Dolev-Yao attacker model. The intruder's capabilities for network messages are described by the deduction rules in Figure 1.

Operational semantics. We define a transition system with states (tr, th, σ), where

- tr is a trace consisting of a sequence of pairs of thread identifiers and events,
- $th : \textit{TID} \rightharpoonup \mathcal{R} \times \textit{Role}$ is a thread pool denoting executing role instances, and
- $\sigma : \mathcal{V}^{\sharp} \cup \mathcal{R}^{\sharp} \to \mathcal{N}_P$ is a substitution with network messages as its range.

The trace tr as well as the executing role instance are symbolic (with terms in $\mathcal{M}_P^{\sharp}$). The separate substitution σ instantiates these messages to (ground) network messages. The ground trace associated with such a state is $tr\sigma$.

We define the (symbolic) intruder knowledge $IK(tr)$ derived from a trace tr as the set of terms in the send events on tr, i.e., $IK(tr) = \{t \mid \exists i. \, (i, \mathsf{snd}(t)) \in tr\}$.

$$\frac{th(i) = (R, \mathsf{snd}(t) \cdot tl)}{(tr, th, \sigma) \to (tr \cdot (i, \mathsf{snd}(t)), th[i \mapsto (R, tl)], \sigma)} \; SEND$$

$$\frac{th(i) = (R, \mathsf{rcv}(t) \cdot tl) \quad IK(tr)\sigma \cup IK_0 \vdash t\sigma}{(tr, th, \sigma) \to (tr \cdot (i, \mathsf{rcv}(t)), th[i \mapsto (R, tl)], \sigma)} \; RECV$$

Fig. 2. Operational semantics

We associate with each protocol P a fixed ground initial knowledge IK_0 and assume that $\mathcal{C} \cup \mathcal{A} \cup \mathcal{F}^\bullet \subseteq IK_0$. In particular, nil $\in IK_0$.

In our model, the substitution σ is chosen non-deterministically in the initial state. The set of initial states $Init_P$ of protocol P contains all (ϵ, th, σ) satisfying

$$\forall i \in dom(th). \; \exists R \in \mathcal{R}_P. \; th(i) = (R, inst_i(P(R))) \wedge \sigma(\mathcal{R}^\sharp) \subseteq \mathcal{A},$$

where $inst_i$ is applied to all terms in the respective protocol role.

The state transitions are defined by the rules in Figure 2. In both the $SEND$ and $RECV$ rules, the first premise states that a send or receive event is in the first position of the role script of thread i. The executed event is removed from the role script and added together with the thread identifier to the trace tr. Transitions do not change the substitution σ, which is fixed in the initial state. The second premise of the $RECV$ rule requires that the network message $t\sigma$ matching the term t in the receive event is derivable from $IK(tr)\sigma \cup IK_0$, i.e., the intruder's (ground) knowledge derived from tr and his initial knowledge IK_0.

2.4   Type System

We introduce a type system that extends Arapinis and Duflot's [2] with type variables, but is equivalent to theirs for ground types. In this type system, all roles and agent names have the same type α and similarly with each kind of long-term key (e.g., $\mathsf{pk}(\alpha)$ is the type of public keys). Each fresh value $f \in \mathcal{F}$ and constant $c \in \mathcal{C}$ has its own type: β_f and γ_c. This enables a fine-grained control in our message transformations. The types of composed terms follow the structure of the terms.

Let $\mathcal{V}_{ty}$ be an infinite set of type variables disjoint from $\mathcal{V}$. We define the set of types by $\mathcal{Y} = \mathcal{T}(\mathcal{V}_{ty}, \{\alpha\}, \{\beta_f \mid f \in \mathcal{F}\}, \{\gamma_c \mid c \in \mathcal{C}\})$. A *typing environment* is a partial function $\Gamma : \mathcal{V} \rightharpoonup \mathcal{Y}$ assigning types to (message) variables. Typing judgements are of the form $\Gamma \vdash t : \tau$, where Γ is a typing environment, t is a term, and τ is a type. The derivable typing judgements are determined by the inference rules in Figure 3. The first row displays the rules for variables, fresh values, and constants. The first two rules assign the types given by the typing environment to plain and instantiated variables. The last three rules in the first row give a type to each fresh value or constant. In the second row, the

$$\frac{(X,\tau) \in \Gamma}{\Gamma \vdash X : \tau} \qquad \frac{(X,\tau) \in \Gamma \quad i \in TID}{\Gamma \vdash X^i : \tau} \qquad \frac{f \in \mathcal{F}}{\Gamma \vdash f : \beta_f} \qquad \frac{f^\ell \in \mathcal{F}^\sharp \cup \mathcal{F}^\bullet}{\Gamma \vdash f^\ell : \beta_f} \qquad \frac{c \in \mathcal{C}}{\Gamma \vdash c : \gamma_c}$$

$$\frac{U \in \mathcal{R} \cup \mathcal{R}^\sharp \cup \mathcal{A}}{\Gamma \vdash U : \alpha} \qquad \frac{U \in \mathcal{R} \cup \mathcal{R}^\sharp \cup \mathcal{A}}{\Gamma \vdash \mathsf{pk}(U) : \mathsf{pk}(\alpha)} \qquad \frac{U \in \mathcal{R} \cup \mathcal{R}^\sharp \cup \mathcal{A}}{\Gamma \vdash \mathsf{pri}(U) : \mathsf{pri}(\alpha)} \qquad \frac{U, V \in \mathcal{R} \cup \mathcal{R}^\sharp \cup \mathcal{A}}{\Gamma \vdash \mathsf{sh}(U,V) : \mathsf{sh}(\alpha,\alpha)}$$

$$\frac{\Gamma \vdash t : \tau}{\Gamma \vdash h(t) : h(\tau)} \qquad \frac{\Gamma \vdash t_1 : \tau_1 \quad \Gamma \vdash t_2 : \tau_2}{\Gamma \vdash \langle t_1, t_2 \rangle : \langle \tau_1, \tau_2 \rangle} \qquad \frac{\Gamma \vdash t_1 : \tau_1 \quad \Gamma \vdash t_2 : \tau_2}{\Gamma \vdash \{\!|t_1|\!\}_{t_2} : \{\!|\tau_1|\!\}_{\tau_2}}$$

Fig. 3. Type system

first rule assigns the agent type α to role names and agents and the remaining rules assign types to long-term keys. The third row shows the typing rules for composed terms, i.e., hashes, pairs, and encryptions.

The abbreviation $\mathcal{Y}_P = \mathcal{T}(\mathcal{V}_{ty}, \{\alpha\}, \{\beta_f \mid f \in \mathcal{F}_P\}, \{\gamma_c \mid c \in \mathcal{C}_P^{\mathrm{nil}}\})$, defines the set of types of a protocol P. We derive the canonical typing environment $\Gamma_P : \mathcal{V}_P \rightharpoonup \mathcal{Y}_P$ for the protocol P from the honest substitution δ_P as $\Gamma_P = \{(X,\tau) \mid X \in dom(\delta_P) \wedge \emptyset \vdash X\delta_P : \tau\}$. Note that Γ_P ranges over ground types.

Proposition 1 (Type inference). *Let P be a protocol and $t \in \mathcal{M}_P^\square$. Then there is unique ground type $\tau \in \mathcal{Y}_P$ such that $\Gamma_P \vdash t : \tau$.*

By this proposition, we can extend Γ_P to all terms $t \in \mathcal{M}_P^\square$, i.e., we have $\Gamma_P(t) = \tau$ if and only if $\Gamma_P \vdash t : \tau$. We say that a substitution is well-typed if the terms in its range respect the types of the variables in its domain.

Definition 4 (Well-typed substitutions). *A substitution θ is well-typed with respect to a typing environment Γ iff $\Gamma \vdash X : \tau$ implies that $\Gamma \vdash X\theta : \tau$ for all $X \in dom(\theta)$.*

In this paper, we assume that it is sufficient to consider attacks with well-typed substitutions. There are multiple ways to achieve this. For example, tagging can be used in protocols that can fully decrypt all messages, in which case tag checking is sufficient to prevent all ill-typed attacks. Alternatively, we can use a result along the lines of [10,12,2,1] stating that there is a well-typed attack for any ill-typed one under certain conditions (e.g., sufficient tagging or well-formedness, which prevents the confusion of ciphertexts with different types).

3 Protocol Transformations

Following Hui and Lowe [11], we distinguish two kinds of protocol transformations: *message-based* and *structural* transformations. Message-based transformations are functions on protocol messages, which we lift to events and protocol roles. In contrast, structural transformations apply directly to protocol roles.

We cover essentially the same structural transformations for splitting and relaying as [11]. The splitting transformation splits selected events with pairs into two events and the relaying transformation removes a rcv(X) and a subsequent snd(X) event from a protocol role. In Section 1, they together justify the step from protocol K5 to K3. The other abstractions, from K4 to K5, from K3 to K2, and from K2 to K1 are obtained by message-based transformations. Here, we mainly focus on message-based protocol transformations. However, structural transformations are discussed in the full version of this paper [15].

In Section 3.1, we introduce a class of message transformations, which includes the following operations on messages: (1) remove encryptions and hashes, (2) remove fields from an encrypted message, (3) pull fields outside of an encryption, (4) split encryption into several ones, and (5) project and reorder pairs.

Consider a logical language $\mathcal{L}$ to express security properties. We will define such a language in Section 4. We want to achieve three main properties for our transformations f (both message-based and structural) and formulas ϕ.

Well-definedness. If P is a protocol then so is $f(P)$, i.e., the three conditions of Definition 3 are preserved by f.

Simulation. f preserves reachability, i.e., if the state (tr, th, σ) is reachable in P then the transformed state $(f(tr), f(th), f(\sigma))$ is reachable in $f(P)$.[1]

Attack preservation. For a state (tr, th, σ) reachable in P such that $(tr, th, \sigma) \not\models \phi$ we have $(f(tr), f(th), f(\sigma)) \not\models f(\phi)$.

The proofs of these three properties hinge on two more basic properties: the preservation of unifiers and of message deducibility. Unifier preservation is needed for well-definedness (the existence of an honest substitution) and attack preservation (for message equalities). Formally, this is expressed as follows.

$$t\theta = u\theta \implies f(t)f(\theta) = f(u)f(\theta) \tag{1}$$

Deducibility preservation is required for the simulation of receive events (see second premise of $RECV$ rule) and attack preservation (for formulas expressing the intruder's knowledge). Formally, this property is stated as follows.

$$T\theta \cup IK_0 \vdash u\theta \implies f(T)f(\theta) \cup f(IK_0) \vdash f(u)f(\theta) \tag{2}$$

We further reduce the properties (1) and (2) to two simpler properties. First, we show in Section 3.2 deducibility preservation for ground terms: $T \vdash u$ implies $f(T) \vdash f(u)$ if all terms in $T \cup \{u\}$ are ground and the set T satisfies an additional mild condition. Second, we establish the substitution property:

$$f(t\theta) = f(t)f(\theta). \tag{3}$$

This property (as well as (1) and (2)) does not hold for all transformations. The problem stems from the application of f to terms with variables: a term t and its instantiation $t\theta$ may be transformed in different ways (see Example 1 below).

---

[1] For now, you can read $f(\theta)$ as the composed substitution $f \circ \theta$.

We solve this problem by typing variables and restricting θ to well-typed substitutions. In Section 3.3, we thus introduce a restricted class of type-based message transformations, where a message's type uniquely determines how it is transformed. We use the type system from Section 2.4, which enables a fine-grained control over the transformations. In Section 3.4, we show that the substitution property (3) holds for type-based transformations f and well-typed substitutions. Then we lift these transformations to protocols and establish well-definedness and the simulation property. Section 4 treats attack preservation.

3.1 Message Transformations

We now introduce a class of message-based transformations. In these transformations, the constant nil plays a special role for the removal of (sub)terms. We remove variables and atoms by mapping them to nil and we rely on the following normalization function to remove the resulting nil-subterms and eliminate trivial encryptions (with key nil).

Definition 5 (Normalization).

$$
\begin{aligned}
nf(t) &= t \qquad \textit{if } t \textit{ is a variable or an atom} \\
nf(h(t)) &= \text{if } nf(t) = \text{nil then nil else } h(nf(t)) \\
nf(\langle t_1, t_2 \rangle) &= \text{if } nf(t_1) = \text{nil then } nf(t_2) \\
&\quad \text{else if } nf(t_2) = \text{nil then } nf(t_1) \\
&\quad \text{else } \langle nf(t_1), nf(t_2) \rangle \\
nf(\{\!|t|\!\}_u) &= \text{if } nf(t) = \text{nil then nil} \\
&\quad \text{else if } nf(u) = \text{nil then } nf(t) \\
&\quad \text{else } \{\!|nf(t)|\!\}_{nf(u)}
\end{aligned}
$$

We say that a term t is in normal form *iff $nf(t) = t$.*

Note that nil can only occur in a normal-form term t if t equals nil. We now formally define message transformations.

Definition 6 (Message transformation). *A function $f : \mathcal{T} \to \mathcal{T}$ is a message transformation on $\mathcal{T}$ if the following conditions hold:*

1. *for all non-normal form terms $t \in \mathcal{T}$, $f(t) = f(nf(t))$,*
2. *if $t \in nf(\mathcal{T})$ is a variable or an atom, then $f(t) = t$ or $f(t) = \text{nil}$. Moreover, if t is an asymmetric key then $f(t) = \text{nil}$ if and only if $f(t^{-1}) = \text{nil}$.*
3. *if $h(u) \in nf(\mathcal{T})$, then $f(h(u)) \in \{nf(h^a(f(u))) \mid a \geq 0\} \cup \{\text{nil}\}$.*
4. *if $\langle u_1, u_2 \rangle \in nf(\mathcal{T})$, then $f(\langle u_1, u_2 \rangle) = nf(\langle f(t_1), \ldots, f(t_n) \rangle)$ for some terms t_i, $1 \leq i \leq n$, such that $\mathcal{P}(\langle u_1, u_2 \rangle, \langle t_1, \ldots, t_n \rangle)$ and $|t_i| < |\langle u_1, u_2 \rangle|$.*
5. *if $\{\!|u|\!\}_k \in nf(\mathcal{T})$, then for some t_i, $1 \leq i \leq n$ s.t. $\mathcal{P}(u, \langle t_1, \ldots, t_n \rangle)$, $|t_i| \leq |u|$, $a_i \geq 0$, and $b \geq 0$, $f(\{\!|u|\!\}_k) = nf(\{\!|\langle \{\!|f(t_1)|\!\}_{f(k)^{a_1}}, \ldots, \{\!|f(t_n)|\!\}_{f(k)^{a_n}} \rangle|\!\}_{f(k)^b})$.*

where $\mathcal{P}(u, t) = split(t) \sqsubseteq split(u) \wedge set(split(t)) = set(split(u))$ and $\{\!|m|\!\}_{k^a}$ denotes the a-fold encryption of message m with the key k.

Condition 1 ensures that we only transform normal-form terms. Conditions 2-5 put restrictions on the transformation of the different kinds of messages. Note that we normalize the result of each transformation step. By Condition 2 we can either remove variables and atoms or keep them unchanged. Moreover, an asymmetric key and its inverse must be both removed or kept. This is necessary to achieve that f respects key inversion, i.e., $f(t^{-1}) = f(t)^{-1}$ for all terms t. We need this property to prove deducibility preservation. Condition 3 enables two types of transformations for hashes: we can (a) add or remove hash function applications or (b) map it to nil (i.e., remove it completely).

Condition 4 allows us to arbitrarily rearrange the components of a pair provided that (a) every component of $\langle t_1, \ldots, t_n \rangle$ is also in $\langle u_1, u_2 \rangle$ but possibly with a smaller number of occurrences (expressed using $\mathcal{P}$) and (b) each term t_i is smaller than the pair $\langle u_1, u_2 \rangle$. This ensures the well-foundedness of our definition and enables inductive proofs on term sizes. Similarly, Condition 5 describes the transformation of encryptions by splitting its plaintext into an arbitrary number of smaller terms t_i (compared to the size of the plaintext). The terms $f(t_i)$ may be encrypted zero or more times with $f(k)$. This enables splitting and selective removal of encryptions.

3.2   Deducibility Preservation

As mentioned above, our proof of deducibility preservation requires that f respects key inversion. However, the conditions discussed above are not sufficient. For instance, we may have $f(\mathsf{h}(\mathsf{pk}(a))) = \mathsf{pk}(a)$ and therefore $f(\mathsf{h}(\mathsf{pk}(a))^{-1}) = \mathsf{pk}(a) \neq \mathsf{pri}(a) = f(\mathsf{h}(\mathsf{pk}(a)))^{-1}$. This shows that we must restrict the transformation of arbitrary terms into asymmetric keys. Therefore, we now introduce the notion of simple terms and we show that message transformations respect key inversion on simple ground terms.

Definition 7 (Simple terms and simple-keyed term sets). *A ground term $t \in \mathcal{T}$ is simple if it is an atom or it contains asymmetric keys only in key positions of encryptions. A set of ground terms T is simple-keyed if k is simple for all $\{\!|u|\!\}_k \in St(T)$.*

Lemma 1. *Let $f \colon \mathcal{T} \to \mathcal{T}$ be a message transformation and $t \in \mathcal{T}$ be a simple ground term. Then f respects key inversion, i.e., $f(t^{-1}) = f(t)^{-1}$.*

Using this lemma, we establish deducibility preservation for simple-keyed sets of network messages.

Theorem 1 (Deducibility preservation). *Let f be a message transformation on $\mathcal{N}_P$, $T \subseteq \mathcal{N}_P$ be a simple-keyed set of network messages and let $u \in \mathcal{N}_P$. Then $T \vdash u$ implies $f(T) \cup \{\mathsf{nil}\} \vdash f(u)$.*

We next present a more syntactic, type-based definition of message transformations for which the substitution property holds.

3.3   Type-Based Protocol Transformations

We want to extend our message transformations to protocols. However, a simple lifting from messages to events, roles, and protocols will not work, since protocol roles contain variables and we cannot guarantee that a pair of matching send and receive events still matches after the transformation. Technically, this problem manifests itself as a failure of the substitution property (3) and unifier preservation (1) for some message transformations. Before giving an example, we extend message transformations to substitutions.

Definition 8. $f: \mathcal{T} \to \mathcal{T}$ be a message transformation on $\mathcal{T}$ and $\theta : \mathcal{V} \rightharpoonup \mathcal{T}$. Then we define the substitution $f(\theta) = \{(x, f(\theta(x))) \mid x \in dom(\theta) \land f(x) = x\}$.

Note that $dom(f(\theta)) \subseteq dom(\theta)$ as f may map some variables in $dom(\theta)$ to nil.

Example 1. Let X be a variable and θ a ground substitution such that $f(X) =$ nil. For the substitution property to hold for X and θ, i.e., $f(X)f(\theta) = f(X\theta)$, we need $f(X\theta) =$ nil. Since θ is arbitrary so is $\theta(X)$. Hence, f would have to map all terms to nil, thus reducing f to a trivial transformation. Similarly, $f(X)$ and $f(X\theta)$ are unifiable only if $f(X\theta) =$ nil. Hence, unifier preservation also fails.

In order to solve this problem we introduce type-based message transformations and restrict our attention to well-typed substitutions. Intuitively, in the typed setting, we can ensure that (1) a term and its (well-typed) instances have the same type and (2) all terms with the same type are transformed in a uniform way. We will guarantee this by having the type of a term alone determine how the term is transformed. This excludes situations like in Example 1 and enables us to establish the substitution property for well-typed substitutions (Section 3.4). Moreover, since the terms in matching send and receive events will have the same type, the typing ensures that the transformed events also match. This enables the lifting of type-based transformations to protocols.

The type system from Section 2.4 is well-suited for our purposes because it gives us a fine-grained control over the transformation of messages. More precisely, since each fresh value and constant has a different type, we can transform messages of similar shapes, but with different types in different ways. For example, we can remove the nonce n_A from $\langle A, n_A \rangle$, while $\langle A, n_B \rangle$ remains unchanged.

Specifying Type-Based Transformations In order to guarantee the uniform transformation of messages with the same type, our definition of type-based message transformations consists of two parts. The first part determines which terms are mapped to nil and therefore removed. It is specified as a set of types. The second part determines how composed messages are transformed and is specified using pattern matching on terms and types. In both cases, we have to ensure that it is only the type of a term, which determines how it is transformed. We define the semantics of these transformations as a functional program.

To avoid the need to introduce fresh variables in transformations, we now restrict our attention to protocols without variables of pair types. This is not a limitation, since we assume that protocol roles can always decompose pairs.

Definition 9. A protocol P is splitting iff, for all $X \in \mathcal{V}_P$, $X\delta_P$ is not a pair.

Function specifications. Let $\mathcal{V}_{pt}$ be an infinite set of *pattern variables* distinct from $\mathcal{V}$ and $\mathcal{V}_{ty}$. We construct term patterns from pattern variables using hashing, pairing and, encryption. Type patterns are types which contain (type) variables.

Definition 10. *The set of term patterns is defined by* $\mathcal{P} = \mathcal{T}(\mathcal{V}_{pt}, \emptyset, \emptyset, \emptyset)$. *A term pattern* $p \in \mathcal{P}$ *is* linear *if each pattern variable occurs at most once in* p.

We introduce a simple generic form of recursive function specifications. Based on these we will then define type-based transformations. Below, we use typing environments of the form $\Gamma : \mathcal{V}_{pt} \rightharpoonup \mathcal{Y}_P$ with pattern variables rather than message variables in the domain. Otherwise, the type system remains the same.

Definition 11. *Let* f *be an unary function symbol. A function specification for* f *with respect to a typing environment* $\Gamma : \mathcal{V}_{pt} \rightharpoonup \mathcal{Y}_P$ *is a list of equations*

$$E_f = [f(p_1 : \pi_1) = u_1, \ldots, f(p_n : \pi_n) = u_n],$$

where each $p_i \in \mathcal{P}$ *is a linear term pattern and* $\pi_i \in \mathcal{Y}_P$ *is a type pattern such that* $\Gamma \vdash p_i : \pi_i$. *The* u_i *are terms, built from the pattern variables in* p_i, *cryptographic operations, and the function symbol* f.

We introduce the notion of a complete set of type patterns to ensure that each term's type matches some type pattern of a function specification. The use of type variables is essential to achieve this.

Definition 12. *A set of type patterns* $S \subseteq \mathcal{Y}_P$ *is* complete *w.r.t. a set of ground types* T *if, for all* $\tau \in T$, *there is* $\pi \in S$ *such that* $\tau = \pi\theta$ *for some* $\theta : \mathcal{V}_{ty} \rightharpoonup \mathcal{Y}_P$.

Example 2. We define $E_0(f)$, the "homomorphic" function specification for f with respect to $\Gamma_0(f) = \{(X, \mathcal{X}), (X', \mathcal{X}')\}$ below. Clearly, any set of patterns including the set $\{h(\mathcal{X}), \{\!|\mathcal{X}|\!\}_{\mathcal{X}'}, \langle \mathcal{X}, \mathcal{X}' \rangle\}$ is complete with respect to composed ground types in $\mathcal{Y}_P$.

$$E_0(f) = [f(h(X) : h(\mathcal{X})) = h(f(X)), \ f(\{\!|X|\!\}_{X'} : \{\!|\mathcal{X}|\!\}_{\mathcal{X}'}) = \{\!|f(X)|\!\}_{f(X')},$$
$$f(\langle X, X' \rangle : \langle \mathcal{X}, \mathcal{X}' \rangle) = \langle f(X), f(X') \rangle]$$

Transformation specifications. We can now make the two parts of the specification of a type-based transformation for a function symbol f more precise. The first part is given by a set T_f of atomic and ground hash types. The intention is that all terms composed from terms of these types by hashing, pairing, and encryption map to nil and are therefore removed. The second part handles composed terms and is given as a function specification E_f for f with respect to a Γ_f. By posing conditions on the term and type patterns, we ensure that the matching clause only depends on the term's type and that the restrictions on message shapes required for protocol transformations are satisfied.

Definition 13 (Type-based message transformation). *A type-based message transformation for a splitting protocol* P *and function symbol* f *is a triple* $S_f = (T_f, \Gamma_f, E_f)$ *satisfying the following conditions:*

1. $T_f \subseteq \mathcal{Y}_P \setminus \{\alpha\}$ is a set of atomic and ground hash types such that $\mathsf{pk}(\alpha) \in T_f$ if and only if $\mathsf{pri}(\alpha) \in T_f$,
2. $E_f = [f(p_1 : \pi_1) = u_1, \ldots, f(p_n : \pi_n) = u_n]$ is a function specification for f with respect to $\Gamma_f : \mathcal{V}_{pt} \rightharpoonup \mathcal{Y}_P$ such that
   (a) $\{\pi_1, \ldots, \pi_n\}$ is a complete set of patterns with respect to composed ground types, i.e., the ground types in the set $\mathcal{Y}_P \setminus atoms(\mathcal{Y}_P)$, and
   (b) p_i is not deeper than π_i for each $1 \leq i \leq n$, i.e., each term position in p_i is also a position in π_i.
   Moreover, for all $(f(p : \pi) = u) \in E_f$ one of the following holds:
   - $p = \mathsf{h}(q)$ and $u = \mathsf{h}^a(f(q))$, where $q \in \mathcal{V}_{pt}$ and $a \geq 0$,
   - $p = \langle q, r \rangle$ and $u = \langle f(t_1), \ldots, f(t_m) \rangle$, where $set(split(\langle q, r \rangle)) \subseteq \mathcal{V}_{pt}$, $split(\langle t_1, \ldots, t_m \rangle) = split(\langle q, r \rangle)$ and $|t_i| < |\langle q, r \rangle|$ for $1 \leq i \leq m$, or
   - $p = \{\!| q |\!\}_r$ and $u = \{\!| \langle \{\!| f(t_1) |\!\}_{f(r)^{a_1}}, \ldots, \{\!| f(t_m) |\!\}_{f(r)^{a_m}} \rangle |\!\}_{f(r)^b}$, where $set(split(q)) \cup \{r\} \subseteq \mathcal{V}_{pt}$, $a_i, b \geq 0$, $split(\langle t_1, \ldots, t_m \rangle) = split(q)$, and $|t_i| \leq |q|$ for $1 \leq i \leq m$.

We forbid $\alpha \in T_f$, since this would result in the removal of all role names from a protocol, which does not make much sense. The type of public and private keys can only be included together in T_f. For the case of pairs and encryptions, the linearity of the patterns p_i implies that the subsumption relation $\mathcal{P}$ between two term tuples from Definition 6 reduces to an equality here.

Transformation semantics. Before defining the semantics of type-based transformations, we formalize the set of types of those terms that we want to remove.

Definition 14. *For a set of ground types G, we define the removable types $rem(G)$ as the least set closed under the following rules.*

- *if $\tau \in G$ then $\tau \in rem(G)$,*
- *if $\tau \in rem(G)$ then $h(\tau) \in rem(G)$,*
- *if $\tau_1, \tau_2 \in rem(G)$ then $\langle \tau_1, \tau_2 \rangle \in rem(G)$, and*
- *if $\tau \in rem(G)$ then $\{\!| \tau |\!\}_{\tau'} \in rem(G)$ for all ground types τ'.*

Definition 15 (Semantics of typed-based transformations). *The semantics of a type-based transformation S_f for a splitting protocol P and function symbol f is given by Program 1.*

As said earlier, the main motivation for type-based setting is to achieve uniform transformations based on types, i.e., the type $\tau = \Gamma_P(t)$ of a term t uniquely determines how t is transformed (τ is well-defined by Proposition 1). We achieve this by ensuring that both (1) term removal and (2) pattern matching for composed types only depend on the type τ. The program ensures point (1) by removing terms with types in $rem(T_f)$ (line 3). The lemma below guarantees that $rem(T_f)$ describes precisely these terms.

Lemma 2. *Let P be a splitting protocol and $S_f = (T_f, \Gamma_f, E_f)$ be a type-based message transformation. Suppose $t \in nf(\mathcal{M}_P^\square) \setminus \{nil\}$ and $\Gamma_P \vdash t : \tau$. Then $\tau \in rem(T_f)$ iff $f(t) = nil$.*

```
1   fun f^{rec}(t) =
2     let τ = Γ_P(t) in
3       if τ ∈ rem(T_f) then nil
4       else if t ∈ vars(M_P^□) ∪ atoms(M_P^□) then t
5       else case (t, τ) of
6         (p_1, π_1) ⇒ nf(u_1[f^{rec}/f])
7       | ⋯
8       | (p_n, π_n) ⇒ nf(u_n[f^{rec}/f])
9
10  fun f(t) = f^{rec}(nf(t))
```

Program 1. Functional program resulting from specification $S_f = (T_f, \Gamma_f, E_f)$

Point (2) is guaranteed by Conditions (2a) and (2b) of Definition 13. A composed term's type uniquely determines a non-empty set of matching term-type patterns of E_f. This is expressed in the following lemma, which together with Lemma 2 will allow us to establish the substitution property.

Lemma 3. *Let P be a splitting protocol and $S_f = (T_f, \Gamma_f, E_f)$ be a type-based message transformation for P, where $E_f = [f(p_1 : \pi_1) = u_1, \ldots, f(p_n : \pi_n) = u_n]$, and let $S(t, \tau) = \{i \mid \exists \theta. (p_i, \pi_i)\theta = (t, \tau)\}$. Then $S(t_1, \tau) = S(t_2, \tau) \neq \emptyset$ for all composed terms $t_1, t_2 \in M_P^□$ of ground type τ in environment Γ_P.*

As expected, type-based message transformations are indeed message transformation, as stated in the following proposition.

Proposition 2. *Let P be a splitting protocol and S_f be a type-based message transformation. Then f is a message transformation on $M_P^□$ and also on N_P.*

Transforming protocols We extend type-based transformations to events, roles and protocols. Transformed events with nil arguments are removed from roles.

Definition 16 (Protocol transformations). *Let S_f be a type-based message transformation. We define $f(s(m)) = s(f(m))$ for events $s(m) \in Event$ and, for event sequences,*

$$f(\epsilon) = \epsilon \qquad f(e \cdot tl) = \text{if } term(f(e)) = \text{nil then } f(tl) \text{ else } f(e) \cdot f(tl)$$

For protocols P, $f(P)(R) = f(P(R))$ for $R \in dom(P)$ and undefined otherwise.

Next, we present two examples of type-based message transformations formalizing some transformations from Section 1. The first one pulls a message out of an encryption and the second one removes some atoms from messages.

Example 3 (K4 to K5). We formalize the protocol K4 as follows (where $c \in \mathcal{C}$).

$\mathsf{K4}(A) = \mathsf{snd}(A, B, n_A) \cdot \mathsf{rcv}(\{\!\!\{B, T_S, n_A, K_{AB}, X\}\!\!\}_{\mathsf{sh}(A,S)}) \cdot$
$\qquad\quad \mathsf{snd}(X, \{\!\!\{c, t_A\}\!\!\}_{K_{AB}}) \cdot \mathsf{rcv}(\{\!\!\{t_A\}\!\!\}_{K_{AB}})$
$\mathsf{K4}(S) = \mathsf{rcv}(A, B, N_A) \cdot \mathsf{snd}(\{\!\!\{B, t_S, N_A, k_{AB}, \{\!\!\{A, t_S, k_{AB}\}\!\!\}_{\mathsf{sh}(B,S)}\}\!\!\}_{\mathsf{sh}(A,S)})$
$\mathsf{K4}(B) = \mathsf{rcv}(\{\!\!\{A, T'_S, K'_{AB}\}\!\!\}_{\mathsf{sh}(B,S)}, \{\!\!\{c, T_A\}\!\!\}_{K'_{AB}}) \cdot \mathsf{snd}(\{\!\!\{T_A\}\!\!\}_{K'_{AB}})$

The type-based message transformation $S_{f_4} = (T_{f_4}, \Gamma_{f_4}, E_{f_4})$, where $T_{f_4} = \emptyset$ and E_{f_4} is defined using list concatenation @ and $E_0(f)$ from Example 2 as follows.

$$E_{f_4} = [f_4(\{|X_1, X_2, X_3, X_4, X_5|\}_K : \{|\mathcal{X}_1, \mathcal{X}_2, \mathcal{X}_3, \mathcal{X}_4, \mathcal{X}_5|\}_{\mathsf{sh}(\alpha,\alpha)})$$
$$= \langle\{|f_4(X_1, X_2, X_3, X_4)|\}_K, f_4(X_5)\rangle] \ @ \ E_0(f_4)$$

Applying f_4 to K4 yields K5 $= f_4$(K4) as follows. In this and the next example, we omit roles that are unchanged by the respective transformations.

$\mathsf{K5}(A) = \mathsf{snd}(A, B, n_A) \cdot \mathsf{rcv}(\{|B, T_S, n_A, K_{AB}|\}_{\mathsf{sh}(A,S)}, X) \cdot$
$\qquad\quad\ \mathsf{snd}(X, \{|c, t_A|\}_{K_{AB}}) \cdot \mathsf{rcv}(\{|t_A|\}_{K_{AB}})$
$\mathsf{K5}(S) = \mathsf{rcv}(A, B, N_A) \cdot \mathsf{snd}(\{|B, t_S, N_A, k_{AB}|\}_{\mathsf{sh}(A,S)}, \{|A, t_S, k_{AB}|\}_{\mathsf{sh}(B,S)})$

Example 4 (K3 to K2). Recall that K3 results from K5 by structural transformations f_5 eliminating the forwarding of B's ticket by A. In K3, defined below, there are therefore separate events for the server sending A and B's ticket and for B receiving his ticket (from S) and the authenticator (from A).

$\mathsf{K3}(A) = \mathsf{snd}(A, B, n_A) \cdot \mathsf{rcv}(\{|B, T_S, n_A, K_{AB}|\}_{\mathsf{sh}(A,S)}) \cdot$
$\qquad\quad\ \mathsf{snd}(\{|c, t_A|\}_{K_{AB}}) \cdot \mathsf{rcv}(\{|t_A|\}_{K_{AB}})$
$\mathsf{K3}(S) = \mathsf{rcv}(A, B, N_A) \cdot \mathsf{snd}(\{|B, t_S, N_A, k_{AB}|\}_{\mathsf{sh}(A,S)}) \cdot \mathsf{snd}(\{|A, t_S, k_{AB}|\}_{\mathsf{sh}(B,S)})$
$\mathsf{K3}(B) = \mathsf{rcv}(\{|A, T'_S, K'_{AB}|\}_{\mathsf{sh}(B,S)}) \cdot \mathsf{rcv}(\{|c, T_A|\}_{K'_{AB}}) \cdot \mathsf{snd}(\{|T_A|\}_{K'_{AB}})$

The type-based message transformation $S_{f_3} = (T_{f_3}, \Gamma_{f_3}, E_{f_3})$ is defined by $T_{f_3} = \{\beta_{t_A}, \gamma_c\}$ and $E_{f_3} = E_0(f_3)$. Applying f_3 to K3 yields protocol K2 $= f_3$(K3) where the key confirmation messages have been removed.

$$\mathsf{K2}(A) = \mathsf{snd}(A, B, n_A) \cdot \mathsf{rcv}(\{|B, T_S, n_A, K_{AB}|\}_{\mathsf{sh}(A,S)})$$
$$\mathsf{K2}(B) = \mathsf{rcv}(\{|A, T'_S, K'_{AB}|\}_{\mathsf{sh}(B,S)})$$

A further abstraction, f_2, removes t_S and n_A from K2, resulting in protocol K1.

3.4 Well-Definedness and Simulation

We are now in a position to establish the substitution property for splitting protocols and well-typed substitutions. Its proof uses Lemmas 2 and 3 above together the following lemma stating that well-typed substitutions preserve types.

Lemma 4. *Let θ be a well-typed substitution with respect to a typing environment Γ. Then for all terms $t \in \mathcal{T}$, $\Gamma \vdash t : \tau$ implies that $\Gamma \vdash t\theta : \tau$.*

Theorem 2 (Substitution property). *Let P be a splitting protocol and S_f be a type-based protocol transformation and θ be a well-typed substitution with respect to Γ_P. Then for all $t \in \mathcal{M}_P^{\square}$, we have $f(t\theta) = f(t)f(\theta)$.*

The first application of the substitution property is to establish well-definedness.

Proposition 3 (Well-definedness). *Let P be a splitting protocol and S_f be a type-based protocol transformation. Then $f(P)$ is a protocol with honest substitution $\delta_{f(P)} = f(\delta_P)$.*

Next, we lift deducibility preservation (Theorem 1) to non-ground terms and establish the simulation property. Since protocol descriptions contain non-ground terms, we restrict our attention to simple-keyed protocols, for which the set of (ground) *types* of the protocol's terms is simple-keyed. Hereafter, IK_0 and IK'_0 denote the intruder's initial knowledge associated with P and $f(P)$, respectively.

Definition 17. *A protocol P is* simple-keyed *if the set of types $\Gamma_P(Rt_P)$ is simple-keyed.*

Lemma 5. *If P is a simple-keyed protocol, $T \subseteq Rt_P^\sharp$ and θ is well-typed ground substitution with respect to Γ_P, then $T\theta$ is a simple-keyed set of terms.*

Proposition 4. *Let P be a simple-keyed, splitting protocol, S_f a type-based message transformation, and θ a well-typed ground substitution with respect to Γ_P. Assume that IK_0 is simple-keyed and $f(IK_0) \subseteq IK'_0$. Then, for all $T \subseteq Rt_P^\sharp$ and $u \in \mathcal{M}_P^\sharp$, we have $T\theta \cup IK_0 \vdash u\theta$ implies $f(T)f(\theta) \cup IK'_0 \vdash f(u)f(\theta)$.*

Theorem 3 (Simulation). *Let P be a simple-keyed, splitting protocol and let S_f be a type-based message transformation. Assume that IK_0 is simple-keyed and $f(IK_0) \subseteq IK'_0$. Then for all states (tr, th, σ) reachable in P such that σ is well-typed w.r.t. Γ_P, then $(f(tr), f(th), f(\sigma))$ is a reachable state of $f(P)$ and $f(\sigma)$ is well-typed w.r.t. $\Gamma_{f(P)}$.*

4   Property Language and Soundness

We introduce a specification language for security properties including secrecy and authentication. We extend our transformations to formulas of the property language and establish the preservation of well-typed attacks (and hence soundness) for protocols and formulas satisfying certain injectiveness conditions.

4.1   Security Properties

Our property specification language is an instance of first-order logic with formulas in negation normal form (negation occurs only in front of atomic formulas).

$$\phi ::= A \mid \neg A \mid \phi_1 \wedge \phi_2 \mid \phi_1 \vee \phi_2 \mid \forall i.\, \phi' \mid \exists i.\, \phi'$$

Here, A are atomic predicates and the quantified variables i represent thread identifiers. An atomic predicate or negated atomic predicate is called a *literal*. The atomic predicates and their meaning are as follows, where $m, m' \in \mathcal{M}_P^\sharp$ are messages, e, e' are events, i, j are thread-id variables, and R is a role name.

$$
\begin{array}{ll}
A ::= i = j & \text{thread } i \text{ and thread } j \text{ are equal} \\
\mid\ m = m' & \text{messages } m \text{ and } m' \text{ are equal} \\
\mid\ role(i, R) & \text{thread } i \text{ executes role } R \\
\mid\ honest(i, R) & \text{the agent playing role } R \text{ in thread } i\text{'s view is honest} \\
\mid\ steps(i, e) & \text{thread } i \text{ has executed event } e \\
\mid\ (i, e) \prec (j, f) & \text{thread } i \text{ has executed } e \text{ before thread } j \text{ has executed } f \\
\mid\ secret(m) & \text{the intruder does not know } m
\end{array}
$$

To achieve attack preservation, we focus on the fragment of this logic where the predicate $secret(m)$ only occurs positively. We call this language $\mathcal{L}_P$. A *property* is a closed formula of $\mathcal{L}_P$. In examples, we freely use standard abbreviations (e.g., for implication) if there is an equivalent negative normal form in $\mathcal{L}_P$.

Recall that $\mathcal{A}_H$ denotes the set of honest agents. Let ϑ be a substitution such that $range(\vartheta) \subseteq dom(th)$. We define formula satisfaction, $(tr, th, \sigma, \vartheta) \vDash \phi$, as follows (omitting the standard cases for the boolean operators and the dual existential quantifier):

$$
\begin{array}{ll}
(tr, th, \sigma, \vartheta) \vDash i = j & \text{iff } \vartheta(i) = \vartheta(j) \\
(tr, th, \sigma, \vartheta) \vDash m = m' & \text{iff } m\sigma = m'\sigma \\
(tr, th, \sigma, \vartheta) \vDash role(i, R) & \text{iff } \exists seq \in Event^*. \, th(\vartheta(i)) = (R, seq) \\
(tr, th, \sigma, \vartheta) \vDash honest(i, R) & \text{iff } R^{\vartheta(i)}\sigma \in \mathcal{A}_H \\
(tr, th, \sigma, \vartheta) \vDash steps(i, e) & \text{iff } (\vartheta(i), e) \in tr \\
(tr, th, \sigma, \vartheta) \vDash (i, e) \prec (j, e') & \text{iff } (\vartheta(i), e) \prec_{tr} (\vartheta(j), e') \\
(tr, th, \sigma, \vartheta) \vDash secret(m) & \text{iff } IK(tr)\sigma \cup IK_0 \vdash m\sigma \text{ is not derivable} \\
(tr, th, \sigma, \vartheta) \vDash \forall i. \, \phi' & \text{iff } (tr, th, \sigma, \vartheta[i \mapsto tid]) \vDash \phi' \text{ for all } tid \in dom(th)
\end{array}
$$

where $a \prec_{tr} b$ ("a occurs before b on tr") holds if $tr = tr_1 \cdot a \cdot tr_2 \cdot b \cdot tr_3$ for some tr_1, tr_2, tr_3. We write $(tr, th, \sigma, \vartheta) \nvDash \phi$ if $(tr, th, \sigma, \vartheta) \vDash \phi$ does not hold. If ϕ is a closed formula, we write $(tr, th, \sigma) \vDash \phi$ instead of $(tr, th, \sigma, \vartheta) \vDash \phi$.

Definition 18 (Attack). *We say that a state $s = (tr, th, \sigma)$ is an attack on ϕ if $s \nvDash \phi$. The state (attack) s is well-typed if σ is well-typed.*

We extend transformations f to formulas $\phi \in \mathcal{L}_P$ as follows:

$$
\begin{array}{ll}
f(i = i') = i = i' & f(secret(m)) = secret(f(m)) \\
f(m = m') = f(m) = f(m') & f(\neg A) = \neg f(A) \\
f(role(i, R)) = role(i, f(R)) & f(\phi_1 \wedge \phi_2) = f(\phi_1) \wedge f(\phi_2) \\
f(honest(i, R)) = honest(i, f(R)) & f(\phi_1 \vee \phi_2) = f(\phi_1) \vee f(\phi_2) \\
f(steps(i, e)) = steps(i, f(e)) & f(\forall i. \, \phi') = \forall i. \, f(\phi') \\
f((i, e) \prec (j, e')) = (i, f(e)) \prec (j, f(e')) & f(\exists i. \, \phi') = \exists i. \, f(\phi')
\end{array}
$$

Example 5 (Secrecy and authentication). Consider the initiator and responder roles of the core Kerberos IV protocol K4 as specified in Example 3.

$$
\begin{aligned}
\mathsf{K4}(A) &= \mathsf{snd}(A, B, n_A) \cdot \mathsf{rcv}(\{\!| B, T_S, n_A, K_{AB}, X |\!\}_{\mathsf{sh}(A,S)}) \cdot \\
&\quad \mathsf{snd}(X, \{\!| c, t_A |\!\}_{K_{AB}}) \cdot \mathsf{rcv}(\{\!| t_A |\!\}_{K_{AB}}) \\
\mathsf{K4}(B) &= \mathsf{rcv}(\{\!| A, T'_S, K'_{AB} |\!\}_{\mathsf{sh}(B,S)}, \{\!| c, T_A |\!\}_{K'_{AB}}) \cdot \mathsf{snd}(\{\!| T_A |\!\}_{K'_{AB}})
\end{aligned}
$$

We express the secrecy of the session key k_{AB} for role A by

$$
\phi_s = \forall i. \, (role(i, A) \wedge honest(i, [A, B]) \wedge steps(i, \mathsf{rcv}(t_2))) \Rightarrow secret(K^i_{AB}).
$$

where $t_2 = \{\!| B, T_S, n_A, K_{AB}, X |\!\}_{\mathsf{sh}(A,S)}$ and $honest(i, [A, B])$ abbreviates the obvious conjunction. We abstract this property to verify it on the simplified protocol $K1 = g(K4)$, where $g = f_2 \circ f_3 \circ f_5 \circ f_4$ is the composition of all transformations in our running example. Hence, we derive $\phi'_s = g(\phi_s)$, yielding

$$\phi'_s = \forall i. \ (role(i, A) \wedge honest(i, [A, B]) \wedge steps(i, \mathsf{rcv}(t'_2))) \Rightarrow secret(K^i_{AB}).$$

where $t'_2 = \{\!|B, K_{AB}|\!\}_{\mathsf{sh}(A,S)}$. Next, we formalize non-injective agreement of B with A on the key k_{AB} and the timestamp t_A. This property is based on the authenticator.

$$\phi_a = \forall i. \ (role(i, B) \wedge honest(i, [A, B]) \wedge steps(i, \mathsf{rcv}(u_1, u_2)))$$
$$\Rightarrow \exists j. \ role(j, A) \wedge steps(j, \mathsf{snd}(X, \{\!|c, t_A|\!\}_{K_{AB}}))$$
$$\wedge \langle A^i, B^i, K'^i_{AB}, T^i_A \rangle = \langle A^j, B^j, K^j_{AB}, t^j_A \rangle$$

where $u_1 = \{\!|A, T'_S, K'_{AB}|\!\}_{\mathsf{sh}(B,S)}$ and $u_2 = \{\!|c, T_A|\!\}_{K'_{AB}}$. For the simplified protocol $K3 = f_5 \circ f_4(K4)$, we check the abstracted formula $\phi'_a = f_5 \circ f_4(\phi_a)$, where B's ticket and the associated variable X of role A have been removed.

$$\phi'_a = \forall i. \ (role(i, B) \wedge honest(i, [A, B]) \wedge steps(i, \mathsf{rcv}(u_2)))$$
$$\Rightarrow \exists j. \ role(j, A) \wedge steps(j, \mathsf{snd}(\{\!|c, t_A|\!\}_{K_{AB}}))$$
$$\wedge \langle A^i, B^i, K'^i_{AB}, T^i_A \rangle = \langle A^j, B^j, K^j_{AB}, t^j_A \rangle$$

4.2 Soundness

We now show that if there exists a well-typed attack on a property ϕ of a protocol P, then the transformed attack state constitutes an attack on property $f(\phi)$ of protocol $f(P)$. In other words, we can say that the protocol P is at least as secure as $f(P)$.

However, attack preservation does not hold for all properties ϕ and type-based message transformations f. For example, attacks on properties involving protocol events may not be preserved if f maps two different events of P to a single one in $f(P)$. Similarly, if f identifies messages then attacks on equality are not preserved. These atomic predicates typically appear in authentication properties.

Our soundness result is therefore restricted to a subset of (P, f)-*safe* formulas of $\mathcal{L}_P$. We first define some auxiliary notions. Let $T^+_{eq}(\phi)$ be the set of pairs (m, m') such that the equation $m = m'$ occurs positively in ϕ and let $T_{evt}(\phi)$ $(T^+_{evt}(\phi))$ be the set of events $s(m), s'(m')$ such that $(i, s(m)) \prec (j, s'(m'))$ or $steps(i, s(m))$ occurs (positively) in ϕ.

Definition 19 ((P, f)-safe formulas). *Let P be a protocol and S_f be a type-based message transformation for P and function symbol f. A formula $\phi \in \mathcal{L}_P$ is (P, f)-safe if*

1. $m\sigma \neq m'\sigma$ *implies* $f(m\sigma) \neq f(m'\sigma)$ *for all* $(m, m') \in T^+_{eq}(\phi)$ *and well-typed ground substitutions* σ,
2. $m \neq m'$ *implies* $f(m) \neq f(m')$ *for all* $s(m) \in T^+_{evt}(\phi)$ *and* $s(m') \in Event^\sharp_P$, *and*
3. $f(m) \neq \mathsf{nil}$ *for all* $s(m) \in T_{evt}(\phi)$.

Table 1. Experimental verification results for Kerberos (times in seconds); the abstraction level increases from left to right columns; (*) denotes highest abstraction level for marked properties

protocol	K4/6			K5/6			K3/6			K2/6		K1/6
property	sec	aut	kc	sec	aut	kc	sec	aut	kc*	sec	aut*	sec*
time [sec]	1.45	1.31	1.16	20.65	20.5	18.27	1.44	1.31	1.18	0.95	0.85	0.14
#clauses/1000	15.4	13.8	12.1	188.9	486.2	165.6	15.9	14.2	12.6	10.0	8.8	1.1
#atoms/1000	2.0	1.9	1.9	33.0	32.9	32.8	2.0	2.0	1.9	1.4	1.3	0.4

Theorem 4 (Attack preservation). *Let P be a simple-keyed, splitting protocol, S_f a type-based message transformation for P and function symbol f, and $\phi \in \mathcal{L}_P$ a (P, f)-safe property. Assume that IK_0 is simple-keyed and $f(IK_0) \subseteq IK_0'$. Then, for all well-typed states (tr, th, σ) reachable in P, we have that $(f(tr), f(th), f(\sigma))$ is a well-typed reachable state of $f(P)$, and if $(tr, th, \sigma) \not\models \phi$ then $(f(tr), f(th), f(\sigma)) \not\models f(\phi)$.*

Example 6. Consider the protocol K4 and the typed-based message transformation S_{f_4} from Example 3. We check that ϕ_s and ϕ_a from Example 5 are $(K4, f_4)$-safe, i.e., satisfy the three conditions of Definition 19. The first condition holds for ϕ_s, since $T_{eq}^+(\phi_s) = \emptyset$. It also holds for ϕ_a, since $f_4(t) = t$ for all t of the form $\langle t_1, t_2, t_3, t_4 \rangle$ such that $\Gamma_{K4} \vdash t : \langle \alpha, \alpha, \beta_{k_{AB}}, \beta_{t_A} \rangle$. The second condition holds trivially for ϕ_s and it holds for ϕ_a, since f_4 does not identify the only term $\langle X, \{\!\{c, t_A\}\!\}_{K_{AB}}\rangle \in T_{evt}^+(\phi_a)$ in its conclusion is not identified with another protocol event term. The third condition holds, since f_4 does not map any term appearing in a *steps* predicate of ϕ_s or ϕ_a to nil. Hence, the properties ϕ_s and ϕ_a are both $(K4, f_4)$-safe. Since the protocol K4 is splitting and simple-keyed, Theorem 4 guarantees that the transformation f_4 preserves well-typed attacks on these properties.

4.3 Experimental Results

We applied abstractions analogous to those described in this paper for the four-message core versions of Kerberos IV and V, K4 and K5, to the full six-message version of these protocols, K4/6 and K5/6. For the resulting protocols we have verified several secrecy and authentication properties using SATMC [3]. Our results are summarized in Table 1.

The columns denote the protocols and the properties verified. We grouped the properties into three classes: session key secrecy from the perspective of each role (*sec*), authentication properties involving a Kerberos server (*aut*), and key confirmation (*kc*). Those columns where the highest degree of abstraction for a given property class is achieved are marked with a star (*). The rows show the verification time and the number of clauses and atoms of the SAT encoding (in thousands). The verification time is dominated by the encoding into a SAT problem whereas the SAT solving time is negligible.

We observe a slowdown from K4/6 to K5/6. We attribute this to the unencrypted responder ticket in K5/6, which increases the intruder's possibilities to interfere with the ticket variable X. The performance on K3/6 is similar to the one on K4/6. More interesting are the performance gains obtained by the further abstractions and the overall speedups that we achieve for the protocols K4 and K5. For example, verifying secrecy on K1/6 is 148 times faster than on K5/6 and still 10.4 times faster than on K4/6.

Additionally, we also used SATMC to verify a variant of the ISO/IEC 9798-3 three-pass mutual authentication protocol (ISO) and both secrecy and authentication for the TLS protocol (TLS). For both protocols we observed an enormous performance gain. For ISO, verification time for the initiator dropped from 107s to 0.2s (factor 535) by removing the responder's nonce and similarly for the responder. For TLS, we have reduced the verification for each property from more than 120s to less than 0.8s (factor 150) by removing fields that are irrelevant for the verified properties such as the cipher suite offer, session id, and certificate verification.

5   Related Work

We can classify existing work on protocol transformations into syntactic and semantic approaches. Syntactic approaches use syntactic criteria to delimit a class of transformations for which soundness can be established a priori. Hui and Lowe [11] define several kinds of transformations similar to ours with the aim improving the performance of the CASPER/FDR model checker. They prove soundness of each kind of transformations based on general soundness criteria for secrecy and authentication. Their protocol model is restricted to atomic keys and they establish their results only for ground messages. We work in a more general setting and discuss in detail the non-trivial issue of handling terms with variables as they appear in protocol specifications. Other works [16,7,6] propose a set of syntactic transformations without however formally establishing their soundness.

Semantic approaches generally cover a larger class of transformations, but each transformation requires a separate proof for its justification. Examples are classical refinement and using abstract channels with security properties [17,4] and Guttman's protocol transformations based on strand spaces [9,8]. Sprenger and Basin [17] have recently proposed a refinement strategy for security protocols that spans several different abstraction levels (including, e.g., confidential and authentic channels). The transformations in the present paper belong to their most concrete level of cryptographic protocols. Guttman [9,8] studies the preservation of security properties by a rich class of protocol transformations in the strand space model. His approach to property preservation is based on the simulation of protocol analysis steps instead of execution steps. Each analysis step explains the origin of a received message. However, he does not provide syntactic conditions for the transformations' soundness.

6   Conclusions

We presented a large class of protocol transformations which is useful both for abstraction and refinement. We have shown its soundness with respect to an expressive property language. Our results constitute a significant extension of Hui and Lowe's work [11]. To validate our approach, we used our transformations to simplify the Kerberos, ISO, and TLS protocols. As a result, we achieved substantial performance improvements for SATMC. We also showed how to use our transformations in the other direction to refine the abstract protocol K1 into the core Kerberos IV and V protocols.

To handle terms with variables as they occur in protocol specifications, our transformations employ the type system given by Arapinis and Duflot [2]. The use of a type system is also motivated by the fact that there are type-flaw attacks that can be fixed by simple transformations that we would like to cover. For example, Meadows [13] presents such an attack on the full seven-message Needham-Schroeder-Lowe protocol, which can be fixed by swapping the components of a pair. Transformations fixing type-flaw attacks are obviously unsound. In a typed model, this problem is avoided since attacks based on type confusion are ruled out. In practice, well-typedness can be achieved by using appropriate tagging schemes [12,10]. Arapinis and Duflot [2] show that for secrecy properties of well-formed protocols it is sufficient to consider well-typed attacks. Well-formedness can be achieved by a lightweight tagging scheme. In her PhD thesis [1] (in French), Arapinis extends this result to a fragment of PS-LTL.

In future work, we want to formally justify the restriction to well-typed attacks for all properties expressible in our language $\mathcal{L}_P$. This could be achieved either by embedding our property language $\mathcal{L}_P$ into PS-LTL or by directly proving a similar result for $\mathcal{L}_P$. We also envision several other extensions. First, tool support to automate the abstraction process is needed. This should include automatic abstraction-refinement to find an appropriate abstraction for a given protocol and property. Second, we want to support additional transformations such as the context-dependent removal of message fields and the transformation of composed messages into atomic ones other than nil (e.g., to turn a Diffie-Hellmann exponentiation into a nonce). This will require the inclusion of freshness arguments in the soundness proof. Finally, extensions of the message algebra with equational theories and the adversary model would be useful (e.g., for modeling forward secrecy for Diffie-Hellmann protocols). However, it is not clear how to extend the typed setting to equational theories.

Acknowledgements. We are grateful to David Basin, Ognjen Maric, and Cas Cremers for their useful comments on earlier drafts of this paper. We also thank the anonymous reviewers for their helpful feedback.

References

1. Arapinis, M.: Sécurité des protocoles cryptographiques: décidabilité et résultats de réduction. PhD thesis, Université Paris-Est (November 2008)
2. Arapinis, M., Duflot, M.: Bounding Messages for Free in Security Protocols. In: Arvind, V., Prasad, S. (eds.) FSTTCS 2007. LNCS, vol. 4855, pp. 376–387. Springer, Heidelberg (2007)
3. Armando, A., Compagna, L.: SAT-based model-checking for security protocols analysis. International Journal of Information Security 7(1), 3–32 (2008)
4. Bieber, P., Boulahia-Cuppens, N.: Formal development of authentication protocols. In: Sixth BCS-FACS Refinement Workshop (1994)
5. Cervesato, I., Meadows, C., Pavlovic, D.: An encapsulated authentication logic for reasoning about key distribution protocols. In: CSFW 2005: Proceedings of the 18th IEEE Workshop on Computer Security Foundations, Washington, DC, USA, pp. 48–61 (2005)
6. Datta, A., Derek, A., Mitchell, J.C., Pavlovic, D.: Abstraction and refinement in protocol derivation. In: Proc. 17th IEEE Computer Security Foundations Workshop, CSFW (2004)
7. Datta, A., Derek, A., Mitchell, J.C., Pavlovic, D.: A derivation system and compositionl logic for security protocols. Journal of Computer Security 13, 423–482 (2005)
8. Guttman, J.D.: Transformations between Cryptographic Protocols. In: Degano, P., Viganò, L. (eds.) ARSPA-WITS 2009. LNCS, vol. 5511, pp. 107–123. Springer, Heidelberg (2009)
9. Guttman, J.D.: Security Goals and Protocol Transformations. In: Mödersheim, S., Palamidessi, C. (eds.) TOSCA 2011. LNCS, vol. 6993, pp. 130–147. Springer, Heidelberg (2012)
10. Heather, J., Lowe, G., Schneider, S.: How to prevent type flaw attacks on security protocols. Journal of Computer Security 11(2), 217–244 (2003)
11. Hui, M.L., Lowe, G.: Fault-preserving simplifying transformations for security protocols. Journal of Computer Security 9(1/2), 3–46 (2001)
12. Li, Y., Yang, W., Huang, C.-W.: Preventing type flaw attacks on security protocols with a simplified tagging scheme. In: Waldron, J. (ed.) ISICT. ACM International Conference Proceeding Series, vol. 90, pp. 244–249. Trinity College Dublin (2004)
13. Meadows, C.A.: Analyzing the Needham-Schroeder Public-Key Protocol: A Comparison of Two Approaches. In: Bertino, E., Kurth, H., Martella, G., Montolivo, E. (eds.) ESORICS 1996. LNCS, vol. 1146, pp. 351–364. Springer, Heidelberg (1996)
14. Meier, S., Cremers, C.J.F., Basin, D.A.: Strong invariants for the efficient construction of machine-checked protocol security proofs. In: Proc. 23th IEEE Computer Security Foundations Symposium, CSF, pp. 231–245 (2010)
15. Nguyen, B.T., Sprenger, C.: Sound security protocol transformations. Technical Report 781, Department of Computer Science, ETH Zurich (2012)
16. Pavlovic, D., Meadows, C.: Deriving Secrecy in Key Establishment Protocols. In: Gollmann, D., Meier, J., Sabelfeld, A. (eds.) ESORICS 2006. LNCS, vol. 4189, pp. 384–403. Springer, Heidelberg (2006)
17. Sprenger, C., Basin, D.: Refining key establishment. In: Proc. 25th IEEE Computer Security Foundations Symposium, CSF, pp. 230–246 (2012)

Logical Foundations of Secure Resource Management in Protocol Implementations

Michele Bugliesi[1], Stefano Calzavara[1], Fabienne Eigner[2], and Matteo Maffei[2]

[1] Università Ca' Foscari Venezia
[2] Saarland University

Abstract. Recent research has shown that it is possible to leverage general-purpose theorem proving techniques to develop powerful type systems for the verification of a wide range of security properties on application code. Although successful in many respects, these type systems fall short of capturing resource-conscious properties that are crucial in large classes of modern distributed applications. In this paper, we propose the first type system that statically enforces the safety of cryptographic protocol implementations with respect to authorization policies expressed in affine logic. Our type system draws on a novel notion of "exponential serialization" of affine formulas, a general technique to protect affine formulas from the effect of duplication. This technique allows to formulate an expressive logical encoding of the authentication mechanisms underpinning distributed resource-aware authorization policies. We further devise a sound and complete type checking algorithm. We discuss the effectiveness of our approach on a case study from the world of e-commerce protocols.

1 Introduction

Verifying the security of modern distributed applications is an important and complex challenge, which has attracted the interest of a growing research community audience over the last decade. Among various static analysis approaches, security type systems have played a major role, since they are able to statically provide security proofs for an unbounded number of concurrent executions, even in presence of an active attacker; they are modular, and scale remarkably well in practice. Recent research has shown that it is possible to leverage general-purpose theorem proving techniques to develop powerful type systems for the verification of a wide range of security properties on application code, thus narrowing the gap between the formal model designed for the analysis and the actual implementation of the protocols [4,2,26]. The integration between type systems and theorem proving is achieved by resorting to a form of dependent types, known as *refinement* types. A refinement type $\{x : T \mid F(x)\}$ qualifies the structural information of the type T with a property specified by the logical formula F: a value M of this type is a value of type T such that $F(M)$ holds.

Authorization systems based on refinement types use the refinement formulas to express (and gain static control of) the credentials associated with the data and the cryptographic keys involved in the authorization checks. Clearly, the expressiveness of the resulting analysis hinges on the choice of the underlying logic, and indeed several logics have been proposed for the specification

D. Basin and J.C. Mitchell (Eds.): POST 2013, LNCS 7796, pp. 105–125, 2013.
© Springer-Verlag Berlin Heidelberg 2013

and verification of security properties [14]. A number of proposals have thus set logic *parametricity* as a design goal, to gain modularity and scalability of the resulting systems. Though parametricity is in principle a sound and wise choice, current attempts in this direction draw primarily (if not exclusively) on classical (or intuitionistic) logical frameworks. Classical logic, however, is unsuitable to express several interesting resource-aware authorization policies, such as those based on consumable credentials, or predicating over access counts and/or usage bounds [16,10]. The natural choice for expressing and reasoning about such classes of policies are instead *substructural* logics, such as linear and affine logic [17,29]. On the other hand, integrating substructural logics with existing refinement type systems for distributed authorization is challenging, as one must build safeguards against the ability of an attacker to duplicate the data exchanged over the network, and correspondingly duplicate the associated credentials, thus undermining their bounded nature [13].

Contributions. In this paper, we present an *affine refinement type system* for RCF [4], a concurrent λ-calculus which can be directly mapped to a large subset of a real functional programming language like F#. The type system guarantees that well-typed programs comply with any given authorization policy expressed in affine logic, even in the presence of an active opponent.

This type system draws on the novel concept of *exponential serialization*, a general technique to protect affine formulas from the effect of duplication. This technique makes it possible to factor the authorization-relevant invariants of the analysis out of the type system, and to characterize them directly as proof obligations for the underlying affine logical system. This leads to a rather general and modular design of the system, and sheds new light on the logical foundations of standard cryptographic patterns underpinning distributed authorization frameworks. Furthermore, the concept of serialization enhances the expressiveness of the type system, capturing programming patterns out of the scope of many substructural type systems.

The clean separation between typing and logical entailment has the additional advantage of enabling the formulation of an algorithmic version of our system, in which the non-deterministic proof search distinctive of substructural type systems can be dispensed with and expressed in terms of a single proof obligation to be discharged to an external theorem prover. This is the key to achieve an efficient implementation of our analysis technique. We prove the algorithmic version sound and complete.

We show the effectiveness of the type system on a realistic case study, namely the *EPMO* electronic purchase protocol proposed in [20]. The proof obligation generated by the type derivation for the customer code is validated by the linear logic theorem prover `llprover` [27] in less than 20 ms.

Related work. Several papers develop expressive type systems for (variants of) RCF [6,4,15,2,26] but, with the exception of F* [26], they do not support resource-aware authorization policies: in fact, even for simple linearity properties like injective agreement they rely on hand-written proofs [5]. F* [26] is a dependently typed functional language for secure distributed programming, featuring refinement types to reason about authorization policies and affine types to reason about stateful computations on affine *values*. Similarly to companion proposals for RCF, the type system of F^* assumes the existence of the contraction rule in the underlying logic, hence it does not support authorization policies built over affine *formulas*. While some simple authentication patterns (e.g., basic nonce handshakes) may certainly be expressed by encoding affine predicates in terms of affine values, other more complex authentication mechanisms are much harder to handle in these terms. The *EPMO* protocol we analyze in Section 6 provides one such case, as (*i*) the nonce it employs may not be construed as an affine value because it is used twice, and (*ii*) the logical formulas justified by crypto-graphic message exchanges are more structured than simple predicates. Though it might be possible to come up with sophisticated encodings of these authenti-cation mechanisms in the programming language (by resorting to, e.g., pairs of affine tokens to encode a double usage of the same nonce and special functions to eliminate logical implications), such encodings are hard to formulate in a general manner and, we argue, are much better expressed in terms of policy annotations than in some ad-hoc programming pattern.

Bhargavan et al. [7] propose a technique for the verification of F# protocol implementations by automatically extracting ProVerif models [9]. Remarkably, the framework can deal with injective agreement. On the other hand, the analysis carried out with ProVerif is not modular and has been shown less robust and scalable than type-checking [6]. Furthermore, the fragment of F# considered is rather restrictive: for instance, it does not include higher-order functions and admits only very limited uses of recursion and state.

A formal account on the integration of refinement types and substructural logics was first proposed by Mandelbaum et al. [21] with a system for local reasoning about program state built around a fragment of intuitionistic linear logic. Later, Bierhoff and Aldrich developed a framework for modular type-state checking of object-oriented programs [8,25,23]. Contrary to our proposal, none of these type systems deals with the presence of hostile (or untyped) program components, or attackers, a feature that would require fundamental changes in these systems and has deep impact on the type rules and the analysis technique.

Tov and Pucella [28] have recently shown how to use behavioral contracts to link code written in an affine language to code in a conventionally typed language. The idea is to coerce affine values to non-affine ones that can be shared with the context, but can still be reasoned about safely using dynamic access counts. There are intriguing similarities between this approach and the usage of nonces and session keys to enforce freshness in a distributed setting, which are worth investigating in the future. The two type systems are, however, fundamentally different, since our present work deals with an affine refinement logic and considers an adversarial setting, which makes a precise comparison hard to formulate.

There exist a number of types and effects systems targeted at the analysis of authenticity properties of cryptographic protocols [18,19,11]. These type systems incorporate ad-hoc mechanisms to deal with nonce handshakes and, thus, to enforce injective agreement properties. Our exponential serialization technique can be seen as a logic-based generalization of such mechanisms, independent of the language and type system. As a consequence, our type system is similarly able to verify authenticity in terms of injective agreement, while allowing for expressing also a number of more sophisticated properties involving access counts and usage bounds. As a downside, the current formulation of our type system does not allow to validate some specific nonce-handshake idioms, like the SOSH scheme [19]. Still, this can be recovered by extending our type system with union and intersection types, as shown in [2].

In a previous work [13], we made initial steps towards the design of a sound system for resource-sensitive authorization, drawing on techniques from type systems for authentication and an affine extension of existing refinement type systems for the applied pi-calculus [1]. That work aims at analyzing crypto-graphic protocols as opposed to their implementations. Furthermore, the type system is designed around a specific cryptographic library: the consequence is that extending the analysis to new primitives requires significant changes in the soundness proof of the type system. In contrast, the usage of RCF in this work allows us to encode cryptography in the language using a standard sealing mech-anism (cf. Section 5.8), which makes the analysis technique easily extensible to new cryptographic primitives. Finally, the non-standard nature of our previous type system makes it difficult to devise an efficient algorithmic variant.

Structure of the paper. Section 2 overviews the challenges and the most impor-tant aspects of our theory on a simple example. Section 3 presents the meta-theory of exponential serialization. Section 4 reviews RCF. Section 5 outlines the type system and our treatment of formal cryptography. Section 6 presents the case study. Section 7 discusses the algorithmic version of our type system. Section 8 concludes. Due to space constraints, we refer to the long version [12] for the complete formalization of the type system and its algorithmic variant, full proofs, and a discussion on a further case study (the Kerberos protocol).

2   Overview of the Framework

We give an intuitive overview of our approach, based on a simple example of a distributed protocol involving a streaming service S and a client C that sub-scribes to the service and pays for watching a movie, chosen from a database of available contents.

Verifying the protocol with a refinement type system requires to first dec-orate the protocol with security annotations, structured as *assumptions* and *assertions*. The former introduce logical formulas which are assumed to hold at a given point (and express the credentials available at the client's side); the latter specify logical formulas which are expected to be entailed by the previ-ously introduced assumptions (and are employed as guards for the resources at the server end). For our example, we start by assuming the authorization policy encoded by the formula below:

$$\forall x, y.(\mathsf{Paid}(x, \$1) \Rightarrow \mathsf{Watch}(x, y))$$

This is a first-order logic formula stating that each client paying one dollar can watch any movie from the database. We can then encode C and S in RCF as follows, using some standard syntactic sugar to enhance readability:

$$C \triangleq \lambda x_C.\, \lambda x_{addS}.\, \lambda x_m.\, \lambda x_k.\, \text{assume Paid}(x_C, \$1);$$
$$\text{let } x_{msg} = \text{sign } (x_C, x_m)\, x_k \text{ in send } x_{addS}\, x_{msg}$$
$$S \triangleq \lambda x_S.\, \lambda x_{addS}.\, \lambda x_{vk}.\, \text{let } y_{msg} = \text{recv } x_{addS} \text{ in}$$
$$\text{let } (z_C, z_m) = \text{verify } y_{msg}\, x_{vk} \text{ in assert Watch}(z_C, z_m)$$

C and S are structured as functions abstracting over the parameters defined by the protocol specification. Initially, C makes the assumption $\text{Paid}(x_C, \$1)$, invokes the function sign to produce a signed request for movie x_m under her private key x_k, and sends it to S on channel x_{addS}. When S receives the message, she invokes the function verify to check the signature using the public key x_{vk}, retrieves the two components of the request z_C and z_m, and asserts the formula $\text{Watch}(z_C, z_m)$. Crucially, the assertion by S is done in terms of the variables z_C and z_m occurring in her code, not of the variables x_C and x_m reported in the code of C. The specification will be judged safe if for all protocol runs the assertion made at the server side is entailed by the assumption made at the client and the underlying authorization policy.

Indeed, the specification can be proved safe, but a closer look shows that the authorization policy is too liberal to enforce the expected access constraints. In fact, we have $\forall x, y.(\text{Paid}(x, \$1) \Rightarrow \text{Watch}(x, y)), \text{Paid}(C, \$1) \vdash \text{Watch}(C, m) \wedge \text{Watch}(C, m')$, i.e., a single payment by C allows her to arbitrarily access the movie database for unboundedly many movies. In other words, the policy does not protect against replay attacks (to which the protocol is indeed exposed).

Affine logic for specification. As we noted earlier, the problem may be addressed by resorting to substructural logics, which capture the intended interpretation of $\text{Paid}(x, \$1)$ as a consumable credential (i.e., a resource).

We focus on a simple, yet expressive, fragment of intuitionistic affine logic [29]:

$$F ::= A \mid F \otimes F \mid F \multimap F \mid \forall x.F \mid \,!F \mid \mathbf{0}$$
$$A ::= p(t_1, \ldots, t_n) \mid t = t' \quad p \text{ of arity } n \text{ in } \Sigma$$
$$t ::= x \mid f(t_1, \ldots, t_n) \quad f \text{ of arity } n \text{ in } \Sigma$$

This is the multiplicative fragment of affine logic with conjunction ($\otimes$) and implication ($\multimap$), the universal quantifier ($\forall$), the exponential modality (!) to express persistent truths, false ($\mathbf{0}$) to express negation, and equality. We presuppose an underlying signature Σ of predicate symbols, ranged over by p, and function symbols, ranged over by f. The set of terms, ranged over by t, is defined by variables and function symbols as expected. We mention here that RCF terms can be encoded into the logic using the locally nameless representation of syntax with binders, as shown by Bengtson et al. [4]. The true boolean predicate is written $\mathbf{1}$ and encoded as $() = ()$, where $()$ is the nullary function symbol encoding the RCF unit value. Atomic formulas, noted A in the above productions, consist of predicates and equalities.

We show some selected rules of our entailment relation in Table 1. Intuitively, proofs in affine logic must use each formula in the environment *at most* once. The duplication of resources is prevented by the splitting of environments among the premises of each rule. The presence of the *weakening* rule distinguishes our

Table 1. The entailment relation $\Delta \vdash F$ (selected rules)

$$\text{(Weak)} \quad \frac{\Delta \vdash F'}{\Delta, F \vdash F'} \qquad \text{(Contr)} \quad \frac{\Delta, !F, !F \vdash F'}{\Delta, !F \vdash F'} \qquad \text{($\otimes$-Left)} \quad \frac{\Delta, F_1, F_2 \vdash F'}{\Delta, F_1 \otimes F_2 \vdash F'} \qquad \text{($\otimes$-Right)} \quad \frac{\Delta_1 \vdash F_1 \quad \Delta_2 \vdash F_2}{\Delta_1, \Delta_2 \vdash F_1 \otimes F_2}$$

$$\text{($\multimap$-Left)} \quad \frac{\Delta_1 \vdash F_1 \quad \Delta_2, F_2 \vdash F'}{\Delta_1, F_1 \multimap F_2, \Delta_2 \vdash F'} \qquad \text{($\multimap$-Right)} \quad \frac{\Delta, F_1 \vdash F_2}{\Delta \vdash F_1 \multimap F_2} \qquad \text{(!-Right)} \quad \frac{\Delta \vdash F \quad \Delta = !F_1, \ldots, !F_n}{\Delta \vdash !F}$$

relation from linear logic, in which all formulas in the environment have to be used *exactly* once in the proof.

We can then re-express the authorization policy for our example as the persistent formula: $!\forall x, y.(\mathsf{Paid}(x, \$1) \multimap \mathsf{Watch}(x, y))$, stating that each payment grants access to a *single* movie. In affine logic, given the environment $\forall x, y.(\mathsf{Paid}(x, \$1) \multimap \mathsf{Watch}(x, y)), \mathsf{Paid}(C, \$1)$, one can derive $\mathsf{Watch}(C, m)$ but not $\mathsf{Watch}(C, m) \otimes \mathsf{Watch}(C, m')$, since the latter derivation would require a double usage of the affine hypothesis $\mathsf{Paid}(C, \$1)$.

Affine refinement types for verification. We move on to typing the previous RCF code, to illustrate how refinement types are employed to provide a static account of the transfer of credentials required for authorization. In our example, this amounts to showing how to statically transfer the payment assumption made by C to S. That assumption is needed by S to justify (i.e., type-check) her assertion according to the underlying authorization policy; the transfer of the assumption, in turn, is achieved by giving x_k and x_{vk} suitable types.

Namely, assuming $x_c : T_1$ and $x_m : T_2$, the existing refinement type systems would give x_k type $\mathsf{SigKey}(x : T_1 * \{y : T_2 \mid \mathsf{Paid}(x, \$1)\})$, formalizing that x_k is a private key intended to sign a pair bearing the expected formula as a refinement; x_{vk}, instead, would be given the corresponding verification key type[1]. The type of x_k requires C to assume the formula $\mathsf{Paid}(x_C, \$1)$ upon signing, while the type of x_{vk} allows S to retrieve the formula $\mathsf{Paid}(z_C, \$1)$ upon verification, which is enough to entail $\mathsf{Watch}(z_C, z_m)$ and make the protocol type-check.

With affine formulas, however, such a solution deserves some special care [13], since if $\mathsf{Paid}(z_C, \$1)$ is extracted with no additional constraint by the type of x_{vk}, a replay attack mounted by an opponent could fool S into reusing the formula multiple times. We discuss next how to deal with such issues.

2.1 Exponential Serialization

There are various possibilities to protect the previous protocol against replay attacks. Here, we decide to run the protocol on top of a nonce-handshake, leading to the following updated RCF code:

---

[1] In RCF we do not have any primitive notion of cryptography and, therefore, we do not have types for cryptography in our type system. We still use this notation to simplify the presentation and we discuss the encoding of these types in Section 5.8.

$$C \triangleq \lambda x_C. \lambda x_{addC}. \lambda x_{addS}. \lambda x_m. \lambda x_k.$$

let $y_n =$ recv x_{addC} in assume $\mathsf{Paid}(x_C, \$1)$;

let $x_{msg} =$ sign (x_C, x_m, y_n) x_k in send x_{addS} x_{msg}

$$S \triangleq \lambda x_{addS}. \lambda x_{addC}. \lambda x_{vk}.\ \text{let } x_n = \mathsf{mkNonce}(\,)\ \text{in send } x_{addC}\ x_n;$$

let $y_{msg} =$ recv x_{addS} in let $(z_C, z_m, z_n) =$ verify y_{msg} x_{vk} in

if $x_n = z_n$ then assert $\mathsf{Watch}(z_C, z_m)$

$\mathsf{mkNonce} \triangleq \lambda\_\ :\ \mathsf{unit}.\ \text{let } x_f = \mathsf{mkFresh}()\ \text{in assume } \mathsf{N}(x_f); x_f$

We assume to be given access to a function $\mathsf{mkFresh} : \mathsf{unit} \to \mathsf{bytes}$, which generates fresh bit-strings. The function $\mathsf{mkNonce} : \mathsf{unit} \to \{x : \mathsf{bytes} \mid \mathsf{N}(x)\}$ is a wrapper around $\mathsf{mkFresh}$, which additionally assumes the formula $\mathsf{N}(x_f)$ over the return value x_f of such a function. This new assumption is reflected by the refined return type of $\mathsf{mkNonce}$. Then, the typing of the key x_k may be structured as follows:

$$x_k : \mathsf{SigKey}(x : T_1 * y : T_2 * \{z : \mathsf{bytes} \mid\ !\, (\mathsf{N}(z) \multimap \mathsf{Paid}(x, \$1))\})$$

to protect the affine formula $\mathsf{Paid}(x_C, \$1)$ with the guard $\mathsf{N}(x_n)$: if $\mathsf{N}(x_n)$ can be proved only once, also $\mathsf{Paid}(x_C, \$1)$ can be extracted only once, irrespectively of the number of signature verifications performed. Remarkably, the guarded version of $\mathsf{Paid}(x_C, \$1)$ is an exponential formula, i.e., a stable truth: as such, it can be safely transmitted over the network, unaffected by replay attacks.

There is one problem left: the assumption $\mathsf{Paid}(x_C, \$1)$ available at the client C does not entail the guarded, exponential formula $!\, (\mathsf{N}(x_n) \multimap \mathsf{Paid}(x_C, \$1))$, which C needs to prove in order to use the key x_k to transmit her request. This is indeed the most intriguing bit of our construction: to construct the desired proof, we may introduce a *serializer* for $\mathsf{Paid}(x_C, \$1)$ among the assumptions of C, to automatically provide for the creation of the guarded version of $\mathsf{Paid}(x_C, \$1)$. The serializer has the form:

$$!\,\forall x, y.(\mathsf{Paid}(x, \$1) \multimap\ !(\mathsf{N}(y) \multimap \mathsf{Paid}(x, \$1)))$$

that is, an exponential and universally quantified formula, serving for multiple communications of different predicates built over Paid. Serializers may be generated automatically for any given affine formula, and introducing them as additional assumptions is sound, in that it does not affect the set of entailed assertions, as we discuss in the next section. Furthermore, serializers capture a rather general class of mechanisms for ensuring timely communications, like session keys or timestamps, which are all based on the consumption of an affine resource to assess the freshness of an exchange.

3 Metatheory of Exponential Serialization

In principle, the introduction of serializers among the assumed hypotheses could alter the intended semantics of the authorization policy, due to the subtle interplay of formulas through the entailment relation. Here, we isolate sufficient conditions under which exponential serialization leads to a sound protection mechanism for affine formulas.

We presuppose that the signature Σ of predicate symbols is partitioned in two sets Σ_A and Σ_C. Atomic formulas A have the form $p(t_1, \ldots, t_n)$ for some $p \in \Sigma_A$; control formulas C have the same form, though with $p \in \Sigma_C$. We identify various categories of formulas defined by the following productions.

$$
\begin{array}{lll}
B ::= A \mid B \otimes B \mid B \multimap B \mid \forall x.B \mid\ !B & \text{base formulas} \\
P ::= B \mid C \mid P \otimes P & \text{payload formulas} \\
G ::= C \multimap P \mid\ !G & \text{guarded formulas}
\end{array}
$$

Base formulas B are formulas of an authorization policy, which are used as security annotations in the application code. For simplicity, we dispense in this section with equalities and $\mathbf{0}$, since they are used in the analysis but they are never assumed in the code. (Notice that compromised principals can be modelled also without negation [4].) Payload formulas P are formulas which we want to serialize for communication over the untrusted network. Importantly, payload formulas comprise also control formulas, which allows, e.g., for the transmission of fresh nonces to remote verifiers: this pattern is present in several authentication protocols [18]. Finally, guarded formulas G are used to model the serialized version of payload formulas, suitable for transmission. We let S denote an arbitrary serializer of the form $!\forall \tilde{x}.(P \multimap !(C \multimap P))$ and we write $\Delta \vdash F^n$ for $\Delta \vdash F \otimes \ldots \otimes F$ (n times), with the proviso that $\Delta \vdash F^0$ stands for $\Delta \nvdash F$.

Given a multiset of assumptions Δ, the extension of Δ with the serializers $S_1, \ldots, S_n$ is sound if Δ and its extension derive the same payload formulas. As it turns out, this is only true when Δ satisfies additional conditions, which we formalize next.

Definition 1 (Rank). *Let* $rk : \Sigma_C \to \mathbb{N}$ *be a total, injective function. Given a formula* F, *we define the* rank *of* F *with respect to* rk, *noted* $rk(F)$, *as follows:*

$$
\begin{array}{lll}
rk(p(t_1, \ldots, t_n)) = rk(p) & & \text{if } p \in \Sigma_C \\
rk(F_1 \otimes F_2) \quad = min\ \{rk(F_1), rk(F_2)\} & & \\
rk(F) \qquad\qquad = +\infty & & \text{otherwise}
\end{array}
$$

Definition 2 (Stratification). *A formula* F *is* stratified *with respect to a rank function* rk *if and only if: (i)* $F = C \multimap P$ *implies* $rk(C) < rk(P)$; *(ii)* $F = P \multimap G$ *implies that* G *is stratified; (iii)* $F = \forall x.F'$ *implies that* F' *is stratified; (iv)* $F = !F'$ *implies that* F' *is stratified. We assume* F *to be stratified in all the other cases. A multiset of formulas* Δ *is* stratified *if and only if there exists a rank function* rk *such that each formula in* Δ *is stratified with respect to* rk.

For instance, the multiset $C_1 \multimap C_2, C_2 \multimap C_3$ is stratified, given an appropriate choice of a rank function, while the multiset $C_1 \multimap C_2, C_2 \multimap C_1$ is not stratified. Stratification is required precisely to disallow such circular dependencies among control formulas in the proof of our soundness result, Theorem 1 below. To prove that result, we need a further definition:

Definition 3 (Guardedness). *Let* $\Delta = P_1, \ldots, P_m, S_1, \ldots, S_n$ *be a stratified multiset of formulas. We say that* Δ *is* guarded *if and only if* $\Delta \vdash C^k$ *implies* $k \leq 1$ *for any control formula* C.

Table 2. Syntax of RCF

$$M, N ::= x \mid () \mid (M, N) \mid \lambda x.\, E \mid h\, M \qquad\qquad \text{values } (h \in \{\mathsf{inl}, \mathsf{inr}, \mathsf{fold}\})$$
$$D, E ::= M \mid M\, N \mid M = N \mid \mathsf{let}\ x = E\ \mathsf{in}\ E' \mid \qquad \text{expressions}$$
$$\mathsf{let}\ (x, y) = M\ \mathsf{in}\ E \mid$$
$$\mathsf{match}\ M\ \mathsf{with}\ h\ x\ \mathsf{then}\ E\ \mathsf{else}\ E' \mid$$
$$(\nu a) E \mid E \upharpoonright E' \mid a!M \mid a? \mid \mathsf{assume}\ F \mid \mathsf{assert}\ F$$

The intuition underlying guardedness may be explained as follows. Consider a multiset Δ, a payload formula P such that $\Delta \vdash P$ and let $S = !\forall \tilde{x}.(P \multimap !(C \multimap P))$ be a serializer for P. Now, the only way that S may affect derivability is by allowing the duplication of the payload formula P via the exponential implication $!(C \multimap P)$. However, this effect is prevented if we are guaranteed that the control formula C guarding P is derived at most once in Δ: that is precisely what the guardedness condition ensures.

Theorem 1 (Soundness of Exponential Serialization). *Let $\Delta = P_1, \ldots, P_m$. If $\Delta' = \Delta, S_1, \ldots, S_n$ is guarded and $\Delta' \vdash P$, then $\Delta \vdash P$ for all P.*

While guardedness is convenient to use in the proof of Theorem 1, it is clearly an undecidable condition. Fortunately, it is not difficult to isolate a sufficient criterion to decide whether a multiset of formulas is guarded based on a simple syntactic check.

Proposition 1. *If $\Delta = P_1, \ldots, P_m, S_1, \ldots, S_n$ is stratified and the control formulas occurring in $P_1, \ldots, P_m$ are pairwise distinct, then Δ is guarded.*

4 Review of RCF

The syntax of values and expressions of RCF [4] is overviewed in Table 2. We assume collections of names (a, b, c, m, n) and variables (x, y, z). Values include variables, unit, pairs, functions and constructions; constructors account for the creation of standard sum types and iso-recursive types. Expressions of RCF include standard λ-calculus constructs like values, applications, equality checks, lets, pair splits, and pattern matching, as well as primitives for concurrent, message-passing computations. For space reasons, we keep the presentation intuitive and mostly informal (we refer to [4] and the long version for complete details). The semantics of expressions is standard, so we just discuss the RCF-specific constructs. Expression $(\nu a) E$ generates a fresh channel name a and then behaves as E. Expression $E \upharpoonright E'$ evaluates E and E' in parallel, and returns the result of E'. Expression $a!M$ asynchronously outputs M on channel a and returns $()$. Expression $a?$ waits until a term N is available on channel a and returns N.

Definition 4 (Safety). *A closed expression E is safe if and only if, in all evaluations of E, the conjunction of the asserted formulas is entailed by the introduced assumptions.*

We let an *opponent* be any closed expression of RCF which does not contain any assumption or assertion. Our goal is to guarantee that safety holds, despite the best efforts of an active opponent.

Definition 5 (Robust Safety). *A closed expression E is* robustly safe *if and only if, for any opponent O, the application $O\,E$ is safe[2].*

5   The Type System

Our refinement type system builds on previous work by Bengtson et al. [4], extending it to guarantee the correct usage of affine formulas and to enforce our revised notion of (robust) safety.

5.1   Types, Typing Environments, and Base Judgements

The syntax of types is defined as follows. The unit value is given type unit. Sum types have form $T + U$, iso-recursive types are denoted by $\mu\alpha.\,T$. Type variables are denoted by α. There exist various forms of dependent types: a function of type $x : T \to U$ takes as an input a value M of type T and returns a value of type $U\{M/x\}$; a pair (M, N) has type $x : T * U$ if M has type T and N has type $U\{M/x\}$; a value M has a refinement type $\{x : T \mid F\}$ if M has type T and the formula $F\{M/x\}$ holds true. We use type $\mathsf{Un} \triangleq \mathsf{unit}$ to model data that may come from, or be sent to the opponent, as it is customary for security type systems. Type $\mathsf{bool} \triangleq \mathsf{unit} + \mathsf{unit}$ is inhabited by $\mathsf{true} \triangleq \mathsf{inl}()$ and $\mathsf{false} \triangleq \mathsf{inr}()$.

Our type system comprises several typing judgements of the form $\Gamma; \Delta \vdash \mathcal{J}$, where $\Gamma; \Delta$ is a typing environment collecting all the information which can be used to derive $\mathcal{J}$. In particular, Γ contains the type bindings, while Δ comprises logical formulas that are known to hold at run-time. Formally, we let Γ be an ordered list of entries $\mu_1, \ldots, \mu_n$ and Δ be a multiset of affine logic formulas. Each entry μ_i in Γ denotes either a type variable (α), a kinding annotation ($\alpha :: k$), or a type binding for channels ($a \updownarrow T$) or variables ($x : T$).

We use the judgement $\Gamma; \Delta \vdash \diamond$ to denote that the typing environment $\Gamma; \Delta$ is well-formed, i.e., it satisfies some standard syntactic conditions (for instance, it does not contain duplicate type bindings for the same variable). The only remarkable point in the definition of $\Gamma; \Delta \vdash \diamond$ is that we forbid variables in Γ to be mapped to a refinement type: indeed, when extending a typing environment with a new type binding $x : T$, we use the function ψ to place the structural type information in Γ and the function *forms* to place the associated refinements in Δ. As an example, we have $\psi(\{y : \mathsf{unit} \mid F(y)\}) = \mathsf{unit}$ and *forms*$(x : \{y : \mathsf{unit} \mid F(y)\}) = F(x)$.

Finally, we use the judgement $\Gamma; \Delta \vdash F$ to denote that the formulas in Δ entail F. The formal definition also syntactically checks that $\Gamma; \Delta$ is well-formed.

5.2   Environment Rewriting

All the type information stored in Γ can be used arbitrarily often in the derivation of any judgement of our type system. The treatment of the formulas in Δ, instead, is subtler, since affine resources must be used at most once during type-checking. In particular, we need to split environment Δ among subderivations

---

[2] Here, the notation $O\,E$ is standard syntactic sugar for let $x = O$ in let $y = E$ in $x\,y$.

to avoid the duplication of resources. The general structure of the rules of our system will thus be the following:

$$\frac{\Gamma; \Delta_1 \vdash \mathcal{J}_1 \quad \cdots \quad \Gamma; \Delta_n \vdash \mathcal{J}_n \quad \Gamma; \Delta \hookrightarrow \Gamma; \Delta_1, \ldots, \Delta_n}{\Gamma; \Delta \vdash \mathcal{J}}$$

where $\Gamma; \Delta \hookrightarrow \Gamma; \Delta'$ denotes the *environment rewriting* of $\Gamma; \Delta$ to $\Gamma'; \Delta'$.

The environment rewriting relation is defined as:

$$\text{(REWRITE)}$$
$$\frac{\Delta \vdash \Delta' \quad \Gamma; \Delta \vdash \diamond \quad \Gamma; \Delta' \vdash \diamond}{\Gamma; \Delta \hookrightarrow \Gamma; \Delta'}$$

where we write $\Delta \vdash F_1, \ldots, F_n$ to denote that $\Delta \vdash F_1 \otimes \ldots \otimes F_n$, with the proviso that $\Delta \vdash \emptyset$ stands for $\Delta \vdash 1$. The adoption of the environment rewriting relation as an house-keeping device for the formulas of Δ greatly improves the expressiveness of the type system in a very natural way. Interestingly, all the non-determinism introduced by the application of the rewriting rules and the splitting of the logical formulas among the premises can be effectively tamed by the algorithmic type system presented in Section 7.

5.3   Kinding and Subtyping

Security type systems often rely on a kinding relation to discriminate whether or not messages of a specific type may be known to the attacker or received from it. The kinding judgement $\Gamma; \Delta \vdash T :: k$ denotes that type T is of kind k. Kind $k = \mathsf{pub}$ denotes public messages which may be sent to the attacker, while kind $k = \mathsf{tnt}$ characterizes tainted message which may come from the attacker. The type Un is both public and tainted.

The subtyping judgment $\Gamma; \Delta \vdash T <: U$ expresses the fact that T is a subtype of U and, thus, values of type T can be used in place of values of type U. The subtyping judgment makes public types subtype of tainted types and further describes standard subtyping relations for types sharing the same structure (e.g., pair types are covariant and function types contra-variant in their arguments).

Our treatment of kinding and subtyping resembles other security type systems [4,2] and only differs in the management of affine formulas, which is similar to the one we employ for typing values and expressions (see below).

5.4   Typing Values

The typing judgement $\Gamma; \Delta \vdash M : T$ denotes that value M is given type T under environment $\Gamma; \Delta$. Some selected rules for assigning types to values are given in the top part of Table 3.

Rule (VAL REFINE) is a natural adaptation to an affine setting of the standard rule for refinement types. Rules (VAL FUN) and (VAL PAIR) are more interesting: notice that our type system does not incorporate affine types, in that the type information in Γ is propagated to all the premises of a typing rule. It is thus crucial for soundness that both pairs and functions are type-checked in an *exponential* environment, i.e., an environment of the form $!\Delta = !F_1, \ldots, !F_n$. For instance, using an affine formula F from the typing environment to give a pair (M, N) type $x : T * \{y : U \mid F\}$ would lead to an unbounded usage of F upon replicated pair splitting operations on (M, N), as we discuss in Section 5.7. Allowing for affine refinements but forbidding affine types confines the problem of resource management to the formula environment, which simplifies the system but might seem overly restrictive. In Section 5.7 we explain how the exponential serialization technique can be leveraged to encode affine types in our framework and, thereby, enhance its expressiveness.

5.5   Typing Expressions

The typing judgement $\Gamma; \Delta \vdash E : T$ denotes that expression E is given type T under environment $\Gamma; \Delta$. Some selected typing rules for expressions are given in the bottom part of Table 3.

Rule (EXP SUBSUM) is a standard subsumption rule for expressions. In rule (EXP SPLIT) we exploit the logic to keep track of the performed pair splitting operation and make type-checking more precise. Rule (EXP ASSERT) is standard and requires an asserted formula F to be derivable from the formulas collected by the environment.

The most complex rule is (EXP FORK): intuitively, when type-checking the parallel expressions $E_1 \upharpoonright E_2$, assumptions in E_1 can be used to type-check assertions in E_2 and vice-versa. On the other hand, we need to prevent an affine assumption in E_1 from being used twice to justify assertions in both E_2 *and* E_1. This is achieved through the *extraction* relation, i.e., through the premises of the form $E_i \rightsquigarrow [\Delta_i \mid D_i]$: the extraction operation destructively collects all the assumptions from the expression E_i and returns the expression D_i obtained by purging E_i of its assumptions. The typing environment is then extended with the collected assumptions and partitioned to type-check the purged expressions D_1 and D_2 respectively. The extraction relation is reported in Table 4. Notice that we prevent formulas containing free names from being extracted outside of the scope of the respective binders (cf. EXTR ASSUME).

The extraction relation is also used to type-check any expression possibly containing active assumptions, i.e., lets, restrictions, and assumptions themselves.

5.6   Formal Results

The main soundness result of our type system is reported below.

Theorem 2 (Robust Safety). *If* $\varepsilon; \emptyset \vdash E : \mathsf{Un}$, *then* E *is robustly safe.*

Theorem 2 above and Theorem 1 in Section 3 (establishing the soundness of exponential serialization) constitute the two building blocks of our static verification technique, which we may finally summarize as follows.

Given any expression E, we identify the payload formulas assumed in E, and construct the corresponding exponential serializers $S_1, \ldots, S_n$ for those formulas. Let then $E^\star = \mathsf{assume}\ S_1 \otimes \cdots \otimes S_n \upharpoonright E$. By Theorem 2, if $\varepsilon; \emptyset \vdash E^\star : \mathsf{Un}$, then $E^\star$ is robustly safe. By Theorem 1, so is the original expression E, provided that a further invariant holds for $E^\star$, namely that all multisets of formulas

Table 3. Typing values and expressions (selected rules)

(VAL VAR)
$$\frac{\Gamma; \Delta \vdash \diamond \qquad (x : T) \in \Gamma}{\Gamma; \Delta \vdash x : T}$$

(VAL FUN)
$$\frac{\Gamma, x : \psi(T); !\Delta', forms(x : T) \vdash E : U \qquad \Gamma; \Delta \hookrightarrow \Gamma; !\Delta'}{\Gamma; \Delta \vdash \lambda x. E : x : T \to U}$$

(VAL PAIR)
$$\frac{\Gamma; !\Delta_1 \vdash M : T \qquad \Gamma; !\Delta_2 \vdash N : U\{M/x\} \qquad \Gamma; \Delta \hookrightarrow \Gamma; !\Delta_1, !\Delta_2}{\Gamma; \Delta \vdash (M, N) : x : T * U}$$

(VAL REFINE)
$$\frac{\Gamma; \Delta_1 \vdash M : T \qquad \Gamma; \Delta_2 \vdash F\{M/x\} \qquad \Gamma; \Delta \hookrightarrow \Gamma; \Delta_1, \Delta_2}{\Gamma; \Delta \vdash M : \{x : T \mid F\}}$$

(EXP SUBSUM)
$$\frac{\Gamma; \Delta_1 \vdash E : T \qquad \Gamma; \Delta_2 \vdash T <: T' \qquad \Gamma; \Delta \hookrightarrow \Gamma; \Delta_1, \Delta_2}{\Gamma; \Delta \vdash E : T'}$$

(EXP LET)
$$\frac{E \leadsto^{\emptyset} [\Delta' \mid E'] \qquad \Gamma; \Delta_1 \vdash E' : T \qquad \Gamma, x : \psi(T); \Delta_2, forms(x : T) \vdash D : U \qquad x \notin fv(U) \qquad \Gamma; \Delta, \Delta' \hookrightarrow \Gamma; \Delta_1, \Delta_2}{\Gamma; \Delta \vdash \text{let } x = E \text{ in } D : U}$$

(EXP SPLIT)
$$\frac{\Gamma; \Delta_1 \vdash M : x : T * U \qquad \Gamma, x : \psi(T), y : \psi(U); \Delta_2, forms(x : T), forms(y : U), !((x, y) = M) \vdash E : V \qquad \{x, y\} \cap fv(V) = \emptyset \qquad \Gamma; \Delta \hookrightarrow \Gamma; \Delta_1, \Delta_2}{\Gamma; \Delta \vdash \text{let } (x, y) = M \text{ in } E : V}$$

(EXP ASSUME)
$$\frac{\Gamma; \Delta, F \vdash \text{assume } \mathbf{1} : T \qquad F \neq \mathbf{1}}{\Gamma; \Delta \vdash \text{assume } F : T}$$

(EXP TRUE)
$$\frac{\Gamma; \Delta \vdash \diamond}{\Gamma; \Delta \vdash \text{assume } \mathbf{1} : \text{unit}}$$

(EXP ASSERT)
$$\frac{\Gamma; \Delta \vdash F}{\Gamma; \Delta \vdash \text{assert } F : \text{unit}}$$

(EXP FORK)
$$\frac{E_1 \leadsto^{\emptyset} [\Delta_1 \mid D_1] \qquad E_2 \leadsto^{\emptyset} [\Delta_2 \mid D_2] \qquad \Gamma; \Delta'_1 \vdash D_1 : T_1 \qquad \Gamma; \Delta'_2 \vdash D_2 : T_2 \qquad \Delta, \Delta_1, \Delta_2 \hookrightarrow \Delta'_1, \Delta'_2}{\Gamma; \Delta \vdash E_1 \upharpoonright E_2 : T_2}$$

Notation: For $\Delta = F_1, \dots, F_n$ we write $!\Delta$ to denote $!F_1, \dots, !F_n$.

assumed during the evaluation of $E^{\star}$ are guarded. While this latter invariant is not enforced by our type system, the desired guarantees may be achieved by requiring that the assumption of control formulas be confined within system code packaged into library functions providing certified access and management of the capabilities associated with those formulas. The certification of the system code provided by the library function, in turn, may be achieved with limited effort, based on the syntactic guardedness condition provided by Proposition 1.

5.7 Encoding Affine Types

Here we discuss how we can take advantage of exponential serialization to encode affine types and, thus, enhance the expressiveness of our type system. For the sake of simplicity, we focus on the encoding of affine pairs.

Table 4. Extraction

(EXTR FORK)

$$\frac{E_1 \leadsto^{\widetilde{a}} [\Delta_1 \mid D_1] \qquad E_2 \leadsto^{\widetilde{a}} [\Delta_2 \mid D_2]}{E_1 \mathbin{\upharpoonright} E_2 \leadsto^{\widetilde{a}} [\Delta_1, \Delta_2 \mid D_1 \mathbin{\upharpoonright} D_2]}$$

(EXTR LET)

$$\frac{E_1 \leadsto^{\widetilde{a}} [\Delta \mid D_1]}{\mathsf{let}\ x = E_1\ \mathsf{in}\ E_2 \leadsto^{\widetilde{a}} [\Delta \mid \mathsf{let}\ x = D_1\ \mathsf{in}\ E_2]}$$

(EXTR RES)

$$\frac{E \leadsto^{a,\widetilde{b}} [\Delta \mid D]}{(\nu a)E \leadsto^{\widetilde{b}} [\Delta \mid (\nu a)D]}$$

(EXTR ASSUME)

$$\frac{F \neq 1 \qquad fn(F) \cap \{\widetilde{a}\} = \emptyset}{\mathsf{assume}\ F \leadsto^{\widetilde{a}} [F \mid \mathsf{assume}\ 1]}$$

(EXTR EXP)

$$\frac{\text{no other rule applies}}{E \leadsto^{\widetilde{a}} [\emptyset \mid E]}$$

Consider the typing environment $\Gamma; \Delta \triangleq x : \mathsf{Un}, y : \mathsf{Un}; A(x), B(y)$. Standard refinement type systems as [4] allow for the following type judgement:

$$\Gamma; \Delta \vdash (x, y) : \{x : \mathsf{Un} \mid A(x)\} * \{y : \mathsf{Un} \mid B(y)\}$$

If the formulas $A(x)$ and $B(y)$ are interpreted as affine resources, however, the previous type assignment is sound only as long as the pair (x, y) can be split only once, since every application of rule (EXP SPLIT) for pair destruction introduces the formulas $A(x), B(y)$ into the typing environment. Since our type system does not feature affine types and has no way to enforce a single deconstruction of a pair, it conservatively forbids the previous type judgement, in that the premises of rule (VAL PAIR) require an exponential typing environment.

Nevertheless, the following type judgement is allowed by our type system:

$$x : \mathsf{Un}, y : \mathsf{Un}; A(x), B(y), S_1, S_2 \vdash (x, y) : \{x : \mathsf{Un} \mid A'(x)\} * \{y : \mathsf{Un} \mid B'(y)\}$$

where $A'(x) \triangleq\ !(P_1(x) \multimap A(x))$ and $B'(y) \triangleq\ !(P_2(y) \multimap B(y))$ are the serialized variants of $A(x)$ and $B(y)$ respectively, while $S_1 \triangleq\ !\forall x.(A(x) \multimap A'(x))$ and $S_2 \triangleq\ !\forall y.(B(y) \multimap B'(y))$ are the corresponding serializers. Here, the main idea for type-checking is to appeal to environment rewriting to consume the affine formulas $A(x)$ and $B(y)$, and introduce their exponential counterparts $A'(x)$ and $B'(y)$ into the environment before assigning a type to the pair components.

The interesting point now is that the pair (x, y) can be split arbitrarily often, but the affine formulas $A(x)$ and $B(y)$ can be retrieved at most once, as long as the control formulas $P_1(x)$ and $P_2(y)$ are assumed at most once in the application code. In this way, we recover the expressiveness provided by affine types. We actually even go beyond that, allowing for a liberal usage of the value itself, as opposed to enforcing the affine usage of any data structure which contains an affine component, as dictated by many earlier substructural frameworks.

5.8 Encoding Cryptography

Formal cryptography can be encoded inside RCF in terms of *sealing* [22,24]. A *seal* k for a type T is a pair of functions: a sealing function $T \to \mathsf{Un}$ and an unsealing function $\mathsf{Un} \to T$. For symmetric cryptography, these functions model encryption and decryption operations, respectively. A payload of type T can be

Table 5. A variant of the *EPMO* protocol

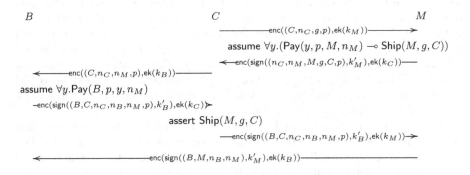

sealed to type Un and sent over the untrusted network; conversely, a message retrieved from the network with type Un can be unsealed to its correct type T.

The sealing/unsealing mechanism is implemented in terms of a list of pairs, which is stored in a global reference that can only be accessed using the sealing and unsealing functions. Upon sealing, the payload is paired with a fresh, public value (the *handle*) representing its sealed version, and the pair is stored in the list; conversely, the unsealing function looks for the handle in the list and returns the associated payload. Different cryptographic primitives, like public key encryptions and signature schemes, can be encoded following such a recipe.

One interesting benefit of our exponential serialization technique is that we can directly leverage the sealing-based cryptographic library proposed by Bengtson et al. [4]. The reason is that we never apply cryptography directly on messages with affine refinements, but we rely on their exponentially serialized variants. Without the serialization, we would need to define a different implementation of the sealing/unsealing mechanism: namely, we would have to enforce that an affine payload is never extracted more than once from the list stored in the global reference, i.e., the unsealing function would have to remove the payload from the list upon invocation. This would complicate the sealing-based abstraction of cryptography and require additional reasoning to justify its soundness.

6   Example: Electronic Purchase

We consider a variant of *EPMO*, a nonce-based e-payment protocol proposed by Guttman et al. [20]. The protocol narration is reported in Table 5.

Initially, a customer C contacts a merchant M to buy some goods g for a given price p; the request is encrypted under the public key of the merchant, $\mathsf{ek}(k_M)$, and includes a fresh nonce, n_C. If M agrees to proceed in the transaction by providing a signed response, C informs her bank B to authorize the payment. The bank replies by providing C a receipt of authorization, called the *money order*, which is then forwarded to M. Now M can verify that C is entitled to pay for the goods and complete the transaction by sending a signed request to B to cash the money order. At the end of the run, the bank transfers the funds and the merchant ships the goods.

A peculiarity of the protocol is that the identifier n_C is employed by C to authenticate *two* different messages, namely the replies by M and B. This pattern cannot be validated by most existing type systems, since the mechanisms hardcoded therein to deal with nonce-handshakes enforce the freshness of each nonce to be checked only once. Our framework, instead, allows for a very natural treatment of such authentication pattern, whose implementation can be written mostly oblivious of the security verification process based on lightweight logical annotations. For space reasons, we focus only on the aspects of the verification connected to the guarantees provided to C.

We define two predicates used in the analysis: $\mathsf{Pay}(B, p, M, n_M)$ states that B authorizes the payment p to M in reference to the order identified by n_M, while $\mathsf{Ship}(M, g, C)$ formalizes that M can ship the goods g to C. The protocol code for the customer, enriched with the most interesting type annotations, is reported below[3].

```
type MsgMC = MsgMC of (xnC: Un * xnM: Un * xM: Un * xg: Un * xC: Un * xp: Un)
  {!(N1(xnC) --o forall y.(Pay(y,xp,xM,xnM) --o Ship(xM,xg,xC))}

type MsgBC = MsgBC of (yB: Un * yC: Un * ynC: Un * ynB: Un * ynM: Un * yp: Un)
  {!(N2(ynC) --o forall y.(Pay(yB, yp, y, ynM))}

let (mkTid : unit -> {x: bytes | N1(x) times N2(x)}) () =
  let xf = mkFresh () in assume (N1(xf) times N2(xf)); xf

let cust C addC M addM B addB g p kC ekM ekB
         (vkM: (MsgMC, MsgMB) either VerKey) (vkB: MsgBC VerKey) =
  let nC = mkTid () in
  let msgCM1 = encrypt (C, nC, g, p) ekM in send addM msgCM1;
  let signMC = decrypt (receive addC) kC in
  let plainMC = verify signMC vkM in
  match plainMC with MsgMC (=nC, xnM, =M, =g, =C, =p) ->
      let msgCB = encrypt (C, nC, xnM, p) ekB in send addB msgCB;
      let signBC = decrypt (receive addC) kC in
      let plainBC = verify signBC vkB in
        match plainBC with MsgBC (=B, =C, =nC, xnB, =xnM, =p) ->
          assert Ship(M, g, C);
          let msgCM2 = encrypt signBC ekM in send addM msgCM2
```

Initially, we let the customer call the library function mkTid, which generates a fresh transaction identifier, corresponding to n_C in the protocol specification, and provides via its return type two distinct capabilities $\mathsf{N}_1(n_C)$ and $\mathsf{N}_2(n_C)$, later employed to authenticate two different messages received by C. Since the signing key of M is used to certify messages of two different types, at steps 2 and 6 of the protocol, the corresponding verification key available to the customer through the variable vkM refers to a sum type. We present only the MsgMC component of such type, since it is the one needed to type-check the code of C: the corresponding refined formula in the type definition describes the promise by M to ship the goods as soon as the requested payment has been authorized by any bank. We then use vkB to convey the other formula which is needed to type-check C, namely a statement that B authorizes the payment to any merchant to whom C wishes to transfer the money order. The hypotheses collected by C are

---

[3] For the sake of readability, we use F#- like syntax and some syntactic sugar like tuples and pattern matching to present code snippets from our example: these can be encoded in RCF using standard techniques [4].

enough to prove her assertion, i.e., to be sure that the request by M has been fulfilled and the goods will be shipped, hence the implementation is well-typed.

7 Algorithmic Typing

The type system presented in Section 5 includes several non-deterministic rules, which make it hard to implement an efficient decision procedure. In this section, we present an algorithmic version, which we prove sound and complete.

7.1 Algorithmic Type System

While standard sources of non-determinism like subtyping or refining value types can be eliminated using type annotations, the rewriting of logical environments, the distinctive source of non-determinism of our system, is harder to deal with. The core idea underlying the algorithmic version of the type system is to dispense with logical environments and to construct bottom-up a single logical formula that characterizes all the proof obligations that would normally be introduced along the type derivation. More in detail, every typing judgment of the form $\Gamma; \Delta \vdash \mathcal{J}$ is matched by an algorithmic counterpart of the form $\Gamma \vdash_{\mathsf{alg}} \mathcal{J}; F$. Intuitively, typing an expression algorithmically constitutes of two steps:

1. The expression (decorated with type annotations whenever needed) is type-checked using the algorithmic type system. This process is fully deterministic and in case of success yields *one* proof obligation F.
2. The proof obligation is verified, e.g., using an external theorem prover.

If both steps succeed, then the expression is well-typed.

In the remainder of this section we focus on selected rules for typing values and expressions: the remaining rules follow along the same lines.

7.2 Typing Values and Expressions

We present some selected algorithmic typing rules in Table 6.

Following standard practice, we rely on typing annotations to deal with non-structural rules. For instance, we explicitly annotate values that are expected to be given a refinement type (cf. VAL REF (ALG)) and expressions whose type should be derived using subtyping (cf. EXP SUBSUM (ALG)). In this way, every possible syntactic form is matched exactly by a single type rule.

We now exemplify the general concepts underlying our technique by contrasting the standard typing rule (VAL FUN) with its algorithmic counterpart (VAL FUN (ALG)). The main source of non-determinism in (VAL FUN) is the rewriting of Δ to $!\Delta'$. As previously mentioned, our goal is to dispense with logical environments and their rewriting, by collecting a single proof obligation that accounts for the proof obligations generated in the original type system. In the algorithmic version, the proof obligation obtained by giving $\lambda x : T. E$ type $V := x : T \to U$ in Γ is $!\forall x.(forms(x : T) \multimap F')$, where F' is the proof obligation collected by giving E type U in $\Gamma, x : \psi(T)$. In the following, we briefly justify why this

Table 6. Selected algorithmic rules for typing values and expressions

(VAL VAR (ALG))

$$\frac{\Gamma \vdash_{\mathsf{alg}} \diamond \qquad (x : T) \in \Gamma}{\Gamma \vdash_{\mathsf{alg}} x : T; 1}$$

(VAL FUN (ALG))

$$\frac{\Gamma, x : \psi(T) \vdash_{\mathsf{alg}} E : U; F' \qquad \mathit{fnfv}(T) \subseteq \mathit{dom}(\Gamma) \cup \{x\}}{\Gamma \vdash_{\mathsf{alg}} \lambda x : T. E : (x : T \to U); !\forall x.(\mathit{forms}(x : T) \multimap F')}$$

(VAL PAIR (ALG))

$$\frac{\Gamma \vdash_{\mathsf{alg}} M : T; F_1 \qquad \Gamma \vdash_{\mathsf{alg}} N : U\{M/x\}; F_2}{\Gamma \vdash_{\mathsf{alg}} (M, N) : x : T * U; !F_1 \otimes !F_2}$$

(VAL REF (ALG))

$$\frac{\Gamma \vdash_{\mathsf{alg}} M : T; F' \qquad \mathit{fnfv}(F) \subseteq \mathit{dom}(\Gamma) \cup \{x\}}{\Gamma \vdash_{\mathsf{alg}} M_{\{x:\_ \mid F\}} : \{x : T \mid F\}; F' \otimes F\{M/x\}}$$

(EXP SUBSUM (ALG))

$$\frac{\Gamma \vdash_{\mathsf{alg}} E : T; F_1 \qquad \Gamma \vdash_{\mathsf{alg}} T <: T'; F_2}{\Gamma \vdash_{\mathsf{alg}} E_{\_<:T'} : T'; F_1 \otimes F_2}$$

(EXP LET (ALG))

$$\frac{E \leadsto^\emptyset [\Delta' \mid E'] \qquad \Gamma \vdash_{\mathsf{alg}} E' : T; F_1 \qquad \Gamma, x : \psi(T) \vdash_{\mathsf{alg}} D : U; F_2 \qquad x \notin \mathit{fv}(U) \qquad \mathit{fnfv}(\Delta') \subseteq \mathit{dom}(\Gamma)}{\Gamma \vdash_{\mathsf{alg}} \mathsf{let}\ x = E\ \mathsf{in}\ D : U; \Delta' \multimap (F_1 \otimes \forall x.(\mathit{forms}(x : T) \multimap F_2))}$$

Notation: In logical formulas, we write $F_1, \ldots, F_n$ to denote $F_1 \otimes \ldots \otimes F_n$.

approach is sound, i.e., we argue why $\Gamma; \Delta \vdash \lambda x. E : V$ for any Δ such that $\Gamma; \Delta \vdash !\forall x.(\mathit{forms}(x : T) \multimap F')$ (i.e., Δ entails $!\forall x.(\mathit{forms}(x : T) \multimap F')$ and both are well-formed with respect to Γ). From $\Gamma; \Delta \vdash !\forall x.(\mathit{forms}(x : T) \multimap F')$, using the rules of the logic, we can show that there exists Δ' such that $\Gamma; \Delta \hookrightarrow \Gamma; !\Delta'$ and $\Gamma; !\Delta' \vdash \forall x.\mathit{forms}(x : T) \multimap F'$. Intuitively, this means that we can eliminate the exponential modality by rewriting the logical environment in exponential form. Furthermore, the well-formedness of $\Gamma; !\Delta'$ ensures that $x \notin \mathit{fv}(!\Delta')$: in this case, we can further eliminate the universal quantification, adding a type binding for x in order to keep the logical environment well-formed (the actual type is not relevant from the logic point of view), i.e., $\Gamma, x : \psi(T); !\Delta' \vdash \mathit{forms}(x : T) \multimap F'$. Using rule ($\multimap$-LEFT), we can finally prove $\Gamma, x : \psi(T); !\Delta', \mathit{forms}(x : T) \vdash F'$. By inductive reasoning, $\Gamma, x : \psi(T); !\Delta', \mathit{forms}(x : T) \vdash E : U$. Finally, (VAL FUN) allows us to derive $\Gamma; \Delta \vdash \lambda x. E : V$. The algorithmic variant is similarly proved complete.

If a typing rule contains multiple premises, then we combine the proof obligations obtained from the premises conjunctively (cf. VAL PAIR (ALG)). Whenever a typing rule relies on extraction (e.g., EXP LET) and adds the extracted environment Δ' to the environment before rewriting, the algorithmic variant of the rule (e.g., EXP LET (ALG)) creates a proof obligation of the form $\Delta' \multimap F$, where F is the proof obligation obtained by combining the proof obligations of the premises using the techniques described above.

7.3 Main Results

Let $\langle E \rangle$ denote the expression obtained from E by erasing all typing annotations.

Theorem 3 (Soundness and Completeness of Algorithmic Typing).

1. *If $\Gamma \vdash_{\mathsf{alg}} E : T; F$ and $\Gamma; \Delta \vdash F$, then $\Gamma; \Delta \vdash \langle E \rangle : T$.*
2. *If $\Gamma; \Delta \vdash E : T$, then there exists E', F such that $\langle E' \rangle = E$, $\Gamma \vdash_{\mathsf{alg}} E' : T; F$, and $\Gamma; \Delta \vdash F$.*

7.4   Typing the Example

The proof obligation assigned to the `cust` function in Section 6 is shown below.

$\forall$C.$\forall$M.$\forall$B.$\forall$G.$\forall$p.
  $\forall$nC.((N1(nC) $\otimes$ N2(nC)) $\multimap$
    $\forall$xnM.(!(N1(nC) $\multimap$ ($\forall$y.Pay(y,p,M,xnM) $\multimap$ Ship(M,g,C))) $\multimap$
      !(N2(nC) $\multimap$ ($\forall$z.Pay(B,p,z,xnM))) $\multimap$
      Ship(M,g,C)))

For the sake of readability we removed all unnecessary occurrences of **1** and unused quantified variables.

In this example, as well as in all other protocols we considered, the problem of solving equalities is reduced to the unification of variables[4]. This allows us to use the `llprover` [27] theorem prover, which at the moment does not support equality theories. The above formula is discharged in less than 20 ms.

8   Conclusion

We presented the first type system for statically enforcing the (robust) safety of cryptographic protocol implementations with respect to authorization policies expressed in affine logic. Our type system benefits from the novel concept of exponential serialization to achieve a general and flexible treatment of affine resources. We further proposed an efficient algorithmic variant of the type system.

We are currently working on the mechanization of our theory by implementing a type-checker based on the algorithmic typing rules. We plan to facilitate type-checking and reduce the need for manual type annotations by taking advantage of recent research on type inference in intuitionistic linear logic [3].

References

1. Abadi, M., Fournet, C.: Mobile values, new names, and secure communication. In: Proc. 28th Symposium on Principles of Programming Languages, POPL, pp. 104–115. ACM (2001)
2. Backes, M., Hriţcu, C., Maffei, M.: Union and Intersection Types for Secure Protocol Implementations. In: Mödersheim, S., Palamidessi, C. (eds.) TOSCA 2011. LNCS, vol. 6993, pp. 1–28. Springer, Heidelberg (2012)

---

[4] Equalities are introduced by pattern-matching, a syntactic sugar which we encode in our system using standard techniques [4].

3. Baillot, P., Hofmann, M.: Type Inference in Intuitionistic Linear Logic. In: PPDP 2010, pp. 219–230. ACM (2010)
4. Bengtson, J., Bhargavan, K., Fournet, C., Gordon, A.D., Maffeis, S.: Refinement Types for Secure Implementations. TOPLAS 33(2), 8 (2011)
5. Bhargavan, K., Corin, R., Deniélou, P.M., Fournet, C., Leifer, J.J.: Cryptographic Protocol Synthesis and Verification for Multiparty Sessions. In: CSF 2009, pp. 124–140. IEEE (2009)
6. Bhargavan, K., Fournet, C., Gordon, A.D.: Modular Verification of Security Protocol Code by Typing. In: POPL 2010, pp. 445–456. ACM (2010)
7. Bhargavan, K., Fournet, C., Gordon, A.D., Tse, S.: Verified Interoperable Implementations of Security Protocols. TOPLAS 31(1) (2008)
8. Bierhoff, K., Aldrich, J.: Modular typestate checking of aliased objects. In: OOPSLA 2007, pp. 301–320. ACM (2007)
9. Blanchet, B.: An Efficient Cryptographic Protocol Verifier Based on Prolog Rules. In: CSFW 2001, pp. 82–96. IEEE (2001)
10. Bowers, K.D., Bauer, L., Garg, D., Pfenning, F., Reiter, M.K.: Consumable Credentials in Linear-Logic-Based Access-Control Systems. In: NDSS 2007. Internet Society (2007)
11. Bugliesi, M., Focardi, R., Maffei, M.: Dynamic Types for Authentication. JCS 15(6), 563–617 (2007)
12. Bugliesi, M., Calzavara, S., Eigner, F., Maffei, M.: Logical Foundations of Secure Resource Management in Protocol Implementations (Long Version), http://www.lbs.cs.uni-saarland.de/affine-rcf/
13. Bugliesi, M., Calzavara, S., Eigner, F., Maffei, M.: Resource-Aware Authorization Policies for Statically Typed Cryptographic Protocols. In: CSF 2011, pp. 83–98. IEEE (2011)
14. Chapin, P.C., Skalka, C., Wang, X.S.: Authorization in Trust Management: Features and Foundations. ACM Computing Surveys 40(3) (2008)
15. Fournet, C., Kohlweiss, M., Strub, P.Y.: Modular Code-Based Cryptographic Verification. In: CCS 2011, pp. 341–350. ACM (2011)
16. Garg, D., Bauer, L., Bowers, K.D., Pfenning, F., Reiter, M.K.: A Linear Logic of Authorization and Knowledge. In: Gollmann, D., Meier, J., Sabelfeld, A. (eds.) ESORICS 2006. LNCS, vol. 4189, pp. 297–312. Springer, Heidelberg (2006)
17. Girard, J.Y.: Linear Logic: Its Syntax and Semantics. In: Advances in Linear Logic. London Mathematical Society LNS, vol. 22, pp. 1–42. Cambridge University Press (1995)
18. Gordon, A.D., Jeffrey, A.: Authenticity by Typing for Security Protocols. JCS 11(4), 451–519 (2003)
19. Gordon, A.D., Jeffrey, A.: Types and Effects for Asymmetric Cryptographic Protocols. JCS 12(3), 435–484 (2004)
20. Guttman, J.D., Thayer, F.J., Carlson, J.A., Herzog, J.C., Ramsdell, J.D., Sniffen, B.T.: Trust Management in Strand Spaces: A Rely-Guarantee Method. In: Schmidt, D. (ed.) ESOP 2004. LNCS, vol. 2986, pp. 325–339. Springer, Heidelberg (2004)
21. Mandelbaum, Y., Walker, D., Harper, R.: An effective theory of type refinements. In: ICFP 2003, pp. 213–225. ACM (2003)
22. Morris, J.: Protection in Programming Languages. CACM 16(1), 15–21 (1973)
23. Naden, K., Bocchino, R., Aldrich, J., Bierhoff, K.: A Type System for Borrowing Permissions. In: POPL 2012, pp. 557–570. ACM (2012)
24. Sumii, E., Pierce, B.: A Bisimulation for Dynamic Sealing. TCS 375(1-3), 169–192 (2007)

25. Sunshine, J., Naden, K., Stork, S., Aldrich, J., Tanter, E.: First-Class State Change in Plaid. In: OOPSLA 2011, pp. 713–732. ACM (2011)
26. Swamy, N., Chen, J., Fournet, C., Strub, P.Y., Bhargavan, K., Yang, J.: Secure Distributed Programming with Value-Dependent Types. In: ICFP 2011, pp. 266–278. ACM (2011)
27. Tomura, N.: llprover - A Linear Logic Prover,
    `http://bach.istc.kobe-u.ac.jp/llprover/`
28. Tov, J.A., Pucella, R.: Stateful Contracts for Affine Types. In: Gordon, A.D. (ed.) ESOP 2010. LNCS, vol. 6012, pp. 550–569. Springer, Heidelberg (2010)
29. Troelstra, A.S.: Lectures on Linear Logic. CSLI Stanford, LNS, vol. 29 (1992)

Keys to the Cloud: Formal Analysis and Concrete Attacks on Encrypted Web Storage

Chetan Bansal[1], Karthikeyan Bhargavan[2],
Antoine Delignat-Lavaud[2], and Sergio Maffeis[3,*]

[1] BITS Pilani-Goa
[2] INRIA Paris-Rocquencourt
[3] Imperial College London

Abstract. To protect sensitive user data against server-side attacks, a number of security-conscious web applications have turned to client-side encryption, where only encrypted user data is ever stored in the cloud. We formally investigate the security of a number of such applications, including password managers, cloud storage providers, an e-voting website and a conference management system. We find that their security relies on both their use of cryptography and the way it combines with common web security mechanisms as implemented in the browser. We model these applications using the WebSpi web security library for ProVerif, we discuss novel attacks found by automated formal analysis, and we propose robust countermeasures.

Keywords: Web Security, Formal Methods, Protocol Verification.

1 Application-Level Cryptography on the Web

Many web users routinely store sensitive data online, such as bank accounts, health records and private correspondence. Servers that store such data are a tempting target for cybercrime: a single attack can yield valuable data, such as credit card numbers, for millions of users. As websites move to using cloud-based data storage, the confidentiality of user data and the trustworthiness of the hosting servers has come further into question.

Transport layer security (TLS) as provided by HTTPS [21] does not fully address these concerns. TLS protects sensitive data over the wire as it travels between a browser and a website. However, it does not protect data at rest, when it is stored on the client or the server, where it can be accessed by an attacker stealing a laptop or hacking into a server. To protect from these risks, web applications use a combination of application-level cryptography and browser-based security mechanisms to securely handle user data. Our goal is to formally investigate the effectiveness of these mechanisms and their concrete deployments.

Application-level cryptography. To protect data from hackers, websites like Dropbox [2] systematically encrypt all files before storing them on the cloud. However,

---

* Maffeis is supported by EPSRC grant EP/I004246/1.

D. Basin and J.C. Mitchell (Eds.): POST 2013, LNCS 7796, pp. 126–146, 2013.
© Springer-Verlag Berlin Heidelberg 2013

since the decryption keys must be accessible to the website, this architecture still leaves user data vulnerable to dishonest administrators and website vulnerabilities. A more secure alternative, used by storage services like SpiderOak and password managers like 1Password, is *client-side encryption*: encrypt all data on the client before uploading it to the website. Using sophisticated cryptographic mechanisms, the server can still perform limited computations on the encrypted data [19]. For example, web applications such as ConfiChair [7] and Helios [4] combine client-side encryption with server-side zero-knowledge constructions to achieve stronger user privacy goals.

These application-level cryptographic mechanisms deserve close formal analysis, lest they provide a false sense of security to their users. In particular, it is necessary to examine not just the cryptographic details (i.e. what is encrypted), but also how the decryption keys are managed on the the browser.

Browser-based security mechanisms. Even with client-side encryption, the server is still responsible for access control to the data it stores. Web authentication and authorization typically rely on password-based login forms. Some websites use single sign-on protocols like OAuth [17] to delegate user authentication to third parties. After login, the user's session is managed using cookies known only to the browser and server. JavaScript is then used to interact with the user, make AJAX requests to download data over HTTPS, store secrets in HTML5 local storage, and present decrypted data to the user.

The security of the application thus depends on both the server and on browser-based mechanisms like cookies and JavaScript. That is dangerous, considering the prevalence of web vulnerabilities such as Cross-Site Scripting (XSS), Cross-Site Request Forgery (CSRF), open redirectors or phishing, even on major websites. In previous work, our survey of encrypted storage services [11] uncovered many such vulnerabilities and showed how can be exploited to bypass both client-side and server-side cryptographic protections. However, these attacks were found by manual inspection aided by tracing tools. Can we search for such attacks systematically and exhaustively? More importantly, can we evaluate any proposed countermeasures to ensure that they are not vulnerable to variations of the same attacks? In response to both these questions, we follow [8] in advocating the automated formal analysis of web security mechanisms.

Formal analysis of cryptographic web applications. Standard cryptographic attacker models employ a crude notion of compromise: if a client or server performs any action outside the description of the protocol, it is considered compromised. This characterization is too strong for web applications which may contain dozens of pages, among which only a few are security-sensitive. We need a new attacker model that allows honest websites to have *some* vulnerable pages.

In previous work [8], we proposed WebSpi, a formal model of web attackers and browser-based security mechanisms, written as a library for ProVerif [12]. We used WebSpi to analyze web authorization and single sign-on applications against a limited set of web attacks including CSRF and open redirectors. Here,

Table 1. Example encrypted web storage applications

Name	Key Derivation	Encryption	Integrity	Metadata Integrity	Sharing
Wuala	PBKDF2	AES, RSA	HMAC	✓	✓(PKI)
SpiderOak	PBKDF2	AES, RSA	HMAC	✓	✓
BoxCryptor	PBKDF2	AES	None	✗	✗
CloudFogger	PBKDF2	AES, RSA	None	✗	✓(PKI)
1Password	PBKDF2-SHA1	AES	None	✗	✓
LastPass	PBKDF2-SHA256	AES, RSA	None	✗	✓
PassPack	SHA256	AES	None	✓	✓
RoboForm	PBKDF2	AES, DES	None	✗	✓
Clipperz	SHA256	AES	SHA256	✓	✗
ConfiChair	PBKDF2	RSA, AES	SHA1	✓	✓(PKI)
Helios	N/A	El Gamal	SHA256	Zero-Knowledge Proof	N/A

we extend WebSpi to cover additional browser mechanisms such as local storage, AJAX, and the associated same origin policy, as well as to account for new attacks such as XSS, insecure cookies or JSONP-based CSRF.

The analysis of [8] did not address cryptographic issues. Here we extend WebSpi to study a series of commercial and academic cryptographic web applications. Our analysis reveals several new web-based attacks that expose flaws in their cryptographic designs, and formally reconstructs attacks previously reported in [11]. These attacks have been responsibly disclosed, and most were fixed in accordance with our suggestions. Our formal analysis suggests new countermeasures that are more robust in the face of web vulnerabilities. We verify these designs against attackers modeled in WebSpi. In summary, our work extends the state of the art by combining symbolic cryptographic protocol analysis with a realistic web attacker model. All the WebSpi scripts referenced in this paper are available online at http://prosecco.inria.fr/webspi/.

Related Work. A number of cryptographic protocols underlying real-world web applications have been verified for sophisticated security properties. Closely related to this paper are the symbolic analyses of ConfiChair [7], Helios [4], and Plutus [13]. However, none of these consider web attacks like CSRF and XSS, and as we show for ConfiChair and Helios, their security guarantees can be broken by such standard web vulnerabilities.

Various attacks have previously been found on encrypted storage applications: on their cryptographic design [10], on their web deployment [5], and on combinations of the two [11]. Such attacks are typically found using ad hoc tracing tools, and these works do not offer any positive guarantees for countermeasures. These attacks serve as motivation for our fomal analysis.

Several works propose formal models of browser-based security mechanisms [24,15,6,16]. Closely related to our work are the models of [6], which capture many of the same web vulnerabilities, and can be analyzed using Alloy [18]. However, they do not generally consider cryptography, whereas our use of ProVerif enables a combination of cryptographic and web security analysis.

2   Encrypted Web Storage Applications

We study encrypted web storage, a core functionality of many security-conscious web applications. More specifically, we evaluate the design, implementation, and use of client-side encryption in the web applications of Table 1. The general architecture of such applications is depicted on the right. They fall in three categories:

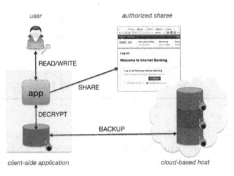

File storage services, such as Wuala and SpiderOak, offer a remote encrypted backup folder synchronized across various user devices with options to share folders and files with non-registered users by sending web links.

Password managers, such as 1Password and LastPass, integrate with a browser to store user login credentials for different websites. When the user browses to a known website, the password manager offers to automatically fill in the login form. The password database is kept encrypted on the client and backed up remotely, and can be synchronized across the user's devices.

Privacy-conscious websites, such as ConfiChair for conference management and Helios for electronic voting use client-side encryption to protect users against powerful attackers who may obtain control over the website itself.

All these applications implement an encrypted storage protocol and then use it to build more advanced features. We begin by describing one such protocol.

2.1   An Encrypted Storage Protocol

Suppose a user u has some sensitive data db with metadata m that she wishes to backup on a storage server. For example, db may be a local file with name m, or db may contain a password for the website m. u uses some client software a to communicate with the server b. When u creates or modifies db, a encrypts the data and sends it to the storage server. Periodically, a downloads and synchronizes its local copy of the encrypted db with the storage server. u does not know or trust the storage server, we assume it is somewhere in the cloud. We describe these two protocols below.

Notation. The cryptographic primitives crypt and decrypt represent symmetric encryption and decryption (e.g. AES in CBC mode); mac represents MACing (e.g. HMAC with SHA256); kdf represents password-based key derivation (e.g. PBKDF2). We model a TLS channel c with some server b as follows: an outgoing message m is denoted $\mathsf{TLS}_c^{\to b}(m)$ and an incoming message is denoted $\mathsf{TLS}_c^{\leftarrow b}(m)$.

Update and Synchronization protocols. Assume that u and b share a secret $\mathrm{secret}_{u,b}$ and that a has a local encryption key K and MAC key K' that it never sends to the server. These three secrets are stored on the client and may be encrypted under a password for additional security.

Update Cloud Storage: Update(u,m,db)

---

	a and b establish TLS connection c: $\mathsf{TLS}_c^{\to b}(-)$, $\mathsf{TLS}_c^{\leftarrow b}(-)$
1. $a \to b$	$\mathsf{TLS}_c^{\to b}(\mathsf{Authenticate}(u, \mathsf{secret}_{u,b}))$
	b verifies $\mathsf{secret}_{u,b}$ and associates c with u
	a updates encdb to (m,e=crypt K db,h=mac K' (m,e))
2. $a \to b$	$\mathsf{TLS}_c^{\to b}(\mathsf{Upload}(\mathsf{m}, \mathsf{e}, \mathsf{h}))$
	b updates storage[u] to (m,e,h)

In the protocol above, $\mathsf{Authenticate}(a, \mathsf{secret}_{a,b})$ denotes a tagged message requesting authentication of user u with password $\mathsf{secret}_{u,b}$. Similarly, message $\mathsf{Upload}(\mathsf{m}, \mathsf{e}, \mathsf{h})$ requests to upload the metadata m with the encryption e of the database db under the key K, and the MAC h of m and e under the MAC key K'. Hence, this protocol protects the confidentiality and ciphertext integrity of db, and the metadata integrity of m. Some applications in Table 1 do not provide metadata integrity; in Section 4.3 we show how this leads to a password recovery attack on 1Password.

The user data db is stored encrypted on the client. If an authorized user requests to read it, the client a will verify the MAC, decrypt encdb, and display the plaintext. The synchronization protocol authenticates the user, downloads the most recent copy of the encrypted database, and verifies its integrity.

Synchronize with Cloud Storage: Synchronize(u)

---

	a and b establish TLS connection c: $\mathsf{TLS}_c^{\to b}(-)$, $\mathsf{TLS}_c^{\leftarrow b}(-)$
1. $a \to b$	$\mathsf{TLS}_c^{\to b}(\mathsf{Authenticate}(u, \mathsf{secret}_{u,b}))$
	b verifies $\mathsf{secret}_{u,b}$ and associates c with u
	b retrieves storage[u] = (m,e,h)
3. $b \to a$	$\mathsf{TLS}_c^{\leftarrow b}(\mathsf{Download}(\mathsf{m}, \mathsf{e}, \mathsf{h}))$
	a checks that mac K' (m, e) = h
	a updates encdb to (m,e,h)

Attacker Model. The protocols described above protect the user from *compromised servers, network attackers* and *stolen devices*. In particular: an attacker gaining control of a storage server, or of a device on which the client application is installed but not running, must be unable to recover any plaintext or information about user credentials; a user must be able to detect any tampering with the stored data; a network attacker must be unable to eavesdrop or tamper with communications through the cloud. Under reasonable assumptions on the cryptographic primitives, one can show that the reference protocol described above preserves the confidentiality of user data (see, for example [7]). However, such proofs do not reflect the actual deployment of web-based encrypted storage applications, leading to attacks that break the stated security goals, despite the formal verification of their cryptographic protocols.

2.2 Deploying Encrypted Storage Protocols over the Web

Although encrypted storage protocols can be deployed using custom clients and servers, a big advantage of deploying it through a website is portability. The storage service may then be accessed from any device that has a web browser without the need for platform-specific software. This raises the challenge that the developer now needs to consider additional web-based attack vectors that affect websites and browsers. Consider an encrypted storage protocol where the client a is a browser and the server b is a website. We discuss the main design questions raised by this deployment architecture.

Password-based Key Derivation. Browser a must be able to obtain the secret $secret_{u,b}$ to authenticate to the server. Then it must be able to obtain the encryption key K and MAC key K'. The usual solution is that all three of these secrets are derived from a passphrase, sometimes called a master password. The key derivation algorithm (e.g. PBKDF2) typically requires a salt and an iteration count. Choosing a high iteration count *stretches* the entropy of the passphrase by making brute-force attacks more expensive, and choosing different salts for each user reduces the effectiveness of pre-computed tables [20]. In the following, we assume that each of the three secrets is derived with a different user-dependent constant (A_u, B_u, C_u) and a high iteration count (iter).

User Authentication and Cookie-based Sessions. To access a storage service a user must log in with the secret $secret_{u,b}$ derived from her passphrase. Upon login, a session is created on the server and associated with a fresh session identifier $sid_{u,b}$ sent back to the browser as a cookie. The browser sends back the cookie with every subsequent request, so the server can correlate all the user actions on the website even if these actions were taken in separate tabs, over different HTTPS connections. This login protocol can be described as follows.

Web Login and Key Derivation: $\mathsf{Login}(u,p,b)$

	user on browser a navigates to `https://b/login`
	a and b establish TLS connection c: $\mathsf{TLS}_c^{\to b}(-)$, $\mathsf{TLS}_c^{\leftarrow b}(-)$
1. $a \to b$	$\mathsf{TLS}_c^{\to b}(\mathsf{Request}(\texttt{/login}))$
2. $b \to a$	$\mathsf{TLS}_c^{\leftarrow b}(\mathsf{Response}(\mathsf{LoginForm}))$
	user enters username u and passphrase p
	a derives and stores $K = \mathsf{kdf}\ p\ A_u$ iter, $K' = \mathsf{kdf}\ p\ B_u$ iter
	a derives $secret_{u,b} = \mathsf{kdf}\ p\ C_u$ iter
3. $a \to b$	$\mathsf{TLS}_c^{\to b}(\mathsf{Request}(\texttt{/login}, \textbf{user} = \texttt{u}\&\textbf{secret} = secret_{u,b}))$
	b verifies that $\textbf{secret} = secret_{u,b}$
	b generates a cookie $sid_{u,b}$
	b stores $(sid_{u,b}, u)$
4. $b \to a$	$\mathsf{TLS}_c^{\leftarrow b}(\mathsf{Response}[sid_{u,b}](\mathsf{LoginSuccess}()))$
	a stores $(b, sid_{u,b})$

We write $\mathsf{Response}[sid_{u,b}](\mathsf{LoginSuccess}())$ to mean that the server sends an HTTP response with a header containing the cookie $sid_{u,b}$ and a body containing the page representing successful login. All subsequent requests from the browser to the server will have this cookie attached to it, written $\mathsf{Request}[\mathsf{sid}_{u,b}](\cdots)$.

Browser-based Cryptography and Key Storage. The login protocol above and the subsequent actions of the client role a of the encrypted storage protocol require a to generate keys, store them, and use them in cryptographic operations. To execute this logic in a browser, typical websites use JavaScript, either as a script embedded in web pages or in an isolated browser extension. In some applications, the cryptography is also implemented in JavaScript (e.g. LastPass). In others, the cryptography is provided by a Java applet but invoked through JavaScript (e.g. ConfiChair). In both cases, the keys must be stored in a location accessible to the script. Sometimes such cryptographic materials are stored in the browser's localStorage which provides a private storage area to each website and to each browser extension.

When the performance or reliability of JavaScript is considered inadequate, a few storage applications (such as SpiderOak) instead cache decryption keys on the server and perform all decryptions on the server side; these keys are discarded upon logout. In the rest of this paper, we generally assume that all cryptography is implemented on the client unless explicitly specified.

Releasing plaintext to authorized websites. In addition to update and synchronize, some storage services offer advanced sharing mechanisms. For example, password managers offer a *form fill* feature whereby user data is automatically retrieved, decrypted, and released to authorized websites. This feature is implemented by a browser extension or bookmarklet and activated when a user visits a login page; the extension automatically fills the login form with the user's credentials for that page. In the protocol description below, the encrypted storage client holding the database and its decryption keys is the browser extension x.

Automatic Form Filling for Web Login: Fill(b)

	user on browser a navigates to `https://b/login`
	a and b establish TLS connection c: $\mathsf{TLS}_c^{\to b}(-)$, $\mathsf{TLS}_c^{\leftarrow b}(-)$
1. $a \to b$	$\mathsf{TLS}_c^{\to b}(\mathsf{Request}(/\texttt{login}))$
2. $b \to a$	$\mathsf{TLS}_c^{\leftarrow b}(\mathsf{Response}(\mathsf{LoginForm}))$
	a triggers browser extension x with the current page hostname
3. $a \to x$	$\mathsf{Lookup}(b)$
	x looks up encdb for $(b, \mathsf{e}, \mathsf{h})$
	x checks that mac K' $(b, \mathsf{e}) = \mathsf{h}$
	x computes $(u, p) = $ decrypt K e
4. $x \to a$	$\mathsf{Result}(b, u, p)$
	a fills LoginForm with (u, p)

Sharing with a web link. File storage services often allow a user to share a file or folder with others, even if they do not have an account with the service. This works by sending the recipient a web link that contains within it the decryption key for the shared file. The receiver can access the file by following the link.

URL-based File Sharing: Share(u,m)

---

          user u sends to v the link U=`https://b/?user=`u`&file=`m`&key=`K

          user v on browser a navigates to U

1. $a \to b$ $\mathsf{TLS}_c^{\to b}(\mathsf{Request}[](\mathsf{U}))$

          b retrieves $\mathsf{storage}[u] = (m, e, h)$

          b decrypts $f = \mathsf{decrypt}\ K\ e$

2. $b \to a$ $\mathsf{TLS}_c^{\leftarrow b}(\mathsf{Response}[](\mathsf{Download}(f)))$

Sending decryption keys in plaintext links is clearly a security risk since the key can easily be leaked. As a result, even services that offer link-based sharing do not use the same key for shared files as they do for private files. For instance, SpiderOak creates a fresh encryption key for each shared folder and re-encrypts its contents. When the owner needs to access and decrypt her own shared files, she must first retrieve this shared key from the server. We model this protocol in more detail in Section 4. Other applications such as Wuala or CloudFogger use a more secure sharing scheme that relies on a public key infrastructure, allowing the decryption key to be sent wrapped under the recipient's public key.

2.3   Web Attacker Model

An encrypted storage application that uses JavaScript and cookie-based sessions is exposed to, and must protect against, a range of web attack vectors.

Code delivery. In typical website deployments, the JavaScript code that performs client-side encryption is itself downloaded from the web. If the attacker controls the server hosting the JavaScript, he may corrupt the application code in order to leak keys back to himself. Alternatively, if the code is downloaded over plain HTTP, a network attacker may tamper with the script.

XSS. In its simplest form, an attacker may be able to exploit unsanitized user input in the application to inject JavaScript that gets inlined in the website HTML and run along with trusted JavaScript. This may give the attacker complete control over a web page in the browser and to all cryptographic materials available to that page. Even carefully written security-conscious applications, such as Dropbox, LastPass, and ConfiChair, may still contain such weaknesses, as we show in Section 5. New browser security mechanisms are being proposed to address this issue [23].

Session Hijacking. Once a session is established, the associated cookie is the only proof of authentication for further actions. If an attacker gets hold of the session cookie, he can perform the same set of operations with the server as the user. In Section 5 we describe attacks of this kind that we found in several applications (including ConfiChair), even if they normally use HTTPS. A solution is for applications to set the cookie in *secure mode*, disallowing the browser to send it over an unencrypted connection.

CSRF. When an action can be triggered by accessing some URL, for example changing the current user's email address or his role in the session, a malicious site can force its users to access this URL and perform the action on their behalf, with attacker-controlled parameters. Although it is up to the application to prevent these kind of attacks, various varieties of CSRF remain common, even in security-oriented web services [9]. A common solution is to use an unguessable authorization token bound to the user session and require it to be sent with every security-sensitive request.

Phishing and Open Redirectors. Features involving third parties may introduce new attack vectors. For instance, in the automatic form filling protocol above, an untrusted website may try feeding the extension a fake URL instead of the legitimate login URL, to trick the extension into retrieving the user's password for a different website. Similarly, open redirectors such as URL `http://b/?redir=x`, that redirect the user to an external website x, facilitate phishing attacks where the website x may fool users into thinking that they are visiting a page on b when in fact they are on website x.

In summary, the design of cryptographic web applications must account for prevalent web vulnerabilities, not just the formal cryptographic attacker of Section 2.1. Next, we introduce our methodology for analyzing such applications.

3   Automated Verification of Web Cryptography

We describe the WebSpi library for ProVerif, and discuss how it is used to model and verify web applications. We show our extensions to WebSpi to model new JavaScript-based attacks. For details on ProVerif, see the official manual [14].

3.1   Processes

The language underlying ProVerif is a variant of applied pi-calculus [3]. Computations are described as the interaction of message-passing processes that communicate over asynchronous named channels. Knowing the name of a channel is enough to be able to send or receive messages on it. The name of a channel defined as private to a process cannot be guessed by other processes, so the creator controls its scope (that can be extended by sending the channel name to other processes). Processes have access to local databases where they can store and retrieve messages. Atomic messages, typically ranged over by $a, b, c, h, k, ...$ are tokens of basic types. Basic types are channels, bitstrings or user-defined. Messages can be composed by pairing (M, N) or by applying n-ary data constructors and destructors $f(M_1, ..., M_n)$. Constructors and destructors are particularly useful for cryptography, as described below. Pattern matching $= M$ is extensively used to parse messages.

ProVerif models *symbolic* cryptography: cryptographic algorithms are treated as perfect black-boxes whose properties are abstractly encoded using constructors and destructors. Consider authenticated encryption:

```
fun aenc(bitstring,symkey): bitstring.
reduc forall b:bitstring,k:symkey; adec(aenc(b,k),k) = b.
```

Given a bit-string b and a symmetric key k, the term aenc(b,k) stands for the bitstring obtained by encrypting b under k. The destructor adec, given an authenticated encryption and the original symmetric key, evaluates to the original bit-string b. ProVerif constructors are collision-free (one-one) functions and are, by default, only reversible if equipped with a corresponding destructor. Hence, MACs and hashes are modeled as irreversible constructors, and asymmetric cryptography is modeled using public and private keys:

```
fun hash(bitstring) : bitstring.
fun pk(privkey):pubkey.
fun sign(bitstring,privkey): bitstring.
reduc forall b:bitstring,sk:privkey; verify(sign(b,sk),pk(sk)) = b.
```

These and other standard cryptographic operations are part of the ProVerif library. Users can define other primitives where necessary. Such primitives can be used for example to build detailed models of applications like ConfiChair [7].

The WebSpi library defines data types related to the HTTP protocol and provides interfaces to the core functionality of browsers and web servers, in the form of a set of private channels. Application-layer protocols are expressed as processes linked to this channel interface. The rest of the network, including potential attackers, can be thought of as arbitrary processes with access to net and any other public channel.

3.2   WebSpi Architecture

In our model, *users* surf the web by interacting with web *pages* on *browsers* that communicate on the public channel net over HTTP(S) with *servers* that host web *applications*.

Users. Users are endowed with, or can acquire, username/password credentials to access applications. Applications are identified by a host name and a path within that host. The behaviour of specific web page users can be modeled by defining a UserAgent process that uses the browser interface described below.

Servers. Servers possess private and public keys used to implement encrypted TLS connections with browsers. These are stored in the serverIdentities table together with the server name (protocol and host) and a flag xdr specifying if cross-domain requests are accepted. The WebSpi implementation of a server is given by the HttpServer process below. HttpServer handles HTTP(S) messages (and encryption/decryption when necessary) and routes parsed messages to the corresponding web applications on the channels httpServerRequest and httpServerResponse. To model the server-side handler of a web application one needs to write a process that uses this interface to send and receive messages.

```
let HttpServer() =
   in(net,(b:Browser,o:Origin,m:bitstring));
   get serverIdentities(=o,pk_P,sk_P,xdr) in
   let (k:symkey,httpReq(u,hs,req)) = reqdec(o,m,sk_P) in
   if origin(u) = o then
   let corr = mkCorrelator(k) in
```

```
out(httpServerRequest,(u,hs,req,corr));
in(httpServerResponse,(=u,resp:HttpResponse,cookieOut:CookiePair,=corr));
out(net,(o,b,respenc(o,httpResp(resp,cookieOut,xdr),k))).
```

Browsers. Each browser has an identifier b and is associated with a user. The WebSpi implementation of a browser is given by the HttpClient process (we inline some fragments below). Cookies and local storage are maintained in global tables indexed by browser, page origin and, only for cookies, path. JavaScript running on a page can access cookies and storage associated with the page origin using the private channels getCookieStorage and setCookieStorage, in accordance to the Same Origin Policy. Cookies can be flagged as *secure* or *HTTP-only.* Secure cookies are sent only on HTTPS connections and HTTP-only cookies are not exposed to pages via the CookieStorage channel. For example, the HttpClient code that gets triggered when the JavaScript of page p on browser b wants to set cookies dc and store ns in local storage is:

```
in (setCookieStorage(b),(p:Page,dc:Cookie,ns:Data));
get pageOrigin(=p,o,h,ref) in get cookies(=b,=o,=h,ck) in
insert cookies(b,o,h,updatedomcookie(ck,securejs(dc),insecurejs(dc)));
insert storage(b,o,ns)
```

Here, the function updatedomcookie prevents JavaScript from updating the HTTP-only cookies of the cookie record ck.

The main role of the browser process is to handle requests generated by users and web pages, and their responses. The location bar is modeled by channel browserRequest, which can be used by to navigate to a specific webpage. Location bar request have an empty referrer header. Hyperlink clicks or JavaScript GET/POST requests are modeled by the pageClick channel. The browser attaches relevant headers (referrer and cookies) and sends the request on the network. When it receives the response, it updates the cookies and creates a new page with the response data. Process HttpClient also takes care of encrypting HTTPS requests, decrypting HTTPS responses, and handling redirection responses. AJAX requests are sent to the browser on channel ajaxRequest. When the browser receives the response to an AJAX request it passes on the relevant data to the appropriate web page. (Although we abstract away the tree-like structure of the DOM, we do represent its main features salient to modeling web interactions: cookies, hyperlinks, location bar, forms, etc.) We give the HttpClient code for sending a request req to URI u from page p, with referrer ref and AJAX flag aj:

```
let o = origin(u) in let p = path(u) in
get cookies(=b,=o,=slash(),cs) in get cookies(=b,=o,=p,cp) in
let header = headers(ref, cookiePair(cs,cp), aj) in
get publicKey(=o,pk_host) in
let m = httpReq(u,header,req) in
let (k:symkey,e:bitstring) = reqenc(o,m,pk_host) in
out(net,(b, o, e));
```

The request header is obtained concatenating the referrer, the cookies cs for path "/" and cp for path p and the AJAX flag aj. If needed one could extend the model by including additional headers such as `Origin` [9]. Note how the code retrieves the public key pk_host of the destination server, which is used to create the symmetric key k and the encrypted message e. The origin parameter o passed to the encryption function reqenc specifies if the chosen protocol is HTTP or HTTPS. In the former case, e equals m.

To model the client side of a web application, one needs to write a process that can access the private browser interface channels pageClick, ajaxRequest, getCookieStorage and setCookieStorage.

Web Attacker Model. Representing the network as a public channel net enables the standard Dolev-Yao *network attacker*, that can intercept and inject messages but is not able to break cryptography. To model a *compromised server*, we simply release its private key on a public channel so that an arbitrary attacker process can impersonate the server. We enable XSS and *code injection* attacks by defining a process AttackerProxy that receives messages on a public channel (available to the attacker) and forwards them on the browser's private channels. The parameters sent on these channels include the browser and page ids, which are normally secret. We can selectively enable the compromise of a specific page on a specific browser by releasing the corresponding ids to the environment. CSRF attacks are enabled by the willingness of the user to visit attacker websites and by the ability of our model to represent GET/POST requests and attach the corresponding cookies.

Verification in WebSpi. The verification model of WebSpi is the same as in ProVerif. Security goals in ProVerif are typically written as correspondence assertions between events embedded in the code [12]. The command event e(M1,...,Mn) inserts an *event* e(M1,...,Mn) in the trace of the process being executed. A script in fact contains processes and *queries* of the form $\forall M_1, ... M_k. e(M_1, ... M_k) \Rightarrow \phi$. ProVerif tries to prove that whenever the event e is reachable, the formula ϕ is true (ϕ can contain conjunctions or disjunctions). In Section 4 we will show concrete security queries.

The soundness properties of ProVerif [12] also hold for our security policies. If an expect is satisfied, then it is satisfied in all traces of running the applied-pi processes defined in the script in parallel with any arbitrary attacker processes. If ProVerif proves that an expect is not satisfied, it outputs a proof derivation that explains how an attacker can trigger an event that violates the policy.

Although very expressive, WebSpi is not a complete model of the web. For example, our model of the Same Origin Policy does not include `<iframe>` tags from different origins within the same page, and we do not model several HTTP headers such as `Origin` and `ETag`. Hence, our main focus is on discovering attacks, which can be validated in the real world, rather than on providing positive guarantees, which may be violated in practice due to omissions in our model.

4   Analyzing Encrypted Web Storage Services

In this section, we analyze three web applications that use the cloud to store encrypted secrets. We show how to model these applications using WebSpi and verify them using ProVerif against realistic web attackers. We show how web vulnerabilities enable concrete attacks that leak secrets to a web attacker. It is difficult to completely eradicate such vulnerabilities from complex, real-world web applications. For that reason we propose countermeasures that harden such applications even in the presence of vulnerabilities.

4.1   ConfiChair

ConfiChair [7] is a cloud-based conference management system that seeks to offer stronger security and privacy guarantees than current systems like EasyChair and EDAS. Each conference has a chair, authors, and a program committee (of reviewers). Once a user logs in at the login page, she is forwarded to a Conferences page where she may choose a conference to participate in. The user may choose her role in the conference by clicking on "change role" which forwards her to the role page. Papers and reviews are stored encrypted on the web server, and each

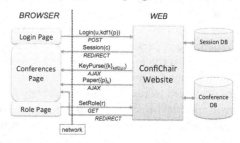

user holds keys to all papers and reviews she is allowed to read in a *keypurse*. For example, each paper has an encryption key (generated by the author) that is stored in the author's and conference chair's keypurses. Each conference has a private key stored only in the chair's keypurse and a shared reviewer key that is stored in each reviewer's keypurse. Each user's keypurse is also stored encrypted on the web server under a key derived from her password. The password itself is not stored there, instead a separate key derived from the password is used to authenticate the user. The web server authenticates users before sending them their keypurses and enforces role-based access control to conference actions and per-user access control to papers and reviews. All the cryptography for decrypting and encrypting keypurses, papers, and reviews is performed in the browser using a combination of JavaScript and a Java applet.

WebSpi Analysis.   We model and evaluate paper downloads using WebSpi.

Login. We model the login page using two processes: LoginApp represents a server-side webpage listening for requests on `https://confichair.org/login`, and LoginUserAgent represents the client-side JavaScript and HTML downloaded from this URL. These processes implement the web login protocol of Section 2.2, but do not yet derive the encryption and MAC keys.

The process LoginUserAgent downloads a login form, waits for the user to type her username and password, derives an authentication credential from the password and sends the username and credential to LoginApp over HTTPS (through the network channel between the browser and HTTP server processes):

```
let loginURI = uri(https(), confichair, loginPath(), nullParams()) in
out(browserRequest(b),(loginURI, httpGet()));
in (newPage(b),(p:Page,=loginURI,d:bitstring));
```

```
get userData(=confichair, uid, pwd, paper) in
let cred = kdf1(pwd) in
in (getCookieStorage(b),(=p,cookiePair(cs,ch),od:Data));
out (setCookieStorage(b),(p,ch,storePassword(pwd)));
event LoginInit(confichair, b, uid);
out(pageClick(b),(p,loginURI,httpPost(loginFormReply(uid,cred))))
```

Notably, the process stores the password in the HTML5 local storage corresponding to the current origin https://confichair.org, making it available to any page subsequently loaded from this origin. When the user logs out, the local storage is purged.

The server process LoginApp is dual to the LoginUserAgent. It checks that the credential provided by the user in the login form is valid (by consulting a server-side database modeled as a table) and creates a session id passed to the browser as a cookie for all pages on the website, before redirecting the user to the conferences page.

Paper Download. We model all the conference pages using a server-side process ConferenceApp and a client-side process ConferenceUserAgent. The process ConferencesUserAgent first makes an AJAX request to retrieve the encrypted keypurse of the logged in user. It then decrypts the keypurse using a key derived from the cached password and stores the decrypted keypurse in local storage for the current origin (https://confichair.org).

```
let keypurseURI = uri(https(), confichair, keyPursePath(), nullParams()) in
out (ajaxRequest(b),(p,keypurseURI,httpGet()));
in (ajaxResponse(b),(=p,=keypurseURI,JSON(x)));
in (getCookieStorage(b),(=p,cookiePair(cs,ch),storePassword(pwd)));
let keypurse(k) = adec(x, kdf2(pwd)) in
out (setCookieStorage(b),(p,ch,storeKeypurse(k))))
```

For simplicity, the keypurse contains a single key, meant for decrypting the current user's papers. Subsequently, the user may at any point ask to download a paper and decrypt the downloaded PDF with the keypurse.

```
let paperURI = uri(https(), h, paperPath(), nullParams()) in
out (ajaxRequest(b),(p,paperURI,httpGet()));
in (ajaxResponse(b),(=p,=paperURI,JSON(y)));
in (getCookieStorage(b),(=p,cookiePair(cs,ch),storeKeypurse(k)));
let paper = adec(y,k) in event PaperReceived(paper))
```

Security Goals. We model two simple security goals for our ConfiChair website model. First, the login mechanism should authenticate the user. This is modeled as a correspondence query:

```
event(LoginAuthorized(confichair,id,u,c)) ⟹event(LoginInit(confichair,b,id))
```

Second, that a user's papers must remain syntactically secret. We model this using an oracle process that raises an event when the attacker successfully guesses the contents of a paper

```
in(paperChannel, paper:bitstring);
get userData(h, uId, k, =paper) in event PaperLeak(uId,paper).
```

We then ask whether the event PaperLeak is ever reachable. The queries written here are quite simple. More generally, they must account for compromised users whose passwords are known to the attacker. For the login and conferences processes above, these queries do indeed hold against an adversary who controls the network, some other websites that honest users may visit, and some set of compromised users.

Attacker Model: XSS on Role Page. Our security analysis found a number of web vulnerabilities. Here we describe how the change-role functionality on the ConfiChair webpage is vulnerable to an XSS attack. If an attacker can trick a user into visiting the URL `http://confichair.org/?set-role=<script>S</script>`, ConfiChair returns an error page that embeds the HTML tag `<script>S</script>`, causing the tainted script S to run. We model this attack as part of the client-side process RoleUserAgent for the role page: after loading the page, the process leaks control of the page to the adversary by publicly disclosing its identifier:

```
let roleURI = uri(https(), h, changeRolePath(), roleParams(x)) in
out(browserRequest(b),(roleURI, httpGet()));
in (newPage(b),(p:Page,=roleURI,y:bitstring));
out(pub, p)
```

The attacker may subsequently use this page identifier p to make requests on behalf of the page, read the cookies, and most importantly, the local storage for the page's origin.

Attacks on Authentication and Paper Secrecy. If we add this RoleUserAgent to our ConfiChair model ProVerif finds several attacks against our security goals. First, the XSS attacker may now read the current user's password from local storage and send it to a malicious website. This breaks our authentication goal since from this point onwards the attacker can pretend to be the user. Second, the XSS attacker may read the current user's keypurse from local storage and send it to a malicious website. This breaks our paper secrecy goal since the attacker can decrypt the user's papers.

These attacks have been experimentally confirmed on the ConfiChair website (along with some others described in Section 5). They break the stated security goals of ConfiChair by leaking the user's papers and reviews to an arbitrary website. The previous ProVerif analysis of ConfiChair [7] did not cover browser-based key management or XSS attacks: its security proofs remain valid in the cloud-based attacker model.

Mitigations and Countermeasures. An obvious mitigation is to eliminate the XSS attack on the change-role functionality. A more interesting design question is how to change the ConfiChair website to be more robust in the presence of such XSS attacks. We focus on countermeasures that keep the current workflow.

First, there is no need for the website to store the cleartext password in local storage, where an XSS attacker can obtain it. Storing just the decryption key is enough. Second, we propose to use a fresh session-specific wrapping key to encrypt both the decryption key and the keypurse before storing them in local storage. The website can then decide which pages need access to these keys and expose the wrapping key in a secure cookie only for those pages. For example, suppose all pages that need access to the wrapping key are served from the sub-domain `secure.confichair.org`, whereas all other pages are served from the parent domain `confichair.org`. The wrapping key can then be set as a cookie for the sub-domain, pages in the parent domain will not be able to access it. In this design, the website never has both the key and the encrypted data. During login the browser has the password and the website has the encrypted data. After login, the browser has a re-encrypted keypurse and the website has the fresh encryption key. With these changes our secrecy and authentication queries are verified by ProVerif. That is, if the login and conferences pages are hosted on the secure sub-domain and are XSS-free, then XSS attacks on other pages do not impact the security of the application. Whether this countermeasure is practical or even resistant to more sophisticated iframe-based attacks requires further investigation.

4.2 SpiderOak

SpiderOak is a commercial cloud-based backup, synchronization and sharing service. It advertises itself as "zero-knowledge", that is, the SpiderOak servers only store encrypted data, but never the associated decryption keys. Users typically use downloaded client software to connect to SpiderOak and synchronize their local folders with cloud-based encrypted backups. However, SpiderOak also provides its users with a web front end to access their data so that they can read or download their files on a machine where they have not installed SpiderOak.

When a user logs into the SpiderOak website, her decryption keys are made available to the web server so that it can decrypt a user's files on her behalf. These keys are to be thrown away when the user logs out. However, if the user shares a folder using a web link with someone else, the decryption key is treated differently. The key is embedded in the web link, and it is also stored on the website for the file owner's use. We focus on modeling this management of shared folders (called shared rooms) on SpiderOak.

WebSpi Analysis. The SpiderOak login process is similar to ConfiChair, except that besides the derived authentication credential it sends also the plaintext password to the server. After login, the user is forwarded to his root directory, from where he may choose to open one of his shared folders (called shared rooms).

The process SharedRoomUserAgent models the client-side JavaScript triggered when the user accesses a shared folder. It makes an AJAX request to retrieve the URL, file names, and decryption key for the folder. It then constructs a web link consisting of the URL, file name, and the decryption key and uses the URL-based sharing protocol of Section 2.2 to retrieve its files. The server-side process SharedRoomApp responds to the AJAX request from the user: it authenticates the user based on her login cookie, retrieves the folder URL, file names, and decryption key from a database and sends it back in a JSON formatted message. It also responds to GET requests for files, but in this case the user does not have to be logged in; she can instead provide the name of the file and the decryption key as parameters in the URI.

Similarly to ConfiChair, we set two security goals: user authentication and syntactic file secrecy. ProVerif is able to show that our SpiderOak model preserves login authentication but it fails to prove file secrecy as we explain below.

JSONP CSRF Attack on Shared Rooms. The SpiderOak shared rooms page is vulnerable to a CSRF attack on its AJAX call for retrieving shared room keys. If a user visits a malicious website while logged into SpiderOak, that website can trigger a cross-site request to retrieve the shared room key for the currently logged-in user. The browser automatically adds the user's login cookie to the request and since the server relies only on the cookie for authentication, it will send back the JSON response to the attacker. The attacker can then retrieve the file by constructing a web link and making a GET request.

This CSRF attack only works if the target website explicitly enables crossdomain AJAX requests, as we found to be the case for SpiderOak. In our SpiderOak model, the SharedRoomsApp page sets the xdr flag, and ProVerif finds the CSRF attack (as a violation of file secrecy).

Mitigations and Countermeasures. We experimentally confirmed the attack on the SpiderOak website and on our advice, SpiderOak removed cross-domain access to shared rooms. As in ConfiChair, we consider whether a different design of SpiderOak would make it resistant to attack even if it had a CSRF vulnerability.

One countermeasure is to encrypt the shared room key with the owner's password. Hence, only the owner can decrypt the key, but that is adequate since other shares are given the key in the web link anyway. ProVerif shows that with this fix the attacker is no longer able to obtain the file, even though the CSRF attack is still enabled. The attacker can get the file URL but not the key.

4.3   1Password

1Password is a password manager that uses the cloud only as an encrypted store. Typically, it uses Dropbox to backup and replicate a user's encrypted password database. To protect these passwords in transit, on Dropbox, and on each device, the password database is always encrypted on the client before uploading. Even though 1Password does not host any website, we show that it is nonetheless vulnerable to web-based attacks.

Password managers such as 1Password provide a browser extension that makes it easier for users to manage their passwords. The first time a user visits a login page and enters his password, the browser extension offers to remember the password. On future visits, 1Password offers to automati-

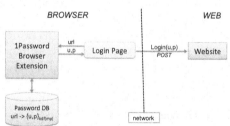

cally fill in the password. Concretely, the extension looks at the origin of the page and uses it to lookup its database. If a password is found, it is decrypted and filled into the login form.

WebSpi Analysis. We model 1Password and its browser extension as a process that waits for messages from a page on a channel extensionChannel; it then looks

Table 2. Web vulnerabilities in cloud storage websites

Name	Alternate Login	Insecure Cookie	XSS	CSRF	Open Redirector	Frameable
Dropbox	OAuth	✗	✓	✓	✗	✗
SpiderOak	HTTP Auth	✗	✗	✓	✗	✗
LastPass	YubiKey	✗	✓	✓	✗	✗
PassPack	YubiKey	✗	✗	✓	✗	✓
ConfiChair	None	✓	✓	✓	✓	✓
Helios	OAuth, OpenID	✓	✓	✓	✓	✓

for an entry for the current origin in the password database (called a keychain store). If it finds an entry, it asks the user for a master password, uses it to decrypt the username and password, and returns them on the extension channel to the requesting page. This protocol corresponds to the automatic form filling protocol of Section 2.2, except that 1Password does not include a MAC with the encrypted data. We compose this extension process with a standard login application, for example, as in the SpiderOak model, to obtain a simple model for 1Password. Login authentication and password secrecy are the security goals.

Metadata Tampering on the Password Database. 1Password is designed to be resistant to attacks on Dropbox and to an attacker who has stolen a user's device. We model an attacker with read/write access to the encrypted password database. Each password entry in 1Password is stored as a separate text file in Dropbox, so our model captures attackers who can read or write to these files. When composed with this attacker and a malicious website, ProVerif finds that password secrecy is violated (hence, so is login authentication).

The attack proceeds as follows: the attacker reads the entry for (say) SpiderOak from the database and replaces the hostname SpiderOak with the name of his own server, Mallory. Since the origin is not encrypted or integrity-protected in the database, this modification remains undetected. The next time the user visits Mallory's website, the page requests a password for Mallory and the 1Password extension instead provides the password for SpiderOak, which gets leaked to Mallory. We call this attack a metadata tampering attack since the attacker manages to modify the metadata surrounding an encrypted password. Similar attacks are applicable in other storage services.

Mitigations and Countermeasures. The metadata tampering attack only applies if the attacker has write access to the encrypted database. Hence, one countermeasure is to make the database inaccessible to the attacker. A more robust solution is to add metadata integrity protection to the password database. As in the protocols of Section 2.2, we propose that both the ciphertext and all metadata in a keychain should be MACed with a key derived from the master password. ProVerif verified that this prevents metadata tampering, and hence password leaks, even if the password database is stored in an insecure location.

5   Concrete Attacks on Encrypted Web Storage Services

We have shown how to formally analyze core components of three encrypted web storage services using WebSpi and ProVerif. In each case, we found that the security provided by cryptography was circumvented by a web-based attack. For illustration, Table 2 summarizes vulnerabilities on storage websites found by us and by others. Besides XSS and CSRF, this table notes websites that did not use secure cookies and were thus vulnerable to session hijacking, those that had open redirectors that may lead to phishing, and those that were framable and thus vulnerable to clickjacking. These vulnerabilities are ubiquitous on the web and seem difficult to avoid on realistic websites. We now explain the impact of such vulnerabilities on our target applications. All the attacks below were discovered and reported by us, either during this work, or in [11].

Metadata Tampering. Encrypted storage services such as BoxCryptor, Cloud-fogger, and 1Password aim to be resilient to the tampering of encrypted data on DropBox. However, these applications failed to protect metadata integrity, so an attacker could confuse users about their stored data. For example, one could rename an encrypted file in BoxCryptor and replace an encrypted file in CloudFogger without these modifications being detected.

User Impersonation. Both ConfiChair and Helios can be attacked if a logged-in user visits a malicious website. If a logged-in conference chair visits a malicious website, the website may use a series of CSRF and clickjacking attacks to close submissions or release referee reports to authors. On Helios, the problem is more serious. If a user authenticates on Helios using Facebook (a common usage pattern), any malicious website she subsequently visits may steal her authentication token and impersonate her, even if she logged out of Helios. The attack relies on an open redirector on Helios and the OAuth 2.0 protocol implemented by Facebook, and corresponds to a token redirection attack previously found using WebSpi [8]. This attack undermines voter authentication on Helios, and lets an attacker modify election settings by impersonating the election administrator.

Password Phishing. Password managers are vulnerable to a variety of phishing attacks where malicious websites try to fool them into releasing passwords for trusted websites. Metadata tampering, as shown for 1Password, also applies to Roboform. Another attack vector is to use carefully crafted URLs that are incorrectly parsed by the password manager. A typical example is `http://a:b@c:d`, which means that the user a with password b wants to access website c at port d, but may be incorrectly parsed by a password manager as a user accessing website a at port b. We found such vulnerabilities in 1Password and many popular JavaScript URL parsing libraries. We also found that password managers like LastPass that use bookmarklets are vulnerable to JavaScript rootkits [5].

6   Conclusions

In this paper, we formally analyzed 3 encrypted web storage applications, and described concrete security attacks in 7 more. Our reports resulted in security updates for Wuala, 1Password, LastPass, and SpiderOak, and security advisories for the ConfiChair and Helios websites, others are being discussed. WebSpi is a useful tool for evaluating web applications and for experimenting with their design to make them more resilient to standard web vulnerabilities. As Web-Spi is not complete, we leave the task of modeling even more attacks, such as framing [22], JavaScript rootkits [5], and other scenarios [1], to future work.

References

1. Browser security handbook, http://code.google.com/p/browsersec
2. How secure is Dropbox?, https://www.dropbox.com/help/27/en
3. Abadi, M., Fournet, C.: Mobile values, new names, and secure communication. SIGPLAN Not. 36, 104–115 (2001)
4. Adida, B.: Helios: Web-based open-audit voting. In: USENIX Security Symposium, pp. 335–348 (2008)
5. Adida, B., Barth, A., Jackson, C.: Rootkits for JavaScript environments. In: Workshop on Offensive Technologies, WOOT (2009)
6. Akhawe, D., Barth, A., Lam, P.E., Mitchell, J., Song, D.: Towards a formal foundation of web security. In: CSF, pp. 290–304 (2010)
7. Arapinis, M., Bursuc, S., Ryan, M.: Privacy Supporting Cloud Computing: ConfiChair, a Case Study. In: Degano, P., Guttman, J.D. (eds.) POST 2012. LNCS, vol. 7215, pp. 89–108. Springer, Heidelberg (2012)
8. Bansal, C., Bhargavan, K., Maffeis, S.: Discovering concrete attacks on website authorization by formal analysis. In: CSF, pp. 247–262 (2012)
9. Barth, A., Jackson, C., Mitchell, J.C.: Robust defenses for cross-site request forgery. In: CCS, pp. 75–88 (2008)
10. Belenko, A., Sklyarov, D.: "Secure Password Managers" and "Military-Grade Encryption" on Smartphones: Oh, Really? Technical report, Elcomsoft Ltd. (2012)
11. Bhargavan, K., Delignat-Lavaud, A.: Web-based attacks on host-proof encrypted storage. In: Workshop on Offensive Technologies, WOOT (2012)
12. Blanchet, B.: Automatic verification of correspondences for security protocols. Journal of Computer Security 17(4), 363–434 (2009)
13. Blanchet, B., Chaudhuri, A.: Automated formal analysis of a protocol for secure file sharing on untrusted storage. In: IEEE Symposium on Security & Privacy (2008)
14. Blanchet, B., Smyth, B.: ProVerif: Automatic Cryptographic Protocol Verifier, User Manual and Tutorial, http://www.proverif.inria.fr/manual.pdf
15. Bohannon, A., Pierce, B.C.: Featherweight Firefox: Formalizing the core of a web browser. In: WebApps (2010)
16. Groß, T.R., Pfitzmann, B., Sadeghi, A.-R.: Browser Model for Security Analysis of Browser-Based Protocols. In: De Capitani di Vimercati, S., Syverson, P.F., Gollmann, D. (eds.) ESORICS 2005. LNCS, vol. 3679, pp. 489–508. Springer, Heidelberg (2005)
17. Hammer-Lahav, E., Recordon, D., Hardt, D.: The OAuth 2.0 Authorization Protocol. IETF Internet Draft (2011)
18. Jackson, D.: Alloy: A Logical Modelling Language. In: Bert, D., Bowen, J.P., King, S., Waldén, M. (eds.) ZB 2003. LNCS, vol. 2651, p. 1. Springer, Heidelberg (2003)
19. Kamara, S., Lauter, K.: Cryptographic Cloud Storage. In: Sion, R., Curtmola, R., Dietrich, S., Kiayias, A., Miret, J.M., Sako, K., Sebé, F. (eds.) FC 2010 Workshops. LNCS, vol. 6054, pp. 136–149. Springer, Heidelberg (2010)

20. Kelsey, J., Schneier, B., Hall, C., Wagner, D.: Secure Applications of Low-Entropy Keys. In: Okamoto, E., Davida, G., Mambo, M. (eds.) ISW 1997. LNCS, vol. 1396, pp. 121–134. Springer, Heidelberg (1998)
21. Rescorla, E.: HTTP over TLS. Request for Comments 2818, IETF (2000)
22. Rydstedt, G., Bursztein, E., Boneh, D., Jackson, C.: Busting frame busting: a study of clickjacking vulnerabilities at popular sites. In: Web 2.0 S&P (2010)
23. Stearne, B., Barth, A. (eds.): Content Security Policy 1.0. W3C Working Draft (2012)
24. Yoshihama, S., Tateishi, T., Tabuchi, N., Matsumoto, T.: Information-Flow-Based Access Control for Web Browsers. IEICE Transactions E92-D(5), 836–850 (2009)

Lazy Mobile Intruders[*]

Sebastian Mödersheim, Flemming Nielson, and Hanne Riis Nielson

DTU Compute, Denmark

Abstract. We present a new technique for analyzing platforms that execute potentially malicious code, such as web-browsers, mobile phones,
or virtualized infrastructures. Rather than analyzing given code, we ask
what code an intruder could create to break a security goal of the platform. To avoid searching the infinite space of programs that the intruder
could come up with (given some initial knowledge) we adapt the lazy
intruder technique from protocol verification: the code is initially just a
process variable that is getting instantiated in a demand-driven way during its execution. We also take into account that by communication, the
malicious code can learn new information that it can use in subsequent
operations, or that we may have several pieces of malicious code that can
exchange information if they "meet". To formalize both the platform and
the malicious code we use the mobile ambient calculus, since it provides
a small, abstract formalism that models the essence of mobile code. We
provide a decision procedure for security against arbitrary intruder processes when the honest processes can only perform a bounded number
of steps and without path constraints in communication. We show that
this problem is NP-complete.

1 Introduction

Mobile Intruder. With *mobile intruder* we summarize the problem of executing
code from an untrusted source in a trusted environment. The most common
example is executing code from untrusted websites in a web browser (e.g., in
Javascript). We trust the web browser and surrounding operating system (at
least in its initial setup), we have a security policy for executing code (e.g.,
on access to cookies in web-browsers), and we want to verify that an intruder
cannot design any piece of code that would upon execution lead to a violation
of our security policy [11]. There are many similar examples where code from an
untrusted source is executed by an honest host such as mobile phones or virtual
infrastructures.

Related Problems. The mobile intruder problem is in a sense the dual of the
mobile agents problem where "honest" code is executed by an untrusted environment [3]. The mobile intruder problem has also similarities with the proof-
carrying-code (PCC) paradigm [15]. In PCC we also want to convince ourselves

---

[*] The research presented in this paper has been partially supported by MT-LAB, a
VKR Centre of Excellence for the Modelling of Information Technology. The authors
thank Luca Viganò and the anonymous reviewers for helpful comments.

D. Basin and J.C. Mitchell (Eds.): POST 2013, LNCS 7796, pp. 147–166, 2013.
© Springer-Verlag Berlin Heidelberg 2013

that a piece of code that comes from an untrusted source will not violate our policy. In contrast to PCC, we do not consider a concrete given piece of code, but verify that our environment securely executes *every* piece of code. Also, of course, we do *not* require code to be equipped with a proof of its security.

The Problem and a Solution. The difficulty in verifying a given architecture for running potentially malicious code lies in the fact that there is an infinite number of programs that the intruder can come up with (given some initial knowledge). Even bounding the size of programs (which is hard to justify in general), the number of choices is vast, so that naively searching this space of programs is infeasible.

Our key observation is that this problem is very similar to a problem in protocol verification and that one may use similar verification methods to address it. The similar problem in protocol verification is that the intruder can at any point send arbitrary messages to honest agents. Also here, we have an infinite choice of messages that the intruder can construct from a given knowledge, leading to an infinitely branching transition relation of the system to analyze. While in many cases we can bound the choice to a finite one without restriction [4], the choice is still prohibitively large for a naive exploration.

In order to deal with this problem of large or infinite search spaces caused by the "prolific" intruder, a popular technique in model checking security protocols is a constraint-based approach that we call *the lazy intruder* [12,13,16,6]. In a state where the intruder knows the set of messages K, he can send to any agent any term t that he can craft from this knowledge, written $K \vdash t$. To avoid this naive enumeration of choices, the lazy intruder instead makes a *symbolic* transition where we represent the sent message by a *variable* x and record the constraint $K \vdash x$. During the state exploration, variables may be instantiated and the constraints must then be checked for satisfiability. The search procedure thus determines the sent message x in a demand-driven, lazy way.

A basic idea is now that code can be seen as a special case of a message and that we may use the lazy intruder to lazily generate intruder code for us. There are of course several differences to the problem of intruder-generated message, because code has a dynamic aspect. For instance the code can in a sense "learn" messages when it is communicating with other processes and use the learned messages in subsequent actions. Another aspect is that we want to consider mobility of code, i.e., the code may move to another location and continue execution there. We may thus consider that code is bundled with its local data and move together with it, as it is the case for instance on migration operations in virtual infrastructures. As a result, when two pieces of intruder-generate code are able to communicate with each other, then they can exchange all information they have gathered. An example is that an intruder-generated piece of code is able to enter a location, gather some secret information there, and return to the intruder's home base with this information.

Contribution. The key idea of this paper is to use the lazy intruder for the malicious mobile code problem: in a nutshell, the code initially written by the intruder is just a variable x and we explore in a *demand driven, lazy* way what this code could look like more concretely in order to achieve an attack.

Like in the original lazy intruder technique, we do not limit the choices of the intruder, but verify the security for the infinite set of programs the intruder could conceive. Also, like in the lazy intruder for security protocols, this yields only a semi-decision procedure for insecurity, because there can be an unbounded number of interactions between the intruder and the environment; this is powerful enough to simulate Turing machines. However by bounding the number of steps that honest processes can perform, we obtain a decision procedure. We show that this problem is NP-complete.

For such a result, we need to use a formalism to model the mobile intruder code—or several such pieces of code—and the environment where the code is executed. In this paper we choose the mobile ambient calculus, which is an extension of common process calculi with a notion of mobility of the processes and a concept of boundaries around them, the ambients. The reason for this choice is that we can develop our approach very abstractly and demonstrate how to deal with each fundamental aspect of mobile code without committing to a complex formalization of a concrete environment such as a web-browser running Javascript or the like. In fact, mobile ambients can be regarded as a "minimal" formalism for mobility. Moreover, it has a well-defined semantics which is necessary to formally prove the correctness of our lazy mobile intruder technique. We therefore avoid a lot of technical problems that are immaterial to our ideas, and neither do we tie our approach to one particular application field.

2   The Ground Model

2.1   The Ambient Calculus

We use the ambient calculus as defined by Cardelli and Gordon [8]. There is a basic version and an extension with communication primitives; we present the ambient calculus right away with communication and only mention that our method also works, mutatis mutandis, for the basic ambient calculus. Fig. 1 contains the syntax of the ambient calculus, and Fig. 2 and 3 give the semantics by defining a structural congruence $\equiv$ and reduction relation $\rightarrow$, respectively. In these figures, we have already omitted some primitives that we do not consider in this paper, namely replication, name restriction, and path constraints; we discuss these restrictions in Sec. 2.5.

The ambient calculus is an extension of standard process calculi with the usual constructs 0 for the inactive process, $P \mid Q$ for the parallel composition of processes P and Q, as well as input $(x).P$—binding the variable x in P—and output $\langle M \rangle$. In addition we have a concept of a process running within a boundary, or *ambient*, denoted $n[P]$, and this ambient has the name n. For instance one may model by $m[P \mid v_1[R] \mid v_2[Q]]$ a situation where a process P is running on a physical machine m together with virtual machines v_1 and v_2 that host processes R and Q, respectively. The communication rule (4) in Fig. 3

$$
\begin{array}{llll}
P, Q ::= & \text{processes} & M ::= & \text{capabilities} \\
0 & \text{inactivity} & x & \text{variable} \\
P \mid Q & \text{composition} & n & \text{name} \\
M[P] & \text{ambient} & in\ M & \text{can enter } M \\
M.P & \text{capability action} & out\ M & \text{can exit } M \\
(x).P & \text{input action} & open\ M & \text{can open } M \\
\langle M \rangle & \text{output action} & &
\end{array}
$$

Fig. 1. Considered fragment of the ambient calculus

$$
P \equiv P \qquad \frac{P \equiv Q}{Q \equiv P} \qquad \frac{P \equiv Q \quad Q \equiv R}{P \equiv R} \qquad \frac{P \equiv Q}{P \mid R \equiv Q \mid R}
$$

$$
\frac{P \equiv Q}{M[P] \equiv M[Q]} \qquad \frac{P \equiv Q}{M.P \equiv M.Q} \qquad \frac{P \equiv Q}{(x).P \equiv (x).Q} \qquad P \mid Q \equiv Q \mid P
$$

$$
(P \mid Q) \mid R \equiv P \mid (Q \mid R) \qquad P \mid 0 \equiv P
$$

Fig. 2. Structural congruence relation

for instance says that processes can communicate when they run in parallel, but not when they are separated by ambient boundaries. Process can move with the operations *in n* and *out n* according to rules (1) and (2); also one process can dissolve the boundary $n[\cdot]$ of another parallel running ambient by the action *open n* according to rule (3). In all positions where names can be used, we may also use arbitrary capabilities M, e.g., one may have strange ambient names like *in in n*, but this is merely because we do not enforce any typing on the communication rules, and we will not consider this in examples.

We require that in all processes where two input actions $(x).P$ and $(y).P$ occur, different variable symbols $x \neq y$ are used. This is not a restriction since we do not have the replication operator and can therefore make all variables disjoint initially by α-renaming.

2.2 Transition Relation

The definition of the reduction relation $\rightarrow$ in Fig. 3 is standard, however there is a subtlety we want to point out that is significant later when we go to a symbolic relation $\Rightarrow$. The point is that, to be completely precise, the symbols n, m, P, Q, R, P', and Q' in these rules are *meta-variables* ranging over names and processes, respectively. When applying a rule, these variables are supposed to be *matched* with the process they are applied to.

To work with the symbolic approach later more easily, let us reformulate this and make explicit the matching by interpreting rules as *rewriting* rules. In this

$$n[in\ m.P \mid Q] \mid m[R] \rightarrow m[n[P \mid Q] \mid R] \quad (1)$$

$$\frac{P' \equiv P \quad P \rightarrow Q \quad Q \equiv Q'}{P' \rightarrow Q'}$$

$$m[n[out\ m.P \mid Q] \mid R] \rightarrow n[P \mid Q] \mid m[R] \quad (2)$$

$$\frac{P \rightarrow Q}{n[P] \rightarrow n[Q]}$$

$$open\ n.P \mid n[Q] \rightarrow P \mid Q \quad\quad (3)$$

$$\frac{P \rightarrow Q}{P \mid R \rightarrow Q \mid R}$$

$$(x).P \mid \langle M \rangle \rightarrow P\{x \mapsto M\} \quad\quad (4)$$

Fig. 3. Reduction relation of the ambient calculus

view, the rules (1)–(4) of Fig. 3 define the essential behavior of the *in*, *out*, and *open* operators and communication, while the other rules simply tell us to which *subterms* of a process the rules may be applied. For instance, the process $M.P$ does not admit a reduction, even if the subterm P does. We can capture that by an *evaluation context* defined as follows:

$$
\begin{array}{lll}
C[\cdot] ::= & & \text{context} \\
& \cdot & \text{empty context} \\
& C[\cdot] \mid P & \text{parallel context} \\
& M[C[\cdot]] & \text{ambient context}
\end{array}
$$

We define that each rule $r = L \rightarrow R$ of the first four rules of Fig. 3 (where the processes L and R have free (meta-) variables on the left-hand and right-hand side) induces a transition relation on *closed* processes as follows: $S \rightarrow_r S'$ holds iff there is an evaluation context $C[\cdot]$ and a substitution σ for all the variables of r such that $S \equiv C[\sigma(P)]$ and $S' := C[\sigma(R)]$.[1]

2.3   Ground Intruder Theory

We now define how the intruder can construct processes from a given knowledge K, which is simply a set of *ground* capabilities (i.e. without variables). This model is defined in the style of Dolev-Yao models of protocol verification as the least closure of K under the application of some operators. These operators are encryption and the like for protocol verification, and here they are the following constructors of processes and capabilities (written with their arguments for readability):

$$\Sigma_p = \{0\,,\ P \mid Q\,,\ M[P]\,,\ M.P\,,\ \langle M \rangle\,,\ in\ M\,,\ out\ M\,,\ open\ M\}$$

We here leave out the input $(x).P$ because it is treated by a special rule.

Fig. 4 inductively defines the *ground intruder deduction relation* $K \vdash_V T$ where K is a set of ground capabilities, T ranges over capabilities and processes,

---

[1] One may additionally allow here that S' can be rewritten modulo $\equiv$ to match the rules of Fig. 3 precisely, but it is not necessary because when applying further transition rules, this is done modulo $\equiv$.

$$\frac{}{K \vdash M} \ M \in K \ \text{(Axiom)} \qquad \frac{K \vdash P \quad P \equiv Q}{K \vdash Q} \ \text{(Str.Cong.)}$$

$$\frac{K \vdash_{V_1} T_1 \quad \ldots \quad K \vdash_{V_n} T_n}{K \vdash_{\cup_{i=1}^n V_i} f(T_1, \ldots, T_n)} \ f \in \Sigma_p \ \text{(Public Operation)}$$

$$\frac{}{K \vdash_{\{x\}} x} \ x \in \mathcal{V} \ \text{(Use variables)} \qquad \frac{K \vdash_V P}{K \vdash_{V \setminus \{x\}} (x).P} \ \text{(Input)}$$

Fig. 4. Ground intruder deduction rules

and V is a set of variables such that $V = fv(T)$ the *free variables* of T. We require that the knowledge K of the intruder contains at least one name k_0, so the intruder can always say *something*. For $V = \emptyset$ we also write simply $K \vdash T$. Let $\mathcal{V}$ denote the set of all variable symbols. The (Axiom) and (Str.Cong.) express that the derivable terms contain all elements of the knowledge K and are closed under structural congruence. The (Public Operation) rule says that derivability is closed under all the operators from Σ_p; here the free variables of the resulting term are the union of the free variables of the subterms. The rule (Use variables) and (Input) together allow the intruder to generate processes that read an input and then use it.

As an example, given intruder knowledge $K = \{in \ n, m\}$ we can derive for instance $K \vdash m[(x).in \ n.out \ x.\langle open \ m \rangle]$.

We use the common term "ground intruder" and later "ground transition system" from protocol verification, suggesting we work with terms that contain no variables. However, we allow the intruder to create processes like $(x).P$ where P may freely contain x, and only require that the intruder processes at the end of the day are *closed* terms (without free variables). We may thus correctly call it "closed intruder" and "closed transition system" but we prefer to stick to the established terms.

2.4 Security Properties

We are now interested in security questions of the following form: given an honest process and a position within that process where the intruder can insert some *arbitrary* code that he can craft from his knowledge, can he break a security goal of the honest process? This is made precise by the following definition:

Definition 1. *Let us specify security goals via a predicate attack(P) that holds true for a process P when we consider P to be successfully attacked. We then also call P an attack state. Let C[·] be an (evaluation) context without free variables that represents the honest processes and the position where the intruder can insert code. Let finally K_0 be a set of ground capabilities. Then the question we want to answer is whether there exist processes P_0 and P such that $K_0 \vdash P_0$, $C[P_0] \rightarrow^* P$ and attack(P).*

We generalize this form of security questions as expected to the case where the intruder can insert several pieces of code $P_0, \ldots, P_k$ in different locations, and they are generated from different knowledges $K_0, \ldots, K_k$, respectively.

There are many ways to define security goals for the ambient calculus, and we have opted here for state-based safety properties rather than observational equivalences. In fact, the most simple goal is that no intruder process may ever learn a secret name s. We can thus describe an attack predicate that holds true for states where a secret s has been leaked to the intruder. To do that, let us label all output actions $\langle M \rangle$ that are part of the intruder generated code with superscript i like $\langle M \rangle^i$. We formalize that an intruder-generated process has learned the secret s in a state S:

$$\mathsf{leak}_s(S) \text{ iff } \langle s \rangle^i \sqsubseteq S.$$

Here $\sqsubseteq$ denotes the subterm relation.

Another goal is that the intruder code cannot reach a given position of the honest platform. This can be reduced to a secrecy goal—at the destination waits a process that writes out a secret. A more complex goal is containment: a sandbox may host an intruder code and give that code some secret s to compute with, but the intruder code should not be able to get s out of the sandbox. This can again be reduced to secrecy (of another value s') if outside the sandbox a special ambient $k_0[open\ s.\langle s' \rangle]$ is waiting. From this ambient an intruder process (who initially knows the name k_0) can obtain secret s' if it was able to learn s and get out of the sandbox.

Example 1. As an example let us consider the firewall example from [8]:

$$Firewall \equiv w[k[out\ w.in\ k'.in\ w] \mid open\ k'.open\ k''.\langle s \rangle]$$

The goal is that the firewall can only be entered by an ambient that knows the three passwords k, k', and k'' (in fact having capability $open\ k$ instead of k is sufficient). Here the ambient $k[\cdot]$ acts as a pilot that can move out of the firewall, fetch a client ambient (that needs to authenticate itself) and move it into the firewall. Suppose we run $Firewall \mid P$ for some process P that the intruder generated from knowledge K and define as an attack a state in which leak_s holds. If K includes $open\ k, k', k''$, then we have an attack, since the intruder can generate the process $P \equiv k'[open\ k.k''[(x).\langle x \rangle^i]]$ from K. An attack is reached as follows:

$$Firewall \mid P$$
$$\rightarrow w[open\ k'.open\ k''.\langle s \rangle] \mid k[in\ k'.in\ w] \mid P$$
$$\rightarrow w[open\ k'.open\ k''.\langle s \rangle] \mid k'[k[in\ w] \mid open\ k.k''[(x).\langle x \rangle^i]]$$
$$\rightarrow w[open\ k'.open\ k''.\langle s \rangle] \mid k'[in\ w \mid k''[(x).\langle x \rangle^i]]$$
$$\rightarrow w[open\ k'.open\ k''.\langle s \rangle \mid k'[k''[(x).\langle x \rangle^i]]]$$
$$\rightarrow w[\langle s \rangle \mid (x).\langle x \rangle^i]$$
$$\rightarrow w[\langle s \rangle^i]$$

If the knowledge K from which the intruder process is created does not include $open\ k$ (or k), k' and k'', then no attack is possible. Also containment of the secret s in the firewall holds.

2.5 The Considered Fragment

For the automation, we have made some restrictions w.r.t. the original ambient calculus. The replication operator $!P \equiv P \mid !P$ together with the creation of new names allows for simulating arbitrary Turing machines and thus prevents a decision procedure for security. Similar to the lazy intruder in protocol verification, we thus bound the steps that honest processes can perform and do this by simply disallowing the replication operator for honest processes. Without replication, one of the main reasons for the name restriction operator $\nu n.P$ is gone, since we can α-rename all restricted names so that they are unique throughout the processes. Note that the name restriction is also useful for goals of observational equivalence, which are essential for privacy goals [1,2] but which we do not consider in this paper.

Note that we do not bound the size of processes that the intruder creates: the derivation relation $K \vdash P$ allows him to make arbitrary use of all constructors. It may appear as if the intruder were bounded because $K \vdash P$ does not include the replication operator either, but this is not true: an attack always consists of a finite number of steps (as violation of a safety property) and thus every attack that can be achieved by an intruder process with replication can be achieved by one without replication (just by "unrolling" the replication as much as necessary for the particular attack). The difference between unbounded intruder processes and bounded honest processes thus stems from the fact that we ask questions of the form: "can a concrete honest process (of fixed size) be attacked by *any* dishonest process (of arbitrary size)?"

We do not need to give the intruder the ability to create arbitrary new names. The reason is that we have no inequality checks in the ambient calculus, i.e., no process can check upon receiving a capability n that it is different from all names it knows (e.g. to prevent replays). Thus, whatever attack works when the intruder uses different self-created names works similarly with always using the same intruder name k_0 that we give the intruder initially.

Finally, the extension of the mobile ambient calculus with communication includes so-called *path constraints* of the form $M.M'$ that can be communicated as messages. Note that this is not ordinary concatenation of messages (which the symbolic techniques we use can easily handle) but sequences of instructions and only after the first has been successfully executed, the next one becomes available, and so the paths cannot be decomposed. Since this includes several problems that would complicate our method, we have excluded them.

3 Symbolic Ambients

We now introduce the symbolic, constraint-based approach that is at the core of this paper. To efficiently answer the kind of security questions we formalized in the previous paragraph, we want to avoid search the space of all processes that an intruder can come up with. To that end, we use the basic idea of the symbolic, constraint-based approach of protocol verification, also known as the lazy intruder [12,13,16,6].

When an agent in a protocol wants to receive a message of the form t—a term that contains variables—we avoid enumerating the set of all messages that the intruder can generate and that are instances of t (because this set is often very large or infinite). Rather we remember the constraint $K \vdash t$ where K is the set of messages that the intruder knows at the point when he sends the instance of t. We then proceed with states that have free variables, namely the variables of t (and of other messages as they sent and received). The allowed values for these variables are governed by the constraints. For a fixed number of agents and sessions, this gives us a symbolic finite-state transition system. An important ingredient of this symbolic approach is checking satisfiability of the $K \vdash t$ constraints. The complexity of the satisfiability problem has been studied for a variety of algebraic theories of the operators involved, e.g. [9,10]; in the easiest theory, the free algebra, the problem is NP-complete [16]. One can check satisfiability of the constraints on-the-fly and prune the search tree when a state has unsatisfiable constraints. Thus during the search messages get successively instantiated with more concrete messages in a demand-driven, lazy way. Hence the name.

Now we carry over this idea to the ambient calculus and apply it to the processes that were written by the intruder, i.e. lazily creating the intruder-generated processes during the search. Recall that in the previous section we defined security problems as reachability of an attack state from $C[P_0]$ where $C[\cdot]$ is a given honest agent and $K_0 \vdash P_0$ is any intruder process generated from a given initial knowledge K_0. We could thus simply work with a symbolic state $C[x]$ where x is a variable and we have the constraint $K_0 \vdash x$.

There are some inconveniences attached to using variables like this for representing processes. First, with every transition the process changes and we therefore need to introduce new variables and relate them to the old ones. Second, the processes can learn new information by communication with others, so the available knowledge changes. For these two reasons we follow a more convenient option and simply represent an intruder generated process by writing $\boxed{K}$ where K is the knowledge from which it was created. K is a set of capabilities and intuitively $\boxed{K}$ represents *any* process that can be created from K. If a process contains two occurrences of $\boxed{K}$ for the same K, they may represent different processes. K may contain variables because we will also handle the communication between processes with the lazy intruder technique. We thus extend the syntax of processes P, Q of Fig. 1 by $\boxed{K}$, and we consider symbolic security problems as reachability of a symbolic attack state (defined in Section 3.2) from an initial state $C[\boxed{K}]$ where $C[\cdot]$ is an honest environment that the intruder code is running in.

A symbolic process will also be equipped with constraints which have the following syntax:

$$
\begin{array}{lll}
\phi, \psi ::= & & \text{constraints} \\
& K \vdash M & \text{intruder deduction constraint} \\
& x = M & \text{substitution} \\
& \phi \wedge \psi & \text{conjunction}
\end{array}
$$

Intuitively, $K \vdash M$ means that capability/message M can been generated by the intruder from knowledge K. In fact, will not use in the symbolic constraints $K \vdash P$ for a process P, since we have no construct for sending processes and all processes the intruder generates are thus covered by the $\boxed{K}$ notation.

Semantics. We define the semantics for pairs (S, ϕ) of symbolic processes and constraints as a (usually infinite) set of closed processes. An *interpretation* $\mathcal{I}$ is a mapping from all variables to ground capabilities. We extend this to a morphism on capabilities, processes, and sets of processes as expected, where $\mathcal{I}$ substitutes only free occurrences of variables. We define the model relation as follows:

$$
\begin{aligned}
\mathcal{I} &\models K \vdash M &\text{iff}\quad & \mathcal{I}(K) \vdash \mathcal{I}(M) \\
\mathcal{I} &\models x = M &\text{iff}\quad & \mathcal{I}(x) = \mathcal{I}(M) \\
\mathcal{I} &\models \phi \wedge \psi &\text{iff}\quad & \mathcal{I} \models \phi \text{ and } \mathcal{I} \models \psi
\end{aligned}
$$

The semantics of (S, ϕ) is the set of possible instantiation of all variables and intruder code pieces $\boxed{K}$ with closed processes:

$$
\begin{aligned}
[\![P, \phi]\!] &= \{Q \mid \mathcal{I} \models \phi \wedge Q \in ext(\mathcal{I}(P))\} \\
ext(\boxed{K}) &= \{P \mid K \vdash P\} \\
ext(x) &= \{x\} \\
ext(n) &= \{n\} \\
ext(f(T_1, \ldots, T_n)) &= \{f(T_1', \ldots, T_n') \mid T_1' \in ext(T_1) \wedge \ldots \wedge T_n' \in ext(T_n)\}
\end{aligned}
$$

Here the T_i range over capabilities and processes and f ranges over all constructors of capabilities and processes. Note the case $ext(x)$ can only occur when processing a subterm of a process where x is bound, so no free variables occur in any $S_0 \in [\![P, \phi]\!]$.

Lazy Intruder Constraint Reduction. A decision procedure for satisfiability of $K \vdash M$ constraints can be designed straightforwardly in the style of [13,6], since we just need to handle the constructors for capabilities, namely *in*, *out*, and *open*, and we have no destructors (or algebraic properties). The only subtlety here is that we have in general several intruder processes that may learn new capabilities independent of each other and may be unable to exchange with each other what they learned—a *multi-intruder problem*. That means we cannot rely on the *well-formedness* assumption often used in the lazy intruder for protocol verification. Suppose the knowledge K in a constraint contains a variable x, then well-formedness says that there exists an constraint $K_0 \vdash M_0$ with $K_0 \subseteq K$ and M_0 contains x, i.e., x is part of a term the intruder generated earlier. Without this assumption, constraint satisfiability is more difficult to check in general [5], however the main problem is the analysis of knowledge K in constraints. This is not an issue because we have no analysis rules for the intruder here. For more details, see the proof of Theorem 1.

3.1   Symbolic Transition Rules

We now define a symbolic transition relation on symbolic processes with constraints of the form $(S, \phi) \Rightarrow (S', \phi \wedge \psi)$. Note that the constraints are *augmented* in every step, i.e., all previous constraints ϕ remain and new constraints ψ may be added.

We first want to lift the standard transition rules on ground processes of Section 2.2 to the symbolic level. The idea is to replace the rule *matching* defined above with rule *unification*. Recall that above we have essentially defined a transition rule $r = L \to R$ to be applicable to state S if $S = C[\sigma(L)]$ for some substitution σ and evaluation context $C[\cdot]$. For the symbolic level we have that S may contain free variables that need to be substituted as well. Suppose the rule r does not contain any variables that occur in the symbolic state (S, ϕ) (which is achieved by α-renaming the rule variables). Thus define that $(S, \phi) \Rightarrow_r (S', \phi \wedge \psi)$ holds iff there is an evaluation context $C[\cdot]$ and a term T such that:

- $S \equiv C[T]$;
- σ is a most general unifier of T and L modulo $\equiv$, i.e., $\sigma(T) \equiv \sigma(L)$ and for no generalization τ of σ it holds that $\tau(T) \equiv \tau(L)$; and
- $S' = \sigma(C[\sigma(R)])$ and $\psi = eq(\sigma)$

where $eq(\sigma)$ is the formula $x_1 = t_1 \wedge \ldots x_n = t_n$ if $\sigma = [x_1 \mapsto t_1, \ldots, x_n \mapsto t_n]$. Observe σ may now replace also variables that occur in S and thus σ is applied also to $C[\cdot]$. Moreover for a given (S, ϕ) and rule r there can only be finitely many most general unifiers σ as discussed in the proof of Theorem 1.

Example 2. Using the *in* rule, we can now make the following symbolic transition: $(x[P] \mid y[in\ z.Q], \phi) \Rightarrow (z[P \mid y[Q]], \phi \wedge x = z)$

Similarly, also $(x[P] \mid y[in\ z.\boxed{K}], \phi) \Rightarrow (z[P \mid y[\boxed{K}]], \phi \wedge x = z)$ is possible for an intruder generated piece of code $\boxed{K}$.

So far, however, the rules do not allow us to make an *in* transition on the following state: $(x[P] \mid y[\boxed{K}], \phi)$ even if the intruder can generate a process of the form *in* $z.Q$ from knowledge K. We will see below how to add appropriate rules for intruder-generated processes, so that for instance in the above state a variant of the in-rule is applicable.

It is immediate that the described symbolic transitions are sound (i.e., all states that are reachable in the symbolic model represent states that are reachable in the standard ground model). There are however not yet complete: in the condition $S \equiv C[T]$ above we restrict the application of rule r to contexts that exist in S—without instantiating intruder code like $\boxed{K}$ first. Giving a complete set of rules for intruder processes is the subject of the rest of this subsection.

Intruder-written Code. We now come to the very core of the approach: lazily instantiating a piece of code $\boxed{K}$ that the intruder generated from knowledge K with a more concrete term in a demand-driven way. This is basically what is missing after the lifting of the ground rules that we have just described, namely when an "abstract" piece of intruder-written code $\boxed{K}$ prevents the application of a rule that would be applicable when replacing $\boxed{K}$ with some more concrete process P such that $K \vdash P$. Obviously we would like to identify such situations without enumerating all processes P that can be generated from K.

In the example $x[P] \mid y[\boxed{K}]$ we discussed above, we have the following possibility: if the intruder code marked $\boxed{K}$ were to have the shape *in x.Q*, we could apply the *in* rule and get to the state $x[y[\boxed{K}]] \mid P]$, assuming $K \vdash in\ x$. Note the residual code (inside $y[\cdot]$ after the move) is again something generated from knowledge K.

There is a systematic way to obtain all rules that are necessary to achieve completeness, namely by answering the following question: given a symbolic process with constraints (S, ϕ), any ground process $S_0 \in [\![S, \phi]\!]$, and a transition $S_0 \to S_0'$ what rule do we need on the symbolic level to perform an analogous transition? Thus, we want to reach an $(S', \phi \land \psi)$ (in zero or more steps) such that $S_0' \in [\![(S', \phi \land \psi)]\!]$. Of course, the rule should also be sound (i.e. all $S_0' \in [\![(S', \phi \land \psi)]\!]$ are reachable with ground transition rules from some $S_0 \in [\![(S, \phi)]\!]$). Soundness is relatively easy to see, because we need to consider rules only in isolation. We now systematically derive rules for each case of (S, ϕ), S_0, and S_0' that can occur and thereby achieve a sound and complete set of symbolic transition rules.

Recall that by the definition, for a transition from S_0 to S_0' with rule $r = L \to R$, we need to have an evaluation context $C_0[\cdot]$ and a substitution σ of the rule variables such that $S_0 = C[\sigma(L)]$ and $S_1 = C[\sigma(R)]$.

The symbolic transition rules we have defined above already handle the case that the symbolic state S has the form $S = C'[T]$ where $\sigma(C'[cot]) = C[\cdot]$ and $\sigma(L) \equiv \sigma(T)$ (as shown in the examples previously) where at a corresponding position a similar rule (under renaming) can be applied without instantiating intruder code. This includes the case that a rule variable P of type process is unified with a piece $\boxed{K}$ of intruder code.

Another case that does not require further work is when the rule match in S_0 is for a subterm of intruder-generated code, i.e. that is subsumed by some $\boxed{K}$ in the symbolic term S. Here we use the fact that intruder deduction is closed under evaluation: if $K \vdash P$ and $P \to P'$, then also $K \vdash P'$.

Therefore all remaining cases that we need to handle are where one or more proper subterms of the redex $\sigma(L)$ in S_0 are intruder-written code that are not trivial, i.e. represent a variable in L. We make a case distinction

- by the different transition rules for $\to$, namely (1)–(4),
- and by how S relates to the matching subterm in S_0.

In-Rule. Let us mark three positions in the *in* rule which could be intruder-written code and that are not yet handled:

$$\overbrace{n[\underbrace{in\ m.P}_{p2}\ |\ Q]}^{p1}\ |\ \underbrace{m[R]}_{p3} \to m[n[P\ |\ Q]\ |\ R]$$

In fact, this notation contains a simplification: for instance looking at position p_2, we could also have the variant that the intruder code is of the form $in\ m.P\ |\ P'$. In such a case, the intruder code piece $\boxed{K}$ in the symbolic state would not exactly correspond to a subterm of the matched rule, but only after "splitting" $\boxed{K}$ into $\boxed{K}\ |\ \boxed{K}$. Such a splitting rule would obviously be sound, but we do not want to include it, and rather perform such splits only in a demand driven way (as the following cases show)—and to keep the notation simple for the positions in the rules. So all positions indicated here are considered under the possibility that the intruder code itself is a parallel composition; note also we are matching/unifying modulo $\equiv$.

In rule with intruder code at position p_1. The first case we consider is when only at p_1 is intruder code, i.e., we have some intruder code running in parallel with an ambient $m[R]$; then the intruder code may be able to enter m if it has the capability $in\ m$. As said before, we could have the case that the intruder code first splits into two parts and only one part enters m while the other part stays outside. This can be helpful if the intruder code does not have the capability *out m*. Since the intruder code can always be trivially 0 if there is nothing to do, it is not a restriction to make the split, so we avoid giving two rules. We obtain:

$$\boxed{K}\ |\ m[R] \Rightarrow \boxed{K}\ |\ m[x[\boxed{K}]\ ]\ |\ R] \text{ and } \psi = K \vdash in\ m \wedge K \vdash x \qquad (5)$$

Here we denote with ψ the new constraints that should be added to the symbolic successor state. x is a new variable symbol (that does not occur so far). The reason for introducing this new symbol x is that a process cannot move without being surrounded by an ambient $n[\cdot]$ construct; as the $n[\cdot]$ of the normal *in* rule has now become part of the $\boxed{K}$ code, we need to say that the intruder himself created the ambient. As there is no obligation to pick a particular name for that ambient, we simply leave it open and just require the intruder can construct it from knowledge K. Note that it would be unsound in general to simplify the right-hand side to $m[\boxed{K}\ |\ R]$ because the intruder cannot get rid of the surrounding $x[\cdot]$ (even though self-chosen) without another process performing *open x*.

To see the soundness of this rule, consider that the intruder code matched on the left-hand side of the rule should have the form $P_1\ |\ x[in\ m.P_2]$ for some processes P_1 and P_2 generated from knowledge K. These are then represented by the two $\boxed{K}$ pieces on the right-hand side of the rule.

In rule with intruder code at position p_2. Here, intruder code is running inside ambient n that runs in parallel with ambient m. The intruder code can move ambient n into m, if it has the capability *in m*:

$$n[\boxed{K}\ |\ Q]\ |\ m[R] \Rightarrow m[n[\boxed{K}\ |\ Q]\ |\ R] \text{ and } \psi = K \vdash in\ m \qquad (6)$$

Note that we could have again the situation that the intruder code is a parallel composition, i.e. of the form $in\ m.P_1 \mid P_2$. However, then after the move we still have $P_1 \mid P_2$ and we thus do not make the split explicit, because this case is still subsumed by $\boxed{K}$ on the right-hand side.

In rule with intruder code at position p_3. Now we consider the situation that an honest ambient $n[in\ m.P \mid Q]$ that wants to enter an ambient m that runs in parallel with intruder code. If the intruder code has name m, it can provide the ambient that the honest process can then enter:

$$n[in\ m.P \mid Q] \mid \boxed{K} \Rightarrow m[n[P \mid Q] \mid \boxed{K}] \mid \boxed{K} \text{ and } \psi = K \vdash m \qquad (7)$$

Here we have again an explicit split of the intruder process into two parts. This is because the concrete intruder process that is partially matched by the left-hand side may have the form $m[R_1] \mid R_2$, i.e. not entirely running within m, and we thus need to denote that residual process explicitly on the right-hand side.

In rule with intruder code at several positions. If the intruder code is at several positions of the rule, we get the following situations. Obviously we do not need to consider the combination $(p_1) + (p_2)$ because (p_2) is a sub-position of (p_1). The case $(p_1) + (p_3)$ means that we have two intruder processes (in general with different knowledge) to run in parallel: $\boxed{K} \mid \boxed{K'}$. We will show below (when we treat communication) that what they can achieve together is to pool their knowledge and join to one process $\boxed{K \cup K'}$.

What is left is the combination $(p_2) + (p_3)$ which means that one intruder process runs inside an ambient n and that runs in parallel with another intruder process. This case we can express by the following rule:

$$n[\boxed{K} \mid Q] \mid \boxed{K'} \Rightarrow x[n[\boxed{K} \mid Q] \mid \boxed{K'}] \mid \boxed{K'} \text{ and } \psi = K \vdash in\ x \wedge K' \vdash x \ (8)$$

Note that the two processes that we start with may not have the same knowledge (here K and K'). Again, we have an explicit split on the side of the K'-generated process into a part that is entered by $n[\cdot]$ and one that remains outside. Also, again, this rule has a new variable x for the name of the ambient that is entered by $n[\cdot]$; this name needs to be part of K' while K only needs to have the $in\ x$ capability.

This rule is a problem for the termination of our approach. Observe that the left-hand side ambient $n[\cdot]$ occurs identically as a subterm on the right side; so the rule "packs in" the $n[\cdot]$ ambient into another $x[\cdot]$ ambient. We will therefore later show that we can limit the application of this rule without loosing attacks.

Out Rule. For the *out* rule we have two positions of intruder code to consider:

$$m[\overbrace{n[\underbrace{out\ m.P}_{p2} \mid Q]}^{p1} \mid R] \to n[P \mid Q] \mid m[R]$$

Out Rule with intruder code at position p_1. Here we have the situation that the intruder code is within an ambient m and has the capability *out m*. To move parts of the code, the intruder must put it within some ambient x (where x is again a new variable symbol):

$$m[\boxed{K} \mid R] \Rightarrow x[\boxed{K}] \mid m[\boxed{K} \mid R] \text{ and } \psi = K \vdash out\ m \wedge K \vdash x \qquad (9)$$

Out rule with intruder code at p_2. This situation is similar except that the intruder code is already contained within an ambient n. We then have:

$$m[n[\boxed{K} \mid Q] \mid R] \Rightarrow n[\boxed{K} \mid Q] \mid m[R] \text{ and } \psi = K \vdash out\ m \qquad (10)$$

This subsumes also the case that there is intruder code at both in m and in n (i.e. also within what is matched as R here).

Open-Rule. The open rule has also just two positions for intruder code, the opening code and the opened code:

$$\underbrace{open\ n.P}_{p1} \mid \underbrace{n[Q]}_{p2} \to P \mid Q$$

The rules for the intruder code at p_1 and at p_2, respectively are immediate:

$$\boxed{K} \mid n[Q] \Rightarrow \boxed{K} \mid Q \text{ and } \psi = K \vdash open\ n \qquad (11)$$

$$open\ n.P \mid \boxed{K} \Rightarrow P \mid \boxed{K} \text{ and } \psi = K \vdash n \qquad (12)$$

The case $(p1) + (p2)$ is again the case of two parallel communicating processes that is treated next.

Communication Rule. Again there are two possible positions where intruder code could reside, namely as the sender or as the receiver:

$$\underbrace{(x).P}_{p1} \mid \underbrace{\langle M \rangle}_{p2} \to P[x \mapsto M]$$

Communication with the intruder receiving. The intruder can receive a message M from an honest process running in parallel:

$$\boxed{K} \mid \langle M \rangle \Rightarrow \boxed{K \cup \{M\}} \qquad (13)$$

Here the resulting intruder process has the message M simply added to its knowledge. The idea is that the remaining process can behave like any process that the intruder could have created, if he initially knew $K \cup \{M\}$. To see that this is sound, consider that the intruder process would have the form $(x).P$ for a new variable x that can occur arbitrarily in P. Thus if this process reads M, the resulting $P[x \mapsto M]$ is is a process that can be generated from knowledge $K \cup \{M\}$ if P was created from knowledge K.

Communication with the intruder sending. For the case that intruder code sends out a message that is received by an honest process, we can be *truly lazy*:

$$(x).P \mid \boxed{K} \Rightarrow P \mid \boxed{K} \text{ and } \psi = K \vdash x \qquad (14)$$

Here, we do not instantiate the message x that is being received, we simply add the constraint that x must be something the intruder can generate from knowledge K. This is in fact the classic case of the lazy intruder—postponing the choice of a concrete message that the intruder sends to an agent. Since the intruder knowledge contains at least one name, there is always "something to say", but what it is will only be determined if the variable x gets unified later upon applying some rule (which can render the $K \vdash x$ constraint unsatisfiable).

Communication with the intruder both sending and receiving. Finally we have the rule that was mentioned above already: when two intruder processes meet they can exchange their knowledge and work together further on:

$$\boxed{K} \mid \boxed{K'} \Rightarrow \boxed{K \cup K'} \qquad (15)$$

This is sound because every $k \in K \setminus K'$ can be sent from the first to the second process until we have $\boxed{K} \mid \boxed{K \cup K'}$ and then the second part subsumes the first, so we can simplify it to $\boxed{K \cup K'}$. Observe that this rule can also be used when we restrict ourselves to the pure ambient calculus without communication: we then simply have two processes in parallel with capabilities K and K', respectively, and what they can achieve is anything a process with capabilities $K \cup K'$ can achieve (even without communication).

As part of the proof of Theorem 1, we formally show that the set of rules we gave for the symbolic transition system are sound and complete, i.e., they represent exactly the reachable states of the original ground transition system. This proof is found in the extended version of this paper [14], but our systematic development of the rules (i.e., covering each possible case) in this subsection serves as a proof sketch for completeness (and the soundness is straightforward to check for each rule).

3.2   Security Properties in the Symbolic System

Before we can state our main result, we need to formally define the properties we can check for in the symbolic system. Right now, we limit ourselves to secrecy goals as a very basic property, and leave the extension to further security properties for future work.

In general for any property that we want to check, we need to be able to express them for both ground and symbolic states, and these definitions for ground and symbolic states must correspond to each other:

Definition 2. *We say that a predicate* attack(S_0) *on closed processes* S_0 *and a predicate* ATTACK(S, ϕ) *on symbolic processes* (S, ϕ) *correspond iff for every* (S, ϕ) *it holds that*

$$\text{ATTACK}(S, \phi) \text{ iff exists } S_0 \in [\![S, \phi]\!] \text{ such that } \text{attack}(S_0)$$

Recall that the attack predicate for secrecy on the ground level was defined as $\text{leak}_s(S_0)$ *iff* $\langle s \rangle^i \sqsubseteq S_0$. *Define the corresponding predicate on the symbolic level:*

$\text{LEAK}_s(S, \phi)$ *iff exists* K *such that* $\boxed{K} \sqsubseteq S$ *and* $K \vdash s \wedge \phi$ *is satisfiable.*

It is immediate that leak_s and LEAK_s correspond: given any (S, ϕ) then

$$\begin{aligned}
\text{LEAK}_S(S, \phi) \text{ iff } & \text{exist } K, \mathcal{I}. \ \boxed{K} \sqsubseteq S, \quad \mathcal{I} \models K \vdash s \wedge \phi \\
\text{iff } & \text{exist } K, \mathcal{I}. \ \boxed{K} \sqsubseteq S, \quad \mathcal{I}(K) \vdash s, \mathcal{I} \models \phi \\
\text{iff } & \text{exist } \mathcal{I}, C[\cdot]. \ C[\langle s \rangle^i] \in ext(\mathcal{I}(S)) \\
\text{iff } & \text{exists } S_0. \ S_0 \in [\![S, \phi]\!] \text{ and } \text{leak}_s(S_0)
\end{aligned}$$

3.3   Main Result

We can now use the symbolic transition system that we have developed using the lazy intruder technique to give a decision procedure for secrecy in our fragment of the ambient calculus without bounding the intruder.

Theorem 1. *The following problem is NP-complete. Given*

- *a name* s,
- *a closed process* $C_0[\cdot]$ *(in our the supported fragment),*
- *and a finite set* K *of ground capabilities as initial intruder knowledge;*

exist P *and* S_0 *such that* $K \vdash P$, $C_0[P] \rightarrow^* S_0$ *and* $\text{leak}_s(S_0)$?

The full proof is found in the extended version [14] and we give here only a proof sketch. We can first show that symbolic transition system we have defined is sound and complete, i.e., representing exactly the reachable states of the standard ground transition system. It is immediate that satisfiability of the constraints of our system is in NP (simple guess and check) and that we can polynomially reduce satisfiability of Boolean formulae to satisfiability of constraints. A similar reduction is possible from satisfiability of Boolean formulae to reachability of leak-states in the ground system, showing that this problem is NP-hard. For containment in NP it remains to show that we can restrict the exploration of the (still infinite-state) symbolic transition system such that the length of explored traces is bounded by a polynomial and such that the explored space contains a LEAK_s state iff one is reachable at all. The idea for this termination proof is that most rules "consume" an action of an honest agent (limiting their applicability); the rules (5) and (9) can be seen as *spreading intruder knowledge* and this can be bounded because there is an upper bound on what the intruder can learn from honest agents; the application of the rule (8) can be bounded to the number of actions that the honest agents can do (since all other applications are covered by (5) and (9)); and finally the rules (6) and (10) alone cannot be applied indefinitely often without producing a state repetition.

3.4 Examples

Let us reconsider the firewall example from before, and see how a lazy intruder process would find the attack. In contrast to the original specification, we leave open how the intruder process P exactly works, and rather specify that it is some process generated from the initial knowledge $K = \{in\ k, k', k''\}$:

$$(Firewall \mid \boxed{K}, true)$$
$$\Rightarrow (w[open\ k'.open\ k''.\langle s\rangle] \mid k[in\ k'.in\ w] \mid \boxed{K}, true) \quad \text{by rule (2)}$$
$$\Rightarrow (w[open\ k'.open\ k''.\langle s\rangle] \mid k'[k[in\ w] \mid \boxed{K}] \mid \boxed{K}, \phi_1) \quad \text{by rule (7)}$$
$$\Rightarrow (w[open\ k'.open\ k''.\langle s\rangle] \mid k'[in\ w \mid \boxed{K}] \mid \boxed{K}, \phi_2) \quad \text{by rule (11)}$$
$$\Rightarrow (w[open\ k'.open\ k''.\langle s\rangle \mid k'[\boxed{K}]] \mid \boxed{K}, \phi_2) \quad \text{by rule (1)}$$
$$\Rightarrow (w[open\ k''.\langle s\rangle \mid \boxed{K}] \mid \boxed{K}, \phi_2) \quad \text{by rule (3)}$$
$$\Rightarrow (w[\langle s\rangle \mid \boxed{K}] \mid \boxed{K}, \phi_3) \quad \text{by rule (12)}$$
$$\Rightarrow (w[\boxed{K \cup \{s\}}] \mid \boxed{K}, \phi_3) \quad \text{by rule (13)}$$

where we have collected the constraints $\phi_1 = K \vdash k'$, $\phi_2 = \phi_1 \wedge K \vdash open\ w$, and $\phi_3 = \phi_2 \wedge K \vdash k''$. These constraints are satisfiable. This corresponds to the attack we had described on the ground model, only here we found it *lazily* during the search, rather than specifying the process up front. Another difference to the original trace is that we have an intruder process $\boxed{K}$ remaining at the outermost level the entire time. This reflects that the intruder process could be a parallel composition of two parts only one of which enters the firewall—the position outside the does not have to be "given up" by the intruder.

Ambient in the Middle. The previous example has basically identified how an honest client (authenticating itself by the knowledge of the keys k, k', and k'') is supposed to behave, namely $Client \equiv k'[open\ k.k''[C_0]]$ for some process C_0. We now consider the case that such an honest client and firewall execute in the presence of an intruder process K:

$$(Firewall \mid Client \mid \boxed{K}, true)$$
$$\Rightarrow (Firewall \mid k'[open\ k.k''[C_0] \mid x[\boxed{K}]] \mid \boxed{K}, \phi_1)$$
$$\Rightarrow (w[open\ k'.open\ k''.\langle s\rangle] \mid k[in\ k'.in\ w] \mid k'[open\ k.k''[C_0] \mid x[\boxed{K}]] \mid \boxed{K}, \phi_1)$$
$$\Rightarrow (w[open\ k'.open\ k''.\langle s\rangle] \mid k'[k[in\ w] \mid open\ k.k''[C_0] \mid x[\boxed{K}]] \mid \boxed{K}, \phi_1)$$
$$\Rightarrow (w[open\ k'.open\ k''.\langle s\rangle] \mid k'[in\ w \mid k''[C_0] \mid x[\boxed{K}]] \mid \boxed{K}, \phi_1)$$
$$\Rightarrow (w[open\ k'.open\ k''.\langle s\rangle \mid k'[k''[C_0] \mid x[\boxed{K}]]] \mid \boxed{K}, \phi_1)$$
$$\Rightarrow (w[open\ k''.\langle s\rangle \mid k''[C_0] \mid x[\boxed{K}]] \mid \boxed{K}, \phi_1)$$
$$\Rightarrow (w[\langle s\rangle \mid k''[C_0] \mid \boxed{K}] \mid \boxed{K}, \phi_2)$$

where $\phi_1 = K \vdash in\ k' \wedge K \vdash x$ and $\phi_2 = K \vdash in\ k' \wedge K \vdash k''$. Note that in the one but last step we apply the open action to the intruder ambient $x[\boxed{K}]$ (unifying $x = k_0$). Thus, the intruder can inject code into the firewall (without being isolated by $x[\cdot]$, and so he can obtain s) if he knows only $in\ k'$ and k''. The *open k* capability is not needed, since this is done by the client after the intruder has infected it.

A Communication Example. As an example where capabilities are communicated consider the process $n_1[\,\boxed{K_1}\,\mid n_2[in\ n_3.\langle in\ n_4\rangle]]\mid n_5[n_4[\,\boxed{K_2}\,\mid\langle out\ n_5\rangle]]$ where $K_1=\{n_3, open\ n_2\}$ and $K_2=\{open\ n_1\}$. Let the goal be that there is no intruder process who will know both $open\ n_1$ and $open\ n_2$. The lazy mobile ambient technique finds an attack as follows:

$$(n_1[\,\boxed{K_1}\,\mid n_3[\,\boxed{K_1}\,\mid n_2[\langle in\ n_4\rangle]]]\mid n_5[n_4[\,\boxed{K_2}\,\mid\langle out\ n_5\rangle]],\mathit{true})$$

$\Rightarrow (n_1[\,\boxed{K_1}\,\mid n_3[\,\boxed{K_1}\,\mid\langle in\ n_4\rangle]]\mid n_5[n_4[\,\boxed{K_2}\,\mid\langle out\ n_5\rangle]],\phi_1)$ by rule (11)

$\Rightarrow (n_1[\,\boxed{K_1}\,\mid n_3[\,\boxed{K_1\cup\{in\ n_4\}}\,]]\mid n_5[n_4[\,\boxed{K_2}\,\mid\langle out\ n_5\rangle]],\phi_1)$ by rule (13)

$\Rightarrow (n_1[\,\boxed{K_1}\,\mid\,\boxed{K_1\cup\{in\ n_4\}}\,]\mid n_5[n_4[\,\boxed{K_2}\,\mid\langle out\ n_5\rangle]],\phi_2)$ by rule (11)

$\Rightarrow (n_1[\,\boxed{K_1\cup\{in\ n_4\}}\,]\mid n_5[n_4[\,\boxed{K_2}\,\mid\langle out\ n_5\rangle]],\phi_2)$ by rule (15)

$\Rightarrow (n_1[\,\boxed{K_1\cup\{in\ n_4\}}\,]\mid n_4[\,\boxed{K_2}\,]\mid n_5[0],\phi_2)$ by rule (2)

$\Rightarrow (n_4[\,\boxed{K_2}\,\mid n_1[\,\boxed{K_1\cup\{in\ n_4\}}\,]]\mid n_5[0],\phi_3)$ by rule (6)

$\Rightarrow (n_4[\,\boxed{K_2}\,\mid\,\boxed{K_1\cup\{in\ n_4\}}\,]\mid n_5[0],\phi_4)$ by rule (11)

$\Rightarrow (n_4[\,\boxed{K_2\cup K_1\cup\{in\ n_4\}}\,]\mid n_5[0],\phi_4)$ by rule (15)

where we the following satisfiable constraints: $\phi_1=K_1\vdash open\ n_2$, $\phi_2=\phi_1\wedge K_1\vdash open\ n_3$, $\phi_3=\phi_2\wedge K_1\cup\{in\ m_4\}\vdash in\ m_4$, and $\phi_4=\phi_3\wedge K_2\vdash open\ n_1$. We have reached a state where an intruder process knows both $open\ n_1$ and $open\ n_2$.

4   Conclusions

We have transferred the symbolic lazy intruder technique from protocol verification to a different problem: an intruder who creates malicious code for execution on some honest platform. This gives us an efficient method to check whether the platform achieves its security goals for *any* intruder code, because we avoid the naive search of the space of possible programs that the intruder can come up with. Instead we determine this code in a demand-driven, lazy way.

Our approach is closest to a model-checking technique. In contrast to static analysis approaches, it works without over-approximation, but requires a bounding of the number of steps that honest agents can perform. The symbolic nature however allows to work without any bound on the size of programs that the intruder can generate. This is similar to the original use of the lazy intruder in protocol verification [12,13,16,6].

We have used a fragment of the mobile ambient calculus with communication as a small and succinct formalism to model both the platform and the mobile code [8]. We have omitted the replication operator in order to bound honest processes (though not the intruder). We have omitted the path constraints because they induce considerable complications for our approach and leave their integration for future work. We also plan to consider the extension of boxed ambients introduced by Bugliesi et al. [7] which add interesting means for access control and communication. Moreover it is possible to extend the ambient calculus and our method to support cryptographic operators (like encryption and signing) in the communication of processes.

We believe that the approach we have presented here is generally applicable to the formal analysis of platforms that host mobile code. The key elements can be summarized as follows. First, the code can be lazily developed by exploring at each step which operations can be performed next and what data is needed. This data is handled lazily as well. Second, the intruder code has a notion of knowledge that it can use in further operations and communications, and every received message adds to this knowledge. Third, the code may be able to move to other locations; two pieces of intruder code that meet then pool their knowledge.

References

1. Abadi, M., Fournet, C.: Mobile values, new names, and secure communication. In: ACM Symposium on Principles of Programming Languages, pp. 104–115 (2001)
2. Abadi, M., Fournet, C.: Private Authentication. Theoretical Computer Science 322(3), 427–476 (2004)
3. Algesheimer, J., Cachin, C., Camenisch, J., Karjoth, G.: Cryptographic security for mobile code. In: IEEE Symposium on Security and Privacy, pp. 2–11 (2001)
4. Arapinis, M., Duflot, M.: Bounding Messages for Free in Security Protocols. In: Arvind, V., Prasad, S. (eds.) FSTTCS 2007. LNCS, vol. 4855, pp. 376–387. Springer, Heidelberg (2007)
5. Avanesov, T., Chevalier, Y., Rusinowitch, M., Turuani, M.: Intruder deducibility constraints with negation. CoRR, abs/1207.4871 (2012)
6. Basin, D., Mödersheim, S., Viganò, L.: OFMC: A symbolic model checker for security protocols. International Journal of Information Security 4(3), 181–208 (2005)
7. Bugliesi, M., Castagna, G., Crafa, S.: Access control for mobile agents: The calculus of boxed ambients. ACM Trans. Program. Lang. Syst. 26(1), 57–124 (2004)
8. Cardelli, L., Gordon, A.D.: Mobile ambients. Theor. Comput. Sci. 240(1), 177–213 (2000)
9. Chevalier, Y., Küsters, R., Rusinowitch, M., Turuani, M.: Deciding the Security of Protocols with Diffie-Hellman Exponentiation and Products in Exponents. In: Pandya, P.K., Radhakrishnan, J. (eds.) FSTTCS 2003. LNCS, vol. 2914, pp. 124–135. Springer, Heidelberg (2003)
10. Delaune, S., Lafourcade, P., Lugiez, D., Treinen, R.: Symbolic protocol analysis for monoidal equational theories. Inf. Comput. 206(2-4), 312–351 (2008)
11. Groß, T., Pfitzmann, B., Sadeghi, A.-R.: Browser Model for Security Analysis of Browser-Based Protocols. In: De Capitani di Vimercati, S., Syverson, P.F., Gollmann, D. (eds.) ESORICS 2005. LNCS, vol. 3679, pp. 489–508. Springer, Heidelberg (2005)
12. Huima, A.: Efficient infinite-state analysis of security protocols. In: Proc. FLOC 1999 Workshop on Formal Methods and Security Protocols (1999)
13. Millen, J.K., Shmatikov, V.: Constraint solving for bounded-process cryptographic protocol analysis. In: Proceedings of CCS 2001, pp. 166–175. ACM Press (2001)
14. Mödersheim, S., Nielson, F., Nielson, H.R.: Lazy mobile intruders (extended version). Technical Report IMM-TR-2012-13, DTU Informatics (2012), imm.dtu.dk/~samo
15. Necula, G.C.: Proof-carrying code. In: POPL, pp. 106–119 (1997)
16. Rusinowitch, M., Turuani, M.: Protocol insecurity with a finite number of sessions, composed keys is NP-complete. Theor. Comput. Sci. 1(299), 451–475 (2003)

On Layout Randomization for Arrays and Functions

Martín Abadi[1,2] and Jérémy Planul[3]

[1] Microsoft Research Silicon Valley
[2] University of California, Santa Cruz
[3] Stanford University

Abstract. Low-level attacks often rely on guessing absolute or relative memory addresses. Layout randomization aims to thwart such attacks. In this paper, we study layout randomization in a setting in which arrays and functions can be stored in memory. Our results relate layout randomization to language-level protection mechanisms, namely to the use of abstract locations (rather than integer addresses). They apply, in particular, when each abstract location can hold an entire array which, concretely, compilation implements with a memory buffer at a random base address.

1 Introduction

Many attacks on software systems rely on predicting the absolute or relative locations of particular pieces of data in memory. For instance, in a system without proper bounds checking, if an attacker has access to one buffer b in the heap and can guess that an immediately contiguous buffer b' contains some sensitive data, then the attacker may try to tamper with the data in b' by overflowing b. The data in b' might for example be an authentication flag that indicates whether the attacker has been properly authenticated, and then the tampering may toggle it from false to true (e.g., [4]). The data in b' might also be a function (or a function pointer), and then the tampering may replace it so that code of the attacker's choice is executed later, when control is transferred to b'.

Layout randomization aims to thwart attacks that guess locations in this manner (e.g., [5, 6, 13]). Basically, layout randomization consists in placing data in memory at random addresses, which may for example be chosen at load time, and which will vary from system to system.

In practice, layout randomization is often an imperfect mitigation (e.g., [16]). In particular, for performance or compatibility reasons, only parts of the memory layout are randomized, typically at a fairly coarse granularity. Moreover, information about the layout sometimes leaks to attackers through various channels. Finally, layout randomization can prove ineffective against attacks that target large regions of memory, such as heap-spraying attacks.

Despite these limitations, layout randomization is widely used in systems, and it has been beneficial. Furthermore, layout randomization resembles other

D. Basin and J.C. Mitchell (Eds.): POST 2013, LNCS 7796, pp. 167–185, 2013.
© Springer-Verlag Berlin Heidelberg 2013

attractive forms of randomization [8] (such as in-place code randomization [12]) and also cryptographic protection (via the analogy between locations and encryption keys). Therefore, we believe that there is value in trying to understand its power, to characterize it precisely, and to compare it to other protection techniques.

In this spirit, recent research [3, 9, 15] relates layout randomization to the use of language-level protection mechanisms. In the present paper we aim to contribute to this line of work. Specifically, we treat layout randomization in a setting in which arrays and functions can be stored in memory—so overflows on arrays can affect other arrays and modify functions, much as in the example above.

We consider a high-level language with an abstract notion of location and a lower-level language with integer memory addresses. Both languages support functions and arrays. In the high-level language, a location can hold an entire array, while in the lower-level language array elements are stored at consecutive addresses in memory. We also consider a translation from the former language to the latter one that maps locations to randomly chosen base addresses for memory buffers. The choice is random but not necessarily uniform. For instance, all base addresses may be chosen to satisfy alignment constraints. On the other hand, the randomization is not done at the finer granularity of individual array entries, nor is the layout within arrays randomized; although conceptually tractable, such variants could have a disastrous impact on performance.

Our translation also embodies two additional precautions that complement layout randomization:

- Even with a random memory layout, it is possible that two buffers are contiguous in memory. Much as in some practical systems (e.g. [10, 17]), we can eliminate this possibility entirely by imposing the introduction of "guard regions" between buffers. Such guard regions contribute to the security guarantees that we establish.
- In the high-level language, an assignment such as $l := M$ completely overwrites the value in l. Therefore, in the low-level language, it is important that a corresponding assignment do not leave any observable traces of that value, even if M is shorter. We introduce a dynamic check to treat this point; other solutions (e.g., with special padding) may be viable.

We study the correctness and security of the translation. Viewing attackers as contexts, we prove that low-level contexts (with integer addresses) correspond to high-level contexts (with abstract locations), thus showing that the translation does not enable any new attacks [1]. We also prove that the translation preserves security properties that can be expressed as program equivalences. Both of these results are probabilistic, with probabilities that approach 1 for suitable distributions on memory layouts.

In the next section, Section 2, we discuss some small examples, informally. We define the high-level language and the low-level language in Sections 3 and 4, respectively. In Section 5, we consider probability distributions on memory layouts. In Section 6, we define and study the translation. Throughout, our approach is often analogous to that of Abadi and Plotkin [3]. We discuss this and other related work in Section 7, and then we conclude with brief comments on further work. Because of space constraints, we leave auxiliary results and proofs to an online version of this paper [2].

2   Examples

As a small introductory example, we consider the following program, which (to first approximation) we can express in both the high-level language and the low-level language defined below:

$$\lambda x.\ l_1 := M;$$
$$l_2 := x;$$
$$N$$

This program inputs a value x, executes M and stores the result in the location l_1, then stores x in the location l_2, and finally executes N. For instance, M might be an array with two locations, the first location could hold a function f and the second an integer n, and N could apply f to the input x and to n after extracting f and n from l_1 and x from l_2. In that case, the program would be:

$$\lambda x.\ l_1 := [f; n];$$
$$l_2 := x;$$
$$(1\, \mathtt{ith}\, !l_1)(!l_2)(2\, \mathtt{ith}\, !l_1)$$

Here, $[f; n]$ forms an array with two elements; $!l_1$ and $!l_2$ return the contents of l_1 and l_2, respectively; and $1\, \mathtt{ith}$ and $2\, \mathtt{ith}$ extract the first and the second elements of an array, respectively.

In the high-level language, we view l_1 and l_2 as two independent, abstract locations, so (under call-by-value semantics) we would expect that this code would behave just like the result of in-lining f, n, and x, namely:

$$\lambda x.\ l_1 := [f; n];$$
$$l_2 := x;$$
$$f(x)(n)$$

In the low-level language, on the other hand, the locations are integer addresses in memory, so we need to worry about buffer overflows and similar errors. In particular, when the value of x is too large to fit into the space allocated for l_2, the input may cause an error. If the error is not caught, it is possible that some of the value of x will clobber the contents of memory including l_1, and then $(1\, \mathtt{ith}\, !l_1)(!l_2)(2\, \mathtt{ith}\, !l_1)$ may not behave like $f(x)(n)$. In that case, an attacker that chooses the value of x may well be able to execute a function of their choice instead of f.

Layout randomization can however ensure that an overflow on l_2 will clobber the contents of l_1 only with a small probability, thus countering the attack. Thus, layout randomization can imply that properties that hold when l_1 and l_2

are two independent, abstract locations continue to hold when they are mapped to concrete memory addresses. Our theorems capture this preservation of properties. The properties could easily fail if instead l_1 and l_2 were mapped to fixed, contiguous memory addresses, and if bounds checking was not done properly, as the attack above indicates.

Some of the same themes appear in many other examples. For instance, consider a piece of code where the location l_1 holds a flag that indicates whether some security check has been completed satisfactorily. For instance, l_1 could hold an authentication flag, as mentioned at the start of the Introduction, and much as in the code of an SSH implementation that Chen et al. attacked [4]. The flag is initially false. After some input x is stored in another location l_2, the security checks are performed, and the flag is set to true if the checks are successful. Later, various sensitive operations may be permitted if the flag is true.

$$\lambda x.\ l_1 := \texttt{false};$$
$$l_2 := x;$$
$$\textbf{if } some\ checks\ \textbf{then}\, l_1 := true;$$
$$\dots$$
$$\textbf{if }!l_1\textbf{ then } do\ some\ sensitive\ operation$$

The security of this code depends on the integrity of the contents of l_1. Layout randomization can protect this integrity, thwarting direct writes to l_1 by attackers who would try to guess its absolute address in memory and also writes via overflows on l_2 and other locations. Our results account for this application of layout randomization.

In the examples above, we are primarily concerned about an adversary that may provide a dangerous input, but which need not modify locations such as l_1 and l_2 directly. In general, however, we are also interested in adversaries that have direct access to some locations, which we call public locations. We refer to other locations as private locations. At the high level, we restrict adversaries so that they cannot refer to private locations; at the low level, we study the protection of the private locations via layout randomization. For instance, letting l be a private location and l' a public location, we may consider the following program:

$$\lambda f.\, l := 0; l' := 0; f(1)$$

At the high level, if an adversary provides an input function f, this function may read or write l', but it cannot read or write l since l is private. Therefore, when $f(1)$ terminates, l should hold the value 0. So, with respect to such adversaries, the program is equivalent to:

$$\lambda f.\, l' := 0; f(1)$$

At the low level, l will be mapped to an integer memory address. If this mapping is predictable, then the adversary may be able to read or write l, either via an absolute address or via a relative address with an offset from l'. With proper layout randomization, on the other hand, l will be mapped to a random address, and the offset between l and l' will be random as well, so the adversary will not be able to find and to access l, with high probability. Therefore, the program equivalence will be preserved, at least in a probabilistic sense.

Furthermore, adversaries may do more than provide a single input. They may be contexts that interact with the systems that we wish to protect, for example invoking them multiple times with different inputs, and accessing public locations before and after those invocations. Our approach addresses such interactions.

3   The High-Level Language

In this section, we define our high-level language. In this language, memory locations are symbolic names, and the semantics uses an abstract store to link locations to values.

3.1   Syntax and Informal Semantics

The high-level language is a call-by-value λ-calculus with natural numbers, arrays, and location-labeled dereference and assignment operations. For general background on the λ-calculus, see [11, 14].

The terms of our language are defined by:

$$M ::= x \mid c \mid [M; \dots; M] \mid \lambda x. M \mid MM$$
$$c ::= * \mid n \mid + \mid =_{\mathtt{nat}} \mid \dots$$
$$\mid \ \mathtt{ith} \mid \mathtt{length}$$
$$\mid !_{\mathtt{loc}} l_{\mathtt{loc}} \mid l_{\mathtt{loc}} :=_{\mathtt{loc}}$$

where M and N range over terms, c ranges over a set of constants, and l ranges over a finite set Loc of locations. The terms include variables, constants, arrays, abstractions, and applications. The constants include $*$ (the "unit" value); the usual arithmetic constants, operations, and relations (such as the numerals n, addition $+$, and equality $=_{\mathtt{nat}}$); array access $\mathtt{ith}$ and length measurement $\mathtt{length}$; and constants for accessing locations $!_{\mathtt{loc}} l_{\mathtt{loc}}$ and $l_{\mathtt{loc}} :=_{\mathtt{loc}}$.

We adopt standard notions of free and bound variables, of closed terms, and of the capture-avoiding substitution $M[N/x]$ of a term N for all free occurrences of a variable x in a term M. We also adopt standard infix notations, for example sometimes writing $M \, \mathtt{ith} \, N$ instead of $\mathtt{ith} \ M \ N$.

Intuitively, $!_{\mathtt{loc}} l_{\mathtt{loc}}$ outputs the contents of location l and $l_{\mathtt{loc}} :=_{\mathtt{loc}}$ writes its argument in location l. Each location can hold arrays of a given length, and writing produces an error if the argument is not an array of the appropriate length. So, for simplicity, we do not allow storing integers and functions directly into memory, but we do allow storing one-element arrays that contain integers and functions, and in examples we may for instance write $l_{\mathtt{loc}} :=_{\mathtt{loc}} 0$ as an abbreviation for $l_{\mathtt{loc}} :=_{\mathtt{loc}} [0]$. We allow nested arrays (such as $[[M; N]]$) but consider only the top level for calculating lengths, and do not differentiate "short" vs. "long" elements in an array (so for example $[0]$, $[\lambda x. x(x7)]$, and $[[M; N]]$ all have length 1). A more elaborate definition could be introduced, and would make sense provided corresponding adjustments are made in the compilation function (see Section 6).

The subscript in $!_{\mathrm{loc}} l_{\mathrm{loc}}$ and $l_{\mathrm{loc}} :=_{\mathrm{loc}}$ is intended to differentiate these constants from the syntax of the low-level language of Section 4. We omit the subscripts sometimes, when they are clear from context or when we wish to discuss both the high-level and the low-level language, as in the examples of Section 2.

Note that l_{loc} is not itself a term in this language, so locations are not first-class values. This restriction constitutes a simplification (see [3, Section 2]), and contributes to the gap between the high-level language and the low-level language of the next section (in which addresses are first-class values). On the other hand, functions for reading and writing locations can be passed as arguments, returned as results, and stored in memory, so encodings of locations as first-class values are straightforward.

Various other standard abbreviations and encodings are convenient. These include encodings of booleans and other datatypes, and recursive function definitions, as usual in untyped call-by-value lambda calculus. Using these, we can program control constructs, including loops of the form `for` $i = 1$ `to` e `do` e' `done`. We sometimes write `skip` for $*$, and $M; N$ for `let` x `be` M `in` N (where x is not free in N). We also use `raise_error` as syntactic sugar for an error-raising term, for instance $j\ k$ where j and k are integers.

For simplicity, this language does not support dynamic allocation, which could perhaps be handled as in the work of Jagadeesan et al. [9], at least in the bounded form that they consider. Treating more general memory-management and scoping facilities remains a challenging subject for further research.

3.2   Values

We designate a subset of the expression of the programming language as *values*:

$$V ::= d \mid e \mid [V; \ldots; V] \mid \lambda x.\, M$$
$$d ::= * \mid n \mid + \mid =_{\mathrm{nat}} \mid \ldots$$
$$\mid \mathtt{ith} \mid \mathtt{length}$$
$$\mid l_{\mathrm{loc}} :=_{\mathrm{loc}}$$
$$e ::= n + \mid n\ =_{\mathrm{nat}} \mid \ldots$$
$$\mid n\ \mathtt{ith}$$

Values can be thought of as (syntax for) completed computations. We include all constants in the set of values, except for the constants for reading locations. We also include partially evaluated binary operators. We write $\mathbb{HV}$ for the set of values of the high-level language.

Values of the form $[V_1; \ldots; V_n]$ are *array values*. We define their length by: $|[V_1; \ldots; V_n]| = n$.

3.3   Memory Model

The semantics of the high-level language is based on a simple model of memory.

We assume a fixed mapping $\mathrm{sig} : \mathrm{Loc} \to \mathbb{N}$ that, intuitively, gives the length of each location. We call such a mapping a *signature*.

A *store* is a mapping $s : \text{Loc} \to \mathbb{HV}$ that sends locations to values of the high-level language, such that $s(l)$ is an array value and $|s(l)| = \text{sig}(l)$ for every $l \in \text{Loc}$.

In order to consider security properties, we assume that the set of locations Loc is the disjoint union of two sets, PubLoc and PriLoc, of *public* and *private* locations. As explained in Section 2 and in Section 6.3, below, we model attackers as programs that have direct access to public locations (but not, by default, to private locations).

3.4   Operational Semantics

We define a small-step operational semantics of the high-level language in the style of Felleisen and Friedman [7].

Redexes include terms of the forms:

$$(\lambda x.\, M)V \qquad V\,\texttt{ith}\,[V; \ldots; V] \qquad \texttt{length}\,[V; \ldots; V]$$
$$!_{\text{loc}}l_{\text{loc}} \qquad l_{\text{loc}} :=_{\text{loc}} V$$

and other redexes that involve the various arithmetic constants, operations, and relations, such as $0 =_{\text{nat}} 0$. Redexes also include "ill-typed" constructions, such as the application 00; these redexes will raise errors. (For brevity, we do not list all these ill-typed constructions.) We define a reduction relation $R \to M$ between redexes and terms, and an error property $R \downarrow_{\text{error}}$ on redexes:

$$(\lambda x.\, M)V \to M[V/x]$$
$$i\,\texttt{ith}\,[V_1; \ldots; V_n] \to V_i \qquad \texttt{length}\,[V_1; \ldots; V_n] \to n$$
$$i\,\texttt{ith}\,[V_1; \ldots; V_n] \downarrow_{\text{error}} \qquad \text{for } i = 0 \text{ and } i > n$$

$$\ldots$$

where the ellipses indicate missing arithmetic and error transitions, such as:

$$0 =_{\text{nat}} 0 \to \texttt{true} \qquad 0 + 1 \to 1 \qquad 00 \downarrow_{\text{error}}$$

We define *evaluation contexts* by:

$$E ::= [-] \mid [V; \ldots; V; E; \ldots; M] \mid EM \mid VE$$

We write $E[M]$ for the term obtained by replacing the "hole" $[-]$ in an evaluation context E with the term M. For every term M, either M is a value, or M can be analyzed uniquely in the form $E[R]$, with R a redex.

A *configuration* is a pair (s, M) with s a store and M a term. The small-step semantics consists of a transition relation and two error properties on configurations:

$$(s, M) \to (s', M') \qquad (s, M) \downarrow_{\text{error}} \qquad (s, M) \downarrow^{l}_{\text{error}}$$

The error property $(s, M) \downarrow^{l}_{\text{error}}$ distinguishes buffer-overflow errors, to which we give a specific treatment below.

For redexes, we set:

$$(s, !_{\text{loc}} l_{\text{loc}}) \to (s, V) \qquad (\text{if } s(l) = V)$$
$$(s, l_{\text{loc}} :=_{\text{loc}} V) \to (s[l \mapsto V], \text{skip}) \qquad (\text{if } |V| = \text{sig}(l))$$
$$(s, l_{\text{loc}} :=_{\text{loc}} V) \downarrow_{\text{error}} \qquad (\text{if } |V| < \text{sig}(l))$$
$$(s, l_{\text{loc}} :=_{\text{loc}} V) \downarrow^{l}_{\text{error}} \qquad (\text{if } |V| > \text{sig}(l))$$

and:

$$\frac{R \to M'}{(s, R) \to (s, M')} \qquad \frac{R \downarrow_{\text{error}}}{(s, R) \downarrow_{\text{error}}}$$

The general case follows via three rules:

$$\frac{(s, R) \to (s', M')}{(s, E[R]) \to (s', E[M'])} \qquad \frac{(s, R) \downarrow_{\text{error}}}{(s, E[R]) \downarrow_{\text{error}}} \qquad \frac{(s, R) \downarrow^{l}_{\text{error}}}{(s, E[R]) \downarrow^{l}_{\text{error}}}$$

We can also define a corresponding big-step semantics by:

$$(s, M) \Rightarrow (s', V) \iff (s, M) \to^* (s', V)$$
$$(s, M) \Downarrow_{\text{error}} \iff \exists s', M'.\, (s, M) \to^* (s', M') \downarrow_{\text{error}}$$
$$(s, M) \Downarrow^{l}_{\text{error}} \iff \exists s', M'.\, (s, M) \to^* (s', M') \downarrow^{l}_{\text{error}}$$
$$(s, M) \Uparrow \iff \forall n.\, \exists s', M'.\, (s, M) \to^n (s', M')$$

These relations and properties are mutually exclusive. The relation $(s, M) \Rightarrow (s', V)$ holds if M evaluates to the value V with final store s' when the initial store is s; the property $(s, M) \Downarrow^{l}_{\text{error}}$ holds if the term M causes a buffer-overflow error on location l when the initial store is s, and $(s, M) \Downarrow_{\text{error}}$ holds if M results in a different error; the property $(s, M) \Uparrow$ holds if M diverges when the initial store is s.

4   The Low-Level Language

Our low-level language, which we define in this section, mainly differs from the high-level language in employing integer addresses.

4.1   Syntax and Informal Semantics

The syntax of the low-level language is a variant of that of the high-level language in which we replace high-level constants for accessing locations by distinguished locations and memory-access constants:

$$M ::= x \mid c \mid [M; \ldots; M] \mid \lambda x.\, M \mid MM$$
$$c \;\; ::= * \mid n \mid + \mid =_{\text{nat}} \mid \ldots$$
$$\mid \text{ith} \mid \text{length}$$
$$\mid l_{\text{nat}} \mid !_{\text{nat}} \mid :=_{\text{nat}}$$

where l ranges over the finite set Loc of locations.

Informally, the constant l_nat evaluates to the index of location l; it returns an integer. The constant $!_\mathsf{nat}$, when applied to an integer n, reads the contents of memory at address n. The constant $:=_\mathsf{nat}$, when applied to a first argument and an integer n, writes the first argument at address n. (So, with infix notation, we write $N := M$ for $:= M\ N$.)

Because each constant l_nat is a first-class, legal expression on its own, we can write programs that pass these constants and that store them in memory, such as $l_\mathsf{nat} :=_\mathsf{nat} l'_\mathsf{nat}$. Moreover, $!_\mathsf{nat}$ and $:=_\mathsf{nat}$ are legal expressions even when they are not applied to location constants (unlike the corresponding notations in the high-level language). Thus, we can write not only $!_\mathsf{nat} l_\mathsf{nat}$ and $l_\mathsf{nat} :=_\mathsf{nat} 0$, but also for example $!_\mathsf{nat} x$, $!_\mathsf{nat}(x+1)$, $(x+1) :=_\mathsf{nat} 8$, or $(x + l_\mathsf{nat}) :=_\mathsf{nat} (x + l'_\mathsf{nat})$, where l is a location and x is a variable. As these small examples illustrate, addresses can be the result of integer computations, on variables and constants (including location constants). This flexibility could allow an attacker to try to access memory at a computed offset from a known location, for instance.

We assume that each address in memory is either used to hold a value or unused, and assume that access to an unused address results in an immediate fatal error. These assumptions are as in the "fatal-error model" of Abadi and Plotkin [3]. It should be possible to adapt our work to the alternative "recoverable-error model".

Both the high-level language and the low-level language allow storing a program in memory, retrieving it, then invoking it. In particular, an attacker may be able to inject code into memory via a direct assignment. On the other hand, neither language allows computing on the code of programs, nor confusing natural numbers with programs. In this respect, the low-level language remains fairly high-level. For example, in the low-level language, after the assignment $l_\mathsf{nat} :=_\mathsf{nat} (\lambda x.\, !_\mathsf{nat} l'_\mathsf{nat})$, an attacker that can read the contents of l_nat would be able to execute $(\lambda x.\, !_\mathsf{nat} l'_\mathsf{nat})$, but not extract l'_nat from it, nor the syntax tree of $(\lambda x.\, !_\mathsf{nat} l'_\mathsf{nat})$. It seems unlikely that one could obtain strong guarantee without some such restrictions.

4.2   Values

As in the high-level language, we designate a subset of the expression of the programming language as *values*. In particular, we take $!_\mathsf{nat}$ and $:=_\mathsf{nat}$ to be values:

$$V ::= d \mid e \mid [V; \ldots; V] \mid \lambda x.\, M$$
$$d ::= * \mid n \mid + \mid =_\mathsf{nat} \mid \cdots$$
$$\mid \texttt{ith} \mid \texttt{length}$$
$$\mid !_\mathsf{nat} \mid :=_\mathsf{nat}$$
$$e ::= n + \mid n =_\mathsf{nat} \mid \cdots$$
$$\mid n\ \texttt{ith}$$
$$\mid :=_\mathsf{nat} V$$

We write $\mathbb{LV}$ for the set of values of the low-level language.

4.3 Memory Model

Concretely, we let a *memory* be a mapping $m : \text{Mem} \rightarrow (\mathbb{LV} + \{\varepsilon\})$, where:

- Mem is the set $0, \ldots, \kappa$ of memory addresses, for a given $\kappa \geq 0$,
- we assume that $|\sum_{l \in \text{Loc}} \text{sig}(l)| \leq \kappa + 1$,
- $\mathbb{LV} + \{\varepsilon\}$ is the disjoint union of $\mathbb{LV}$ and $\{\varepsilon\}$, and
- $m(a) = \varepsilon$ indicates that a is an unused address of m.

Since the low-level language contains location constants, its semantics depends on how these are laid out in memory. A *memory layout* is an injective mapping $w : \text{Loc} \hookrightarrow \text{Mem}$. Such a memory layout connects the abstract and the concrete memory models. A location that stores an array in the abstract model corresponds to a range of memory addresses in the concrete model. For a location l, that range starts at address $w(l)$ and includes $\text{sig}(l)$ consecutive address. We restrict attention to those memory layouts that do not cause range overflows or overlaps, that is, such that there exist no $l_1 \in \text{Loc}$ such that $w(l_1) \leq \kappa < w(l_1) + \text{sig}(l_1) - 1$, and no distinct $l_1, l_2 \in \text{Loc}$ such that $w(l_1) \leq w(l_2) < w(l_1) + \text{sig}(l_1)$. We let $\text{Ran}(w)$ be the set $\{a \in \text{Mem} \mid \exists l.\, w(l) \leq a < w(l) + \text{sig}(l)\}$.

A *public layout* $w_p : \text{PubLoc} \hookrightarrow \text{Mem}$ maps public locations to addresses. We assume that one public layout is fixed throughout, and we consider only those memory layouts that extend it.

We also define stores for the low-level language; we call them low-level stores to distinguish them from those of the high-level language, to which they are directly analogous. Thus, a *low-level store* is a mapping $s : \text{Loc} \rightarrow \mathbb{LV}$ that sends locations to values of the low-level language, such that $s(l)$ is an array value and $|s(l)| = \text{sig}(l)$ for every $l \in \text{Loc}$. For every low-level store s and memory layout w, there is a corresponding memory $\text{mem}(s, w)$ defined by:

$$
\text{mem}(s, w)(a) = \begin{cases} s(l).(i) & \text{if there exists } i \in 1..\text{sig}(l) \text{ such that } w(l) + i - 1 = a \\ \varepsilon & \text{otherwise } (a \notin \text{Ran}(w)) \end{cases}
$$

where $s(l).(i)$ is the ith element of the array value $s(l)$. The mapping $s \mapsto \text{mem}(s, w)$ is 1-1, from low-level stores to memories, but not onto. We say that m *has the form* $\text{mem}(s, w)$ if it equals $\text{mem}(s, w)$ for some w. We abbreviate $\text{mem}(s, w)$ to s_w.

4.4 Operational Semantics

The operational semantics resembles that of the high-level language in its treatment of functions and numbers. In particular, the redexes and the reduction relation between redexes and terms are both much as in the high-level language, but with

$$l_{\text{nat}} \quad (\text{for } l \in \text{Loc}) \qquad !_{\text{nat}} V \qquad V :=_{\text{nat}} V$$

as redexes. Evaluation contexts are as in the high-level language.

A configuration is a pair (m, M) of a memory m and a term M. The semantics consists of a transition relation and two error properties on configurations, all relative to the memory layout chosen:

$$w \models (m, M) \rightarrow (m', M')$$

$$w \models (m, M) \downarrow_{\text{error}} \qquad w \models (m, M) \downarrow_{\text{error}}^a$$

The error property $w \models (m, M) \downarrow_{\text{error}}^a$ distinguishes accesses to out-of-range or unused addresses; in particular, if $w \models (m, M) \downarrow_{\text{error}}^a$ and m has the form s_w, then $a \notin \text{Ran}(w_p)$.

For redexes, the transition relation and error properties are given by the rules:

$$\frac{R \rightarrow M'}{w \models (m, R) \rightarrow (m, M')} \qquad \frac{R \downarrow_{\text{error}}}{w \models (m, R) \downarrow_{\text{error}}}$$

together with:

$$w \models (m, l_{\text{nat}}) \rightarrow (m, w(l)) \qquad (\text{for } l \in \text{Loc})$$

and:

$$
\begin{array}{ll}
w \models (m, !_{\text{nat}} a) \rightarrow (m, V) & (\text{if } a \in \text{Mem and } m(a) = V) \\
w \models (m, !_{\text{nat}} a) \downarrow_{\text{error}}^a & (\text{if } a \notin \text{Mem or } m(a) = \varepsilon) \\
w \models (m, a :=_{\text{nat}} V) \rightarrow (m[a \mapsto V], \text{skip}) & (\text{if } a \in \text{Mem and } m(a) \neq \varepsilon) \\
w \models (m, a :=_{\text{nat}} V) \downarrow_{\text{error}}^a & (\text{if } a \notin \text{Mem or } m(a) = \varepsilon)
\end{array}
$$

The general case follows by the rules:

$$\frac{w \models (m, R) \rightarrow (m', M')}{w \models (m, E[R]) \rightarrow (m', E[M'])}$$

and:

$$\frac{w \models (m, R) \downarrow_{\text{error}}}{w \models (m, E[R]) \downarrow_{\text{error}}} \qquad \frac{w \models (m, R) \downarrow_{\text{error}}^a}{w \models (m, E[R]) \downarrow_{\text{error}}^a}$$

Much as in the high-level language, too, this small-step semantics induces a big-step semantics:

$$
\begin{array}{ll}
w \models (m, M) \Rightarrow (m', V) & \Longleftrightarrow \quad w \models (m, M) \rightarrow^* (m', V) \\
w \models (m, M) \Downarrow_{\text{error}} & \Longleftrightarrow \quad \exists m', M'.w \models (m, M) \rightarrow^* (m', M') \downarrow_{\text{error}} \\
w \models (m, M) \Downarrow_{\text{error}}^a & \Longleftrightarrow \quad \exists m', M'.w \models (m, M) \rightarrow^* (m', M') \downarrow_{\text{error}}^a \\
w \models (m, M) \Uparrow & \Longleftrightarrow \quad \forall n. \exists m', M'. w \models (m, M) \rightarrow^n (m', M')
\end{array}
$$

These relations and properties are mutually exclusive.

5   Layout Distributions

The effectiveness of layout randomization requires the use of unpredictable layouts. In this section, we define distributions on layouts, and introduce several quantities that below we employ in quantitative security bounds.

Let d be a probability distribution over the layouts that extend w_p. When $\varphi(w)$ is a statement, we write $P_d(\varphi(w))$ for the probability that it holds with respect to the distribution d. For example, $\varphi(w)$ might be the assertion that, with the layout w, an execution that starts from a particular low-level configuration (m, M) will produce an error. In that case, $P_d(\varphi(w))$ is the probability that such an execution will produce an error for a random layout chosen according to d.

For any $n \in \mathbb{N}$, we write $w\#n$ as an abbreviation for $n \notin (\mathrm{Ran}(w) \backslash \mathrm{Ran}(w_p))$. Informally, when we think of n as an address that an attacker is guessing (not out of the memory bounds, and not at public locations, since the attacker knows those), $w\#n$ means that the attacker does not guess the address of a private location. Then $P_d(w\#n)$ is the corresponding probability, for w chosen according to d. Furthermore, we define:

$$\delta_d = \min\{P_d(w\#n) \mid n \in \mathrm{Mem} \setminus \mathrm{Ran}(w_p)\}$$

For example, suppose that l is the only private location and that $\mathrm{sig}(l) = 1$. If layouts chosen according to d always map l to the integer 5, then $\delta_d = 0$, simply because $P_d(w\#5) = 0$. Obviously, such layouts enable an attacker to access the contents of l, trivially, via the address 5. On the other hand, if layouts chosen according to d map l to each of $\mathrm{Mem} \setminus \mathrm{Ran}(w_p)$ with uniform probability, then $\delta_d = 1 - (1/|\mathrm{Mem} \setminus \mathrm{Ran}(w_p)|)$.

As these examples illustrate, a small value for δ_d indicates a lack of security. Therefore, we consider lower bounds on δ_d for certain choices of d. These lower bounds approach 1 as the size of memory grows, thus indicating that attacker guesses should succeed with vanishing probability in the limit.

In particular, a system may map all public locations to contiguous addresses starting at address 0, and all private locations to contiguous addresses starting at some random base address in the remaining space. There are $|\mathrm{Mem}| - \sum_{l \in \mathrm{Loc}} \mathrm{sig}(l) + 1$ possible positions for the base address. Moreover, any address is the image of a private location with at most $\sum_{l \in \mathrm{PriLoc}} \mathrm{sig}(l)$ of those possible positions. Hence, for this simple distribution, we can show that:

$$\delta_d \geq 1 - \frac{\sum_{l \in \mathrm{PriLoc}} \mathrm{sig}(l)}{|\mathrm{Mem}| - \sum_{l \in \mathrm{Loc}} \mathrm{sig}(l) + 1}$$

assuming $\sum_{l \in \mathrm{Loc}} \mathrm{sig}(l) \leq |\mathrm{Mem}|$. Even with such a coarse scheme, δ_d approaches 1 as $|\mathrm{Mem}|$ grows. For example, if there is no public location, the private locations have total length 2^{32} (which represents a reasonable volume to hold in an actual memory), and the size of memory is 2^{64} (as in a large virtual address space), then this bound is $\delta_d \geq (1 - (2^{32}/(2^{64} - 2^{32} + 1)))$, roughly $(1 - 2^{-32})$.

Much more sophisticated arrangements are possible, in particular ones that map each private location independently. Overall, it is fairly easy to pick distributions on layouts that ensure that δ_d approaches 1. Basically, with such distributions, when an attacker looks for private locations in a large enough memory, getting only one try, the attacker is almost certain to miss provided the memory is large enough.

Similarly, for any $l \in \mathrm{Loc}$, we write $w\#l$ as an abbreviation for $w(l) + \mathrm{sig}(l) \notin \mathrm{Ran}(w)$. Thus, $w\#l$ holds precisely when the end of the array located in l is not contiguous to any other location in use. When this property holds, direct buffer overflows from l will raise an error in the implementation, even without proper bounds checking. We define:

$$\varrho_{\mathrm{d}} = \min\{\mathrm{P_d}(w\#l) \mid l \in \mathrm{Loc}\}$$

As for δ_{d}, we would like ϱ_{d} to be large. Fortunately, assuming that memory is large enough, we can easily focus attention on layouts w such that $w\#l$ for all l, so $\varrho_{\mathrm{d}} = 1$. In such layouts, all arrays are separated by unused locations. These unused locations are analogous to the "guard zones" or "guard regions" that appear in practical systems (e.g. [10, 17]).

Moreover, the wishes for δ_{d} that approaches 1 and for $\varrho_{\mathrm{d}} = 1$ are compatible. For instance, a system may keep all public memory together starting at address 0, and private memory together at some random base address in the remaining space, but separate any two arrays with one unused location.

Our results hold for any probability distribution d. For the rest of the paper, we fix a choice of d, and write $\mathrm{P}(\varphi(w))$, δ, and ϱ as abbreviations for $\mathrm{P_d}(\varphi(w))$, δ_{d}, and ϱ_{d}, respectively.

6 Compilation and Its Properties

In this section we define the translation discussed in the introduction. We then prove its correctness and its security.

6.1 The Translation

We translate terms M of the high-level language to terms $M^{\downarrow}$ of the low-level language. Crucially, this translation maps abstract locations to their low-level counterparts. Since these are interpreted relatively to a memory layout, and since this memory layout is chosen according to a probability distribution, the translation embodies layout randomization.

The translation is trivial for all constructs of the high-level language with the exception of the constants $!_{\mathrm{loc}}l_{\mathrm{loc}}$ and $l_{\mathrm{loc}} :=_{\mathrm{loc}}$, which we compile as follows:

$$(!_{\mathrm{loc}}l_{\mathrm{loc}})^{\downarrow} = [!_{\mathrm{nat}}l_{\mathrm{nat}}; !_{\mathrm{nat}}l_{\mathrm{nat}} + 1; \ldots; !_{\mathrm{nat}}l_{\mathrm{nat}} + \mathrm{sig}(l) - 1]$$
$$(l_{\mathrm{loc}} :=_{\mathrm{loc}})^{\downarrow} = \lambda x.\, \mathtt{for}\ i = 1\ \mathtt{to}\ \mathtt{length}\, x\ \mathtt{do}\ l_{\mathrm{nat}} + i - 1 :=_{\mathrm{nat}}\ i\ \mathtt{ith}\, x;\ \mathtt{done};$$
$$\mathtt{if}\ i < \mathrm{sig}(l)\ \mathtt{then}\ \mathtt{raise\_error}$$

Both $(!_{\mathrm{loc}}l_{\mathrm{loc}})^{\downarrow}$ and $(l_{\mathrm{loc}} :=_{\mathrm{loc}})^{\downarrow}$ employ the signature $\mathrm{sig}(l)$. In the case of $(!_{\mathrm{loc}}l_{\mathrm{loc}})^{\downarrow}$, this signature indicates how much to read from memory. In the case of $(l_{\mathrm{loc}} :=_{\mathrm{loc}})^{\downarrow}$, it serves to ensure that what is being written to memory is not too short. Alternatively, as suggested in the Introduction, we could add distinguished padding values to fill the space available.

However, $(l_{\mathtt{loc}} :=_{\mathtt{loc}})^{\downarrow}$ does not check whether its argument (the data being written to memory) is too long. This absence of bounds checking leads to the possibility of buffer overflows. Although the absence of bounds checking is deliberate in this definition, it models common mistakes (poor design decisions or implementation blunders). In general, without layout randomization or other mitigations, such mistakes could jeopardize security. Nevertheless, our security results (presented below) apply despite these buffer overflows. (Note that, in addition to the buffer overflows that the translation may introduce, contexts may attempt other problematic operations, such as accessing memory at an offset from a known location, as in $(l_{\mathtt{nat}} + 256) :=_{\mathtt{nat}} 0$; our results still apply.)

Since high-level stores may contain functions, and those may contain occurrences of the constructs $!_{\mathtt{loc}}l_{\mathtt{loc}}$ and $l_{\mathtt{loc}} :=_{\mathtt{loc}}$, we extend the translation so that it maps each high-level store s to a low-level store $s^{\downarrow}$. We define $s^{\downarrow}$ by setting, for every $l \in \mathrm{Loc}$,

$$s^{\downarrow}(l) = s(l)^{\downarrow}$$

Given a layout w, we can then obtain a memory $s_w^{\downarrow}$.

6.2   Correctness

The translation is correct in the sense that $M^{\downarrow}$ simulates M, under the corresponding big-step semantics:

Proposition 1. *Suppose that M is a term of the high-level language, and w a layout. Then:*

1. *If $(s, M) \Rightarrow (s', V)$ then, $w \models (s_w^{\downarrow}, M^{\downarrow}) \Rightarrow (s_w'^{\downarrow}, V^{\downarrow})$.*
2. *If $(s, M) \Downarrow_{\mathrm{error}}$ then $w \models (s_w^{\downarrow}, M^{\downarrow}) \Downarrow_{\mathrm{error}}$.*
3. *If $(s, M) \Downarrow_{\mathrm{error}}^{l}$ then, if $w(l) + \mathrm{sig}(l) \notin \mathrm{Ran}(w)$, $w \models (s_w^{\downarrow}, M^{\downarrow}) \Downarrow_{\mathrm{error}}^{w(l)+\mathrm{sig}(l)}$.*
4. *If $(s, M) \Uparrow$ then $w \models (s_w^{\downarrow}, M^{\downarrow}) \Uparrow$.*

Fixing a distribution on layouts, we can derive a probabilistic statement from Proposition 1:

Proposition 2. *Suppose that M is a term of the high-level language. Then:*

1. *If $(s, M) \Rightarrow (s', V)$, then, for every w, $w \models (s_w^{\downarrow}, M^{\downarrow}) \Rightarrow (s_w'^{\downarrow}, V^{\downarrow})$.*
2. *If $(s, M) \Downarrow_{\mathrm{error}}$ then, for every w, $w \models (s_w^{\downarrow}, M^{\downarrow}) \Downarrow_{\mathrm{error}}$.*
3. *If $(s, M) \Downarrow_{\mathrm{error}}^{l}$ then $\mathrm{P}(w \models (s_w^{\downarrow}, M^{\downarrow}) \Downarrow_{\mathrm{error}}^{w(l)+\mathrm{sig}(l)}) \geq \varrho$.*
4. *If $(s, M) \Uparrow$ then, for every w, $w \models (s_w^{\downarrow}, M^{\downarrow}) \Uparrow$.*

Further, we can restate the correctness of compilation in terms of a coarse notion of evaluation. For any store s and term M of the high-level language, we define $\mathrm{Eval}(M, s)$ by:

$$\mathrm{Eval}(M, s) = \begin{cases} \checkmark & \text{if } (s, M) \Rightarrow (s', V) \text{ for some } (s', V) \\ \mathrm{E} & \text{if } (s, M) \Downarrow_{\mathrm{error}}^{u} \\ \Omega & \text{if } (s, M) \Uparrow \end{cases}$$

Here, $(s, M) \Downarrow_{error}^u$ means that $(s, M) \Downarrow_{error}$ or $(s, M) \Downarrow_{error}^l$ for some l, and $\checkmark$, E, and Ω are tokens that indicate normal termination, error, and divergence, respectively. Similarly, for any low-level term M, memory m, and layout w, we define $\mathrm{Eval}_w(M, m)$ by:

$$\mathrm{Eval}_w(M, m) = \begin{cases} \checkmark & \text{if } w \models (m, M) \Rightarrow (m', V) \text{ for some } (m', V) \\ \mathrm{E} & \text{if } w \models (m, M) \Downarrow_{error}^u \\ \Omega & \text{if } w \models (m, M) \Uparrow \end{cases}$$

where $w \models (m, A) \Downarrow_{error}^u$ means that $w \models (m, A) \Downarrow_{error}$ or $w \models (m, A) \Downarrow_{error}^a$ for some a. We obtain:

Proposition 3. *Let M be a high-level term and s a high-level store. Then:*

$$\mathrm{P}(\mathrm{Eval}(M, s) = \mathrm{Eval}_w(M^\downarrow, s_w^\downarrow)) \geq \varrho$$

This statement is simpler and weaker than those above. It expresses that evaluating M from a store s and $M^\downarrow$ from a corresponding memory $s_w^\downarrow$ lead to the same outcome with probability at least ϱ. Here, an outcome is, coarsely, normal termination, error, or divergence. Note that the probability does not depend on δ; since (as explained in Section 5) we can often take $\varrho = 1$, we can then have that evaluating M from a store s and $M^\downarrow$ from a corresponding memory $s_w^\downarrow$ lead to the same outcome with probability 1.

6.3   Security: Mapping Contexts

Although we cannot hope to establish that every program of the high-level language is secure in some absolute sense, we would like to argue that compiling a program from the high-level language to the low-level language does not introduce vulnerabilities. In other words, we regard programs of the high-level language as security specifications, and expect that the corresponding programs of the low-level language conform to those specifications.

Our notion of security relies on the distinction between public and private locations (much as in [3]). As stated in Section 3, we assume that the set of locations Loc is the disjoint union of two sets, PubLoc and PriLoc, of *public* and *private* locations. We then say that a high-level (respectively low-level) term is *public* if all its occurrences of $!_{loc}l_{loc}$ and $l_{loc} :=_{loc}$ (respectively l_{nat}) are with $l \in$ PubLoc. We model attackers as public contexts, that is, as programs of our languages that interact with the programs that we aim to protect, and that have direct access to public locations.

Contexts (both public contexts and general contexts) have different capabilities in each language. In particular, in the high-level language, contexts can refer to abstract locations, while in the low-level language contexts can use integer addresses, and this might permit exploits that rely on guessing integer addresses, perhaps using offset calculations. So, if the contexts of the low-level language were much more expressive than those of the high-level language, security might be jeopardized. We aim to show that, in fact, the extra flexibility of the low-level language does not affect security, at least with high probability.

Therefore, we show that a low-level term $M^\downarrow$ is as secure as its high-level counterpart M by arguing that the behavior $M^\downarrow$ in each public context C of the low-level language corresponds to the behavior of M in some corresponding public context $C^\uparrow$ of the high-level language. Since we model attackers as public contexts, this result indicates that, for every low-level attack, there is a corresponding high-level attack with the same effect.

In order to relate behaviors at the two levels, we introduce *pure* stores. A store is *pure* if it contains no location, assignment, or dereference. Therefore, every pure store is both a high-level and a low-level public store. For simplicity, in what follows, we consider only pure initial stores.

We obtain the following theorem:

Theorem 1. *Suppose that M is a high-level term and C is a public low-level term. Then $CM^\downarrow$ is a public low-level term, and there exists a public high-level term $C^\uparrow$ such that one of the following three mutually exclusive statements holds for any pure store s:*

- *there exist s', s'', V', and V'' such that, for all w, $w \models (s_w, CM^\downarrow) \Rightarrow (s'_w, V')$ and $(s, C^\uparrow M) \Rightarrow (s'', V'')$,*
- *$P(w \models (s_w, CM^\downarrow) \Downarrow^u_{error}) \geq min(\delta, \varrho)$ and $(s, C^\uparrow M) \Downarrow^u_{error}$, or*
- *for all w, $w \models (s_w, CM^\downarrow) \Uparrow$ and $(s, C^\uparrow M) \Uparrow$.*

The probability bound as a function of δ and ϱ arises, basically, because a non-public, low-level memory access is made independently of the layout.

Using the coarse evaluation function again, we derive a weaker but simpler statement:

Corollary 1. *Suppose that M is a high-level term and C is a public low-level term. Then there exists a public high-level term $C^\uparrow$ such that, for any pure store s, we have:*

$$P(\text{Eval}(C^\uparrow M, s) = \text{Eval}_w(CM^\downarrow, s_w)) \geq min(\delta, \varrho)$$

Intuitively, for every attack (represented by C) on $M^\downarrow$ there is a corresponding attack (represented by $C^\uparrow$) on M that leads to the same outcome (normal termination, error, or divergence).

6.4   Security: Preservation of Equivalences

We introduce a relation $\approx_{h,p}$ of *public (contextual) operational equivalence* for the high-level language, and a relation $\approx_{l,p}$ of *public (contextual) operational partial equivalence* for the low-level language. These two relations refine the corresponding standard relations of operational equivalence. Much as in other settings, they can be used for capturing security properties, such as those discussed informally in Section 2. Therefore, we aim to show that compilation preserves equivalences, at least in a probabilistic sense.

We define $\approx_{h,p}$ by setting, for any two high-level terms M_0 and N_0:

$$M_0 \sim_{h,p} N_0 \iff \forall \text{pure } s. \, \text{Eval}(M_0, s) = \text{Eval}(N_0, s)$$

and then, for any two high-level terms M and N:

$$M \approx_{h,p} N \iff \forall \text{public high-level } C. \, CM \sim_{h,p} CN$$

Thus, $M_0 \sim_{h,p} N_0$ means that M_0 and N_0 yield the same outcome from all pure high-level stores, and $M \approx_{h,p} N$ means the same in an arbitrary public context.

Although Eval produces only a coarse outcome, and although the definition of $\sim_{h,p}$ focuses on pure stores, the quantification over all public contexts leads to fine distinctions between terms. For instance, when n and n' are two different numbers, we have $n \sim_{h,p} n'$, but we do not have $n \approx_{h,p} n'$, simply because a context C may compare its argument to n, terminate if the comparison succeeds, and diverge otherwise. Similarly, we do not have $(l_{\text{loc}} :=_{\text{loc}} n) \approx_{h,p} (l_{\text{loc}} :=_{\text{loc}} n')$ if l is a public location, because a context C may read from l_{loc}, compare the result to n, terminate if the comparison succeeds, and diverge otherwise. On the other hand, the equivalence $(l'_{\text{loc}} :=_{\text{loc}} n) \approx_{h,p} (l'_{\text{loc}} :=_{\text{loc}} n')$ does hold when l' is a private location, and captures a secrecy property.

Note that this equivalence would not hold if we had quantified over arbitrary stores rather than pure stores in the definition of $M_0 \sim_{h,p} N_0$. Let s be a store that maps the public location l to the function $\lambda x.\,!_{\text{loc}}l'_{\text{loc}}$. Let C be a context that consumes an argument, reads from l_{loc}, applies its contents to $*$, compares the result to n, terminates if the comparison succeeds, and diverges otherwise. Then $\text{Eval}(C(l'_{\text{loc}} :=_{\text{loc}} n), s)$ and $\text{Eval}(C(l'_{\text{loc}} :=_{\text{loc}} n'), s)$ yield different outcomes ($\checkmark$ and Ω, respectively).

As this small example illustrates, the quantification over pure stores (rather than arbitrary stores) in the definition of $M_0 \sim_{h,p} N_0$ is crucial because stores may contain functions. In particular, in an arbitrary store, a public location l could contain functions that, when invoked, read or write private locations; a context could then read from l and use those functions to access private locations. Thus, assuming that there is at least one public location l, removing the restriction to pure stores would effectively erase the distinction between public and private locations, and would yield a standard relation of contextual equivalence.

Analogously, for the low-level language, for any M_0 and N_0, we say that $M_0 \sim_{l,p} N_0$ holds if and only if, for every pure store s, at least one of the following three possibilities holds:

- there exist s', s'', V', and V'' such that, for all w, $w \models (s_w, M_0) \Rightarrow (s'_w, V')$ and $w \models (s_w, N_0) \Rightarrow (s''_w, V'')$,
- $P(w \models (s_w, M_0) \Downarrow^u_{\text{error}}) \geq min(\delta, \varrho)$ and $P(w \models (s_w, N_0) \Downarrow^u_{\text{error}}) \geq min(\delta, \varrho)$, or
- for all w, $w \models (s_w, M_0) \Uparrow$ and $w \models (s_w, N_0) \Uparrow$.

This relation is a partial equivalence; as in [3], reflexivity may fail (because terms that branch on the concrete addresses of private locations do not behave identically for all layouts). If $\delta > 0$ and $\varrho > 0$ then the three possibilities are mutually exclusive; also, if the first of them holds, then s', s'', V', and V'' are uniquely determined. Further, for any two low-level terms M and N, we set:

$$M \approx_{l,p} N \iff \forall \text{public low-level } C. CM \sim_{l,p} CN$$

The following theorem shows that compilation preserves and reflects equivalences:

Theorem 2. *Let M and N be high-level terms. If $M \approx_{h,p} N$, then $M^{\downarrow} \approx_{l,p} N^{\downarrow}$. The converse holds as well if $\delta > 0$ and $\varrho > 0$.*

7   Related and Further Work

The pioneering work of Pucella and Schneider treats a small C-like language with arrays, and relates obfuscation and type systems [15]. Their theorems focus on integrity properties, and do not explicitly mention probabilities. As explained by Abadi and Plotkin, those theorems basically pertain to protection from a potentially dangerous input, while we consider more general attackers, represented by arbitrary contexts, and also treat program equivalences that can express integrity and secrecy properties.

Our approach is most similar to that of Abadi and Plotkin (specifically, in their "fatal error" model) [3], though with several substantial differences. In particular, we treat a dynamically typed language (rather than a statically typed language), which gives us additional flexibility in the typing of memory. Furthermore, we allow arrays and functions to be stored in memory (rather than just integers). This extension enables the formulation of examples suggested by practical attacks. It also entails a number of complications and opportunities, such as the compilation of array operations, the quantification over pure stores in defining equivalences, and the consideration of guard regions.

The choice of an untyped language and the possibility of storing functions in memory appear also in the work of Jagadeesan et al. [9]. Their programming languages include not only functions but also continuations, a bounded form of local state, and some novel, non-standard constructs. In particular, they do not view addresses as integers even in low-level systems, but pointer arithmetic is available via encodings. On the other hand, the languages do not include arrays, nor the resulting concerns about overflows that appear prominently in this paper.

Despite these distinctions, all these works aim to contribute to the understanding of randomization in the context of programming languages and their implementations. There remain opportunities for research towards this goal. In particular, further work may treat additional constructs and models of computation, such as concurrency. It may also consider combinations of layout randomization with other techniques. Our use of guard regions, in this paper, is a small step in that direction. Other relevant techniques include stack canaries for protecting return addresses and various inline reference monitors that aim to guarantee control-flow integrity. All these techniques may be used in concert in practical systems; a principled study may be able to shed light on their synergies and overlaps.

Acknowledgments. We are grateful to Úlfar Erlingsson and to Gordon Plotkin for discussions on this work. Jérémy Planul's work is supported by DARPA PROCEED.

References

1. Abadi, M.: Protection in Programming-Language Translations. In: Larsen, K.G., Skyum, S., Winskel, G. (eds.) ICALP 1998. LNCS, vol. 1443, pp. 868–883. Springer, Heidelberg (1998)
2. Abadi, M., Planul, J.: On layout randomization for arrays and functions (2013), Long version of this paper, at http://www.msr-inria.inria.fr/~jplanul/libraries-long.pdf
3. Abadi, M., Plotkin, G.D.: On protection by layout randomization. ACM Transactions on Information and System Security 15(2), 8:1–8:29 (2012)
4. Chen, S., Sezer, E.C., Xu, J., Gauriar, P., Iyer, R.K.: Non-control-data attacks are realistic threats. In: Proceedings of the Usenix Security Symposium, pp. 177–192 (2005)
5. Druschel, P., Peterson, L.L.: High-performance cross-domain data transfer. Technical Report TR 92-11, Department of Computer Science, The University of Arizona (March 1992)
6. Erlingsson, Ú.: Low-Level Software Security: Attacks and Defenses. In: Aldini, A., Gorrieri, R. (eds.) FOSAD 2007. LNCS, vol. 4677, pp. 92–134. Springer, Heidelberg (2007)
7. Felleisen, M., Friedman, D.P.: Control operators, the secd-machine, and the lambda-calculus. In: 3rd Working Conference on the Formal Description of Programming Concepts, pp. 193–219 (1986)
8. Forrest, S., Somayaji, A., Ackley, D.H.: Building diverse computer systems. In: 6th Workshop on Hot Topics in Operating Systems, pp. 67–72 (1997)
9. Jagadeesan, R., Pitcher, C., Rathke, J., Riely, J.: Local memory via layout randomization. In: Proceedings of the 24th IEEE Computer Security Foundations Symposium, pp. 161–174 (2011)
10. McCamant, S., Morrisett, G.: Evaluating SFI for a CISC architecture. In: Proceedings of the 15th USENIX Security Symposium, pp. 209–224 (2006)
11. Mitchell, J.: Foundations for Programming Languages. MIT Press (1996)
12. Pappas, V., Polychronakis, M., Keromytis, A.D.: Smashing the gadgets: Hindering return-oriented programming using in-place code randomization. In: IEEE Symposium on Security and Privacy, pp. 601–615 (2012)
13. PaX Project. The PaX project (2004), http://pax.grsecurity.net/
14. Pierce, B.: Types and Programming Languages. MIT Press (2002)
15. Pucella, R., Schneider, F.B.: Independence from obfuscation: A semantic framework for diversity. Journal of Computer Security 18(5), 701–749 (2010)
16. Sotirov, A., Dowd, M.: Bypassing browser memory protections: Setting back browser security by 10 years (2008), https://www.blackhat.com/presentations/bh-usa-08/Sotirov_Dowd/bh08-sotirov-dowd.pdf
17. Wahbe, R., Lucco, S., Anderson, T.E., Graham, S.L.: Efficient software-based fault isolation. In: Proceedings of the Fourteenth ACM Symposium on Operating Systems Principles, pp. 203–216 (1993)

A Theory of Agreements and Protection

Massimo Bartoletti[1], Tiziana Cimoli[1], and Roberto Zunino[2]

[1] Università degli Studi di Cagliari, Italy
[2] Università di Trento and COSBI, Italy

Abstract. We present a theory of contracts. Contracts are interacting processes with an explicit notion of obligations and objectives. We model processes and their obligations as event structures. We define a general notion of *agreement*, by interpreting contracts as multi-player concurrent games. A participant agrees on a contract if she has a strategy to reach her objectives (or make another participant chargeable for a violation), whatever the moves of her adversaries. We then tackle the problem of *protection*. A participant is protected by a contract when she has a strategy to defend herself in all possible contexts, even in those where she has not reached an agreement. We show that, in a relevant class of contracts, agreements and protection mutually exclude each other. We then propose a novel formalism for modelling contractual obligations: event structures with circular causality. Using this model, we show how to construct contracts which guarantee both agreements and protection.

1 Introduction

The lack of precise guarantees about the reliability and security of cloud services is a main deterrent for industries wishing to move their applications and business to the cloud [1]. A key problem is how to drive safe and fair interactions among distributed participants which are possibly mutually distrusted, and have possibly conflicting individual goals. In addition to the well-known difficulties of distributed software systems (distribution, concurrency, heterogeneity, mobility, *etc.*), cloud components and infrastructures are often under the governance of different providers, possibly competing among each other. Analysis and verification techniques can be applied only on the software components under one's control, while no assumptions can be made about the components made available by other providers. Therefore, standard compositional techniques have to be adapted to cope with the situation where providers fail to keep the promises made, or even choose not to.

We envision a *contract-oriented computing* paradigm [3], where reliable interactions are driven by contracts which formalise Service-Level Agreements. Contracts specify the behavior of a software component, from the point of view of the interactions it may participate in, and the goals it tries to reach. Differently from most of the approaches based on behavioural types [15], which use contracts only in the "matchmaking" phase, a contract-oriented component is not supposed to be *honest*, in that it may not keep the promises made.

D. Basin and J.C. Mitchell (Eds.): POST 2013, LNCS 7796, pp. 186–205, 2013.
© Springer-Verlag Berlin Heidelberg 2013

In a contract-oriented application, participants advertise their contracts to some *contract brokers*, which are the contract-oriented analogous of service repositories in the Web Service paradigm. Then, participants wait until the contract broker finds an *agreement* among the contracts in its hands. When this happens, a session is created among the participants involved in the contract, so that they can interact. Agreement is a property of contracts which guarantees that each honest participant may reach her objectives, provided that the other participants cooperate honestly. Moreover, if an honest participant does not reach her goals, then some other participant can be blamed. An external judge may then inspect the contract and the status of the session. In case a violation is found, the judge will eventually provide the prescribed compensations/punishments.

The underlying assumption of this view is that participants trust in the contract broker. In a context populated by attackers, it may happen that a dishonest contract broker creates a fraudulent session, making participants interact in the absence of an agreement. In this way, the contract broker may allow an accomplice to swindle an unaware participant. Note that the accomplice may perform his scam while adhering to his contract, and so he will not be liable for violations.

A crucial problem is how to devise contracts which protect participants from malicious contract brokers, while at the same time allowing honest brokers to find agreements. A good contract should allow a participant to reach her goals in contexts where the other participants are cooperative, and prevent her from performing imprudent actions which could be exploited by malicious participants.

In this paper we propose a foundational model for contracts. We specify the behaviour of participants as event structures [21], a basic semantic model for interactive systems. We then provide a formal definition for the two key notions intuitively introduced above, i.e. *agreement* and *protection*. To do that, we borrow techniques from game theory, by interpreting contracts as multi-player concurrent games. By abstracting away from the concrete details of contract languages, our model is a first step towards a unifying framework for reasoning about contracts, in the same spirit that event structures can be used as an underlying semantics for a variety of concrete models of concurrency.

A first result is that agreement and protection cannot coexist for a broad class of objectives. That is, if we are given the objectives of a set of participants, it is impossible to construct a contract which protects them all, and at the same time admits an agreement. Roughly, the problem is that, when the offers of the participants mutually depend on their requests, the participant which risks in doing the first step is not protected.

To overcome this negative result, we extend event structures with a new notion of causality. While in classical event structures an action a which causally depends on an action b can only be performed after b, in our extension we also consider a relaxed version of causality, which allows a to happen before b, under the (legally binding) promise that b will be eventually performed.

The main result of the paper is that, using this model for contracts, it is possible for a wide class of objectives to construct a set of contracts which protect their participants and still admit an agreement.

2   Contracts

At an abstract level, contracts are concurrent systems, enriched with a notion of *obligation* (what I must do in a given state) and *objective* (what I expect to obtain in a given state). Event structures (ES) are one of the classical models for concurrency [21]. Notwithstanding the variety of formalisations, ES are at least equipped with an *enabling* relation modelling causality (usually written $\vdash$), and another relation modelling non-determinism (usually written #). ES can provide a basic semantic model for contractual clauses, by interpreting the enabling $\{b\} \vdash a$ as: "I am obliged to do a *after* you have done b".

2.1   Event Structures

Event structures [21] have a deep theory. Here we only report some basic definitions, which are needed in our technical development. We assume an enumerable universe of *events*, ranged over by $a, b, e, \ldots$. For a set of events X, the predicate $CF(X)$ is true iff X is *conflict-free*, i.e. $CF(X) \triangleq (\forall e, e' \in X : \neg(e\#e'))$.

Definition 1 (Event structure [21]). *An event structure $\mathcal{E}$ is a triple $\langle E, \#, \vdash \rangle$, where (1) E is a set of events, (2) $\# \subseteq E \times E$ is an irreflexive and symmetric conflict relation (3) $\vdash \subseteq \{X \subseteq_{fin} E \mid CF(X)\} \times E$ is the enabling relation, which is saturated, i.e. $\forall X \subseteq Y \subseteq_{fin} E. \ X \vdash e \wedge CF(Y) \implies Y \vdash e$.*

An ES is *finite* when E is finite; it is *conflict-free* when the conflict relation is empty. We shall often use the following shorthands: $X \vdash Y$ for $\forall e \in Y. X \vdash e$, $a \vdash b$ for $\{a\} \vdash b$, and $\vdash e$ for $\emptyset \vdash e$.

Definition 2 (Persistent conflict). *An event $e \in E$ is persistently conflictable in $\mathcal{E}$ iff the set $\{\bar{e} \in E \mid e\#\bar{e}\}$ is infinite. A set $X \subseteq E$ is persistently conflictable iff some $e \in X$ is persistently conflictable.*

For a sequence $\sigma = \langle e_0 \, e_1 \cdots \rangle$ in E (possibly infinite), we write $\bar{\sigma}$ for the set of elements in σ; we write σ_i for the subsequence $\langle e_0 \cdots e_{i-1} \rangle$. If $\sigma = \langle e_0 \cdots e_n \rangle$, we write σe for the sequence $\langle e_0 \cdots e_n e \rangle$. The empty sequence is denoted by ε. For a set S, we denote with S^* the set of finite sequences over S, and with S^ω the set of finite and infinite sequences over S.

A configuration C is a "snapshot" of the behaviour of the system modeled by an ES, where for each event $e \in C$ it is possible to find a finite justification, *i.e.* a sequence of events containing all the causes of e.

Definition 3 (Configuration [21]). *For an ES $\mathcal{E} = \langle E, \#, \vdash \rangle$, a set $C \subseteq E$ is a configuration of $\mathcal{E}$ iff $CF(C)$, and*

$$\forall e \in C. \ \exists \sigma = \langle e_0 \cdots e_n \rangle. \ e \in \bar{\sigma} \subseteq C \wedge \forall i \leq n. \, \overline{\sigma_i} \vdash e_i$$

The set of all configurations of $\mathcal{E}$ is denoted by $\mathfrak{F}_{\mathcal{E}}$.

Definition 4 (LTS of an ES). *For an ES $\mathcal{E}$, the labelled transition system* $\mathrm{LTS}_\mathcal{E} = \langle \wp_{fin}(E), E, \to_\mathcal{E} \rangle$ *is defined as follows:*

$$C \xrightarrow{e}_\mathcal{E} C \cup \{e\} \qquad\qquad iff\ C \vdash e,\ e \notin C\ and\ CF(C \cup \{e\})$$

Definition 5. *For two ES $\mathcal{E}, \mathcal{E}'$, we define $\mathcal{E} \sqcup \mathcal{E}'$ as the pointwise union of $\mathcal{E}, \mathcal{E}'$.*

2.2 An Event-Based Model of Contracts

A contract (Def. 6) specifies the obligations and the objectives of a set of participants. The atomic entities of a contract are the *events*, which are uniquely associated to participants through a labelling π. Obligations are modelled as an event structure. Intuitively, an enabling $X \vdash e$ models the fact that, if all the events in X have happened, then e is an obligation for $\pi(e)$. Such obligation may be discharged only by performing e, or any event in conflict with e. For instance, consider an internal choice between two events a and b. This is modelled by an ES with enablings $\vdash a$, $\vdash b$ and conflict $a\#b$. After the choice (say, of a), the obligation b is discharged. Objectives are modelled as a function Φ, which associates each participant A and each trace of events σ to a *payoff* $\Phi A\sigma$. We assume a rather coarse notion of payoffs: we only have three possible outcomes which represent, respectively, success (1), failure (-1), and tie (0).

Definition 6 (Contract). *A contract $\mathcal{C}$ is a 4-tuple $\langle \mathcal{E}, \mathcal{A}, \pi, \Phi \rangle$, where:*

- $\mathcal{E} = \langle E, \#, \vdash \rangle$ *is an event structure;*
- $\mathcal{A}$ *is a set of* participants *(ranged over by $\mathsf{A}, \mathsf{B}, \ldots$);*
- $\pi : E \to \mathcal{A}$ *associates each event with a participant;*
- $\Phi : \mathcal{A} \rightharpoonup E^\omega \to \{-1, 0, 1\}$ *associates each participant and trace with a* payoff.

Hereafter, we shall assume that contracts respect two basic requirements. For all $X \vdash e$ in $\mathcal{E}$, we ask that (*i*) $\Phi(\pi(e)) \neq \bot$, and (*ii*) e is not persistently conflictable in $\mathcal{E}$. Notice that Φ is a partial function (from $\mathcal{A}$ to functions), hence a contract does not need to define payoffs for all the participants in $\mathcal{A}$ (typically, when A advertises her contract, she will not speculate about the objectives of B). Constraint (*i*) asks that if a contract defines some obligations for A, then A must also declare in $\mathcal{C}$ her payoffs. Constraint (*ii*) rules out those ill-formed contracts where some obligations can be persistently discharged.

Example 1. Suppose there are two kids who want to play together. Alice has a toy airplane, while Bob has a bike. Both kids are willing to share their toys, but they do not trust each other. Thus, before starting to play they advertise the following contracts. Alice will lend her airplane only *after* Bob has allowed her ride his bike. Bob will lend his bike without conditions. We model the events "Alice lends her airplane" and "Bob lends his bike" as a and b, respectively. The obligations of Alice and Bob are modelled by the following event structures:

$$\mathcal{E}_\mathsf{A} : \{b\} \vdash a \qquad\qquad \mathcal{E}_\mathsf{B} : \emptyset \vdash b$$

The objectives of the two kids are modelled by the functions Φ_A (which establishes Alice's payoff) and Φ_B (for Bob). Alice has a positive payoff in those traces where b has been performed, while she has a negative payoff when she performs a while not obtaining b in return. The payoffs of Bob are dual. Formally:

$$\Phi_A A \;=\; \lambda\sigma.\begin{cases} 1 & \text{if } b \in \overline{\sigma} \\ 0 & \text{if } a, b \notin \overline{\sigma} \\ -1 & \text{otherwise} \end{cases} \qquad \Phi_B B \;=\; \lambda\sigma.\begin{cases} 1 & \text{if } a \in \overline{\sigma} \\ 0 & \text{if } b, a \notin \overline{\sigma} \\ -1 & \text{otherwise} \end{cases}$$

Summing up, the contracts of Alice and Bob are $\mathcal{C}_A = \langle \mathcal{E}_A, \mathcal{A}, \pi, \Phi_A \rangle$ and $\mathcal{C}_B = \langle \mathcal{E}_B, \mathcal{A}, \pi, \Phi_B \rangle$, respectively, where $\mathcal{A} = \{A, B\}$, $\pi(a) = A$, and $\pi(b) = B$. $\square$

Observe that the definition of payoff functions in Def. 6 is quite liberal. Indeed, it also allows for uncomputable functions, which are of little use in doing anything with a contract. One may then be interested in considering relevant subclasses of payoff functions, in the same spirit of the rich classification of winning conditions in game theory [9].

Assume that participant A has a sequence $\langle O^0\, O^1 \cdots \rangle$ of sets of events, and a sequence $\langle R^0\, R^1 \cdots \rangle$ of the same cardinality. The sets O^i are called *offers*, while R^i are the *requests*. A function Φ is an *Offer-Request (O-R) payoff* for A if, whenever A performs in σ some offer O^i (in whatever order), then σ also contains the corresponding request R^i. For instance, the payoff functions Φ_A and Φ_B in Ex. 1 are O-R payoffs for A and B. The offers and the requests of A and B are, respectively $O_A^0 = \{a\} = R_B^0$ and, dually, $O_B^0 = \{b\} = R_A^0$.

Definition 7 (Offer-Request payoff). *Let $\pi : E \to \mathcal{A}$. We say that Φ is a Offer-Request payoff for A iff there exist (possibly infinite) sequences $(O^i)_i$, $(R^i)_i$ of equal cardinality such that for all i, $O^i \subseteq \pi^{-1}(A)$, $\emptyset \neq R^i \subseteq E \setminus \pi^{-1}(A)$, and*

$$\Phi A \;=\; \lambda\sigma.\begin{cases} 1 & \text{if } (\exists i.\ R^i \subseteq \overline{\sigma}) \wedge (\forall j.\ O^j \subseteq \overline{\sigma} \implies R^j \subseteq \overline{\sigma}) \\ 0 & \text{if } (\forall i.\ R^i \not\subseteq \overline{\sigma} \wedge O^i \not\subseteq \overline{\sigma}) \\ -1 & \text{otherwise} \end{cases}$$

A contract $\mathcal{C} = \langle \mathcal{E}, \mathcal{A}, \pi, \Phi \rangle$ has O-R payoffs iff Φ is a O-R payoff for all $A \in \mathcal{A}$. If, additionally, all the sets O^i (resp. R^i) are finite for all $A \in \mathcal{A}$, we say that $\mathcal{C}$ has finite offers (resp. finite requests). If Φ has a finite number of finite offers-request, then Φ is finite.

Example 2. In [8] contracts are modelled in a variant of CCS which includes prefixing, internal/external choice, and recursion. Consider e.g. a server A which repeatedly offers to her clients a choice between two actions a and b. The client B internally chooses one of his (co-)actions $\overline{a}$ and $\overline{b}$. This is modelled in [8] as:

$$c_A = rec\, X.\, (a.X + b.X) \qquad c_B = rec\, Y.\, (\overline{a}.Y \oplus \overline{b}.Y)$$

In our theory we model c_A and c_B as the contracts $\mathcal{C}_A$ and $\mathcal{C}_B$, defined below. For all $i \geq 0$, let a_i, b_i be events of A, and let $\overline{a_i}, \overline{b_i}$ be events of B. The event structures of A and B have the following enablings and conflicts, for all $i \geq 0$:

$\mathcal{E}_A : \quad \overline{a_i} \vdash a_i, \quad \overline{b_i} \vdash b_i, \quad a_i \# b_i$

$\mathcal{E}_B : \quad \vdash \overline{a_0}, \quad \vdash \overline{b_0}, \quad a_i \vdash \overline{a_{i+1}}, \quad a_i \vdash \overline{b_{i+1}}, \quad b_i \vdash \overline{a_{i+1}}, \quad b_i \vdash \overline{b_{i+1}}, \quad \overline{a_i} \# \overline{b_i}$

The payoff of a A is positive in a play σ if A has no obligations; similarly for B.

$$\Phi_P P = \lambda \sigma. \begin{cases} 1 & \text{if } \nexists e \in \pi^{-1}(P). \ \sigma \xrightarrow{e} \mathcal{E}_P \\ -1 & \text{otherwise} \end{cases} \qquad \square$$

Given two contracts $\mathcal{C}, \mathcal{C}'$, we denote with $\mathcal{C} \mid \mathcal{C}'$ their composition. If $\mathcal{C}'$ is the contract written by an adversary of $\mathcal{C}$, then a naïve composition of the two contracts could easily lead to an attack, e.g. when Mallory's contract says that Alice is obliged to give him her airplane. To prevent from such kinds of attacks, contract composition is a partial operation. We do *not* compose contracts which assign payoffs to the same participant, neither those which disagree on the association between events and participants.

Definition 8 (Composition of compatible contracts). *Two contracts* $\mathcal{C} = \langle \mathcal{E}, \mathcal{A}, \pi, \Phi \rangle$ *and* $\mathcal{C}' = \langle \mathcal{E}', \mathcal{A}', \pi', \Phi' \rangle$ *are* compatible *whenever:*

$$\forall e \in \mathcal{E} \cap \mathcal{E}'. \ e = e' \implies \pi(e) = \pi'(e) \qquad (1)$$

$$\forall A \in \mathcal{A} \cup \mathcal{A}'. \ \Phi(A) = \bot \ \lor \ \Phi'(A) = \bot \qquad (2)$$

If $\mathcal{C}, \mathcal{C}'$ *are compatible, we define their composition as:*

$$\mathcal{C} \mid \mathcal{C}' = \langle \mathcal{E} \sqcup \mathcal{E}', \mathcal{A} \cup \mathcal{A}', \pi \sqcup \pi', \Phi \sqcup \Phi' \rangle$$

Two contracts which both assign obligations to A are not compatible.

Lemma 1. *If* $\mathcal{C} = \langle \mathcal{E}, \mathcal{A}, \pi, \Phi \rangle$ *and* $\mathcal{C}' = \langle \mathcal{E}', \mathcal{A}', \pi', \Phi' \rangle$ *are compatible, then:*

$$X \vdash e \in \mathcal{E} \ \land \ X' \vdash e' \in \mathcal{E}' \implies \pi(e) \neq \pi'(e') \ \land \ e \neq e'$$

Example 3. The contracts $\mathcal{C}_A$ and $\mathcal{C}_B$ in Ex. 1 are compatible, and their composition is the contract $\mathcal{C} = \mathcal{C}_A \mid \mathcal{C}_B = \langle \mathcal{E}, \mathcal{A}, \pi, \Phi \rangle$ defined as follows:

$$\begin{aligned} \mathcal{E} : \quad & \{b\} \vdash a, \quad \emptyset \vdash b \\ \mathcal{A} : \quad & \{A, B\} \\ \pi : \quad & \pi(a) = A, \quad \pi(b) = B \end{aligned} \qquad \Phi P = \begin{cases} \Phi_A A & \text{if } P = A \\ \Phi_B B & \text{if } P = B \end{cases} \qquad \square$$

2.3   Agreements

A crucial notion on contracts is that of *agreement*. Intuitively, when Alice agrees on a contract $\mathcal{C}$, then she can safely initiate an interaction with the other participants, and be guaranteed that the interaction will not "go wrong" — even in the presence of attackers. This does not mean that Alice will always succeed in all interactions: in case Bob is dishonest, we do not assume that an external authority (e.g. Bob's mother) will lend the bike to Alice. We intend that Alice agrees on a contract where, in all the interactions where she does not succeed, then some other participant must be found dishonest. That is, we consider Alice satisfied if she can blame another participant. In real-world applications, a judge may provide compensations to Alice, or impose a punishment to the participant who has violated the contract. Here, we shall not explicitly model the judge, and we shall focus instead on how to formalise the agreement property.

We interpret a contract $\mathcal{C} = \langle \mathcal{E}, \mathcal{A}, \pi, \Phi \rangle$ as a nonzero-sum concurrent multiplayer game. The game involves the players in $\mathcal{A}$ concurrently performing events in order to reach the objectives defined by Φ. A *play* of $\mathcal{C}$ is a (finite or infinite) sequence of events of $\mathcal{E}$. We postulate that the permitted moves after a (finite) sequence of steps σ are exactly the events enabled by $\mathcal{E}$ in $\overline{\sigma}$, i.e. e is permitted in σ iff $\overline{\sigma} \xrightarrow{e}_{\mathcal{E}}$. A *strategy* Σ for A is a function which associates to each finite play σ a set of events of A (possibly empty), such that if $e \in \Sigma(\sigma)$ then σe is still a play. A play $\sigma = \langle e_0 \, e_1 \cdots \rangle$ *conforms* to a strategy Σ for A if, for all $i \geq 0$, if $e_i \in \pi^{-1}(\mathsf{A})$, then $e_i \in \Sigma(\sigma_i)$.

As usual in concurrency, we shall only consider those *fair* plays where an event permanently enabled is eventually performed. Indeed, contracts would make little sense in the presence of unfair plays, because an honest participant willing to perform a promised action could be perpetually prevented (by an unfair scheduler) from keeping her promise.

Definition 9 (Fair play). *A play* $\sigma = \langle e_0 \, e_1 \cdots \rangle$ *is* fair *w.r.t. strategy* Σ *iff:*

$$\forall i \leq |\sigma|. \left(\forall j : i \leq j \leq |\sigma|. \, e \in \Sigma(\sigma_j) \right) \implies \exists h \geq i. \, e_h = e$$

Our notion of agreement takes into account whether participants behave honestly in their plays. Informally, a participant is *innocent* in a play if she always keeps the promises made. An innocent participant has no persistently enabled events, i.e. all her enabled events are either performed or conflicted.

Definition 10 (Innocence). *We say that* A *is* innocent in σ *iff:*

$$\forall i \geq 0. \, \forall e \in \pi^{-1}(\mathsf{A}). \left(\overline{\sigma_i} \xrightarrow{e}_{\mathcal{E}} \implies \exists j \geq i. \, e_j \# e \, \vee \, e_j = e \right)$$

If A *is not innocent in* σ, *then we say she is* culpable.

There always exist strategies which guarantee A to be innocent in every (fair) play. The greatest of such strategies is the *eager strategy*, which prescribes A to do all her enabled events.

Lemma 2. *Say a strategy* Σ *for* A *is* innocent *iff* A *is innocent in all fair plays which conform to* Σ. *The eager strategy* $\Sigma_{\mathsf{A}}^e = \lambda \sigma. \{e \in \pi^{-1}(\mathsf{A}) \mid \overline{\sigma} \xrightarrow{e}_{\mathcal{E}} \}$ *is the greatest innocent strategy for* A.

We now define when a participant *wins* in a play. If A is culpable, then she loses. If A is innocent, but some other participant is culpable, then A wins. Otherwise, if all participants are innocent, then A wins if she has a positive payoff in the play. This is formalised as the function $\mathcal{W}$ in Def. 11 below.

Definition 11 (Winning play). *Define* $\mathcal{W} : \mathcal{A} \rightharpoonup E^\omega \to \{1, 0, -1\}$ *as:*

$$\mathcal{W}\mathsf{A}\sigma = \begin{cases} \Phi\mathsf{A}\sigma & \textit{if all participants are innocent in } \sigma \\ -1 & \textit{if } \mathsf{A} \textit{ is culpable in } \sigma \\ +1 & \textit{otherwise} \end{cases}$$

For a participant A *and a play* σ, *we say that* A *wins (resp. loses) in* σ *iff* $\mathcal{W}\mathsf{A}\sigma > 0$ *(resp.* $\mathcal{W}\mathsf{A}\sigma < 0$*).*

We can now define when a participant *agrees* on a contract. Intuitively, A is happy to participate in an interaction regulated by contract $\mathcal{C}$ when she has a strategy Σ which allows her to win in all fair plays conform to Σ. More formally, we say that Σ is *winning* (resp. *losing*) for A iff A wins (resp. loses) in every fair play which conforms to Σ.

Definition 12 (Agreement). *A participant* A *agrees on a contract* $\mathcal{C}$ *if and only if* A *has a winning strategy in* $\mathcal{C}$. *A contract* $\mathcal{C}$ *admits an agreement whenever all the involved participants agree on* $\mathcal{C}$.

Example 4. The contract $\mathcal{C}$ of Ex. 3 admits an agreement. The winning strategies for A and B are, respectively:

$$\Sigma_\mathsf{A}(\sigma) = \begin{cases} \{a\} & \text{if } b \in \bar{\sigma} \text{ and } a \notin \bar{\sigma} \\ \emptyset & \text{otherwise} \end{cases} \qquad \Sigma_\mathsf{B}(\sigma) = \begin{cases} \{b\} & \text{if } b \notin \bar{\sigma} \\ \emptyset & \text{otherwise} \end{cases}$$

For A, the only fair plays conform to Σ_A are ε and $\langle b\,a \rangle$. B is culpable in ε, while in $\langle b\,a \rangle$ the payoff of A is positive. For B, the only fair plays conform to Σ_B are $\langle b \rangle$ and $\langle b\,a \rangle$. A is culpable in $\langle b \rangle$, while in $\langle b\,a \rangle$ the payoff of B is positive. $\square$

Example 5. The contracts in Ex. 2 above admit an agreement. The winning strategies for A and B are the eager strategies Σ_A^e and Σ_B^e, respectively. $\square$

Example 6. Note that Σ_A^e is not necessarily winning for A. For instance, consider the contract with $\vdash a$, $\vdash b$, $a\#b$, $\pi^{-1}(\mathsf{A}) = \{a, b\}$, and $\Phi\mathsf{A}\sigma = 1$ iff $a \in \bar{\sigma}$. We have that $\Sigma_\mathsf{A}^e(\varepsilon) = \{a, b\}$, but A is losing in the fair play $\sigma = \langle b \rangle$. However, A agrees on $\mathcal{C}$, because the strategy $(\lambda\sigma. \text{if } \bar{\sigma} \overset{a}{\nrightarrow} \text{ then } \{a\} \text{ else } \emptyset)$ is winning for A.

Example 7. The union of two winning strategies is not necessarily a winning strategy. For instance, consider the contract with enablings $\vdash a$, $\vdash b$, $\{a\} \vdash a'$, $\{b\} \vdash b'$, and conflicts $a\#b'$, $a'\#b$ (all the events are of participant A). Let:

$$\Sigma_a(\sigma) = \begin{cases} \{a\} & \text{if } \bar{\sigma} \overset{a}{\nrightarrow} \\ \{a'\} & \text{if } \bar{\sigma} \overset{a'}{\nrightarrow} \\ \emptyset & \text{otherwise} \end{cases} \qquad \Sigma_b(\sigma) = \begin{cases} \{b\} & \text{if } \bar{\sigma} \overset{b}{\nrightarrow} \\ \{b'\} & \text{if } \bar{\sigma} \overset{b'}{\nrightarrow} \\ \emptyset & \text{otherwise} \end{cases}$$

and let $\Phi\mathsf{A}\sigma$ be positive if either $a, a' \in \bar{\sigma}$, or $b, b' \in \bar{\sigma}$. Both Σ_a and Σ_b are winning strategies for A in $\mathcal{C}$, but their union $\Sigma = \lambda\sigma.\Sigma_a(\sigma) \cup \Sigma_b(\sigma)$ is not. Indeed, $\Sigma(a) = \{a', b\}$, and so $\sigma = \langle a\,b \rangle$ is a fair play w.r.t. Σ such that $\Phi\mathsf{A}\sigma \leq 0$.

We now define the composition $\sqcup$ of a set of strategies. Unlike for the union of winning strategies, their $\sqcup$-composition is guaranteed to be winning (Lemma 3).

Definition 13. *For a set of strategies $\mathcal{S}$, we define the strategy $\bigsqcup \mathcal{S}$ as:*

$$(\bigsqcup \mathcal{S})(\sigma) = \bigcup \{\Sigma(\sigma) \mid \Sigma \in \mathcal{S} \wedge \sigma \text{ conforms to } \Sigma\}$$

Lemma 3. *Let $\mathcal{S} = \{\Sigma_1, \ldots, \Sigma_n\}$ be a set of strategies. Then:*

(a) A play σ conforms to $\bigsqcup \mathcal{S}$ iff σ conforms to Σ_i, for some i.
(b) If all Σ_i are winning for A in $\mathcal{C}$, then $\bigsqcup \mathcal{S}$ is a winning strategy for A in $\mathcal{C}$.

The following lemma gives a necessary condition for reaching an agreement on a contract with O-R payoffs. The ES must have a configuration containing at least a request set, and all the offers are matched by the respective requests.

Lemma 4. *Let $\mathcal{C} = \langle \mathcal{E}, \mathcal{A}, \pi, \Phi \rangle$ be a contract with O-R payoff $\Phi A = \lambda \sigma. \phi(\overline{\sigma})$ for A. If A agrees on $\mathcal{C}$, then there exists $C \in \mathcal{F}_{\mathcal{E}}$ such that $\phi(C) > 0$.*

The following theorem establishes a sufficient condition for reaching agreements in conflict-free contracts with O-R payoffs. If there exists a configuration C in $\mathcal{C}$ which contains all the requests of A, then A agrees on $\mathcal{C}$. Since the ES of $\mathcal{C}$ is conflict-free, if the strategy of A prescribes to do all her enabled events in C, then the other participants are obliged to do their events in C. Eventually, either some participant $B \neq A$ is culpable, or a state is reached where the payoff of A is positive.

Theorem 1. *Let $\mathcal{C}$ be a contract with O-R payoff for A. If $\mathcal{E}$ is conflict-free and $\bigcup_i R_A^i \subseteq C$ for some $C \in \mathcal{F}_{\mathcal{E}}$, then A agrees on $\mathcal{C}$.*

Example 8. Note that conflict-freeness is necessary in Theorem 1. Consider e.g. the contract $\mathcal{C}$ with O-R payoff for A given by $O_A^0 = \{a\}$ and $R_A^0 = \{b\}$. Assume that $\pi^{-1}(A) = \{a\}$, and $\pi^{-1}(B) = \{b, b'\}$. The ES of $\mathcal{C}$ has enablings $\vdash a$, $\vdash b$, $\vdash b'$, and conflict $b \# b'$. The set $\{a, b\}$ is a configuration, but A does not agree on $\mathcal{C}$. Indeed, either A does no events, or she performs a. In the first case, A is culpable, while in the second one she will have a negative payoff if B does b'.   □

2.4   Protection

In contract-oriented interactions [3], mutually distrusted participants advertise their contracts to a contract broker. The broker composes contracts which admit an agreement, and then establishes a session among the participants involved in such contracts. When a participant agrees on a contract, she is guaranteed that — even in the presence of malicious participants — no interaction driven by the contract will ever go wrong. At worst, if A does not reach her objectives, then some other participant will be found culpable of an infringement.

This model of interaction works fine under the hypothesis that contract brokers are honest, i.e. they never establish a session in the absence of an agreement among all the participants. Suppose Alice is willing to lend her airplane in exchange of Bob's bike. In her contract, she could promise to lend the airplane (unconditionally), and declare that her objective is to obtain the bike. A malicious contract broker could construct an attack by establishing a session between Alice and Mallory, whose contract just says to take the airplane and give nothing in exchange. Mallory is *not* culpable, because her contract declares no obligations, and so Alice loses.

Formally, a contract $\mathcal{C}_A$ *protects* A if, whatever contract $\mathcal{C}$ is composed with $\mathcal{C}_A$, A has a way to non-lose in the composed contract.

Definition 14 (Protection). *A contract $\mathcal{C}_A$ protects participant A if and only if, for all contracts $\mathcal{C}$ compatible with $\mathcal{C}_A$, A has a non-losing strategy in $\mathcal{C}_A \mid \mathcal{C}$.*

Notice that if A agrees with $\mathcal{C}$, then not necessarily $\mathcal{C}$ protects A. For instance, Mallory could join $\mathcal{C}$ with her contract $\mathcal{C}_M$, and prevent Alice from borrowing Bob's bike in $\mathcal{C} \mid \mathcal{C}_M$. A sufficient (yet hardly realistic) criterion for protection is to declare nonnegative payoffs for all σ. Less trivially, the following example shows a contract with possible negative payoffs which still offers protection.

Example 9. The contract $\mathcal{C}_B$ of Ex. 1 does *not* protect Bob. To prove that, consider e.g. the attacker contract $\mathcal{C}' = \langle \mathcal{E}', \mathcal{A}, \pi, \Phi_{\mathcal{C}'} \rangle$, where $\mathcal{A}$ and π are as in Ex. 1, while we define $\mathcal{E}'$ with no enablings, and $\Phi_{\mathcal{C}'}$ is immaterial except for being undefined on B (otherwise $\mathcal{C}'$ and $\mathcal{C}_B$ are not compatible). Consider then the contract $\mathcal{C}' \mid \mathcal{C}_B$. There are only two possible strategies for B:

$$\Sigma_B = \lambda\sigma.\emptyset \qquad\qquad \Sigma'_B = \lambda\sigma. \begin{cases} \{b\} & \text{if } b \notin \overline{\sigma} \\ \emptyset & \text{otherwise} \end{cases}$$

The strategy Σ_B is losing for B, because B is not innocent under Σ_B. The strategy Σ'_B is losing as well, because in the fair play $\sigma = \langle b \rangle$ we have that $\Phi B\sigma = -1$, but no participant is culpable in σ. By Def. 14, B is not protected by $\mathcal{C}_B$.

On the other hand, the contract $\mathcal{C}_A$ protects Alice. To show that, consider a contract $\mathcal{C}$ compatible with $\mathcal{C}_A$. Let Σ_A be the following strategy for A:

$$\Sigma_A = \lambda\sigma. \begin{cases} \{a\} & \text{if } b \in \overline{\sigma} \text{ and } a \notin \overline{\sigma} \\ \emptyset & \text{otherwise} \end{cases}$$

Let σ be a fair play in $\mathcal{C} \mid \mathcal{C}_A$ conforming to Σ_A. There are two cases:

- $b \in \overline{\sigma}$. Then, since σ is fair, by definition of Σ_A there must exist i such that $a \in \overline{\sigma}_i$, and so A is innocent in σ. Furthermore, we have that $\Phi A\sigma = 1$.
- $b \notin \overline{\sigma}$. By definition of $\mathcal{C}_A$, A is not culpable in σ. Also, since $b \notin \overline{\sigma}$ and $a \notin \overline{\sigma}$, then $\Phi A\sigma = 0$.

In both cases, Σ_A is non-losing for A. Therefore, $\mathcal{C}_A$ protects A. $\qquad\square$

The following theorem establishes sufficient conditions for protection in contracts with O-R payoffs. Essentially, A is protected if, whenever she enables an offer O_A^i, the corresponding request R_A^i has been already satisfied.

Theorem 2. *A contract* $\mathcal{C}_A = \langle \mathcal{E}, \mathcal{A}, \pi, \Phi \rangle$ *with O-R payoffs for* A *protects* A *if*
$\forall i, Y. \; Y \vdash O_A^i \implies R_A^i \subseteq Y.$

We now consider a relevant subclass of Offer-Request payoffs, where the requests of all participants mutually depend on their offers. An O-R payoff is *circular* when it is not possible to satisfy requests from all participants without each participant doing some offer (item (3)), and each combination of the requests is covered by a set of offers (item (4)). For instance, the payoffs of Alice and Bob in Ex. 1 are circular, because their requests (e.g. a and b, respectively) match exactly their offers.

Definition 15. *An O-R payoff* Φ *for participants* $\mathcal{A}$ *is* circular *when:*

$$\forall \mathcal{J} : \mathcal{A} \to \mathbb{N}. \; \exists \mathcal{L} : \mathcal{A} \to \mathbb{N}. \; \bigcup_{A \in \mathcal{A}} O_A^{\mathcal{L}A} \subseteq \bigcup_{A \in \mathcal{A}} R_A^{\mathcal{J}A} \tag{3}$$

$$\forall \mathcal{J} : \mathcal{A} \to \mathbb{N}. \; \exists \mathcal{L} : \mathcal{A} \to \mathbb{N}. \; \bigcup_{A \in \mathcal{A}} O_A^{\mathcal{L}A} \supseteq \bigcup_{A \in \mathcal{A}} R_A^{\mathcal{J}A} \tag{4}$$

Example 10 (Dining retailers [5]). Around a table, n cutlery retailers are about to have dinner. At the center of the table, there is a large dish of food. Despite the food being delicious, the retailers cannot start eating right now. To do that, and follow the proper etiquette, each retailer needs a complete cutlery set, consisting of n pieces of different kinds. Each of the n retailers owns a distinct set of n piece of cutlery, all of the same kind. The retailers start discussing about trading their cutlery, so that they can finally eat.

We formalise this scenario as follows. Each retailer A_i initially owns n pieces of kind i. For all $j \neq i$, the event $e_{i,j}$ models A_i giving a piece of cutlery to retailer A_j. Thus, $\pi^{-1}(A_i) = \{e_{i,j} \mid j \neq i\}$. Retailer A_i offers $n-1$ pieces of his cutlery of kind i in exchange for $n-1$ pieces of cutlery of the other kinds.

$$O_i = \{e_{i,j} \mid j \neq i\} \qquad\qquad R_i = \{e_{j,i} \mid j \neq i\}$$

By Def. 15, the payoff Φ_i of each retailer is a finite O-R circular payoff. □

Agreement and protection can coexist in contracts with *infinite* circular O-R payoffs (see Ex. 11). Intuitively, when an infinite offer O_A has to match an infinite request R_B, participants A and B may take turns in doing event in $O_A \cup R_B$. This strategy is winning for both participants (hence they have an agreement), and protection follows because no participant completes her offer before receiving the corresponding request.

Example 11. Let $\mathcal{C}_A = \langle \mathcal{E}_A, \mathcal{A}, \pi, \Phi_A \rangle$ and $\mathcal{C}_B = \langle \mathcal{E}_B, \mathcal{A}, \pi, \Phi_B \rangle$ be contracts with circular O-R payoffs (with infinite offers/requests) defined as follows:

$$O_A = \{e_i \mid i \in \mathbb{N}\} = R_B \qquad\qquad R_A = \{\overline{e_i} \mid i \in \mathbb{N}\} = O_B$$

and let $\mathcal{A} = \{A, B\}$, $\pi(e_i) = A$, $\pi(\overline{e_i}) = B$ for all $i \in \mathbb{N}$. Let the ES $\mathcal{E}_A$ and $\mathcal{E}_B$ be defined by the following enablings (and empty conflicts):

$$\mathcal{E}_A : \; \{\vdash e_0\} \cup \{\overline{e_i} \vdash e_{i+1} \mid i \geq 0\} \qquad\qquad \mathcal{E}_B : \; \{e_i \vdash \overline{e_i} \mid i \geq 0\}$$

The contract $\mathcal{C} = \mathcal{C}_A \mid \mathcal{C}_B$ admits an agreement. We prove separately that A and B agree on $\mathcal{C}$. Let Σ_A^e be the eager strategy for A. Let σ be a fair play of $\mathcal{C}$ conform to Σ_A^e. We prove that A wins in σ. By Lemma 2, the strategy Σ_A^e makes A innocent in σ. There are two subcases. If B is not innocent in σ, then A wins. Otherwise, the play σ must be infinite, i.e. $\overline{\sigma} = \{e_i\}_{i \in \mathbb{N}} \cup \{\overline{e_i}\}_{i \in \mathbb{N}}$. Therefore, $R_A \subseteq \overline{\sigma}$, and so A wins. To prove that B has a winning strategy in $\mathcal{C}$ we proceed similarly, by choosing the eager strategy Σ_B^e for B.

We now show that $\mathcal{C}_A$ protects A. Let $\mathcal{C}'$ be compatible with $\mathcal{C}_A$. The eager strategy Σ_A^e is non-losing for A. Indeed, in every fair play σ conform to Σ_A^e, if there exists $\overline{e_i} \in R_A \not\subseteq \overline{\sigma}$ then $e_{i+1} \in O_A \not\in \overline{\sigma}$, and so $\Phi A \sigma \geq 0$. To prove that $\mathcal{C}_B$ protects B, we proceed similarly, by choosing the eager strategy Σ_B^e for B.   □

A remarkable feature of *finite* circular payoffs is that, in each play where all participants win, at some point there exists a participant A which has performed all the offers in O_A^i before having obtained all the requests in R_A^i. Intuitively, the participant A which makes this "first step" is not protected. The proof technique exploited by Lemma 5 is similar to that used in [11] to prove that fair exchange is impossible without a trusted third party.

Lemma 5. *Let $\mathcal{C}$ be a contract with finite circular O-R payoffs. If σ is a winning play for all participants in $\mathcal{A}$, then there exists a prefix η of σ and a participant $A \in \mathcal{A}$ such that $\Phi A \eta < 0$.*

Our main result in this section is Theorem 3 below. It states that if a set of contracts with finite circular O-R payoffs admits an agreement, then some of the participants are not protected, and *vice versa*.

Theorem 3. *Let $\mathcal{C}_1, \ldots, \mathcal{C}_n$ be contracts with circular finite O-R payoffs for $A_1, \ldots, A_n$, respectively. Then, at most one of the following statements is true:*

(a) $\mathcal{C}_1 \mid \cdots \mid \mathcal{C}_n$ admits an agreement;
(b) for all $i \in 1..n$, $\mathcal{C}_i$ protects A_i.

3   Reconciling Agreement with Protection

In the previous section we have shown that agreement and protection cannot coexist in a relevent class of contracts (Theorem 3). As made evident by Theorem 2, to protect herself A must obtain all her requests R_A^i before doing all her offers O_A^i. If all participants adhere to this principle, agreement is not possible. For instance, Alice and Bob in Ex. 1 would be protected by contracts with enablings $a \vdash b$ and $b \vdash a$, but no agreement would be possible because nobody risks doing the first step.

To reconcile agreements with protection, A could relax her contract, i.e. she could do a in change of the *promise* of B to do b. In this case A can safely do the first step, because either B does b, or he will be culpable of a contract violation.

To model this kind of "conditional" enabling, we propose an extension of Winskel's event structures with a new *circular causality* relation ($\Vdash$). The enabling $b \Vdash a$ (intuitively, "I will do a if you *promise* to do b") together with the other prescription $a \Vdash b$ has a configuration where both a and b have happened, despite of the circular dependencies. We call our extension *ES with circular causality* (CES in short).

In Sect. 3.1 we introduce CES and we state some basic properties. In Sect. 3.2 we reformulate our theory of contracts by using CES in place of ES. Finally, in Sect. 3.3 we show how CES allow for reconciling agreement with protection.

3.1   Event Structures with Circular Causality

Definition 16. *An event structure with circular causality is an ES enriched with a (saturated) circular enabling relation* $\Vdash \subseteq \{X \subseteq_{fin} E \mid CF(X)\} \times E$.

We conservatively extend the notion of configuration in [21] to deal with circular causality. Intuitively, for all events e_i in the sequence $\langle e_0 \cdots e_n \rangle$, e_i can either be $\vdash$-enabled by its predecessors, or $\Vdash$-enabled by the *whole* sequence. Note that if C is a finite configuration, and $\{e_0 \ldots e_n\}$ is an enumeration of C which satisfies all the enablings, not necessarily $\{e_0 \ldots e_{n-1}\}$ is a configuration as well (see *e.g.*, $\mathcal{E}_2$ in Fig. 1). To reason compositionally about configurations, Def. 17 defines a slightly more general notion of configurations.

In an *X-configuration* C, the set C can contain an event e even in the absence of a justification of e through a standard/circular enabling — provided that e belongs to X. This allows, given an X-configuration, to add/remove any event and obtain an Y-configuration, possibly with $Y \neq X$. We shall say that the events in X have been taken "on credit", to remark the fact that they may have been performed in the absence of a causal justification. Configurations (i.e., $\emptyset$-configurations) play a crucial role, as they represent sets of events where all the credits have been honoured.

Definition 17 (Configuration). *Let* $\mathcal{E} = (E, \#, \vdash, \Vdash)$ *be a CES. A conflict-free sequence* $\sigma = \langle e_0 \ldots e_n \rangle \in E^*$ *without repetitions is an X-trace of* $\mathcal{E}$ *iff:*

$$\forall i \leq n. \, (e_i \in X \ \vee \ \overline{\sigma_i} \vdash e_i \ \vee \ \overline{\sigma} \Vdash e_i)$$

For all $C, X \subseteq E$ *we say that* C *is an X-configuration of* $\mathcal{E}$ *iff* $CF(C)$ *and:*

$$\forall e \in C. \, \exists \sigma \ X\text{-trace.} \ e \in \overline{\sigma} \subseteq C$$

The set of all X-configurations of $\mathcal{E}$ *is denoted by* $\mathcal{F}_{\mathcal{E}}(X)$, *or just* $\mathcal{F}_{\mathcal{E}}$ *when* $X = \emptyset$.

Example 12. Consider the four CES in Fig. 1.

(1) $\mathcal{E}_1$ has enablings $\emptyset \vdash a$, $\emptyset \Vdash b$, and conflict $a\#b$. By Def. 17 we have $\emptyset, \{a\}, \{b\} \in \mathcal{F}_{\mathcal{E}_1}$, but $\{a, b\} \notin \mathcal{F}_{\mathcal{E}_1}$.
(2) $\mathcal{E}_2$ has enablings $\{a\} \vdash b$ and $\{b\} \Vdash a$. Here $\emptyset, \{a, b\} \in \mathcal{F}_{\mathcal{E}_2}$, $\{b\} \in \mathcal{F}_{\mathcal{E}_2}(\{b\})$ and $\{a\} \in \mathcal{F}_{\mathcal{E}_2}(\{a\})$, while neither $\{a\}$ nor $\{b\}$ belong to $\mathcal{F}_{\mathcal{E}_2}(\emptyset)$.
(3) $\mathcal{E}_3$ has enablings $\{a\} \vdash b$, $\{a\} \vdash c$, $\{b\} \Vdash a$, $\{c\} \vdash a$, and conflict $b\#c$. The only non-empty configuration of $\mathcal{E}_3$ is $\{a, b\}$.

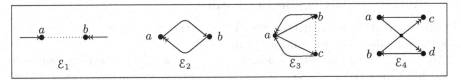

Fig. 1. CES are denoted as directed hypergraphs, where nodes stand for events. An hyperedge from a set of nodes X to node e denotes an enabling $X \circ e$, where $\circ = \vdash$ if the edge has a single arrow, and $\circ = \Vdash$ if the edge has a double arrow. A conflict $a\#b$ is represented by a dotted line between a and b.

(4) $\mathcal{E}_4$ has enablings $\{a,b\} \Vdash c$, $\{a,b\} \Vdash d$, $\{c\} \vdash a$, and $\{d\} \vdash b$. We have that $\{a,b,c,d\} \in \mathcal{F}_{\mathcal{E}_4}$. Note that, were one (or both) of the $\Vdash$ turned into a $\vdash$, then the only configuration would have been the empty one.   □

According to Winskel's axiom of finite causes, all events in a configuration (except those taken on credit) have a finite justification. Thus, an event cannot be justified through an infinite chain of events, i.e. in the CES with enablings $\{e_{i+1}\} \Vdash e_i$ for all $i \geq 0$, the set $\{e_i \mid i \geq 0\}$ is *not* a configuration.

The configurations of CES do still enjoy the finiteness and coherence properties of classical ES, though they are not coincidence-free, which is correct from our point of view because of the presence of circular dependencies. A subset A of a set F is *pairwise compatible* iff $\forall e, e' \in \bigcup A.\ \exists C \in F.\ e, e' \in C$.

Theorem 4. *For all CES $\mathcal{E}$, and for all $X \subseteq E$, the set $\mathcal{F}_{\mathcal{E}}(X)$ satisfies:*

- *(Coherence) If F is a pairwise compatible subset of $\mathcal{F}_{\mathcal{E}}(X)$, then $\bigcup F \in \mathcal{F}$.*
- *(Finiteness) $\forall C \in \mathcal{F}.\ \forall e \in C.\ \exists C_0 \in \mathcal{F}.\ e \in C_0 \subseteq_{fin} C$*

We define below an operational semantics of CES. This is given in terms of an LTS, the states of which are pairs (C, X). The first element is the set of events occurred so far; the second element is a set of events taken "on credit".

Definition 18 (LTS of a CES). *For a CES $\mathcal{E}$, we define $\mathrm{LTS}_{\mathcal{E}} = \langle S, E, \rightarrow_{\mathcal{E}} \rangle$, where $S = \wp_{fin}(E) \times \wp_{fin}(E)$, and $\rightarrow_{\mathcal{E}}$ is defined by the following rule:*

$$\frac{e \notin C \qquad CF(C \cup \{e\})}{(C,X) \xrightarrow{e}_{\mathcal{E}} (C \cup \{e\}, \Delta(C,X,e))}$$

where for all $C, X \subseteq E$ and for all $e \in E$, we define:

$$\Delta(C,X,e) = (X \setminus \{x \in X \mid C \cup \{e\} \Vdash x\}) \cup \begin{cases} \{e\} & \text{if } C \cup \{e\} \not\Vdash e \wedge C \not\vdash e \\ \emptyset & \text{otherwise} \end{cases}$$

The set $\Delta(C, X, e)$ defines how credits change when firing e in a play where the current credits are X, and the events C have already been performed.

The following theorem relates traces of $\mathrm{LTS}_{\mathcal{E}}$ to configurations of $\mathcal{E}$.

Theorem 5. *For all CES $\mathcal{E}$, for all $C, X \subseteq E$:*

$$C \in \mathcal{F}(X) \iff \forall D \subseteq_{fin} C.\ \exists X_0 \subseteq X.\ \exists C_0.\ D \subseteq C_0 \subseteq C \wedge (\emptyset, \emptyset) \rightarrow^* (C_0, X_0)$$

3.2   Agreement in CES-Based Contracts

In this section we conservatively extend the contract theory of Sect. 2, by allowing the component $\mathcal{E}$ of a contract to be a CES.

By Def. 18, a conflict-free sequence $\langle e_0\, e_1 \cdots \rangle$ without repetitions uniquely identifies a trace $(\emptyset, \emptyset) \xrightarrow{e_0}_{\mathcal{E}} (C_1, X_1) \xrightarrow{e_1}_{\mathcal{E}} \cdots$ in $\mathrm{LTS}_{\mathcal{E}}$. We denote with $(C_k^{\sigma}, X_k^{\sigma})$ the state of $\mathrm{LTS}_{\mathcal{E}}$ reached after k steps of the sequence σ. A *play* of a contract $\mathcal{C}$ is a (finite or infinite) sequence σ of events such that $(\emptyset, \emptyset) \xrightarrow{\sigma}_{\mathcal{E}}$. The notions of *strategy* and *conformance* to a strategy are as in Sect. 2.

The key difference between ES-based and CES-based contracts is the notion of innocence. In the ES-based model, a participant A is culpable in a play σ when some event e of A is enabled in σ. Here, in addition to enabled events, we consider obligations those events which can be done "on credit", under the guarantee that they will be eventually honoured, whatever events are done later on by the other participants. These events are said *prudent*. The definition of prudent strategies and of innocent participants is mutually coinductive. A participant A is innocent in σ when she has no persistently prudent events. Hence, if the strategy of A tells to do all her prudent events, then in all fair plays these events must either become imprudent, or be fired, or be conflicted. Formally (although a bit counter-intuitively), fired and conflicted events are imprudent: therefore, A is innocent when all her prudent events eventually become imprudent.

Definition 19 (Prudence). *A strategy Σ for A is* prudent *if, for all finite plays σ, for all $e \in \Sigma(\sigma)$ such that σe conforms to Σ, and for all fair plays $\sigma' = \sigma e \eta$ conform to Σ where all $B \neq A$ are innocent,*

$$\exists k > |\sigma|.\ X_k^{\sigma'} \cap \pi^{-1}(A) \subseteq X_{|\sigma|}^{\sigma'}$$

An event e is prudent in σ *if there exists a prudent strategy Σ such that σ conforms to Σ and $e \in \Sigma(\sigma)$.*
A participant A is innocent in $\sigma = \langle e_0\, e_1 \cdots \rangle$ *iff:*

$$\forall e \in \pi^{-1}(A).\ \forall i \geq 0.\ \exists j \geq i.\ e \text{ is imprudent in } \sigma_j$$

Example 13. Recall the CES from Ex. 12. In $\mathcal{E}_1$, both a and b are prudent in the empty play ε, because they are enabled in $\emptyset$. In $\mathcal{E}_2$, a is prudent in ε, while b is *not* prudent in ε, yet it is prudent in $\langle a \rangle$. Now consider the CES $\mathcal{E}_3$, and assume that $\pi(a) = A$ and $\pi(b) = \pi(c) = B$. We have that a is *not* prudent in ε, because if B chooses to do c, then the credit a can no longer be honoured. Instead, both b and c are prudent in $\langle a \rangle$.

Notice that, after Lemma 6 below, the new definition of innocence conservatively extends that in Def. 10. That is, an event enabled in σ is prudent.

Lemma 6. *For all σ and $e \notin \overline{\sigma}$, if $\overline{\sigma} \vdash e$ or $\overline{\sigma} \cup \{e\} \Vdash e$ then e is prudent in σ.*

Lemma 7. *Let $\mathcal{S}$ be a finite set of prudent strategies. Then, $\bigsqcup \mathcal{S}$ is prudent.*

Lemma 8. *For a contract $\mathcal{C} = \langle \mathcal{E}, \cdots \rangle$, where $\mathcal{E}$ is a finite CES, the strategy $\Sigma_A^p = \lambda \sigma.\ \{e \in \pi^{-1}(A) \mid e \text{ is prudent in } \sigma\}$ is the greatest prudent strategy for A.*

Lemma 9. Σ_A^p *is an innocent strategy for* A.

For a CES $\mathcal{E}$ and a set of events C, we say that e is *reachable from C* iff there exists η such that $e \in \overline{\eta}$ and $(C, \emptyset) \xrightarrow{\eta} (C', \emptyset)$. Theorem 6 states that in conflict-free CES which have only circular enablings, the set of prudent events in σ coincides with the set $\mathcal{R}_{\mathcal{E}}^{\overline{\sigma}}$ of events reachable from $\overline{\sigma}$.

Theorem 6. *If $\mathcal{E}$ is conflict-free and $\vdash$-free, then for all plays σ of $\mathcal{C} = \langle \mathcal{E}, \cdots \rangle$:*

$$e \in \mathcal{R}_{\mathcal{E}}^{\overline{\sigma}} \iff e \text{ prudent in } \sigma$$

We now refine the notion of winning strategy given in Def. 11. The items are similar to the corresponding items in Def. 11, except that the definitions of innocence now takes into account the events performed on credit.

Definition 20 (Winning play). *Define the function $\widetilde{W}$ as follows:*

$$\widetilde{W}A\sigma = \begin{cases} \Phi A\sigma & A \text{ is credit-free and all participants are innocent in } \sigma \\ +1 & \text{if } A \text{ is innocent, and some } B \neq A \text{ is culpable in } \sigma \\ -1 & \text{otherwise} \end{cases}$$

where we say that A *is* credit-free *in* σ *iff*

$$\forall e \in \pi^{-1}(A). \ \forall i \geq 0. \ \exists j \geq i. \ e \notin X_j^{\sigma}$$

The notions of winning/losing play/strategy, agreement and protection are the same as in Sect. 2, except that $\widetilde{W}$ is now used in place of $\mathcal{W}$.

Lemma 10. *Let Σ_A be a prudent strategy for* A. *For all fair plays σ conform to Σ_A, either* A *is credit-free in σ, or some* B $\neq$ A *is culpable in σ.*

Example 14. In Ex. 9 we have shown that the contract $\mathcal{C}_A$ protects Alice, while $\mathcal{C}_B$ does not protect Bob. Suppose now to change Bob's contract into a contract $\mathcal{C}_B'$ where Bob relaxes his requirements. The contract $\mathcal{C}_B'$ differs from $\mathcal{C}_B$ only in the event structure $\mathcal{E}_B'$, which contains exactly one circular enabling: $\{a\} \Vdash b$. Similarly to Ex. 4, the contract $\mathcal{C}_A \mid \mathcal{C}_B'$ admits an agreement. To show that, let Σ_A and Σ_B be the following strategies for A and B, respectively:

$$\Sigma_A(\sigma) = \begin{cases} \{a\} & \text{if } b \in \overline{\sigma} \text{ and } a \notin \overline{\sigma} \\ \emptyset & \text{otherwise} \end{cases} \qquad \Sigma_B(\sigma) = \begin{cases} \{b\} & \text{if } b \notin \overline{\sigma} \\ \emptyset & \text{otherwise} \end{cases}$$

Roughly, the only fair play which conforms to Σ_A and Σ_B where both A and B are innocent is $\sigma = \langle ba \rangle$, which gives rise to the following trace in LTS$_{\mathcal{E}}$:

$$(\emptyset, \emptyset) \xrightarrow{b} (\{b\}, \{b\}) \xrightarrow{a} (\{a, b\}, \emptyset)$$

We have that A and B win in σ, because $\widetilde{W}A\sigma = 1 = \widetilde{W}B\sigma$. Thus, Σ_A and Σ_B are winning strategies for A and B, respectively, and so $\mathcal{C}$ admits an agreement. $\square$

3.3   Protection in CES-Based Contracts

In this section we show that CES-based contracts allow for both agreements and protection in contracts with circular finite O-R payoffs. Before presenting the formal results, we give some intuition through our working example.

Example 15. Differently from the contract $\mathcal{C}_B$ in Ex. 9, the contract $\mathcal{C}'_B$ in Ex. 14 protects Bob. Let $\mathcal{C}'$ be a contract compatible with $\mathcal{C}'_B$. Consider the strategy Σ^p_B for B, as defined in Lemma 9. Let ν be a fair play of $\mathcal{C}'_B \mid \mathcal{C}'$ conform to Σ^p_B. By contradiction, assume that B loses in ν. By Lemma 9, B is innocent in ν, and so it must be $\Phi B \nu < 0$. By definition, the payoff of B is negative only when $b \in \overline{\nu}$ and $a \notin \overline{\nu}$. Assume that $\nu = \eta\,b\,\eta'$. By definition of Σ^p_B, the event b was prudent in η, and we have the transition $(\overline{\eta}, X^0) \xrightarrow{b} (\overline{\eta} \cup \{b\}, X^0 \cup \{b\})$. After B has performed b, its only strategy is the empty one. By Def. 19, for all plays $e_0 e_1 \cdots$ starting from $(\overline{\eta} \cup \{b\}, X^0 \cup \{b\})$, there exists some $k > 0$ such that $b \notin X^k$. This means that b has been honoured, and the only way to do that is to perform a. Therefore, $a \in \overline{\nu}$ — contradiction.   □

We now construct a CES from an O-R payoff with finite responses. For all clauses (O, R), the CES contains the enablings $R \Vdash O$. Lemma 11 below reveals a key feature of circularity: the CES obtained from a circular O-R payoff has a configuration which comprises all the responses of all participants. Together with Theorem 7, this will allow for constructing a contract which admits an agreement. Theorems 7 and 8 are the CES counterpart of Theorems 1 and 2 for ES-based contracts, respectively.

Definition 21. *For an O-R payoff Φ with clauses $(O^i, R^i)_i$ and finite R^i, define $\mathcal{E}(\Phi)$ as the conflict-free CES with (saturated) enablings $\{R^i \Vdash O^i\}_i$.*

Lemma 11. *Let Φ be a finite circular O-R payoff for $\mathcal{A}$ such that $\Phi A = \lambda\sigma.\,\phi_A\overline{\sigma}$ for all $A \in \mathcal{A}$. Then, $\exists C \in \mathcal{F}_{\mathcal{E}(\Phi)}.\ \forall A \in \mathcal{A}.\ \bigcup_i R^i_A \subseteq C$.*

Theorem 7. *Let $\mathcal{C}$ be a contract with O-R payoff for A. If $\mathcal{E}$ is conflict-free and $\vdash$-free, and $\bigcup_i R^i_A \subseteq C$ for some $C \in \mathcal{F}_{\mathcal{E}}$, then A agrees on $\mathcal{C}$.*

Theorem 8. *For a finite CES $\mathcal{E}$ and an O-R payoffs Φ for A, the contract $\langle \mathcal{E}, \mathcal{A}, \pi, \Phi \rangle$ protects A if: $\forall i, Y.\ (\forall e \in O^i_A.\ Y \vdash e \lor Y \Vdash e) \implies R^i_A \subseteq Y$.*

Theorem 9 below states that agreements and protection can coexist in CES-based contracts with circular finite O-R payoffs. Recall that Theorem 3 excluded this possibility for ES-based contracts. Condition (5) in Theorem 9 is technical, yet it makes the theorem applicable to a broad class of contracts with O-R payoffs (e.g. the dining retailers scenario, see Ex. 17). Ex. 16 shows that when condition (5) is not satisfied, Theorem 9 does not hold in general.

Theorem 9. *Let $\Phi_1, \ldots, \Phi_n$ be finite circular O-R payoffs for $A_1, \ldots, A_n$, respectively, and such that, for all $A \in \{A_1, \ldots, A_n\}$:*

$$\forall P \subseteq \mathbb{N}.\ \forall j.\ O^j_A \subseteq \bigcup_{i \in P} O^i_A \implies R^j_A \subseteq \bigcup_{i \in P} R^i_A \tag{5}$$

Then, there exist contracts $\mathcal{C}_i = \langle \mathcal{E}_i, \mathcal{A}, \pi, \Phi_i \rangle$ for $i \in 1..n$ such that:

(a) $\mathcal{C}_1 \mid \cdots \mid \mathcal{C}_n$ admits an agreement;
(b) for all $i \in 1..n$, $\mathcal{C}_i$ protects A_i;
(c) for all plays σ of $\mathcal{C}_1 \mid \cdots \mid \mathcal{C}_n$, $\forall e \in \overline{\sigma}.\ \exists i.\ e \in O^i_{\pi(e)}$.

Example 16. Consider the O-R payoff Φ_A of participant A defined by:

$$O^0 = \{a_0, a_1\} \quad\quad O^1 = \{a_1, a_2\} \quad\quad O^2 = \{a_0, a_2\}$$
$$R^0 = \{b_0\} \quad\quad\quad R^1 = \{b_1\} \quad\quad\quad R^2 = \{b_0, b_1\}$$

Condition (5) of Theorem 9 is satisfied, hence the contract with CES $\mathcal{E}(\Phi_A)$ protects A, and allows A to reach an agreement with other participants whenever the overall payoff satisfies the conditions of the theorem.

Suppose now to change Φ_A, by requiring $R^2 = \{b_2\}$. Notice that such modified payoff no longer satisfies condition (5). Indeed, by choosing $P = \{0, 1\}$ and $j = 2$ we have that $\{a_0, a_2\} = O^2 \subseteq O^0 \cup O^1$, but $\{b_2\} = R^2 \not\subseteq R^0 \cup R^1$. So, Theorem 9 does not apply. The CES $\mathcal{E}(\Phi_A)$ contains the enablings $\{b_0\} \Vdash \{a_0, a_1\}$, $\{b_1\} \Vdash \{a_1, a_2\}$, and $\{b_2\} \Vdash \{a_0, a_2\}$. Now A is *not* protected. Indeed, an attacker B could perform b_0 and b_1 to oblige A to do a_0, a_1, a_2. A would lose, because to be innocent she has to do all the offers in O^2, but doing so she is not guaranteed to obtain R^2. As a matter of facts, there exists no CES which guarantees both agreement and protection for the payoff Φ_A. □

Example 17. Recall the dining retailers scenario from Ex. 10. The payoff Φ_i of each retailer is a finite O-R circular payoff, and condition (5) is trivially satisfied. Therefore, Theorem 9 allows for constructing contracts which admit an agreement and protects all retailers. The CES of contract $\mathcal{C}_i$ of retailer A_i has enablings $\{e_{j,i} \mid i \neq j\} \Vdash \{e_{i,j} \mid i \neq j\}$. The idea is simple: A_1 offers his pieces of cutlery, in exchange of the commitment of the other retailers to do the same. Since all retailers commit to the analogous contract, we have an agreement. □

4 Related Work and Conclusions

We have studied contracts from a foundational perspective. Our formalisation of contracts builds upon a very abstract model of concurrent computations, namely event structures, to provide general notions of agreement and protection. We expect that specific formalisations of agreement, e.g. the one in [8], can be interpreted as instances of our general notion, in the same spirit that event structures can provide semantics to more concrete models of concurrency, e.g. CCS, π-calculus and Petri nets [21].

An abstract model of contracts is fundamental for the development of the contract-oriented paradigm. In addition to the possibility of relating different formalisations of contracts, such an abstract model would also allow for reasoning uniformly about the properties of contract-based systems. For instance, the static/dynamic notions of *honesty* of a process, which in [4] were specific for the contracts of [8], could be generalised to a broader class of contracts.

Aiming at generality, we have almost neglected some relevant issues, e.g. devising efficient decision procedures for agreements. Although in the most general setting (infinite event structures, arbitrary payoff functions) we come up against the problem of undecidability, such kind of results can be obtained by considering suitable subclasses of event structures/payoff functions (e.g. model checking temporal logic on finite representations of infinite event structures, as in [18]).

A heterogeneous ecosystem of formalisms for contracts has appeared in the literature. Citing a few recent approaches, these formalisms include logics [5,19], behavioural types [6,8], Petri nets [20], multi-player games [13], domain-specific languages [16], c-semirings [7], *etc.*

Most of the existing models do not explicitly deal with the circularity issue, which instead has been a main subject of study in this paper. An exception is [5], where circularity is dealt with at a proof-theoretic level. The logic PCL presented in [5] extends propositional intuitionistic logic with a new connective, that weakens the standard implication →, somehow similarly to the way our ⊩ weakens the standard enabling ⊢. CES and PCL are strongly related: preliminary results suggest that finite conflict-free CES correspond to Horn PCL formulae.

In [2] some preliminary work on event structures with circular causality is presented. In the simplified model of [2], where event structures are finite and conflict-free, and the goals are O-R payoffs without offers, it is shown how to decide agreements through an encoding of event structures into PCL formulae.

In [14] event structures are extended with a *response* relation. A relation $a \bullet\!\!\rightarrow b$ models the fact that, whenever event a is present in a trace, then b must eventually occur after a. This is quite different from a circular enabling $a \Vdash b$, which instead does not impose any ordering between a and b (it suffices that b is honoured somehow). Also, augmenting the number of ⊩-enablings increases the number of configurations, while adding more response relations reduces it.

Liability issues are the focus of [16,12]. Given a contract and an execution trace, the problem is to establish evidence about the occurrence of a contract violation, and in particular to assign blame to misbehaving participants. While [16,12] are not concerned about how an agreement is found (they just consider the contract as already agreed upon), they explore issues not explicitly modelled in our framework. The notion of liability in [16] takes into account time constraints. Extending our contract model with temporal deadlines and, more in general, with quantitative aspects (like e.g. probabilities) seems to be feasible, along the lines of analogous extensions of events structures [17].

Our model adopts a draconian notion of innocence, in that a participant omitting to perform a single due event in a play is considered culpable, regardless of the fact that the other participants could equally be satisfied with that play. Establishing finer-grained notions of causality between a violation and the resulting failure, as done e.g. in [12], seems a plausible extension of our work.

Our notion of winning play (Def. 11 and Def. 20) is a sort of lexicographic objective, similarly to those in [10]. The secure equilibria introduced in [10] require that a player cannot increase her payoff while decreasing the payoff of the other player. This is stronger than our notion of agreement, where we just require that strategies exist which yield a positive payoff for all players. Indeed, such strategies do not even have to form a Nash equilibrium.

Acknowledgments. Work partially supported by Aut. Region of Sardinia under grants L.R.7/2007 CRP2-120 (TESLA), CRP-17285 (TRICS), P.I.A. 2010 Project "Social Glue", and by MIUR PRIN 2010-11 project "Security Horizons".

References

1. Armbrust, M., et al.: A view of cloud computing. Comm. ACM 53(4), 50–58 (2010)
2. Bartoletti, M., Cimoli, T., Pinna, G.M., Zunino, R.: An event-based model for contracts. In: Proc. PLACES (2012)
3. Bartoletti, M., Tuosto, E., Zunino, R.: Contract-oriented computing in CO_2. Scientific Annals in Computer Science 22(1), 5–60 (2012)
4. Bartoletti, M., Tuosto, E., Zunino, R.: On the Realizability of Contracts in Dishonest Systems. In: Sirjani, M. (ed.) COORDINATION 2012. LNCS, vol. 7274, pp. 245–260. Springer, Heidelberg (2012)
5. Bartoletti, M., Zunino, R.: A calculus of contracting processes. In: LICS (2010)
6. Bravetti, M., Zavattaro, G.: Towards a Unifying Theory for Choreography Conformance and Contract Compliance. In: Lumpe, M., Vanderperren, W. (eds.) SC 2007. LNCS, vol. 4829, pp. 34–50. Springer, Heidelberg (2007)
7. Buscemi, M.G., Montanari, U.: CC-Pi: A Constraint-Based Language for Specifying Service Level Agreements. In: De Nicola, R. (ed.) ESOP 2007. LNCS, vol. 4421, pp. 18–32. Springer, Heidelberg (2007)
8. Castagna, G., Gesbert, N., Padovani, L.: A theory of contracts for web services. ACM Transactions on Programming Languages and Systems 31(5) (2009)
9. Chatterjee, K., Henzinger, T.A.: A survey of stochastic ω-regular games. J. Comput. Syst. Sci. 78(2), 394–413 (2012)
10. Chatterjee, K., Henzinger, T.A., Jurdzinski, M.: Games with secure equilibria. Theor. Comput. Sci. 365(1-2), 67–82 (2006)
11. Even, S., Yacobi, Y.: Relations among public key signature systems. Technical Report 175, Computer Science Department, Technion, Haifa (1980)
12. Gössler, G., Le Métayer, D., Raclet, J.-B.: Causality Analysis in Contract Violation. In: Barringer, H., Falcone, Y., Finkbeiner, B., Havelund, K., Lee, I., Pace, G., Roşu, G., Sokolsky, O., Tillmann, N. (eds.) RV 2010. LNCS, vol. 6418, pp. 270–284. Springer, Heidelberg (2010)
13. Henriksen, A.S.: Adversarial Models for Cooperative Interactions. PhD thesis, Department of Computer Science, University of Copenhagen (2011)
14. Hildebrandt, T.T., Mukkamala, R.R.: Declarative event-based workflow as distributed dynamic condition response graphs. In: Proc. PLACES (2010)
15. Honda, K., Yoshida, N., Carbone, M.: Multiparty asynchronous session types. In: POPL (2008)
16. Hvitved, T., Klaedtke, F., Zălinescu, E.: A trace-based model for multiparty contracts. JLAP 81(2), 72–98 (2012)
17. Katoen, J.-P.: Quantitative and qualitative extensions of event structures. PhD thesis, University of Twente (1996)
18. Penczek, W.: Model-Checking for a Subclass of Event Structures. In: Brinksma, E. (ed.) TACAS 1997. LNCS, vol. 1217, pp. 145–164. Springer, Heidelberg (1997)
19. Prisacariu, C., Schneider, G.: A Formal Language for Electronic Contracts. In: Bonsangue, M.M., Johnsen, E.B. (eds.) FMOODS 2007. LNCS, vol. 4468, pp. 174–189. Springer, Heidelberg (2007)
20. van der Aalst, W.M.P., Lohmann, N., Massuthe, P., Stahl, C., Wolf, K.: Multiparty contracts: Agreeing and implementing interorganizational processes. Comput. J. 53(1), 90–106 (2010)
21. Winskel, G.: Event Structures. In: Brauer, W., Reisig, W., Rozenberg, G. (eds.) APN 1986. LNCS, vol. 255, pp. 325–392. Springer, Heidelberg (1987)

Computational Soundness of Symbolic Zero-Knowledge Proofs: Weaker Assumptions and Mechanized Verification

Michael Backes[1,2], Fabian Bendun[1], and Dominique Unruh[3]

[1] Saarland University, Saarbrücken, Germany
{backes,bendun}@cs.uni-saarland.de
[2] MPI-SWS, Saarbrücken, Germany
[3] University of Tartu, Tartu, Estonia
unruh@ut.ee

Abstract. The abstraction of cryptographic operations by term algebras, called symbolic models, is essential in almost all tool-supported
methods for analyzing security protocols. Significant progress was made
in proving that symbolic models offering basic cryptographic operations
such as encryption and digital signatures can be sound with respect
to actual cryptographic realizations and security definitions. Even abstractions of sophisticated modern cryptographic primitives such as zero-
knowledge (ZK) proofs were shown to have a computationally sound
cryptographic realization, but only in ad-hoc formalisms and at the cost
of placing strong assumptions on the underlying cryptography, which
leaves only highly inefficient realizations.

In this paper, we make two contributions to this problem space. First,
we identify weaker cryptographic assumptions that we show to be sufficient for computational soundness of symbolic ZK proofs. These weaker
assumptions are fulfilled by existing efficient ZK schemes as well as generic
ZK constructions. Second, we conduct all computational soundness proofs
in CoSP, a recent framework that allows for casting computational soundness proofs in a modular manner, independent of the underlying symbolic
calculi. Moreover, all computational soundness proofs conducted in CoSP
automatically come with mechanized proof support through an embedding of the applied π-calculus.

1 Introduction

Proofs of security protocols are known to be error-prone and, owing to the
distributed-system aspects of multiple interleaved protocol runs, awkward for
humans to make. Hence work towards the automation of such proofs started
soon after the first protocols were developed. From the start, the actual cryptographic operations in such proofs were idealized into so-called symbolic models,
following [18, 19, 29], e.g., see [23, 33, 1, 26, 11]. This idealization simplifies proof
construction by freeing proofs from cryptographic details such as computational
restrictions, probabilistic behavior, and error probabilities. It was not at all clear

D. Basin and J.C. Mitchell (Eds.): POST 2013, LNCS 7796, pp. 206–225, 2013.
© Springer-Verlag Berlin Heidelberg 2013

whether symbolic models are a sound abstraction from real cryptography with its computational security definitions. Existing work has largely bridged this gap for symbolic models offering the core cryptographic operations such as encryption and digital signatures, e.g., see [2, 9, 24, 30, 16, 14].

While symbolic models traditionally comprised only basic cryptographic operations, recent work has started to extend them to more sophisticated primitives with unique security features that go far beyond the traditional goal of cryptography to solely offer secrecy and authenticity of communication. Zero-knowledge (ZK) proofs[1] constitute arguably the most prominent such primitive. This primitive's unique security features, combined with the recent advent of efficient cryptographic implementations of this primitive for special classes of problems, have paved the way for its deployment in modern applications. For instance, ZK proofs can guarantee authentication yet preserve the anonymity of protocol participants, as in the Civitas electronic voting protocol [15] or the Pseudo Trust protocol [27], or they can prove the reception of a certificate from a trusted server without revealing the actual content, as in the Direct Anonymous Attestation (DAA) protocol [13]. More recently, ZK proofs have been used to develop novel schemes for anonymous webs of trust [5] as well as privacy-aware proof-carrying authorization [28].

A symbolic abstraction of (non-interactive) ZK proofs has been put forward in [7]. The proposed abstraction is suitable for mechanized proofs [7, 4] and was already successfully used to produce the first fully mechanized proof of central properties of the DAA protocol. A computational soundness result for such symbolic ZK proofs has recently been achieved as well [10]. However, this work imposes strong assumptions on the underlying cryptographic implementation of zero-knowledge proofs: Among other properties, the zero-knowledge proof is required to satisfy the notion of extraction zero-knowledge; so far, only one (inefficient) scheme is known that fulfills this notion [22]. Thus the vast number of recently proposed, far more efficient zero-knowledge schemes, and particularly those schemes that stem from generic ZK constructions, are not comprised by this result. Hence they do not serve as sound instantiations of symbolic zero-knowledge proofs, leaving all actually deployed ZK protocols without any computational soundness guarantee. In addition, the result in [10] casts symbolic ZK proofs within an ad-hoc formalism that is not accessible to existing formal proof tools.

1.1 Our Contribution

In this paper, we make the following two contributions to this problem space:

- First, we identify weaker cryptographic assumptions that we show to be sufficient for obtaining a computational soundness result for symbolic ZK proofs.

---

[1] A zero-knowledge proof [20] consists of a message or a sequence of messages that combines two seemingly contradictory properties: First, it constitutes a proof of a statement x (e.g, $x =$ "the message within this ciphertext begins with 0") that cannot be forged, i.e., it is impossible, or at least computationally infeasible, to produce a zero-knowledge proof of a wrong statement. Second, a zero-knowledge proof does not reveal any information besides the bare fact that x constitutes a valid statement.

Essentially, we show that the strong notion of extraction zero-knowledge required in [10] can be replaced by the weaker notion of simulation-sound extractability. In contrast to extraction zero-knowledge, simulation-sound extractability constitutes an established property that many existing cryptographic constructions satisfy. In particular, there exist generic constructions for transforming any non-interactive ZK proof into a ZK proof that satisfies simulation-sound extractability (and the remaining properties that we impose for computational soundness) [31], as well as several efficient schemes that are known to satisfy simulation-sound extractability (and the remaining properties), e.g., [25, 21, 32]. Thus requiring simulation-sound extractability instead of extraction zero-knowledge greatly extends the pool of cryptographic constructions for ZK proofs that constitute sound implementations, and it for the first time enables the computationally sound deployment of efficient ZK realizations.

- Second, we conduct all computational soundness proofs in CoSP [3], a recent framework that allows for casting computational soundness proofs in a conceptually modular and generic way: proving x cryptographic primitives sound for y calculi only requires $x + y$ proofs (instead of $x \cdot y$ proofs without this framework), and the process of embedding calculi is conceptually decoupled from computational soundness proofs of cryptographic primitives. In particular, computational soundness proofs conducted in CoSP are automatically valid for the applied π-calculus, and hence accessible to existing mechanized verification techniques.

  The conduction in CoSP has the drawback that the computational soundness is shown for trace properties. However, trace properties are sufficient to verify weak anonymity. Consequently, we can show central properties of the DAA protocol.

1.2 Outline of the Paper

First, we introduce our symbolic abstraction of (non-interactive) ZK proofs within CoSP in Section 2. Section 3 contains the weaker cryptographic assumptions that we show to be sufficient for achieving computational soundness of ZK proofs. Our main theorem is presented in Section 4 for which we give a proof overview in Section 5. Section 6 concludes and outlines future work.

2   Symbolic Model for Zero-Knowledge

In this section, we describe our symbolic abstraction of zero-knowledge proofs.

Terms and Constructors. We model nonces, probabilistic public-key encryption and signatures, pairs, strings, and zero-knowledge proofs. Except for the latter, our modeling closely follows that of [3]. The following grammar describes the set **T** of all terms that may occur in the symbolic model:

$$\mathbf{T} ::= \text{enc}(\text{ek}(N), t, N) \mid \text{ek}(N) \mid \text{dk}(N) \mid \text{sig}(\text{sk}(N), t, N) \mid \text{vk}(N) \mid \text{sk}(N) \mid$$
$$\text{crs}(N) \mid \text{ZK}(\text{crs}(N), t, t, N) \mid \text{pair}(t, t) \mid S \mid N \mid$$
$$\text{garbage}(N) \mid \text{garbageEnc}(t, N) \mid \text{garbageSig}(t, N) \mid \text{garbageZK}(t, t, N)$$
$$S ::= \text{empty} \mid \text{string}_0(S) \mid \text{string}_1(S)$$

Here N represents nonces and ranges over $\mathbf{N}_P \cup \mathbf{N}_E$, two disjoint infinite sets of nonces, the protocol nonces and adversary nonces, respectively. $\text{ek}(N), \text{dk}(N)$, $\text{vk}(N), \text{sk}(N)$ represent encryption, decryption, verification, and signing keys. $\text{enc}(\text{ek}(N_1), t, N_2)$ represents an encryption under public key $\text{ek}(N_1)$ of plaintext t using algorithmic randomness N_2. (Symbolically, the algorithmic randomness just allows to distinguish different encryptions of the same plaintext; computationally, it will actually be the randomness used by the encryption algorithm.) $\text{sig}(\text{sk}(N_1), t, N_2)$ is a signature of t under signing key $\text{sk}(N_1)$ with algorithmic randomness N_2. Bitstrings can be expressed using terms matching the nonterminal S. $\text{garbage}(N)$ represents invalid terms, $\text{garbageEnc}(t, N)$ and $\text{garbageSig}(t, N)$ represent invalid encryptions and signatures (but which at a first glance seem to be valid encryptions/signatures with public key t).

Zero-Knowledge Proofs. The interesting part are the zero-knowledge proofs. To understand the meaning of a term $\text{ZK}(\text{crs}(N), x, w, M)$, we first need to introduce the relation $R_{\text{adv}}^{\text{sym}}$. This relation is part of the symbolic modeling, but all our results are parametric in $R_{\text{adv}}^{\text{sym}}$. (I.e., our result holds for any choice of $R_{\text{adv}}^{\text{sym}}$, as long as $R_{\text{adv}}^{\text{sym}}$ satisfies certain constraints.) $R_{\text{adv}}^{\text{sym}}$ specifies what a valid witness for a particular statement would be. For example, if we wish to show that we know a decryption key w that decrypts a given ciphertext x, then we define $R_{\text{adv}}^{\text{sym}} := \{(x, w) : \exists N, M, t.x = \text{enc}(\text{ek}(N), t, M), w = \text{dk}(N)\}$.[2] The term $\text{ZK}(\text{crs}(N), x, w, M)$ then represents a zero-knowledge proof constructed with respect to a common reference string $\text{crs}(N)$ with statement x and witness w and using algorithmic randomness M. A valid proof satisfies $(x, w) \in R_{\text{adv}}^{\text{sym}}$. Note that our symbolic model does not ensure that any term $\text{ZK}(\text{crs}(N), x, w, M)$ is a valid proof. Instead, we provide a destructor $\text{verify}_{\text{ZK}}$ below that allows to check the validity. As we will see below, the statement x can be extracted from a proof, but the witness w is hidden.

Destructors. Protocol operations on terms are described by a set of destructors. These are partial functions from $\mathbf{T}^n$ to $\mathbf{T}$ (where n depends on the destructor). The destructors are specified in Figure 1. Note that there are a number of destructors that do not modify their input ($\text{isek}, \text{iszk}, \text{equals}, \dots$). These are useful for testing properties of terms: The protocol can, e.g., compute $\text{isek}(t)$ and then branch depending on whether the destructor succeeds. We only describe the destructors related to ZK proofs. $\text{getPub}(t)$ returns the statement x proven by a ZK proof t. getPub does not check whether the proof is actually valid; for this, we have $\text{verify}_{\text{ZK}}(t_1, t_2)$ which checks whether t_2 is a valid proof with respect to

---

[2] Notice that it is no restriction that we use the same relation for all ZK-proofs: To encode relations $R_1, \dots, R_n$, we define a relation $R := \{((a, x), w) : \exists i.a = a_i \wedge (x, w) \in R_i\}$ where a_i are distinct terms.

$$dec(dk(t_1), enc(ek(t_1), m, t_2)) = m$$

$$verify_{sig}(vk(t_1), sig(sk(t_1), t_2, t_3)) = t_2$$

$$isek(ek(t)) = ek(t)$$

$$isvk(vk(t)) = vk(t)$$

$$isenc(enc(ek(t_1), t_2, t_3)) = enc(ek(t_1), t_2, t_3)$$

$$isenc(garbageEnc(t_1, t_2)) = garbageEnc(t_1, t_2)$$

$$issig(sig(sk(t_1), t_2, t_3)) = sig(sk(t_1), t_2, t_3)$$

$$issig(garbageSig(t_1, t_2)) = garbageSig(t_1, t_2)$$

$$iscrs(crs(t_1)) = crs(t_1)$$

$$iszk(ZK(t_1, t_2, t_3, t_4)) = ZK(t_1, t_2, t_3, t_4)$$

$$iszk(garbageZK(t_1, t_2, t_3))$$
$$= garbageZK(t_1, t_2, t_3)$$

$$ekof(enc(ek(t_1), t_2, t_3)) = ek(t_1)$$

$$ekof(garbageEnc(t_1, t_2)) = t_1$$

$$crsof(ZK(crs(t_1), t_2, t_3, t_4)) = crs(t_1)$$

$$crsof(garbageZK(t_1, t_2, t_3)) = t_1$$

$$vkof(sig(sk(t_1), t_2, t_3)) = vk(t_1)$$

$$vkof(garbageSig(t_1, t_2)) = t_1$$

$$fst(pair(t_1, t_2))) = t_1$$

$$snd(pair(t_1, t_2)) = t_2$$

$$unstring_0(string_0(s)) = s$$

$$unstring_1(string_1(s)) = s$$

$$getPub(ZK(t_1, t_2, t_3, t_4)) = t_2$$

$$getPub(garbageZK(t_1, t_2, t_3)) = t_2$$

$$equals(x, x) = x$$

$$verify_{ZK}(crs(t_1), ZK(crs(t_1), t_2, t_3, t_4))$$
$$= ZK(crs(t_1), t_2, t_3, t_4) \text{ if } (t_2, t_3) \in R_{adv}^{sym}$$

Fig. 1. Definition of destructors. If no rule matches, a destructor returns $\bot$.

the CRS t_1. If so, t_2 is returned (and can, e.g., be fed into getPub); otherwise $\bot$ is returned. $iscrs(t)$ and $iszk(t)$ allow us to test if t is a CRS or a (possibly invalid) zero-knowledge proof.

Protocols. We use the protocol model from the CoSP framework [3]. There, a protocol is modeled as a (possibly infinite) tree of nodes. Each node corresponds to a particular protocol action such as receiving a term from the adversary, sending a previously computed term to the adversary, applying a constructor or destructor to previously computed terms (and branching depending on whether the application is successful), or picking a nonce. We do not describe the protocol model in detail here, but it suffices to know that a protocol can freely apply constructors and destructors (computation nodes), branch depending on destructor success, and communicate with the adversary. Despite the simplicity of the model, it is powerful enough to embed powerful calculi such as the applied π-calculus (shown in [3]) or RCF, a core calculus for F# (shown in [8]). (In the Appendix C, we present our computational soundness result in the applied π-calculus.)

Protocol Conditions. The protocols we consider are subject to a number of conditions, listed in Figure 2. The most interesting protocol condition is *valid proofs condition*: During the symbolic execution of the protocol, whenever the protocol constructs a ZK proof $ZK(c, x, w, N)$ we have $(x, w) \in R_{honest}^{sym}$. Here R_{honest}^{sym} is some fixed but arbitrary relation with $R_{honest}^{sym} \subseteq R_{adv}^{sym}$ (like in R_{adv}^{sym}, our results are parametric in R_{honest}^{sym}). In the simplest case, we would have $R_{honest}^{sym} :=$ R_{adv}^{sym}. Then the valid proofs condition simply requires that the protocol never tries to construct a ZK-proof with an invalid witness. (We only impose this condition on the honest protocol, not on the adversary.) In some cases, however, it may be advantageous to let R_{honest}^{sym} be strictly smaller than R_{adv}^{sym}. This permits us to model a certain asymmetry in guarantees given by a zero-knowledge proof system: To honestly generate a valid proof, we need a witness with $(x, w) \in R_{\text{honest}}^{\text{sym}}$, but given a malicious prover, we only have the guarantee that the prover knows a witness with $(x, w) \in R_{\text{adv}}^{\text{sym}}$. We call $R_{\text{honest}}^{\text{sym}}$ the *usage restriction*.

The Adversary. The capabilities of the adversary are described by a deduction relation $\vdash$. $S \vdash t$ means that from the terms S, the adversary can deduce t. $\vdash$ is defined by the following rules:

$$\frac{m \in S}{S \vdash m} \qquad \frac{N \in \mathbf{N}_E}{S \vdash N} \qquad \frac{S \vdash t_1, \ldots, t_n \qquad t_1, \ldots, t_n \in \mathbf{T} \qquad F \text{ constructor or destructor} \qquad F(t_1, \ldots, t_n) \in \mathbf{T}}{S \vdash F(t_1, \ldots, t_n)}$$

Note that the adversary cannot deduce protocol nonces. These are secret until explicitly revealed. The capabilities of the adversaries with respect to the network (intercept/modify messages) are modeled explicitly by the protocol: if the adversary is allowed to intercept a message, the protocol explicitly communicates it through the adversary.

Protocol Execution. Given a particular protocol Π (modeled as a tree), the set of possible protocol traces is defined by traversing the tree: in case of an input node the adversary nondeterministically picks a term t with $S \vdash t$ where S are the terms sent so far through output nodes; at computation nodes, a new term is computed by applying a constructor or destructor to terms computed/received at earlier nodes; then the left or right successor is taken depending on whether the destructor succeeded. The sequence of nodes we traverse in this fashion is called a *symbolic node trace* of the protocol. By specifying sets of node traces, we can specify trace properties for a given protocol. We refer to [3] for details on the protocol model and its semantics.

3   Computational Implementation

We now describe how to implement the constructors and destructors from the preceding section computationally. Following [3], we do so by specifying a partial deterministic function $A_F : (\{0, 1\}^*)^n \to \{0, 1\}^*$ (the *computational implementation of F*) for each constructor or destructor $F : \mathbf{T}^n \to \mathbf{T}$. Intuitively, A_F should behave as F, only on bitstrings, e.g., $A_{\text{enc}}(ek, m, r)$ should encrypt m using encryption key ek and algorithmic randomness r. The distribution A_N specifies the distribution according to which nonces are picked. In Appendix A.1 we give the full list of implementation conditions that the computational implementation must fulfill. These are mostly simple syntactic conditions (such as $A_{\text{fst}}(A_{\text{pair}}(x, y)) = x$). Furthermore, we require that A_{enc} and A_{sig} correspond to an IND-CCA secure encryption scheme and a strongly unforgeable signature scheme. These conditions are essentially the same as in [3]. Here, we will only discuss the cryptographic properties the implementation of ZK proofs should satisfy.

Properties of ZK Proofs. In [10], it was shown that for getting computational soundness of (non-interactive) zero-knowledge proofs, we need at least the following properties:[3] *Completeness* (if prover and verifier are honest, the proof is

---

[3] It was not shown that these are the minimal properties, but it was shown that none of these properties can be dropped without suitable substitute.

accepted), *extractability* (given a suitable trapdoor, one can get a witness out of a valid proof – this models the fact that the prover knows the witness), *zero-knowledge* (given a suitable trapdoor and a true statement x, a ZK-simulator can produce proofs without knowing a witness that are indistinguishable from normally generated proofs for x), *unpredictability* (two proofs are equal only with negligible probability), *length-regularity* (the length of a proof only depends on the length of statement and witness), and some variant of *non-malleability* (see below). Furthermore, they required for convenience that the verification and the extraction algorithm are deterministic.

The interesting property is non-malleability: Intuitively, non-malleability means that given a proof for some statement x, it is not possible to derive a proof for some other statement x', even if x logically entails x'. (For example, given a proof that the ciphertext c contains a plaintext $i < 5$ it should not be possible to construct a proof that c contains $i < 6$.) There are several variants of non-malleability; [10] used the notion of *extraction zero-knowledge* which is a strong variant of extractability (we are aware of only one scheme in the literature that has this property [22]). They left it as an open problem whether weaker variants also lead to computational soundness. We answer this question positively. We use the weaker and more popular notion of *simulation-sound extractability*. In a nutshell, this notion guarantees that the adversary cannot produce proofs from which no witness can be extracted, even when given access to a ZK-simulator.

We actually need an even weaker property: *honest simulation-sound extractability*. Here the adversary may ask the ZK-simulator to produce a simulated proof for x if he knows a witness w for x.

In the symbolic model, we have distinguished two relations R_{adv}^{sym} and R_{honest}^{sym}, the first modeling what the adversary is able to do, the second modeling what honest participants are allowed to do. Similarly, our definition of *weakly symbolically-sound zero-knowledge proof* distinguishes two relations $R_{adv}^{comp} \supseteq R_{honest}^{comp}$. All conditions assume that honest participants use $(x, w) \in R_{honest}^{comp}$. ("Weakly" distinguishes our notion from that in [10] which requires extraction ZK.)

Definition 1 (Weakly Symbolically-Sound ZK Proofs). *A weakly symbolically-sound zero-knowledge proof system for relations $R_{honest}^{comp}, R_{adv}^{comp}$ is a tuple of polynomial-time algorithms $(\mathbf{K}, \mathbf{P}, \mathbf{V})$ such that there exist polynomial-time algorithms $(\mathbf{E}, \mathbf{S})$ and the following properties hold:*

- Completeness: *Let a polynomial-time adversary $\mathcal{A}$ be given. Let $(\text{crs}, \text{simtd}, \text{extd}) \leftarrow \mathbf{K}(1^\eta)$. Let $(x, w) \leftarrow \mathcal{A}(1^\eta, \text{crs})$. Let proof $\leftarrow \mathbf{P}(x, w, \text{crs})$. Then with overwhelming probability in η, it holds $(x, w) \notin R_{adv}^{comp}$ or $\mathbf{V}(x, \text{proof}, \text{crs}) = 1$.*
- Zero-Knowledge: *Fix a polynomial-time oracle adversary $\mathcal{A}$. For given crs, simtd, let $\mathcal{O}_{\mathbf{P}}(x, w) := \mathbf{P}(x, w, \text{crs})$ if $(x, w) \in R_{honest}^{comp}$ and $\mathcal{O}_{\mathbf{P}}(x, w) := \bot$ otherwise, and let $\mathcal{O}_{\mathbf{S}}(x, w) := \mathbf{S}(x, \text{crs}, \text{simtd})$ if $(x, w) \in R_{honest}^{comp}$ and $\mathcal{O}_{\mathbf{S}}(x, w) := \bot$ otherwise. Then*

$$|\Pr[\mathcal{A}^{\mathcal{O}_{\mathbf{P}}}(1^\eta, \text{crs}) = 1 : (\text{crs}, \dots) \leftarrow \mathbf{K}(1^\eta)] -$$
$$\Pr[\mathcal{A}^{\mathcal{O}_{\mathbf{S}}}(1^\eta, \text{crs}) = 1 : (\text{crs}, \dots) \leftarrow \mathbf{K}(1^\eta)]|$$

is negligible in η.

- Honest simulation-sound extractability: *Let a polynomial-time oracle adversary $\mathcal{A}$ be given. Let* $(\text{crs}, \text{simtd}, \text{extd}) \leftarrow \mathbf{K}(1^\eta)$. *Let* $\mathcal{O}(x, w) := \mathbf{S}(x, \text{crs}, \text{simtd})$ *if* $(x, w) \in R_{\text{honest}}^{\text{comp}}$ *and* $\perp$ *otherwise. Let* $(x, \text{proof}) \leftarrow \mathcal{A}^{\mathcal{O}}(1^\eta, \text{crs})$. *Let* $w \leftarrow \mathbf{E}(x, \text{proof}, \text{extd})$. *Then with overwhelming probability, if* $\mathbf{V}(x, \text{proof}, \text{crs}) = 1$ *and* proof *was not output by* $\mathcal{O}$ *then* $(x, w) \in R_{\text{adv}}^{\text{comp}}$.
- Unpredictability: *Let a polynomial-time adversary $\mathcal{A}$ be given. Let* $(\text{crs}, \text{simtd}, \text{extd}) \leftarrow \mathbf{K}(1^\eta)$. *Let* $(x, w, \text{proof}') \leftarrow \mathcal{A}(1^\eta, \text{crs}, \text{simtd}, \text{extd})$. *Then with overwhelming probability, it holds* proof$' \neq \mathbf{P}(x, w, \text{crs})$ *or* $(x, w) \notin R_{\text{honest}}^{\text{comp}}$.
- Length-regularity: *Let two witnesses w and w', and statements x and x' be given such that* $|x| = |x'|$, *and* $|w| = |w'|$. *Let* $(\text{crs}, \text{simtd}, \text{extd}) \leftarrow \mathbf{K}(1^\eta)$. *Then let* proof $\leftarrow \mathbf{P}(x, w, \text{crs})$ *and* proof$' \leftarrow \mathbf{P}(x', w', \text{crs})$. *Then we get* $|\text{proof}| = |\text{proof}'|$ *with probability 1.*
- Deterministic verification and extraction: *The algorithms V and E are deterministic.*

(We do not explicitly list soundness because it is implied by honest simulation-sound extractability.) $\diamond$

We then require that $A_{\text{crs}}, A_{\text{ZK}}, A_{\text{verify}_{\text{ZK}}}$ correspond to the key generation $\mathbf{K}$, prover $\mathbf{P}$, and verifier $\mathbf{V}$ of a weakly symbolically-sound ZK proof system for some relations $R_{\text{honest}}^{\text{comp}}, R_{\text{adv}}^{\text{comp}}$. We stress that using the the construction in [31] on a length-regular and extractable NIZK leads to weakly symbolically-sound ZK proof system. The proof is postponed to the Appendix B.

The Relations. It remains to specify what conditions we place on the relations $R_{\text{honest}}^{\text{comp}}, R_{\text{adv}}^{\text{comp}}$. Obviously, we cannot expect computational soundness if we allow arbitrary $R_{\text{honest}}^{\text{comp}}, R_{\text{adv}}^{\text{comp}}$. Instead, we need to formulate the fact that $R_{\text{honest}}^{\text{comp}}, R_{\text{adv}}^{\text{comp}}$ somehow correspond to the symbolic relations $R_{\text{honest}}^{\text{sym}}, R_{\text{adv}}^{\text{sym}}$. We thus give minimal requirements on the relationship between those relations. Essentially, we want that whenever $(x, w) \in R_{\text{honest}}^{\text{sym}}$ then for the corresponding computational bitstrings m_x, m_w we have $(m_x, m_w) \in R_{\text{honest}}^{\text{comp}}$; this guarantees that if symbolically, we respect the usage restriction $R_{\text{honest}}^{\text{sym}}$, then computationally we only use witnesses the honest protocol is allowed to use. And whenever $(m_x, m_w) \in R_{\text{adv}}^{\text{comp}}$ we have $(x, w) \in R_{\text{adv}}^{\text{sym}}$; this guarantees that a computational adversary will not be able to prove statements m_x that do not also correspond to statements x that can be proven symbolically. (Formally, these conditions are used to show Lemmas 4 and 6 in the computational soundness proof below.) To model correspondence between the symbolic terms x, w and the bitstrings m_x, m_w, we define a function img_η that translates a term to a bitstring (essentially by applying A_F for each constructor F). The function img_η depends on an environment η, a partial function $\mathbf{T} \to \{0,1\}^*$ that assigns bitstrings to nonces and adversary-generated terms. We use the definition of a *consistent environment* that lists various natural properties an environment will have (such as mapping ZK-terms to bitstrings of the right type); the definition of consistent environments is deferred to Appendix C.1. Given these notions, we can formalize the conditions $R_{\text{honest}}^{\text{comp}}, R_{\text{adv}}^{\text{comp}}$ should satisfy:

Definition 2 (Implementation of Relations). *A pair of relations $R_{\text{honest}}^{\text{comp}}$, $R_{\text{adv}}^{\text{comp}}$ on $\{0,1\}^*$ implement a relation $R_{\text{adv}}^{\text{sym}}$ on $\mathbf{T}$ with usage restriction $R_{\text{honest}}^{\text{sym}}$ if the following conditions hold for any consistent $\eta \in \mathcal{E}$:*

(i) $(x, w) \in R_{\text{honest}}^{\text{sym}}$ and $\text{img}_\eta(x) \neq \bot \neq \text{img}_\eta(w) \implies (\text{img}_\eta(x), \text{img}_\eta(w)) \in R_{\text{honest}}^{\text{comp}}$

(ii) $(\text{img}_\eta(x), \text{img}_\eta(w)) \in R_{\text{adv}}^{\text{comp}} \implies (x, w) \in R_{\text{adv}}^{\text{sym}}$

(iii) $R_{\text{honest}}^{\text{sym}} \subseteq R_{\text{adv}}^{\text{sym}}$ and $R_{\text{honest}}^{\text{comp}} \subseteq R_{\text{adv}}^{\text{comp}}$ ◇

In the Appendix C.5 we give some practical examples satisfying this definition.

Protocol Execution. The CoSP framework specifies semantics for executing a given protocol in the computational model given a computational implementation A_F. The execution is analogous to the symbolic execution, except that computation nodes apply functions A_F instead of constructors and destructors (with branching depending on $A_F(\ldots) \overset{?}{=} \bot$). Input and output nodes receive and send bitstrings to a probabilistic polynomial-time adversary. This probabilistic process yields a trace of nodes, the *computational node trace*. Details are specified in [3].

4   Computational Soundness

Using the definitions from Section 2 and 3, we can finally state our main result. A *trace property* is a prefix-closed, efficiently decidable set $\mathcal{P}$ of node traces. We say a protocol Π *symbolically satisfies* $\mathcal{P}$ if every symbolic node trace (see page 211) of Π is in $\mathcal{P}$. We say Π *computationally satisfies* $\mathcal{P}$ if the computational node trace (see page 214) is in $\mathcal{P}$ with overwhelming probability.

Theorem 1 (Computational Soundness of ZK Proofs). *Let Π be a protocol satisfying the protocol conditions listed in figure 2. Let A_F be a computational implementation satisfying the implementation conditions from Section 3. Then for any node trace $\mathcal{P}$, if Π symbolically satisfies $\mathcal{P}$, then Π computationally satisfies $\mathcal{P}$.*   ◇

We describe the proof in Section 5.

5   The Proof

In this section, we describe our proof of computational soundness (Theorem 1). First, we describe how the computational soundness proof for encryptions and signatures is done in the CoSP framework (Section 5.1). To understand our proof it is essential to understand that proof first. Then, we sketch how computational soundness of zero-knowledge proofs that have the extraction zero-knowledge property was shown in [10] (Section 5.2). It is instructive to compare their approach to ours. In Section 5.3, we describe the idea underlying our proof (using simulation-sound extractability instead of extraction-zero knowledge). Finally, in Section 5.4 we give an overview of our proof. The full proof is given in appendix C.3. The lemmas in this overview are simplified for readability and informal.

1. The annotation of each crs-node, each key-pair (ek, dk) and (vk, sk) is a fresh nonce. which does not occur anywhere else.

2. There is no node annotated with a garbage, garbageEnc, garbageSig, garbageZK, or $N \in \mathbf{N}_E$ constructor in the protocol.

3. The last argument of a enc, sig, ZK constructor are fresh nonces. These nonces are not used anywhere else except in case of enc and sig as part of a subterm of the third argument in a ZK-node.

4. A dk-node is only used as first argument for dec-node or as subterm of the third argument in a ZK-node.

5. A sk-node is only used as first argument for sig-node or as subterm of the third argument in a ZK-node.

6. The first argument of a dec-computation node is a dk-node.

7. The first argument of a sig-computation node is a sk-node.

8. The first argument of a ZK-computation is a crs-computation node which is annotated by a nonce $N \in \mathbf{N}_P$. This nonce is only used as annotation of this crs node and nowhere else.

9. The first argument of a verify$_{ZK}$-computation is a crs-computation node which is annotated by a nonce $N \in \mathbf{N}_P$. This nonce is only used as annotation of this crs node and nowhere else.

10. The protocol respects the usage restriction $R_{\text{honest}}^{\text{sym}}$ in the following sense: In the symbolic execution of the protocol, whenever a ZK-computation-node ν is reached, then $(f(\nu_x), f(\nu_w)) \in R_{\text{honest}}^{\text{sym}}$ where f is the function mapping nodes to terms (cf. the definition of the symbolic execution in [3]) and ν_x and ν_w are the second and third argument of ν.

11. For the relation $R_{\text{adv}}^{\text{sym}}$ it holds: There is an efficient algorithm **SymbExtr**, that given a term M together with a set S of terms , outputs a term N, such that $S \vdash N$ and $(N, M) \in R_{\text{adv}}^{\text{sym}}$ or outputs $\perp$ if there is no such term N. We call a relation satisfying this property symbolically extractable.

12. The relation $R_{\text{adv}}^{\text{sym}}$ is efficiently decidable.

Fig. 2. Protocol conditions

5.1 Computational Soundness Proofs in CoSP

Remember that in the CoSP framework, a protocol is modeled as a tree whose nodes correspond to the steps of the protocol execution; security properties are expressed as sets of node traces. Computational soundness means that for any polynomial-time adversary A the trace in the computational execution is, except with negligible probability, also a possible node trace in the symbolic execution. The approach for showing this is to construct a so-called simulator Sim. The simulator is a machine that interacts with a symbolic execution of the protocol Π on the one hand, and with the adversary A on the other hand; we call this a hybrid execution. The simulator has to satisfy the following two properties:

- Indistinguishability: The node trace in the hybrid execution is computationally indistinguishable from that in the computational execution with adversary A.
- Dolev-Yaoness: The simulator Sim never (except for negligible probability) sends terms t to the protocol with $S \nvdash t$ where S is the list of terms Sim received from the protocol so far.

The existence of such a simulator then guarantees computational soundness: Dolev-Yaoness guarantees that only node traces occur in the hybrid execution that are possible in the symbolic execution, and indistinguishability guarantees that only node traces occur in the computational execution that can occur in the hybrid one.

How to Construct a Simulator? In [3], the simulator Sim is constructed as follows: Whenever it gets a term from the protocol, it constructs a corresponding bitstring and sends it to the adversary, and when receiving a bitstring from the adversary it parses it and sends the resulting term to the protocol. Constructing bitstrings is done using a function β, parsing bitstrings to terms using a function τ. The simulator picks all random values and keys himself: For each protocol nonce N, he initially picks a bitstring r_N. He then translates, e.g., $\beta(N) := r_N$ and $\beta(\mathrm{ek}(N)) := A_{\mathrm{ek}}(r_N)$ and $\beta(\mathrm{enc}(\mathrm{ek}(N), t, M)) := A_{\mathrm{enc}}(A_{\mathrm{ek}}(r_N), \beta(t), r_M)$. Translating back also is natural: Given $m = r_N$, we let $\tau(m) := N$, and if c is a ciphertext that can be decrypted as m using $A_{\mathrm{dk}}(r_N)$, we set $\tau(c) := \mathrm{enc}(\mathrm{ek}(N), \tau(m), M)$. However, in the last case, a subtlety occurs: what nonce M should we use as symbolic randomness in $\tau(c)$? Here we distinguish two cases: If c was earlier produced by the simulator: Then c was the result of computing $\beta(t)$ for some $t = \mathrm{enc}(\mathrm{ek}(N), t', M)$ and some nonce M. We then simply set $\tau(c) := t$ and have consistently mapped c back to the term it came from.

If c was not produced by the simulator: In this case it is an adversary generated encryption, and M should be an adversary nonce to represent that fact. We could just use a fresh nonce $M \in \mathbf{N}_E$, but that would introduce the need of additional bookkeeping: If we compute $t := \tau(c)$, and later $\beta(t)$ is invoked, we need to make sure that $\beta(t) = c$ in order for the Sim to work consistently (formally, this is needed in the proof of the indistinguishability of Sim). And we need to make sure that when computing $\tau(c)$ again, we use the same M. This bookkeeping can be avoided using the following trick: We identify the adversary nonces with symbols N^m annotated with bitstrings m. Then $\tau(c) := \mathrm{enc}(\mathrm{ek}(N), \tau(m), N^c)$, i.e., we set $M := N^c$. This ensures that different c get different randomness nonces N^c, the same c is always assigned the same N^c, and $\beta(t)$ is easy to define: $\beta(\mathrm{enc}(\mathrm{ek}(N), m, N^c)) := c$ because we know that $\mathrm{enc}(\mathrm{ek}(N), m, N^c)$ can only have been produced by $\tau(c)$. To illustrate, here are excerpts of the definitions of β and τ (the first matching rule counts):

- $\tau(c) := \mathrm{enc}(\mathrm{ek}(M), t, N)$ if c has earlier been output by $\beta(\mathrm{enc}(\mathrm{ek}(M), t, N))$ for some $M \in \mathbf{N}, N \in \mathbf{N}_P$
- $\tau(c) := \mathrm{enc}(\mathrm{ek}(M), \tau(m), N^c)$ if c is of type ciphertext and $\tau(A_{\mathrm{ekof}}(c)) = \mathrm{ek}(M)$ for some $M \in \mathbf{N}_P$ and $m := A_{\mathrm{dec}}(A_{\mathrm{dk}}(r_M), c) \neq \perp$
- $\beta(\mathrm{enc}(\mathrm{ek}(N), t, M)) := A_{\mathrm{enc}}(A_{\mathrm{ek}}(r_N), \beta(t), r_M)$ if $M \in \mathbf{N}_P$
- $\beta(\mathrm{enc}(\mathrm{ek}(M), t, N^m)) := m$ if $M \in \mathbf{N}_P$

Bitstrings m that cannot be suitably parsed are mapped into terms garbage(N^m) and similar that can then be mapped back by β using the annotation m.

Showing Indistinguishability. Showing indistinguishability essentially boils down to showing that the functions β and τ consistently translate terms back and forth. More precisely, we show that $\beta(\tau(m)) = m$ and $\tau(\beta(t)) = t$. Furthermore, we need to show that in any protocol step where a constructor or destructor F is applied to terms $t_1, \ldots, t_n$, we have that $\beta(F(t_1, \ldots, t_n)) = A_F(\beta(t_1), \ldots, \beta(t_n))$. This makes sure that the computational execution (where A_F is applied) stays in sync with the hybrid execution (where F is applied and the result is translated using β). The proofs of these facts are lengthy (involving case distinctions over all constructors and destructors) but do not provide much additional insight; they are very important though because they are responsible for most of the implementation conditions that are needed for the computational soundness result.

Showing Dolev-Yaoness. The proof of Dolev-Yaoness is where most of the actual cryptographic assumptions come in. In this sketch, we will slightly deviate from the original proof in [3] for easier comparison with the proof in the present paper. The differences are, however, inessential. Starting from the simulator Sim, we introduce a sequence of simulators Sim_4, Sim_5, Sim_f. (We start the numbering with 4 because we later introduce additional simulators.)

In Sim_4, we change the function β as follows: When invoked as $\beta(\text{enc}(\text{ek}(N), t, M))$ with $M \in \mathbf{N}_P$, instead of computing $A_{\text{enc}}(A_{\text{ek}}(r_N), \beta(t), r_M)$, β invokes an encryption oracle $\mathcal{O}_{\text{enc}}^N$ to produce the ciphertext c. Similarly, $\beta(\text{ek}(N))$ returns the public key provided by the oracle $\mathcal{O}_{\text{enc}}^N$. The hybrid executions of Sim and Sim_4 are then indistinguishable. (Here we use that the protocol conditions guarantee that no randomness is used in two places.) Also, the function τ is changed to invoke $\mathcal{O}_{\text{enc}}^N$ whenever it needs to decrypt a ciphertext while parsing. Notice that if c was returned by $\beta(t)$ with $t := \text{enc}(\dots)$, then $\tau(c)$ just recalls the term t without having to decrypt. Hence $\mathcal{O}_{\text{enc}}^N$ is never asked to decrypt a ciphertext it produced.

In Sim_5, we replace the encryption oracle $\mathcal{O}_{\text{enc}}^N$ by a fake encryption oracle $\mathcal{O}_{fake}^N$ that encrypts zero-plaintexts instead of the true plaintexts. Since $\mathcal{O}_{\text{enc}}^N$ is never asked to decrypt a ciphertext it produced, IND-CCA security guarantees that the hybrid executions of Sim_4 and Sim_5 are indistinguishable. Since the plaintexts given to $\mathcal{O}_{fake}^N$ are never used, we can further change $\beta(\text{enc}(N, t, M))$ to never even compute the plaintext $\beta(t)$.

Finally, in Sim_f, we additionally change β to use a signing oracle in order to produce signatures. As in the case of Sim_4, the hybrid executions of Sim_5 and Sim_f are indistinguishable.

Since the hybrid executions of Sim and Sim_f are indistinguishable, in order to show Dolev-Yaoness of Sim, it is sufficient to show Dolev-Yaoness of Sim_f.

The first step to showing this is to show that whenever Sim_f invokes $\beta(t)$, then $S \vdash t$ holds (where S are the terms received from the protocol). This follows from the fact that β is invoked on terms t_0 sent by the protocol (which are then by definition in S), and recursively descends only into subterms that can be deduced from t_0. In particular, in Sim_5 we made sure that $\beta(t)$ is not invoked by $\beta(\text{enc}(\text{ek}(N), t, M))$; t would not be deducible from $\text{enc}(\text{ek}(N), t, M)$. Next we prove that whenever $S \nvdash t$, then t contains a visible subterm t_{bad} with $S \nvdash t_{bad}$ such that t_{bad} is a protocol nonce, or a ciphertext $\text{enc}(\dots, N)$ where N is a protocol nonces, or a signature, or a few other similar cases. (Visibility is a purely syntactic condition and essentially means that t_{bad} is not protected by an honestly generated encryption.)

Now we can conclude Dolev-Yaoness of Sim_f: If it does not hold, Sim_f sends a term $t = \tau(m)$ where m was sent by the adversary A. Then t has a visible subterm t_{bad}. Visibility implies that the recursive computation of $\tau(m)$ had a subinvocation $\tau(m_{bad}) = t_{bad}$. For each possible case of t_{bad} we derive a contradiction. At this point we use the cryptographic arguments like for example unforgeability of signature schemes. Thus, Sim_f is Dolev-Yao, hence Sim is indistinguishable and Dolev-Yao. Computational soundness follows.

5.2 Computational Soundness Based on Extraction ZK

We now describe how computational soundness for zero-knowledge proofs was shown in [10], based on the strong assumption of extraction zero-knowledge. Our presentation strongly deviates from the details of the proof in [10]; we explain what their proof would be like if recast in the CoSP framework. This makes it easier to compare the proof to our proof and the proof described in the preceding section.

Extraction zero-knowledge is a strong property that guarantees the following: It is not possible to distinguish a prover-oracle from the a simulator-oracle, even when given access to an extraction oracle that extracts the witnesses from arbitrary proofs except the ones produced by the prover/simulator-oracle. Notice that there is a strong analogy to IND-CCA secure encryption. The prover-oracle corresponds to an encryption-oracle, the witness to the plaintext, the simulator-oracle to a fake encryption-oracle encrypting zero-plaintexts, and the extractor-oracle to a decryption-oracle.

This analogy allows us to adapt the idea for proving computational soundness of encryptions to the case of ZK proofs. As in the proof described in Section 5.1, we construct a simulator Sim with translation functions τ and β. We extend β and τ to deal with ZK proofs analogue to the cases of encryptions in Section 5.1.

The proof of indistinguishability is analogous to that in Section 5.1, except that we use the extractability property of the proof system to make sure that the simulator does not abort when invoking the extraction algorithm while trying to parse a ZK proof z in $\tau(z)$. Notice that plain extractability (as opposed to simulation-sound extractability) can be used here since we do not use a ZK-simulator in the construction of Sim.

To prove Dolev-Yaoness, we proceed as in Section 5.1, except that we introduce three more intermediate simulators Sim_1, Sim_2, and Sim_3. (See Figure 3.) In Sim_1, we invoke a prover-oracle $\mathcal{O}_{\text{ZK}}^N$ with statement $\beta(t)$ and witness $\beta(t')$ in $\beta(\text{ZK}(\text{crs}(N), t, t', M))$ instead of computing $A_{\text{ZK}}(A_{\text{crs}}(r_N), \beta(t), \beta(t'), r_M)$. (This is analogous to Sim_4 above.) $\mathcal{O}_{\text{ZK}}^N$ aborts if the witness is not valid.

Fig. 3. Simulators used in the proof. An arrow marked DY means Dolev-Yaoness is propagated from one simulator to the other. An arrow marked ZK means ZK-breaks are propagated (needed in Section 5.4).

In Sim_2, we replace the prover-oracle $\mathcal{O}_{\text{ZK}}^N$ by a ZK-simulator-oracle $\mathcal{O}_{\text{sim}}^N$. That oracle runs the ZK-simulator (after checking that the witness is valid).

Extraction zero-knowledge guarantees that this replacement leads to an indistinguishable hybrid execution. (We need that the witness is checked before running the simulator because extraction zero-knowledge gives no guarantees in the case of invalid witnesses, even if the witness is not actually used by the ZK-simulator.) Finally, in Sim_3 we modify the ZK-simulator-oracle $\mathcal{O}_{\mathrm{sim}}^N$ such that it does not check the witness any more. A protocol condition guarantees that this check would succeed anyway, so this change leads to an indistinguishable hybrid execution. Furthermore, since witnesses given to $\mathcal{O}_{\mathrm{sim}}^N$ are never used, we can further change $\beta(\mathrm{ZK}(\mathrm{crs}(N), t, t', M))$ to never even compute the witness $\beta(t')$.

The rest of the proof is analogous to that in Section 5.1. I.e., we continue with the simulator $\mathrm{Sim}_3, \mathrm{Sim}_4, \mathrm{Sim}_f$ as described there and show that Sim_f is Dolev-Yao.

Note that this computational soundness proof crucially depends on the extraction ZK property. We need to use the extractor in the construction of τ, and we need to replace the prover-oracle by a ZK-simulator-oracle in order to make sure that β does not descend into witnesses. And that replacement takes place in a setting where the parsing function τ and thus the extractor is used.

5.3   Proof Idea

We now describe the idea of our approach that allows us to get rid of extraction ZK. As explained in Section 5.2, we cannot use the extractor as part of the parsing function τ if we do not have extraction ZK. However, the following observation shows that we might not need to run the extractor: Although in the computational setting, the only way to compute a witness is to extract it (unless the relation is trivial), in the symbolic setting, given a symbolic statement x, it is typically easy to compute a corresponding symbolic witness w. (E.g., when proving the knowledge of a secret key that decrypts a term $c = \mathrm{enc}(\mathrm{ek}(N), t, M)$, then the witness is $\mathrm{dk}(N)$ which can just be read off c.) We stress that we do not claim that the witness can be deduced (in the sense of $\vdash$) from x, only that its symbolic representation can be efficiently computed from the statement.

Thus, for an adversary-generated proof z with CRS $A_{\mathrm{crs}}(r_N)$ and statement m_x and that passes verification, we define $\tau(z)$ as follows: We run $w :=$ **SymbExtr**(S, x) and return $\tau(z) := \mathrm{ZK}(\mathrm{crs}(N), x, w, N^z)$. Here S is the list of terms send by the protocol so far, **SymbExtr**(S, x) denotes an arbitrary witness w satisfying the following two conditions: w is a valid witness for x (i.e., $(x, w) \in R_{\mathrm{adv}}^{\mathrm{sym}}$) and $S \vdash w$. (Our result assumes that $w = $ **SymbExtr**(S, x) is efficiently computable whenever w exists, this will be the case for most natural relations.)

The condition $S \vdash w$ is necessary since otherwise the simulator Sim would produce a proof that the adversary could not have deduced (since he could not have deduced the witness), and thus the simulator would not be Dolev-Yao.

Assume for the moment that **SymbExtr**(S, x) always succeeds (i.e., in the hybrid execution, there always is a w with $(x, w) \in R_{\mathrm{adv}}^{\mathrm{sym}}$ and $S \vdash w$). In this case, we can finish the proof analogously to that in Section 5.2: Indistinguishability of Sim follows by carefully checking all cases, and the Dolev-Yaoness by the same sequence of simulators as in Section 5.2. We do not need extraction zero-knowledge when going from Sim_1 to Sim_2, though, because in Sim_1, no extractor is used (we use symbolic extraction instead). Thus the zero-knowledge property is sufficient instead of extraction zero-knowledge.

But how to show that $\mathbf{SymbExtr}(S, x)$ always succeeds? Two things might go wrong. First, no valid witness w with $(x, w) \in R_{\text{adv}}^{\text{sym}}$ might exist. Note that the extractability property only guarantees that computationally, a valid witness for the computational statement m_x exists. This does not necessarily imply that translating that witness into a term (e.g., using τ) yields a valid symbolic witness. Second, there might be a valid witness w, but that witness is not deducable ($S \not\vdash w$). Again, extractability only guarantees that the adversary "knows" a witness in the computational setting, this does not imply deducability in the symbolic setting.

In essence, to show that $\mathbf{SymbExtr}(S, x)$ succeeds, we need a kind of computational soundness result: Whenever computationally, the adversary knows a valid witness, then symbolically, the adversary knows a valid witness. This seems problematic, because it seems that we need to use a computational soundness result within our proof of computational soundness – a seeming circularity. Fortunately, this circularity can be resolved: The fact that $\mathbf{SymbExtr}(S, x)$ succeeds is used only when proving that Sim is indistinguishable (i.e., mimics the computational execution well). But the fact that $\mathbf{SymbExtr}(S, x)$ succeeds does not relate to the computational execution at all. In fact, it turns out to be closely related to the Dolev-Yaoness and can be handled in the same proof. And that proof does not use the fact that symbolic extraction succeeds.

5.4   Proof Overview

We now give a more detailed walk-through through our proof. This exposition can also be seen as a guide through the full proof in appendix C.3.

The Simulator. The first step is to define the simulator Sim, i.e., the translation function β and τ. Here, we only present the parts of the definition related to ZK proofs (the first matching rule counts):

1. $\tau(z) := \text{ZK}(\text{crs}(N_1), t_1, t_2, N_2)$ if z has earlier been output by $\beta(\text{ZK}(\text{crs}(N_1), t_1, t_2, N_2))$ for some $N_1, N_2 \in \mathbf{N}_P$
2. $\tau(z) := \text{ZK}(\text{crs}(N), x, w, N^z)$ if z is of type zero-knowledge proof and $\tau(z)$ was computed earlier and has output $\text{ZK}(\text{crs}(N), x, w, N^z)$
3. $\tau(z) := \text{ZK}(\text{crs}(N), x, w, N^z)$ if z is of type zero-knowledge proof, $\tau(A_{\text{crsof}}(z)) = \text{crs}(N)$ for some $N \in \mathbf{N}_P$, $A_{\text{verify}_{\text{ZK}}}(A_{\text{crsof}}(z), z) = z$, $m_x := A_{\text{getPub}}(z) \neq \bot$, $x := \tau(m_x) \neq \bot$ and $w := \mathbf{SymbExtr}(S, x)$ where S is the set of terms sent to the adversary so far.
4. $\tau(z) := \text{garbageZK}(c, x, N^z)$ if z is of type zero-knowledge proof, $c := \tau(A_{\text{crsof}}(z))$ and $x := \tau(A_{\text{getPub}}(z))$.
5. $\beta(\text{ZK}(\text{crs}(N_1), t_1, t_2, N_2)) := A_{\text{ZK}}(A_{\text{crs}}(r_{N_1}), \beta(t_1), \beta(t_2), r_{N_2})$ if $N_1, N_2 \in \mathbf{N}_P$
6. $\beta(\text{ZK}(\text{crs}(t_0), t_1, t_2, N^s)) := s$
7. $\beta(\text{garbageZK}(t_1, t_2, N^z)) := z$

Here $\mathbf{SymbExtr}(S, x)$ returns a witness w with $(x, w) \in R_{\mathrm{adv}}^{\mathrm{sym}}$ and $S \vdash w$ if such w exists, and $\perp$ otherwise. A key point is what to do when $\mathbf{SymbExtr}(S, x)$ fails. We will later show that this happens with negligible probability only, but for now we need to specify the behavior in this case: When $\mathbf{SymbExtr}(S, x)$ returns $\perp$ in the rule 3), we say an *extraction failure* occurred. In this case, the simulator runs the extractor (using the extraction trapdoor corresponding to $A_{\mathrm{crs}}(r_N)$) to get a (computational) witness m_w for m_x. Then Sim computes $w := \tau^*(m_w)$ where τ^* is defined like τ, except that the rule 3) is dropped (hence τ^* will map an adversary-generated ZK-proof always to a garbageZK-term). Then the simulator aborts. If $(x, w) \notin R_{\mathrm{adv}}^{\mathrm{sym}}$, we say a *ZK-break* occurred.

The reader may wonder why we let the simulator compute a symbolic witness w in case of an extraction failure even though w is never used. The reason is that we later show that this w always has $(x, w) \in R_{\mathrm{adv}}^{\mathrm{sym}}$ and $S \vdash w$, which contradicts the fact that we get an extraction failure in the first place. The reason for using τ^* instead of τ is that we have to avoid getting extraction failures within extraction failures. We use the same sequence of simulator modifications as in Section 5.2 (see Figure 3). The only difference is that the simulator Sim handles zero-knowledge proofs as defined above.

We can now show that Sim_f is Dolev-Yao. The proof of this fact is analogous to the case the proof sketched in Section 5.2. We even show something slightly stronger, namely that neither τ nor τ^* outputs an undeducable term:

Lemma 1 (Sim_f is Dolev-Yao). *For any invocation $t := \tau(m)$ or $t := \tau^*(m)$, we have $S \vdash t$ where S are the terms sent to the simulator so far. In particular, Sim_f is Dolev-Yao.* ◇

As in Section 5.2, we show Sim is Dolev-Yao iff Sim_f is Dolev-Yao. We will also need preservation of the property that ZK-breaks occur with negligible probability.

Lemma 2 (Preservation of Simulator-Properties). • Sim *is Dolev-Yao iff* Sim_f *is.* • *In the hybrid execution of* Sim *extraction failures occur with negligible probability iff the same holds for* Sim_f. • *In the hybrid execution of* Sim_2 *(not* Sim!) *ZK-breaks occur with negligible probability iff the same holds for* Sim_f. ◇

Dolev-Yaoness, extraction failures, and ZK-breaks carry over from Sim_3 to Sim_4 and from Sim_5 to Sim_f because the randomness used in encrypting and signing is not re-used by protocol condition 3. (Notice that randomness might have occurred within a witness, but due to the change in Sim_3, we do not invoke $\beta(w)$ on witnesses any more.) Dolev-Yaoness, extraction failures, and ZK-breaks carry over from Sim_4 to Sim_5 due to the IND-CCA property. Dolev-Yaoness and extraction failures carry over from Sim to Sim_1 because the randomness used for constructing ZK-proofs is not reused by protocol condition 3.

Furthermore, Dolev-Yaoness and extraction failures carry over from Sim_1 to Sim_2 because of the zero-knowledge property of the proof system. There is a subtlety here: Sim_1 does use the extractor (namely after an extraction failure). So usually, we would not be allowed to apply the zero-knowledge property (we

would need extraction ZK). But fortunately, after an extraction failure, no terms
are sent by the simulator. Thus, anything that happens after an extraction failure
has no impact on whether the simulator is Dolev-Yao or not. Thus, for analyzing
whether Dolev-Yaoness carries over from Sim_1 to Sim_2, we can assume that those
simulators abort directly after incurring an extraction failure (without invoking
the extractor afterwards). Then no extractions occur in the simulator, and we
can use the zero-knowledge property. Analogously, extraction failures carry over
from Sim_1 to Sim_2.

Notice that we cannot use the same trick to show that ZK-breaks carry over
from Sim_1 to Sim_2: Whether ZK-breaks occur is determined after the invocation
of the extractor. Fortunately, we only need that ZK-breaks carry over from Sim_2
to Sim_f.

To show Lemma 2, it remains to show that Dolev-Yaoness, extraction failures,
and ZK-breaks carry over from Sim_2 to Sim_3. The only difference between these
simulators is that Sim_3 does not check whether the witness m_w given to the
ZK-simulation-oracle is valid (i.e., $(\beta(t_1), \beta(t_2)) \in R_{\text{honest}}^{\text{comp}}$ in rule 5). Thus, to
conclude the proof of Lemma 2, we need to show that the probability that the
ZK-simulation-oracle is called with an invalid witness is negligible.

No Invalid Witnesses. To show that the ZK-simulation-oracle is only called by
Sim_2 with valid computational witnesses $\beta(t_1)$, we need to show two things:

Lemma 3 (No Invalid Symbolic Witnesses). *If Sim_3 is Dolev-Yao, then
in rule 5), we have $(t_1, t_2) \in R_{\text{honest}}^{\text{sym}}$ with overwhelming probability. The same
holds for Sim.*   ◇

Lemma 4 (Relating the Relations, Part 1). *In an execution of Sim_3
the following holds with overwhelming probability: if $(x, w) \in R_{\text{honest}}^{\text{sym}}$ then
$(\beta(x), \beta(w)) \in R_{\text{honest}}^{\text{comp}}$. The same holds for Sim.*   ◇

Once we have these lemmas, Lemma 2 follows: We know from Lemma 1 that
Sim_f is Dolev-Yao. We have already shown that this property carries over to
Sim_3. Thus by Lemmas 3 and 4, $(\beta(t_1), \beta(t_2)) \in R_{\text{honest}}^{\text{comp}}$ in rule 5).

To show Lemma 3, we observe the following: If the simulator sends only terms
that are deducible (i.e., that a symbolic adversary could also have sent), then in
the hybrid execution, no execution trace occurs that could not have occurred in
the symbolic execution either. By protocol condition 10, in a symbolic execution,
$(t_1, t_2) \in R_{\text{honest}}^{\text{sym}}$ whenever the protocol constructs an $\text{ZK}(\text{crs}(N), t_1, t_2, M)$-term.
Since rule 5) only applies to such protocol-generated terms (ZK-terms from τ
have $M \in \mathbf{N}_E$), it follows that $(t_1, t_2) \in R_{\text{honest}}^{\text{sym}}$ in rule 5). Lemma 3 follows.
Lemma 4 follows because we required that $R_{\text{honest}}^{\text{comp}}, R_{\text{adv}}^{\text{comp}}$ implement $R_{\text{adv}}^{\text{sym}}$ with
usage restriction $R_{\text{honest}}^{\text{sym}}$; Definition 2 was designed to make Lemma 4 true.

Thus, Lemmas 3 and 4 hold, thus Lemma 2 follows. Since Sim_f is Dolev-Yao
by Lemma 1, it follows with Lemma 2 that Sim is Dolev-Yao. It remains to show
that Sim is indistinguishable.

Indistinguishability of Sim. As described in Section 5.1, to show indistinguishability of Sim, the main subproof is to show (a) that $\beta(F(t_1, \ldots, t_n))$

$= A_F(\beta(t_1), \ldots, \beta(t_n))$ when the protocol computes $F(t_1, \ldots, t_n)$. And, of course, we need (b) that the simulator does not abort. The proof of (a) is, as before, done by careful checking of all cases. The only interesting case is $F = \text{verify}_{\text{ZK}}$. Here we need that an honestly-generated ZK proof with statement x and witness w passes verification symbolically $(x, w \in R_{\text{honest}}^{\text{sym}})$ iff it passes verification computationally $((\beta(x), \beta(w)) \in R_{\text{honest}}^{\text{comp}})$. Fortunately, we have already derived all needed facts: By Lemmas 1 and 3, $(x, w) \in R_{\text{honest}}^{\text{sym}}$ with overwhelming probability. And then by Lemma 4, $(\beta(x), \beta(w)) \in R_{\text{honest}}^{\text{sym}}$.

To show (b), we need to show that extraction failures occur with negligible probability. The approach for this is a bit roundabout, we first analyze Sim_2:

Lemma 5 (No ZK-Breaks). *In the hybrid execution of* Sim_2, *ZK-breaks occur with negligible probability.*   ◇

To show this, we use the simulation-sound extractability property of the proof system to show that the values m_x, m_w extracted by the extractor after an extraction failure satisfy $(m_x, m_w) \in R_{\text{adv}}^{\text{comp}}$. And then it follows that $(x, w) \in R_{\text{adv}}^{\text{sym}}$ with $x := \tau(m_x)$, $w := \tau^*(m_w)$ by the converse of Lemma 4:

Lemma 6 (Relating the Relations, Part 2). *In an execution of* Sim_2 *the following holds with overwhelming probability: if* $(m_x, m_w) \in R_{\text{adv}}^{\text{comp}}$ *then* $(\tau(m_x), \tau^*(m_w)) \in R_{\text{adv}}^{\text{sym}}$.   ◇

Thus Lemma 5 is shown. From this, with Lemma 2 we get that ZK-breaks occur with negligible probability also for Sim_f. Based on this fact, we can show the following lemma:

Lemma 7 (No Extraction Failures). *In the hybrid execution of* Sim_f, *extraction failures occur with negligible probability.*   ◇

To see this, we use that ZK-breaks only occur with negligible probability in the execution of Sim_f. Thus, by definition of ZK-breaks, this means that $(x, w) \in R_{\text{adv}}^{\text{sym}}$ for the terms $x := \tau(m_x)$ and $w := \tau(m_w)$ computed after the extraction failure. Furthermore, by Lemma 1, it follows that $S \vdash w$. But then, by definition, **SymbExtr**(x, S) would have output a w or another witness, but not $\bot$. Thus the extraction failure would not have occurred. This shows Lemma 7.

Finally, from Lemmas 5 and 2 we get that extraction failures occur with negligible probability in the execution of Sim, too. Thus property (b) also holds, thus we have shown Sim to be indistinguishable.

Notice that the roundabout way through Sim_2 and Sim_f to show that extraction failures occur with negligible probability in the execution of Sim is necessary: We cannot directly show Lemma 5 for Sim_f because Sim_f uses the simulator to prove untrue statements (e.g., it may prove that a ciphertext contains a certain value, but since we use a fake encryption oracle, that ciphertext actually contains a zero-plaintext), so simulation-sound extractability cannot be applied. Also, we cannot use the fact $S \vdash \tau^*(x)$ directly on Sim because this fact cannot be propagated from Sim_f to Sim (since τ^* is executed after the extractor is used, we would need extraction ZK to bridge from Sim_2 to Sim_1).

Concluding the Proof. We have shown that Sim is Dolev-Yao and indistinguishable. From [3, Thm. 1] we then immediately get Theorem 1.

6   Conclusions

In this paper, we have shown that computational soundness of symbolic ZK proofs can be achieved under realistic cryptographic assumptions for which efficient realizations and generic constructions are known. The computational soundness proof has been conducted in CoSP, and hence it holds independent of the underlying symbolic calculi and comes with mechanized proof support.

We conclude by highlighting two open questions that we consider as future work. First, current abstractions model non-interactive ZK proofs, i.e., a ZK proof constitutes a message that can forwarded, put into other terms, etc. Developing a symbolic abstraction to reflect (the more common) interactive ZK proofs thus requires a conceptually different approach, as such proofs cannot be replayed, put into other terms, etc. We plan to draw ideas from a recently proposed symbolic abstraction for (interactive) secure multi-party computation [6] to reflect this behavior. Second, soundness proofs of individual primitives have typically been proved in isolation, without a guarantee that the soundness result prevails when composed. We plan to build on recent work on composable soundness notions [17] to establish a composable soundness result for ZK proofs.

References

1. Abadi, M., Gordon, A.D.: A calculus for cryptographic protocols: The spi calculus. In: ACM CCS (1997)
2. Abadi, M., Rogaway, P.: Reconciling two views of cryptography (the computational soundness of formal encryption). Journal of Cryptology 15(2) (2002)
3. Backes, M., Hofheinz, D., Unruh, D.: Cosp: A general framework for computational soundness proofs. In: ACM CCS (2009)
4. Backes, M., Hriţcu, C., Maffei, M.: Type-checking zero-knowledge. In: ACM CCS (2008)
5. Backes, M., Lorenz, S., Maffei, M., Pecina, K.: Anonymous Webs of Trust. In: Atallah, M.J., Hopper, N.J. (eds.) PETS 2010. LNCS, vol. 6205, pp. 130–148. Springer, Heidelberg (2010)
6. Backes, M., Maffei, M., Mohammadi, E.: Computationally sound abstraction and verification of secure multi-party computations. In: FSTTCS (2010)
7. Backes, M., Maffei, M., Unruh, D.: Zero-knowledge in the applied pi-calculus and automated verification of the direct anonymous attestation protocol. In: IEEE S&P (2008)
8. Backes, M., Maffei, M., Unruh, D.: Computationally sound verification of source code. In: ACM CCS (2010)
9. Backes, M., Pfitzmann, B.: Symmetric encryption in a simulatable Dolev-Yao style cryptographic library. In: IEEE CSFW (2004)
10. Backes, M., Unruh, D.: Computational soundness of symbolic zero-knowledge proofs. Journal of Computer Security 18(6) (2010)

11. Basin, D., Mödersheim, S., Viganò, L.: OFMC: A symbolic model checker for security protocols. International Journal of Information Security (2004)
12. Blanchet, B.: An Efficient Cryptographic Protocol Verifier Based on Prolog Rules. In: 14th IEEE CSFW (2001)
13. Brickell, E.F., Camenisch, J., Chen, L.: Direct anonymous attestation. In: ACM CCS (2004)
14. Canetti, R., Herzog, J.: Universally Composable Symbolic Analysis of Mutual Authentication and Key-Exchange Protocols. In: Halevi, S., Rabin, T. (eds.) TCC 2006. LNCS, vol. 3876, pp. 380–403. Springer, Heidelberg (2006)
15. Clarkson, M.R., Chong, S., Myers, A.C.: Civitas: Toward a Secure Voting System. In: IEEE S&P (2008)
16. Cortier, V., Warinschi, B.: Computationally Sound, Automated Proofs for Security Protocols. In: Sagiv, M. (ed.) ESOP 2005. LNCS, vol. 3444, pp. 157–171. Springer, Heidelberg (2005)
17. Cortier, V., Warinschi, B.: A composable computational soundness notion. In: Proc. 18th ACM CCS (2011)
18. Dolev, D., Yao, A.C.: On the security of public key protocols. IEEE Transactions on Information Theory 29(2) (1983)
19. Even, S., Goldreich, O.: On the security of multi-party ping-pong protocols. In: IEEE CSF (1983)
20. Goldwasser, S., Micali, S., Rackoff, C.: The knowledge complexity of interactive proof systems. SIAM Journal on Computing 18(1) (1989)
21. Groth, J.: Simulation-Sound NIZK Proofs for a Practical Language and Constant Size Group Signatures. In: Lai, X., Chen, K. (eds.) ASIACRYPT 2006. LNCS, vol. 4284, pp. 444–459. Springer, Heidelberg (2006)
22. Groth, J., Ostrovsky, R.: Cryptography in the Multi-string Model. In: Menezes, A. (ed.) CRYPTO 2007. LNCS, vol. 4622, pp. 323–341. Springer, Heidelberg (2007)
23. Kemmerer, R., Meadows, C., Millen, J.: Three systems for cryptographic protocol analysis. Journal of Cryptology 7(2) (1994)
24. Laud, P.: Symmetric encryption in automatic analyses for confidentiality against active adversaries. In: IEEE S&P (2004)
25. Li, H., Li, B.: An Unbounded Simulation-Sound Non-interactive Zero-Knowledge Proof System for NP. In: Feng, D., Lin, D., Yung, M. (eds.) CISC 2005. LNCS, vol. 3822, pp. 210–220. Springer, Heidelberg (2005)
26. Lowe, G.: Breaking and Fixing the Needham-Schroeder Public-Key Protocol Using FDR. In: Margaria, T., Steffen, B. (eds.) TACAS 1996. LNCS, vol. 1055, pp. 147–166. Springer, Heidelberg (1996)
27. Lu, L., Han, J., Liu, Y., Hu, L., Huai, J.-P., Ni, L., Ma, J.: Pseudo trust: Zero-knowledge authentication in anonymous p2ps. IEEE Trans. Parallel Distrib. Syst. (2008)
28. Maffei, M., Pecina, K.: Position paper: Privacy-aware proof-carrying authorization. In: PLAS (2011)
29. Merritt, M.: Cryptographic Protocols. PhD thesis, Georgia Tech (1983)
30. Micciancio, D., Warinschi, B.: Soundness of Formal Encryption in the Presence of Active Adversaries. In: Naor, M. (ed.) TCC 2004. LNCS, vol. 2951, pp. 133–151. Springer, Heidelberg (2004)
31. Sahai, A.: Non-malleable non-interactive zero knowledge and adaptive chosen-ciphertext security. In: FOCS (1999)
32. Sahai, A.: Simulation-sound non-interactive zero knowledge. Technical report, IBM Research Report RZ 3076 (2001)
33. Schneider, S.: Security properties and CSP. In: IEEE S&P (1996)

Proving More Observational Equivalences
with ProVerif

Vincent Cheval[1] and Bruno Blanchet[2]

[1] LSV, ENS Cachan & CNRS & INRIA Saclay Île-de-France, France
[2] INRIA Paris-Rocquencourt, France

Abstract. This paper presents an extension of the automatic protocol
verifier PROVERIF in order to prove more observational equivalences.
PROVERIF can prove observational equivalence between processes that
have the same structure but differ by the messages they contain. In
order to extend the class of equivalences that PROVERIF handles, we
extend the language of terms by defining more functions (destructors)
by rewrite rules. In particular, we allow rewrite rules with inequalities as
side-conditions, so that we can express tests "if then else" inside terms.
Finally, we provide an automatic procedure that translates a process
into an equivalent process that performs as many actions as possible inside terms, to allow PROVERIF to prove the desired equivalence. These
extensions have been implemented in PROVERIF and allow us to automatically prove anonymity in the private authentication protocol by
Abadi and Fournet.

1 Introduction

Today, many applications that manipulate private data incorporate a cryptographic protocol, in order to ensure that such private information is never disclosed to anyone but the entitled entities. However, it has been shown that some
currently used cryptographic protocols are flawed, e.g., the e-passport protocols [5]. It is therefore essential to obtain as much confidence as possible in the
correctness of security protocols. To this effect, several tools have been developed
to automatically verify security protocols. Until recently, most tools focused on
reachability properties (or trace properties), such as authentication and secrecy,
which specify that the protocols cannot reach a bad state. However, privacy-type
properties cannot be naturally formalised as reachability properties and require
the notion of behavioural equivalence, in order to specify the indistinguishability between several instances of the protocols. In the literature, the notion of
may-testing equivalence was first introduced in [16] and has been studied for
several calculi, e.g., the spi-calculus [3,13]. Typically, two processes P and Q
are may-testing equivalent if for any process O, the processes $P \mid O$ and $Q \mid O$
can both emit on the same channels. However, the high difficulty of deciding
this equivalence led to the introduction of stronger equivalences such as *observational equivalence* that additionally checks the bisimilarity of the process P
and Q. This notion was the focus of several works, e.g., [7,12]. In this paper, we
focus on the automation of the proofs of observational equivalence.

D. Basin and J.C. Mitchell (Eds.): POST 2013, LNCS 7796, pp. 226–246, 2013.
© Springer-Verlag Berlin Heidelberg 2013

Related Work. The first algorithms to verify equivalence properties for security protocols dealt with a bounded number of sessions, a fixed set of basic primitives, and no else branches [14,13], but their complexity was too large for practical implementations. [6] showed that diff-equivalence, a strong equivalence between processes that have the same structure but differ by the terms they contain, is also decidable for bounded processes without else-branches; this result applies in particular to the detection of off-line guessing attacks against password-based protocols and to the proof of strong secrecy. However, the procedure does not seem to be well-suited for an implementation. Recently, a more practical algorithm was designed for bounded processes with else branches, non-determinism, and a fixed set of primitives [9] but there is no available implementation. These techniques rely on a symbolic semantics [8,12,15]: in such a semantics, the messages that come from the adversary are represented by variables, to avoid an unbounded case distinction on these messages.

To our knowledge, only three works resulted in automatic tools that verify equivalence properties for security protocols: PROVERIF [7], SPEC [17], and AKISS [10]. The tool SPEC provides a decision procedure for observational equivalence for processes in the spi-calculus. The tool AKISS decides a weaker equivalence close to the may-testing equivalence for a wide variety of primitives. The scope of these two tools is limited to bounded determinate processes without non-trivial else branches, that is, processes whose executions are entirely determined by the adversary inputs. At last, the tool PROVERIF was first a protocol analyser for trace properties but, since [7], it can also check the diff-equivalence between processes written in the applied pi calculus [1]. Although the diff-equivalence is stronger than observational equivalence, it still allows one to express many interesting properties such as anonymity and unlinkability, and it is much easier to prove than observational equivalence. Furthermore, PROVERIF is the only tool that accepts unbounded processes with else branches and any cryptographic primitives that can be represented by an equational theory and/or rewrite rules. Even if it does not always terminate, it was shown very efficient for many case studies (e.g., proving the absence of guessing attacks in EKE, proving the core security of JFK [7] or proving anonymity and unlinkability of the Active Authentication protocol of the electronic passport [4]). Hence the present paper focuses on the tool PROVERIF.

Motivation. Since the notion of equivalence proved by PROVERIF is stronger than observational equivalence, it may yield false attacks. Indeed, PROVERIF proves equivalences $P \approx Q$ in which P and Q are two variants of the same process obtained by selecting different terms for P and Q. Moreover, PROVERIF requires that all tests yield the same result in both processes, in particular the tests of conditional branchings. Thus, for a protocol that does not satisfy this condition, PROVERIF will fail to prove equivalence. Unfortunately, many indistinguishable processes do not satisfy this condition. Consider for example the processes:

$$P \stackrel{def}{=} c(x).\text{if } x = \text{pk}(sk_A) \text{ then } \overline{c}\langle\{s\}_{\text{pk}(sk_A)}\rangle \text{ else } \overline{c}\langle\{N_p\}_{\text{pk}(sk_A)}\rangle$$
$$Q \stackrel{def}{=} c(x).\text{if } x = \text{pk}(sk_B) \text{ then } \overline{c}\langle\{s\}_{\text{pk}(sk_B)}\rangle \text{ else } \overline{c}\langle\{N_q\}_{\text{pk}(sk_B)}\rangle$$

where all names but c are private and the public keys $\mathsf{pk}(sk_A)$ and $\mathsf{pk}(sk_B)$ are public. The protocol P is simply waiting for the public key of the agent A ($\mathsf{pk}(sk_A)$) on a channel c. If P receives it, then he sends some secret s encrypted with A's public key; otherwise, he sends a fresh nonce N_p encrypted with A's public key on channel c. On the other hand, the protocol Q does similar actions but is waiting for the public key of the agent B ($\mathsf{pk}(sk_B)$) instead of A. Assuming that the attacker does not have access to the private keys of A and B, then the two protocols are equivalent since the attacker cannot differentiate $\{s\}_{\mathsf{pk}(sk_A)}$, $\{N_p\}_{\mathsf{pk}(sk_A)}$, $\{s\}_{\mathsf{pk}(sk_B)}$, and $\{N_q\}_{\mathsf{pk}(sk_B)}$.

However, if the intruder sends the public key of the agent A ($\mathsf{pk}(sk_A)$), then the test of the conditional branching in P will succeed ($\mathsf{pk}(sk_A) = \mathsf{pk}(sk_A)$) whereas the test of the same conditional branching in Q will fail ($\mathsf{pk}(sk_A) \neq \mathsf{pk}(sk_B)$). Since this test does not yield the same result in both processes, PROVERIF will fail to prove the equivalence between P and Q. This false attack also occurs in more realistic case studies, e.g., the private authentication protocol [2] and the Basic Access Control protocol of the e-passport [5].

Our Contribution. Our main contribution consists in addressing the issue of false attacks due to conditional branchings. In particular, we allow function symbols defined by rewrite rules with inequalities as side-conditions, so that we can express tests of conditional branchings directly inside terms (Section 2). Therefore, we still consider equivalences between processes that differ by the terms they contain, but our term algebra is now richer as it can express tests. Hence, we can now prove equivalences between processes that take different branches in internal tests, provided that what they do after these tests can be merged into a single process. We show how the original Horn clauses based algorithm of PROVERIF can be adapted to our new calculus (Sections 3 and 4). Moreover, we provide an automatic procedure that transforms a process into an equivalent process that contains as few conditional branchings as possible, which allows PROVERIF to prove equivalence on a larger class of processes. In particular, the implementation of our extension in PROVERIF allowed us to automatically prove anonymity of the private authentication protocol for an unbounded number of sessions (Section 5). Anonymity was already proven by hand in [2] for the private authentication protocol; we automate this proof for a slightly simplified model. We eliminated some false attacks for the Basic Access Control protocol of the e-passport; however, other false attacks remain so we are still unable to conclude for this protocol. Our implementation is available as PROVERIF 1.87beta, at http://proverif.inria.fr. A long version with additional details and proofs is available at http://www.lsv.ens-cachan.fr/~cheval/(BC)POST13.pdf.

2   Model

This section introduces our process calculus, by giving its syntax and semantics. As mentioned above, our work extends the behaviour of destructor symbols, so our syntax and semantics of terms change in comparison to the original calculus of PROVERIF [7]. However, we did not modify the syntax of processes thus the

$$M ::= \qquad\qquad\qquad\qquad\qquad \text{message}$$

x, y, z	variables
a, b, c	names
$\mathsf{f}(M_1, \ldots, M_n)$	constructor application

$$U ::= \qquad\qquad\qquad\qquad\qquad \text{may-fail message}$$

M	message
fail	failure
u	may-fail variable

$$D ::= \qquad\qquad\qquad\qquad\qquad \text{term evaluation}$$

U	may-fail message
eval $\mathsf{h}(D_1, \ldots, D_n)$	function evaluation

$$P, Q, R ::= \qquad\qquad\qquad\qquad\qquad \text{processes}$$

0	nil
$M(x).P$	input
$\overline{M}\langle N \rangle.P$	output
$P \mid Q$	parallel composition
$!P$	replication
$(\nu a)P$	restriction
let $x = D$ in P else Q	term evaluation

Fig. 1. Syntax of terms and processes

semantics of processes differs only due to changes coming from the modifications in the semantics of terms.

2.1 Syntax

The syntax of our calculus is summarised in Fig. 1. The messages sent on the network are modelled using an abstract term algebra. We assume an infinite set of names $\mathcal{N}$ and an infinite set of variables $\mathcal{X}$. We also consider a signature Σ consisting of a finite set of function symbols with their arity. We distinguish two categories of function symbols: constructors f and destructors g. Constructors build terms; destructors, defined by rewrite rules, manipulate terms, as detailed below. We denote by h a constructor or a destructor. *Messages* M are terms built from variables, names, and constructors applied to terms.

We define an *equational theory* by a finite set of equations $M = N$, where M, N are terms without names. The equational theory is then obtained from these equations by reflexive, symmetric, and transitive closure, closure under application of function symbols, and closure under substitution of terms for variables. By identifying an equational theory with its signature Σ, we denote $M =_\Sigma N$ an equality modulo the equational theory, and $M \neq_\Sigma N$ an inequality modulo the equational theory. We write $M = N$ and $M \neq N$ for syntactic equality and inequality, respectively. In this paper, we only consider consistent equational theories, i.e., there exist terms M and N such that $M \neq_\Sigma N$.

Destructors. In [7], the rewrite rules describing the behaviour of destructors follow the usual definition of a rewrite rule. However, as previously mentioned, we want to introduce tests directly into terms and more specifically into the definition of destructors. Hence, we introduce *formulas* on messages in order to express these tests. We consider formulas ϕ of the form $\bigwedge_{i=1}^n \forall \tilde{x}_i.M_i \neq_\Sigma N_i$, where $\tilde{x}$ stands for a sequence of variables $x_1, \ldots, x_k$. We denote by $\top$ and $\bot$ the *true* and *false* formulas, respectively corresponding to an empty conjunction ($n = 0$) and to $x \neq_\Sigma x$, for instance. Formulas will be used as side conditions for destructors. We denote by $fv(\phi)$ the free variables of ϕ, i.e., the variables that are not universally quantified. Let σ be a substitution mapping variables to ground terms. We define $\sigma \vDash \phi$ as follows: $\sigma \vDash \bigwedge_{i=1}^n \forall \tilde{x}_i.M_i \neq_\Sigma N_i$ if and only if for $i = 1, \ldots n$, for all σ_i of domain $\tilde{x}_i$, $\sigma\sigma_i M_i \neq_\Sigma \sigma\sigma_i N_i$.

In [7], destructors are partial functions defined by rewrite rules; when no rewrite rule can be applied, we say that the destructor fails. However, this formalism does not allow destructors to succeed when one of their arguments fails. We shall need this feature in order to include as many tests as possible in terms. Therefore, we extend the definition of destructors by defining *may-fail messages*, denoted by U, which can be messages M, the special value fail, or a variable u. We separate fail from ordinary messages M so that the equational theory does not apply to fail. May-fail messages represent the possible arguments and result of a destructor. We differentiate variables for may-fail messages, denoted u, v, w from variables for messages, denoted x, y, z. A may-fail variable u can be instantiated by a may-fail term while a message variable x can be instantiated only by a message, and so cannot be instantiated by fail.

For two ground may-fail messages U_1 and U_2, we say that $U_1 =_\Sigma U_2$ if and only if $U_1 = U_2 =$ fail or U_1, U_2 are both messages, denoted M_1, M_2, and $M_1 =_\Sigma M_2$. Given a signature Σ, a destructor $\mathbf{g}$ of arity n is defined by a finite set of rewrite rules $\mathbf{g}(U_1, \ldots, U_n) \to U \parallel \phi$ where $U_1, \ldots, U_n, U$ are may-fail messages that do not contain any name, ϕ is a formula as defined above that does not contain any name, and the variables of U and $fv(\phi)$ are bound in $U_1, \ldots, U_n$. Note that all variables in $fv(\phi)$ are necessarily message variables. Variables are subject to renaming. We omit the formula ϕ when it is $\top$. We denote by $\mathrm{def}_\Sigma(\mathbf{g})$ the set of rewrite rules describing $\mathbf{g}$ in the signature Σ.

Example 1. Consider a symmetric encryption scheme where the decryption function either properly decrypts a ciphertext using the correct private key, or fails. To model this encryption scheme, we consider, in a signature Σ, the constructor senc for encryption and the destructor sdec for decryption, with the following rewrite rules:

- sdec(senc$(x, y), y) \to x$ (decryption succeeds)
- sdec$(x, y) \to$ fail $\parallel \forall z.x \neq_\Sigma$ senc(z, y) (decryption fails, because x is not a ciphertext under the correct key)
- sdec(fail, $u) \to$ fail, sdec$(u,$ fail$) \to$ fail (the arguments failed, the decryption also fails)

Let $U_1, \ldots, U_n$ be may-fail messages and $\mathbf{g}$ be a destructor of arity n. We say that $\mathbf{g}$ rewrites $U_1, \ldots, U_n$ into U, denoted $\mathbf{g}(U_1, \ldots, U_n) \to U$, if there exist

$g(U'_1, \ldots, U'_n) \to U' \parallel \phi$ in $\text{def}_\Sigma(g)$, and a substitution σ such that $\sigma U'_i =_\Sigma U_i$ for all $i = 1 \ldots n$, $\sigma U' = U$ and $\sigma \vDash \phi$. At last, we ask that, given a signature Σ, for all destructors g of arity n, $\text{def}_\Sigma(g)$ satisfies the following properties:

P1. For all ground may-fail messages $U_1, \ldots, U_n$, there exists a may-fail message U such that $g(U_1, \ldots, U_n) \to U$.

P2. For all ground may-fail messages $U_1, \ldots, U_n, V_1, V_2$, if $g(U_1, \ldots, U_n) \to V_1$ and $g(U_1, \ldots, U_n) \to V_2$ then $V_1 =_\Sigma V_2$.

Property P1 expresses that all destructors are total while Property P2 expresses that they are deterministic (modulo the equational theory). By Property P2, a destructor cannot reduce to fail and to a message at the same time.

In Example 1, the destructor sdec follows the classical definition of the symmetric decryption. However, thanks to the formulas and the fact that the arguments of a destructor can fail, we can describe the behaviour of new primitives.

Example 2. We define a destructor that tests equality and returns a boolean by:

$$\text{eq}(x, x) \to \text{true} \qquad\qquad \text{eq}(x, y) \to \text{false} \parallel x \neq_\Sigma y$$
$$\text{eq}(\text{fail}, u) \to \text{fail} \qquad\qquad \text{eq}(u, \text{fail}) \to \text{fail}$$

This destructor fails when one of its arguments fails. This destructor could not be defined in PROVERIF without our extension, because one could not test $x \neq_\Sigma y$.

From Usual Destructors to our Extension. From a destructor defined, as in [7], by rewrite rules $g(M_1, \ldots, M_n) \to M$ without side conditions and such that the destructor is considered to fail when no rewrite rule applies, we can build a destructor in our formalism. The algorithm is given in Lemma 1 below.

Lemma 1. *Consider a signature Σ. Let g be a destructor of arity n described by the set of rewrite rules $S = \{g(M_1^i, \ldots, M_n^i) \to M^i \mid i = 1, \ldots, m\}$. Assume that g is deterministic, i.e., S satisfies Property P2. The following set $\text{def}_\Sigma(g)$ satisfies Properties P1 and P2:*

$$\text{def}_\Sigma(g) = S \cup \{g(x_1, \ldots, x_n) \to \text{fail} \parallel \phi\}$$
$$\cup \{g(u_1, \ldots, u_{k-1}, \text{fail}, u_{k+1}, \ldots, u_n) \to \text{fail} \mid k = 1, \ldots, n\}$$

where $\phi = \bigwedge_{i=1}^m \forall \tilde{y}_i.(x_1, \ldots, x_n) \neq_\Sigma (M_1^i, \ldots, M_n^i)$ and $\tilde{y}_i$ are the variables of $(M_1^i, \ldots, M_n^i)$, and $x_1, \ldots, x_n$ are message variables.

The users can therefore continue defining destructors as before in PROVERIF; the tool checks that the destructors are deterministic and automatically completes the definition following Lemma 1.

Generation of Deterministic and Total Destructors. With our extension, we want the users to be able to define destructors with side conditions. However, these destructors must satisfy Properties P1 and P2. Instead of having to verify these properties a posteriori, we use a method that allows the user to provide precisely the destructors that satisfy P1 and P2: the user inputs a sequence of rewrite rules $g(U_1^1, \ldots, U_n^1) \to V^1$ otherwise $\ldots$ otherwise $g(U_1^m, \ldots, U_n^m) \to V^m$ where U_k^i, V^i are may-fail messages, for all i, k. Intuitively, this sequence indicates that when reducing terms by the destructor g, we try to apply the rewrite rules in the order of the sequence, and if no rule is applicable then the destructor fails. To model the case where no rule is applicable, we add the rewrite rule $g(u_1, \ldots, u_n) \to \text{fail}$ where $u_1, \ldots, u_n$ are distinct may-fail variables, at the end of the previous sequence of rules. Then, the obtained sequence is translated into a set S of rewrite rules with side conditions as follows

$$S \stackrel{\text{def}}{=} \left\{ g(U_1^i, \ldots, U_n^i) \to V^i \;\|\; \bigwedge_{j<i} \forall \tilde{u}^j.(U_1^i, \ldots, U_n^i) \neq_\Sigma (U_1^j, \ldots, U_n^j) \right\}_{i=1..m+1}$$

where $\tilde{u}^j$ are the variables of $U_1^j, \ldots, U_n^j$. We use side-conditions to make sure that rule i is not applied if rule j for $j < i$ can be applied. Notice that, in the set S defined above, the formulas may contain may-fail variables or the constant fail. In order to match our formalism, we instantiate these variables by either a message variable or fail, and then we simplify the formulas.

Term Evaluation. A *term evaluation* represents the evaluation of a series of constructors and destructors. The term evaluation eval $h(D_1, \ldots, D_n)$ indicates that the function symbol h will be evaluated. While all destructors must be preceded by eval, some constructors might also be preceded by eval in a term evaluation. In fact, the reader may ignore the prefix eval since eval h and h have the same semantics with the initial definition of constructors with equations. However, eval becomes useful when we convert equations into rewrite rules (see Section 4.1). The prefix eval is used to indicate whether a term has been evaluated or not. Even though we allow may-fail messages in term evaluations, since no construct binds may-fail variables in processes, only messages M and fail may in fact occur. In order to avoid distinguishing constructors and destructors in the definition of term evaluation, for f a constructor of arity n, we let $\text{def}_\Sigma(f) = \{f(x_1, \ldots, x_n) \to f(x_1, \ldots, x_n)\} \cup \{f(u_1, \ldots, u_{i-1}, \text{fail}, u_{i+1}, \ldots, u_n) \to \text{fail} \mid i = 1, \ldots, n\}$. The second part of the union corresponds to the failure cases: the constructor fails if, and only if, one of its arguments fails.

Processes. At last, the syntax of processes corresponds exactly to [7]. A trailing 0 can be omitted after an input or an output. An else branch can be omitted when it is else 0.

Even if the condition if $M = N$ then P else Q is not included in our calculus, it can be defined as let $x = \text{equals}(M, N)$ in P else Q, where x is a fresh variable and equals is a binary destructor with the rewrite rules $\{\text{equals}(x, x) \to x, \text{equals}(x, y) \to \text{fail} \;\|\; x \neq_\Sigma y, \text{equals}(\text{fail}, u) \to \text{fail}, \text{equals}(u, \text{fail}) \to \text{fail}\}$. The destructor equals succeeds if and only if its two arguments are equal messages modulo the equational theory and different from fail. We always include this destructor in the signature Σ. An evaluation context C is a closed context built from $[\,]$, $C \mid P$, $P \mid C$, and $(\nu a)C$.

Example 3. We consider a slightly simplified version of the private authentication protocol given in [2]. In this protocol, a participant A is willing to engage in communication and reveal its identity to a participant B, without revealing it to other participants. The cryptographic primitives used in this protocol are the asymmetric encryption and pairing. Expressed in PROVERIF syntax, the participants A and B proceed as follows:

$$A(sk_a, sk_b) \stackrel{def}{=} (\nu n_a)\overline{c}\langle \mathsf{aenc}(\langle n_a, \mathsf{pk}(sk_a)\rangle, \mathsf{pk}(sk_b))\rangle.c(x).0$$

$$
\begin{aligned}
B(sk_b, sk_a) \stackrel{def}{=}\ & (\nu n_b)c(y).\mathsf{let}\ x = \mathsf{adec}(y, sk_b)\ \mathsf{in} \\
& \mathsf{let}\ xn_a = \mathsf{proj}_1(x)\ \mathsf{in} \\
& \quad \mathsf{let}\ z = \mathsf{equals}(\mathsf{proj}_2(x), \mathsf{pk}(sk_a))\ \mathsf{in} \\
& \quad\quad \overline{c}\langle \mathsf{aenc}(\langle xn_a, \langle n_b, \mathsf{pk}(sk_b)\rangle\rangle, \mathsf{pk}(sk_a))\rangle\rangle.0 \\
& \quad \mathsf{else}\ \overline{c}\langle \mathsf{aenc}(n_b, \mathsf{pk}(sk_b))\rangle\rangle.0 \\
& \mathsf{else}\ \overline{c}\langle \mathsf{aenc}(n_b, \mathsf{pk}(sk_b))\rangle\rangle.0 \\
& \mathsf{else}\ \overline{c}\langle \mathsf{senc}(n_b, \mathsf{pk}(sk_b))\rangle\rangle.0
\end{aligned}
$$

$$System(sk_a, sk_b) \stackrel{def}{=} A(sk_a, sk_b)\ |\ B(sk_b, sk_a)$$

where sk_a and sk_b are the respective private keys of A and B, proj_1 and proj_2 are the two projections of a pairing denoted by $\langle\ ,\ \rangle$, aenc and adec are the asymmetric encryption and decryption, and $\mathsf{pk}(sk)$ is the public key associated to the private key sk.

In other words, A first sends to B a nonce n_a and its own public key $\mathsf{pk}(sk_a)$ encrypted with the public key of B, $\mathsf{pk}(sk_b)$. After receiving this message, B checks that the message is of the correct form and that it contains the public key of A. If so, B sends back to A the "correct" message composed of the nonce n_a he received, n_b a freshly generated nonce, and his own public key ($\mathsf{pk}(sk_b)$), all this encrypted with the public key of A. Otherwise, B sends back a "dummy" message, $\mathsf{aenc}(n_b, \mathsf{pk}(sk_b))$. From the point of view of the attacker, this dummy message is indistinguishable from the "correct" one since the private keys sk_a and sk_b are unknown to the attacker, so the attacker should not be able to tell whether A or another participant is talking to B. This is what we are going to prove formally.

2.2 Semantics

The semantics of processes and term evaluations is summarised in Fig. 2. The formula $D \Downarrow_\Sigma U$ means that D evaluates to U. When the term evaluation corresponds to a function h preceded by eval, the evaluation proceeds recursively by evaluating the arguments of the function and then by applying the rewrite rules of h in $\mathsf{def}_\Sigma(h)$ to compute U, taking into account the side-conditions in ϕ.

The semantics of processes in PROVERIF is defined by a *structural equivalence*, denoted $\equiv$, and some *internal reductions*. The structural equivalence $\equiv$ is the smallest equivalence relation on extended processes that is closed under α-conversion of names and variables, by application of evaluation contexts, and

$U \Downarrow_\Sigma U$

eval $h(D_1, \ldots, D_n) \Downarrow_\Sigma \sigma U$

  if $h(U_1, \ldots, U_n) \to U \parallel \phi$ is in $\mathrm{def}_\Sigma(h)$ and σ is such

  that for all i, $D_i \Downarrow_\Sigma V_i$, $V_i =_\Sigma \sigma U_i$ and $\sigma \vDash \phi$

$\overline{N}\langle M \rangle.Q \mid N'(x).P \to_\Sigma Q \mid P\{^M/_x\}$	if $N =_\Sigma N'$	(Red I/O)
let $x = D$ in P else $Q \to_\Sigma P\{^M/_x\}$	if $D \Downarrow_\Sigma M$	(Red Fun 1)
let $x = D$ in P else $Q \to_\Sigma Q$	if $D \Downarrow_\Sigma \mathsf{fail}$	(Red Fun 2)
$!P \to_\Sigma P \mid !P$		(Red Repl)
$P \to_\Sigma Q \Rightarrow P \mid R \to_\Sigma Q \mid R$		(Red Par)
$P \to_\Sigma Q \Rightarrow (\nu a)P \to_\Sigma (\nu a)Q$		(Red Res)
$P' \equiv P,\ P \to_\Sigma Q,\ Q \equiv Q' \Rightarrow P' \to_\Sigma Q'$		(Red $\equiv$)

Fig. 2. Semantics of terms and processes

satisfying some further basic structural rules such as $P \mid 0 \equiv P$, associativity and commutativity of $\mid$, and scope extrusion. However, this structural equivalence does not substitute terms equal modulo the equational theory and does not model the replication. Both properties are in fact modelled as internal reduction rules for processes. This semantics differs from [7] by the rule (Red Fun 2) which previously corresponded to the case where the term evaluation D could not be reduced whereas D is reduced to fail in our semantics.

Both relations $\equiv$ and $\to_\Sigma$ are defined only on closed processes. We denote by $\to_\Sigma^*$ the reflexive and transitive closure of $\to_\Sigma$, and by $\to_\Sigma^* \equiv$ its composition with $\equiv$. When Σ is clear from the context, we abbreviate $\to_\Sigma$ to $\to$ and $\Downarrow_\Sigma$ to $\Downarrow$.

3   Using Biprocesses to Prove Observational Equivalence

In this section, we recall the notions of observational equivalence and biprocesses introduced in [7].

Definition 1. *We say that the process P emits on M $(P\downarrow_M)$ if and only if $P \to_\Sigma^* \equiv C[\overline{M'}\langle N \rangle.R]$ for some evaluation context C that does not bind $\mathrm{fn}(M)$ and $M =_\Sigma M'$.*

Observational equivalence, denoted $\approx$, is the largest symmetric relation $\mathcal{R}$ between closed processes such that $P \mathcal{R} Q$ implies:

1. *if $P\downarrow_M$, then $Q\downarrow_M$;*
2. *if $P \to_\Sigma^* P'$, then $Q \to_\Sigma^* Q'$ and $P' \mathcal{R} Q'$ for some Q';*
3. *$C[P] \mathcal{R} C[Q]$ for all closed evaluation contexts C.*

Intuitively, an evaluation context may represent an adversary, and two processes are observationally equivalent when no adversary can distinguish them. One of the most difficult parts of deciding the observational equivalence between two processes directly comes from the second item of Definition 1. Indeed, this

$$\overline{N}\langle M\rangle.Q \mid N'(x).P \;\rightarrow\; Q \mid P\{^M/_x\} \qquad\qquad \text{(Red I/O)}$$
$$\text{if } \mathsf{fst}(N) =_\Sigma \mathsf{fst}(N') \text{ and } \mathsf{snd}(N) =_\Sigma \mathsf{snd}(N')$$

$$\mathsf{let}\ x = D\ \mathsf{in}\ P\ \mathsf{else}\ Q \rightarrow P\{^{\mathsf{diff}[M_1,M_2]}/_x\} \qquad \text{(Red Fun 1)}$$
$$\text{if } \mathsf{fst}(D)\Downarrow_\Sigma M_1 \text{ and } \mathsf{snd}(D)\Downarrow_\Sigma M_2$$
$$\mathsf{let}\ x = D\ \mathsf{in}\ P\ \mathsf{else}\ Q \rightarrow Q \qquad\qquad\qquad \text{(Red Fun 2)}$$
$$\text{if } \mathsf{fst}(D)\Downarrow_\Sigma \mathsf{fail} \text{ and } \mathsf{snd}(D)\Downarrow_\Sigma \mathsf{fail}$$

Fig. 3. Generalized rules for biprocesses

condition indicates that each reduction of a process has to be matched in the second process. However, we consider a process algebra with replication, hence there are usually infinitely many candidates for this mapping.

To solve this problem, [7] introduces a calculus that represents pairs of processes, called *biprocesses*, that have the same structure and differ only by the terms and term evaluations that they contain. The grammar of the calculus is a simple extension of the grammar of Fig. 1 with additional cases so that $\mathsf{diff}[M, M']$ is a term and $\mathsf{diff}[D, D']$ is a term evaluation.

Given a biprocess P, we define two processes $\mathsf{fst}(P)$ and $\mathsf{snd}(P)$, as follows: $\mathsf{fst}(P)$ is obtained by replacing all occurrences of $\mathsf{diff}[M, M']$ with M and $\mathsf{diff}[D, D']$ with D in P, and similarly, $\mathsf{snd}(P)$ is obtained by replacing $\mathsf{diff}[M, M']$ with M' and $\mathsf{diff}[D, D']$ with D' in P. We define $\mathsf{fst}(D)$, $\mathsf{fst}(M)$, $\mathsf{snd}(D)$, and $\mathsf{snd}(M)$ similarly. A process or context is said to be *plain* when it does not contain diff.

Definition 2. *Let P be a closed biprocess. We say that P satisfies observational equivalence when $\mathsf{fst}(P) \approx \mathsf{snd}(P)$.*

The semantics of biprocesses is defined as in Fig. 2 with generalized rules (Red I/O), (Red Fun 1), and (Red Fun 2) given in Fig. 3.

The semantics of biprocesses is such that a biprocess reduces if and only if both sides of the biprocess reduce in the same way: a communication succeeds on both sides; a term evaluation succeeds on both sides or fails on both sides. When the two sides of the biprocess reduce in different ways, the biprocess blocks. The following lemma shows that, when both sides of a biprocess always reduce in the same way, then that biprocess satisfies observational equivalence.

Lemma 2. *Let P_0 be a closed biprocess. Suppose that, for all plain evaluation contexts C, all evaluation contexts C', and all reductions $C[P_0] \rightarrow^* P$,*

1. *if $P \equiv C'[\overline{N}\langle M\rangle.Q \mid N'(x).R]$ then $\mathsf{fst}(N) =_\Sigma \mathsf{fst}(N')$ if and only if $\mathsf{snd}(N) =_\Sigma \mathsf{snd}(N')$;*
2. *if $P \equiv C'[\mathsf{let}\ x = D\ \mathsf{in}\ Q\ \mathsf{else}\ R]$ then $\mathsf{fst}(D)\Downarrow_\Sigma\mathsf{fail}$ if and only if $\mathsf{snd}(D)\Downarrow_\Sigma\mathsf{fail}$.*

Then P_0 satisfies observational equivalence.

Intuitively, the semantics for biprocesses forces that each reduction of a process has to be matched by the same reduction in the second process. Hence, verifying the second item of Definition 1 becomes less problematic since we reduce to one the number of possible candidates Q'.

Example 4. Coming back to the private authentication protocol detailed in Example 3, we want to verify the anonymity of the participant A. Intuitively, this protocol preserves anonymity if an attacker cannot distinguish whether B is talking to A or to another participant A', assuming that A, A', and B are honest participants and furthermore assuming that the intruder knows the public keys of A, A', and B. Hence, the anonymity property is modelled by an observational equivalence between two instances of the protocol: one where B is talking to A and the other where B is talking to A', which is modelled as follows:

$$(\nu sk_a)(\nu sk'_a)(\nu sk_b)\overline{c}\langle \mathsf{pk}(sk_a)\rangle.\overline{c}\langle \mathsf{pk}(sk'_a)\rangle.\overline{c}\langle \mathsf{pk}(sk_b)\rangle.System(sk_a, sk_b)$$
$$\approx (\nu sk_a)(\nu sk'_a)(\nu sk_b)\overline{c}\langle \mathsf{pk}(sk_a)\rangle.\overline{c}\langle \mathsf{pk}(sk'_a)\rangle.\overline{c}\langle \mathsf{pk}(sk_b)\rangle.System(sk'_a, sk_b)$$

Since the "dummy" message and the "correct" one are indistinguishable from the point of view of the attacker, this equivalence holds. To prove this equivalence using PROVERIF, we first have to transform this equivalence into a biprocess. This is easily done since only the private keys ska and ska' change between the two processes. Hence, we define the biprocess P_0 as follows:

$$(\nu sk_a)(\nu sk'_a)(\nu sk_b)\overline{c}\langle \mathsf{pk}(sk_a)\rangle.\overline{c}\langle \mathsf{pk}(sk'_a)\rangle.\overline{c}\langle \mathsf{pk}(sk_b)\rangle.System(\mathsf{diff}[sk_a, sk'_a], sk_b)$$

Note that $\mathsf{fst}(P_0)$ and $\mathsf{snd}(P_0)$ correspond to the two protocols of the equivalence. For simplicity, we only consider two sessions in this example but our results also apply to an unbounded number of sessions (for the definition of anonymity of [5]).

4 Clause Generation

In [7], observational equivalence is verified by translating the considered biprocess into a set of Horn clauses, and using a resolution algorithm on these clauses. We adapt this translation to our new destructors.

4.1 From Equational Theories to Rewrite Rules

Equational theories are a very powerful tool for modeling cryptographic primitives. However, for a practical algorithm, it is easier to work with rewrite rules rather than with equational theories. Hence in [7], a signature Σ with an equational theory is transformed into a signature Σ' with rewrite rules that models Σ, when Σ has the finite variant property [11]. These rewrite rules may rewrite a term M into several irreducible forms (the variants), which are all equal modulo Σ, and such that, when M and M' are equal modulo Σ, M and M' rewrite to at least one common irreducible form. We reuse the algorithm from [7] for generating Σ', adapting it to our formalism by just completing the rewrite rules of constructors with rewrite rules that reduce to fail when an argument is fail.

4.2 Patterns and Facts

In the clauses, the messages are represented by patterns, with the following grammar:

$p ::=$	pattern		$mp ::=$	may-fail pattern
x, y, z, i	variables		p	pattern
$f(p_1, \ldots, p_n)$	constructor application		u, v	may-fail variables
$a[p_1, \ldots, p_n]$	name		fail	failure

The patterns p are the same as in [7]. The variable i represents a session identifier for each replication of a process. A pattern $a[p_1, \ldots, p_n]$ is assigned to each name of a process P. The arguments $p_1, \ldots, p_n$ allow one to model that a fresh name a is created at execution of (νa). For example, in the process $!\, c'(x).(\nu a)P$, each name created by (νa) is represented by $a[i, x]$ where i is the session identifier for the replication and x is the message received as input in $c'(x)$. Hence, the name a is represented as a function of i and x. In two different sessions, (i, x) takes two different values, so the two created instances of a $(a[i, x])$ are different.

Since we introduced may-fail messages to represent the possible failure of a destructor, we also define *may-fail patterns* to represent the failure in clauses. As in messages and may-fail messages, a may-fail variable u can be instantiated by a pattern or fail, whereas a variable x cannot be instantiated by fail.

Clauses are built from the following predicates:

$F ::=$	facts
$\mathsf{att}'(mp, mp')$	attacker knowledge
$\mathsf{msg}'(p_1, p_2, p'_1, p'_2)$	output message p_2 on p_1 (resp. p'_2 on p'_1)
$\mathsf{input}'(p, p')$	input on p (resp. p')
$\mathsf{formula}(\bigwedge_i \forall \tilde{z}_i . p_i \neq_\Sigma p'_i)$	formula
bad	bad

Intuitively, $\mathsf{att}'(mp, mp')$ means that the attacker may obtain mp in $\mathsf{fst}(P)$ and mp' in $\mathsf{snd}(P)$ by the same operations; the fact $\mathsf{msg}'(p_1, p_2, p'_1, p'_2)$ means that message p_2 may be output on channel p_1 by the process $\mathsf{fst}(P)$ while p'_2 may be output on channel p'_1 by the process $\mathsf{snd}(P)$ after the same reductions; $\mathsf{input}'(p, p')$ means that an input is possible on channel p in $\mathsf{fst}(P)$ and on channel p' in $\mathsf{snd}(P)$. Note that both facts msg' and input' contain only patterns and not may-fail patterns. Hence channels and sent terms are necessarily messages and so cannot be fail. The fact $\mathsf{formula}(\phi)$ means that ϕ has to be satisfied. At last, bad serves in detecting violations of observational equivalence: when bad is not derivable, we have observational equivalence.

4.3   Clauses for the Attacker

The capabilities of the attacker are represented by clauses adapted from the ones in [7] to fit our new formalism. We give below the clauses that differ from [7].

$$\mathsf{att}'(\mathsf{fail}, \mathsf{fail}) \qquad\qquad\qquad\qquad\qquad\qquad\qquad \text{(Rfail)}$$

For each function h, for each pair of rewrite rules

$$\mathsf{h}(U_1, \ldots, U_n) \to U \parallel \phi \text{ and } \mathsf{h}(U_1', \ldots, U_n') \to U' \parallel \phi'$$
$$\text{in def}_{\Sigma'}(\mathsf{h}) \text{ (after renaming of variables),} \tag{Rf}$$
$$\mathsf{att}'(U_1, U_1') \wedge \ldots \wedge \mathsf{att}'(U_n, U_n') \wedge \mathsf{formula}(\phi \wedge \phi') \to \mathsf{att}'(U, U')$$

$$\mathsf{input}'(x, x') \wedge \mathsf{msg}'(x, z, y', z') \wedge \mathsf{formula}(x' \neq_\Sigma y') \to \mathsf{bad} \tag{Rcom}$$

$$\mathsf{att}'(x, \mathsf{fail}) \to \mathsf{bad} \tag{Rfailure}$$

plus the symmetric clauses (Rcom') and (Rfailure') obtained from (Rcom) and (Rfailure) by swapping the first and second arguments of att' and input', and the first and third arguments of msg'.

Clauses (Rf) apply a constructor or a destructor on the attacker's knowledge, given the rewrite rules in $\mathrm{def}_{\Sigma'}(\mathsf{h})$. Since our destructors may return fail, by combining (Rf) with (Rfailure) or (Rfailure'), we can detect when a destructor succeeds in one variant of the biprocess and not in the other. We stress that, in clauses (Rfailure) and (Rcom), x, x', y, y' are message variables and so they cannot be instantiated by fail. (The messages sent on the network and the channels are never fail.)

4.4   Clauses for the Protocol

To translate the protocol into clauses, we first need to define evaluation on open terms, as a relation $D \Downarrow' (U, \sigma, \phi)$, where σ collects instantiations of D obtained by unification and ϕ collects the side conditions of destructor applications. More formally, the relation $D \Downarrow' (U, \sigma, \phi)$ specifies how instances of D evaluate: if $D \Downarrow' (U, \sigma, \phi)$, then for any substitution σ' such that $\sigma' \vDash \phi$, we have $\sigma'\sigma D \Downarrow_{\Sigma'} \sigma'U$. There may be several (U, σ, ϕ) such that $D \Downarrow' (U, \sigma, \phi)$ in case several instances of D reduce in a different way. This relation is defined as follows:

$$U \Downarrow' (U, \emptyset, \top)$$

$$\begin{aligned}
&\mathsf{eval}\ \mathsf{h}(D_1, \ldots, D_n) \Downarrow' (\sigma_u V, \sigma_u \sigma', \sigma_u \phi' \wedge \sigma_u \phi) \\
&\quad \text{if } (D_1, \ldots, D_n) \Downarrow' ((U_1, \ldots, U_n), \sigma', \phi'), \\
&\quad \mathsf{h}(V_1, \ldots, V_n) \to V \parallel \phi \in \mathrm{def}_{\Sigma'}(\mathsf{h}) \text{ and} \\
&\quad \sigma_u \text{ is a most general unifier of } (U_1, V_1), \ldots, (U_n, V_n)
\end{aligned}$$

$$\begin{aligned}
&(D_1, \ldots, D_n) \Downarrow' ((\sigma_n U_1, \ldots, \sigma_n U_{n-1}, U_n), \sigma_n \sigma, \sigma_n \phi \wedge \phi_n) \\
&\quad \text{if } (D_1, \ldots, D_{n-1}) \Downarrow' ((U_1, \ldots, U_{n-1}), \sigma, \phi) \text{ and } \sigma D_n \Downarrow' (U_n, \sigma_n, \phi_n)
\end{aligned}$$

The most general unifier of may-fail messages is computed similarly to the most general unifier of messages, even though specific cases hold due to may-fail variables and message variables: there is no unifier of M and fail, for any message M (including variables x, because these variables can be instantiated only by messages); the most general unifier of u and U is $\{{}^U/_u\}$; the most general unifier of fail and fail is the identity; finally, the most general unifier of M and M' is computed as usual.

The translation $[\![P]\!]\rho sH$ of a biprocess P is a set of clauses, where ρ is an environment that associates a pair of patterns with each name and variable, s

is a sequence of patterns, and H is a sequence of facts. The empty sequence is written $\emptyset$; the concatenation of a pattern p to the sequence s is written s, p; the concatenation of a fact F to the sequence H is written $H \wedge F$. Intuitively, H represents the hypothesis of the clauses, ρ represents the names and variables that are already associated with a pattern, and s represents the current values of session identifiers and inputs. When ρ associates a pair of patterns with each name and variable, and f is a constructor, we extend ρ as a substitution by $\rho(f(M_1, \ldots, M_n)) = (f(p_1, \ldots, p_n), f(p'_1, \ldots, p'_n))$ where $\rho(M_i) = (p_i, p'_i)$ for all $i \in \{1, \ldots, n\}$. We denote by $\rho(M)_1$ and $\rho(M)_2$ the components of the pair $\rho(M)$. We let $\rho(\text{diff}[M, M']) = (\rho(M)_1, \rho(M')_2)$.

The definition of $[\![P]\!]\rho s H$ is directly inspired from [7]. We only present below the case $[\![\text{let } x = D \text{ in } P \text{ else } Q]\!]\rho s H$.

$$[\![\text{let } x = D \text{ in } P \text{ else } Q]\!]\rho s H =$$

$$\bigcup \{[\![P]\!]((\sigma\rho)[x \mapsto (p, p')])(\sigma s, p, p')(\sigma H \wedge \text{formula}(\phi))$$

$$\mid (\rho(D)_1, \rho(D)_2) \Downarrow' ((p, p'), \sigma, \phi)\}$$

$$\cup \bigcup \{[\![Q]\!](\sigma\rho)(\sigma s)(\sigma H \wedge \text{formula}(\phi)) \mid (\rho(D)_1, \rho(D)_2) \Downarrow' ((\text{fail}, \text{fail}), \sigma, \phi)\}$$

$$\cup \{\sigma H \wedge \text{formula}(\phi) \rightarrow \text{bad} \mid (\rho(D)_1, \rho(D)_2) \Downarrow' ((p, \text{fail}), \sigma, \phi)\}$$

$$\cup \{\sigma H \wedge \text{formula}(\phi) \rightarrow \text{bad} \mid (\rho(D)_1, \rho(D)_2) \Downarrow' ((\text{fail}, p'), \sigma, \phi)\}$$

This formula is fairly similar to the one in [7]: when both $\rho(D)_1$ and $\rho(D)_2$ succeed, the process P is translated, instantiating terms with the substitution σ and taking into account the side-condition ϕ, to make sure that $\rho(D)_1$ and $\rho(D)_2$ succeed; when both fail, the process Q is translated; and at last when one of $\rho(D)_1$, $\rho(D)_2$ succeeds and the other fails, clauses deriving bad are generated. Since may-fail variables do not occur in D, we can show by induction on the computation of $\Downarrow'$ that, when $(\rho(D)_1, \rho(D)_2) \Downarrow' ((mp_1, mp_2), \sigma, \phi)$, mp_1 and mp_2 are either fail or a pattern, but cannot be a may-fail variable, so our definition of $[\![\text{let } x = D \text{ in } P \text{ else } Q]\!]\rho s H$ handles all cases.

4.5   Proving Equivalences

Let $\rho_0 = \{a \mapsto (a[], a[]) \mid a \in fn(P_0)\}$. We define the set of clauses that corresponds to biprocess P_0 as $\mathcal{R}_{P_0} = [\![P_0]\!]\rho_0 \emptyset \emptyset \cup \{(\text{Rfail}), \ldots, (\text{Rfailure}')\}$. The following theorem enables us to prove equivalences from these clauses.

Theorem 1. *If* bad *is not a logical consequence of* $\mathcal{R}_{P_0}$, *then* P_0 *satisfies observational equivalence.*

This theorem shows the soundness of the translation. The proof of this theorem is adapted from the proof of Theorem 3 of [7]. Furthermore, since we use almost the same patterns and facts as in [7], we also use the algorithm proposed in [7] to automatically check if bad is a logical consequence of $\mathcal{R}_{P_0}$, with the only change that we use the unification algorithm for may-fail patterns.

5   Automatic Modification of the Protocol

In this section, we first present the kind of false attack that we want to avoid and then propose an algorithm to automatically generate, from a biprocess P, equivalent biprocesses on which PROVERIF will avoid this kind of false attack.

5.1   Targeted False Attacks

We present a false attack on the anonymity of the private authentication protocol due to structural conditional branching.

Example 5. Coming back to the private authentication protocol (see Example 4), we obtained a biprocess P_0 on which we would ask PROVERIF to check the equivalence. Unfortunately, PROVERIF is unable to prove the equivalence of P_0 and yields a false attack. Indeed, consider the evaluation context C defined as follows:

$$C \stackrel{def}{=} \_ \mid (\nu n_i)c(x_{sk_a}).c(x_{sk_{a'}}).c(x_{sk_b}).\overline{c}\langle\mathsf{aenc}(\langle n_i, x_{sk_a}\rangle, x_{sk_b})\rangle$$

The biprocess $C[P_0]$ can be reduced as follows:

$$\begin{aligned}
C[P_0] \rightarrow_\Sigma^* \ & (\nu n_i)(\nu sk_a)(\nu sk_{a'})(\nu sk_b) \\
& (\overline{c}\langle\mathsf{aenc}(\langle n_i, \mathsf{pk}(sk_a)\rangle, \mathsf{pk}(sk_b))\rangle \mid System(\mathsf{diff}[sk_a, sk_{a'}], sk_b)) \\
\rightarrow_\Sigma^* \ & (\nu n_i)(\nu sk_a)(\nu sk_{a'})(\nu sk_b)(A(\mathsf{diff}[sk_a, sk_{a'}], sk_b) \mid \\
& \quad \mathsf{let}\ z = \mathsf{equals}(\mathsf{proj}_2(\langle n_i, \mathsf{pk}(sk_a)\rangle)), \mathsf{pk}(\mathsf{diff}[sk_a, sk_{a'}]))\ \mathsf{in} \\
& \quad \overline{c}\langle\mathsf{aenc}(\langle n_i, \langle n_b, \mathsf{pk}(sk_b)\rangle\rangle, \mathsf{pk}(\mathsf{diff}[sk_a, sk_{a'}]))\rangle \\
& \quad \mathsf{else}\ \overline{c}\langle\mathsf{aenc}(n_b, \mathsf{pk}(sk_b))\rangle\rangle
\end{aligned}$$

However from this point, the biprocess gets stuck, i.e., no internal reduction rule is applicable. More specifically, neither the internal rule (Red Fun 1) nor (Red Fun 2) is applicable. Indeed, if we denote $D = \mathsf{equals}(\mathsf{proj}_2(\langle n_i, sk_a\rangle))$, $\mathsf{pk}(\mathsf{diff}[sk_a, sk_{a'}]))$, we have that $\mathsf{snd}(D) \Downarrow_\Sigma \mathsf{fail}$ and $\mathsf{fst}(D) \Downarrow_\Sigma \mathsf{pk}(sk_a)$, which contradicts Item 2 of Lemma 2. So PROVERIF cannot prove the equivalence. But, although a different branch of the let is taken, the process outputs the message $\mathsf{aenc}(\langle n_b, \langle n_a, \mathsf{pk}(sk_b)\rangle\rangle, \mathsf{pk}(sk_a))$ in the first variant (in branch of the let) and the message $\mathsf{aenc}(n_b, \mathsf{pk}(sk_b))$ in the second variant (else branch of the let). Intuitively, these two messages are indistinguishable, so in fact the attacker will not be able to determine which branch of the let is taken, and observational equivalence still holds.

In order to avoid the false attacks similar to Example 5, we transform term evaluations let $x = D$ in $\overline{c}\langle M_1\rangle$ else $\overline{c}\langle M_2\rangle$ into a computation that always succeeds let $x = D'$ in let $m = D''$ in $\overline{c}\langle m\rangle$. The term evaluation D' will correspond to the value of the evaluation of D when the latter succeeds and a new constant c_{fail} when D fails. Thus we ensure that D' never fails. Moreover, the term evaluation D'' computes either M_1 or M_2 depending on the value of D', i.e., depending on whether D succeeds or not. The omitted else 0 branches are never taken.

Since the same branch is always taken, the false attack disappears. To do that, we introduce three new destructors catchfail, letin, notfail and a constant c_{fail}, which rely on the side conditions that we have added to destructors. These new destructors are defined as follows:

$$
\begin{aligned}
&\text{def}_\Sigma(\text{catchfail}) = &&\text{def}_\Sigma(\text{letin}) = &&\text{def}_\Sigma(\text{notfail}) = \\
&\quad \text{catchfail}(x) \to x &&\quad \text{letin}(x, u, v) \to u \parallel x \neq_\Sigma c_{fail} &&\quad \text{notfail}(x) \to \text{fail} \\
&\quad \text{catchfail}(\text{fail}) \to c_{fail} &&\quad \text{letin}(c_{fail}, u, v) \to v &&\quad \text{notfail}(\text{fail}) \to c_{fail} \\
& &&\quad \text{letin}(\text{fail}, u, v) \to \text{fail} &&
\end{aligned}
$$

One can easily check that $\text{def}_\Sigma(\text{catchfail})$, $\text{def}_\Sigma(\text{letin})$, and $\text{def}_\Sigma(\text{notfail})$ satisfy Properties P1 and P2. Intuitively, the destructor catchfail evaluates its argument and returns either the result of this evaluation when it did not fail or else returns the new constant c_{fail} instead of the failure constant fail. The destructor letin will get the result of catchfail as first argument and return its third argument if catchfail returned c_{fail}, and its second argument otherwise. Importantly, catchfail never fails: it returns c_{fail} instead of fail. Hence, let $x = D$ in $\overline{c}\langle M_1 \rangle$ else $\overline{c}\langle M_2 \rangle$ can be transformed into let $x = \text{eval catchfail}(D)$ in let $m = \text{eval letin}(x, M_1, M_2)$ in $\overline{c}\langle m \rangle$: if D succeeds, x has the same value as before, and $x \neq c_{fail}$, so $\text{letin}(x, M_1, M_2)$ returns M_1; if D fails, $x = c_{fail}$ and $\text{letin}(x, M_1, M_2)$ returns M_2. The destructor notfail inverts the status of a term evaluation: it fails if and only if its argument does not fail. This destructor will be used in the next section.

Example 6. Coming back to Example 5, the false attack occurs due to the following term evaluation:

$$
\begin{aligned}
&\text{let } z = \text{equals}(\text{proj}_2(x), \text{pk}(\text{diff}[ska, ska'])) \text{ in} \\
&\quad \overline{c}\langle \text{aenc}(\langle n_i, \langle n_b, \text{pk}(sk_b) \rangle \rangle, \text{pk}(\text{diff}[sk_a, sk_{a'}])) \rangle \\
&\text{else } \overline{c}\langle \text{aenc}(n_b, \text{pk}(sk_b)) \rangle
\end{aligned}
$$

We transform this term evaluation as explained above:

$$
\text{let } z = \text{letin}(\text{catchfail}(\text{equals}(\text{proj}_2(x), \text{pk}(\text{diff}[ska, ska']))), M, M') \text{ in } \overline{c}\langle z \rangle
$$

where $M = \text{aenc}(\langle n_i, \langle n_b, \text{pk}(sk_b) \rangle \rangle, \text{pk}(\text{diff}[sk_a, sk_{a'}]))$, $M' = \text{aenc}(n_b, \text{pk}(sk_b))$. Note that with $x = \langle n_i, \text{pk}(sk_a) \rangle$ (see Example 5), if D is the term evaluation $D = \text{letin}(\text{catchfail}(\text{equals}(\text{proj}_2(x), \text{pk}(\text{diff}[ska, ska']))), M, M')$, we obtain that:

- $\text{fst}(D) \Downarrow \text{aenc}(\langle n_i, \langle n_b, \text{pk}(sk_b) \rangle \rangle, \text{pk}(sk_a))$
- $\text{snd}(D) \Downarrow \text{aenc}(n_b, \text{pk}(sk_b))$

which corresponds to what $\text{fst}(P_0)$ and $\text{snd}(P_0)$ respectively output. Thanks to this, if we denote by P_0' our new biprocess, we obtain that $\text{fst}(P_0) \approx \text{fst}(P_0')$ and $\text{snd}(P_0) \approx \text{snd}(P_0')$. Furthermore, ProVerif will be able to prove that the biprocess P_0' satisfies equivalence, i.e., $\text{fst}(P_0') \approx \text{snd}(P_0')$ and so $\text{fst}(P_0) \approx \text{snd}(P_0)$.

The transformation proposed in the previous example can be generalised to term evaluations that perform actions other than just a single output. However, it is possible only if the success branch and the failure branch of the term evaluation both input and output the same number of terms. For example, the biprocess let $x = D$ in $\bar{c}\langle M\rangle.\bar{c}\langle M'\rangle$ else $\bar{c}\langle N\rangle$ cannot be modified into a biprocess without else branch even with our new destructors. On the other hand, the success or failure of D can really be observed by the adversary, by tracking the number of outputs on the channel c, so the failure of the proof of equivalence corresponds to a real attack in this case.

5.2 Merging and Simplifying Biprocesses

To automatically detect and apply this transformation, we define two functions, *merge* and *simpl*. The function *merge*, defined in Fig. 4, is partial. It takes two biprocesses as arguments and detects if those two biprocesses can be merged into one biprocess. If the merging is possible, it returns the merged biprocess. This merged biprocess is expressed using a new operator branch, similar to diff: branch$[D, D']$ is a term evaluation and we introduce functions fst$'$ and snd$'$ such that fst$'(P)$ (resp. snd$'(P)$) replaces each branch$[D, D']$ with D (resp. D') in P.

Case (Mout) detects that both biprocesses output a message while case (Min) detects that both biprocesses input a message. We introduce a *let* for the channels and messages so that they can later be replaced by a term evaluation. Case (Mpar) uses the commutativity and associativity of parallel composition to increase the chances of success of *merge*. Cases (Mres) and (Mres$'$) use $Q \approx (\nu a)Q$ when $a \notin fn(Q)$ to allow merging processes even when a restriction occurs only on one side. Case (Mrepl2) is the basic merging of replicated processes, while Case (Mrepl1) allows merging $!!P$ with $!P'$ (case $n = 0$) because $!P \approx !!P$, and furthermore allows restrictions between the two replications, using $Q \approx (\nu a)Q$. Case (Mlet1) merges two processes that both contain term evaluations, by merging their success branches together and their failure branches together. On the other hand, Cases (Mlet2), (Mlet2$'$) also merge two processes that contain term evaluations, by merging the success branch of one process with the failure branch of the other process. Cases (Mlet3), (Mlet3$'$), (Mlet4), (Mlet4$'$) allow merging a term evaluation with another process P', by merging P' with either the success branch or the failure branch of the term evaluation. This merging is useful when PROVERIF can prove that the resulting process satisfies equivalence, hence when both sides of the obtained *let* succeed simultaneously. Therefore, rule (Mlet3) is helpful when D always succeeds, and rule (Mlet4) when D always fails. When no such case applies, merging fails.

The function *simpl* is total. It takes one biprocess as argument and simplifies it by replacing all subprocesses of the form let $x = D$ in P else P', where $merge(P, P')$ succeeds, with

$$\text{let } x = \text{eval catchfail}(D) \text{ in } Q\{^{\text{eval letin}(x,D_1,D_2)}/_{\text{branch}[D_1,D_2]}\} \text{ else } 0$$

for some $Q = merge(P, P')$. This replacement is performed bottom up, so that P and P' have already been simplified when we transform let $x = D$ in P else P'.

$$merge(0,0) \overset{def}{=} 0 \tag{Mnil}$$

$$merge(\overline{M}\langle N\rangle.P, \overline{M'}\langle N'\rangle.P') \overset{def}{=}$$
$$\text{let } x = \mathsf{branch}[M, M'] \text{ in let } x' = \mathsf{branch}[N, N'] \text{ in } \overline{x}\langle x'\rangle.merge(P, P') \tag{Mout}$$
$$\text{where } x \text{ and } x' \text{ are fresh variables}$$

$$merge(M(x).P, M'(x').P') \overset{def}{=}$$
$$\text{let } y = \mathsf{branch}[M, M'] \text{ in } y(y').merge(P\{^y/_x\}, P'\{^y/_{x'}\}) \tag{Min}$$
$$\text{where } y \text{ and } y' \text{ are fresh variables}$$

$$merge(P_1 \mid \ldots \mid P_n, P'_1, \mid \ldots \mid P'_n) \overset{def}{=} Q_1 \mid \ldots \mid Q'_n$$
$$\text{if } (i_1, \ldots, i_n) \text{ is a permutation of } (1, \ldots, n) \tag{Mpar}$$
$$\text{and for all } k \in \{1, \ldots, n\}, Q_k = merge(P_k, P'_{i_k})$$

$$merge((\nu a)P, Q) \overset{def}{=} (\nu a)merge(P, Q) \tag{Mres}$$
$$\text{after renaming } a \text{ such that } a \notin fn(Q)$$

$$merge(!(\nu a_1)\ldots(\nu a_n)! P, ! P') \overset{def}{=} !(\nu a_1)\ldots(\nu a_n)merge(! P, ! P') \tag{Mrepl1}$$
$$\text{after renaming } a_1, \ldots, a_n \text{ such that } a_1, \ldots, a_n \notin fn(P')$$

$$merge(! P, ! P') \overset{def}{=} ! merge(P, P')$$
$$\text{if there is no } P_1, a_1, \ldots, a_n \text{ such that } P = (\nu a_1)\ldots(\nu a_n)! P_1 \tag{Mrepl2}$$
$$\text{and no } P'_1, a'_1, \ldots, a'_m \text{ such that } P' = (\nu a'_1)\ldots(\nu a'_m)! P'_1$$

$$merge(\text{let } x = D \text{ in } P_1 \text{ else } P_2, \text{let } x' = D' \text{ in } P'_1 \text{ else } P'_2) \overset{def}{=}$$
$$\text{let } y = \mathsf{branch}[D, D'] \text{ in } Q_1 \text{ else } Q_2 \text{ if } y \text{ is a fresh variable}, \tag{Mlet1}$$
$$Q_1 = merge(P_1\{^y/_x\}, P'_1\{^y/_{x'}\}), \text{ and } Q_2 = merge(P_2, P'_2)$$

$$merge(\text{let } x = D \text{ in } P_1 \text{ else } P_2, \text{let } x' = D' \text{ in } P'_1 \text{ else } P'_2) \overset{def}{=}$$
$$\text{let } y = \mathsf{branch}[D, \mathsf{notfail}(D')] \text{ in } Q_1 \text{ else } Q_2 \text{ if } y \text{ is a fresh variable}, \tag{Mlet2}$$
$$x' \notin fv(P'_1), Q_1 = merge(P_1\{^y/_x\}, P'_2), \text{ and } Q_2 = merge(P_2, P'_1)$$

$$merge(\text{let } x = D \text{ in } P_1 \text{ else } P_2, P') \overset{def}{=} \text{let } y = \mathsf{branch}[D, \mathsf{c_{fail}}] \text{ in } Q \text{ else } P_2 \tag{Mlet3}$$
$$\text{if } y \text{ is a fresh variable and } Q = merge(P_1\{^y/_x\}, P')$$

$$merge(\text{let } x = D \text{ in } P_1 \text{ else } P_2, P') \overset{def}{=} \text{let } y = \mathsf{branch}[D, \mathsf{fail}] \text{ in } P_1\{^y/_x\} \text{ else } Q \tag{Mlet4}$$
$$\text{if } y \text{ is a fresh variable and } Q = merge(P_2, P')$$

plus symmetric cases (Mres'), (Mrepl1'), (Mlet2'), (Mlet3'), and (Mlet4') obtained from (Mres), (Mrepl1), (Mlet2), (Mlet3), and (Mlet4) by swapping the first and second arguments of *merge* and branch.

Fig. 4. Definition of the function *merge*

The notation $Q\{^{\text{eval letin}(x,D_1,D_2)}/_{\text{branch}[D_1,D_2]}\}$ means that we replace in Q every instance of $\text{branch}[D_1, D_2]$, for some D_1, D_2, with eval $\text{letin}(x, D_1, D_2)$. The function *simpl* performs the transformation of term evaluations outlined in Section 5.1, when we can merge the success and failure branches.

Both functions are non-deterministic; the implementation may try all possibilities. In the current implementation of PROVERIF, we apply the rules (Mlet3) and (Mlet4) only if the rules (Mlet1) and (Mlet2) are not applicable. Moreover, we never merge 0 with a process different from 0. This last restriction is crucial to reduce the number of biprocesses returned by *merge* and *simpl*. Typically, we avoid that 0 and let $x = M$ in P else 0 are merged by the rule (Mlet4).

5.3   Results

Lemma 3 below shows that observational equivalence is preserved by the functions *merge* and *simpl*. In this lemma, we consider biprocesses P and P' that are not necessarily closed. We say that a context C is closing for P when $C[P]$ is closed. Moreover, given two biprocesses P and Q, we say that $P \approx Q$ if, and only if, $\text{fst}(P) \approx \text{fst}(Q)$ and $\text{snd}(P) \approx \text{snd}(Q)$.

Lemma 3. *Let P and P' be two biprocesses. If $merge(P, P') = Q$ then, for all contexts C closing for P, $C[P] \approx C[\text{fst}'(Q)]$ and, for all contexts C closing for P', $C[P'] \approx C[\text{snd}'(Q)]$. For all contexts C closing for P, $C[P] \approx C[simpl(P)]$.*

From the previous lemma, we can derive the two main results of this section.

Theorem 2. *Let P be a closed biprocess. If $simpl(P)$ satisfies observational equivalence, then $\text{fst}(P) \approx \text{snd}(P)$.*

From Theorem 2, we can extract our algorithm. Given a biprocess P as input, we compute $simpl(P)$. Since *simpl* is total but non-deterministic, we may have several biprocesses as result for $simpl(P)$. If PROVERIF proves equivalence on at least one of them, then we conclude that $\text{fst}(P) \approx \text{snd}(P)$.

Theorem 3. *Let P and P' be two closed processes that do not contain diff. Let $Q = merge(simpl(P), simpl(P'))$. If the biprocess $Q\{^{\text{diff}[D,D']}/_{\text{branch}[D,D']}\}$ satisfies observational equivalence, then $P \approx P'$.*

The previous version of PROVERIF could only take a biprocess as input. However, transforming two processes into a biprocess is usually not as easy as in the private authentication example. Theorem 3 automates this transformation.

6   Conclusion

In this paper, we have extended PROVERIF with destructors defined by rewrite rules with inequalities as side-conditions. We have proposed a procedure relying on these new rewrite rules to automatically transform a biprocess into equivalent biprocesses on which PROVERIF avoids the false attacks due to conditional branchings. Our extension is implemented in PROVERIF, which is available at http://proverif.inria.fr. Experimentation showed that the automatic transformation of a biprocess is efficient and returns few biprocesses. In particular, our extension automatically proves anonymity as defined in [5] for the private authentication protocol for an unbounded number of sessions.

However, PROVERIF is still unable to prove the unlinkability of the UK e-passport protocol [5] even though we managed to avoid some previously existing false attacks. This is a consequence of the matching by PROVERIF of traces with the same scheduling in the two variants of the biprocesses. Thus we would like to relax the matching of traces, e.g., by modifying the replication identifiers on the left and right parts of biprocesses. This would allow us to prove even more equivalences with PROVERIF and in particular the e-passport protocol.

Another direction for future research would be to define equations with inequalities as side-conditions. It may be possible to convert such equations into rewrite rules with side-conditions, like we convert equations into rewrite rules.

Acknowledgments. This work has been partially supported by the ANR projects PROSE (decision ANR 2010-VERS-004) and JCJC VIP n° 11 JS02 006 01, as well as the grant DIGITEO API from Région Île-de-France. It was partly done while the authors were at Ecole Normale Supérieure, Paris.

References

1. Abadi, M., Fournet, C.: Mobile values, new names, and secure communication. In: POPL 2001, pp. 104–115. ACM, New York (2001)
2. Abadi, M., Fournet, C.: Private authentication. Theoretical Computer Science 322(3), 427–476 (2004)
3. Abadi, M., Gordon, A.D.: A calculus for cryptographic protocols: The spi calculus. Information and Computation 148(1), 1–70 (1999)
4. Arapinis, M., Cheval, V., Delaune, S.: Verifying privacy-type properties in a modular way. In: CSF 2012, pp. 95–109. IEEE, Los Alamitos (2012)
5. Arapinis, M., Chothia, T., Ritter, E., Ryan, M.: Analysing unlinkability and anonymity using the applied pi calculus. In: CSF 2010, pp. 107–121. IEEE, Los Alamitos (2010)
6. Baudet, M.: Sécurité des protocoles cryptographiques: aspects logiques et calculatoires. Ph.D. thesis, LSV, ENS Cachan (2007)
7. Blanchet, B., Abadi, M., Fournet, C.: Automated verification of selected equivalences for security protocols. Journal of Logic and Algebraic Programming 75(1), 3–51 (2008)
8. Borgström, J., Briais, S., Nestmann, U.: Symbolic Bisimulation in the Spi Calculus. In: Gardner, P., Yoshida, N. (eds.) CONCUR 2004. LNCS, vol. 3170, pp. 161–176. Springer, Heidelberg (2004)
9. Cheval, V., Comon-Lundh, H., Delaune, S.: Trace equivalence decision: Negative tests and non-determinism. In: CCS 2011, pp. 321–330. ACM, New York (2011)
10. Ciobâcă, Ş.: Automated Verification of Security Protocols with Applications to Electronic Voting. Ph.D. thesis, LSV, ENS Cachan, France (2011)

Formal Verification of e-Auction Protocols

Jannik Dreier, Pascal Lafourcade, and Yassine Lakhnech

Université Grenoble 1, CNRS, Verimag, France
firstname.lastname@imag.fr

Abstract. Auctions have a long history, having been recorded as early as 500 B.C.. With the rise of Internet, electronic auctions have been a great success and are increasingly used. Many cryptographic protocols have been proposed to address the various security requirements of these electronic transactions. We propose a formal framework to analyze and verify security properties of e-Auction protocols. We model protocols in the Applied π-Calculus and define privacy notions, which include secrecy of bids, anonymity of the participants, receipt-freeness and coercion-resistance. We also discuss fairness, non-repudiation and non-cancellation. Additionally we show on two case studies how these properties can be verified automatically using ProVerif, and discover several attacks.

1 Introduction

Auctions are a simple method to sell goods and services. Typically a *seller* offers a good or a service, and the *bidders* make offers. Depending on the type of auction, the offers might be sent using sealed envelopes which are opened at the same time to determine the winner (the "sealed-bid" auction), or an *auctioneer* could announce prices decreasingly until one bidder is willing to pay the announced price (the "dutch auction"). Additionally there might be several rounds, or offers might be announced publicly directly (the "English" or "shout-out" auction). The winner usually is the bidder submitting the highest bid, but in some cases he might only have to pay the second highest offer as a price (the "second-price"- or "Vickrey"-Auction). In general a bidder wants to win the auction at the lowest possible price, and the seller wants to sell his good at the highest possible price. For more information on different auction methods see [1].

Depending on the type of auction and the application different security properties might be interesting to realize in an auction protocol and have been discussed in the literature. We identify the following main security properties of auction protocols:

- **Fairness:** We propose the three following fairness properties: Firstly a fair auction protocol should not *leak* any information about the other participants and their offers until the bidding phase is over (so as to prohibit unfair tactics based on leaked information). We call this *Weak* or *Strong Noninterference*, depending on if the number of bidders is leaked or not. Thirdly a protocol should not allow anybody to win although they did not submit the highest price, i.e. ensure that the *Highest Price Wins*. Otherwise a losing bidder could try to cheat to win.
- **Authentication**: For the seller it is crucial to ensure *Non-Repudiation*, i.e. that – after the winner has been announced – the winning bidder cannot claim that he did not submit the winning bid. Additionally we might want to ensure *Non-Cancellation*,

D. Basin and J.C. Mitchell (Eds.): POST 2013, LNCS 7796, pp. 247–266, 2013.
© Springer-Verlag Berlin Heidelberg 2013

i.e. that a bidder cannot cancel a submitted offer before the winner is announced, to have binding bids.

- **Privacy:** We distinguish several different notions: *Secrecy of Bids*, *Anonymity of Bidders*, *Receipt-Freeness* and *Coercion-Resistance*. Secrecy of Bids guarantees that the losing bids remain secret, or at least cannot be linked to the participants. Anonymity of Bidders means that the participants, in particular the winner, remain anonymous. Privacy is important in sealed-bid auctions to also prevent information leakage after the auction is over, for example if an auction is organized in several rounds. Receipt-Freeness ensures that bidders are unable to prove to an attacker (which might be another bidder trying to force them to submit a low bid so that he wins) that they bid a certain offer, and Coercion-Resistance means that even when interacting with a coercer, the bidders can still bid a price of their choice.
- **Verifiability**: A verifiable protocol should allow the bidders to verify that the winner was correctly determined, in particular if they lost. Additionally it might be desirable to give the bidders the ability to contest if they think that their offers were not taken into account correctly. We do not consider verifiability in this paper.

Related Work: Many electronic auction (e-Auction) protocols have been proposed in the literature (see e.g. [2–5] for an overview). As case studies, we use the protocol by Curtis et al. [6], which uses a trusted registrar and pseudonyms, and the protocol by Brandt [3], which is entirely distributed using secure multi-party computation.

The different security properties have been discussed since the early publications on e-Auctions, e.g. Franklin and Reiter [7] discuss secrecy of bids, anonymity of bidders, fairness, non-repudiation and non-cancellation. Further publications [8–11] have used and refined these notions, also adding verifiability. Abe and Suzuki [12] introduced and motivated Receipt-Freeness for e-Auctions. Cancellation of bids was also discussed by Stubblebine and Syverson [13] who proposed a protocol implementing cancellation as a feature, and another protocol ensuring non-cancellation. Still, all definitions given in these papers are informal.

Although there has been much work on developing auction protocols and discussing properties, there is considerably less work on their formal definition and analysis. Subramanian [14] proposed an auction protocol and analyzed it using a BAN-style logic to show some security properties. In particular he showed the atomicity of the transaction, weak secrecy of private keys and a form of anonymity modeled as weak secrecy of the public key of the bidder. More recently Dong et al. [15] analyzed a receipt-free auction protocol in the Applied π-Calculus. They only considered privacy, in particular secrecy of the bidding price and receipt-freeness, but only for losing bidders. Verifiability and accountability was formalized by Kuesters et al. [16].

In the context of electronic voting there has been much more work on formal verification, in particular in the area of privacy [17–23]. Some notions are similar, yet there are some fundamental differences to auctions: In the case of voting the published result is the sum of all votes, hence there is a certain leakage of information about all voters. For example if a candidate received no votes at all, this increases the attackers knowledge about the voters' votes as he can exclude this previously possible option. Yet ideally there should always be some uncertainty about the votes, i.e. no voter's privacy should entirely compromised (apart from pathological cases such as an unanimous vote). In the case of auctions, the public outcome is the winning bid(der), who loses all privacy. In some cases he might stay anonymous, e.g. the well known "bidder on the phone", but at least the winning price will be public. The other bid(der)s however can remain completely private/anonymous – we only know that the offers are inferior. Fairness also is a requirement in electronic voting as well as e-Auctions, but properties such as Non-Repudiation and Non-Cancellation are specific to e-Auctions.

There has been a lot of work on Non-Repudiation in the context of contract signing protocols (e.g. [24, 25]). We rely on the work by Klay et al. [24] who propose many different flavors of non-repudiation based on agent knowledge or authentication. We only consider "Non-Repudiation of Origin", i.e. that the bidder cannot deny that he made an offer, implemented as a form of authentication.

Contributions: We provide the following main contributions: i) We give a formal framework in the Applied π-Calculus [26] to model and analyze e-Auction protocols. ii) We define the discussed fairness, privacy and authentication properties in our model and analyze their relationship. iii) We provide two case studies: The protocol by Curtis et al. [6] and a protocol by Brandt [3]. We show how both can be modeled in the Applied π-Calculus and verified using Proverif [27–29]. We discover several flaws on these protocols and explain how some of their shortcomings can be addressed. Due to the space limitations we cannot give the full proofs here, they are available in [30], and the ProVerif code used in the case studies is available in [31].

Outline: In Section 2, we recall the Applied π-Calculus and model auction protocols. In Section 3, we formally define the security properties. In Section 4, we analyze two protocols in our model before concluding in the last section.

2   Preliminaries

We recall the Applied π-Calculus and introduce our model of auction protocols.

2.1   Applied π-Calculus

The Applied π-Calculus [26] is a formal language to describe concurrent processes. The calculus consists of *names* (which typically correspond to data or channels), *variables*, and a *signature* Σ of *function symbols* which can be used to build *terms*. Functions typically include encryption and decryption – for example enc(*message*, *key*), dec(*message*, *key*) – hashing, signing etc. Terms are correct (i.e. respecting arity and sorts) combinations of names and functions. We distinguish the type "channel" from other *base* types. To model equalities we use an equational theory E which defines a relation $=_E$. A classical example which describes the correctness of symmetric encryption is dec(enc(*message*, *key*), *key*) $=_E$ *message*. Processes are constructed using the grammars detailed in Figure 1.

The substitution $\{M/x\}$ replaces the variable x with term M. We denote by $fv(A)$, $bv(A)$, $fn(A)$, $bn(A)$ the free variables, bound variables, free names or bound names respectively. A process is *closed* if all variables are bound or defined by an active substitution. The *frame* $\Phi(A)$ of an active process A is obtained by replacing all plain

$P, Q, R :=$	plain processes
0	null process
$P \mid Q$	parallel composition
$!P$	replication
$\nu n.P$	name restriction ("new")
if $M = N$ then P	conditional
else Q	
$\text{in}(u, x).P$	message input
$\text{out}(u, x).P$	message output

(a) Plain process

$A, B, C :=$	active processes
P	plain process
$A \mid B$	parallel composition
$\nu n.A$	name restriction
$\nu x.A$	variable restriction
$\{M/x\}$	active substitution

(b) Extended process

Fig. 1. Grammars for *plain* and *extended* or *active processes*

processes in A by 0. This frame can be seen as a representation of what is statically known to the exterior about a process. The domain $\text{dom}(\Phi)$ of a frame Φ is the set of variables for which Φ defines a substitution. An evaluation context $C[\_]$ denotes an active process with a hole for an active process that is not under replication, a conditional, an input or an output. In the rest of the paper we use the following usual notions of equivalence and bisimilarity based on the original semantics [26].

Definition 1. *Two terms M and N are equal in the frame ϕ, written $(M = N)\phi$, if and only if $\phi \equiv \nu \tilde{n}.\sigma$, $M\sigma = N\sigma$, and $\{\tilde{n}\} \cap (fn(M) \cup fn(N)) = \emptyset$ for some names $\tilde{n}$ and some substitution σ.*

Definition 2. *Two closed frames ϕ and ψ are statically equivalent, written $\phi \approx_s \psi$, when $\text{dom}(\phi) = \text{dom}(\psi)$ and when for all terms M and N we have $(M = N)\phi$ if and only if $(M = N)\psi$. Two extended processes A and B are statically equivalent $(A \approx_s B)$ if their frames are statically equivalent.*

The intuition is that two processes are statically equivalent if the messages exchanged with the environment cannot be distinguished by an attacker (i.e. all operations on both sides give the same results). This idea can be extended to *labeled bisimilarity*.

Definition 3. Labeled bisimilarity *is the largest symmetric relation $\mathcal{R}$ on closed active processes, such that $A \mathcal{R} B$ implies: i) $A \approx_s B$, ii) if $A \to A'$, then $B \to^* B'$ and $A' \mathcal{R} B'$ for some B', iii) if $A \xrightarrow{\alpha} A'$ and $fv(\alpha) \subseteq \text{dom}(A)$ and $bn(\alpha) \cap fn(B) = \emptyset$, then $B \to^* \xrightarrow{\alpha} \to^* B'$ and $A' \mathcal{R} B'$ for some B'.*

In this case each interaction on one side can be simulated by the other side, and the processes are statically equivalent at each step during the execution, thus an attacker cannot distinguish both sides.

2.2 Modeling Auction Protocols

We model auction protocols in the Applied π-Calculus as follows.

Definition 4. *An auction protocol is defined by a tuple $(B, S, A_1, \ldots, A_m, \tilde{n})$ where B is the process that is executed by the bidders, S is the process executed by the seller,* *and the A_j's are the processes executed by the authorities (for example an auctioneer, a registrar etc.), and $\tilde{n}$ is a set of private channels. We also assume the existence of a particular public channel res that is only used to publish the winning bid(der).*

Note that we have only one process for the bidders. This means that different bidders will execute the same process, but with different variable values (e.g. the keys, the bids etc.). To reason about privacy, we talk about instances of an auction protocol, which we call *auction processes*.

Definition 5. *An instance of an auction protocol $(B, S, A_1, \ldots, A_m, \tilde{n})$ is called an auction process, which is a closed process $\nu\tilde{n}'.(B\sigma_{id_1}\sigma_{b_1} | \ldots | B\sigma_{id_k}\sigma_{b_k} | S | A_1 | \ldots | A_l)$, where $l \leq m$, $\tilde{n}'$ includes the secret channel names $\tilde{n}$, $B\sigma_{id_i}\sigma_{b_i}$ are the processes executed by the k bidders, σ_{id_i} is a substitution assigning the identity to the i-th bidder[1], σ_{b_i} specifies the i-th bid and A_j's are the auction authorities which are required to be honest. In our definitions we use the context $AP'[\cdot]$ which allows us to reason about bidders inside the auction process AP, for example if we want to explicit bidders l and o, we rewrite AP as $AP'[B\sigma_{id_l}\sigma_{b_l} | B\sigma_{id_o}\sigma_{b_o}]$.*

The restricted channel names model private channels. Note that we only model the honest authorities as unspecified parties are subsumed by the attacker.

By abuse of notation we write $b_l > b_o$ to express that the bidding price determined by the substitution σ_{b_l} is greater than the one assigned by σ_{b_o}, and $\max_i\{b_i\}$ denotes the maximal price assigned by any substitution σ_{b_i}.

In order to reason about reachability and authentication properties we will use *events*. Events are annotations, hence we extend the above plain process grammar as follows: $P = \text{event } e(M_1, \ldots, M_n).P$ where e is the name of the event, and the terms $M_1, \ldots, M_n$ are parameters. These events do not change the behavior of the processes, but allow us to verify properties such as "event bad is unreachable" or "on every trace event a is preceded by event b". We use the following events: bid(p,id): When a bidder id bids the price p the event bid(p,id) is emitted. recBid(p,id): When a bid at price p by bidder id is recorded by the auctioneer/bulletin board[2]/etc. the event recBid(p,id) is called. This will be used to model Non-Cancellation, i.e. from this point on a bid is considered binding. won(p,id): When a bidder id wins the auction at price p, the event won(p,id) is emitted.

We use the following transformation introduced in [18] that turns a process P into another process P^{ch} that reveals all its inputs and secret data on the channel ch.

Definition 6. *Let P be a plain process and ch be a channel name. P^{ch} is defined by:*

- $0^{ch} \doteq 0$,
- $(P|Q)^{ch} \doteq P^{ch}|Q^{ch}$,
- $(\nu n.P)^{ch} \doteq \nu n.\text{out}(ch, n).P^{ch}$ *if n is a name of base type,* $(\nu n.P)^{ch} \doteq \nu n.P^{ch}$ *otherwise,*
- $(\text{in}(u, x).P)^{ch} \doteq \text{in}(u, x).\text{out}(ch, x).P^{ch}$ *if x is a variable of base type,* $(\text{in}(u, x).P)^{ch} \doteq \text{in}(u, x).P^{ch}$ *otherwise,*

---

[1] This determines for example the secret keys.
[2] A bulletin board is a central append-only noticeboard that is often used for communication in protocols.

- $(\mathtt{out}(u, M).P)^{ch} \triangleq \mathtt{out}(u, M).P^{ch}$,
- $(\mathtt{if}\ M = N\ \mathtt{then}\ P\ \mathtt{else}\ Q)^{ch} \triangleq \mathtt{if}\ M = N\ \mathtt{then}\ P^{ch}\ \mathtt{else}\ Q^{ch}$.
- $(!P)^{ch} \triangleq !P^{ch}$,

In the remainder we assume that $ch \notin fn(P) \cup bn(P)$ before applying the transformation. We need another transformation of [18] that does not only reveal the secret data, but also takes orders from an outsider before sending a message or branching. This models a completely corrupted party.

Definition 7. *Let P be a plain process and c_1, c_2 be channel names. P^{c_1,c_2} is defined as follows:*

- $0^{c_1,c_2} \triangleq 0$,
- $(P|Q)^{c_1,c_2} \triangleq P^{c_1,c_2}|Q^{c_1,c_2}$,
- $(\nu n.P)^{c_1,c_2} \triangleq \nu n.\mathtt{out}(c_1, n).P^{c_1,c_2}$ *if n is a name of base type, $(\nu n.P)^{c_1,c_2} \triangleq \nu n.P^{c_1,c_2}$ otherwise,*
- $(\mathtt{in}(u, x).P)^{c_1,c_2} \triangleq \mathtt{in}(u, x).\mathtt{out}(c_1, x).P^{c_1,c_2}$ *if x is a variable of base type, $(\mathtt{in}(u, x).P)^{c_1,c_2} \triangleq \mathtt{in}(u, x).P^{c_1,c_2}$ otherwise,*
- $(\mathtt{out}(u, M).P)^{c_1,c_2} \triangleq \mathtt{in}(c_2, x).\mathtt{out}(u, x).P^{c_1,c_2}$ *where x is a fresh variable,*
- $(!P)^{c_1,c_2} \triangleq !P^{c_1,c_2}$,
- $(\mathtt{if}\ M = N\ \mathtt{then}\ P\ \mathtt{else}\ Q)^{c_1,c_2} \triangleq \mathtt{in}(c_2, x).\mathtt{if}\ x = true\ \mathtt{then}\ P^{c_1,c_2}\ \mathtt{else}\ Q^{c_1,c_2}$ *where x is a fresh variable and true is a constant.*

To hide the output of a process, we use the following definition of [18].

Definition 8. *Let A be an extended process, $A^{\backslash out(ch,\cdot)}$ is defined by $\nu ch.(A|!\mathtt{in}(ch, x))$.*

3 Security Requirements

3.1 Fairness Properties

A fair auction protocol should not leak any information about any participant until the bidding phase is over and the winning bid is announced, and hence some information is inevitably leaked. We propose the following two definitions:

Definition 9. *An auction protocol ensures Strong Noninterference (SN) if for any two auction processes AP_A and AP_B that halt at the end of the bidding phase (i.e. where we remove all code after the last recBid event) we have $AP_A \approx_l AP_B$.*

This notion is very strong: Any two instances, independently of the participants and their offers, are required to be bisimilar until the end of the bidding phase. This would also require two instances with a different number of participants to be bisimilar, which will probably not hold on many protocols. A more realistic notion is the following:

Definition 10. *An auction protocol ensures Weak Noninterference (WN) if for any two auction processes $AP_A = \nu\tilde{n}'.(B\sigma_{id_1}\sigma_{b_{1,A}} | \ldots | B\sigma_{id_k}\sigma_{b_{k,A}} | S | A_1 | \ldots | A_l)$ and $AP_B = \nu\tilde{n}'.(B\sigma_{id_1}\sigma_{b_{1,B}} | \ldots | B\sigma_{id_k}\sigma_{b_{k,B}} | S | A_1 | \ldots | A_l)$ that halt at the end of the bidding phase (i.e. where we remove all code after the last recBid event) we have $AP_A \approx_l AP_B$.*

This only requires any two instances with the same participants $B\sigma_{id_i}$ to be bisimilar, however bids may still change. It is easy to see that (SN) implies (WN).

Another important fairness property is that there is no strategy that allows a malicious participant to win the auction at a chosen price, independently of the other bids.

Definition 11. *An auction protocol ensures* Highest Price Wins (HPW) *if for any auction process AP we have for $AP'[B\sigma_{id_A}\sigma_{b_A} \mid (B\sigma_{id_B}\sigma_{b_B})^{c_1,c_2}]$ where b_A is the highest bid, there is no trace containing the event won for bidder id_B with a lower bid.*

The idea is the following: We have an honest bidder $B\sigma_{id_A}$ who submits the highest bid. The attacker has completely corrupted another bidder $B\sigma_{id_B}$ and should be unable to win the auction on his behalf on a lower bid.

Note that these definitions can be applied independently of trust assumptions, and that different assumptions can lead to different results: For example, a protocol might ensure (HPW) if the auctioneer is trusted, but not otherwise.

3.2 Authentication Properties

The first authentication property we want to define is *Non-Repudiation*, i.e. that – once the winner has been announced – a winning bidder cannot claim that the winning bid was not send by him. As discussed in [24], Non-Repudiation can be expressed as form of authentication.

Definition 12. *An auction protocol ensures the property of* Non-Repudiation (NR) *if for every auction process AP on every possible execution trace the event* won(p, id) *is preceded by a corresponding event* bid(p, id).

The intuition is simple: If there was a trace on which a bidder would win without submitting the winning bid, he could try to claim that he did not submit the winning bid even in a case where he rightfully won.

Note two subtleties with this definition: Firstly, since only honest parties are explicitly modeled, it is clear that only honest parties can emit events. Hence one could think that our definition implicitly assumes some parties to be honest – however, this is not the case: If we do not trust the party that would normally emit for example the event won, we can simply remove this party from the model and replace it with a new party that receives the parameters on a special channel, and then emits the event using these parameters. This gives the adversary total control about the events, as it would be the case for a distrusted authority. Secondly we need to have session-dependent identifiers for the bidders in our events. This is to ensure that the protocol only accepts bids that were submitted in a the same instance, and that an attacker cannot submit a bid from a different session.

The second authentication property we model is *Non-Cancellation*, i.e. that a bidder cannot cancel a submitted bid before the winner is announced.

Definition 13. *An auction protocol ensures the property of* Non-Cancellation (NC) *if for any auction process AP which contains a bidder $(B\sigma_{id_i}\sigma_{b_i})^{chc}$, i.e. a bidder which reveals his secret data on channel chc (see Def. 6), and which submits the highest bid, i.e. $\forall j \neq i : b_i > b_j$, there is no trace containing the events* recBid(b_i, id_i) *and* won(b_w, id_w) *for another, lower bid, i.e. $b_w < b_i$.*

The idea is the following: The bidder id_i submits the highest bid, so he should win. If however there is the possibility that even though his bid was correctly received he did not win, this would mean that the intruder was able to cancel the bidder's bid even after reception. We require the bidder to reveal all his secret data to the intruder to capture the fact that the bidder himself might want to cancel his offer, in which case he could use his private data (keys etc.) to do so.

Note that technically we only defined Non-Cancellation for the winning bidder. This is sufficient since in a first-price auction the other bids do not influence the outcome. Additionally it can be generalized to other auction types by simply requiring that the winning price must be correct on all traces. This is to ensure that no other bids that influence the result can be canceled.

Both properties are independent: A protocol may implement the cancellation of bids as an official feature, for example after all bids have been submitted, bidders could be allowed to cancel their bids for a certain period of time, before the winner is finally announced. At the same time, such a protocol may ensure non-repudiation of the winner using e.g. signatures. Similarly a protocol may ensure Non-Cancellation but no Non-Repudiation if the submitted bids cannot be canceled, but are not authenticated, so that the winner can successfully claim not having submitted the winning bid. Again, a protocol might ensure Non-Cancellation or Non-Repudiation for a certain trust setting, but not for another.

3.3   Privacy Properties

We consider Privacy, Receipt-Freeness and Coercion-Resistance, and at each level two independent axes: i) the winner may stay anonymous or not, ii) the bids may stay completely private or there might be list of all bids, which are however unlinkable to the bidders.

These definitions are expressed for protocols implementing a first-price sealed-bid auction. We also provide the generalized notions (P), (RF) and (CR), which can also be applied to other types of auctions such as second-price auctions. We show that if a pro-

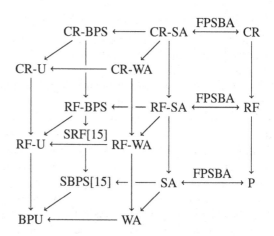

Fig. 2. Relations among the privacy notions. $A \xrightarrow{C} B$ means that under the assumption C a protocol ensuring A also ensures B.

tocol correctly implements a First-Price Sealed-Bid Auction (FPSBA), these notions coincide with the corresponding Strong Anonymity-notions (SA), (RF-SA) and (CR-SA). Figure 2 provides an overview of the different notions.

Privacy. The first privacy notion we consider was proposed by Dong et al. [15].

Definition 14. *An electronic auction protocol ensures* Strong Bidding-Price Secrecy (SBPS) *if for an auction process AP and any bids* $b_A, b_B < b_C$ *we have*

$$AP' \left[B\sigma_{id_A}\sigma_{b_A} | B\sigma_{id_C}\sigma_{b_C} \right] \approx_l AP' \left[B\sigma_{id_A}\sigma_{b_B} | B\sigma_{id_C}\sigma_{b_C} \right]$$

The intuition is the following: If the losing bids are private, a losing bidder may change his bid for another losing one without this being noticeable to an attacker. This is expressed as an observational equivalence between two situations where a losing bidder changes his bid. Note that $B\sigma_{id_C}$ does not necessarily win since in AP' there might be a bidder offering a higher price, but $b_A, b_B < b_C$ guarantees that $B\sigma_{id_A}$ loses.

We propose the following, weaker notion of Bidding-Price Unlinkability, which allows the losing bids to be public, however their link to the bidders have to be secret.

Definition 15. *An e-Auction protocol ensures* Bidding-Price Unlinkability (BPU) *if for an auction process AP and any bids* $b_A, b_B < b_C$ *we have*

$$AP' \left[B\sigma_{id_A}\sigma_{b_A} | B\sigma_{id_B}\sigma_{b_B} | B\sigma_{id_C}\sigma_{b_C} \right] \approx_l AP' \left[B\sigma_{id_A}\sigma_{b_B} | B\sigma_{id_B}\sigma_{b_A} | B\sigma_{id_C}\sigma_{b_C} \right]$$

In this definition we require two situations in which two losing bidders swap their bids to be bisimilar. This might be the case if the bids are public, but the real identity of the bidders is hidden, e.g. through the use of pseudonyms.

Note that the previous two notions only concern the losing bids, yet we might also want to preserve the anonymity of the winning bidder.

Definition 16. *An electronic auction protocol ensures* Strong Anonymity (SA) *if for an auction process AP and any bids* $b_A, b_B \leq b_C$ *we have*

$$AP' \left[B\sigma_{id_A}\sigma_{b_A} | B\sigma_{id_C}\sigma_{b_C} \right] \approx_l AP' \left[B\sigma_{id_A}\sigma_{b_C} | B\sigma_{id_C}\sigma_{b_B} \right]$$

Here we require two situations to be bisimilar where two different bidders win using the same offer, and the losing bidders may also use different bids in the two cases. This is stronger than Strong Bidding-Price Secrecy (SBPS).

A slightly weaker notion is Weak Anonymity, which allows the bids to be public, however their link to the bidders have to be secret, even for the winner.

Definition 17. *An electronic auction protocol ensures* Weak Anonymity (WA) *if for an auction process AP and any bids* $b_A \leq b_C$ *we have*

$$AP' \left[B\sigma_{id_A}\sigma_{b_A} | B\sigma_{id_C}\sigma_{b_C} \right] \approx_l AP' \left[B\sigma_{id_A}\sigma_{b_C} | B\sigma_{id_C}\sigma_{b_A} \right]$$

Here again two different bidders win using the same bid, but the losing bidder cannot choose his bid freely as above - the two bidders swap their bids. This corresponds for example to a situation with a public list of bids in clear, but where it is private which bidder submitted which bid. Weak Anonymity (WA) is stronger than Bidding-Price Unlinkability (BPU) as even the winner remains anonymous. All these definitions are only meaningful for first-price auctions. To also deal with second-prices sealed-bid auctions, we can use the following generalization based on the published result.

Definition 18. *Let* $P|_c = \nu\tilde{ch}.P$ *where* $\tilde{ch}$ *are all channels except for c, i.e. we hide all channels except for c.*

Definition 19. *An electronic auction protocol ensures* Privacy (P) *if for any two auction processes* $APA = \nu\tilde{n}'.(B\sigma_{id_1}\sigma_{b_1,A} \mid \ldots \mid B\sigma_{id_k}\sigma_{b_k,A} \mid S \mid A_1 \mid \ldots \mid A_l)$ *and* $APB = \nu\tilde{n}'.(B\sigma_{id_1}\sigma_{b_1,B} \mid \ldots \mid B\sigma_{id_k}\sigma_{b_k,B} \mid S \mid A_1 \mid \ldots \mid A_l)$ *we have*

$$AP_1|_{res} \approx_l AP_2|_{res} \Rightarrow AP_1 \approx_l AP_2$$

The intuition is quite simple: any two instances (consisting of the same bidders) which give the same result, i.e. the same winning bid, have to be bisimilar.

It turns out that for a correct first-price sealed-bid auction protocol which only publishes the winning price, this coincides with Strong Anonymity.

Definition 20. *An electronic auction protocol implements a* First-Price Sealed-Bid Auction (FPSBA) *if for any auction processes* $APA = \nu\tilde{n}'.(B\sigma_{id_1}\sigma_{b_1,A} \mid \ldots \mid B\sigma_{id_k}\sigma_{b_k,A} \mid S \mid A_1 \mid \ldots \mid A_l)$ *and* $APB = \nu\tilde{n}'.(B\sigma_{id_1}\sigma_{b_1,B} \mid \ldots \mid B\sigma_{id_k}\sigma_{b_k,B} \mid S \mid A_1 \mid \ldots \mid A_l)$ *we have*

$$APA|_{res} \approx_l APB|_{res} \Leftrightarrow \max_i b_{i,A} = \max_i b_{i,B}$$

This definition requires the protocol to announce the same result if and only if the maximum among the submitted bids is the same, independently of which bidder submitted which bid. It is easy to see that this is true in the case of a correct first-price sealed-bid auction protocol. This allows us to prove the equivalence of (P) and (SA).

Theorem 1. *If an electronic auction protocol implements a First-Price Sealed-Bid Auction (FPSBA), then Privacy (P) and Strong Anonymity (SA) are equivalent.*

Proof. Sketch: Assume we have two instances that give the same result, by (FPSBA) they have the same maximal bid. This bid may have been submitted by another bidder, and the other bids might have changed, but $AP_1 \approx_l AP_2$ can be proved using successive applications of (SA). Similarly if we assume two instances as in the definition of (SA), it is easy to see that they have the same maximal offer. Hence the result will be the same, and we can apply (P) to conclude.   □

Receipt-Freeness. A first Receipt-Freeness definition for auction protocols was proposed by Dong et al. [15]. It is a generalization of Strong Bidding-Price Secrecy (SBPS).

Definition 21. *An electronic auction protocol ensures* Simple Receipt-Freeness (SRF) *if for an auction process* AP *and any bids* $b_A, b_B < b_C$ *there exists a process* B' *such that* $B'^{\setminus out(chc,\cdot)} \approx_l B\sigma_{id_A}\sigma_{b_B}$ *and*

$$AP'\left[(B\sigma_{id_A}\sigma_{b_A})^{chc} \mid B\sigma_{id_C}\sigma_{b_C}\right] \approx_l AP'\left[B' \mid B\sigma_{id_C}\sigma_{b_C}\right]$$

The intuition behind this definition is a follows: If the protocol is receipt-free, an attacker cannot distinguish between a situation where a losing bidder bids b_A and reveals all his secret data on a channel chc, and a situation where the bidder bids b_B and only pretends to reveal his secret data (the fake strategy, modeled by process B'). Note that Simple Receipt-Freeness (SRF) implies Strong Bidding-Price Secrecy (SBPS).

This definition has several shortcomings: Firstly, it ensures receipt-freeness only for one losing bidder, whereas in reality several bidders might be under attack. Secondly, it does not necessary ensures the privacy of other bidders: Consider for example a protocol that allows a losing bidder to create a fake receipt for himself (e.g. using a trapdoor to generate a different decryption key), and that reveals all submitted bids to the participating bidders (e.g. to enable verifiability). Such a protocol would be secure according to above definition, but it would imply that a coercer can ask to a bidder to reveal the other participants bids, violating their privacy. To address these issues, we propose the following notions, inspired by some definitions developed for electronic voting [20] and the above privacy notions.

Definition 22. *An electronic auction protocol ensures* **RF-XXX** *if for any two auction processes* $AP_A = \nu\tilde{n}'.(B\sigma_{id_1}\sigma_{b_1,A} \mid \ldots \mid B\sigma_{id_k}\sigma_{b_k,A} \mid S \mid A_1 \mid \ldots \mid A_l)$ *and* $AP_B = \nu\tilde{n}'.(B\sigma_{id_1}\sigma_{b_1,B} \mid \ldots \mid B\sigma_{id_k}\sigma_{b_k,B} \mid S \mid A_1 \mid \ldots \mid A_l)$ *such that*

- *if XXX=BPS* (Bidding-Price-Secrecy), *there exists a* j *with* $b_{j,A} = b_{j,B} = \max_i b_{i,A}$ $= \max_i b_{i,B}$ *and for any subset* $I \subset \{1, \ldots, j-1, j+1, \ldots k\}$,
- *if XXX=U* (Unlinkability), *there exists* j *with* $b_{j,A} = b_{j,B} = \max_i b_{i,A} = \max_i b_{i,B}$ *and a permutation* Π *with* $\forall i : b_{i,B} = b_{\Pi(i),A}$, *and for any subset* $I \subset \{1, \ldots, j-1, j+1, \ldots k\}$,
- *if XXX=SA* (Strong Anonymity), $\max_i b_{i,A} = \max_i b_{i,B}$ *and for any subset* $I \subset \{1, \ldots, k\}$,
- *if XXX=WA* (Weak Anonymity), *here exists a permutation* Π *with* $\forall i : b_{i,B} = b_{\Pi(i),A}$, *and for any subset* $I \subset \{1, \ldots, k\}$,

there exist processes B_i' *such that we have* $\forall i \in I : B_i'^{\backslash out(chc_i, \cdot)} \approx_l B\sigma_{id_i}\sigma_{b_i,B}$ *and*

$$AP_A'\left[\mid_{i \in I} (B\sigma_{id_i}\sigma_{v_i,A})^{chc_i}\right] \approx_l AP_B'\left[\mid_{i \in I} B_i'\right]$$

Consider the first case, (RF-BPS): In this definition any subset of losing bidders may create fake receipts at the same time, and the other bidders can also change their bids. It is easy to see that this definition implies Simple Receipt-Freeness (SRF).

Similarly to our privacy definitions, we can also weaken (RF-BPS) and only consider cases where the bids are merely unlinkable to the bidders, by only considering permutations of the bids: We obtain (RF-U).

The third notion (RF-SA) is stronger in the sense that we also allow the winning bidder to be under attack, i.e. a winner needs to be able to create a fake receipt that proves that he lost, and a losing bidder needs to be able to create a fake receipt that proves that he won. Note that an attacker might ask a losing bidder to prove that he bid a certain price before the auction is over. If the bidder decides to bid less and create a fake receipt, the attacker may notice that he got a fake receipt if for example the winning bid is less than the price on the receipt. This is however an inherent problem of auctions, but our definition guarantees that a losing bidder can create a fake receipt for the winning price once the auction is over and the winning price is known.

Again, we can define a weaker version where the list of prices may be public, but it has to be unlinkable to the bidders, even for the winner: (RF-WA). It is easy to see that

(RF-SA) implies (RF-BPS) and (RF-WA), and that both (RF-BPS) and (RF-WA) imply (RF-U). Note that this definition implicitly assumes that all bidders not under attack are honest. If one also wants to consider corrupted bidders, this can be modeled by replacing some of the honest bidders $B\sigma_{id_i}\sigma_{b_i,X}$ by corrupted bidders $(B\sigma_{id_i}\sigma_{b_i,X})^{c_1^i,c_2^i}$.

Finally, the following definition is a generalization of Receipt-Free Strong Anonymity (RF-SA) (analogous to (P) and (SA)): Any two instance giving the same result have to be bisimilar, even if bidders are under attack.

Definition 23. *A auction protocol ensures* Receipt-Freeness (RF) *if for any two auction processes* $APA = \nu\tilde{n}'.(B\sigma_{id_1}\sigma_{b_{1,A}} \mid \ldots \mid B\sigma_{id_k}\sigma_{b_{k,A}} \mid S \mid A_1 \mid \ldots \mid A_l)$ *and* $APB = \nu\tilde{n}'.(B\sigma_{id_1}\sigma_{b_{1,B}} \mid \ldots \mid B\sigma_{id_k}\sigma_{b_{k,B}} \mid S \mid A_1 \mid \ldots \mid A_l)$ *and any subset* $I \subset \{1,\ldots,k\}$, *there exist processes* B'_i *such that we have* $\forall i \in I : B_i^{\prime\backslash out(chc_i,\cdot)} \approx_l B\sigma_{id_i}\sigma_{b_i,B}$ *and*

$$AP_A|_{res} \approx_l AP_B|_{res} \Rightarrow AP'_A \left[\underset{i\in I}{|} (B\sigma_{id_i}\sigma_{v_i,A})^{chc_i}\right] \approx_l AP'_B \left[\underset{i\in I}{|} B'_i\right].$$

Similarly to Privacy (P), we prove that for protocols implementing a First-Price Sealed-Bid Auction (First-Price Sealed-Bid Auction), Receipt-Free Strong Anonymity (RF-SA) and Receipt-Freeness coincide.

Coercion-Resistance. Coercion-Resistance is a stronger property than receipt-freeness: The intruder may not only ask for a receipt, but is also allowed to interact with the bidder during the bidding process and to give orders. We can generalize the previously discussed Receipt-Freeness notions to Coercion-Resistance as follows.

Definition 24. *An electronic auction protocol ensures* CR-XXX *if for any two auction processes* $APA = \nu\tilde{n}'.(B\sigma_{id_1}\sigma_{b_{1,A}} \mid \ldots \mid B\sigma_{id_k}\sigma_{b_{k,A}} \mid S \mid A_1 \mid \ldots \mid A_l)$ *and* $APB = \nu\tilde{n}'.(B\sigma_{id_1}\sigma_{b_{1,B}} \mid \ldots \mid B\sigma_{id_k}\sigma_{b_{k,B}} \mid S \mid A_1 \mid \ldots \mid A_l)$ *such that*

- *if XXX=BPS (Bidding-Price Secrecy): there exists a j with $b_{j,A} = b_{j,B} = \max_i b_{i,A} = \max_i b_{i,B}$ and for any subset* $I \subset \{1,\ldots,j-1,j+1,\ldots k\}$,
- *if XXX=U (Unlinkability): there exists a j with $b_{j,A} = b_{j,B} = \max_i b_{i,A} = \max_i b_{i,B}$ and there exists a permutation Π with $\forall i : b_{i,B} = b_{\Pi(i),A}$ and for any subset* $I \subset \{1,\ldots,j-1,j+1,\ldots k\}$,
- *if XXX=SA (Strong Anonymity): $\max_i b_{i,A} = \max_i b_{i,B}$ and for any subset* $I \subset \{1,\ldots,k\}$,
- *if XXX=WA (Weak Anonymity): there exists a permutation Π with $\forall i : b_{i,B} = b_{\Pi(i),A}$ and for any subset* $I \subset \{1,\ldots,k\}$,

there exist processes B'_i *such that for any contexts* $C_i, i \in I$ *with* $C_i = \nu c_1.\nu c_2.(\_|P_i)$, $\tilde{n} \cap fn(C) = \emptyset$ *and* $AP'_A \left[\underset{i\in I}{|} C_i \left[(B\sigma_{id_i}\sigma_{b_i,A})^{c_1,c_2}\right]\right] \approx_l AP'_A \left[\underset{i\in I}{|} (B\sigma_{id_i}\sigma_{b_i,A})^{chc_i}\right]$ *we have* $\forall i \in I : C_i [B'_i]^{\backslash out(chc_i,\cdot)} \approx_l B\sigma_{id_i}\sigma_{v_i,B}$ *and*

$$AP'_A \left[\underset{i\in I}{|} C_i \left[(B\sigma_{id_i}\sigma_{v_i,A})^{c_1,c_2}\right]\right] \approx_l AP'_B \left[\underset{i\in I}{|} C_i [B'_i]\right]$$

The difference to the previous receipt-freeness definitions is that the attacked bidders do not only reveal their data on channel c_1, but also take orders on channel c_2. The context

C_i models the attacker that tries to force them to bid the price $b_{i,A}$ (this is expressed by the condition on C_i). The protocol is hence coercion-resistant if there exists a counter-strategy B' which allow the bidders to bid $b_{i,B}$ instead without the attacker noticing. For non sealed-bid first-price auction, we obtain the following definition.

Definition 25. *An auction protocol ensures* Coercion-Resistance (CR) *if for any two auction processes* $AP_A = \nu\tilde{n}'.(B\sigma_{id_1}\sigma_{b_1,A} \mid \dots \mid B\sigma_{id_k}\sigma_{b_k,A} \mid S \mid A_1 \mid \dots \mid A_l)$ *and* $AP_B = \nu\tilde{n}'.(B\sigma_{id_1}\sigma_{b_1,B} \mid \dots \mid B\sigma_{id_k}\sigma_{b_k,B} \mid S \mid A_1 \mid \dots \mid A_l)$ *and any subset* $I \subset \{1,\dots,k\}$, *there exists processes* B_i' *such that for any contexts* $C_i, i \in I$ *with* $C_i = \nu c_1.\nu c_2.(\_|P_i)$, $\tilde{n} \cap fn(C) = \emptyset$ *and*

$$AP_A'\left[\left.\underset{i\in I}{\big|}\, C_i\left[(B\sigma_{id_i}\sigma_{b_i,A})^{c_1,c_2}\right]\right]\right. \approx_l AP_A'\left[\left.\underset{i\in I}{\big|}\, (B\sigma_{id_i}\sigma_{b_i,A})^{chc_i}\right]\right.$$

we have $\forall i \in I : C_i\left[B_i'\right]^{\backslash out(chc_i,\cdot)} \approx_l B\sigma_{id_i}\sigma_{v_i,B}$ *and*

$$AP_A|_{res} \approx_l AP_B|_{res} \Rightarrow AP_A'\left[\left.\underset{i\in I}{\big|}\, C_i\left[(B\sigma_{id_i}\sigma_{v_i,A})^{c_1,c_2}\right]\right]\right. \approx_l AP_B'\left[\left.\underset{i\in I}{\big|}\, C_i\left[B_i'\right]\right]\right.$$

Again we can prove that for protocols implementing a First-Price Sealed-Bid Auction (FPSBA), Coercion-Resistant Strong Anonymity (CR-SA) and Coercion-Resistance (CR) coincide.

4   Case Studies

We applied the previously explained definitions on two case studies using ProVerif [27–29]: the protocol by Curtis et al. [6], and the protocol by Protocol by Brandt [3].

4.1   Protocol by Curtis, Pierprzyk and Seruga [6]

The protocol by Curtis et al. [6] was designed to support sealed-bid first- and second price auctions while guaranteeing fairness, privacy, verifiability and non-repudiation.

Informal Description. The main idea of the protocol is the following: The bidders register with a trusted Registration Authority (RA) using a Public-Key Infrastructure (PKI), which issues pseudonyms that will then be used for submitting bids to the Seller (S). It is split into three phases: Registration, Bidding, and Winner determination.

- *Registration:* Each bidder sends his identity, a hash of his bidding price b_i and a signature of $h(b_i)$ to the RA. The RA checks the identity and the signature using the PKI, and replies with an encrypted (using the bidder's public key) and signed message containing a newly generated pseudonym p and the hashed bid $h(b_i)$.
- *Bidding:* The RA generates a new symmetric key k. Each bidder will send $c = Enc_{pk_S}(b_i)$, his bid b_i encrypted with the seller's public key, and a signature of c, together with his pseudonym to the RA. The RA will reply with a signature on c, and encrypts the bidders message, together with the hashed bid $h(b_i)$ from phase one, using the symmetric key k. This encrypted message is then send to the seller.

– *Winner determination:* After all bids have been submitted, the RA will reveal the symmetric key k to the seller. The seller can then decrypt the bids, verify the correctness of the hash and determine the winner. To identify the winner using the pseudonym he can ask the RA to reveal the true identity.

Formal Model. We modeled the protocol in ProVerif using a standard equational theory for symmetric encryption (functions senc and sdec), asymmetric encryption (functions enc, dec and pubkey – which generates the public key corresponding to a secret key) and signatures (functions sign, checksign and getmessage):

$$\mathrm{sdec}(\mathrm{senc}(m, key), key) = m$$
$$\mathrm{dec}(\mathrm{enc}(m, \mathrm{pubkey}(sk)), sk) = m$$
$$\mathrm{checksign}(\mathrm{sign}(m, sk), \mathrm{pubkey}(sk)) = m$$
$$\mathrm{getmessage}(\mathrm{sign}(m, sk)) = m$$

Due to space limitations we cannot include the full model here, the ProVerif code is available on our website [31].

Analysis. We assume a honest RA and an honest seller.

Non-Repudiation (NR): To prove (NR), we have to show that on each possible trace the event won(p,id) is preceded by the event bid(p,id). ProVerif can verify such properties using queries, in this case using the query

```
query p:price,id:identity;
event(won(p,id)) ==> event(bid(p,id)).
```

This query means that for any value p of type price and any id of type identity, if the event won(p,id) is recorded, it is preceded by the event bid(p,id). ProVerif finds the following attack: Since the channel between the Registration Authority and the Seller is not protected, anybody can pretend to be the RA and submit false bids, encrypted with a self-chosen symmetric key. After all false bids are submitted, the attacker reveals the symmetric key and the seller will decrypt the bogus bids. Hence the event won(p,id) can be emitted on a trace without any event bid(p,id). We propose a solution to address this problem: If the messages from the RA to the seller are signed, the attacker cannot impersonate RA any more and ProVerif is able to prove Non-Repudiation for the accordingly modified protocol.

Non-Cancellation (NC): Here we have to show that even if a bidder reveals his secret data to the intruder, the intruder cannot cancel a submitted bid, i.e. there is no trace with the events recBid(p_1,id_a) and won(p_2,id_b) where $p\_1 > p\_2$. To verify this we need to model at least two distinct prices, which can be implemented using constants, i.e. by setting p_1 = max_price and p_2 = smaller_price, where max_price and smaller_price are two constants such that max_price > smaller_price[3]. Then we want to test the conjunction (not the precedence as above)

---

[3] Note that most auction protocols assume a finite number of possible prices anyway, which we can model using a list of constants.

of two events, which is not possible directly in ProVerif. A well-known solution is to replace the underlying events with messages over a private channel to a newly added processes which will call a conjunction event recBid_and_won once he received all the messages. Then we can use the following query:

```
query event(recBid_and_won(max_price, id_a,
           smaller_price, id_b)).
```

where the first two parameters are from the event recBid(p_1,id_a) and the second from the event won(p_2,id_b), here instantiated with price constants as explained above and two constants for two different bidders. For the original protocol, ProVerif finds a similar attack to the one described above: An attacker can delete the messages sent by the the RA to the seller, and choose a symmetric key and send bogus messages containing prices of his choice instead. When he reveals the symmetric key, a bidder of his choice will win, hence there will be an event won(smaller_price,id_b) for a smaller price than the one recorded by recBid(max_price,id_a). Even if we add signatures as proposed above, ProVerif still comes up with an attack: A dishonest bidder might submit a first bid triggering the event recBid for this bid, delete the forwarded message to the seller, and then submit a second bid at a different price. A first attempt to fix this issue would be – as proposed in the original paper – by including the number of bids in the message where the RA reveals the symmetric key. This would allow the seller to verify if he received the correct number of bids. However the attack still works if two auctions take place in parallel: Since the RA uses the same PKI in both cases, he will use the same keys. The malicious bidder could register in the second auction, obtain the signed bid and replace his original bid with this message. The new message will include a different pseudonym, but the seller has no means of verifying if a pseudonym corresponds to the current auction. A solution would be to use different keys for different auctions (which need to be set up in a secure way), but we were unable to verify the resulting protocol because of some limitations of ProVerif: For example the counting of messages requires to maintain state information for the RA.

Noninterference: It is clear that the protocol does not ensure Strong Noninterference (SN) since an attacker can simply count the number of messages to determine the number of participants. However we can check Weak Noninterference (WN), i.e. that any two instances containing the same bidders and only differing in the bids are bisimilar up to the end of the bidding phase, using the following query in ProVerif:

```
noninterf b_1, ..., b_n.
```

This query will ask ProVerif to verify strong secrecy of the variables b_1, ..., b_n., i.e. to check that any two instances of the protocol that only differ in these variables are bisimilar. For the original protocol ProVerif finds an attack which is based on the first message, which includes the hashed bidding price. An attacker simply hashes the possible values and compares the result. If we encrypt this message using the RA's public key, ProVerif is able to prove Weak Noninterference (WN). This modification was proposed in the original paper to achieve anonymity of bidders, but turns out to be also necessary to ensure fairness.

Highest Price Wins (HPW): Here we have to show that a malicious bidder cannot win the auction at a chosen price, even if another bidder submitted a higher bid. Again, we will assume that we have a finite number of possible prices. Then we can check the property using ProVerif by modeling two bidders, the first one bidding max_price, and the second one is corrupted by the adversary (according to Def. 7). To prevent the adversary from just winning using the highest possible price (which would not necessarily correspond to an attack), we declare the constant max_price private[4]. We also have to be sure that the protocol does not leak max_price before the end of the bidding phase (which would contradict the intention of declaring it private). As we already showed Weak Noninterference (WN), we can be sure that this is not the case. Hence we can check if the event won is reachable for the corrupted bidder id_B using the following query

```
query p:price; event(won(p, id_B)).
```

Since bidder id_A submitted the highest possible price and the attacker cannot access and submit this value, he should be unable to make id_B win the auction. For the original protocol – only corrected with added encryption of the first bid to ensure Weak Noninterference –, ProVerif finds an attack again using the fact that the messages from the RA to the Seller are not authenticated, hence an attacker can pretend to be RA and submit bids of his choice to win the auction at a price of his choice. If we add signatures again, ProVerif still comes up with an attack: A dishonest bidder might register twice and then replace the message from the RA to the seller containing the correct bid with his own, bogus bid obtained using the second registration. As above, this could probably be circumvented by counting the messages and using different keys for different auction, but we hit again the limitations of ProVerif when trying to model and verify the resulting protocol.

Privacy: The authors claim in the original paper that if the first message is encrypted, their protocol ensures anonymity of the bidders. Yet we can see that it does not ensure Strong Anonymity (SA) since after the symmetric key has been published, an attacker can obtain a list with hashes of all bids, which allows to distinguish $h(b_A)$, $h(b_C)$ from $h(b_B)$, $h(b_C)$. Hence we checked Weak Anonymity (WA) using the choice[] operator in ProVerif, which verifies if the processes obtained by instantiating a variable with two different values are bisimilar. More precisely, we can check if for two swapping bidders (the first bidder bids b_A = choice[b_1,b_2], the second b_B = choice[b_2,b_1]) the resulting processes are bisimilar. This query leads to another possible attack: The intruder might delay the messages from the second bidder. He waits until the first bidder sent his final message and this was relayed to the seller by the RA. This allows the attacker to link this message to the first bidder and distinguish both cases based on the hash after decrypting the message using the published symmetric key. This type of attack is well-known in electronic voting [18]. As a solution, we have to ensure that both messages to the seller are sent at exactly the same time using

---

[4] In the definition we did not require A to submit the highest possible bid, but only a higher bid than anybody else. We could model the existence of higher prices by defining additional private constants, but this would not change the verification task since they are never used by any honest participants and are not accessible to the attacker.

synchronization. Inspired by some techniques used in ProSwapper [32], we prove that the accordingly modified protocol ensures Weak Anonymity (WA).

It is also clear that the protocol is neither Receipt-Free nor Coercion-Resistant for any of the proposed notions since the hashed bidding price in the first message can be used as a receipt. Even if this message is encrypted, the data used to encrypt (keys, random values) can be used as a receipt. Note that for all properties ProVerif responds in less than a second on a standard PC.

4.2 Protocol by Brandt [3]

The protocol by Brandt [3] was designed to ensure full privacy in a completely distributed way. It exploits the homomorphic properties of a distributed El-Gamal Encryption scheme for a secure multi-party computation of the winner.

Informal Description. The participating bidders and the seller communicate using a bulletin board, i.e. an append-only memory accessible for everybody. The bids are encoded as bit-vectors where each entry corresponds to a price. The protocol then uses linear algebra operations on the bid vectors to compute a function f_i, which returns a vector containing one zero if the bidder i submitted the highest bid, and only random numbers otherwise. To be able to compute this function in a completely distributed way, and to guarantee that no coalition of malicious bidders can break privacy, these computations are performed on the encrypted bids using homomorphic properties of a distributed El-Gamal Encryption.

In a nutshell, the protocol realizes the following steps:

1. Firstly, the distributed key is generated: each bidder chooses his part of the secret key and publishes the corresponding part of the public key on the bulletin board.
2. Each bidder then computes the joint public key, encrypts his offer using this key and publishes it on the bulletin board.
3. Then the auction function f is calculated for every bidder using some operations exploiting the homomorphic property of the encryption scheme.
4. The outcome of this computation (n encrypted values) are published on the bulletin board, and each bidder partly decrypts each value using his secret key.
5. These shares are posted on the bulletin board, and can be combined to obtain the result.

Formal Model. Modeling the exchanged messages is straightforward (see [31] for the ProVerif code). Modeling the distributed encryption scheme and the distributed computations is a more challenging task since a too abstract model might miss attacks, whereas a too fine-grained model can lead to non-termination or false attacks.

The protocol assumes a finite set of possible prices, which we will model as constants $p\_1, \ldots, p\_n$. Assuming q bidders, we can define the following equational theory to model steps 3 and 4 of the protocol:

$$f(\text{enc}(b\_1, \text{pkey}, r\_1), ..., \text{enc}(b\_q, \text{pkey}, r\_q), \text{sk\_i})$$
$$= \text{share}((\max_i\{b\_i\}, \arg\max_i\{b\_i\}), (b\_1, ..., b\_q), \text{pkey}, \text{sk\_i}, g(r\_1, .., r\_q))$$

This equation models the following properties of the function f: If we have bids b_1, ..., b_q encrypted using the same joint public key pkey, some random values r_1, ... ,r_q, and a part sk_i of the secret key we obtain a share of the function outcome, i.e. the tuple (winning price, id of the winner), for the same public and secret keys and a function of the used random values. Since the share will look slightly different depending on the bids even if winning bid is the same, we also include b_1, ... , b_q in the share. This is necessary to avoid false attacks in ProVerif. The next equation corresponds to step 5 of the protocol and uses the function combine(pk(k_1), ..., pk(k_q)) which models the computation of the joint public key based on the individual ones.

$$\mathrm{dec}(\mathrm{share}(m, x\_1, \mathrm{combine}(\mathrm{pk}(k\_1), ..., \mathrm{pk}(k\_q))), k\_1, r\_1), ...,$$
$$\mathrm{share}(m, x\_q, \mathrm{combine}(\mathrm{pk}(k\_1), ..., \mathrm{pk}(k\_q))), k\_q, r\_q)) = m$$

The equation models that knowing all shares of the function outcome allows to decrypt it, if

- all shares have been constructed using the same joint public key, which was computed using the function combine from the individual public keys, and
- the individual public keys were computed from the same secret keys that were used to compute the shares.

Since the number of different prices n and the number of participants q are finite, we can enumerate all possible equations. In particular we can list all possible parameters of the function f, which allows us to enumerate all instances and replace the max and arg max functions which their actual values. This yields a convergent equational theory, which allows ProVerif to verify all the tested properties in less than one second.

Analysis. We use the same ProVerif techniques we discussed in the previous section. Essentially the protocol ensures none of the defined properties, mainly due the lack of authentication, even if all parties are trusted. The attacker can simulate a completely different protocol execution towards the seller (i.e. setting up keys, encrypting bids of his choice, doing the calculation, and publishing the shares), which allows attacks on Non-Repudiation (a trace with event won, but without event bid), Non-Cancellation (a trace with event recBid and event won with a different, lower bid from the same bidder) and Highest Price Wins (the event won with a lower bid from a corrupted bidder is reachable).

Although the protocol claims to be fully private, ProVerif finds an attack that allows to completely uncover a bidder's bid: Since there is no authentication, an intruder can simulate all other parties with respect to a participant. He will generate secret keys, publish the according public keys and on reception of the attacked bidder's bid, simply copy it and claim that it is his own bid. Then the joint computation and decryption will take place, and the announced winning price will be attacked bidder's offer, which is hence public. Note that this is not an attack on the security of the computation, but on the structure of the protocol.

It is also clear that the protocol does not ensure Strong Noninterference since the number of participants is public, which allows to distinguish instances with different number of participants. However we prove Weak Noninterference using choice[] (the use of noninterf leads to false attacks). The ProVerif-code is available in [31].

5 Conclusion and Future Work

We provided a framework to formally verify security properties in e-Auction protocols. In particular we discussed how protocols can be modeled in the Applied π-Calculus and how security properties such as different notions of Privacy, Fairness and Authentication can be expressed. We analyzed the relationship between the different notions and detailed a hierarchy of privacy notions (Fig. 2).

Using two case studies [3, 6], we showed how our definitions can be applied on existing protocols and are suitable for automated analysis using ProVerif. The results were surprising: One of the two protocols provided none of our security notions without modifications, the other protocol only one. It was particularly interesting to see that even the protocol by Brandt did not ensure privacy, although it was especially designed with privacy in mind. The discovered flaw is however not an attack on the cryptographic primitive used, but on the protocol architecture. This underlines again the complexity of designing secure protocols: A combination of secure building blocks can be insecure. In case of the protocol by Curtis et al. we also subsequently discussed several modifications to improve security.

As future work, we would like to verify Non-Cancellation and Highest Price Wins on the modified protocol by Curtis et al., which was not possible directly in ProVerif. There exist extensions which allow to model states, e.g. StatVerif [33] which might be used in this case.

References

1. Krishna, V.: Auction Theory. Academic Press (2002)
2. Brandt, F.: A verifiable, bidder-resolved auction protocol. In: Proceedings of the 5th AAMAS Workshop on Deception, Fraud and Trust in Agent Societies, pp. 18–25 (2002)
3. Brandt, F.: How to obtain full privacy in auctions. International Journal of Information Security 5, 201–216 (2006)
4. Brandt, F., Sandholm, T.: On the existence of unconditionally privacy-preserving auction protocols. ACM Trans. Inf. Syst. Secur. 11, 6:1–6:21 (2008)
5. Passch, C., Song, W., Kou, W., Tan, C.-J.: Online Auction Protocols: A Comparative Study. In: Kou, W., Yesha, Y., Tan, C.J.K. (eds.) ISEC 2001. LNCS, vol. 2040, pp. 170–186. Springer, Heidelberg (2001)
6. Curtis, B., Pieprzyk, J., Seruga, J.: An efficient eauction protocol. In: ARES, pp. 417–421. IEEE Computer Society (2007)
7. Franklin, M., Reiter, M.: The design and implementation of a secure auction service. In: Proceedings of the 1995 IEEE Symposium on Security and Privacy, pp. 2–14 (May 1995)
8. Harkavy, M., Tygar, J.D., Kikuchi, H.: Electronic auctions with private bids. In: Proceedings of the 3rd USENIX Workshop on Electronic Commerce, pp. 61–74 (1998)
9. Kikuchi, H., Harkavy, M., Tygar, J.D.: Multi-round anonymous auction protocols. In: Proceedings of the First IEEE Workshop on Dependable and Real-Time E-Commerce Systems, pp. 62–69. Springer (1998)
10. Lee, B., Kim, K., Ma, J.: Efficient Public Auction with One-Time Registration and Public Verifiability. In: Pandu Rangan, C., Ding, C. (eds.) INDOCRYPT 2001. LNCS, vol. 2247, pp. 162–174. Springer, Heidelberg (2001)
11. Omote, K., Miyaji, A.: A Practical English Auction with One-Time Registration. In: Varadharajan, V., Mu, Y. (eds.) ACISP 2001. LNCS, vol. 2119, pp. 221–234. Springer, Heidelberg (2001)

12. Abe, M., Suzuki, K.: Receipt-Free Sealed-Bid Auction. In: Chan, A.H., Gligor, V.D. (eds.) ISC 2002. LNCS, vol. 2433, pp. 191–199. Springer, Heidelberg (2002)

13. Stubblebine, S.G., Syverson, P.F.: Fair On-Line Auctions without Special Trusted Parties. In: Franklin, M.K. (ed.) FC 1999. LNCS, vol. 1648, pp. 230–240. Springer, Heidelberg (1999)

14. Subramanian, S.: Design and verification of a secure electronic auction protocol. In: Proceedings of the 17th IEEE Symposium on Reliable Distributed Systems, SRDS 1998, pp. 204–210. IEEE Computer Society (1998)

15. Dong, N., Jonker, H., Pang, J.: Analysis of a Receipt-Free Auction Protocol in the Applied Pi Calculus. In: Degano, P., Etalle, S., Guttman, J. (eds.) FAST 2010. LNCS, vol. 6561, pp. 223–238. Springer, Heidelberg (2011)

16. Küsters, R., Truderung, T., Vogt, A.: Accountability: definition and relationship to verifiability. In: Proceedings of the 17th ACM Conference on Computer and Communications Security, CCS 2010, pp. 526–535. ACM (2010)

17. Backes, M., Hritcu, C., Maffei, M.: Automated verification of remote electronic voting protocols in the applied pi-calculus. In: CSF 2008, pp. 195–209 (2008)

18. Delaune, S., Kremer, S., Ryan, M.: Verifying privacy-type properties of electronic voting protocols. Journal of Computer Security 17, 435–487 (2009)

19. Dreier, J., Lafourcade, P., Lakhnech, Y.: Vote-Independence: A Powerful Privacy Notion for Voting Protocols. In: Garcia-Alfaro, J., Lafourcade, P. (eds.) FPS 2011. LNCS, vol. 6888, pp. 164–180. Springer, Heidelberg (2012)

20. Dreier, J., Lafourcade, P., Lakhnech, Y.: Defining Privacy for Weighted Votes, Single and Multi-voter Coercion. In: Foresti, S., Yung, M., Martinelli, F. (eds.) ESORICS 2012. LNCS, vol. 7459, pp. 451–468. Springer, Heidelberg (2012)

21. Dreier, J., Lafourcade, P., Lakhnech, Y.: A formal taxonomy of privacy in voting protocols. In: First IEEE International Workshop on Security and Forensics in Communication Systems, ICC 2012 WS - SFCS (2012)

22. Küsters, R., Truderung, T.: An Epistemic Approach to Coercion-Resistance for Electronic Voting Protocols. In: S&P 2009, pp. 251–266. IEEE Computer Society (2009)

23. Smyth, B., Cortier, V.: Attacking and fixing helios: An analysis of ballot secrecy. In: CSF 2011, pp. 297–311. IEEE (2011)

24. Klay, F., Vigneron, L.: Formal aspects in security and trust, pp. 192–209. Springer (2009)

25. Liu, J., Vigneron, L.: Design and verification of a non-repudiation protocol based on receiver-side smart card. Information Security, IET 4(1), 15–29 (2010)

26. Abadi, M., Fournet, C.: Mobile values, new names, and secure communication. In: POPL 2001, pp. 104–115. ACM, New York (2001)

27. Blanchet, B.: An Efficient Cryptographic Protocol Verifier Based on Prolog Rules. In: CSFW 2001, pp. 82–96. IEEE Computer Society, Cape Breton (2001)

28. Blanchet, B.: From Secrecy to Authenticity in Security Protocols. In: Hermenegildo, M.V., Puebla, G. (eds.) SAS 2002. LNCS, vol. 2477, pp. 342–359. Springer, Heidelberg (2002)

29. Blanchet, B., Abadi, M., Fournet, C.: Automated verification of selected equivalences for security protocols. Journal of Logic and Algebraic Programming 75(1), 3–51 (2008)

30. Dreier, J., Lafourcade, P., Lakhnech, Y.: Formal verification of e-auction protocols. Technical Report TR-2012-17, Verimag Research Report (October 2012), http://www-verimag.imag.fr/TR/TR-2012-17.pdf

31. Dreier, J.: The proverif code used to automatically verify the examples is available at http://www-verimag.imag.fr/~dreier/papers/post-code.zip (2012)

32. Klus, P., Smyth, B., Ryan, M.D.: Proswapper: Improved equivalence verifier for proverif (2010), http://www.bensmyth.com/proswapper.php

33. Arapinis, M., Ritter, E., Ryan, M.D.: Statverif: Verification of stateful processes. In: CSF 2011, pp. 33–47. IEEE Computer Society (2011)

Sessions and Separability in Security Protocols*

Marco Carbone[1] and Joshua D. Guttman[2]

[1] IT University of Copenhagen
carbonem@itu.dk
[2] Worcester Polytechnic Institute
guttman@wpi.edu

Abstract. Despite much work on sessions and session types in non-adversarial contexts, session-like behavior given an active adversary has not received an adequate definition and proof methods. We provide a syntactic property that guarantees that a protocol has session-respecting executions. Any uncompromised subset of the participants are still guaranteed that their interaction will respect sessions. A protocol transformation turns any protocol into a session-respecting protocol.

We do this via a general theory of separability. Our main theorem applies to different separability requirements, and characterizes when we can separate protocol executions sufficiently to meet a particular requirement. This theorem also gives direct proofs of some old and new protocol composition results. Thus, our theory of separability appears to cover protocol composition and session-like behavior within a uniform framework, and gives a general pattern for reasoning about independence.

Keywords: Sessions, Security Protocols, Strand Spaces.

1 Introduction

A transaction or protocol respects sessions if the local runs of the individual participants always match up globally in a compatible way. When one participant receives any message in a session σ, it should have been sent by another participant acting *within the same session* σ. Session-respecting behavior is often studied using *session types* [21,22]. However, most work in this tradition studies sessions within a benign execution environment.

We adapt those ideas to environments containing active adversaries, who may control the medium of communication [28,15,4]. We define session-respecting behavior in an adversarial environment, offering syntactic conditions that ensure a protocol's behavior respects sessions. We exhibit a transformation that, given any protocol, yields one with session-respecting behavior.

Our central idea is *separability*. In an execution, an adversary may receive a message from one session and deliver it, or its fragments, into another session. In this case, we would like to *separate* the sessions by removing the connection that

---

* Carbone thanks the Danish Agency for Science, Technology and Innovation, and Guttman thanks the US National Science Foundation under grant CNS-0952287. Extended version at http://www.cs.wpi.edu/~guttman/pubs/CG13_long.pdf.

D. Basin and J.C. Mitchell (Eds.): POST 2013, LNCS 7796, pp. 267–286, 2013.
© Springer-Verlag Berlin Heidelberg 2013

the adversary has created. Separability means we can do this, possibly applying a renaming to one of them so that they involve different parameters. Although the adversary can create connections between different session, these connections are inessential. They can be removed modulo renaming. Hence, anything the adversary can achieve in a session, he can also do without relying on any other session. No successful attack requires unwitting support from participants engaged in a different session.

Session separability clarifies the real world effects of a protocol. Suppose a protocol allows a customer to buy merchandise through a broker, who receives a commission from a manufacturer. Can the broker manipulate the protocol so one interaction with the customer allows two interactions with the manufacturer? Can the broker receive his commission for the same transaction twice?

Suppose a compliant customer and manufacturer interact with a dishonest broker in a separable protocol. If messages from the single customer run reach local runs M_1, M_2 for the manufacturer, they will belong to the same session. Alternatively one run M belongs to no session, i.e. it occurs with no involvement of a customer. These conditions are easy for a protocol designer to analyze. To protect against the first, the manufacturer should contribute a fresh random value ("nonce") to help define the session. Then distinct manufacturer runs always belong to different sessions. To protect against the second, some authentication is needed between manufacturer and customer, a familiar and well-understood problem. Thus, separability reduces the no-double-commission property to simple characteristics of the protocol.

Strand spaces offer a partially ordered model; protocol executions ("bundles") are annotated directed acyclic graphs [30,20,18]. The edges represent causal relations. We interpret separation properties in terms of the absence of causal paths in these graphs, or the ability to find a related graph without them.

Contributions. Our main result, the *Separability Theorem* (Thm. 16), tells how to take an execution of a protocol and modify it into another execution that satisfies separability. It applies to a range of different *separability specifications*. Each separability specification is a partial order that says which kinds of events are allowed to causally affect which others.

Our result about sessions, Thm. 17, says that the syntactic conditions in Def. 8—mainly concerning "session nonces" that serve to define sessions—entail the premise of Thm. 16. Thus, executions can be made to satisfy a separability specification defined in terms of these nonces. We also provide a transformation that strengthens any protocol to one that satisfies these conditions (Thm. 10).

Thm. 16 also applies to other separability specifications. We apply it to protocols with "disjoint encryption" in three slightly different senses (Thms. 19–21), thereby yielding variants, sometimes sharpenings, of a number of results on preserving security goals under protocol composition [19,1,9,8,11]. Thus, the Separability Theorem formalizes a pattern of reasoning with wide applicability in protocol design and analysis. It unites session-oriented reasoning with protocol composition. All proofs are relegated to the extended version http://www.cs.wpi.edu/~guttman/pubs/CG13_long.pdf.

Related Work. Various flavors of sessions and separability have already played roles within protocol analysis and design. Among approaches based on computational methods, a session notion is often used to define the local runs that authentication should connect, as with Bellare and Rogaway [4]; in some models the sessions are defined by a bitstring that may be chosen by the adversary or built out of random contributions from the participants (e.g. Canetti-Krawczyk [7]). The Universal Composability model also assumes a random value that contributes to each cryptographically prepared unit and acts as a session identifier [6]; for a recent and more flexible alternative, see Küsters and Tuengerthal [24].

If different sessions of a protocol can never affect one another, then this simplifies analysis. The designer can explore the outcomes possible with a single instance of each role in the protocol. Indeed, Lowe's original proof that his changes to Needham-Schroeder were correct used a separability argument. He proved that any run could involve at most two non-separable instances of either role, and then model-checked the possible two-instance runs [25]. Lowe and Allaa Kamil [23] use separability to establish properties of TLS, such as that the adversary cannot divert application data from one TLS session to another. Their path-based methods within the strand space framework motivated some of the techniques used below in §4.

Cortier et al. [10] propose a protocol transformation, which they prove correct using session separability. Given a protocol satisfying any security property in an environment with a passive adversary, their transformation returns a new protocol that satisfies that property despite an active adversary. Their transformation adds freshly-generated nonces to the original protocol; this suggested our treatment of nonces in Thm. 10. Their transformation then inserts all of these nonces in with each message of the original protocol, which is signed and then encrypted. Our transformation does not add any additional cryptographic operations, but simply inserts the nonces into any pre-existing cryptographic units. This simpler treatment suffices because we are here exclusively concerned with separability, rather than any particular security goals. Another contrast concerns the adversary model. Their result concerns only sessions in which every participant is compliant, whereas our separability holds for the compliant participants, even in sessions with non-compliant participants.

Arapinis, Delaune, and Kremer [2] also offer a separability argument, leading to a protocol transformation which guarantees secrecy. The transformation adds nonces to each encrypted or signed term, although, together with nonces, it also adds principal names. Only the former is needed for separability; the latter helps with secrecy. Their transformation appears to generalize Lowe's fix to Needham-Schroeder. A subsequent paper with Ryan [12] investigates tagged password-based protocols, where the "tags" are tuples of session parameters hashed in with the key. They show that their composition is resistant to guessing attacks. Their proofs appear to establish particular instances of our Separability Theorem. We conjecture that our methods reconstruct their results, although proving this would require reformulating behavioral equivalences (in addition to trace properties) within our framework.

Deniélou et al. in [5] provide a compiler for generating ML code from multiparty protocol specifications. Their main result (Session Integrity Theorem) shows that there is no interference between multiple instances of the same protocol. Such a result could also be modeled in our framework as a variant of protocol independence. As we have mentioned, our approach also seems to capture the essence of several protocol composition results [19,1,9,8,11].

Separability also allows full verification within the bounded-session model of protocol analysis [29,26,3], rendering many classes of problems decidable.

In [17] we offer a logical language that can formalize the security goals that are preserved when omitting separable local runs.

2   Strand Spaces, with a Session Protocol

We first summarize the strand space terminology we will use in this paper. See [30,18] for more detail on strand spaces and our terminology.

We also introduce an example to illustrate separability, the *Trusted Broker Service*, in which a server S acts as a broker to match clients C_1 and C_2, who are executing different roles. S provides them with a key K to use to initiate an exchange. Clients trust the broker to generate a fresh key; to distribute it only to compliant principals; and to choose an appropriate pairing of clients.

Messages. Let Alg_0 be an algebra equipped with some operators and a set of homomorphisms $\eta\colon \mathsf{Alg}_0 \to \mathsf{Alg}_0$. We call the members of Alg_0 **basic values.**

Alg_0 is the disjoint union of infinite sets of *nonces, basic keys, names,* and *texts.* The operators $\mathsf{sk}(a)$ and $\mathsf{pk}(a)$ map names to signature keys and public encryption keys. K^{-1} maps an asymmetric basic key to its inverse, and a symmetric basic key to itself. Homomorphisms η are maps that that respect sorts and the operators $\mathsf{sk}(a)$, $\mathsf{pk}(a)$, and K^{-1}. An infinite set X disjoint from Alg_0—the **indeterminates**—act like unsorted variables.

The algebra Alg of **messages** is freely generated from $\mathsf{Alg}_0 \cup X$ by two operations: encryption $\{\!|t_0|\!\}_{t_1}$ and tagged concatenation $\mathsf{tag}\ t_0,\ t_1$. The tags tag are drawn from some set TAG. For a distinguished tag nil, we write nil $t_0,\ t_1$ as $t_0,\ t_1$. In $\{\!|t_0|\!\}_{t_1}$, a non-basic key t_1 is a symmetric key. To reduce cases in proofs, we do not introduce digital signature and hashing as separate operations. We can encode hashes $\mathsf{hash}(t)$ as encrypting t with a public key K_h, where no principal holds the inverse decryption key K_h^{-1}. A digital signature $[\![t]\!]_K$ is encoded as the concatenation $t,\ \{\!|\mathsf{hash}(t)|\!\}_K$.

A homomorphism $\alpha = (\eta, \chi)\colon \mathsf{Alg} \to \mathsf{Alg}$ pairs a homomorphism η on basic values and a function $\chi\colon X \to \mathsf{Alg}$; $\alpha(t)$ is defined by the conditions:

$$\begin{aligned}
\alpha(a) &= \eta(a), && \text{if } a \in \mathsf{Alg}_0 & \alpha(\{\!|t_0|\!\}_{t_1}) &= \{\!|\alpha(t_0)|\!\}_{\alpha(t_1)} \\
\alpha(x) &= \chi(x), && \text{if } x \in X & \alpha(\mathsf{tag}\ t_0,\ t_1) &= \mathsf{tag}\ \alpha(t_0),\ \alpha(t_1)
\end{aligned}$$

We call these homomorphisms **substitutions**, and use them to plug in values for parameters. Indeterminates x are blank slots, to be filled by any $\chi(x) \in \mathsf{Alg}$.

Messages t_1, t_2 have a *common instance* when there exist substitutions α, β that identify them: $\alpha(t_1) = \beta(t_2)$. Alg has the most general unifier property. That is, suppose that for $v, w \in \mathsf{Alg}$, there exist any α, β such that $\alpha(v) = \beta(w)$. Then there are α_0, β_0, such that $\alpha_0(v) = \beta_0(w)$, and for all α_1, β_1, if $\alpha_1(v) = \beta_1(w)$, then α_1 and β_1 are of the forms $\gamma \circ \alpha_0$ and $\gamma \circ \beta_0$.

Strands, Ingredients, and Origination. A **strand** is a sequence of local actions called **nodes**, each of which is either a message *transmission*, written $\bullet \rightarrow$, or else a message *reception*, written $\bullet \leftarrow$. Strands may be written vertically, or horizontally as in Fig. 1. This figure shows the behaviors of an initiating client C_1 and a responding client C_2 with a broker or server S. The protocol, which we call TBS, allows the broker to pair requests from suitable pairs of clients, and distribute a session key to them.

If n is a node, and the message t is transmitted or received, then we write $t = \mathsf{msg}(n)$. Double arrows indicate successive events on the same strand, e.g. $\bullet \Rightarrow \bullet \Rightarrow \bullet$. Each role in Fig. 1, and each column in Figs. 3,5 is a strand.

We write $s \downarrow i$ to mean the ith node along s, starting at $s \downarrow 1$. The **parameters** of s are the basic values and indeterminates in any $\mathsf{msg}(s \downarrow i)$.

The **ingredients** of a message are those subterms that may be reached by descending through concatenations, and through the plaintext but not the encryption keys. The values that **occur** in it descend also through encryptions. We write $\sqsubseteq$ ("is an ingredient of") and $\ll$ ("occurs in"), resp., for the smallest reflexive, transitive relation such that

$$t_1 \sqsubseteq (t_1, t_2) \qquad t_2 \sqsubseteq (t_1, t_2) \qquad t_1 \sqsubseteq \{\!|t_1|\!\}_{t_2}$$

$$t_1 \ll (t_1, t_2) \qquad t_2 \ll (t_1, t_2) \qquad t_1 \ll \{\!|t_1|\!\}_{t_2} \qquad t_2 \ll \{\!|t_1|\!\}_{t_2}.$$

We say that t **originates** on a node n if n is a transmission node, and $t \sqsubseteq \mathsf{msg}(n)$, and for all n_0, if $n_0 \Rightarrow^+ n$, then $t \not\sqsubseteq \mathsf{msg}(n)$. A basic value a is *freshly chosen* if it originates just once. We call it **uniquely originating**. In this case, a was chosen by a participant, without the bad luck of any other principal selecting the same value independently. A key is regarded as uncompromised if it originates *nowhere*. We call a basic value a **non-originating** in a set of nodes B if there is no $n \in B$ such that a originates at n. It may still be used in B even if it does not originate anywhere, since the regular strands may receive and send messages encrypted by K or K^{-1}, thus using K for encryption and decryption, resp.

A message t_0 **lies only inside encryptions in t with keys S** iff, in t's abstract syntax tree, every path from the root to an occurrence of t_0 traverses an encryption, and if that occurrence is in the plaintext, then the key is in S.

Protocols. A **protocol** Π is a finite set of strands, called the **roles** of the protocol. A **regular** strand for Π is any instance of one of the roles of Π, i.e. the result $\alpha(\rho)$ of some substitution α on the parameters of a role $\rho \in \Pi$. Fig. 1 is an example protocol. A protocol may also specify some parameters of a role that are always non-originating or uniquely originating. We will also formalize *adversary* behavior by strands (which use inverse). We stipulate a syntactic constraint:

Assumption 1. *If $\rho \in \Pi$, then the key inverse symbol does not appear in any message $\mathsf{msg}(\rho \downarrow i)$. Moreover, $\mathsf{sk}(A) \not\sqsubseteq \mathsf{msg}(\rho \downarrow i)$. If $\{\!|t|\!\}_K \ll \mathsf{msg}(\rho \downarrow i)$ for $\rho \in \Pi$, then K is either a basic value or an encryption (not a concatenation).*

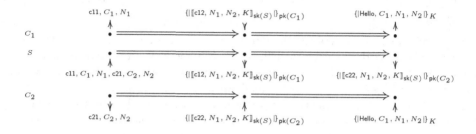

Fig. 1. Trusted Broker Service Protocol, TBS

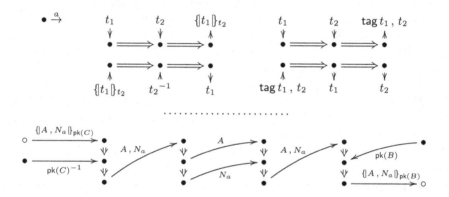

Fig. 2. Part I: Adversary roles to generate basic value a; encrypt and decrypt; concatenate and separate. Part II: A compound adversary activity

The Adversary. Adversary strands consist of zero or more reception nodes followed by one transmission node. The adversary obtains the transmitted value as a function of the values received; or creates it, if there are no reception nodes. The adversary can choose basic values, and operate on complex values using the strands shown above in Fig. 2. These are often used in patterns, e.g. as in Fig. 2 Part II, which transport information along paths. Six strands are shown. Two are of length 1, in which the adversary transmits keys, namely his own private decryption key $\mathsf{pk}(C)^{-1}$ and B's public encryption key $\mathsf{pk}(B)$. Two are a (leftmost) decryption strand and a (rightmost) encryption strand. The second node on a decryption or encryption strand is called the **key node**, since it receives the key used to perform the cryptographic operation.

In the middle are a separation strand that breaks A, N_a into its two parts, followed by a concatenation strand that puts them back together. These strands are unnecessary here. We include them here to illustrate that the adversary can always break a concatenation down to non-concatenated parts, i.e., either basic values or encryptions (see Assumption 3).

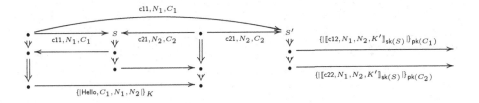

Fig. 3. A bundle of protocol TBS

Adversary strands are closed under substitutions along the strand, as they comprise all the instances of the roles in Fig. 2, Part I. Indeed, this also holds for regular strands, which are all the substitution instances of the roles $\rho \in \Pi$:

Lemma 1. *If α is a substitution and s is an adversary strand or a regular strand of Π, then so is $\alpha(s)$.*

Bundles. An execution is pieced together from a finite set of strands (or their initial segments), where these may be regular strands of Π or adversary strands. Two nodes are connected with a single arrow $\bullet \rightarrow \bullet$ when the former transmits a message, and the latter receives that same message directly from it. A *bundle* is a causally well founded graph built using strands by $\rightarrow$:

Definition 2. *Let $\mathcal{B} = \langle \mathcal{N}, \rightarrow_E \cup \Rightarrow_E \rangle$ be a finite, directed acyclic graph where (i) $n_1 \Rightarrow_E n_2$ implies $n_1 \Rightarrow n_2$, i.e. that n_1, n_2 are successive nodes on the same strand; and (ii) $n_1 \rightarrow_E n_2$ implies that n_1 is a transmission node, n_2 is a reception node, and $\mathsf{msg}(n_1) = \mathsf{msg}(n_2)$. $\mathcal{B}$ is a **bundle** if:*

1. *If $n_1 \Rightarrow n_2$, and $n_2 \in \mathcal{N}$, then $n_1 \in \mathcal{N}$ and $n_1 \Rightarrow_E n_2$; and*
2. *If n_2 is a reception node, there exists a unique $n_1 \in \mathcal{N}$ such that $n_1 \rightarrow_E n_2$.*

*$\mathcal{B}$ is an **open bundle** if, in condition 2, there is at most one $n_1 \in \mathcal{N}$ such that $n_1 \rightarrow_E n_2$, rather than exactly one.*

We write $\mathsf{nodes}(\mathcal{B})$ for the nodes of $\mathcal{B}$, and $\mathsf{regnodes}(\mathcal{B})$ for its regular (non-adversary) nodes; $\mathsf{edges}(\mathcal{B})$ is the set $\Rightarrow_E \cup \rightarrow_E$ of edges of $\mathcal{B}$. $\preceq_\mathcal{B}$ is the causal partial order $(\rightarrow_E \cup \Rightarrow_E)^*$, and $\prec_\mathcal{B} = (\rightarrow_E \cup \Rightarrow_E)^+$.

*A node n is **realized** in an open bundle $\mathcal{B}$ iff n is a transmission node, or else n is a reception node and has an incoming $\rightarrow$ edge, i.e. $n' \rightarrow n$.*

*$(\mathcal{B}, \mathsf{unique}, \mathsf{non})$ is an **annotated** bundle (resp. open bundle) if $\mathcal{B}$ is a bundle (resp. open bundle), unique is a finite set of basic values each originating at most once in $\mathcal{B}$, and non is a finite set of basic values each originating nowhere in $\mathcal{B}$.*

The causal partial order $\preceq$ is well-founded, since $\mathcal{B}$ is finite.

Example: The session-oriented protocol TBS. Fig. 3 is a bundle. TBS defines a session via a nonce from each client, and the server-generated session key. It gathers the two incoming messages to the broker in a single reception,

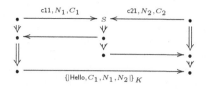 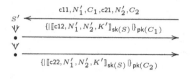

Fig. 4. Open bundle separating Fig. 3

allowing some (untrusted) auxiliary process to propose a matching. In Fig. 3, the adversary reuses the nonces N_1, N_2 to start a second server strand. However, we can fix this, separating the second server strand, just by renaming these nonces to new values N_1', N_2'. This yields the new bundle in Fig. 4, in which the adversary can supply the message coming from the upper right. Fig. 4 is an open bundle, as shown without adversary activity.

These figures are annotated (possibly open) bundles with various choices of unique, non. An interesting choice would be unique $= \{N_1, N_2, K, N_1', N_2'\}$ for Fig. 4 and unique $= \{N_1, N_2, K\}$ for Fig. 3. A relevant choice for both non $= \{\mathsf{sk}(S), \mathsf{pk}(C_1)^{-1}, \mathsf{pk}(C_2)^{-1}, \mathsf{pk}(S)^{-1}\}$.

In studying separability we are interested in bundles equipped with a choice of fresh and uncompromised values. Hence, we will assume that all bundles are annotated with sets of uniquely originating and non-originating values unique, non. When using "bundle" and $\mathcal{B}$, we will mean "annotated bundle" as defined above.

The core pattern for separating a session is:

- removing dependence on an existing session;
- renaming some freshly chosen items in one or more local runs;
- allowing the adversary to supply incoming messages in these runs.

When a protocol ensures that this pattern will succeed in separating behaviors, it has session behavior.

However, this is not always possible. As an example, consider the protocol TBSMINUS, which is just like TBS, except that the session nonces N_1, N_2 are omitted in all the messages. Here we can have the essentially inseparable bundle Fig. 5. No amount of renaming and pruning edges will produce a bundle in which C_2 and C_2' do not both depend on the same strand C_1.

We assume (i) public encryption keys may be freely sent or used by anyone, including the adversary; and (ii) when a value a originates uniquely, and is used on a different regular strand as part of a key for encryption, then it has been received as an ingredient on that strand. When $a \sqsubseteq \mathsf{msg}(m_1)$, this conclusion follows from the definition of unique origination. We also assume (iii) that a basic value is not received from a later transmission when it could be received from an earlier one. If a bundle violates this property, we can fix it by rerouting arrows to start from earlier nodes.

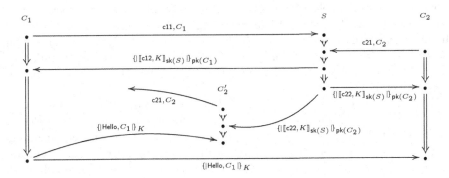

Fig. 5. An inseparable execution of TBSMINUS

Assumption 2. *Let* $(\mathcal{B}, \text{unique}, \text{non})$ *be an annotated bundle.*

1. $\text{pk}(A) \notin \text{unique} \cup \text{non}$ *for all names* A.
2. *Suppose* $a \in \text{unique}$, a *originates on* n_0, *and for some transmission node* m_1, $a \ll K$ *and* $\{|t|\}_K$ *originates at* m_1. *If* n_0, m_1 *lie on different strands, then there is a reception node* $m_0 \Rightarrow^+ m_1$ *such that* $a \sqsubseteq \text{msg}(m_0)$.
3. *If* $a = \text{msg}(n_0) = \text{msg}(n_1) = \text{msg}(n_2)$ *is a basic value, where* n_0, n_1 *are transmission nodes, with* $n_0 \preceq n_1 \preceq n_2$. *Then it is not the case that* $n_1 \to n_2$.

Lemma 3. *Suppose* $\mathcal{B}$ *is a bundle with* $n_0, m_1 \in \text{nodes}(\mathcal{B})$. *If* $a \in \text{unique}$ *originates at* n_0 *and* $a \ll \text{msg}(m_1)$, *then* $n_0 \preceq m_1$.

The "Lies-below" Relation. We now define a relation between bundles (or open bundles) of reducing information. We say that one (open) bundle lies below another when the latter results by adding information to the ordering relation $\preceq$ and adding equations between parameters. The key idea is reducing the ordering relation in a bundle $\mathcal{B}$, possibly renaming some occurrences of parameters, so as to "rename them apart" in a simpler bundle $\mathcal{C}$. We actually formalize this in the other direction, by considering a homomorphism from $\mathcal{C}$ into the richer $\mathcal{B}$. We call this a *local renaming*, because restricted to portions of $\mathcal{C}$ it acts like a renaming. It acts injectively on each portion separately.

Definition 4 (Local Renaming). *Suppose* $\mathcal{C}$ *is an open bundle.*

The sets $S_1, \ldots, S_n$ **partition** $\text{nodes}(\mathcal{C})$ **by strands** *if (i) the* S_i *are disjoint; (ii)* $\bigcup S_i = \text{nodes}(\mathcal{C})$; *and (iii) any two nodes on the same strand are in the same partition class* S_i.

A substitution α *is a* **local renaming of** $\mathcal{C}$ *with respect to* $S_1, \ldots, S_n$ *if the sets partition* $\text{nodes}(\mathcal{C})$ *by strands, and moreover, for every* $j \leq n$, α *restricted to the parameters of the strands in* S_j *is a renaming, i.e. an invertible map from parameters to parameters.*

For instance, in Fig. 4, the part to the left of the white space S_1 and the part to the right S_2 form a partition by strands. The map which sends $N_1' \mapsto N_1$

and $N_2' \mapsto N_2$, and is elsewhere the identity, is a local renaming, which we will write $[N_1' \mapsto N_1, N_2' \mapsto N_2]$. It is a renaming (the identity) when restricted to the parameters that appear in S_1, the left half, since N_1', N_2' do not appear on the left. Moreover, it is a renaming when restricted to S_2, the right half, too, since N_1, N_2 do not appear as parameters on the right. Thus, it is injective on the parameters appearing in S_2.

Every renaming is a local renaming, but a local renaming α is not a true ("global") renaming when $\alpha(x) = \alpha(y)$ holds for parameters x, y to nodes in different partition classes S_j, S_k. We often think of the action of a local renaming backward, viewing its source as the result of "renaming apart" values that are equated in its target. If we view $[N_1' \mapsto N_1, N_2' \mapsto N_2]$ as if it were acting on Fig. 3 to yield Fig. 4, then it is "renaming apart" different occurrences of N_1, N_2.

One open bundle lies below another if, after applying a local renaming forward, their regular nodes are the same, as are their uniquely originating and non-originating values, but one precedence order is a suborder of the other:

Definition 5. 1. $\mathcal{C}$ **lies below** $\mathcal{B}$ **via** α *iff, for some* $S_1, \ldots, S_i$, α *is a local renaming for* $\mathcal{C}$ *with respect to* $S_1, \ldots, S_i$, *and:*
  (a) $\alpha(\mathsf{regnodes}(\mathcal{C})) = \mathsf{regnodes}(\mathcal{B})$;
  (b) *For all* $n_0, n_1 \in \mathsf{regnodes}(\mathcal{C})$, $n_0 \preceq_{\mathcal{C}} n_1$ *implies* $\alpha(n_0) \preceq_{\mathcal{B}} \alpha(n_1)$;
  (c) $\alpha^{-1}(\mathsf{unique}(\mathcal{B})) = \mathsf{unique}(\mathcal{C})$; *and*
  (d) $\alpha^{-1}(\mathsf{non}(\mathcal{B})) = \mathsf{non}(\mathcal{C})$
2. $\mathcal{C}$ **lies below** $\mathcal{B}$ *if it does so via some* α.
3. $\mathcal{B}$ *and* $\mathcal{C}$ *are* **equivalent** *iff each lies below the other via renamings* α, β, *and* $\alpha \circ \beta$ *is the identity on the parameters involved.*

For instance, Fig. 4 lies below Fig. 3 via $[N_1' \mapsto N_1, N_2' \mapsto N_2]$, given the choices of unique, non mentioned after Defn. 2.

If $\mathcal{C}$ lies below $\mathcal{B}$, then $\mathcal{C}$ differs from $\mathcal{B}$ only in having a sparser ordering, and in not yet having equated some parameters that have been equated in $\mathcal{B}$. We can think of $\mathcal{C}$ as a simplified version of $\mathcal{B}$. It is less informative in that the information that these parameters are equal has not yet been added.

Lemma 6. *"Lies below" is a well-founded partial order to within isomorphism:*

1. *"Lies below" is reflexive and transitive.*
2. $\mathcal{C}$ *and* $\mathcal{B}$ *each lie below the other iff their regular parts are isomorphic.*
3. *If* $\langle \mathcal{B}_i \rangle_i$ *is an infinite sequence of bundles such that* $i < j$ *implies* $\mathcal{B}_j$ *lies below* $\mathcal{B}_i$, *then for some* i, k, $i < k$ *and* $\mathcal{B}_i$ *lies below* $\mathcal{B}_k$.

3   Formalizing Sessions

We now turn to defining when TBS and similar session-oriented protocols are separable. Suppose that Π is a protocol, and $P \colon \Pi \to \mathsf{Nonce} \cup \mathsf{Key}$ is a function that chooses a parameter for each role. As an example, if Π is TBS, we would be interested in the function P that assigns N_1 to the first client role; N_2 to the second client role; and K to the server (broker) role.

We say that x is a **session parameter** if $x \in \mathsf{range}(P)$. P associates each role to the session parameter that it chooses. We call $P(\rho)$ ρ's **proper session parameter**, and we require that $P(\rho)$ originates on ρ.

If x is a session parameter, x **is acquired at step** i if $x \ll \rho \downarrow i$ but $x \not\ll \rho \downarrow j$ for $j < i$. It is **acquired by step** k if it is acquired at step i for some $i \leq k$. A parameter x is **key material at step** i if $x \ll K$ and $\{\!|t|\!\}_K \ll \mathsf{msg}(\rho \downarrow i)$.

As a convention, we will assume that the parameters of each role have been chosen (by a renaming if necessary) so that corresponding session parameters on different roles have the same name. We could of course avoid this convention at the cost of added notation, in the form of a function which would supply the necessary correlations.

No Ambiguity. TBS uses the session parameters unambiguously in each encryption. No encryption in the protocol could be misinterpreted by a receiver so as to interchange the session parameters. For instance, N_1 and N_2 always appear in the same order, and K always appears after them or in key position.

No Ambiguity: If encryptions $\{\!|t|\!\}_K \ll \mathsf{msg}(\rho \downarrow i)$ and $\{\!|t'|\!\}_{K'} \ll \mathsf{msg}(\sigma \downarrow j)$ have a common instance $\alpha(\{\!|t|\!\}_K) = \beta(\{\!|t'|\!\}_{K'})$, then ρ and σ have acquired the same session parameters by steps i and j resp., and $\alpha(x) = \beta(x)$ for each of those session parameters.

We here follow our convention that corresponding session parameters on different roles have been given the same parameters names.

Contribution. Every encrypted unit involves the session parameters. This is akin to the tagging property [12], except that the session parameters do not have to contribute to the key. The last message of TBS is $\{\!|\mathsf{Hello}, C_1, N_1, N_2|\!\}_K$. Two session parameters are in the plaintext, while K is the encryption key. All the session parameters could be concentrated in the key; $\{\!|\mathsf{Hello}, C_1|\!\}_{\mathsf{hash}(N_1, N_2, K)}$ would also work. Alternatively, they could all be concentrated in the plaintext, with some public key used for encryption.

In this protocol, the participants agree on all of the session parameters at the start. They then use them throughout the remainder of the protocol. A protocol can also have some participants agree on their session parameters, while other participants join the session later. These "late arrivals" allow for an attractive flexibility in the session-type literature [13]. Of course, the encrypted units *before* the late arrivals are expected to contain only the session parameters that have already been seen at that point.

Contribution to Encryptions: If $\{\!|t|\!\}_K \ll \mathsf{msg}(\rho \downarrow i)$ and session parameter x is acquired by step i, then $x \ll \{\!|t|\!\}_K$.

The No-Vs Property. The observation that session parameters may be acquired piecemeal is an important insight. It implies that "same session," which sounds like an equivalence relation, is in fact misleading. A partially defined session with session parameters $x_1, \ldots, x_i$ may affect any of its possible extensions with an additional session parameter $x_1, \ldots, x_i, x_{i+1}$. However, any one of those extensions is incompatible with those having a different value x'_{i+1}. Indeed, messages from a step with extended session parameters $x_1, \ldots, x_i, x_{i+1}$ should not affect an event with session parameters $x_1, \ldots, x_i$. If they did, the latter could also affect a distinct extension $x_1, \ldots, x_i, x'_{i+1}$. Thus, transitively, there could be effects from an event with parameters $x_1, \ldots, x_i, x_{i+1}$ to one with parameters $x_1, \ldots, x_i, x'_{i+1}$. That would be contrary to the session discipline.

For this reason, we regard the "may influence" relation on partially defined sessions as a partial order (on the sessions) or as a pre-order (on the transmission and reception events within the sessions). We will write $n_1 \rightsquigarrow n_2$ when an event n_1 may influence an event n_2.

We require non-influence to persist, specifically when n_1 selects a fresh value that is a parameter to n_2. We formulate this as a "no Vs" condition. Whenever we have a V in the may-influence relation, this is not an open V, but a closed triangle-like configuration, for any $n_3 \succeq n_2$:

$$
\begin{array}{c}
n_1 \\
 \\
n_2
\end{array}
\rightsquigarrow n_3
\qquad \text{implies} \qquad
\begin{array}{c}
n_1 \\
\downarrow \\
n_2
\end{array}
\rightsquigarrow n_3.
\tag{1}
$$

A node n_2 that I cannot influence cannot influence a later node that I can influence, at least when I have uniquely originated a value found in that node. This no Vs property turns out to be crucial to proving the Separability Theorem, whose proof tries to create new bundles by local renamings.

To see what could go wrong, suppose the TBS server received the two parts of its first incoming message on separate nodes: $(\mathsf{c11}, C_1, N_1) \Rightarrow (\mathsf{c21}, C_2, N_2) \Rightarrow \ldots$. Then an adversary could deliver C_2's nonce N_2 as if it were from C_1, to the first server node n_2. C_2's first node n_1 should not influence n_2, since n_1 has the C_2 nonce defined, whereas n_2 does not; n_2 has only the C_1 nonce parameter defined. However, if the adversary re-delivers the same nonce on the server's second node n_3, then C_2's first node n_1 can influence this second server node n_3. Node n_3 has the same value for the only session parameter defined on n_1. This is precisely the open V situation, where $n_1 \not\rightsquigarrow n_2 \rightsquigarrow n_3$, and $n_1 \rightsquigarrow n_3$.

Acquisition. In order to ensure the no-Vs property syntactically, some properties are needed, constraining how session parameters are acquired. First, some session parameters $\bar{x}$ are received in a principal's first reception. These may be transported without encryption, such as N_1 and N_2 in TBS. This is why S receives both N_1 and N_2 in a single message in its first node. Second, there are no transmissions after a reception and before transmitting a strand's proper session nonce. Third, when a session includes late-arriving participants, values freshly chosen after a late arrival in the session will be transmitted under encryptions that cannot be compromised. Various techniques are available for proving this [20,18], but here we will just use a simple sufficient condition, namely that the decryption key is non-originating. These messages will be received by participants that have already joined the session; i.e. their proper nonces have already been chosen, and must also appear in this encryption by the *Contribution* requirement. This is a per-bundle requirement, for a bundle $\mathcal{B}$.

Parameter Acquisition: Session parameters divide into two groups, $\overline{x}$ and $\overline{y}$.

1. If x in $\overline{x}$ is acquired on reception node $\rho \downarrow i$, then i is the earliest reception node on ρ.
2. If x in $\overline{x}$ is acquired on transmission node $\rho \downarrow i$, and $\rho \downarrow k$ is any reception node with $k < i$, then there is no transmission node between them.
3. Let y in $\overline{y}$ be acquired (by reception or transmission) on $\rho \downarrow i$, and let $k \geq i$. There is a set $\mathsf{LAK}(\mathcal{B})$ of *late-arrival protection keys of* $\mathcal{B}$ such that: (a) If $\alpha(\rho \downarrow k) \in \mathsf{nodes}(\mathcal{B})$, then $\alpha(y)$ lies only inside encryptions in $\mathsf{msg}(\alpha(\rho \downarrow k))$ with keys K where $\alpha(K^{-1}) \in \mathsf{LAK}(\mathcal{B})$.
   (b) If $a \in \mathsf{unique}_{\mathcal{B}}$ is any value acquired on $\alpha(\rho \downarrow k)$, $\alpha(y)$ lies only inside encryptions in $\mathsf{msg}(\alpha(\rho \downarrow k))$ with keys K where $\alpha(K^{-1}) \in \mathsf{LAK}(\mathcal{B})$.

Condition 3 ensures that y always appears together with all previously defined session parameters. We focus on bundles in which, for any late arrivals to the session in a bundle $\mathcal{B}$, the strands still active then are all uncompromised, i.e. $\mathsf{LAK}(\mathcal{B}) \subseteq \mathsf{non}_{\mathcal{B}}$. In TBS, all session parameters belong to the first group $\overline{x}$, as all of the roles acquire them from their peers on their first reception. For protocol design, it is desirable that the session key can double as S's session parameter, traveling in the encrypted messages from the server.

May-Influence Relations. Curiously, the Separability Theorem, Thm. 16 depends only on two properties of a reflexive, transitive *may-influence* relation, namely, the no Vs property, and the fact that forward influence on a strand is always permitted. Because of this generality, we sought to specify various degrees of separability, i.e. to specify how sparse a bundle we would like to obtain in the "lies below" ordering. To parametrize our reasoning, we define a *may-influence* relation to be a pre-ordering $n_1 \rightsquigarrow n_2$ on regular nodes with these two properties. It specifies the upper bound on which nodes of Π may influence each other.

Definition 7. *Let $\mathcal{B}$ be an (annotated) bundle for protocol Π. Then a preorder $\rightsquigarrow$ is a **may-influence relation** for $\mathcal{B}$ iff for all $n_1, n_2, n_3 \in \mathsf{regnodes}(\mathcal{B})$,*

1. *if $n_1 \Rightarrow n_2$ then $n_1 \rightsquigarrow n_2$; and*
2. *"No Vs," Eqn. 1: Suppose (i) $a \in \mathsf{unique}_{\mathcal{B}}$ originates at n_1 and $a \ll \mathsf{msg}(n_2)$ and (ii) $n_2 \rightsquigarrow n_3$ and $n_2 \preceq_{\mathcal{B}} n_3$. If $n_1 \rightsquigarrow n_3$, then $n_1 \rightsquigarrow n_2$.*

   *$\mathcal{B}$ **obeys** $\rightsquigarrow$ iff, for all $m, n \in \mathsf{regnodes}(\mathcal{B})$, $m \preceq_{\mathcal{B}} n$ implies $m \rightsquigarrow n$.*

   *Π **obeys** $\rightsquigarrow$ subject to Φ if, for every Π-bundle $\mathcal{B}$ satisfying Φ, there is a Π-bundle $\mathcal{C}$ satisfying Φ such that $\mathcal{C}$ lies below $\mathcal{B}$ and $\mathcal{C}$ obeys $\rightsquigarrow$.*

When $m \rightsquigarrow n$, we say that m is *permitted to influence* n.

When $m \Rightarrow n$, m must be allowed to influence n, since it is impossible to prevent the influence; hence condition 1 on influence functions. Condition 2 prohibits open, V-shaped configurations. One leg of the V starts at a's origin n_1, and the other at n_2, and the legs join at a jointly influenced n_3. When $a \ll \mathsf{msg}(n_2)$, then n_1 must be permitted to influence n_2. If a's origin n_1 cannot influence n_2, then their causal consequences must remain separated thereafter.

Π obeys $\rightsquigarrow$ if Π-bundles either already obey the ordering constraint, or some bundle lying below is sparse enough to obey it. In weakening the order $\preceq$, we are allowed to select preimages under local renamings. We use the constraints Φ to record assumptions about freshly chosen nonces and uncompromised keys.

Protocols with Session Parameters. We can now define:

Definition 8. *A bundle $\mathcal{B}$ satisfies Φ_s, the **session constraint**, if the late arrival protection keys $\mathsf{LAK}(\mathcal{B}) \subseteq \mathsf{non}_{\mathcal{B}}$ and, for every node $\alpha(\rho \downarrow i) \in \mathsf{nodes}(\mathcal{B})$, where ρ acquires its proper session nonce at step i, $\alpha(P(\rho)) \in \mathsf{unique}_{\mathcal{B}}$.*

*Π has **session parameters** P for $\mathcal{B}$ if No ambiguity, Contribution to encryptions, and Parameter acquisition hold for Π, P, and $\mathcal{B}$.*

*The **session may-influence** relation $\leadsto_s$ holds between Π-nodes n_1 and n_2, written $n_1 \leadsto_s n_2$, iff (i) $n_1 = \alpha(\rho \downarrow i)$ and $n_2 = \beta(\sigma \downarrow j)$ where $\rho, \sigma \in \Pi$; (ii) every session parameter x that has been acquired by step i on ρ has been acquired by step j on σ; and (iii) $\alpha(x) = \beta(x)$ for each session parameter x acquired by step i on ρ.*

Essentially, $n_1 \leadsto_s n_2$ means that the partial function assigning session parameters to values in node n_1 is a subfunction of the partial function assigning session parameters to values in node n_2. The may-influence relation is fixed by the ordering of definedness on these partial functions.

Lemma 9. *If $\mathcal{B}$ is a Π-bundle satisfying Φ_s, and Π has session parameters P in $\mathcal{B}$, then $\leadsto_s$ is a may-influence relation for $\mathcal{B}$.*

A Transformation Yielding Protocols with Session Parameters. A simple transformation can produce protocols with session parameters.

The transformation has two parts. The first part prepends before σ a node that transmits a session parameter, and a node that receives a concatenated tuple containing session nonces from each of the other roles:

$$+N_i \;\Rightarrow\; -(N_1, \ldots, N_{i-1}, N_{i+1}, \ldots, N_k) \;\Rightarrow\; \sigma$$

In the second part, we transform all encrypted units $\{\!|t|\!\}_K$ contained in σ, to $\{\!|t, \tilde{N}|\!\}_K$, where $\tilde{N}$ is the sequence of all the session nonces introduced in the first step. Thus, letting $\mathcal{T}_{\tilde{N}}$ be this transformation,

Theorem 10. *$\mathcal{T}_{\tilde{N}}(\Pi)$ has session parameters for each $\mathcal{T}_{\tilde{N}}(\Pi)$-bundle $\mathcal{B}$.*

It is easy to very that *No Ambiguity*, *Contribution to Encryptions*, and *Parameter Acquisition* are all true, where the late-arriving parameters $\overline{y}$ are vacuous.

4   The Separability Theorem

Penetrator Paths. The ways that adversary strands manipulate messages are tightly constrained by their syntactic forms. We introduce *penetrator paths* to be able to express these relations conveniently.

Definition 11. *A **key node** is the middle node on an adversary encryption or decryption strand, which receives the key to be used (Fig. 2).*

*A **penetrator path** in $\mathcal{B}$ is a sequence $p = \langle n_0, n_1, \ldots, n_k \rangle$ with $k > 0$ and each $n_i \in \mathsf{nodes}(\mathcal{B})$, such that:*

1. *$n_1, \ldots, n_{k-1}$ are all penetrator nodes;*
2. *if n_i is a reception node and $i < k$, then n_{i+1} is a transmission node and $n_i \Rightarrow^+ n_{i+1}$;*
3. *if n_i is a transmission node, then $n_i \to n_{i+1}$ in $\mathcal{B}$.*

We often focus on the penetrator paths that stretch from a regular node to a regular node, traversing penetrator strands. These represent activities of the adversary that extract useful materials from regular transmissions, and use them to construct messages to satisfy regular receptions.

We write $p(i)$ for the node n_i, and $|p|$ for k, the number of arrows traversed by p, so $p(|p|)$ is the last node on p. Two paths are shown in Fig. 2. In both cases, $p(0)$ is the hollow circle at the upper left, indicating an unshown regular node, and $p(9)$ is the hollow circle at lower right. One path traverses the edge A in the middle, and the other traverses N_a. We generally write $\mathsf{first}(p)$ and $\mathsf{last}(p)$ for $p(0)$ and $p(|p|)$.

Definition 12. *The penetrator path p is **direct** if no key node appears in p, except possibly as $\mathsf{last}(p)$.*

*$\mathcal{B}$ is **normal** if, on every direct penetrator path, each destructive penetrator strand (decryption, separation) appears before any constructive strand (encryption, concatenation).*

The penetrator paths in Fig. 2 are direct. We speak of an *extended path* when we wish to emphasize that it may not be direct.

Lemma 13 ([20]). *Every bundle $\mathcal{B}$ has a normal bundle $\mathcal{C}$ lying below $\mathcal{B}$ via the identity Id. If $\mathcal{C}$ is any normal bundle, and p is a direct penetrator path in $\mathcal{C}$, then there is a pair of nodes $p_j \to p_{j+1}$ such that, for all $i \leq j \leq k$:*

1. *$\mathsf{msg}(p(i)) \sqsubseteq \mathsf{msg}(\mathsf{first}(p))$ and $\mathsf{msg}(p(k)) \sqsubseteq \mathsf{msg}(\mathsf{last}(p))$;*
2. *If $p(i)$ is an adversary node, then $p(i)$ lies on a destructive strand (decryption, separation); and*
3. *If $p(k+1)$ is an adversary node, then $p(k+1)$ lies on a constructive strand (encryption, concatenation).*

This lemma still holds in our current context, which includes compound keys, because it is restricted to *direct* paths p. Since a key node in p must be the last node, and we never continue along its encryption or decryption strand, we never encounter any case different from those already shown in the proof in [20].

By this lemma, when proving that there exists a bundle lying below $\mathcal{B}$ with a particular property, it is sound to silently assume that $\mathcal{B}$ is normal.

The **bridge term** of a direct penetrator path p in a normal $\mathcal{B}$ is the message $\mathsf{msg}(p(j))$ on the edge that follows all destructive penetrator strands and precedes all constructive penetrator strands. We will write $\mathsf{bt}(p)$ to refer to the bridge term of p. A single communication edge $\mathsf{first}(p) \to p(1)$, with no adversary strands in between, is a direct path of length 1; $\mathsf{bt}(p) = \mathsf{msg}(\mathsf{first}(p)) = \mathsf{msg}(p(1))$. The two edges leading to n_1 and n_2 in Fig. 3 are examples with the concatenated bridge terms $\mathtt{c}11, N_1, C_1$ and $\mathtt{c}21, N_2, C_2$. The bridge terms for the two direct paths shown in Fig. 2 are A and N_a. The adversary can always break concatenations down in this way:

Assumption 3. *If $p(i) \to p(i+1)$ is a bridge term in bundle $\mathcal{B}$, then $\mathsf{msg}(p(i))$ is either an encryption or a basic value, but not a concatenation.*

For any bundle $\mathcal{C}$, there is an equivalent $\mathcal{B}$ in which the adversary separates every concatenated value to its basic or encrypted parts, and then subsequently reconcatenates these parts, as in Fig. 2, Part II [20, Prop. 9]. Assumption 3 restricts our attention to these equivalent but more convenient $\mathcal{B}$.

The direct paths form a framework that supports the extended paths:

Lemma 14. *Let $\mathcal{B}$ be a bundle, and p an extended penetrator path in $\mathcal{B}$ that is not direct. Let $p(i)$ be the earliest key node along p.*

1. *The part of p leading to $p(i)$ forms a direct path.*
2. *Let $p(j)$ be any key node along p, lying on an encryption or decryption strand s, $m_1 \Rightarrow p(j) \Rightarrow m_3$. There are direct paths q such that m_1, m_3 lie on q.*
3. *If s is an encryption strand, then $\mathsf{msg}(p(j)) \ll \mathsf{msg}(\mathsf{last}(q))$. If s is a decryption strand, then $\mathsf{msg}(p(j)) \ll \mathsf{msg}(\mathsf{first}(q))$.*

The Separability Theorem. An extended path p is *critical* iff its source $\mathsf{first}(p)$ is not permitted to influence its target $\mathsf{last}(p)$.

We wish to remove the critical paths, since this will reduce a bundle to one that obeys the influence specification. If the adversary uses a path to influence a node, contrary to our $\rightsquigarrow$, we want to clip this path. If we can always remove these paths, and replace a Π-bundle containing critical paths with one with no critical paths, then even the adversary gets no advantage from critical paths. No violation of the influence specification is essential. Everything that can happen in Π can happen without violating the influence specification. If this is true in Π, we can assume $\rightsquigarrow$ when analyzing Π; nothing that matters will be left out.

A sufficient condition for this to hold is that Π's executions be "reparable:"

Definition 15. *A path p is $\rightsquigarrow$-critical in $\mathcal{B}$ iff $\mathsf{first}(p) \not\rightsquigarrow \mathsf{last}(p)$.*

$\mathcal{B}$ is $\rightsquigarrow$-reparable iff $\rightsquigarrow$ is a may-influence relation for $\mathcal{B}$, and every $\rightsquigarrow$-critical path p has a bridge $p(i) \to p(i+1)$ where $\mathsf{msg}(p(i)) = a$ is a basic value.

When $\rightsquigarrow$ is understood, we omit it and write "critical" or "reparable." We can assume no bridge term of p is a concatenation by Assumption 3. Thus, when p is reparable, $\mathsf{bt}(p)$ is a basic value. In Fig. 3, the most interesting bridge terms are N_1 and N_2, which are the uniquely originating values.

Theorem 16 (Separability). *For every $\rightsquigarrow$-reparable Π-bundle $\mathcal{B}$, there is a Π-bundle $\mathcal{C}$ lying below $\mathcal{B}$ such that $\mathcal{C}$ obeys $\rightsquigarrow$.*

Separability for Protocols with Session Parameters. We will first apply Thm. 16 to the main case of protocols with session parameters, and $\leadsto_s$. The key thing is to show that every critical path is reparable. The main reason why this is true is that—unless $\mathsf{first}(p) \leadsto_s \mathsf{last}(p)$ and $\mathsf{last}(p) \leadsto_s \mathsf{first}(p)$—all encryptions at the two ends contain different sets of session parameters. Thus, the bridge terms are basic values.

Theorem 17. *If Π is a protocol with session parameters, then every Π-bundle satisfying Φ_s is $\leadsto_s$-reparable. Hence, by Thm. 16, Π obeys $\leadsto_s$ subject to Φ_s.*

If each strand succeeds in choosing its session parameter freshly, then no two instances of the same role are related by the causal order in a reduced bundle, i.e. one obeying $\leadsto_s$. This holds because any two instances supply different values for the session parameter, which are thus incompatible in $\leadsto_s$.

Theorem 18. *Suppose that Π is a protocol with session parameters, and $\mathcal{B}$ obeys $\leadsto_s$ and satisfies Φ_s. Then $s_1 \downarrow i \npreceq s_2 \downarrow j$ when (i) $s_1 = \alpha(\rho)$ and $s_2 = \beta(\rho)$; and (ii) $P(\rho)$ is acquired on ρ by step $\min(i,j)$.*

5 Protocol Independence

We turn now from our focus on sessions to combining protocols. We organize the results by the choice of may-influence relation.

The Discrete May-Influence Relation. Let Π_1 and Π_2 be protocols, i.e. sets of strands satisfying the assumptions mentioned in 2–3. For simplicity assume that the protocols are disjoint, in the sense that no strand (or initial segment) is an instance of a role of Π_1 and also an instance of a role of Π_2. Let $\Pi = \Pi_1 \cup \Pi_2$ be the protocol that contains all the roles of Π_1 and Π_2.

Define $n_1 \leadsto_1 n_2$ to hold for $n_1, n_2 \in \mathsf{regnodes}(\Pi)$ just in case $n_1, n_2 \in \mathsf{regnodes}(\Pi_1)$ or $n_1, n_2 \in \mathsf{regnodes}(\Pi_2)$. That is, nodes of the two source protocols may not influence each other.

We can use this *may-influence* relation to infer a protocol independence result, à la [1,9]. Define Π_1, Π_2 to have *sharply disjoint encryption* if

1. every key used for encryption on any node of either is a basic value; and
2. if e_1 is any encryption occurring in Π_1 and e_2 is any encryption occurring in Π_2, then e_1 and e_2 have no common instance.

The two conditions here are essentially syntactic. Condition 2 says that unification fails for the two encryptions. One way to satisfy condition 2 is using tags. If Π_1, Π_2 may have distinct tags τ_1, τ_2, such that every encryption in Π_i begins with tag τ_i, then condition 2 is certainly satisfied.

Theorem 19. *If Π_1, Π_2 have sharply disjoint encryption, then all $\Pi_1 \cup \Pi_2$ bundles are $\leadsto_1$-reparable. Hence, by Thm. 16, $\Pi_1 \cup \Pi_2$ obeys $\leadsto_1$.*

This is the essential idea behind [1,9]. The clever extension to algebras with convergent subterm rewrite rules in Ciobaca and Cortier's [8] appears to involve related ideas.

In our formalism, condition 1 is in fact unnecessary:

Theorem 20. *Let Π_1, Π_2 satisfy Condition 2 of sharply disjoint encryption, and let $\mathcal{B}$ be any bundle of $\Pi_1 \cup \Pi_2$. There is a bundle $\mathcal{C}$ lying below $\mathcal{B}$ such that $\mathcal{C}$ is $\leadsto_1$-reparable. Hence, by Thm. 16, $\Pi_1 \cup \Pi_2$ obeys $\leadsto_1$.*

This shows a pitfall in interpreting strand-based results in the applied pi-calculus. In applied pi, letting $w = \mathsf{hash}(k_1, k_2)$, the two protocols P_1 and P_2:

$$P_1 = \nu\, k_1 s \,.\, \langle k_1 \rangle \,.\, \langle \{\!|\mathsf{t1}, s|\!\}_w \rangle \qquad P_2 = \nu\, k_2 s \,.\, \langle k_2 \rangle \,.\, \langle \{\!|\mathsf{t2}, s|\!\}_w \rangle$$

compose to yield $\nu\, k_1 k_2 s \,.\, P_1 \mid P_2$. In strands, by contrast, parameters in individual roles are essentially locally bound, since their possible instances are all substitution instances. Thus, there is no sense in which the two roles share the "same" k_1, k_2. Moreover, ν-binding expresses a notion of local choice that is somewhat different from both our unique origination and non-origination. It appears to be that the adversary never originates the ν-bound value. Thus, this result appears to be strong, but not truly comparable to results such as [9].

Another limitation of our result is that it is proved for a particular message algebra, and an adversary model for that, rather than for a class of algebras. We conjecture that there is a substantial class for which the lemmas of §§2, 4 hold, and that our results will hold throughout that class.

A One-Way Influence Relation. Here we consider an asymmetric relation between the protocols Π_1, Π_2. Our goal is to ensure that adding the auxiliary protocol cannot undermine the main protocol Π_1. In many cases, Π_2 consumes cryptographically prepared units such as digital signatures or encrypted tickets (as in Kerberos), for instance, when it resumes sessions created by the main protocol. Thus, the main protocol may influence the auxiliary, but the reverse should not occur [19]. Let $\Pi = \Pi_1 \cup \Pi_2$, and define $n_1 \leadsto_2 n_2$ to hold for $n_1, n_2 \in \mathsf{regnodes}(\Pi)$ just in case $n_1 \in \mathsf{regnodes}(\Pi_1)$ or $n_2 \in \mathsf{regnodes}(\Pi_2)$.

With a more delicate definition of *disjoint encryption*, and stipulating the condition Φ that no uniquely originating value is contributed by Π_2, we obtain:

Theorem 21. *Let Π_1, Π_2 satisfy disjoint encryption, and let $\mathcal{B}$ be any bundle of $\Pi_1 \cup \Pi_2$ satisfying Φ. There is a bundle $\mathcal{C}$ lying below $\mathcal{B}$ such that $\mathcal{C}$ is $\leadsto_2$-reparable. Hence, by Thm. 16, $\Pi_1 \cup \Pi_2$ obeys $\leadsto_2$.*

We may also use this second form of protocol independence to explain the "sequential composition" of Datta et al. [11]. Here, the nodes of the auxiliary protocol are placed after nodes of the primary protocol, but on the same strands; the formalization is unchanged. In particular, h maps nodes of the primary protocol to π_1 and nodes of the secondary protocol to π_2. The Clause 1 in Defn. 7 allows this to work when nodes of the secondary protocol never appear before a node of the primary protocol on any strand.

Vertical Composition. Suppose that a protocol achieves a goal, assuming that it uses channels that provide particular kinds of protection against the adversary, e.g. that the adversary cannot spoof messages on these channels, or cannot snoop on their contents. Does that yield a secure protocol when these channels are replaced by subprotocols that ensure that the assumptions are met? This is the "vertical composition problem" [14,16,27]. Our methods seem highly relevant to this problem, but they require a way to express the channel assumptions as restrictions on the set of relevant bundles. We plan to explore this.

Conclusion. Two further main areas of future work remain. The more substantial is to adapt this approach to cover a notion of observational equivalence. This appears to involve enriching the adversary model to include a strand that detects the equality of two basic values. We also intend to soften the no Vs condition, which is tighter than necessary. For instance, it permits a tuple of messages to be received in a unit, but prohibits these same messages from being received successively, even when there are no intervening transmissions. More careful methods should relax this condition.

Acknowledgments. We are extremely grateful to Véronique Cortier, John Ramsdell, Paul Rowe, and the anonymous referees at POST.

References

1. Andova, S., Cremers, C., Gjøsteen, K., Mauw, S., Mjølsnes, S., Radomirović, S.: Sufficient conditions for composing security protocols. Information and Computation (2007)
2. Arapinis, M., Delaune, S., Kremer, S.: From One Session to Many: Dynamic Tags for Security Protocols. In: Cervesato, I., Veith, H., Voronkov, A. (eds.) LPAR 2008. LNCS (LNAI), vol. 5330, pp. 128–142. Springer, Heidelberg (2008)
3. Armando, A., Basin, D., Boichut, Y., Chevalier, Y., Compagna, L., Cuellar, J., Hankes Drielsma, P., Heám, P.C., Kouchnarenko, O., Mantovani, J., Mödersheim, S., von Oheimb, D., Rusinowitch, M., Santiago, J., Turuani, M., Viganò, L., Vigneron, L.: The AVISPA Tool for the Automated Validation of Internet Security Protocols and Applications. In: Etessami, K., Rajamani, S.K. (eds.) CAV 2005. LNCS, vol. 3576, pp. 281–285. Springer, Heidelberg (2005)
4. Bellare, M., Rogaway, P.: Entity Authentication and Key Distribution. In: Stinson, D.R. (ed.) CRYPTO 1993. LNCS, vol. 773, pp. 232–249. Springer, Heidelberg (1994)
5. Bhargavan, K., Corin, R., Deniélou, P.-M., Fournet, C., Leifer, J.J.: Cryptographic protocol synthesis and verification for multiparty sessions. In: IEEE Computer Security Foundations Symposium (2009)
6. Canetti, R.: Universally composable security: A new paradigm for cryptographic protocols. Technical Report 2000/067, IACR (October 2001), appeared in FOCS (2001)
7. Canetti, R., Krawczyk, H.: Analysis of Key-Exchange Protocols and Their Use for Building Secure Channels. In: Pfitzmann, B. (ed.) EUROCRYPT 2001. LNCS, vol. 2045, pp. 453–474. Springer, Heidelberg (2001)
8. Ciobâcă, Ş., Cortier, V.: Protocol composition for arbitrary primitives. In: CSF, pp. 322–336. IEEE Computer Society Press (July 2010)

9. Cortier, V., Delaune, S.: Safely composing security protocols. Formal Methods in System Design 34(1), 1–36 (2009)
10. Cortier, V., Warinschi, B., Zălinescu, E.: Synthesizing Secure Protocols. In: Biskup, J., López, J. (eds.) ESORICS 2007. LNCS, vol. 4734, pp. 406–421. Springer, Heidelberg (2007)
11. Datta, A., Derek, A., Mitchell, J.C., Pavlovic, D.: A derivation system and compositional logic for security protocols. Journal of Computer Security 13(3), 423–482 (2005)
12. Delaune, S., Kremer, S., Ryan, M.D.: Composition of password-based protocols. In: Proceedings of the 21st IEEE Computer Security Foundations Symposium (CSF 2008), pp. 239–251. IEEE Computer Society Press (June 2008)
13. Deniélou, P.-M., Yoshida, N.: Dynamic multirole session types. In: POPL, pp. 435–446 (2011)
14. Dilloway, C., Lowe, G.: Specifying secure transport channels. In: CSF, pp. 210–223. IEEE (2008)
15. Dolev, D., Yao, A.: On the security of public-key protocols. IEEE Transactions on Information Theory 29, 198–208 (1983)
16. Groß, T., Modersheim, S.: Vertical protocol composition. In: CSF, pp. 235–250. IEEE (2011)
17. Guttman, J.D.: Security Goals and Protocol Transformations. In: Mödersheim, S., Palamidessi, C. (eds.) TOSCA 2011. LNCS, vol. 6993, pp. 130–147. Springer, Heidelberg (2012)
18. Guttman, J.D.: Shapes: Surveying crypto protocol runs. In: Cortier, V., Kremer, S. (eds.) Formal Models and Techniques for Analyzing Security Protocols. Cryptology and Information Security Series, IOS Press (2011)
19. Guttman, J.D., Thayer, F.J.: Protocol independence through disjoint encryption. In: Computer Security Foundations Workshop. IEEE CS Press (2000)
20. Guttman, J.D., Thayer, F.J.: Authentication tests and the structure of bundles. Theoretical Computer Science 283(2), 333–380 (2002)
21. Honda, K., Vasconcelos, V.T., Kubo, M.: Language Primitives and Type Discipline for Structured Communication-Based Programming. In: Hankin, C. (ed.) ESOP 1998. LNCS, vol. 1381, pp. 122–138. Springer, Heidelberg (1998)
22. Honda, K., Yoshida, N., Carbone, M.: Multiparty asynchronous session types. In: Proc. of POPL, vol. 43(1), pp. 273–284. ACM (2008)
23. Kamil, A., Lowe, G.: Analysing TLS in the strand spaces model. Journal of Computer Security 19(5), 975–1025 (2011)
24. Küsters, R., Tuengerthal, M.: Composition theorems without pre-established session identifiers. In: CCS, pp. 41–50. ACM (2011)
25. Lowe, G.: Breaking and Fixing the Needham-Schroeder Public-Key Protocol Using FDR. In: Margaria, T., Steffen, B. (eds.) TACAS 1996. LNCS, vol. 1055, pp. 147–166. Springer, Heidelberg (1996)
26. Millen, J.K., Shmatikov, V.: Constraint solving for bounded-process cryptographic protocol analysis. In: CCS, pp. 166–175. ACM (2001)
27. Mödersheim, S., Viganò, L.: Secure Pseudonymous Channels. In: Backes, M., Ning, P. (eds.) ESORICS 2009. LNCS, vol. 5789, pp. 337–354. Springer, Heidelberg (2009)
28. Needham, R., Schroeder, M.: Using encryption for authentication in large networks of computers. CACM 21(12) (December 1978)
29. Rusinowitch, M., Turuani, M.: Protocol insecurity with finite number of sessions is NP-complete. In: Computer Security Foundations Workshop, pp. 174–187 (2001)
30. Thayer, F.J., Herzog, J.C., Guttman, J.D.: Strand spaces: Proving security protocols correct. Journal of Computer Security 7(2/3), 191–230 (1999)

Author Index